TRANSFORMATION AND TRADITION IN 1960s BRITISH CINEMA

TRANSFORMATION AND TRADITION IN 1960s BRITISH CINEMA

Richard Farmer, Laura Mayne,
Duncan Petrie and Melanie Williams

EDINBURGH
University Press

Edinburgh University Press is one of the leading university presses in the UK. We publish academic books and journals in our selected subject areas across the humanities and social sciences, combining cutting-edge scholarship with high editorial and production values to produce academic works of lasting importance. For more information visit our website: edinburghuniversitypress.com

© Richard Farmer, Laura Mayne, Duncan Petrie and Melanie Williams, 2019, 2021

Edinburgh University Press Ltd
The Tun – Holyrood Road
12 (2f) Jackson's Entry
Edinburgh EH8 8PJ

First published in hardback by Edinburgh University Press 2019

Typeset in 10/12.5 pt Sabon by
Servis Filmsetting Ltd, Stockport, Cheshire

A CIP record for this book is available from the British Library

ISBN 978 1 4744 2311 3 (hardback)
ISBN 978 1 4744 2312 0 (paperback)
ISBN 978 1 4744 2313 7 (webready PDF)
ISBN 978 1 4744 2314 4 (epub)

The right of Richard Farmer, Laura Mayne, Duncan Petrie and Melanie Williams to be identified as authors of this work has been asserted in accordance with the Copyright, Designs and Patents Act 1988 and the Copyright and Related Rights Regulations 2003 (SI No. 2498).

Published with the support of the University of Edinburgh Scholarly Publishing Initiatives Fund.

CONTENTS

List of Figures — vii
Acknowledgements — viii

    Introduction — 1
    Duncan Petrie and Melanie Williams

PART ONE   STRUCTURES AND COMPANIES

1. Distribution and Production: The British Majors — 33
   Duncan Petrie

2. American Involvement in UK Production — 63
   Duncan Petrie

3. Public Support in a Changing Climate — 95
   Duncan Petrie

4. The Vertically Integrated Independent — 119
   Laura Mayne

5. Low-budget Independent Production — 138
   Laura Mayne

PART TWO   CREATIVE AGENCY

6. Screenwriting — 161
   Melanie Williams

7. Directing — 180
   Melanie Williams

8. Production Design — 203
   Melanie Williams

9. Costume Design — 222
   Melanie Williams

10. Cinematography — 241
    Duncan Petrie and Melanie Williams

11. Editing — 259
    Melanie Williams

PART THREE   MEDIA CONVERGENCE

12. Film and Television — 281
    Richard Farmer

13. Film and TV Advertising — 303
    Richard Farmer

14. Film and Pop Music — 327
    Richard Farmer

    Conclusion — 349
    Duncan Petrie and Melanie Williams

Appendices — 354
Bibliography — 365
Index — 380

FIGURES

I.1	Alan Bates and June Ritchie in *A Kind of Loving*	2
1.1	Norman Wisdom continuing to be a Rank Organisation mainstay in *The Early Bird*	34
2.1	Peter O'Toole and Zia Mohyeddin await the arrival of Omar Sharif in *Lawrence of Arabia*	64
3.1	Carol White in the NFFC-supported box-office success *Poor Cow*	96
4.1	The eyes of Catherine Deneuve in *Repulsion*	120
5.1	Colin Campbell and Dudley Sutton in *The Leather Boys*	138
6.1	Frederic Raphael's dialogue for Alan Bates and Denholm Elliott in *Nothing but the Best*	162
7.1	Clive Donner directs Barry Evans directing the participants in *Here We Go Round the Mulberry Bush*	181
8.1	The whitewashed art deco interior created by Assheton Gorton for *The Knack . . . and How to Get It*	204
9.1	A diverse array of feminine fashions created by costume designer Julie Harris for *Casino Royale*	222
10.1	James Fox and Dirk Bogarde clash on the staircase in *The Servant*	242
11.1	Albert Finney as the titular hero of *Tom Jones*	260
12.1	Tony Hancock makes his film debut in *The Rebel*	282
13.1	Orson Welles sells Barley Flakes in London's docklands in *I'll Never Forget What's 'is Name*	304
14.1	Pop fans on the dancefloor in *Gonks Go Beat*	328
C.1	The closing shot of *Carry On Up the Khyber*	349

ACKNOWLEDGEMENTS

This work was supported by the Arts and Humanities Research Council (grant number AH/L014793/1). The research project 'Transformation and Tradition in British Cinema of the 1960s: Industry, Creativity, and National Branding' ran between 2015 and 2017, and is the source of the research underpinning this book.

Our project's advisory board was an important source of guidance and support throughout, so thanks to Richard Paterson, Geoff Andrew, Jo Botting, Pamela Church Gibson, Charles Drazin, Andrew Higson, John Hill, Nick James, Nathalie Morris, Julian Petley, Neil Sinyard, and Sarah Street for their invaluable input.

Other individuals who have been very helpful and supportive in various ways (including providing keynote presentations at our various project events) include James Chapman, Llewella Chapman, Steve Chibnall, Philip Drummond, Liz Eggleston, Sue Harper, Marcus Hearn, Matthew Jones, Richard Lester, Sandy Lieberson, Andy Miller, Robert Murphy, Alison Pierse, David Puttnam, Robert Shail, Alwyn W. Turner, Rita Tushingham, Justin Smith and Melvyn Stokes. Sarah Cronin-Stanley of Talking Pictures TV and Steven Hess of Woodfall Films have been especially supportive of our work and deserve particular thanks. Upekha Bandaranayake (BFI DVD), Martin Cater (Network DVD), Elizabeth Pauker (Criterion), Candy Vincent-Smith (Studio Canal), and the team behind the Indicator label for Powerhouse DVD have all engaged with our research and offered opportunities to disseminate it more widely, for which we are grateful. We would also like to thank the organisers of various research seminars, conferences, symposia, screenings and other public events across the UK for providing us with opportunities to try out and develop our ideas on 1960s British cinema, and get some valuable feedback from a variety of different audiences. Likewise, colleagues who participated in the symposia and conferences we organised as part of our project, which took place in York, Norwich and London, and everyone who wrote for our blog (https://60sbritishcinema.wordpress.com/), or engaged with our project on Facebook and Twitter: thank you for your important contributions to the overall research project from which this book derives.

As the research project's investigators, Duncan would like to thank Ed Braman, Simon van der Borgh, Mike Cordner and Romana Turina at the University of York, and Melanie would like to thank her colleagues in the School of Art, Media and American Studies, and administrative support staff across the Faculty of Arts and Humanities at the University of East Anglia, for their kindness and help throughout the life of the project and during the writing of this book.

The authors would like to acknowledge the following archives and libraries that have been indispensable to their research: the British Film Institute's Reuben Library and the BFI Special Collections material in the National Film and Television Archive (with particular thanks to Nigel Arthur, Jonny Davies, Nathalie Morris, Claire Smith and Peter Todd), the Film Finances Archive (with thanks to Charles Drazin, Thoko Mavolwane, James Shirras, David Korda and Steven Ransohoff), the BECTU British Entertainment History Project (Sue Malden), the Bill Douglas Cinema Museum (Phil Wickham), the History of Advertising Trust (Alistair Moir), the TUC Library (James Goddard), the Cinema and Television History Research Centre at De Montfort University (Steve Chibnall), the Borthwick Archives at the University of York (Gary Brannan), and the National Archives in Kew, the National Library of Scotland and the libraries at the universities of York, East Anglia and Cambridge, and all the very supportive and helpful archivists and librarians working there.

We would also like to thank Gillian Leslie and Richard Strachan at Edinburgh University Press for their enthusiasm and assiduousness throughout the publication process.

Finally, all four authors offer personal thanks to family and friends for their support during the researching and writing of this book.

INTRODUCTION

Duncan Petrie and Melanie Williams

1960s BRITISH CINEMA: CONTESTATION AND CONTRADICTION

Within the history of British cinema, the 1960s is a decade that most scholars and critics agree represented a moment of transformation, as film was caught up in and influenced by a wider process of social and cultural change. Put bluntly, British films – and their protagonists – looked and sounded very different to the way they had in the 1950s. As *Sight and Sound*'s editor Penelope Houston wrote in 1963:

> A few years ago, if the British cinema had an immediately identifiable image, it would have been a shot of Kenneth More, jaw boldly jutting, on the bridge of a destroyer. At the moment, the national cinema would more readily be summed up in a view of a boy and girl wandering mournfully through the drizzle and mist of industrial Britain, looking for a place to live or a place to make love.[1]

A few years on again, British cinema's 'identifiable image' would probably be a colourful gathering of London's beautiful young people; indeed in 1970, Houston was to characterise the industry in terms of 'another jaded party, dragging on exhaustedly into the night in its bedraggled fancy dress, surrounded by its odds and ends of boutique bric-a-brac'.[2] Both situations were far removed from the dominant milieu of 1950s British film. As Raymond Durgnat observed, its middle-class patriotic ethos found itself 'challenged, and

Figure I.1   The emblematic early sixties image of 'a boy and girl wandering mournfully through the drizzle and mist of industrial Britain': Alan Bates and June Ritchie in *A Kind of Loving* (John Schlesinger, 1962).

shattered, by successive waves: anger, satire, Swinging London, hippiedom, Hollywood-led cosmopolitanism' as the 1960s progressed, while the decade's 'sudden changes in morality and taste so baffled film-business professionals as almost to repeat the chaos of the coming of sound'.[3] This was a period in which British film-making was frequently bewildered but also energised by the rapidly changing social and industrial context in which it had to operate. In films, as in popular culture more generally, there was a new emphasis on youth, individualism, vitality and mobility. Philip French described how British cinema of the 1960s seemed to possess 'a feeling for the medium, a drive, a sense of style, a freewheeling vigour, for which there are few previous parallels', and this sense of liberated modernity in both content and form, at its best, still feels fresh half a century on.[4] However, French also acknowledged how some of the medium's outward vitality might be read as symptomatic of 'a desperate energy that seeks to conceal a lack of content behind a battery of tricks', thus setting in train an ongoing ambivalence in the critical response towards 1960s British film.[5]

Subsequent evaluations of the nation's cinematic achievements during the decade have reached some very different conclusions, indicating some of this ambivalence and critical contestation. Robert Murphy concluded his 1992 study of the decade with his bold claim that 'the 1960s saw a greater number of significant and exciting films made in Britain than at any time before or since'.[6] Jeffrey Richards partially concurs with this hypothesis, likewise arguing that the era 'witnessed a revitalisation of British cinema and the emergence of a flourishing and diverse film culture, after what was widely perceived to be the doldrums era of the 1950s'.[7] Ample evidence can be marshalled to support such positive assessments. An influx of Hollywood finance gave British films unprecedented access to international markets, boosting their visibility and earning power, with the United Artists-backed James Bond series, initiated by *Dr No* (1962), providing a perfect example of this new box-office phenomenon, as did United Artists' other big success stories, their films with the Beatles, starting strongly with *A Hard Day's Night* (1964). In addition to their new worldwide commercial success, British films attained new levels of international critical acclaim, winning the Oscar for Best Film on no less than four occasions during the decade: *Lawrence of Arabia* (1962), *Tom Jones* (1963), *A Man for All Seasons* (1966) and *Oliver!* (1968). British actors Peter O'Toole, Paul Scofield, Trevor Howard, Laurence Olivier, Albert Finney, Richard Burton, Rex Harrison, Peter Sellers, Michael Caine, Alan Bates, Ron Moody, Deborah Kerr, Rachel Roberts, Julie Christie, Samantha Eggar, Lynn Redgrave, Vanessa Redgrave, Edith Evans, Maggie Smith, Sarah Miles and Glenda Jackson were all Oscar-nominated or Oscar-winning for their performances in local films. British productions also triumphed at Cannes, winning the Palme d'Or three times with *The Knack ... and How to Get It* (1965), *Blow Up* (1966) and *If ....* (1968). *Accident* (1967) shared the Grand Prix Award, while the previous year *Alfie* (1966) had picked up the Prix du Jury. Rita Tushingham, Samantha Eggar, Vanessa Redgrave, Richard Harris and Terence Stamp all won its acting awards. At the Berlin Film Festival, the Golden Bear was awarded to *A Kind of Loving* (1962) and *Cul-de-sac* (1966), while *Repulsion* (1965) picked up its Jury Grand Prize. Peter Finch and Edith Evans both picked up its acting awards. These festival successes were especially hard won as British productions competed against an international profusion of art cinema.[8]

And yet for Alexander Walker, who provided the first major account of British cinema of this era shortly after it had ended, such ostensible triumphs were ultimately illusory. The conclusion to his book *Hollywood, England* has the tone of a post-mortem rather than a victory celebration when he asserts that:

> it is the inability, or disinclination of even established-name directors in Britain to articulate a view of life and society in freshly conceived and individual terms, and to translate these aesthetically to the screen with an unmistakable signature, that one most feels the absence of during the 1960s.[9]

For Walker, this outcome derived in part from an overdependence on American finance that had only intensified as the decade progressed and, once the cash ceased to flow, would leave British cinema with nothing to fall back on. But he also suggests that the film industry had become caught up in a wider cultural malaise, growing increasingly meretricious, superficial, narcissistic and addicted to excess:

> At its worst it seemed the cinema was a continuous commercial whose dimensions were those of 'sheer fantasy' – the uninhibited sex, the progressive nudity, the frivolous dress, the rhythm of pop music, the visual intensity, the affluent hedonism of all descriptions. Everything was marketable, being sold back to the public who inspired it, or remade in a newer trend when they had sickened of it.[10]

Even the most dispassionate account produced during the decade, *A Competitive Cinema* (1966), written by Terence Kelly, Graham Norton and George Perry for the Institute of Economic Research, presented a picture of a film industry in crisis: struggling with declining audience numbers, dominated by a small number of complacent and self-interested entities, operating restrictive practices and creating barriers to new forms of entrepreneurial and creative activity.[11] This sense of stagnation could also be discerned within state policy towards the industry and it is telling that the list of recommendations produced by Kelly and his co-authors was considerably more thoughtful and ambitious than those contained in a government Monopolies and Mergers Commission report on the industry also published in 1966.[12]

Such wildly differing assessments of British cinema also correspond with divergent accounts of the wider significance and legacy of the 1960s. For historian Arthur Marwick, the decade heralded nothing less than a 'cultural revolution', creating a society that was more modern, vibrant, affluent, youthful, tolerant, diverse, aspirational and self-critical.[13] Numerous aspects of Marwick's analysis, and the characteristics he identifies as central to cultural change in the 1960s, tally with developments in British film. The rise of anti-establishment subcultures and social movements corresponds with the breakthrough of the New Wave; a new stress on individualism and entrepreneurialism can be discerned in the motivations of ambitious and innovative independent producers; the rise of youth is reflected in new kinds of stories and protagonists (and stars playing them), and other production personnel who built careers during the decade. Unprecedented international cultural exchange underpinned the cosmopolitanism of British cinema with its injection of overseas money and talent and a proliferation of co-productions; a greater emphasis on spectacle can be observed in the rising production values of British films and the growing ubiquity of widescreen and colour; increasing liberalism, permissiveness and sexual freedom is evident in the relaxation in censorship and concomitant production and exhibition of more X-certificated films with franker depictions of sex and violence; the new cultural importance of fashion and rock music was likewise directly reflected in the form and content of numerous British films.[14]

Marwick's summation is overwhelmingly positive, but for other commentators the changes associated with that decade were profoundly negative, representing a decline in respect for authority, morality and cultural traditions, heralding nothing less than the end of civilisation. While it is very easy to pigeonhole this as the predictable, reactionary response of an increasingly redundant establishment, some of the key critiques came from individuals who had participated in the decade's process of change, specifically the satire boom which was generally seen as inaugurating the decline of deference towards those in authority. The journalist, critic and broadcaster Bernard Levin, known for his regular appearances on the BBC's *That Was the Week That Was*, began his study of the sixties, *The Pendulum Years*, with a pessimistic summary of its lack of sound judgement:

> It was a credulous age, perhaps the most credulous ever, and the more rational, the less gullible it claimed to be, the less rational, the more gullible it showed itself. Never was it easier to gain a reputation as a seer, never was a following so rapidly and readily acquired.[15]

Meanwhile Christopher Booker, one of the founders of *Private Eye* magazine, a beacon of anti-establishment sentiment, argued in his book *The Neophiliacs* that British culture became caught up in a collective fantasy during this era, obsessed with image, and addicted to novelty and sensation, and its hedonistic party would inevitably have to give way to a crashing hangover:

> When the historians come to look back on the 1960s as a whole, they will perceive a curiously general pattern affecting not just the civilisation of the West, but a great part of the rest of the world. A decade which began with so many bright hopes, growing from the middle Fifties onwards, had presented in many senses an increasingly darkening landscape, ending in years when (despite the many specific exceptions) the prevailing mood was one at least of confusion and disillusionment, if not of considerable gloom.[16]

As Robert Hewison notes, 'both Levin and Booker interpret the period as one of illusion, giving way to reality – the rhetoric of "realism" was to become popular on the political Right'.[17] However, Hewison also acknowledges a more widespread sense of disillusionment that gradually replaced an earlier spirit of optimism as the sixties drew to a close. The thesis of George Melly's *Revolt into Style* charts how the explosion in popular culture during the era – music, art, film, TV, radio and literature – inevitably moved from a form of youthful protest to a commodified and castrated product.[18] Meanwhile, Jeff Nuttall's preface to his celebratory exploration of the rise of the counterculture, *Bomb Culture* notes the turn to violence that came to characterise the student protests of 1968, describing 'an evolutionary convulsion rather than a reformation. Young people are not correcting society. They are regurgitating it.'[19] This is the same narrative of creative promise being squandered, turning sour, or resorting to extremes that permeates Alexander Walker's otherwise measured account of the rise and fall of British cinema during the decade, also written in its immediate wake.

More recently however, historian Dominic Sandbrook (born in the 1970s and therefore not drawing on personal memories of the 1960s unlike most previous chroniclers) has offered a different perspective again on the decade. Sandbrook emphasises the importance of continuity over change, suggesting that 'the sixties are best understood not as a dramatic turning point, interrupting the course of the nation's history and sending it off in a radically new direction, but rather as a stage in a long evolution stretching back into the forgotten past'.[20] And just as Marwick's very different model of what the sixties represented can be applied to British cinema of the era, so too can Sandbrook's arguments. For alongside the lively innovation and the impact of youthful newcomers and cosmopolitan visitors, long-established (and arguably 'old-fashioned') film-makers like David Lean, Carol Reed, Anthony Asquith, Frank Launder and Sidney Gilliat, and the Boulting brothers continued to enjoy high-profile success throughout the decade, while the continuing popularity of *Carry On* comedy owed much to older cultural traditions of music hall and seaside-postcard humour.[21] Although new independent producers like Woodfall Films advocated fresh approaches to film-making, the industry continued to be dominated, and arguably kept in the position of stasis, by the vertically integrated duopoly of Rank and Associated British.

Sandbrook's analysis also offers a sense of the Janus-faced nature of the 1960s, echoing Levin's metaphor of the 'pendulum', simultaneously looking backwards and forwards, that can be discerned in some of the decade's most emblematic and popular cultural products. A fine example is provided by the television series *The Avengers* (1961–9) which, in its most popular guise, offered a crime-fighting double act of an Edwardian-styled gentleman John Steed (Patrick Macnee) and his ultra-modern female counterpart, skilled in martial arts (Honor Blackman as Cathy Gale, then Diana Rigg as Emma Peel), creating what Sandbrook describes as 'a balance between patriotic tradition and swinging modernity, not so very different from the combination offered by James Bond or even the Beatles'.[22] Sandbrook also tempers the more common emphasis on novelty and revolution in accounts of the decade by invoking the equal importance of nostalgia in British culture at this time, with his key examples including the Beatles' mock-Edwardian opus *Sgt Pepper's Lonely Hearts Club Band* (1967), the BBC's literary adaptation *The Forsyte Saga* (1967–8) and its sitcom *Dad's Army* (1968–77) alongside the influence of William Morris on interior design.

Sandbrook's acknowledgement of the 'contradictory impulses' affecting Britain in the 1960s, and the sometimes paradoxical oppositions they created, is echoed in Mark Donnelly's account.[23] These oppositions included: the valorisation of the modern versus an increasing anxiety about the future fuelled by the Cold War and nuclear proliferation; a sense of renewed national self-confidence versus foreboding at Britain's international decline as a world power following the loss of empire; an obsession with youth versus rising moral panic about juvenile delinquency, teenage sexual activity and pregnancy; and a rise in living standards versus the persistence of poverty and deprivation as Britain continued to struggle with economic instability.

There is perhaps occasional evidence in Sandbrook's work of a quasi-Oedipal wish to unseat Marwick as primary explainer of the significance of the 1960s, as well as divergent ideological affiliations between the two historians, which finds expression in Sandbrook's slight overemphasis on the residual aspects of the 1960s at the expense of its emergent aspects, just as Marwick had previously de-emphasised the residual in favour of foregrounding the emergent.[24] This book will nail its colours to neither mast and instead will deal with the conflicting historiography of the period by acknowledging its status as a period riven with ambiguity and contradiction, an era of both continuity and change, tradition and transformation.

Defining our Focus

This study sets out to extend, complement and in some instances complicate existing British cinema scholarship on the 1960s. Alexander Walker's and Robert Murphy's accounts remain indispensable.[25] Despite his ultimate sense of disappointment in 1960s British cinema, coupled with a possible overemphasis on auteurist models of cinema achievement, Walker's consideration of the role of financiers and entrepreneurial producers, in addition to the close attention he pays to key directors and films, provides a very insightful and nuanced account of the functioning and development of the industry, underpinned by interviews with many of the major figures directly responsible not long after the fact. Murphy's concern in *Sixties British Cinema* is more with the shape and organisation of the product, an identification and analysis of popular genres and cycles of films which provides an invaluable – and extraordinarily inclusive – cultural map, sensitively contextualised throughout. Another hugely significant contribution to British film historiography of the period is John Hill's *Sex, Class and Realism: British Cinema 1956–63*, a strongly sociological study of the roots and achievements of the British New Wave and associated works from the 'kitchen sink' and 'social problem' traditions, which reflects the crucial relationship between cinema and wider processes and structures of development and change.[26]

But since the most recent of these studies was published more than twenty-five years ago, the decade felt more than ripe for major scholarly revaluation, particularly because the decades adjacent to the 1960s had received extensive revisionist work in recent years. The early 2000s saw the publication of three books on the 1950s by Christine Geraghty, Ian MacKillop and Neil Sinyard, and Sue Harper and Vincent Porter. [27] Even more books have been published on British cinema of the 1970s, including works by Robert Shail, Paul Newland, Sue Harper and Justin Smith, and Sian Barber, with Leon Hunt and Laurel Forster and Sue Harper also contributing volumes on British popular culture including but not exclusively focusing on films.[28] It therefore made sense to return to what had come in between these two newly reappraised decades, with the benefit of being able to consult and analyse previously unavailable archival resources.

This book is the primary output from a three-year research project, funded by the UK Arts and Humanities Research Council, designed to offer new insights into British cinema of the 1960s (the four co-authors comprise its research team).[29] The project uses the twin concepts of transformation and tradition as a means of navigating some of the complexities and contradictions of British film culture during this decade. Its primary focus is on film production (although it is attentive to the inextricably interlinked realms of film distribution and exhibition, and elements of critical and audience reception too), and it is mainly concerned with mainstream commercial feature films, while acknowledging the lively interaction and creative cross-pollination between diverse areas of film production.[30] Developments in non-fiction and documentary film-making during the decade have been explored by scholars such as Patrick Russell and James Taylor, while its flourishing experimental and avant-garde sectors, whose innovations were frequently co-opted by more commercially minded practitioners, have been chronicled by Margaret Dickinson and Al Rees.[31] It is our contention that mainstream commercial cinema provides the most fruitful territory for exploring an industry in transition, where the crucial tension between transformation and tradition, novelty and continuity, presents itself most readily.

Our study firstly explores the organisation and functioning of an industry in transition. It examines some of the key players operating at its centre and on its margins, including the role of the major British and American distributors who provided the main source of film finance and therefore exercised a great deal of influence over the kind of films that were produced and exhibited in Britain during the period. Of particular interest here is how the situation changed and developed, with the involvement of the Hollywood majors in British cinema intensifying as the decade progressed. This also impacted on state support for indigenous production, as conveyed by the declining significance of the National Film Finance Corporation during the same period. While many smaller companies were forced to close, some independents adapted and were able to take advance of the new climate and examples of these will be profiled in case studies.

Secondly, we examine the development of different creative professional areas in British film production over the course of the decade, tracking the impact of the cultural changes abounding in the 1960s, as well as the more specific shifts within the British film industry, on various individuals' careers. Our primary focus here is on those professional areas responsible for the changing look of sixties films: production design, costume design, cinematography and editing, as well as the bedrock authorial roles of screenwriter and director (the changing sound of sixties films is dealt with in relation to the interaction between pop music and film). Most workers had to accommodate themselves to working on a freelance basis rather than on the studio contracts that previously predominated, but some flourished within the bigger budget, more spectacular milieu of sixties cinema, and relished its opportunities for experimentation and extravagance.

Thirdly, the book considers British cinema's relationship to developments in other cultural industries and forms in the 1960s, as films drew upon and participated in a more widespread atmosphere of creativity revitalising British theatre, fashion and advertising as well as fuelling newer culture forms such as television and pop music. Our focus here is on the especially vibrant cultural domains of advertising, television and pop music, each of which enjoyed a new significance in the sixties, influencing what was going on in film at the time, supplying personnel and ideas, while they in turn drew on the activities of a newly resurgent film industry. This upsurge in creativity reached far beyond the domestic scene to exert an international influence, exemplified by a phenomenon like the 'British invasion', the groups who gained massive popularity in the US and worldwide in the 1960s with their exciting new music, spearheaded by the Beatles. The new pre-eminence of all things British reached its apotheosis in April 1966 with the famous cover of *Time* magazine on which London was proclaimed 'the swinging city'. As journalist Peter Evans would neatly put it: '*Time* magazine set it on the trapeze and wrote the playbill: Swinging London'.[32] And even though this phenomenon was, according to an insider like Evans, 'at heart a beautiful myth; the molten fraud of commerce, and copywriters', it is nonetheless true that at this time London did exert a magnetic pull on creative people, facilitating unprecedented levels of social mixing and professional networking .³³ Myth it may have been, but it had real-world consequences for the British film industry, as Hollywood studios and international film-makers were drawn towards the UK as a new global hub for production, and the economic patterns of film financing underwent dramatic changes which were to have long-term impacts on the development of British cinema for years to come.

In line with 'new film history' approaches prioritising archival research, we make use of a range of previously unavailable or under-explored archive resources in our work here.³⁴ These include the British Film Institute Special Collections held by the National Film and Television Archive, the collections of Bill Douglas Cinema Museum at the University of Exeter, the National Archives, relevant files from the archives of the completion guarantee company Film Finances, the BBFC, the History of Advertising Trust's archives, interviews with industry practitioners for the BECTU oral history project, and other smaller archival collections, each of which provided fresh sources of knowledge and insight into the period. We have also surveyed a wide range of film-related publications from trade journals such as *Kine Weekly* and *The Daily Cinema*, to trade union publications such as *Film and Television Technician* and *The Screenwriter*, industry discussion forums such as the *Journal for the Society of Film and Television Arts,* and film magazines ranging from the more highbrow *Sight and Sound, Movie,* and *Films and Filming*, to the mass-market orientated *Photoplay, ABC Film Review* and *Showtime*, as well as wider press and media coverage of British cinema at the time and various autobiographical accounts, all of which has helped us to build as comprehensive a picture as possible of the period's rich and complex film culture.

Our project also generated a detailed database of British film production in the 1960s, enabling us to track fluctuations and developments in individual careers, in studio provenance, and in genre across the decade and to make some interesting and original observations about its dominant trends and most prolific personnel.

CONTEXT: ANATOMY OF AN INDUSTRY IN TRANSITION

The organisation and functioning of the British film industry during the 1960s is characterised by both continuity and change. The basic framework of the industry remained largely unchanged from the previous decade, with inter-related production, distribution and exhibition sectors comprising mainly a few large vertically integrated companies alongside an array of smaller independent entities. Dominating the landscape were two long-established conglomerates, the Rank Organisation and the Associated British Picture Corporation, whose roots stretched back to the late 1920s.³⁵ Collectively, 'the duopoly' owned Britain's two national cinema circuits, controlled two of the four largest UK distributors (and had a 50 per cent stake in a third) and operated large modern studios at Pinewood and Elstree respectively.[36] The 'third force' in the industry was British Lion, another company with a long history which had become a major player in the 1940s under the leadership of Alexander Korda, operating as a distributor/producer with a large production base at Shepperton studios, but found itself increasingly beleaguered in the 1960s despite numerous prominent individual successes. The fourth substantial British distribution company, Anglo-Amalgamated, was established in 1945 and built its business handling second features including American imports before expanding into low-budget production at the small Merton Park studios in Wimbledon. In 1962 ABPC acquired half of Anglo, effectively bringing the company into the major's fold.

The other large modern studio complex in Britain was the MGM facility at Borehamwood which the Hollywood company had acquired in 1944 from Rank and subsequently rebuilt and expanded. This was just one element of a substantial American presence in the British film industry dating back to the 1910s when several US companies set up UK subsidiaries to distribute their product.[37] By the 1960s six of the Hollywood majors – 20th Century Fox, Columbia, MGM, Paramount, United Artists and Walt Disney – operated their own UK distribution subsidiaries, which also facilitated 'runaway' productions: American-financed films qualifying as British. The enduring popularity of Hollywood movies with British audiences also ensured that the duopoly maintained close relations with the American majors. ABPC had a corporate connection with Warner Brothers, who had acquired 25 per cent of the British corporation in 1940 and was co-owner of Warner Pathé Distributors, established in 1960 to release both companies' films in the UK market. Rank had a similar relationship with Universal dating back to 1936 when the General Cinema Finance Corporation bought a quarter stake in the then ailing Hollywood studio.[38] These connections ensured Warner and Universal product had automatic access to one of the UK's two major cinema circuits. But the other Hollywood majors enjoyed alliances nearly as close, with the ABC chain also handling Paramount and MGM's films, while 20th Century Fox, Columbia, United Artists and Walt Disney had a parallel arrangement with the Rank circuit.

The major issue facing the British film industry during the 1960s was the continuing decline in cinema attendances, which had begun as early as the late 1940s but had hastened precipitously by the later 1950s. Many regarded this as a direct consequence of the rise of television and conceived of various strategies to combat it. However, other commentators have argued that the focus on television obscures the significance of the impact of other changes in post-war leisure patterns, the growth of home ownership and a greater emphasis on domesticity, at least among slightly older demographics.[39] Whatever the reasons, UK cinema admissions were to shrink from 501 million in 1960 to 193 million in 1970, with a corresponding reduction in the number of cinemas from 3,034 to 1,529 over the same period. Total box-office revenue remained more stable however, falling from £63,641,000 to £59,041,000, sustained by higher admission prices and more 'premium ticket' and 'roadshow' presentations of big budget 'epics'.[40] The contraction of the market impacted particularly hard on the smaller and less powerful entities within the industry, including a number of minor cinema chains which often had a strong regional base or concentration. The most significant of these included Solomon Sheckman's Essoldo circuit, which had spread out nationally from the northeast of England; Star Cinemas, the bulk of whose halls were across the north of England; the linked Scottish chains Caledonian and A. B. King; and two circuits located primarily in the Home Counties: Shipman & King and Granada. This meant that more than 50 per cent of cinemas in Britain comprised even smaller local micro-chains and single halls and it was this exhibition sector that was hardest hit by the decline in admissions. And while the abolition of entertainment tax in 1960 was estimated to be worth an additional £7 million to the industry, this proved too little, too late, for many.[41]

However, the picture of overall decline is complicated by the emergence of a number of new companies, notably the Classic Cinema chain, founded in 1961 and subsequently expanded through the acquisition of forty-seven cinemas from Rank in 1968, and Jacey chain which had started out in the Midlands.[42] Alternative kinds of exhibition were also being pioneered in the 1960s, particularly in the specialist or arthouse sector. In 1967 the British Film Institute began rolling out the first phase of a new chain of Regional Film Theatres, based on the model of the National Film Theatre, which within four years had expanded to thirty-six sites.[43] The changing market led many of the surviving exhibitors to begin subdividing their larger cinemas into two or more smaller screens. The first of these was the Odeon Nottingham which had been 'twinned' as early as 1964, followed in 1968 by Rank cinemas in Leeds, Liverpool and Sheffield. ABC followed in 1969 when their Edinburgh theatre was divided into three auditoria.[44]

In terms of distribution, beyond the UK and US majors noted above, and companies with close connections to the dominant players, there were other smaller-scale operators, with around half of the seventy or so companies handling British product in the home market at some point during the 1960s being associated with just one film. Smaller distributors included the group of satellites clustered around British Lion in the early 1960s, the most significant being Bryanston Films, and Elstree Films, set up in 1962 by the Grade Organisation and ABPC, as well as the Children's Film Foundation, specialising in product for under-sixteens and tied to Rank.[45] Several mid-size distributors specialised in low-budget genre cinema, the most significant being Butcher's (low-budget crime films), Planet (crime and horror), Grand National (crime), Compton (sex and exploitation films), Gala (arthouse) and Regal (various), while smaller specialist operators included Miracle, Orb and Richard Schulman Entertainments (who all distributed sex films), and Moral Rearmament and Worldwide (religious films). But the distribution sector was particularly volatile during the decade, with only the UK and American majors, plus a handful of others, operating continually throughout. Around a dozen operators were extinct or dormant by the mid-1960s, among them the eight British Lion satellites, Elstree Films, Butcher's and Regal, while significant newcomers during the latter part of the decade included Tigon, which largely specialised in horror, and the American company Avco–Embassy.

Inter-relations between the different industrial sectors of production, distribution and exhibition render it impossible to consider the fortunes of one in isolation. The most common method of film financing during the 1960s was the provision of distribution guarantees against which producers could borrow money from a bank, an arrangement that made distributors the key driver of British film production. While some companies, primarily the American majors, were prepared to provide 100 per cent financing, otherwise distributors guaranteed 70 per cent of budgets, leaving the producer to raise the remaining 30 per cent from other sources including overseas distributors, loans from the National Film Finance Corporation (NFFC), private investors or through the deferral of fees to themselves and other key individuals involved in the film including the director and the leading actors.

Film production was therefore almost entirely the domain of independent companies by the 1960s, as studio systems on both sides of the Atlantic began to operate more as conduits for independent product than wholesale creators of their slate of films. While the major British distribution companies maintained some 'in-house' activity – most notably the teams of Frank Launder and Sidney Gilliat and the Boulting brothers at British Lion – this still tended to entail multi-picture deals with independent contractors. A good example is provided by Peter Rogers, one of the decade's most prolific producers, whose slate of low-budget comedies for Anglo-Amalgamated including several entries in the successful *Carry On* series. When Anglo boss Nat Cohen terminated the contract in 1966, Rogers and his famous brand simply moved their business to Rank where they remained for the next twelve years. Other successful independents developed close associations with key distributors. Tony Richardson and John Osborne's company Woodfall Films made four features for Bryanston before beginning a long relationship with the Hollywood studio United Artists; Joseph Janni's Vic Films enjoyed a fruitful partnership with Anglo-Amalgamated for most of the decade; while Albert 'Cubby' Broccoli and Harry Saltzman's Eon Films made the successful James Bond films with backing from United Artists.

Most independent producers rented facilities at the four major studios or smaller alternatives such as Twickenham, Beaconsfield and Ardmore in Ireland. But some production companies owned their own studio facilities, necessitating significant levels of ongoing activity that was easier to maintain on modest budgets. The most important of these was Hammer Films which, under the leadership of James Carreras, produced around six features a year from their base at Bray, a combination of the company's trademark horror and fantasy films alongside action adventures and psychological thrillers. Carreras secured finance from a range of sources, including several of the Hollywood majors. The company's growing ambitions, underpinned by a deal involving Seven Arts, 20th Century Fox and Warner Pathé distributors, led Hammer to move production to the larger and more modern facilities at Elstree in 1966, and in 1968 their success was recognised with a Queen's Award to Industry for services to British exports. Elsewhere, Julian Wintle and Leslie Parkyn's production company Independent Artists acquired Beaconsfield studios in 1958 from Sydney Box where they then specialised in a range of low-budget first and second features for Rank, Anglo-Amalgamated and British Lion–Bryanston. Meanwhile the American brothers Edward and Harry Danziger concentrated firmly on second-feature production at their New Elstree base from 1956, making films which were subsequently released through British Lion, Warner Pathé and several of the Hollywood majors, alongside their parallel production of television series such as *The Cheaters* (ABC, 1960–2) and *Richard the Lionheart* (ITV, 1962–3).

Creative agency is a crucial factor in understanding the achievements of British cinema in the 1960s, particularly given the broader association of the decade with individualism and the flourishing of a new entrepreneurial spirit.[46] At the forefront of this is the producer, until recently a rather neglected figure in British cinema history. As Vincent Porter argues, 'film production is, and always has been, an industrial activity, not simply a canvas for individual artists' and it is vital that the 'role of the producer in promoting and sustaining the collective endeavour of film production' should be recognised.[47] The term 'producer' is also notoriously slippery and can be applied to very different kinds of roles including the executives of major production and distribution companies. Thus, Anglo-Amalgamated boss Nat Cohen, Hammer Films' James Carreras and the Compton management team of Michael Klinger and Tony Tenser were all among the most enterprising producers of the decade.[48]

But if we confine the title of producer to the independent operators directly responsible for developing projects, assembling their creative teams, securing finance and overseeing the actual production process, then a different set of names emerge. These include the aforementioned Tony Richardson and John Osborne, Joseph Janni, Cubby Broccoli and Harry Saltzman, Peter Rogers, and the film-making teams the Boulting brothers and Frank Launder and Sidney Gilliatt, alongside Kenneth Harper and Walter Shenson (responsible respectively for the films featuring music stars Cliff Richard and the Beatles), Michael Relph and Basil Dearden, John and James Woolf, Betty Box, Hugh Stewart, Ivan Foxwell, George H. Brown, and esteemed Americans such as Sam Spiegel, Carl Foreman, Charles Schneer, Hal B. Wallis and director/ producers Stanley Kubrick and Stanley Donen. Despite the high-profile work undertaken by many of the above, in fact the most prolific figures tended to be low-budget and 'B' movie producers, among them Jack Greenwood who made almost fifty second features for Anglo-Amalgamated at Merton Park, Hammer film regulars Anthony Nelson Keys, Michael Carreras and Anthony Hinds, the Danziger brothers, Julian Wintle and Leslie Parkyn, Jack Parsons and Harry Allan Towers. The latter specialised in an early form of transnational production by exploiting local opportunities in various parts of the world including South Africa, Ireland and Hong Kong and collaborating with a variety of co-producing partners.[49] One other crucial team was Max Rosenberg and Milton Subotsky's Amicus productions which started in the field of teen musicals before going on to become one of Hammer's main rivals across the horror/ fantasy genres.

The break-up of the old studio system and the proliferation of independent production created new opportunities for ambitious and entrepreneurial individuals to operate in flexible and versatile ways. As in the United States, independence afforded successful actors greater power within the system, and there are examples of individuals setting up production companies to develop, produce and sometimes direct their own projects. The decade began with the formation of a number of independent co-operatives, among them Allied Film Makers which saw actors Bryan Forbes, Richard Attenborough and Jack Hawkins join forces with Basil Dearden, Michael Relph and Guy Green.[50] Actor Stanley Baker produced *Zulu* (1964) and *Sands of the Kalahari* (1965) – both of which he also starred in – with director Cy Endfield before forming Oakhurst Productions with Woodfall alumnus Michael Deeley. This company went on to make several films including *Robbery* (1967), *Where's Jack?* (1969) and *The Italian Job* (1969).[51] Following his success as the star of *Tom Jones*, Albert Finney co-produced *Night Must Fall* (1964) before setting up Memorial Enterprises with Michael Medwin in 1965.[52] The company's subsequent productions included the feature films *Charlie Bubbles* (1967), directed by and starring Finney; Peter Watkins' *Privilege* (1967), Lindsay Anderson's *If . . . .* (1968) and the Bill Naughton adaptation *Spring and Port Wine* (1970), in addition to the BFI funded short features *The Burning* and *Loving Memory*. David Hemmings formed the Hemdale Company in 1967 with John Daly primarily as a way of helping actors avoid high taxes through investments in production. The company became a major independent force in the 1970s and 1980s, although Hemmings left in 1971 to pursue other acting, directing and producing opportunities.

In terms of distinct cycles or genres of film, our analysis indicates that crime and comedy were the most prevalent categories, accounting for almost half of the total number of features made in Britain during the 1960s. However, as a mainstay of 'B' movie production, crime films become markedly less prevalent in the second half of the decade. Drama (a rather broad category) accounts for a further eighth of total production, with fantasy/horror accounting for a similar proportion. Thus almost three quarters of films fall into these four broad generic categories – with musicals (including many featuring pop music and starring musicians in leading roles) and war films the next most significant.[53] In his book, Robert Murphy dedicates chapters to each of these, alongside 'social problem' films and those associated with 'swinging London', while youth films and pop musicals are covered too.[54] This suggests how beyond the familiar generic categories, identifiable cycles of films – sometimes constituting a sub-genre, whose prevalence or popularity was often short-lived and stimulated by wider cultural trends – provide another useful way of differentiating British films during the decade. In addition to the 'kitchen sink'/New Wave cycle, the 'social problem' film, 'pop musicals' and 'swinging London' films, the raft of spy films that followed in the wake of James Bond, fanned by Cold War politics, were also of particular significance.

Sectoral interests and relations were mediated through a small number of key industry bodies. The Cinema Exhibitors Association (CEA) represented the interest of the exhibition sector, while the British Film Producers Association (BFPA) and the Federation of British Film Makers (FBFM) did likewise for those involved in production and to a certain extent, distribution. The Society of Film and Television Arts, the successor to the British Film Academy and forerunner of the present-day BAFTA, promoted cinema's artistic and cultural value and held annual awards recognising practitioners' achievements. Artists and workers were represented by a number of guilds and unions, most notably the Association of Cinema and Television Technicians (ACTT), the National Association of Theatrical and Kine Employees (NATKE), the actors' union, Equity, the Writers' Guild and the Musicians' Union. These organisations also worked together through the Federation of Film Unions (FFU). The unions were a powerful force during the 1960s, membership was largely mandatory and collective agreements were enforced across a wide range of areas including crewing, pay and working conditions.[55]

While ostensibly dictated by the laws of the market and free enterprise, the British film industry was also subject to certain government policy initiatives aimed primarily at protecting local production, reflecting long-standing concerns that the popularity of Hollywood product would otherwise make British film-making unviable. In 1966 Terence Kelly, Graham Norton and George Perry identified a range of factors signifying the importance of the cinema to the nation.[56] Interestingly, only the first of these was industrial and related to the economic value of the industry's earnings and the number of people employed in the sector. The others were either social or cultural: cinema as an amenity and popular entertainment, or cinema's role in communicating national values and ideas, its wider artistic and educational value. This sense of public good had motivated film policy since the 1927 Cinematographic Act when a quota of British films was established for both exhibitors and distributors. By the 1960s this only applied to the former who had to ensure a minimum of 30 per cent of the features they booked were British.

Two other initiatives had both been introduced as responses to the immanent collapse of indigenous film production in the aftermath of World War Two and continued to operate into the 1960s. The National Film Finance Corporation was effectively a specialised bank, established in 1949 with a revolving fund of £6 million to provide loans to producers. The British Film Production Fund was generated via a levy on cinema tickets and subsequently paid out to producers as a proportion of their box-office receipts. Initiated in 1950 as a voluntary measure, the Eady Levy (named after Treasury official Sir Wilfred Eady) became mandatory in 1958 and payments were worth on average an additional 44.3 per cent on top of a film's box-office earnings. This additional income also directly benefitted the NFFC by boosting the chances that films they had invested in were able to turn a profit and thus pay back the loans received from the Corporation.

A further element of state support came in the form of the BFI's production activities.[57] These had begun in 1952 under the auspices of the Experimental Film Fund which during its first decade provided a space for new talent to make films on modest grants, with around fifty short productions supported at a total expenditure of just £30,000.[58] While many of the films produced were documentaries on art, the most significant development was the Fund's support for several Free Cinema documentaries which helped initiate the film careers of Tony Richardson, Lindsay Anderson and Karel Reisz, all key figures in the British cinema of the 1960s. However, by 1963 the Experimental Film Fund's resources had run out and for three years it remained quasi-dormant. It was subsequently revived in 1966 when the BFI received a substantial increase in its grant-in-aid from Jennie Lee, the UK's first minister for the arts who had been appointed by Labour prime minister Harold Wilson. The resurrected Experimental Film Fund was renamed the BFI Production Board, with annual recurring funding of around £12,000 and a full-time production officer, the Australian film-maker Bruce Beresford. The Board continued to be chaired by Michael Balcon and included several major industry figures, among them the producers Lord (John) Brabourne, Carl Foreman and Anthony Havelock Allen, the directors Bryan Forbes and Karel Reisz and the documentarians Edgar Anstey, Jill Craigie, Arthur Elton and Basil Wright.[59] While its resources were still tiny compared with the funds available for mainstream film-making,

Beresford was able to support almost seventy films over a five-year period. This included works by emerging talents like Ridley Scott with *Boy and Bicycle* (1965), Stephen Frears with *The Burning* (1968), and Tony Scott with *One of the Missing* (1968) and *Loving Memory* (1970); although all these films received only limited exhibition. But one of the Board's notable achievements during this period was Don Levy's *Herostratus,* the first full-length experimental feature supported by the BFI Production Board. Made on a budget of less than £10,000 – with funding partners including the BBC and the film's producer, former BFI director James Quinn – it took three years to make and was finally released in May 1968, opening the new cinema at London's Institute of Contemporary Arts.

While overall audience numbers were falling in the 1960s, the most frequent and consistent cinemagoers tended to be young people. If we consider the ratings that films were given by the British Board of Film Censors, the most notable developments are a declining share of U (or Universal) -rated films from around 50 per cent at the beginning of the decade to 30 per cent by the end and a corresponding increase in X-rated films (restricted to audiences aged 16 and over) from 15 per cent to 40 per cent. The A-certificate category (indicating material more suitable for adults, but to which children might be admitted if accompanied by an adult) remained more stable at around 30–35 per cent. This shift is not only a reflection of the liberalisation of censorship (exemplified by John Trevelyan's tenure at the BBFC) and the franker portrayals of sex and violence across a range of media in a period of greater permissiveness, but it is also a symptom of the industry's attempt to differentiate itself from the limitations placed on what could be broadcast on television and to increase cinema's appeal to the demographic which had become its most loyal and committed audience.[60]

In the effort to retain audiences by boosting production values and reinvesting cinema with a sense of spectacle and excitement, the decade saw the decisive eclipse of black and white by colour production (now made more affordable by new colour stock such as Eastmancolor): while black and white was still being used on three out of four British feature productions during the first four years of the decade, by 1966 the proportions had been reversed. By the end of the decade black and white had practically disappeared for all but the occasional arthouse film like *Ulysses* (1967), *The Sailor from Gibraltar* (1967) and *Inadmissible Evidence* (1968), the latter two made by Woodfall. The budgets of British productions also rose significantly during the decade. Leading the way were the James Bond films, produced by Cubby Broccoli and Harry Saltzman. The first film in the series, *Dr No* (1962) cost around £390,000 (or $1.1 million), *From Russia With Love* (1963) was more in the region of £700,000 and *Goldfinger* (1964) over £1 million. By this point the profitability of the series allowed the cost of *Thunderball* (1965) to triple to £3.2 million,

Table I.1 British Board of Film Censors classifications by year for British films

Rating	1960	1961	1962	1963	1964	1965	1966	1967	1968	1969
U	67 (51%)	56 (50%)	61 (50%)	46 (41%)	29 (35%)	32 (39%)	24 (30%)	23 (28%)	26 (28%)	26 (32.5%)
A	44 (33%)	40 (35%)	46 (38%)	44 (39%)	30 (37%)	30 (37%)	28 (34.5%)	29 (35%)	29 (31%)	23 (29%)
X	21 (16%)	17 (15%)	15 (12%)	22 (20%)	23 (28%)	20 (24%)	29 (35.5%)	31 (37%)	39 (41%)	31 (38.5%)

followed by £3.4 million for *You Only Live Twice* (1967), which remained the most expensive Bond production until *The Spy Who Loved Me* (1977).[61] Less spectacular but just as indicative of the overall trend is the gradual rise in the budgets for the *Carry On* films. The first film, *Carry On Sergeant* (1958) cost £78,000, while *Carry On Regardless* (1961), the fifth instalment, came in at around £100,000. Thereafter, budgets continued to increase, reaching a peak of £288,000 with *Carry On Follow That Camel* (1967).

This pattern is repeated elsewhere, with Woodfall's New Wave hit *Saturday Night and Sunday Morning* (1960) costing £116,885, provided by Bryanston and the NFFC, while their period extravaganza, *Tom Jones* (1963) was financed by United Artists at a cost of £410,000, evoking the impact of Hollywood financing on British production and the opportunities it offered to ambitious producers. Similarly, the three films made by John Schlesinger and Joseph Janni for Anglo-Amalgamated – *A Kind of Loving* (1962), *Billy Liar* (1963) and *Darling* (1965) – cost £148,000, £209,600 and £331,000 respectively: a combination of increasing creative ambitions and general inflation. Also notable is the difference between the £141,725 provided by Elstree Films and the NFFC for Joseph Losey's *The Servant* (1963) and the £299,772 cost of his subsequent film *Accident* (1967), shared by London Independent Distributors and the NFFC. Meanwhile, Losey's *Boom!* (1968) cost Universal more than £1.5 million, although half of this was the fee for its stars Richard Burton and Elizabeth Taylor. But despite the general inflationary trend, budgets did not need to be high, as examples such as *Morgan ... A Suitable Case for Treatment* (1966) and *Poor Cow* (1967) show, budgeted at £164,913 and £242,607 respectively. And by the end of the decade the *Carry On* films were also economising, with *Carry On Camping* (1969) costing £208,000.

At the same time 'British' films were being increasingly made for an international market. As Sarah Street points out, British imports accounted for an average of 20 per cent of the total number of foreign films shown at American cinemas during the decade, and fourteen British films also earned more than $10 million at the US box office, conspicuous among them the United Artists-backed James Bond productions *Thunderball* (the most commercially successful British film of the decade), *Goldfinger* and *You Only Live Twice*.[62] While British films had tended to be marketed in America as specialist or arthouse product by distribution companies like Embassy and Continental, the increased involvement by the Hollywood majors in financing British films – as opposed to buying distribution rights for the Western Hemisphere – helped to create a much stronger connection between commercial exploitation and critical success.

KEY ISSUES AND CHALLENGES

For all its apparent dynamism and buoyancy, this was also a period in which the British film industry faced some major challenges and crises. For a long time, concern had been expressed – notably and most consistently by the Federation of British Film Makers, the unions and certain sections of the press – at the increasing concentration of power in the hands of a very small number of companies. The reduction in the number of cinemas caused by the declining audience numbers served to increase the dominance of the duopoly in exhibition. While Rank and ABC had controlled just over 20 per cent of all cinemas in 1952, by 1965 this had risen to 29 per cent; as the majors tended to own the larger and more modern halls, their combined share of cinema seats had almost doubled from 23 per cent to 43.5 per cent during the same period.[63]

Dwindling attendances had led to the distinct Odeon and Gaumont circuits being combined in 1958 as the Rank Release. But subsequent efforts to establish a new National Circuit or 'third release', comprising independents and some minor chains, proved a failure. A key factor was financial viability, in that while an average release on the Rank and ABPC circuits could expect to earn between £85,000–95,000 and £75,000–85,000 respectively, the corresponding forecast for the third release was only £35,000–40,000.[64] Thus producers and distributors sought to get their films into the major circuits, leaving the third release with the leftovers and rejects, which further weakened the business of independent exhibitors, resulting in more cinema closures.

From their relatively secure exhibition base, Rank and ABPC controlled the flow of product in the industry, with their own distribution subsidiaries enjoying guaranteed access to the national cinema chains. This left British Lion, who had no standing arrangements with either chain and was forced to compete alongside all the other distributors for a circuit release, at a significant disadvantage. British Lion had also been forced into public ownership in 1955 following a disastrous period during which £3 million loaned from the NFFC had been irretrievably lost. The duopoly further consolidated their dominance of exhibition through the operation of various restrictive practices, including exercising first refusal on all product and the operation of a block booking and barring system that allowed them to control the wider release of individual films, including any access granted to independent exhibitors. This gave the Rank and ABPC executives in charge of booking films for their respective cinemas considerable power as 'gatekeepers' within the industry.[65]

Independent producers were particularly concerned about their access to the domestic market as the major circuits appeared content to give preference to imported American product. In March 1961 the Federation of British Film Makers called for an increase in the quota from 30 per cent to 50 per cent for the two major circuits, claiming that the monopolistic trend in exhibition was harmful to both independent producers and distributors and against the public interest.[66] While strongly supported by the ACTT, this proposal was rejected by other key industry players. James Carreras of Hammer and Nat Cohen and Stuart Levy of Anglo-Amalgamated argued that such a move would antagonise foreign governments at a point when British producers were seeking to expand their business in overseas markets. They also suggested that a higher quota would lower the standard of British production and precipitate a return to the much-derided 'quota quickie'.[67] *Kine Weekly* was also critical of the FBFM demands, noting that the major circuits were achieving a level of 37 per cent for British product, comfortably in excess of the minimum statutory requirement.[68] This raises a key tension that was to pervade industry debates throughout the decade and beyond: on one hand, a commitment to state protection of the industry in the national interest, on the other, the encouragement of entrepreneurial activity within an acknowledgment of the increasingly international nature of film production and distribution.

Discontent with monopoly control rumbled on until a crisis point was reached in 1963. In September the FBFM identified an increasing problem of producers facing long delays in obtaining a circuit release for completed films. This had serious financial implications as it was estimated some £2.25 million of capital value was frozen in films waiting for a release. The bulk of the delayed films were backed by British Lion and their associated satellite distributors, but while *Kine Weekly* reported that as many as ten features were affected, British Lion's David Kingsley was only prepared to name two: Bryanston's *Ladies Who Do* and Garrick's *The Leather Boys*.[69] The crisis was also impacting on the volume of production activity and by November the ACTT reported that employment in all grades was at its lowest for many years, mainly due to cancellations or postponements of productions alongside the virtual closure of Beaconsfield and Twickenham studios and redundancy of almost one third of the workforce at Elstree.[70]

The FBFM and the ACTT blamed the situation on the restrictive booking practices of the two major circuits and reiterated their wish for an increase in the quota, although this was not supported by the British Film Producers Association whose membership included some of the more powerful players with close connections to the majors. The Federation of Film Unions also called for the creation of a new third circuit or release, equal in booking and revenue power to the duopoly, alongside a bolstering of support for independent producers through increased borrowing powers for the National Film Finance Corporation, and the retention of British Lion in public ownership.[71]

Unsurprisingly the duopoly took a different view, arguing that the problem was essentially one of overproduction in a contracting market. Kenneth Winckles, managing director of Rank's Theatre Division, declared: 'We have come to the end of an era. Many in the industry have been slow to appreciate it. I recognise that most producers are genuinely doing their best on modest budgets, but the market has changed: requirements have changed.'[72] He went on to argue that the public was largely indifferent to the origin of films, caring only for *entertainment* (apparently confirmed by the enduring dominance of Hollywood product on British cinema screens) and therefore all of the protectionist measures being called for, from the re-establishment of a third release to an increased quota, were unrealistic. Winckles' chairman, John Davis, even drew parallels with what was happening at the time to Britain's transport infrastructure: 'Dr Beeching did not want to close railway line, but the public had shown, by not using the lines, that they did not need the services which were offered, with the result that the lines had become uneconomic.'[73] *Kine Weekly* concurred, noting that with British first feature production running at around seventy films a year, and the circuits accepting forty of these, the 'industry has reached the state of over-production for the market as it exists today – unless the average quality is raised to meet all competition'.[74]

This question of quality became a significant issue and appeared to be supported by evidence. Firstly, films that were struggling to secure a release date were overwhelmingly in the low-budget category. Secondly, this sector of British production was already beginning to contract as producers of supporting features either bailed out or moved wholly into television. Thirdly, the number of American-financed British films was increasing; moreover, these tended to be made on higher budgets with correspondingly enhanced production values. While many independent productions continued to cost less than £150,000, John Davis argued that to stand any chance in the marketplace, the budget for an average British feature now had to be in the range of £250,000 to £400,000.[75] Interestingly, the London-based American producer Carl Foreman who specialised in larger films had argued at the beginning of 1963:

> The biggest problem facing the industry is not the shrinkage in cinemas, as painful as this may be for the exhibitors concerned, nor disagreements about the sale of ice cream and peanuts in cinemas, or even controversy about the division or application of the levy, nor TV, but the staggering, ever-increasing spiral of production costs.[76]

Whatever the diagnosis, the situation had profound implications for feature production. The 'B' movie was effectively killed off, with several smaller distributors being forced out of business.

Widespread concerns about the organisation and functioning of the industry finally led to Edward Heath, president of the Board of Trade, announcing in August 1964 that the supply of films to exhibitors would be investigated by the Monopolies Commission. The policy was reaffirmed by the new Labour government which came to office two months later. But this investigation would rumble on for more than two years and culminate in the publication of a report that Alexander Walker dubbed 'a masterpiece of doublethink,' one which appeared to acknowledge the existence of monopoly but failed to come up with any substantial response, calling instead for a voluntary implementation of key measures including flexible booking and the establishment of a trades dispute committee and an appeals tribunal. [77]

By this time, American finance had become the major force driving British film production, rising to a peak in 1968. This had created an intensified level of activity, despite the continuing decline in audiences, with more British films being made on higher budgets and enjoying access to the US market, something that had eluded many ambitious British producers in the past. But by 1969 the cracks were beginning to show as several of the Hollywood majors posted losses or substantially reduced profits. And as the decade drew to a close, the feared retrenchment had begun, plunging the British film industry into a new crisis. The Hollywood withdrawal marked the passing of the brief American fascination with all things British and the revitalisation of US youth culture in which Haight Ashbury became the centre of universe, not the Kings Road. As critic John Russell Taylor astutely observed: 'If *The Graduate* has taught Hollywood anything [. . .], is it not perhaps that they can make their own European-type, intelligent off-beat successes? And if so, what will they want to come to Europe for, now that we no longer have the monopoly in that sort of thing?'[78] Meanwhile British Lion, which was publicly listed in 1968, had substantially reduced their production activities. Rank followed suit as the balance of their overall business shifted increasingly towards non-film activities, notably the hugely profitable Rank Xerox photocopying division. In January 1969 the music company, EMI, acquired a controlling stake in ABPC and initiated a modest but ultimately unsuccessful new production programme at Elstree under the leadership of Bryan Forbes.

US investment had declined from its 1968 peak, but the bell weather for the irrevocable change taking place was MGM's cancellation of Fred Zinnemann's production *Man's Fate* in late 1969, just two days before shooting was due to begin.[79] An article from *The Economist*, 'Hollywood or bust', reprinted in the ACTT journal *Film and Television Technician* in December 1969 (who reported that 400 of its 4,500 members were now unemployed) baldly presented the depressing picture:

> The majors are in a really bad way. MGM has forecast a loss of $25 million for the year; Columbia's profits were down 40 per cent; Paramount, part of the conglomerate Gulf and Western, made a loss; Twentieth Century Fox has just declared a loss of $22 million for the first nine months of the year; Music Corporation of America, which is the Universal parent, made a loss of $7 million just for the third quarter of the year [. . .][80]

In the mid-1960s, Penelope Houston had expressed her fears about an 'occupied industry' in which '[e]verything is fine, in fact, unless and until the Americans move out.'[81] By the end of the decade, she would get an answer to her question, 'What would happen in creative, let alone business, terms if the Americans should decide to hand our production industry back to us?'[82] Thus a period that had seen the profile of British cinema achieve unprecedented levels of visibility and success, ended on a dying fall, and with the inauguration of yet another film industry crisis.

NOTES

1. Penelope Houston, *The Contemporary Cinema* (Harmondsworth: Penguin, 1963), p. 119. The previous year, critic Barrie Pattison had also talked about British films 'replac[ing] the quarter-deck with the bedroom and the village post office with the industrial street covered with real garbage'. Barrie Pattison, 'Taking in the garbage', *Films and Filming*, July 1962, p. 39.
2. Penelope Houston, 'Seventy', *Sight and Sound*, Winter 1969, p. 4.
3. Raymond Durgnat, 'Britannia waives the rules', *Film Comment*, July/August 1976, p. 51, p. 58.
4. Philip French, 'The Alphaville of Admass, or how we learned to stop worrying and love the boom', *Sight and Sound*, Summer 1966, p. 109.
5. Ibid.
6. Robert Murphy, *Sixties British Cinema* (London: BFI, 1992), p. 278.
7. Jeffrey Richards, 'New Waves and Old Myths: British Cinema in the 1960s' in Bart Moore-Gilbert and John Seed (eds), *Cultural Revolution: The Challenge of the Arts in the 1970s* (London: Routledge, 1992), p. 218.
8. See Peter Cowie, *Revolution! The explosion of world cinema in the 60s* (London: Faber, 2004).
9. Alexander Walker, *Hollywood, England: The British Film Industry in the Sixties* (London: Michael Joseph, 1974), p. 462.
10. Ibid. p. 464.
11. Terrence Kelly, Graham Norton and George Perry, *A Competitive Cinema* (London: Institute of Economic Affairs, 1966).
12. Monopolies and Mergers Commission, *A Report on the Supply of Films for Exhibition in Cinemas in the UK* (London: HMSO, 1966).
13. Arthur Marwick, *The Sixties* (Oxford: Oxford University Press, 1998). A similar focus on the 'swinging sixties' as a harbinger of progress and reinvigoration is offered by Brian Masters, *The Swinging 60s* (London: Constable, 1985) and Shawn Levy, *Swinging London and the Invention of Cool* (London: Fourth Estate, 2002).
14. Marwick, *The Sixties*, pp. 16–20. In addition, Marwick's conception of the 'Long Sixties', a period that runs from 1958 to 1974, subdivided into three sub periods: 1958–63 (the first stirrings of a cultural revolution), 1964–9 (the 'High Sixties') and 1969–74 (the follow through and catching up) has relevance to British film historiography. 1958 marked the first stirrings of what became the British New Wave, including the production of *Room at the Top* and the formation of Woodfall Films; 1963 saw the end of this phase and the beginning of a shift toward the idea of 'swinging London' anticipated by films like *Billy Liar* and *Tom Jones*; while a number of key films from the early 1970s, among them *The Go-Between* (1970), *A Clockwork Orange* (1971), *The Devils* (1971), *O Lucky Man!* (1973) and *Don't Look Now*

(1973) continued to extend and develop the thematic and aesthetic preoccupations of the previous era (as well as several being supported by American finance).
15. Bernard Levin, *The Pendulum Years: Britain and the Sixties* (London: Jonathan Cape: 1970), p. 9.
16. Christopher Booker, *The Neophiliacs: A Study of the Revolution in English Life in the Fifties and Sixties* (London: Pimlico, 1992), p. 303
17. Robert Hewison, *Too Much: Art and Society in the Sixties* (London: Methuen, 1986), p. 180.
18. George Melly, *Revolt into Style: The Pop Arts* (London: Faber, 1970, 2012).
19. Jeff Nuttall, *Bomb Culture* (London: Palladin, 1970), p. 7.
20. Dominic Sandbrook, *White Heat: A History of Britain in the Swinging Sixties* (London: Little, Brown, 2006), p. 794.
21. Andy Medhurst, *A National Joke: Popular Comedy and English Identities* (London: Routledge, 2007).
22. Dominic Sandbrook, *Never Had It So Good: A History of Britain from Suez to the Beatles* (London: Little, Brown, 2005), p. 729.
23. Mark Donnelly, *Sixties Britain* (Harlow: Pearson Education, 2005), p. xii.
24. The very useful categories of residual and emergent were first outlined by Raymond Williams in *Marxism and Literature* (Oxford: Oxford University Press, 1977).
25. Also important is the five-part documentary series *Hollywood UK* (BBC, 1993), presented by Richard Lester and featuring contributions from numerous actors, directors, writers, producers and other key individuals from the era.
26. John Hill, *Sex, Class and Realism: British Cinema 1956–1963* (London: BFI, 1986).
27. Christine Geraghty, *British Cinema in the Fifties: Gender, Genre and 'the New Look'* (London: Routledge, 2000). Ian McKillop and Neil Sinyard (eds), *British Cinema of the 1950s: A Celebration* (Manchester: Manchester University Press, 2003). Sue Harper and Vincent Porter, *British Cinema of the 1950s: The Decline of Deference* (Oxford: Oxford University Press, 2003).
28. Robert Shail (ed.), *Seventies British Cinema* (London: BFI/Palgrave Macmillan 2008); Paul Newland (ed.), *Don't Look Now: British Cinema in the 1970s* (Bristol: Intellect, 2010); Paul Newland, *British Films of the 1970s* (Manchester: Manchester University Press, 2013); Sue Harper and Justin Smith (eds), *British Film Culture in the 1970s* (Edinburgh: Edinburgh University Press, 2012); Sian Barber, *The British Cinema in the 1970s: Capital, Culture and Creativity* (Basingstoke: Palgrave Macmillan, 2013); Leon Hunt, *British Low Culture: From Safari Suits to Sexploitation* (Abingdon: Routledge, 1998); Laurel Foster and Sue Harper (eds), *British Culture and Society in the 1970s: The Lost Decade* (Newcastle: Cambridge Scholars Press, 2010).
29. The project's website, including its blog and the database of films compiled by Laura Mayne, is entitled *Transformation and Tradition in Sixties British Cinema*, <https://60sbritishcinema.wordpress.com/>. Several other publications have also derived from work during the project (a full list is provided on the website), and three symposia and a summative conference at BFI Southbank were also held between 2015 and 2017.
30. Another AHRC-funded project has explored film audience memories in the 1960s: 'Remembering 1960s British Cinema-going', <https://www.ucl.ac.uk/cinemamemories> (accessed 17 August 2018).
31. Patrick Russell, *100 British Documentaries* (London: BFI/Palgrave, 2007), Patrick Russell and James Taylor (eds), *Shadows of Progress: Documentary Film in Post War Britain* (London: BFI/Palgrave, 2010). Margaret Dickinson (ed.), *Rogue Reels: Oppositional Film Making in Britain 1945–90* (London: BFI, 1999). Al Rees,

A History of Experimental Film and Video (London: BFI/Palgrave Macmillan, 2011). Nor is British animation a primary focal area, despite its wider importance in the media culture of the period, not least through the work of animators such as Richard Williams and Bob Godfrey.
32. David Bailey and Peter Evans, *Goodbye Baby & Amen: A Saraband for the Sixties* (New York: Coward–McCann, 1969), p. 5.
33. Ibid. p. 10.
34. James Chapman, Mark Glancy and Sue Harper (eds), *The New Film History: Sources, Methods, Approaches* (Basingstoke: Palgrave Macmillan, 2007).
35. Associated British was founded as British International Pictures in 1927 by John Maxwell. While Rank entered the industry in the 1930s, he subsequently acquired the Gaumont British Picture Corporation in 1941 which had been built by Isidore Ostrer through the amalgamation of interests in production, distribution and exhibition during the 1920s.
36. While three new sound stages were opened at Elstree in 1966, Bryan Forbes reports in his autobiography that when he took over as head of production at ABPC in 1969 he found the facilities to be in a rather neglected state, noting, 'Nearly every building on the lot was in dire need of renovation.' *A Divided Life* (London: Mandarin, 1993), p. 65.
37. Thomas Guback, 'Hollywood's International Market', in Tino Balio (ed.), *The American Film Industry*, revised edition (Madison: University of Wisconsin Press, 1985).
38. Geoffrey Macnab, *J. Arthur Rank and the British Film Industry* (London: Routledge, 1993).
39. David Docherty, David Morrison and Michael Tracey, *The Last Picture Show: Britain's Changing Film Audience* (London: BFI, 1987).
40. Linda Wood, *British Film Industry: Information Guide, No. 1* (London: BFI, 1980), p. 2.
41. *The Daily Cinema*, 6 April 1960.
42. On the latter, see Adrian Smith, 'As long as indifferent sexy films are box office they will abound!!: The Jacey cinema chain and independent distribution and exhibition in 1960s Britain', in I. Q. Hunter, Laraine Porter, and Justin Smith (eds), *The Routledge Companion to British Cinema History* (London: Routledge, 2017), pp. 209–19.
43. Melanie Selfe, 'The View from Outside London' in Geoffrey Nowell-Smith and Christoph Dupin (eds), *The British Film Institute, the Government and Film Culture, 1933–2000* (Manchester: Manchester University Press, 2012).
44. Stuart Hanson, *From Silent Screen to Multi Screen: A History of Cinema Exhibition in Britain since 1896* (Manchester: Manchester University Press, 2007), p. 121.
45. R. Agajanian, '"Just for Kids?" Saturday Morning Cinema and Britain's Children's Film Foundation in the 1960s', *Historical Journal of Film, Radio and Television*, 18: 3, 1998.
46. See Arthur Marwick, *The Sixties* and Anthony Sampson, *Anatomy of Britain* (London: Hodder & Stoughton, 1965).
47. Vincent Porter, 'Making and Meaning: The Role of the Producer in British Films', *Journal of British Cinema and Television*, 9: 1, 2012, p. 23.
48. Andrew Spicer and A. T. McKenna, *The Man Who Got Carter: Michael Klinger, Independent Production and the British Film Industry, 1960–1980* (London: I. B. Tauris, 2013); John Hamilton, *Beasts in the Cellar: The Exploitation Film Career of Tony Tenser* (London: FAB Press, 2005).
49. Dave Mann, *Harry Alan Towers: The Transnational Career of a Cinematic Contrarian* (Jefferson, NC: McFarland & Co., 2014).

50. Sally Dux, 'Allied Film Makers: Crime, Comedy and Social Concern', *Journal of British Cinema and Television*, 9: 2, 2012.
51. Baker and Deeley, along with Barry Spikings subsequently took over British Lion and Shepperton Studios in 1973.
52. Reported in *Kine Weekly*, 3 June 1965.
53. Dennis Gifford, *The British Film Catalogue*, 3rd edition (London: Routledge, 2000).
54. The first three of Murphy's genres: 'social problem', 'swinging London' and youth-oriented films can all be accommodated under the broader category of drama. Our own project database indicates a mini boom in such musicals in 1965 when ten films were released, the majority cashing in on the vogue for pop musicians appearing in films following the success of *A Hard Day's Night* (1964) featuring the Beatles.
55. Ian Reid, 'Trade Unions and the British Film Industry: 1930s–1980s, in I. Q. Hunter, Larraine Porter and Justin Smith (eds), *The Routledge Companion to British Cinema History* (London: Routledge, 2017).
56. Terence Kelly et al., *A Competitive Cinema*.
57. Christoph Dupin, 'The BFI and Film Production: Half a Century of Innovative Independent Film-Making' in Geoffrey Nowell-Smith and C. Dupin (eds), *The British Film Institute, the Government and Film Culture, 1933–2000* (Manchester: Manchester University Press, 2012).
58. This funding comprised an initial investment of £12,500 provided by the film trade, a subsequent grant of £10,000 in 1961 from the Gulbenkian Foundation, and subsequent earnings from supported films. Information provided by BFI director James Quinn for a meeting of the Experimental Film Fund Board on 6 November 1961, Michael Balcon Papers, BFI Special Collections, MEB 1946 J/17.
59. Minutes from BFI Production Board Meeting, 15 December 1966, BFI Special Collections, ITM15893. The other board members were art historians John Berger and David Sylvester, theatre director William Gaskill, technical expert Baynham Honri and Walter Lucas of the British Drama League.
60. Figures derived from project database. For more on UK film censorship in the sixties, see Tracey Hargreaves, 'The Trevelyn years: British censorship and 1960s cinema', in Edward Lamberti (ed.), *Behind the Scenes at the BBFC: Film Classification from the Silver Screen to the Digital Age* (London: BFI, 2012), pp. 53–70.
61. Budgets taken from <http://www.the-numbers.com/movies/franchise/James-Bond#tab=summary> and <http://007.lucklaboratories.com/> (both accessed 17 August 2018).
62. Sarah Street, *Transatlantic Crossings: British Feature Films in the United States* (London: Continuum, 2002). Street's complete listings for the 1960s are included as an appendix to this chapter.
63. Terence Kelly et al., *A Competitive Cinema*, p. 47.
64. Ibid. p. 18.
65. During the decade, both Rank and ABPC also continued a corporate strategy of diversification and the development of other activities including some in the leisure sector such as bingo halls, bowling alleys and ballrooms. Kelly et al. note that in the year 1964–5, Rank's film interests contributed only 38.2 per cent of the group's total sales and just 28.8 per cent of profits (£4,380,000 out of £15,191,000), while ABPC's film activities contributed 48 per cent of the group's profits (£2,842,000 out of £5,938,000) during the same year. *A Competitive Cinema*, p. 44.
66. *The Daily Cinema*, 13 March 1961.
67. *Kine Weekly*, 16 March 1961, p. 3.
68. Ibid. p. 4.

69. Film Finances files for *Ladies Who Do* and *The Leather Boys*.
70. 'State of Crisis in the British Film Industry: Six Unions Take Action' *Film and TV Technician*, November 1963, pp. 289–90.
71. Ibid.
72. 'Production Crisis Moves Challenged by Winckles', *Kine Weekly*, 14 November 1963, p. 3.
73. 'Davis Puts the Crisis in Perspective', *Kine Weekly*, 19 December 1963, p. 123.
74. *Kine Weekly*, 3 October 1963, p. 4.
75. 'Davis Puts the Crisis in Perspective', *Kine Weekly*, 19 December 1963, p. 123.
76. Carl Foreman, 'The Revolution in the Film Industry', *The Daily Cinema*, Preview of 1963, January 1963, p. 13
77. Alexander Walker, *Hollywood, England,* p. 332. Lead report that the government has accepted the industry's proposals for voluntary implementation of the Monopolies Commission report, *Kine Weekly*, 10 June 1967.
78. John Russell Taylor, 'Backing Britain', *Sight and Sound*, Summer 1969, p. 113.
79. Michael Wakely, 'Situation hopeless but not serious', *Films and Filming*, May 1970, p. 9.
80. 'Hollywood or bust', *Film and Television Technician*, December 1969, p. 8.
81. Penelope Houston, 'Occupied industry', *Sight and Sound*, Spring 1965, pp. 59–60, and 'England, their England', *Sight and Sound*, Spring 1966, p. 56.
82. Ibid.

PART ONE

STRUCTURES AND COMPANIES

1. DISTRIBUTION AND PRODUCTION: THE BRITISH MAJORS

Duncan Petrie

INTRODUCTION

There were four major British players in film distribution, and by extension production, during the 1960s: Rank, Associated British (whose distribution arm was Warner Pathé), British Lion and Anglo-Amalgamated. Collectively, these companies were involved in distributing around 45 per cent of the total number of British features and thus played a key role in shaping the national cinema. Their involvement with films took one of three different forms: projects developed and produced in-house, distribution guarantees provided to independent producers and completed films picked up for distribution only. The second type of involvement was the most common and the provision of a distribution guarantee (essentially a form of pre-sale) allowed the producer to borrow production finance from a bank. This was increasingly preferable to the old model of in-house production, as cost and risk could be shared with the producer and other investors – a distribution guarantee usually provided only 70 per cent of production costs. But it also underlines the key role of distributors in a post-studio era characterised by one-off rather than slate or rolling production. Rank, ABPC and British Lion also rented their studio facilities – at Pinewood, Elstree and Shepperton respectively – to productions funded by other sources, including the American majors.

The pattern of releases for each of the four major British distributors across the decade is shown on Table 1.1.[1]

What is immediately striking is the rapid decline in the number of films

Figure 1.1 Top-ranking star: Norman Wisdom continuing to be a Rank Organisation mainstay in *The Early Bird* (Robert Asher, 1965).

handled by Anglo-Amalgamated and British Lion after 1963. In both cases this is a direct impact of the production crisis which affected the kind of low-budget films that comprised a large part of each distributor's business. In the case of Anglo, 60 per cent of the company's output between 1960 and 1964 was 'B' films. But the figures for both Rank and Warner Pathé are also misleading in that Universal's British production programme accounts for more than a third of Rank's UK output from 1966 to 1969, while more than half of Warner Pathé's British product during the same period comprised Warner or Warner–Seven Arts films. Given that overall production levels in Britain remained relatively stable from 1964 onwards, the decline in the involvement of the big four is highly significant, a consequence of the increasing Hollywood financing and distribution of British features.

A closer examination of each company provides a more detailed picture of the specific contribution they made to British cinema during the decade.

Rank

During the 1950s the Rank Organisation increasingly came under the control of John Davis, who had succeeded founder J. Arthur Rank as managing director in 1948. Davis's priority was to impose a new level of fiscal discipline on a

Table 1.1 Number of domestic films handled by the four major British distributors by year

Distributor	1960	1961	1962	1963	1964	1965	1966	1967	1968	1969	Total
Anglo-Amalgamated	17	16	19	19	13	11	7	5	1	2	110
British Lion	22	15	25	22	8	4	4	1	2	2	105
Rank	17	15	13	16	3	9	15	12	9	11	120
Warner Pathé	13	5	9	7	7	13	13	13	11	8	99
Total	69	51	66	64	31	37	39	31	23	23	434

company that had lost a great deal of money in the late 1940s and this afforded him the opportunity to consolidate his control over all aspects of the business. In the sphere of production, he quickly sidelined all potential rivals, retaining only the services of his loyal American lieutenant, Earl St John, as production head at Pinewood. Davis's personal control extended to personal approval of all projects and budgets and the deployment of Rank contract artists on individual productions. While acknowledging he was 'a brilliant businessman', Sue Harper and Vincent Porter argue that Davis was also very controlling and ill at ease with creative people: 'Authoritarian in his management style, and conservative in both his politics and his tastes, Davis had no sense of how or when to take creative risks.'[2] They also note 'a dogged persistence in sticking with a formula once it had proved popular.'[3] These characteristics were to be firmly maintained into the following decade, with Davis consolidating his domination of the company in 1962 when he also became chairman following the retirement of J. Arthur Rank.

Rank's most successful films of the 1950s had been comedies, notably the series initiated in 1954 by *Doctor in the House*, directed by Ralph Thomas, produced by Betty Box and starring Dirk Bogarde, Kenneth More and James Robertson Justice.[4] Also popular were the more modestly budgeted series of films starring Norman Wisdom in his famous screen persona as the hapless but loveable 'gump', beginning with *Trouble in Store* (1953). Davis's conservative instincts were reinforced by a failed series of adventure films made on larger budgets for the international market in the late 1950s which resulted in substantial losses in 1958 and 1959. The increasing level of risk arguably influenced Davis's sceptical view of domestic production and encouraged a strategy of diversification into other areas of business. In 1956 a deal was signed with the Halord Company in America for the non-US rights of the Xerox copying process and by 1963 Rank Xerox had become a high profitable subsidiary of the Rank Organisation.

Between 1960 and 1963 Rank Film Distributors handled around fifteen features a year, around two thirds of which were 'A' or first films. This dropped dramatically in 1964 before recovering to around ten to twelve features a year during the second half of the decade. In terms of key producers, Thomas and Box continued to feature strongly with twelve features between 1960 and 1969. Comedy continued to loom large with a further three contributions to the *Doctor* series – *Doctor in Love* (1960), the highest-grossing domestic release that year despite the absence of Dirk Bogarde, *Doctor in Distress* (1963) and *Doctor in Clover* (1966) – in addition to *No, My Darling Daughter* (1961), a romantic comedy featuring Juliet Mills as the precocious daughter of a wealthy industrialist, and the Cold War espionage romp *Hot Enough for June* (1964), starring Bogarde and Sylva Koscina. But Thomas and Box explored other genres and subjects. *Conspiracy of Hearts* (1960) featured the daring rescue of Jewish children by Italian nuns during World War Two, *No Love for Johnnie* (1961) – the first Rank film to receive an X certificate – the opportunism of an ambitious British politician, *The Wild and the Willing* (1962) the racy exploits of a group of undergraduates, which marked the big-screen debuts of Samantha Eggar, John Hurt and Ian McShane and was seen as an attempt by Rank to promote new young talent,[5] and *The High Bright Sun* (1965), another Dirk Bogarde vehicle set against the backdrop of the Cyprus emergency of the late 1950s. In an obvious attempt to cash in on the James Bond phenomenon, Thomas and Box updated H. C. McNeile's special agent Bulldog Drummond in *Deadlier than the Male* (1966), which pitted Richard Johnson's hero against a pair of glamorous female assassins played by Elke Sommer and Sylva Koscina. Johnson returned in the equally outlandish *Some Girls Do* (1969), while *Nobody Runs Forever* (1968) is a more conventional spy thriller featuring Rod Taylor as an Australian policeman in London.[6]

The Norman Wisdom comedies also continued well into the 1960s, appearing regularly in the top ten British domestic releases. Produced by Hugh Stewart and directed by Robert Asher, the films maintained the familiar Wisdom persona and formulaic plots and include *The Bulldog Breed* (1960), *On the Beat* (1962), *A Stitch in Time* (1963), *The Early Bird* (1965), the first of the series in colour, and *Press for Time* (1966) – produced by Robert Hartford Davis and Peter Newbrook.[7] Stewart was an important contract producer for Rank during the decade and his other comedies include *Make Mine Mink* (1960), *In The Doghouse* (1961) and three films starring the popular television team of Eric Morecambe and Ernie Wise: *The Intelligence Men* (1965), *That Riviera Touch* (1966) and *The Magnificent Two* (1967), involving the hapless duo in increasingly outlandish (mis)adventures in exotic foreign locations.

The importance of popular formulaic comedy to Rank's core output was further confirmed when the Corporation acquired the popular *Carry On* series from Anglo-Amalgamated. Producer Peter Rogers had started his career working for Rank's religious film production unit before joining Sydney Box at Gainsborough as a writer. When he graduated to producer he insisted on making his films at Pinewood where he enjoyed good relations with both the studio management and the union works committee.[8] Rogers was married to Betty Box, while his partner, director Gerald Thomas, was the brother of Ralph, tightening the family connections around two of Rank's most prolific and successful production teams. The first *Carry On* film made for Rank (the thirteenth overall) was the French Revolution farce *Don't Lose your Head* (1967) and continued with *Follow That Camel* (1967), at £288,000 the most expensive of the series to date – *Don't Lose Your Head* had been budgeted at £234,086[9] – and featuring American star Phil 'Sgt Bilko' Silvers alongside the *Carry On* regulars in an attempt to broaden the series' transatlantic appeal.

While these two films had deliberately dropped the familiar prefix, this was subsequently reinstated for *Carry On Doctor* (1968) – a send up of the *Doctor* films, followed by *Carry On Up the Khyber* (1968) and *Carry On Camping* (1969), the second highest-grossing general domestic release of the year and the most commercially successful of the *Carry On* films.[10]

Beyond comedies, Rank continued to favour established creative personnel. They included Roy Ward Baker, who directed and produced the racial integration drama *Flame in the Streets* (1961) starring John Mills, and the western *The Singer, Not the Song* (1961), made in Spain, which pitted Mills against fellow Rank contract star Dirk Bogarde. Exotic overseas locations was also provided by Ivan Foxwell's comedy drama *Tiara Tahiti* (Ted Kotcheff, 1962), again starring Mills and James Mason, and by James Bond producer Cubby Broccoli's African-set Bob Hope farce, *Call Me Bwana* (Gordon Douglas, 1963). While more modest domestic fare was provided by Val Guest with the epidemic thriller *80,000 Suspects* (1963) and the beauty pageant exposé *The Beauty Jungle* (1964). Julian Wintle and Leslie Parkyn's Independent Artists supplied a range of first and second features to Rank.[11] Examples of the former include the crime drama *Never Let Go* (1960) and the comedy *Waltz of the Toreadors* (1962), both directed by John Guillermin, produced by Peter de Sarigny and starring Peter Sellers; *Very Important Person* (1961) and *The Fast Lady* (1963), both directed by Ken Annakin who would subsequently make the crime drama *The Informers* (1963) directly for Rank; the comedy *Father Came Too* (Peter Graham Scott, 1963); and Lindsay Anderson's New Wave drama *This Sporting Life* (1963), starring Richard Harris and Rachel Roberts, which, despite critical acclaim, was a commercial failure. Rank's association with Independent Artists ended when Wintle and Parkyn moved into TV-series production in 1963 with *The Human Jungle*,[12] following the lead of Robert Baker and Monty Berman who had three films released through Rank in 1960: *The Flesh and the Fiends*, *The Siege of Sidney Street* and *The Treasure of Monte Cristo*.

Rank's engagement with grittier contemporary subject matter was also facilitated through Allied Film Makers, an independent production collective established in 1960 by the actors Jack Hawkins, Bryan Forbes and Richard Attenborough, the former Ealing director/producer team of Basil Dearden and Michael Relph, and the cinematographer-turned-director, Guy Green. Alexander Walker notes that Rank provided AFM with a guarantee of £143,000 and the end money for all but one of the company's films:

> These arrangements gave the Rank Organisation an extremely favourable deal, since its own cinemas could show the films which it helped to finance and on which it already took a distributor's fee; but it also increased the financial muscle of the film-makers as distinct from the

front-office distributors – the one had assumed some of the functions of the other.[13]

The AFM slate commenced with the series of productions made by Dearden and Relph, beginning auspiciously with the ensemble crime thriller *The League of Gentlemen* (1960), which was the sixth highest-grossing film at the British box office that year; followed by the science-fiction spoof *Man in the Moon* (1961); *All Night Long* (1961), an updated version of Othello set in the London Jazz scene; the critically acclaimed *Victim* (1961) featuring Dirk Bogarde as a closeted homosexual barrister facing blackmail; and *Life for Ruth* (1963), in which a couple's religious beliefs lead them to refuse a life-saving blood transfusion for their daughter. The other two AFM productions were both atmospheric dramas directed by Bryan Forbes and produced by Richard Attenborough: *Whistle Down the Wind* (1961), another commercial hit which starred Alan Bates as a murderer on the run and Hayley Mills as young girl who believes he is a resurrected Jesus, and *Séance on a Wet Afternoon* (1964) featuring Richard Attenborough and the American actress Kim Stanley as a couple who kidnap a young girl in order to blackmail her parents. As Sally Dux points out, the final two AFM productions, *Life for Ruth* and *Séance on a Wet Afternoon* failed to perform at the box office, leaving the company in debt to Rank for a sum between £300,000 and £400,000 and effectively ending their collaboration.[14]

In 1962 Rank distributed two films made by the American company Allied Artists: Peter Ustinov's adaptation of Herman Melville's *Billy Budd* starring Ustinov alongside Robert Ryan and newcomer Terence Stamp in the title role, and *Day of the Triffids*, a sci-fi shocker featuring mutant killer plants, directed by Steve Sekeley and produced by George Pitcher. In addition, between 1960 and 1963 Rank released a number of supporting features supplied by a variety of producers including Independent Artists, Jack Parsons, Lawrence Huntingdon, Lance Comfort, Peter Bezencenet and Jim O'Connolly.

Rank's production policy began to change following the turmoil of the winter of 1963/4, although the only affected production they were involved in was the beatnik thriller *The Party's Over*, directed by Guy Hamilton. The studio subsequently disowned the film following problems with the BBFC and it was finally distributed by Monarch in 1965. John Davis maintained that the turmoil was primarily due to a change in audience tastes:

> ... the public have clearly shown that they do not want films about politics, they don't want a sermon preaching to them, or on the subjects of the kitchen sink and administration of the North of England as it no longer exists. They want to be entertained when they go out for their evening's amusement ...[15]

Kelly et al.[16] point out that by the mid-decade Rank had already started supporting big-budget runaways by guaranteeing a minimum return on distribution in specified territories, notably Samuel Bronston's productions *El Cid* (1961), *55 Days at Peking* (1963), *The Fall of the Roman Empire* (1964) and *The Magnificent Showman* (1964). The growing American presence in British film production was also driving up domestic production costs and in September 1965 Davis announced that the future of the domestic industry now lay predominantly in large-scale co-productions: 'The people do not want little films – of course there are outstanding exceptions – they can have their fill of these on television.'[17] This was made at an international sales convention dinner for the Rank–Columbia co-production *The Heroes of Telemark* (1965), an epic £2 million war film depicting a daring commando raid in Nazi-occupied Norway, directed and produced by the Hollywood veteran Anthony Mann and featuring an all-star cast led by Kirk Douglas and Richard Harris.[18]

Davis used the same conference to promote Rank's new co-production scheme with the National Film Finance Corporation, a more modest partnership with each party investing £500,000 in a slate of films to be selected by the NFFC. While this provided the Corporation with the opportunity to invest in larger-budget films with a greater chance of box-office success and a more favourable *pari passu*[19] recoupment deal (rather than being the last in line), the arrangement allowed Rank to fend off charges that they were no longer interested in supporting British independent producers. Davis was also keen to capitalise on the decision to give the NFFC sole responsibility for the selection of the films to be supported in order to answer accusations of monopolistic practices and Rank's 'empire-building!'[20] The scheme resulted in six features: *I Was Happy Here* (1965) – budgeted at a modest £169,200;[21] *The Sandwich Man* (1966) – £250,253;[22] *Romeo and Juliet* (1966) – £215,000; the Anglo-Australian co-production *They're a Weird Mob* (1966) – with Rank and the NFFC providing £166,925 of a total budget of £234,925;[23] *Maroc 7* (1967) – the most expensive of the slate at £316,000; and *Two Weeks in September* (1967), the first film to be made under the new Anglo-French co-production deal. Also made in collaboration with the NFFC, but outside the official partnership, was the George H. Brown production, *The Trap* (1966), directed by Sidney Hayers largely on location in Canada and on a substantial £355,000 budget. But individually and collectively, these films failed to generate sufficient interest at the box office, both *Maroc 7* and *The Trap* had also gone substantially over budget,[24] and the initiative was quietly shelved.

But co-productions with major American partners continued to dominate Rank's production strategy with budgets steadily climbing. The £300,000 cost of Harry Saltzman's *The Ipcress File* (Sidney J. Furie, 1965)[25], Michael Caine's first outing as Len Deighton's special agent Harry Palmer, was shared with Universal; while for the Thomas–Box production *Deadlier than the Male*, each company provided a guarantee of £275,000 against a total budget of just under £630,000.[26] The same team's *Nobody Runs Forever* was budgeted at £837,920 with Rank guaranteeing £418,960,[27] leaving the balance to be picked up by Cinerama and the American TV network ABC – who were also involved in producer Anatole de Grunwald's feature *Stranger in the House* (Pierre Rouve, 1967). Rank invested just over £478,000 for Ivan Foxwell's Cold War thriller, *The Quiller Memorandum* (Michael Anderson, 1966), with 20th Century Fox providing the balance of the substantial £940,000 budget.[28] While Ken Annakin's *The Long Duel* (1967),[29] a lavish adventure set in India and starring Yul Brynner and Trevor Howard, was initially bankrolled by Rank before being sold to Paramount as part of a two-film deal alongside *Maroc 7*.[30] *Subterfuge* (1968), yet another spy thriller directed by Peter Graham Scott and produced by Peter Snell, was co-financed by Commonwealth United Entertainment.

In September 1968 Davis announced that Rank was curtailing its film-production programme, and while very short on specific reasons the implications were that too many of the films had been making losses.[31] At the same time the Organisation reported after tax profits of £8,642,000, a 60 per cent increase on the previous year,[32] and a reflection of the continuing profitability of Xerox and Rank's involvement in a wide range of leisure activities which including dancing, catering, bowling and the Top Rank Club. Indeed, the profitability of the Rank Xerox operations were more than three times that for the group's combined activities in film, where production and distribution actually posted a loss of £583,000.[33] This prompted the ACTT's Sid Cole to attack the Organisation at the union's annual conference the following spring for 'relegating film production to an even more minor role in an economically irrational group.'[34] Soon afterwards Albert Finney wrote a sarcastic letter to *The Daily Cinema* in which, under the guise of an 'apology' for having criticised Rank's handling of *Charlie Bubbles*, detailed how he waited a year after delivery before his film – which was financed by Universal – was given a very cursory release in the Odeon St Martin's Lane in October 1968.[35] Rank's rather tepid commitment appeared to be confirmed by Davis's announcement in September of the same year – following yet another hike in group profits to £11,258,000[36] – that he had no intention of embarking on any major production programme amid fears of a looming withdrawal of American finance but rather would continue operations at a rate of just four to six features a year.[37]

Davis also took the opportunity to return to a familiar argument that the decline in cinema audiences would not be halted until producers stopped making so many X-rated films. This residual Methodism was increasingly in tension with commercial logic as a number of other companies – from Hammer Films to Woodfall – had exploited the adults-only certificate to entice audiences to both sensational and serious fare. A telling example was Rank's decision to reject Ken Russell and Larry Kramer's adaptation of D. H. Lawrence's *Women in Love* (1969) on grounds of morality.'[38] All of this indicates an organisation increasingly focused on its non-film business and out of step with changing social mores; while Rank had been prepared to occasionally back seriously minded X-rated films, their preference had always been for family entertainment.

Associated British

The production policy of the Associated British Picture Corporation during the 1960s also displayed a significant level of continuity with the previous decade. As Harper and Porter (2003) point out, during the 1950s ABPC had directly invested in between four and six features a year and production at Elstree was run by studio boss Robert Clark with a strong emphasis on economy and efficiency.[39] As at Rank, everything was tightly controlled from the centre with the consequence that very few of ABPC's films demonstrated much creative flair. The involvement of Warner Bros. – who owned 25 per cent of the Corporation – gave the Hollywood studio two seats on the Associated British board and a significant level of influence, and as Vincent Porter shows, the interests of the Warner camp were often in tension with those of Clark and the ABPC chairman, Sir Philip Warter.[40] This came to a head in the late 1950s when Clark was sidelined at the behest of Jack Warner and replaced by R. J. Wallis who in turn reported to the ABPC managing director, and Warners' appointee, C. J. Latta. The American interests within ABPC paved the way for the establishment in 1960 of Warner Pathé distributors to handle films made by both companies.

ABPC operated similar production arrangements to those of Rank and as Porter notes, Latta placed a new emphasis on renting out Elstree studios to independent productions while concentrating Associated British's in-house film-making on modest pot-boiler comedies.[41] These tended to be produced by either W. A. Whitaker or Gordon L. T. Scott and featured popular TV comedians, a reflection of ABPC's business interests in television which began in 1955 when subsidiary ABC became part of the new ITV network, broadcasting on weekends in the Midlands and the North. Whitaker made *The Rebel* (Robert Day, 1960) with Tony Hancock, *The Cracksman* (Peter Graham Scott, 1963) and *Mr Ten Percent* (Scott, 1967) with Charlie Drake and *The Bargee* (Duncan Wood, 1964) with Harry H. Corbett; Scott worked with Drake on *Sands of the Desert* (John Paddy Carstairs, 1960) and *Petticoat Pirates* (David MacDonald, 1961), Hancock on *The Punch and Judy Man* (Jeremy Summers, 1962), Ronald Fraser on *The Pot Carriers* (Peter Graham Scott, 1962) and *Crooks in Cloisters* (Summers, 1964). Another ABPC regular, Thomas Clyde, produced a more varied slate including the thriller *Moment of Danger* (Lásló Benedek, 1960), the comedy *Follow that Horse* (Alan Bromily, 1960) and the drama *Guns of Darkness* (1962) directed by veteran Anthony Asquith.

Beyond this core, a small number of experienced film-makers also worked at Elstree during the early 1960s. Some supplied similar types of comedies such as Mario Zampi with *Bottoms Up!* (1960), Danny Angel with *We Joined the Navy* (Wendy Toye, 1962) and Muriel Box[42] with the Harry H. Corbett vehicle, *Rattle of a Simple Man* (1964), which was to be her last film. But greater variety was provided by director Terence Young's Soho gangster film *Too Hot to Handle* (1960); Michael Balcon's World War Two drama set in Burma, *The Long and the Short and the Tall* (1961), directed by Leslie Norman and adapted by Willis Hall from his stage play; Danny Angel's social drama, *West 11* (1963), set in Notting Hill and directed by newcomer Michael Winner; and Wolf Rilla and Michael Luke's *The World Ten Times Over* (1963), charting the exploits of two young women in the fleshpots of Soho. James Woolf and Peter Glenville's 'social problem' film *Term of Trial* (1962), starring Laurence Olivier and Simone Signoret, was effectively a British Warner Bros. production. Warner Pathé's share of 'B' movies was mainly supplied by the Danziger brothers whose production base was next door at New Elstree studios.

In 1961 ABPC diversified their production strategy, setting up Elstree Distributors in partnership with the Grade Organisation run by producer and agent Leslie Grade and his brother, Bernard Delfont. This resulted in a trio of commercially successful youth-oriented films produced by Kenneth Harper and starring pop sensation Cliff Richard: *The Young Ones* (Sidney J. Furie, 1962), *Summer Holiday* (Peter Yates, 1963) and *Wonderful Life* (Furie, 1964), the first two ranking second highest-grossing domestic releases of their respective years. Harper also produced the comedies *Go to Blazes* (Michael Truman, 1962) and *French Dressing* (1964), the latter the feature debut of director Ken Russell. Elstree Films supported Joan Littlewood's *Sparrows Can't Sing* (1963), providing a distribution guarantee worth 70 per cent of the £100,888 budget.[43] Grade financed Joseph Losey's *The Servant* (1963) a provocative study of class relations scripted by Harold Pinter and starring Dirk Bogarde and James Fox which was made on a modest budget of £141,725.[44] Losey's next feature, the World War One drama *King and Country* (1964), was equally dependent on the support of Danny Angel who invested almost half of the budget of £82,728, with ABPC acquiring the distribution for £20,000.[45] Elstree Films also made the musical comedy *Up Jumped a Swagman* (1965), directed by Christopher Miles and starring the Australian singer Frank Ifield.

Another key development was ABPC's acquisition of 50 per cent of Anglo-Amalgamated in April 1962. The trade press speculated that this merger would encourage producers associated with Anglo to consider more ambitious production for international distribution.[46] From the beginning of the following year Warner Pathé began handling the physical distribution of

Anglo-Amalgamated product in the UK, leaving the latter to concentrate on production and international sales.[47] This was around the time that changes in the market for British films were beginning to reverberate and in August 1963 ABPC chairman Philip Warter expressed serious concerns in his annual statement in *ABC News* 'that the ever-increasing costs of operating the studios and the high costs of film production in general makes this branch of the business, if taken in isolation, unremunerative'.[48] Nevertheless, he conceded that the need to ensure a supply of films for the company's cinemas meant that the Corporation would continue to support British production. The following year ABPC made a loss on its studio operation of £322,000, but by 1965 this had been reduced to £166,000.[49]

Elsewhere ABPC's involvement in television production was proving an increasingly important part of their overall business. In 1963 they provided finance to Julian Wintle and Leslie Parkyn for their first TV drama series, *The Human Jungle*, starring Herbert Lom. Then in September 1964 construction began on three new sound stages at Elstree at a cost of £500,000,[50] reflecting both a growing demand from Hollywood-financed features and television series shot on 35mm film. In November 1966 Warter announced the establishment of a new subsidiary, ABC Television Films Ltd, operating out of Elstree studios with funds of £3.5 million to produce TV films in colour for the world market.[51] Soon afterwards the first colour series of *The Avengers* – which had moved production base from Teddington to Elstree the previous year[52] – was announced at a cost of over £1 million.[53]

By the mid-1960s, Warner Pathé's slate of releases was increasingly dominated by modestly budgeted exploitation films of the kind that Anglo-Amalgamated had been associated with. An example is the slate of productions made by director Frederic Goode and producer Harry Field including the music revue *Pop Gear* (1965), the thriller *Death is a Woman* (1965), the horror film *Hand of Night* (1965) and the African-set adventure *The Syndicate* (1967). In 1965 the company also distributed three films produced by the prolific exploitation specialist Harry Allan Towers, who already had a close association with Anglo: *24 Hours to Kill*, *The Face of Fu Manchu* and *Ten Little Indians*. But even more important was the distributor's association with Hammer Films, a relationship that dated back to the early 1960s with the crime thriller *Hell is a City* (Val Guest, 1960) and the adventure films *The Devil Ship Pirates* (Don Sharp, 1963), *The Scarlet Blade* (John Gilling, 1963) and *The Brigand of Kandahar* (Gilling, 1965). Following the success of *She* (Robert Day, 1965), Hammer's most ambitious project to date, made on a budget of £312,000 which was largely provided by MGM, the company arranged a package deal involving Seven Arts, 20th Century Fox and Warner Pathé.[54] A further eighteen films were made under this agreement, the majority horror and fantasy subjects and including *The Nanny* (Seth Holt, 1965), *Dracula, Prince of Darkness* (Terence

Fisher, 1965), *The Plague of the Zombies* (John Gilling, 1966), *One Million Years BC* (Val Guest, 1966) – featuring stop-motion animation from Ray Harryhausen and at £425,000 the most expensive Hammer production to date but which grossed $8 million worldwide – *The Witches* (Cyril Frankel, 1966), *Frankenstein Created Woman* (Fisher, 1967), *The Mummy's Shroud* (Gilling, 1967), *Quatermass and the Pit* (Roy Ward Baker, 1967) and *The Devil Rides Out* (Fisher, 1968).

In 1968 Seven Arts acquired Warner Bros. in a development that also led to the British music company EMI buying Warners' 25 per cent holding in ABPC for £9.5 million.[55] By this time ABPC owned 74 per cent of Anglo-Amalgamated and had a 50 per cent stake in Thames Television (the result of a merger between ABC TV and Rediffusion) and it quickly became clear that EMI wanted nothing less than a controlling stake in the Corporation. A protracted negotiation was played out in the trade press until February 1969 when *Kine Weekly* announced that EMI had finally acquired 53 per cent of ABPC shares.[56] Within a month Bernard Delfont was named as the new chairman and chief executive and he quickly appointed the writer/director Bryan Forbes as the new head of production at Elstree from May with a £4 million revolving fund to enable a new domestic production programme.[57]

The EMI takeover brought the curtain down on the long-standing association of Robert Clark with ABPC. For despite being sidelined by the Warner Bros. faction at the beginning of the decade, Clark continued to be a force both within the Corporation as chief executive and deputy chairman and in the wider industry, serving as chairman of the British Film Producers Association and becoming the first chair of a new single producers body, the Film Production Association of Great Britain, following the merger of the BFPA with the Federation of British Film Makers in 1967. Clark also chaired an all-industry committee tasked with responding to the recommendations of the 1966 Monopolies Commission report on the supply of films. In another significant development, Nat Cohen, chairman and chief executive of Anglo-Amalgamated, joined the ABPC board in March 1969. Two years later Cohen succeeded Bryan Forbes as head of production after the latter's slate of films proved to be yet another false start.

ANGLO-AMALGAMATED

Along with partner Stuart Levy, Cohen had founded Anglo-Amalgamated in 1945, initially building their company in the 'B' movie market through distributing American product and producing their own films at Merton Park studios.[58] By the mid-1950s Anglo started to expand into 'A' features with crime films like *The Sleeping Tiger* (1954) and *The Intimate Stranger* (1956), both directed by the blacklisted American director Joseph Losey. Cohen and

Levy also demonstrated a keen sense of the changing market and Robert Murphy praises Anglo for being 'sufficiently astute to back the first British teenage film, *The Tommy Steele Story*,'[59] released in 1957 and followed in the same year by *The Duke Wore Jeans*. The company also capitalised on the growing vogue for more lurid horror films stimulated by the success of Hammer, resulting in the Sadian trilogy comprising *Horrors of the Black Museum* (Arthur Crabtree, 1959), *Circus of Horrors* (Sidney Hayers, 1960) and *Peeping Tom* (Michael Powell, 1960).[60] Even more significant was their support for producer Peter Rogers and director Gerald Thomas's low-budget comedy, *Carry On Sergeant* (1958), the first instalment in a series that was to become a national institution, boosting the fortunes of Anglo-Amalgamated considerably in the process. Thus by the beginning of the 1960s the company had become a serious industry player, distributing around half a dozen first features a year and a substantial output of 'B' films produced by Jack Greenwood at Merton Park. Harper and Porter note, 'While Cohen was in charge of project development and production, Levy concentrated on sales and distribution. They also had a phased business plan and a production strategy, far more efficiently conceived than other small outfits.'[61]

Anglo entered the decade riding high on the success of the *Carry On* series – *Carry On Nurse* was Britain's top box-office general release in 1959. This continued to provide a core part of Anglo's business for the next six years with *Carry On Constable* (1960) – the second most-popular film in its year of release – *Carry On Regardless* (1961), *Carry On Cruising* (1962), *Carry On Cabby* (1963), *Carry On Cleo* (1963), *Carry On Jack* (1964), *Carry On Spying* (1964), *Carry On Cowboy* (1965) and *Carry On Screaming* (1966). The series featured an ensemble cast led by Sid James, Kenneth Williams, Joan Sims, Hattie Jacques, Charles Hawtrey and a stable production team, while the comedy relied heavily on a familiar mix of farce and innuendo. Budgets were also kept under tight control despite rising steadily from £82,500 for *Constable* to £197,500 for *Screaming*.[62] *Cruising* and *Cleo* were the first two *Carry On*s to be made in colour, but this did not become standard practice until *Cowboy*.

Rogers and Thomas also produced a substantial number of other low-budget comedies for Anglo, many featuring the same comic style, leading players and production personnel, and including *No Kidding* (1960), *Watch Your Stern* (1960), *Raising the Wind* (1961), *The Iron Maiden* (1962), *Twice Round the Daffodils* (1962), *Nurse on Wheels* (1963) and *The Big Job* (1965). The ambitious Rogers even formed a second production team comprising Jack Hanbury and director Sidney Hayers – whose previous films for Anglo included the horror films *Circus of Horrors* (1960) and *Night of the Eagle* (1962), resulting in the romantic melodrama *This is My Street* (1963) and the musical comedy *Three Hats for Lisa* (1965). Rogers' importance to Anglo was confirmed by an appointment to the company's board of directors in 1960, but by July 1963 heavy production responsibilities forced him to stand down.[63] Beyond the association with Rogers, Anglo's other comedies included a trio of films featuring Bob Monkhouse, an emerging star on radio and television: *Dentist on the Job* (C. M Pennington Richards, 1961), *On the Fiddle* (Cyril Frankel, 1961) and *She'll Have to Go* (1962), directed and produced by Robert Asher.[64]

Also central to Anglo's strategy was the 'B' movie unit run by Jack Greenwood at Merton Park which turned out more than a dozen superior programmers a year until 1963. The bulk of these were adaptations of stories by Edgar Wallace – beginning with *The Clue of the Twisted Candle* (Allan Davies, 1960) – which resulted in some forty-seven one-hour dramas, earning Merton Park a strong identity and a reputation for quality within the sphere of supporting features.[65] As Greenwood explained to *Kine Weekly*, the films were shot in ten or eleven days if made entirely in the studio or twelve to thirteen days if there were a high proportion of locations involved (the *Carry On* films by comparison tended to be made on schedules of six to seven weeks). At least four scripts were ready for production at any given time. Dubbed versions were produced for France, Italy and Germany; in some instances these were exhibited as a first feature by joining two films together with a specially filmed introduction and linking sequences. In addition to the 'B' movies, Greenwood was also responsible for the more highbrow crime drama, *The Criminal* (1960), the third film directed by Joseph Losey for Anglo and starring Stanley Baker and Sam Wanamaker. Another regular supplier of 'B' movies to Anglo was the aforementioned Independent Artists.

Relationships with American companies had always been a key part of Cohen and Levy's business, particularly in relation to productions in the horror and fantasy genres including Herman Cohen's *Konga* (1960) and a series of co-productions with American International Pictures, whose films Anglo regularly distributed in the UK. In July 1962 a deal for films to be made in Britain over the next 12 months on budgets of around £200,000 was announced[66] resulting in four productions: two adaptions of Edgar Allan Poe short stories by Roger Corman starring Vincent Price, *The Masque of Red Death* (1964) and *The Tomb of Ligeia* (1965); *City Under the Sea* (1965), the last film directed by Jacques Tourneur; and *Monster of Terror* (Daniel Haller, 1965) which featured a late appearance of horror veteran Boris Karloff. Anglo also continued to mine the growing market for films featuring pop music with *Catch Us If You Can* (1965), featuring the Dave Clark Five, produced by David Deutsch and directed by newcomer John Boorman, and *Gonks Go Beat* (1965), a blend of science fiction and pop musical from the team of Robert Hartford Davis and Peter Newbrook.

The closer ties with ABPC and Warner Pathé allowed Anglo to devote more time to developing their production ambitions. While plans to co-produce

Stanley Baker and Cy Endfield's imperial adventure *Zulu* (1964) with Joseph Levine's Embassy Pictures came unstuck (the film was eventually made by Embassy in partnership with Paramount on a budget of more than £600,000[67]), Anglo's association with producer Joseph Janni and director John Schlesinger proved a more fruitful collaboration. This began in 1961 when Janni approached Cohen with two New Wave projects, *A Kind of Loving* and *Billy Liar*. Encouraged by the success of the Woodfall films, Anglo offered Janni 100 per cent financing for both films of £148,000 and £209,600 respectively,[68] an unusual but typically bold statement of faith.[69] *A Kind of Loving* (1962) went on to win the Golden Bear at the Berlin Film Festival the following year. Anglo's move into more prestigious film-making was apparently confirmed when the veteran team of Basil Dearden and Michael Relph made *The Mind Benders* (1963), a psychological thriller written by James Kennaway, starring Dirk Bogarde and made on a budget of £210,781 with Anglo guaranteeing the more customary 70 per cent in partnership with the NFFC.[70] The following year, director Clive Donner and producer David Deutsch provided *Nothing but the Best* (1964), a new variant on *Room at the Top* featuring Alan Bates, the star of *A Kind of Loving*, as its ruthless social-climbing anti-hero. The budget this time was £176,500 with Anglo providing £123,550.[71] The third Schlesinger–Janni film was to be one of the most iconic of the era as well as Anglo's most prestigious and successful production. In addition to being a box-office hit, *Darling* made an international star of Julie Christie and won Oscars for Best Actress, Original Screenplay and Costume Design. Cohen and Levy also sold the film to Embassy for a reported $1 million which was almost equivalent to the entire production cost of just under £350,000.[72]

At the beginning of 1965, Nat Cohen announced a new £3 million programme that would confirm Anglo as 'the largest British production firm' in *Kine Weekly*.[73] But within eighteen months Stuart Levy was dead at the age of just fifty-nine and soon afterwards Cohen decided to sever connections with the *Carry On* series, apparently to concentrate on more prestigious productions.[74] As Morris Bright and Robert Ross point out, this decision came soon after Anglo had hosted a huge party to celebrate Peter Rogers's twenty-first production for the company.[75] Anglo went on to develop the lavish Thomas Hardy adaptation, *Far From the Madding Crown* (1967), with Joseph Janni and John Schlesinger which was ultimately financed by MGM to the tune of just under £1 million and featured Julie Christie alongside Terence Stamp, Alan Bates and Peter Finch. Janni's final production for Anglo was the more modest *Poor Cow* (1967), the first theatrical feature directed by Ken Loach, starring Carol White and Terence Stamp. Made on a budget of under £250,000,[76] this was the fifth highest-grossing general release for 1968.

As the decade wore on and the company became more tightly entwined within ABPC, so the number of films released under the Anglo banner declined substantially. The prolific output of independent producer Harry Allan Towers dominated, with nine adventure, fantasy and horror features directed by Don Sharp – *The Brides of Fu Manchu* (1966), *Our Man in Marrakesh* (1966) and *Jules Verne's Rocket to the Moon* (1967); Jeremy Summers – *Five Golden Dragons* (1967), *The Vengeance of Fu Manchu* (1967) and *The Face of Eve* (1968); Lindsay Shonteff – *Sumuaru* (1967); and Jess Franco – *The Blood of Fu Manchu* (1968) and *The Castle of Fu Manchu* (1968). The decade ended with Anglo supporting a small number of contemporary dramas including Christopher Morahan and Leon Clore's *All Neat in Black Stockings* (1969), the thriller *Daddy's Gone a Hunting* (1969), produced and directed by American Mark Robson, and Ted Kotcheff's study of prejudice, *Two Gentlemen Sharing* (1969), a pickup from Paramount who co-financed the film with the NFFC.

The acquisition of ABPC by EMI led Cohen to become controller of EMI's production division by 1971, bringing the story of the company he had built to an end.[77] Alexander Walker describes Cohen as 'a more urbane version of the one-man-bands who used to boss the studios in Hollywood's heyday of the movie moguls'.[78] It is certainly the case that Cohen's approach to the business had more in common with the chutzpah of a Louis B. Mayer than the fiscal caution of a John Davis. Yet, despite his undoubted success in building a company by taking risks and engaging with changing audience tastes for particular genres, Cohen remains a rather neglected figure within British cinema history. But that may also be because Anglo's films only intermittently aspired to traditional British markers of quality and good taste.

British Lion

If Anglo-Amalgamated was the British distributor most closely aligned in temperament and policy to the Americans, then the most doggedly domestic was the aptly named British Lion. The company had a long history but its most significant developments had occurred in the late 1940s and early 1950s when Alexander Korda had presided over an almost textbook boom-to-bust trajectory. As noted elsewhere, when the National Film Finance Corporation was established they immediately invested half of their £6 million fund to keep British Lion afloat. Most of this was lost and in January 1955 British Lion was taken into public ownership with the NFFC becoming the principal shareholder in a new company, British Lion Films, to which it advanced a further £569,000 in return for 60 per cent of its share capital. The company would continue to run Shepperton studios, distribute its own films and offer distribution guarantees to independent producers, mainly in partnership with the NFFC. But as Harper and Porter note, business remained poor with the exceptions of films made by John and Roy Boulting, including *Josephine and Men* (1955) and *Private's Progress* (1956), and by Frank Launder and Sidney

Gilliat such as *Geordie* (1955), *The Constant Husband* (1955) and *The Green Man* (1958).[79] Thus in an attempt to halt the slide, in 1958 the company's new managing director, David Kingsley (who had previously run the NFFC), invited the four to join the British Lion board, thus shifting creative power to active independent film-makers in a way that distinguished British Lion from its principal rivals.

Between 1958 and 1960 the company finally moved into profit, driven largely by the efforts of the new management team. But the reorganisation also placed a new emphasis on reducing British Lion's dependency on speculative financing and as the then chairman, Douglas Collins, indicated: 'we encouraged the formation of new production groups who would use Shepperton studios and distribute their films through British Lion.'[80] This paved the way for the emergence of a number of satellite producer/distributors who released their films through British Lion, the most significant of which was Bryanston Films, a collective of established producers set up and run by Maxwell Setton and Michael Balcon as managing director and chairman respectively.[81] The company made more than thirty films for British Lion, a combination of first and supporting features. As the Bryanston board members included Kenneth and Gerald Shipman, the owners of Twickenham studios, their films had a choice of production bases. A further six satellite distributors emerged – Britannia, Pax, Garrick[82], Magna, Albion and Wessex – prompting *Kine Weekly* to describe 1961 as 'the year of the silk-lined umbrella . . . in which the trend has been for independent producers and directors to form their own distribution-production companies and then step under the protecting brolly of a major distributor for the benefit of both.'[83] Between 1960 and 1963 these satellites provided more than 50 per cent of the product handled by British Lion, prompting the Boulting brothers to affirm their commitment to independents, stating in an interview in May 1963, 'Our activities and those of our co-directors are aimed at liberating film-makers . . . to make their own films in their own way.'[84] In common with Anglo-Amalgamated, British Lion handled significant numbers of 'B' films during the early part of the decade, supplied by Bryanston, ACT Films, Parroch–McCallum and various other producers.

British Lion's new business strategy also included the successful exploitation of films acquired from the old company run by Korda. Secondly, a reduction in operational overheads had been brought about by a joint-selling arrangement in the UK with Columbia, leading to the establishment of BLC Films in 1961 under joint managing directors David Kingsley and Ken Hargreaves.[85] Thirdly, the films made by British Lion's directors continued to be commercially successful. Launder and Gilliat scored box-office hits with the comedies *The Pure Hell of St Trinian's* (1960), *Only Two Can Play* (1962) and *The Great St Trinian's Train Robbery* (1966), while the Boultings had success notable with the Peter Sellers' vehicle *Heaven's Above* (1963) and *The Family Way* (1966),

Bill Naughton's northern sex comedy featuring Hayley Mills and Hywel Bennett as a pair of newlyweds. Other features made by the Boultings alternated between comedies like *A French Mistress* (1960) and *Rotten to the Core* (1965) and thrillers such as *Suspect* (1960) and *Twisted Nerve* (1968), while Launder and Gilliat's output also included *Joey Boy* (1965).[86] In addition, Sidney Gilliat's brother Leslie produced the comedies *The Amorous Prawn* (Anthony Kimmins, 1962) and *Two Left Feet* (Roy Baker, 1963) – another casualty of the 1963 crisis – and the espionage thriller *Ring of Spies* (Robert Tronson, 1963). Other commercial hits include the Peter Sellers vehicles *The Battle of the Sexes* (1960), made by ex-Ealing personnel Charles Crichton and Monja Danischewsky for Bryanston; *Two Way Stretch* (1960), made by Robert Day and E. M. Smedley Ashton, and *The Wrong Arm of the Law* (Cliff Owen, 1962), produced by Aubrey Baring.

Alongside this dependence on rather traditional fare, British Lion also supported more cutting-edge contemporary drama, including Richard Attenborough and Bryan Forbes' first production, *The Angry Silence* (1960) – made before the formation of Allied Film Makers and its deal with Rank – and Forbes' subsequent *The L-Shaped Room* (1962), produced by James Woolf and starring Leslie Caron. British Lion also supported Peter Brook's big-screen translation of William Golding's *Lord of the Flies*, its release delayed by the winter crisis until November 1964, and distributed Clive Donner's adaptation of Harold Pinter's *The Caretaker* (1963), whose tiny £30,000 budget was raised primarily from private investors. More significantly, the relationship with Bryanston made British Lion a key participant in the New Wave through four features made by Tony Richardson and John Osborne's Woodfall Films: *The Entertainer* (1960), *Saturday Night and Sunday Morning* (1960), *A Taste of Honey* (1961) and *The Loneliness of the Long Distance Runner* (1962), the latter three making stars of Albert Finney, Rita Tushingham and Tom Courtenay respectively. *Saturday Night and Sunday Morning* was also to prove Bryanston's biggest commercial success, earning more than £400,000 at the British box office, and Woodfall's significance was acknowledged when Richardson and Osborne joined the collective's board in August 1961.[87]

Bryanston also continued to rely on established talent, including several former colleagues of Balcon's from Ealing, and much of their output comprised rather old-fashioned comedies such as *Light Up the Sky* (Lewis Gilbert, 1960), the George H. Brown productions *The Boy Who Stole a Million* (Charles Crichton, 1960), *Double Bunk* (1961) and *Ladies Who Do* (1963), the last two directed by C. M. Pennington-Richards, and Monja Danischewsky's *Two and Two Make Six* (Freddie Francis, 1962). In addition, Leslie Norman directed the 'social problem' film *Spare the Rod* (1961), Dearden and Relph the crime drama *A Place to Go* (1963) and Michael Truman the murder investigation *Girl in the Headlines* (1963). Bryanston's films tended to be made on very modest budgets of between £100,000 and £150,000 – the exceptions being *The Entertainer* and *A Prize of Arms* (Cliff Owen, 1962) which each cost around £250,000.[88] In a response to the changing market Bryanston also attempted to make higher-budget films through collaboration with the American company Seven Arts, but the fruits of this endeavour all failed at the box office: the African adventure *Sammy Going South* (Alexander Mackendrick, 1963), the only Bryanston film made in colour by Balcon's own production company on a substantially higher budget of £385,000;[89] *The Small World of Sammy Lee* (1963), Ken Hughes's tale of a Soho confidence man played by Anthony Newley which cost a more modest £185,000,[90] and *The Wild Affair* (John Krish, 1963), a satire of contemporary sexual mores starring Nancy Kwan. By the end of 1963 the writing was on the wall and the last film to feature the Bryanston logo was Michael Winner's delinquent youth drama, *The System* (1964).

Of the other satellites the most significant was Britannia, established and run by Steven Pallos, whose output included a number of films produced by Donald Taylor including *City of the Dead* (1960), *Foxhole in Cairo* (1960), *Hands of Orlac* (1960) and the UK–West German co-production *The Devil's Daffodil* (1961), as well as Val Guest's crime drama, *Jigsaw* (1962). Pax was a collaborative initiative by Bryanston and Britannia to support more ambitious productions, although only one significant film resulted: Guest's sci-fi disaster movie, *The Day the Earth Caught Fire* (1961), made on a budget of £190,000.[91] Garrick was responsible for *The Leather Boys* (Sidney J. Furie, 1963), yet another film caught up in the winter crisis. The fact that all of these satellite companies had ceased operations by 1964 indicated the extent to which British Lion appeared increasingly outmanoeuvred by a rapidly changing marketplace and their lack of power vis-à-vis the Rank–ABPC duopoly.

Around the same time, the government decided the moment had come to return British Lion to private ownership. Described elsewhere in this book, the process culminated in March 1964 with a £1.6 million sale to a consortium led by former Bryanston chair, Michael Balcon. This alliance included five production groups: Balcon and the American distributor/exhibitor Walter Reade; Launder–Gilliat and the Boulting brothers; Joseph Janni and John Schlesinger; and Long Distance Films – comprising Tony Richardson, John Osborne, Oscar Lewenstein and James Isherwood of Woodfall Films in partnership with Border TV Ltd and the Beatles' manager Brian Epstein – a very interesting cross-media grouping that was indicative of the wider developments in the entertainment industries. The new British Lion board comprised Balcon as chair, David Kingsley as vice chair, representatives from Hambros bank and Humphries Labs and one from each of the five production units.

Despite the wealth of experience and talent of its owners, the newly privatised company found it difficult to build momentum. A memo to the Board of Trade from July 1965 not only contained a request for restrictions on British Lion negotiating long-term deals with the two major cinema circuits (rather than operating on a film-by-film basis) to be lifted, but also a plea that the government reacquire a financial interest in the company in order to help it compete more effectively at a time of further contraction in the British market and increasing American involvement in domestic production.[92] Soon afterwards, Michael Balcon confirmed that the low number and poor quality of projects being submitted to the company was causing concern, citing that American studios were securing superior projects by providing more attractive funding deals.[93] Moreover, having announced in 1964 that *Modesty Blaise* would be British Lion's first foray into big-budget production, within a year the project had been lost to 20th Century Fox,[94] who were more able to provide the £1 million plus budget it required. This was a rerun of Balcon's previous experience with *Tom Jones* which Bryanston–Seven Arts lost to United Artists for similar reasons. Disappointed at the lack of progress, the British Lion chairman decided to retire in September 1965 and was succeeded by Lord (Arnold) Goodman.[95]

While continued exploitation of assets and the buoyancy of rentals at Shepperton studios allowed British Lion to increase its profits for the year to March 1967, Goodman noted that the company had substantially cut back on their production programme and was facing a very uncertain future.[96] As if to confirm the deepening sense of pessimism, following a decade in charge, managing director David Kingsley resigned in September and was succeeded by John Boulting. But despite the difficulties, the company continued to make interesting modest films such as Karel Reisz and Leon Clore's R. D. Laing-influenced comic-drama, *Morgan – A Suitable Case for Treatment* (1966) and Joseph Strick's adaptation of James Joyce's *Ulysses* (1967), budgeted at £165,000 and £215,000 respectively.[97] Elsewhere, Jack Cardiff's psychedelic *Girl on a Motorcycle* (1968), with Marianne Faithfull and Alain Delon represented British Lion's adjustment to the modish changes sweeping British cinema of the time. But the company's most commercially successful film of 1969 was the big-screen adaptation of the popular TV show, *Till Death Us Do Part*, featuring Jonny Speight's foul-mouth bigot Alf Garnett (Warren Mitchell). Directed by Norman Cohen and produced by Jon Pennington, this was the highest-grossing general release in the UK that year.[98] The company's finances also received a welcome boost by a major sale of British Lion films to the BBC in July 1968 in a deal worth £1,995,000,[99] followed by a new share issue in December which raised a further £931,000.[100] While allowing British Lion to end what had been a very challenging decade on an up note, going public was to open the door for City of London investors more interested in asset-stripping than restoring the company's former glories, paving the way for a new period of crisis during the early 1970s.[101]

CONCLUSION

This consideration of the big four British distributors operating during the 1960s reveals a number of important issues. Immediately striking is the continued reliance on talent and genres that had proven successful during the previous decade. Comedy is particularly important, occupying a central role in the outputs of all four companies. The growing significance of television is also crucial and while the small screen was often regarded as the enemy, the decade also saw a number of films built around the appeal of TV comics like Tony Hancock, Charlie Drake, Sid James, Harry H. Corbett and Morecambe and Wise while the more conspicuously successful translation of *Till Death Us Do Part* to the big screen in 1969 initiated another cycle of TV spin-offs that would continue into the following decade and beyond.

A second key feature is the importance of company connections and alliances, most of which helped the major distributors maintain levels of product and spread risk. Thus British Lion's facilitation of its various satellite companies during the first half of the decade was a defining aspect of that company's much-heralded support for independents. Notable here was Bryanston, which in its support of Woodfall found itself at the cutting edge of a new wave of British cinema. But British Lion's rivals had established their own similar relationships, with Elstree Distributors and Anglo-Amalgamated effectively functioning as satellites of Associated British, while Rank's support for Allied Film Makers and their co-funding initiative with the NFFC served a similar purpose. Such arrangements also helped the pooling of resources and the sharing of risk which was increasingly important in the light of growing American competition for the best projects and rising production costs. But many of these relationships proved short-lived, the victims of a changing marketplace, and the impact is vividly demonstrated by the major contraction in product being handled by British Lion and Anglo, although the latter's gradual incorporation into ABPC was another key factor in that company's changing position.

Differing fortunes were also reflected in the corporate alliances that were established with more powerful American interests. This was clearly a preferred route for Rank, whose ongoing relationship with Universal was extended to co-productions with other Hollywood studios, while ABPC's long-standing connection with Warners and with Seven Arts, which took control of the Hollywood studio in 1967, also proved highly significant, as did Anglo's more limited collaboration with American International Pictures. This was one area where British Lion lost out, beyond the association with Columbia in BLC. The outspoken Boulting brothers had a reputation for their anti-American stance. In an interview published in *Kine Weekly* in December 1969, John Boulting bemoaned the destructive influence of American finance that had driven up costs while the market had contracted:

They function in the same way in America, in Hollywood, and they destroyed themselves there for very roughly the same reasons. You see, they've created a Frankenstein monster that is now turning on its creator and destroying him in the best horror tradition. It's a gallery of Frankensteins![102]

If declining audiences and American money had hastened the demise of the British second feature and the failure of the British Lion satellites, alternative approaches to modest-scale film-making proved more durable. Anglo-Amalgamated often proved more in tune with market trends and opportunities, as their forays into comedy, pop musicals, horror and even social realism suggest, as did Elstree Distributors with their youth-oriented but family-friendly pop films starring Cliff Richard, alongside their courageous support for Joseph Losey's *The Servant*. Meanwhile, the most consistently successful and productive British production company of the decade was Hammer Films, whose showmanship and carefully budgeted horror films, psychological thrillers and action adventures allowed them to strike multi-picture deals with American and British funders, notably Warner Pathé who also continued to release some Hammer films as double bills. This success was recognised in 1968 when the company received a Queen's Award for Service to Industry, with *Kine Weekly* reporting an increase in Hammer's earnings from overseas from 47 per cent in 1965 to 82 per cent in 1967.[103]

But American dominance did ultimately reduce the number of productions supported by the four major British distributors. During the early years of the 1960s their combined output totalled between sixty and seventy films annually, but by the end of decade this had declined to around twenty films a year. Moreover, concerns about the commitment of the two major combines to supporting a thriving indigenous production base continued to rumble on. As Alexander Walker argues in his summing of the decade: 'The major blot on the era is that the wealthy cinema-owners in Britain, left in charge of production, distribution and exhibition, did relatively little except serve their own interests and their shareholders.'[104] There is plenty of evidence suggesting that neither Rank nor ABPC were prepared to take the kind of risks that the Hollywood majors, Anglo-Amalgamated or niche British producers like Hammer, Compton and Tigon routinely did. But arguably the conservatism of John Davis and Robert Clark was more than matched by that of John Boulting, and British Lion would have to wait until the 1970s when a production new team of Michael Deely and Barry Spikings injected a fresh approach. What is certain is that by 1969 the major players in domestic film production in Britain found themselves in an even more depleted and fragmented state than they had begun the decade.

APPENDIX: BUDGETS AND FINANCING DETAILS FOR SELECTED PRODUCTIONS SUPPORTED BY THE MAJOR BRITISH DISTRIBUTORS – FROM FILM FINANCES

BRITISH LION AND SATELLITES

Table 1.A.1 Funding details for selected films distributed by British Lion and satellites (from Film Finances archive)

Title	Budget	Financing deal
Battle of the Sexes (1960)	£135,000	Bryanston: £95,000, Walter Reade: £20,500, deferrals etc.: £19,500
The Boy Who Stole a Million (1960)	£100,000	Bryanston: £49,500, Paramount: £49,500, deferrals: £1,000
City of the Dead (1960)	£45,000	Britannia: £16,000, NFFC: £4,500, US distributor: £22,500
Cone of Silence (1960)	£139,360	Bryanston: £95,900, NFFC: £27,400, producers: £16,060
The Entertainer (1960)	£192,928	Bryanston: £75,000, NFFC: £56,500, Continental: £56,500
Light Up the Sky (1960)	£126,500	Bryanston: £88,550, producer: £22,500, Twickenham: £5,000, others: £10,000
Saturday Night and Sunday Morning (1960)	£117,000	Bryanston: £82,000, NFFC: £28,000, Twickenham Studios: £6,000, Tony Richardson: £1,000 deferral
Two Way Stretch (1960)	£115,500	British Lion: £85,000, producers: £15,000, private investment: £15,000
The Day the Earth Caught Fire (1961)	£190,000	Pax: £133,500, NFFC: £41,500, producer: £15,000
A Taste of Honey (1961)	£120,000	Bryanston: £84,000, Continental: £36,000
Double Bunk (1961)	£106,000	Bryanston: £74,000, NFFC: £26,500, deferrals: £5,500
Two and Two Make Six (1962)	£128,000	Bryanston: £90,000, NFFC: £38,000
The Wrong Arm of the Law (1962)	£221,000	Romulus: £154,700, Walter Reade: £25,000, producer: £20,680, deferrals: £20,620
Ladies Who Do (1963)	£134,500	Bryanston: £94,000, NFFC: £32,500, deferrals: £8,000
Sammy Going South (1963)	£385,000	Bryanston–Seven Arts: £269,500, Seven Arts: £57,750, Enterprise: £57,750
The Small World of Sammy Lee (1963)	£190,067	Bryanston–Seven Arts: £130,200, Seven Arts: £59,867
The Leather Boys (1964)	£106,000	Garrick: £74,000, NFFC: £27,500, deferrals: £4,500
He Who Rides a Tiger (1965)	£65,000	NFFC: £65,000
Morgan ... A Suitable Case for Treatment (1966)	£165,000	British Lion: £115,500, BL equity: £41,000, deferrals: £8,500
Ulysses (1967)	£215,000	British Lion: £150,500, NFFC: £29,500, deferrals: £35,000

ABPC (AND ASSOCIATES)

Table 1.A.2 Funding details for selected films distributed by APBC and associates (from Film Finances archive)

Title	Budget	Financing deal
Sparrows Can't Sing (1963)	£100,888	Elstree Distributors: £70,622, NFFC: £20,266, deferrals: £10,000
The Servant (1963)	£141,725	Elstree Distributors: £99,208, NFFC: £35,017, deferrals: £7,500
French Dressing (1963)	£179,000	ABPC: £139,000, NFFC: £25,000, Universal: £12,500, producers: £2,500
King and Country (1964)	£82,728	ABPC: £20,000, Universal: £18,666, Danny Angel: £37,562, deferrals: £6,500

ANGLO-AMALGAMATED

Table 1.A.3 Funding details for selected films distributed by Anglo-Amalgamated (from Film Finances archive)

Title	Budget	Financing deal
Peeping Tom (1960)	£131,000	Anglo: £101,000 (£51,000 equity, £50,000 guarantee), NFFC: £15,000, private investment: £15,000
A Kind of Loving (1962)	£148,000	Anglo: £148,000
Billy Liar (1963)	£209,600	Anglo: £209,600
The Mind Benders (1963)	£200,000	Anglo: £140,000, NFFC: £50,000, deferrals: £10,000
Nothing But the Best (1964)	£176,500	Anglo: £130,000, NFFC: £41,000, deferral: £5,500
Darling (1965)	£348,415	Anglo: £214,515, NFFC: £95,000, Film Finances: £38,500
Poor Cow (1967)	£242,600	Anglo: £121,300, NFFC: £121,300
All Neat in Black Stockings (1969)	£260,000	Anglo: £182,000, Princes Investments: £65,000, deferrals: £13,000

RANK

Table 1.A.4 Funding details for selected films distributed by Rank (from Film Finances archive)

Title	Budget	Financing deal
Faces in the Dark (1960)	£104,000	Welbeck Film Distributors (Sydney Box): £72,000, NFFC: £26,000, deferrals: £6,000
The League of Gentlemen (1960)	£175,500	Allied Film Makers: £123,000, NFFC: £22,500, deferrals: £30,000
Never Let Go (1960)	£155,000	Rank: £108,500, NFFC: £24,000, deferrals: £22,500
Piccadilly Third Stop (1960)	£92,000	Sydney Box Associates: £50,000, NFFC: £16,750, producer: £11,000, deferrals: £14,250
I Was Happy Here (1965)	£169,200	NFFC–Rank joint fund: £169,200
The Ipcress File (1965)	£309,261	Rank–Universal: £300,000, producers: £9,261
The Sandwich Man (1966)	£214,000	NFFC–Rank joint fund: £214,000
Maroc 7 (1966)	£316,000	NFFC–Rank joint fund: £316,000
They're a Weird Mob (1966)	£235,000	NFFC–Rank joint fund: £167,000, Australian distributor: £68,000
The Trap (1966)	£355,000	Rank: £170,000, Canadian investor: £85,000, NFFC: £85,000, deferrals: £15,000
Deadlier than the Male (1966)	£628,500	Rank: £275,000, Santor Film Productions: £275,000, producers: £38,500, Sydney Box Associates: £40,000 (contingency)
Press for Time (1966)	£272,500	Rank: £175,000, NFFC: £75,000, deferments: £22,500
The Long Duel (1967)	£1,056,211	Rank: £1,056,211
Nobody Runs Forever (1969)	£837,920	Rank: £418,960, Selmur Productions: £418,960

NOTES

1. Figures derived from project database.
2. Sue Harper and Vincent Porter, *British Cinema of the 1950s: The Decline of Deference* (Oxford: Oxford University Press, 2003), p. 56.
3. Ibid.
4. This was followed by *Doctor at Sea* (1955) and *Doctor in the House* (1957).
5. *The Daily Cinema*, 4 June 1962.
6. The executive producer on *Deadlier than the Male* was Betty Box's brother Sydney, whose long association with Rank stretched back to the late 1940s when he ran Gainsborough Productions with his wife Muriel. While a prominent casualty of John Davis's ascendancy, Box continued to be involved in various productions released through Rank including *Faces in the Dark* (1960), directed by David Eady and produced by Jon Pennington, and *Piccadilly Third Stop* (1960), directed by Wolf Rilla and produced by Norman Williams.

7. Two other Wisdom comedies, *There Was a Crooked Man* (1960) and *The Girl on the Boat* (1961) were produced by John Bryan and released by United Artists.
8. Morris Bright and Robert Ross, *The Life and Work of Peter Rogers* (London: BBC, 2000), p. 76–7.
9. 4 February 1967, production cost report on *Don't Lose Your Head*, Gerald Thomas Papers, BFI Special Collections.
10. *Kine Weekly*, 27 September 1969, the film took £165,000 on its London release alone. It was also made very economically at £208,000 making it the cheapest *Carry On* made for Rank.
11. The 1959 slate included *Tiger Bay* (1959), which introduced Hayley Mills, and *Blind Date* (1959), directed by Joseph Losey.
12. Reported in *Kine Weekly*, 5 September 1963.
13. Alexander Walker, *Hollywood, England: The British Film Industry in the Sixties* (London: Michael Joseph, 1974), p. 103.
14. Sally Dux, 'Allied Film Makers: Crime, Comedy and Social Concern', *Journal of British Cinema and Television*, 9: 2, 2012, pp. 198–213.
15. *The Daily Cinema*, 13 December 1963, p. 5.
16. Terence Kelly, Graham Norton and George Perry, *A Competitive Cinema* (London: Institute of Economic Affairs, 1966), p. 51.
17. *Kine Weekly*, 9 September 1965, p. 7.
18. At the same conference Davis announced new investment in Pinewood studios with two new stages being built to accommodate demand for both film and television production.
19. Meaning side by side, at the same rate or on an equal footing.
20. Ibid. p. 19.
21. Film Finances file on *I Was Happy Here*.
22. Film Finances file on *The Sandwich Man*.
23. Film Finances file on *They're a Weird Mob*.
24. *Maroc 7* was budgeted at £316,000 but cost £400,000, while the corresponding figures for *The Trap* were £355,000 and £457,500. In both cases this was in part a consequence of substantial problems on the overseas locations in Morocco and Canada respectively. Film Finances files for *Maroc 7* and *The Trap*.
25. Film Finances file on *The Ipcress File*.
26. Film Finances file on *Deadlier than the Male*. The rest of the budget was covered by an investment of £38,600 from the producers and £40,000 from Sydney Box Associates.
27. Film Finances file on *Nobody Runs Forever*.
28. Film Finances file on *The Quiller Memorandum*.
29. It was reported to be costing £1 million with Rank putting up the entire budget, *The Daily Cinema*, 26 October 1966.
30. Paramount's rights for both films covered the Western Hemisphere and Japan, *The Daily Cinema*, 30 December 1966.
31. *The Daily Cinema*, 25 September 1968.
32. *Kine Weekly*, 7 September 1968.
33. *Kine Weekly*, 28 September 1968.
34. *Kine Weekly*, 19 April 1969, p. 5.
35. *The Daily Cinema*, 27 June 1969, p. 2.
36. *Kine Weekly*, 6 September 1969.
37. *Kine Weekly*, 27 September 1969.
38. The film was subsequently funded by United Artists on a budget of £650,000 and went on to earn a very respectable $4.5 million. Interview with Larry Kramer, *The Daily Cinema*, 13 December 1969.

39. Harper and Porter, *British Cinema of the 1950s: The Decline of Deference*.
40. Vincent Porter, 'All Change at Elstree: Warner Bros., ABPC and British Film Policy 1945–61', *Historical Journal of Film, Radio and Television*, 21: 1, 2002, pp. 5–35. Porter points out that Robert Clark had been a protégé of the ABPC founder, John Maxwell, who died in 1940, while Sir Philip Warter was Maxwell's son-in-law.
41. Ibid.
42. Box's previous association with rank ended when she split from her producer husband Sydney.
43. Film Finances file on *Sparrows Can't Sing*.
44. Film Finances file on *The Servant*.
45. Film Finances file on *King and Country*.
46. *Kine Weekly*, 12 April 1962.
47. *Kine Weekly*, 25 October 1962.
48. Chairman's Statement, *ABC News*, vol. 17, no. 5, August 1963, p. 4.
49. *ABC News*, vol. 19, no. 5, August 1965.
50. *The Daily Cinema*, 16 September 1964.
51. *The Daily Cinema*, 18 November 1966.
52. See James Chapman, *Saints and Avengers: British Adventure Series in the 1960s* (London: I. B. Tauris, 2006), p. 74.
53. *Kine Weekly*, 14 January 1967.
54. David Meikle, *A History of Horrors: The Rise and Fall of the House of Hammer* (Lanham, MD and London: Scarecrow Press, 1996).
55. *Kine Weekly*, 10 February 1968. In the previous year EMI had also taken over the Grade Organisation.
56. *Kine Weekly*, 1 February 1969.
57. Alexander Walker, *Hollywood, England*.
58. See David Ryder, *Making it on Wardour Street* (Leeds: Cinemuseum Publishing, 2007).
59. Robert Murphy, *Sixties British Cinema* (London: BFI, 1992), p. 109.
60. See David Pirie, *A Heritage of Horror: The English Gothic Cinema 1946–72* (London: Gordon Fraser, 1973).
61. Harper and Porter, *British Cinema of the 1950s*, p. 191.
62. There are varying estimates for the budgets of the films, but these all indicate a steady rise with notable jumps from *Regardless* (£200,000) to *Cruising* (£140,000) and between *Spying* (£148,000) and *Cleo* (£194,323). Rogers also utilised a series of different legal entities to facilitate the deals, including Peter Rogers Productions, GHW Productions, Ethiro Productions and Adder Productions.
63. *Kine Weekly*, 25 July 1963.
64. *Kine Weekly*, 1 December 1960.
65. Steve Chibnall and Brian McFarlane (eds) *The British 'B' Film* (Basingstoke: Palgarve Macmillan/BFI, 2009), pp. 236–40. Anglo also made the popular Edgar Lustgarten series of 30-minute programme fillers: *Scotland Yard* (1953–61) and *The Scales of Justice* (1962–7).
66. *Kine Weekly*, 26 July 1962.
67. The film cost £618,876, Film Finances file on *Zulu*.
68. Both went slightly over budget – *A Kind Of Loving* cost £155,902 and *Billy Liar* £236,809. Film Finances files.
69. Alexander Walker, *Hollywood, England*, p. 111.
70. Film Finances file for *The Mind Benders*.
71. Film Finances file for *Nothing But the Best*.

72. Film Finances file on *Darling*. A cost of production statement for 30 June 1965 indicated a final figure of £348,015 (Anglo had provided £214,515, the NFFC £95,000, and, as the film had gone over budget, Film Finances had come in with £38,500.
73. *Kine Weekly*, 21 January 1965, p. 3.
74. Robert Webber, *50 Years of Carry On* (London: Century, 2008), p. 98.
75. Bright and Ross, *The Life and Work of Peter Rogers*, p. 143.
76. The film ended up costing £228,206, Film Finances file on *Poor Cow*.
77. Andrew Spicer, 'Producers and Moguls' in I. Q. Hunter, Laraine Porter and Justin Smith (eds), *The Routledge Companion to British Cinema History* (London: Routledge, 2017).
78. Alexander Walker, *Hollywood, England*, p. 111.
79. Harper and Porter, *British Cinema of the 1950s*.
80. Douglas Collins, *A Nose for Money: How to Make a Million* (London: Michael Joseph, 1963), p. 238.
81. The other investor/partners included Aubrey Baring, David Dent, Julian Wintle, Colin Lesslie, Charles Frend, Charles Leat, Kenneth and Gerald Shipman, George H. Brown, Basil Dearden, Ronald Neame and Monja Danichewsky. A number of other members were affiliated through connections with named directors. These include Michael Relph (with Dearden), Norman Priggen (with Frend), John Bryan and Albert Fennell (with Neame) and Leslie Parkyn (with Wintle). See Duncan Petrie, 'Bryanston Films: An Experiment in Co-Operative Independent Production and Distribution, *Historical Journal of Film, Radio and Television*, 2017.
82. The investors in Garrick included Film Finances (see Drazin 2014: 18).
83. John Champ, 'The British Production Scene: It Was an Umbrella Year', *Kine Weekly*, 14 December 1961. In April 1963 it was announced that a new umbrella group of film-makers, called Nova Film Distributors, had signed with British Lion. This comprised Anthony Havelock-Allan (chairman), Peter de Sarigny and Grahame Tharp (managing directors), with John Bryan, Peter Finch, Sidney J. Furie, Guy Hamilton and Cliff Owen. However by then the situation was deteriorating and nothing came of the initiative.
84. Derek Todd, 'The Boulting Brothers Find Pegs on Which to Hang the World', *Kine Weekly*, 30 May 1963, p. 66.
85. Reported in *Kine Weekly*, 30 March 1961.
86. Some of these productions did good business, notably *Heaven's Above*, *The Great St Trinian's Train Robbery*, and *The Family Way* which all ranked in the top ten domestic hits of the year.
87. They replaced Julian Wintle and Leslie Parkyn who had resigned from the Bryanston board.
88. Figures from Bryanston Summary of Earnings for 31 August 1962, MEB 1957 J/32
89. Bryanston–Seven Arts guaranteed £269,500 with investments of £57,750 each from Enterprise and the main Seven Arts company. Film Finances file on *Sammy Going South*.
90. Film Finances file on *The Small World of Sammy Lee*.
91. Film Finances file on *The Day the Earth Caught Fire*.
92. *Kine Weekly*, 29 July 1965.
93. *Kine Weekly*, 19 August 1965.
94. *The Daily Cinema*, 5 June 1965.
95. Michael Balcon, *Michael Balcon Presents … A Lifetime of Films* (London: Hutchison, 1969), p. 209.

96. *Kine Weekly*, 29 July 1967, p. 6. British Lion's consolidated profits for year to 31 March 1967 were £235,654, an increase on the previous year's figure of £154,880, *Kine Weekly*, 22 July 1967.
97. In the case of *Morgan*, the British Lion distribution guarantee of £115,439 was supplemented by a direct investment of £41,228. The film ended up going 12 days over schedule due to bad weather, forcing Film Finances to provide £37,000. Film Finances file on *Morgan . . . A Suitable Case for Treatment*. In the case of *Ulysses*, British Lion guaranteed £150,500, the NFFC £29,500 with the remainder made up of £35,000 in deferments. Film Finances file on *Ulysses*.
98. The special presentation category continued to be dominated by larger Hollywood funded productions such as *Oliver!*, *Chitty Chitty Bang Bang* and *Where Eagles Dare*.
99. Reported in *Kine Weekly*, 27 July 1968. Profits for the year to March 1969 increased to £575,867, more than doubling the previous year's £247,178. *Kine Weekly*, 12 July 1969.
100. *Kine Weekly*, 14 December 1968, this noted that the proceeds from the sale would be used to purchase Tudor Productions (£410,444) and to reduce the overdraft of £734,713 obtained in June 1967.
101. Derek Threadgall, *Shepperton Studios: An Independent View* (London: BFI, 1994).
102. Derek Todd, 'The Stable Door: after the (US) horse has gone', *Kine Weekly*, 6 December 1969, p. 6.
103. *Kine Weekly*, 1 June 1968.
104. Alexander Walker, *Hollywood, England*, p. 457.

2. AMERICAN INVOLVEMENT IN UK FILM PRODUCTION

Duncan Petrie

INTRODUCTION

Alexander Walker begins his seminal account of the 1960s by establishing that 'to talk of the "British" cinema in these years is to ignore the reality of what underpinned the industry – namely, American finance or the dollar economy of what, for convenience sake, we can call "Hollywood."'[1] This also features strongly in Terence Kelly, Graham Norton and George Perry's study which lists a number of advantages the American involvement afforded British producers including 100 per cent finance deals, little interference in the production process, access to both local and international markets – including all-important US distribution, and 50 per cent of net profits.[2] By 1966, the year when *Time* magazine pronounced London as 'the swinging city',[3] Britain had become, with Hollywood support, a magnet for the international film-making community. Penelope Houston struck a celebratory tone in *Sight and Sound*, declaring the presence of so many major creative talents – including François Truffaut, Michelangelo Antonioni, Stanley Kubrick, Charlie Chaplin, Joseph Losey and Richard Lester – to be 'a very satisfactory situation all round':

> The Americans are not driving the British out of work, they are creating employment. They are not setting out to Americanise British films: they are using a good deal of British talent to develop an international cinema. They are not taking over a communications industry . . . They are simply

Figure 2.1 British cinema broadening its horizons in the 1960s: Peter O'Toole and Zia Mohyeddin await the arrival of Omar Sharif in the US-backed epic *Lawrence of Arabia* (David Lean, 1962).

coming here to make movies. They are not even, as some people seem to think, stealing the Eady money out of the mouths of starving British film-makers: they are getting back a fair share on a big investment.[4]

But this endorsement also belies the existence of more critical viewpoints. The meticulously even-handed Kelly et al. identify negative consequences of the American presence, including higher production costs, making it difficult for UK financiers to compete, and the risks of increasing dependence on non-British sources of support which could be subsequently withdrawn at any time. The long-held fear of American cultural domination that had informed various policies to protect British film-making from the 1920s also reared its head, prompting Kelly et al. to note:

> The dilemma is how to prevent foreign-controlled production dominating our screens and to ensure that there is an adequate supply of films which are British in character as well as in law, while at the same time not adopting Little Englander policies which drive away all the American investment on which the home industry at present depends.[5]

Concerns about the increasing Hollywood control of British film production were articulated perhaps most strongly and consistently by the National Film Finance Corporation, whose existence was being seriously undermined by the American gravy train. By 1968 that domination was starkly apparent with Hollywood supporting 88 per cent of all British first features and providing 90 per cent of the total investment in production.[6]

This chapter will examine American involvement in British film production during the 1960s in order to test the veracity of the standard historical account and to provide a deeper and more detailed analysis by making substantial use of two sources of data. Firstly, the project database allows a more comprehensive survey of the involvement of each of the Hollywood majors which in turn can reveal different corporate strategies and relationships and how these developed over the decade. Secondly, the files of the completion guarantee company Film Finances provide detailed information on the financing and production of several Hollywood-backed British productions that can also indicate important features and differences compared with fully UK-financed films.

Hollywood and British Cinema: The Background Context

The Hollywood presence in the British film industry had long predated the 1960s. The importance of the UK market for American product was recognised as early as 1912 when Vitagraph set up a renting company in London, followed by Fox in 1916 and Famous Lasky Film Service (Paramount) in 1919. The subsequent introduction of a quota in 1927 to protect British production prompted the Hollywood majors to mount their own film-making activities. Some arranged deals with independent producers, Fox and Warner established their own studios at Wembley and Teddington respectively, while MGM ran a high-profile production operation at Denham studios from 1937 to 1939 under the leadership of Michael Balcon. But the key developments that would provide the context for 'Hollywood, England' occurred after the end of the Second World War.

Part of a range of measures aimed at bolstering the recovery of the UK economy, the 1948 Anglo-American Film Agreement resulted in the blocking of a proportion of the revenue earned by Hollywood in Britain. While $17 million could be remitted, plus a sum in dollars equal to the earnings of British films in the United States, this left around $20 million which, as Thomas Guback notes, could be spent 'in Britain to produce films, acquire story rights and buy real estate and studios'.[7] Revisions to the agreement in 1950 increased incentives for American producers by allowing additional blocked currency to be remitted as a bonus equal to 23 per cent of expenditure on film production in Britain and 50 per cent of monies spent on distribution rights for British films.[8] The following year saw the bonus for British production raised to 33.33 per cent. The resulting 'runaway' production was driven by Hollywood investment of some $15 million a year during the first half of the 1950s, representing around 50 per cent of the studios' combined earnings at the British box office.

Another key factor was the Eady Levy, a tax on cinema tickets introduced in 1949 which distributed revenue to producers via the British Film Fund in

65

proportion to their box-office performance. During the 1950s it was estimated that Eady payments could be worth an average of 44.3 per cent on top of a film's box-office earnings. While introduced to encourage British production, the Hollywood studios were able to take advantage of the levy – as they had previously done with the quota – by making films through their UK subsidiaries that qualified as British. Moreover, as Jonathan Stubbs points out, Eady was more generous than similar schemes in France and Italy which led to considerably more runaway productions being made in Britain.[9]

The combined impact of these incentives was substantial. Sue Harper and Vincent Porter estimate that approximately 170 American-backed British films were produced during the 1950s, around half being first features. As 837 films over 72 minutes were registered between 1950 and 1959 this suggests as much as 20 per cent were US-funded.[10] The activities of individual companies took different forms. In 1948 MGM acquired and rebuilt the former Amalgamated studios at Borehamwood, while Warners relocated from their damaged Teddington facility to ABPC's Elstree studios, a move facilitated by their 37.5 per cent ownership of Associated British.[11] 20th Century Fox and Walt Disney – who were encouraged to move beyond animation into the production of live-action family adventures in Britain – beginning with *Treasure Island* (1950) – were also active at the start of the 1950s. Columbia followed in 1953 through their connection with the independent production company Warwick Films run by Americans Irving Allen and Albert 'Cubby' Broccoli.

This American presence was further consolidated when the Eady Levy was made mandatory in 1957, stimulating an increase in the proportion of Hollywood-funded films from 23 per cent to 42 per cent. Columbia led the way through deals with prestige producers like Sam Spiegel – whose *The Bridge on the River Kwai* (1957) directed by David Lean proved hugely profitable – to more modest enterprises such as Hammer Films with whom the studio began a relationship in 1958 when they acquired a 49 per cent stake in Bray studios.[12] Hammer's managing director, James Carreras, understood the advantage of doing business with the Americans and in addition to Columbia he also secured backing from Warners and then, more significantly, Universal which was to cement his company's lucrative association with the horror genre.[13]

These developments were also informed by the response of Hollywood to other major challenges, notably the decline in cinemagoing and the impact of the forced break up of vertical integration that had defined the classical studio system. A key response was the consolidation of the majors as distributors and the growth in the outsourcing of production to independents. Tino Balio has identified United Artists as 'the company that changed the film industry' through their financing of independent producers both at home and abroad.[14] Interestingly, the management team responsible – Arthur Krim and Robert

Benjamin – had previously worked for Eagle Lion, set up in 1946 to distribute British films made by Rank in the United States. What made United Artists different was that they were essentially a distribution company rather than a traditional studio, they offered independent producers autonomy once the main ingredients of a project had been agreed, affording the producer ownership in their picture and allowing production to be set up anywhere in the world. This allowed the company to nurture long-term relationships with producers and so guarantee quality product.[15] United Artists' rivals had studios to fill and so were unable to provide this in the same way. But others slowly began to follow suit, led by Columbia and then Universal – whose fortunes were transformed following the 1962 takeover by MCA whose head, former talent agent, Lew Wasserman, had pioneered the package system that gave producers and stars more power and control.[16]

Thus Hollywood was encouraged to make films with independent producers wherever the conditions were favourable, and by the early 1960s Britain had become a very attractive option for a new and different kind of runaway production. While the Anglo-American Film Agreement may have formally ended on 1 February 1960,[17] removing any compulsion for the studios to reinvest their earnings in British production, by now the other incentives for continued involvement were well understood. Most notably, the American share of the Eady Levy would increase substantially from 10 per cent in 1953 to an estimated 80 per cent by 1966.[18] The spoils could be particularly lucrative for highly performing films such as *Thunderball* (1965), the fourth of the James Bond films, which received a payment of $2.1 million (£750,000), roughly 15 per cent of the entire available fund for that year.[19]

The Operations of Individual Studios

All of the Hollywood majors enjoyed stable relationships with one of the two main circuits and their interests were also strongly represented on various British industry bodies. For example, the executive committee of the Film Production Association of Great Britain, created at the beginning of 1967 by the merger of the British Film Producers Association and the Federation of British Film Makers, included no fewer than eight employees of the UK arms of American companies: Ken Hargreaves (Anglo-Embassy), Norman Katz (Seven Arts), Arvid Griffen (MGM British), Maxwell Setton (Columbia), Harvey Harrison (Paramount), Stuart Lyons (Fox), David Chasman (United Artists) and C. James (Walt Disney).[20] The involvement of the major American distributors in British film production across the entire decade in terms of number of productions (and as a percentage of the total number of films of 55 minutes and over released in Britain from 1960 to 1969) is shown in Table 2.1.[21] The annual breakdown over the decade is shown in Table 2.2.

Table 2.1 Number of British films financed by American distributors, 1960–9

20th Century Fox	Columbia	MGM	Paramount	United Artists	Universal via Rank	Walt Disney	Warners via Warner Pathé	Others	Total
47	93	59	46	83	34	13	27	9	411
4.7%	9.4%	6%	4.6%	8.4%	3.4%	1.3%	2.7%	0.9%	41.4%

Table 2.2 Number of British films financed by American distributors by year

Distributor	1960	1961	1962	1963	1964	1965	1966	1967	1968	1969
20th Century Fox	5	5	4	2	6	6	2	5	7	5
Columbia	14	15	7	10	6	9	6	8	10	8
MGM	2	8	8	7	6	9	3	5	6	5
Paramount	6	0	3	1	2	4	5	10	11	4
United Artists	9	9	10	6	9	5	8	5	12	10
Universal	1	3	3	3	4	0	3	7	5	5
Walt Disney	2	2	2	3	1	1	1	0	1	0
Warner Bros.	1	1	0	0	0	1	3	8	7	6
Others	0	0	0	0	0	0	0	3	3	3
Total US	40	43	37	32	34	35	31	51	62	46
Total all	132	113	122	114	82	83	82	86	96	80
US as % of total	30%	38%	30%	28%	41%	42%	38%	59%	65%	57.5%

These figures yield some very interesting insights. While the trend is clearly towards increased involvement from 1964 onwards, the American share of British production is substantial across the entire decade. This suggests that the significance of the first four years may have been neglected in previous accounts. Moreover, the scale of American dominance during the latter part of the decade is less extreme than suggested by the NFFC reports which claim figures ranging from 64 per cent of all films in 1965 to 88 per cent by 1968.[22]

Given the tendency to treat Hollywood involvement in British cinema as singular or monolithic, it is worth considering the profiles of the individual studios. Over the course of the decade, Columbia and United Artists emerge as the most prolific in terms of number of films supported. A second tier is formed by MGM, Fox and Paramount, followed by a third group comprising Universal, Warners and Walt Disney. But if we consider the level of involvement over time, Columbia and United Artists' dominance owes much to the number of films supported in the early part of the decade, with only MGM – who had their own studio to run – having a similar profile. This would appear to give substance to the argument that the focus on independent producers pioneered by these two studios gave them an initial advantage. While all of the companies (apart from Disney) feature strongly in the latter part of the decade, the substantial increase in the activities of Paramount and Warners (and to a lesser extent Universal) is particularly notable. Around this time both companies were subject to takeovers: Paramount by Gulf + Western in 1966 and Warner Bros. by Seven Arts in 1968 and in each case the new management instigated a change in policy. But, elaborating on the survey approach taken by Robert Murphy in his study of sixties British cinema, a more detailed consideration of each studio's output follows.[23]

Columbia

In addition to supporting more British films than any other Hollywood studio during the decade, Columbia financed some of the most high-profile productions, including three Best Picture Oscar winners: *Lawrence of Arabia* (1962), *A Man for All Seasons* (1966) and *Oliver!* (1968). The studio's presence in the British industry was further consolidated in 1961 with the formation of BLC Films, a joint sales operation with British Lion.[24] The key figure in the story was Mike Frankovich, Columbia's European head of production from 1955 to 1964. Active in runaway production since the early 1950s, Frankovich made several films for the studio as an independent before joining them in an executive capacity. His strong attachment to and deep knowledge of the British industry enhanced Columbia's ability to gain trust and pick winners and *Kine Weekly* described Frankovich's promotion in 1962 to first vice president as 'just recognition of the dynamic which Mike has brought to bear upon the organisation's production activities in Britain and Europe'.[25] The role of European production chief was assumed by Maxwell Setton, a former associate of Frankovich,[26] who joined Columbia from Bryanston Films. But Setton's boss was to remain a key presence, reaffirming his company's commitment to British production in the face of lobbying against runaway production back in United States.[27] When Frankovich relocated to the US at the end of 1963 to head up Columbia's worldwide production activities, he was given a heartfelt send-off from senior members of the British industry.[28] Bernard F. Dick argues that Frankovich's strengths included 'the ability to harmonise the talents of stars, directors and writers',[29] which underpinned the studio's succession of hit films produced on both sides of the Atlantic during the 1960s. Setton was confirmed head of British production in May 1964, where he worked closely with a team that included development head, the actor-turned-agent, John van Eyssen, who in turn would succeed him in 1969 when Setton returned to independent production.

Columbia's British programme is characterised by its stability and was built on their strong relationships with a range of established producers, led by a group of Americans who had moved to London during the previous decade, notably Irving Allen, Sam Spiegel, Carl Foreman and Charles Schneer who provided the company with some of its most prestigious and successful films of the period. These include Foreman's *The Guns of Navarone* (J. Lee Thompson, 1961), *The Victors* (1963) and *Born Free* (James Hill, 1966) and Spiegel's *Lawrence of Arabia* and *The Night of the Generals* (Anatole Litvak, 1967). Following the demise of Warwick Films, Allen continued to focus on action adventures like *The Hellions* (Ken Annakin, 1961), *The Long Ships* (Jack Cardiff, 1963) and *Genghis Khan* (Henry Levin, 1965), while Schneer specialised in fantasy films featuring the talents of animator Ray Harryhausen such as *Mysterious Island* (Cy Endfield, 1961), *Jason and the Argonauts* (Don Chaffey, 1963) and *The First Men on the Moon* (Nathan Juran, 1964). Beyond this core, Columbia backed other high-profile American director/producers resulting in *Dr Strangelove* (Stanley Kubrick, 1964), *Bunny Lake is Missing* (Otto Preminger, 1965), *Lord Jim* (Richard Brooks, 1965), *The Heroes of Telemark* (Anthony Mann, 1965), *A Man for All Seasons* (Fred Zinnemann, 1966), *To Sir With Love* (James Clavell, 1967) and *The Deadly Affair* (Sidney Lumet 1967). Charles K. Feldman's multi-director James Bond spoof, *Casino Royale* (1967), famously ran out of control, but still did reasonable business at the box office. The studio had also facilitated the move into producing by its former head of European publicity, Walter Shenson, with *The Mouse that Roared* (1959) and following a very successful spell working with United Artists he returned to Columbia for the comedies *30 is a Dangerous Age Cynthia* (Joe McGrath, 1967) – a film that Shenson reportedly self-financed to the tune of £200,000[30] – and *Don't Raise the Bridge, Lower the River* (Jerry Paris, 1968).

British talent associated with the studio included Carol Reed, who directed *Our Man in Havana* (1960), *The Running Man* (1963) and the Oscar-winning musical, *Oliver!* The latter was produced by John Woolf whose brother James made *The Pumpkin Eater* (Jack Clayton, 1964), *Life at the Top* (Ted Kotcheff, 1965) and the US production, *King Rat* (1965) for Columbia. The latter film's director, Bryan Forbes, subsequently made *The Wrong Box* (1966), the new production team of John Goldstone and Otto Plaschkes provided the 'swinging London' film *Georgy Girl* (Silvio Narrizano, 1966), while David Deutsch produced *Interlude* (Kevin Billington, 1968) and *Lock up Your Daughters!* (Peter Coe, 1969).

During the early part of the decade Columbia also distributed a significant number of lower-budget and second features. Alongside various 'B' movies produced by Bill Luckwell and the Danzigers, this included eighteen psychological thrillers, adventure films and comedies from Hammer Films including *The Terror of the Tongs* (1960), *Never Take Sweets from a Stranger* (1961), *The Damned* (1961), *The Pirates of Blood River* (1962) and *Watch it Sailor!* (1962); and the first two films made by Milton Subotsky and Max Rosenberg's Amicus Productions, the teen musicals *Its Trad Dad!* (1962), the feature debut of Richard Lester, and *Just for Fun!* (1963).

United Artists

In praising the vision and enterprise of American companies, Kelly et al. argue that 'United Artists' list of British films alone is a devastating comment on the poverty and/or mediocre initiative of British distributors. It has made United Artists by far the strongest distributor in Britain.'[31] But the decade began rather inauspiciously, and with the odd exception such as *Tunes of Glory* (Ronald Neame, 1960) and *The Valiant* (Roy Ward Baker, 1961), low-budget films accounted for the bulk of United Artists' British product until 1963. This included a substantial number of 'B' movies, among them fourteen second features made by American ex-pats Edward and Harry Danziger, including *Spider's Web* (1961), the brothers' first full-length feature in Technicolor made just before they quit film production, and a handful of films produced by George Fowler and directed by the emerging Canadian talent Sidney J. Furie. The studio also backed two films with comedian Norman Wisdom, moonlighting from Rank, produced by John Bryan: *There Was a Crooked Man* (1960) and *Girl on the Boat* (1962).

But United Artists' profile was dramatically transformed by production head George H. 'Bud' Ornstein, who moved to London in June 1961 after several years working for the company in Spain.[32] He subsequently backed the game-changing James Bond series produced by Cubby Broccoli and Harry Saltzman, beginning with *Dr No* (1962) and followed by *From Russia with Love* (1963), *Goldfinger* (1964) *Thunderball* (1965), *You Only Live Twice* (1967) and *On Her Majesty's Secret Service* (1969). In addition to routinely dominating the UK box office, Tino Balio notes that the Bond pictures provided United Artists with some of their best-performing films in the American domestic market between 1957 and 1969, with *Thunderball* ($27 million), *Goldfinger* ($22.5 million) and *You Only Live Twice* ($18 million) in first, third and fifth place respectively.[33]

United Artists backed Tony Richardson and John Osborne's Woodfall Films, beginning with the Oscar-winning *Tom Jones* (1963) and followed by *Girl With Green Eyes* (Desmond Davies, 1964), *One Way Pendulum* (Peter Yates, 1965) and the Palme d'Or-winning *The Knack . . . and How to Get It* (Richard Lester, 1965). The studio also supported the Beatles films *A Hard Day's Night* (1964) and *Help!* (1965), made by the team of Richard Lester and Walter Shenson. Alexander Walker acknowledges the significance of Ornstein's support for *Tom Jones* – a project that had been lost by Bryanston–Seven Arts who were unprepared to take the risk and then rejected by Columbia – as a key moment. Ornstein's insistence on the project 'brought him near to being fired,'[34] but he found an ally in New York in David Picker, the nephew of United Artists vice president Arnold Picker and the resulting film went on to make almost $40 million worldwide, beginning an eight-picture relationship between United Artists and Woodfall. During this period, the studio also signed a deal with Basil Dearden and Michael Relph, resulting in *Masquerade* (1964), *Woman of Straw* (1964) and the Dearden-directed *Khartoum* (1965). Ornstein left United Artists in December 1964, initially joining forces with Beatles manager Brian Epstein in a new independent called Pickfair Films, before moving to Broccoli and Saltzman's company Eon where he was to play a key role in the production of *Thunderball* and *You Only Live Twice*. His successor at United Artists, David Chasman, was a former director of marketing and advertising for the studio in New York who maintained the company's British operations in a similar high-profile manner to the end of the decade.

The main characteristic of United Artists' production strategy was long-term multi-picture deals with independents. In addition to the Bond series, Broccoli made *Chitty Chitty Bang Bang* (Ken Hughes, 1968) and Saltzman *Billion Dollar Brain* (Ken Russell, 1967) and *The Battle of Britain* (Guy Hamilton, 1969). The contract with Woodfall, perhaps the independent that did more than any other to define the era, was dominated by Tony Richardson's projects *Mademoiselle* (1966), *The Sailor from Gibraltar* (1967), *The Charge of the Light Brigade* (1968) and *Laughter in the Dark* (1969), but included the odd exception, such as Ken Loach and Tony Garnett's *Kes* (1969). In addition to the Beatles films, Walter Shenson produced *The Mouse on the Moon* (1963), again directed by Richard Lester who also went on to make *A Funny Thing Happened on the Way to the Forum* (1966), *How I Won the War* (1967) and *The Bed Sitting Room* (1969) without Shenson for United Artists.

The other major independent supplying United Artists during the decade was the Mirisch Corporation, which made films in both the United States and Britain. Their latter productions commenced with the drama *Stolen Hours* (Daniel Petrie, 1963) and include the *Pink Panther* comedies, *A Shot in the Dark* (Blake Edwards, 1964) and *Inspector Clouseau* (Bud Yorkin, 1968); a series of war films: *633 Squadron* (1964), *Attack on the Iron Coast* (1968), *Mosquito Squadron* (1968) and *Submarine X1* (1968); and John Huston's adventure/comedy, *Sinful Davey* (1969). While Balio argues that United Artists' British production ventures 'consisted of a diversified range of product suitable for all markets',[35] there is evidence of a continuing attempt to support risk and innovation as suggested by more unusual productions such as Peter Brook's *Marat/Sade* (1966), Ken Russell's *Women in Love* (1969) – which had been rejected by Rank on moral grounds – and Gerry and Sylvia Anderson's big-screen versions of the popular animated television series, *Thunderbirds are Go!* (1966) and *Thunderbird 6* (1968).

MGM

By comparison, MGM was a much more traditional Hollywood operation, described by Robert Murphy as 'the most conservative, and with its huge, well-equipped Borehamwood studios, the most influential of the American majors.'[36] But the company's ten-stage UK production facility had always been a double-edged sword, giving MGM a prominent place in the industry but saddling it with substantial operating costs and a vulnerability to business volatility. In March 1954, 300 MGM studio employees had to be laid off during a slack period in production, and a similar problem was encountered in autumn 1961 when *Kine Weekly* reported that 117 employees at the studio had been made redundant.[37] Yet a mere six months later it was announced that two new sound stages and a modern new laboratory would be built in anticipation of an increase in production.[38] In terms of key personnel, during the early part of the decade MGM's British production was overseen by Lawrence P. Bachmann, a former associate of producer Pandro S. Berman who made a number of prestige films during the 1950s, while in 1963 Arvid Griffen succeeded Maurice Foster as head of the studio.

The stand-out British-made MGM films of the 1960s are undoubtedly the David Lean epic, *Doctor Zhivago* (1965), Michelangelo Antonioni's *Blow Up* (1966), which was awarded the Palme d'Or in 1967, and Stanley Kubrick's ambitious sci-fi drama, *2001: A Space Odyssey* (1968). Other prestige fare was provided by the Arthur Freed production *Light in the Piazza* (1961), Kubrick's *Lolita* (1962), Robert Wise's *The Haunting* (1963) and a series of productions by the Russian émigré, Anatole de Grunwald: *Come Fly With Me* (1962), *I Thank a Fool* (1962), *The VIPs* (1963) and *The Yellow Rolls Royce* (1964), the last two directed by long-time associate Anthony Asquith, recalling MGM's tradition of star ensemble pics in luxurious surroundings. But once again the production slate for the early part of the decade included several second features produced by the Danziger brothers and Ronald Kinnoch – whose output included *Village of the Damned* (1960), *Invasion Quartet* (1961), *Postman's Knock* (1961) and *Cairo* (1963). MGM also made a series of adaptations of Agatha Christie's Miss Marple novels with Margaret Rutherford as the lady sleuth, including *Murder She Said* (1961), *Murder at the Gallop* (1963), *Murder Ahoy* (1964) and *Murder Most Foul* (1964) – the latter two produced by Ben Arbeid who also made *Private Potter* (1962), *Children of the Damned* (1963) and *The Alphabet Murders* (1965).

While MGM's output for the mid-decade was dominated by their relationship with Carlo Ponti, who in addition to *Doctor Zhivago* and *Blow Up* produced *Operation Crossbow* (Michael Anderson, 1965) and *Lady L* (Peter Ustinov, 1965), the studio's output remained a rather mixed bag. Jack Cardiff directed action-packed films beginning with *Young Cassidy* (1965), which he took over from John Ford, and followed by *The Liquidator* (1965) and *The Mercenaries* (1967) alongside Albert Finney and Karel Reisz's thriller *Night Must Fall* (1964) – a remake of the 1937 MGM British film[39], Kenneth Hyman and Sidney Lumet's *The Hill* (1965), the Joe Janni–John Schlesinger Thomas Hardy adaptation, *Far From the Madding Crowd* (1967), and the pop musical *Mrs Brown, You've got a Lovely Daughter* (1968), produced by Beatles and Rolling Stones associate, Allen Klein and featuring Herman's Hermits. The latter half of the decade saw an important link-up with the American Martin Ransohoff's company Filmways on *Eye of the Devil* (J. Lee Thompson, 1966),

Roman Polanski's *Dance of the Vampires* (1967) and Jack Clayton's *Our Mother's House* (1967); two action-packed World War Two subjects – *The Dirty Dozen* (Robert Aldrich, 1967) and *Where Eagles Dare* (Brian Hutton, 1968), produced by Kenneth Hyman and Elliott Kastner respectively; the big-budget period drama, *Alfred the Great* (Clive Donner, 1969) starring David Hemmings; and the old-fashioned musical *Goodbye Mr. Chips* (Herbert Ross, 1969), featuring Peter O'Toole in the role made famous by Robert Donat in the 1939 MGM British production, which cost almost £3.5 million.[40] While the war films performed very successfully at the box office, the more distinctively 'British' historical productions, despite their thoroughly modern stars, flopped badly.

Towards the end of the decade the studio became caught up in a power struggle. In September 1969 it was announced that the former production chief of Warner–Seven Arts, Kenneth Hyman – who had produced *The Hill* and *The Dirty Dozen* – was to assume a similar position at Culver City.[41] But following the subsequent acquisition of MGM by Kirk Kerkorian, Hyman withdrew, leaving the company to embark on a major reorganisation of its business at a time when spiralling budget costs on the latest David Lean epic *Ryan's Daughter* were causing concern. While rumours in 1969 that the MGM British studios were to close had been dismissed, the following April this came to pass with the remnants of MGM's production activities moving to the neighbouring EMI (formerly ABPC) facility at Elstree.[42] The company also cancelled a number of prestige projects, among them Stanley Kubrick's biopic about Napoleon Bonaparte and Fred Zinnemann's adaptation of André Malraux's novel, *Man's Fate*.

20th Century Fox

Fox began the decade in a relatively strong position, announcing a £7 million British production programme in June 1960,[43] and providing Britain's official entry to the Cannes Film Festival in successive years with the D. H. Lawrence adaptation *Sons and Lovers* (Jack Cardiff, 1960), produced by the American Jerry Wald, followed by the Raymond Stross–Guy Green thriller, *The Mark* (1961). As with all Fox productions during this period, these were made in CinemaScope, the anamorphic widescreen system developed by the company in the early 1950s. At the beginning of the 1960s a key advocate for Fox's British production activity was James Pattinson, the manging director of the studio's UK distribution subsidiary.[44] In an article for *Kine Weekly*, Pattinson noted that while the company's UK production strategy in the 1950s had embraced three different types of product ranging from small local films, to deals with established producers, and big studio pictures: 'Today our production activity here is not designed solely for the British market. It is designed for world market pictures.'⁴⁵ In addition to the two Cannes entries, Fox's British roster included Lewis Gilbert's *Sink the Bismark!* (1960), *The Millionairess* (Anthony Asquith, 1960), produced by Dimitri de Grunwald and starring Peter Sellers, whose own directorial debut, *Mr Topaze* (1961) was also produced by de Grunwald. John Brabourne and Jack Clayton's *The Innocents* (1961), Michael Powell's *The Queen's Guards* (1961), Burt Kennedy's *The Canadians* (1961), Leo McCarey's *Satan Never Sleeps* (1962), Mark Robson's *Nine Hours to Rama* (1962) and Walter Seltzer and Guy Hamilton's *Man in the Middle* (1963) were other key films supported during this period.

In July 1962 the president of 20th Century Fox, Spyros Skouras, was forced to retire due to ill health and was succeeded by Darryl F. Zanuck who appointed his son Richard as head of production. It was then revealed that the studio was in serious financial difficulties, largely due to Walter Wanger's epic production of *Cleopatra,* which began at Pinewood before transferring to Italy and ended up costing a monumental $31 million (£11 million). Zanuck subsequently decreed that future Fox productions would be made at Century City in Los Angeles unless a foreign locale was absolutely necessary.⁴⁶ However, the situation improved and in 1963 Elmo Williams was appointed Fox's new London-based production chief. Having begun his career as an editor before rising to become a production executive, Williams was another highly respected American in the British production scene and he actively sought to develop his company's profile by making films with 'an international viewpoint and international appeal'.⁴⁷

The new slate included the thriller *The Third Secret* (Charles Crichton, 1963), the George H. Brown–John Guillermin military drama *Guns at Batasi* (1964), the sea-faring adventure *A High Wind in Jamaica* (1965) directed by Alexander Mackendrick, Ken Annakin's ambitious ensemble comedy *Those Magnificent Men in Their Flying Machines* (1965), made in 70mm Todd-AO, and the more serious World War One aviation drama, *The Blue Max* (1966), also with Guillermin. But underpinning the studio's renewed vigour was the enormous success of *The Sound of Music* (Robert Wise, 1965), an American production which was the top-grossing film of the entire decade and the first to earn over $100 million. These prestige productions were complemented by a series of cheaper films provided by Robert Lippert, the American 'B' movie producer and distributor who had been closely involved with Fox during the previous decade, including *The Earth Dies Screaming* (1964), directed by Hammer stalwart Terence Fisher, *The Horror of it All* (1964), *Witchcraft* (1964) and *Curse of the Fly* (1965).

In 1966 Williams was recalled to Hollywood, ostensibly to facilitate closer co-ordination in the casting and production of Fox films, but actually a symptom of Richard Zanuck's tightening grip over all aspects of the studio's operations.⁴⁸ His successor in London was André Hakim, supported by Stuart Lyons who moved up to the top job two years later.⁴⁹ The new team steered Fox's British production towards more contemporary subjects and styles, notably reflected in the comic-book spy thriller, *Modesty Blaise* (1966), produced by Joe Janni and directed by Joseph Losey, Brian Forbes' spy drama *Deadfall* (1967), Michael Cacoyannis's *The Day the Fish Came out* (1967), Ronald Neame and Fielder Cooke's *Prudence and the Pill* (1968), Michael Laughlin and Mike Sarne's *Joanna* (1968), and *The Touchables* (1968), directed by photographer Robert Freeman and produced by John Bryan. Stanley Donen made three films for Fox during this period: the comedy-satire *Bedazzled* (1967), the romantic road-movie *Two For the Road* (1967) and the gay-themed comedy drama *Staircase* (1969). High-profile literary adaptations such as Guy Green's version of the John Fowles' novel, *The Magus* (1968), Ivan Foxwell's *Decline and Fall... of a Birdwatcher* (John Krish 1968), an update of Evelyn Waugh's 1920s comic classic, and Ronald Neame's take on Muriel Spark's *The Prime of Miss Jean Brodie* (1969) also featured in the studio's output. Promotion for this slate in the trade press went under the banner 'Think Young! Think 20th Century Fox!' and placed an emphasis on the youthful talent involved, naming several stars, directors and even Richard Zanuck.⁵⁰ However, in *Sight and Sound* John Russell-Taylor criticised the studio's lack of direction or coherence compared with the programmes of rivals like Universal and Paramount.⁵¹ What is clear is that the films failed to perform sufficiently to compensate for the conspicuous failure of the musical fantasy *Dr Doolittle* (1967), which had cost three times its original budget of $6 million, and Fox arrived at the decade's end once again in deep financial trouble.

Paramount

The British production activities of Paramount were effectively insignificant until 1964 which saw the release of two period films: the Stanley Baker–Cy Endfield production *Zulu* and Hal B. Wallis and Peter Glenville's *Becket*. The studio's production representative in London at this point was Howard Harrison, who had replaced Richard Patterson in 1961 when the latter joined Seven Arts.⁵² Between 1960 and 1964 practically all Paramount's British product comprised 'B' movies made by the Danziger brothers, acquired to support the studio's American features on their UK release. The odd exception included Ray Stark's Hong Kong-set *The World of Suzie Wong* (1960), *The Boy Who Stole a Million* (Charles Crichton, 1960), a low-budget co-production with Bryanston, and the two films noted above, *Zulu* being a co-production with Joe Levine's Embassy Pictures. The relationship with Baker and Endfield continued with *The Sands of the Kalahari* (1965), and that year saw Paramount's activities begin to step up with the Marcel Hellman–Terence Young costume drama *The Amorous Adventures of Moll Flanders* (1965),

Martin Ritt's John Le Carré adaptation, *The Spy Who Came in from the Cold* (1965), and the beginning of an association with Amicus which provided a number of low-budget horror and fantasy films including *The Skull* (1965), *The Psychopath* (1966) and *The Deadly Bees* (1967). Their momentum continued into 1966 with Lewis Gilbert's *Alfie*, Harry Saltzman's *Funeral in Berlin* (both starring Michael Caine), the Ray Stark–Ken Hughes *Drop Dead Darling*, and two further collaborations with Embassy, *The Spy With a Cold Nose* and *The Idol*, both directed by Daniel Petrie.

A key development came in 1966 when Paramount were acquired by Gulf + Western and Charles Bluhdorn the new studio boss appointed George Ornstein as his head of European production. *Kine Weekly* announced in November that Paramount were embarking on an ambitious and expanded production programme with the ambition to make fifteen films a year in Britain, 50 per cent of the company's total production.[53] While Ornstein inherited some projects initiated by Harrison, including the musical *Half a Sixpence* (George Sidney, 1967), the increased level of activity under his stewardship produced a wide range of subjects from an equally diverse array of film-makers. Key figures included director Peter Collinson who had made his debut with the claustrophobic thriller, *The Penthouse* (1968) and went on to direct *Up the Junction* (1967), *The Long Day's Dying* (1968) and *The Italian Job* (1969) for Paramount. The second of these was produced by John Brabourne who provided more traditional fare with Franco Zeffirelli's Shakespeare adaptation, *Romeo and Juliet* (1968) and *The Dance of Death* (1968), from the play by Strindberg. Ornstein also backed Stanley Baker and Michael Deeley's *Robbery* (Peter Yates, 1967)[54], Basil Dearden and Michael Relph's *The Assassination Bureau* (1968) and the Michael Powell-produced *Sebastian* (1967), directed by another promising newcomer, David Greene, in addition to Woodfall's *Inadmissible Evidence* (1968), Lindsay Anderson's Palme d'Or winning satire, *If . . . .* (1968), and Richard Attenborough's adaptation of Joan Littlewood's anti-war revue, *Oh! What a Lovely War* (1969). Alexander Walker notes that Paramount also entered into a deal with the NFFC to finance two films on a *pari passu* basis – *Negatives* (Peter Medak, 1968) and *Two Gentlemen Sharing* (Ted Kotcheff, 1969) – although neither was subsequently distributed by the company.[55]

While the emphasis was clearly on new talent and daring subject matter, this slate conspicuously failed to replicate Ornstein's success at United Artists, prompting Walker to note that Paramount's head of production 'sometimes felt he was presiding over the frenzied disintegration of the very trends he had helped to initiate in the early 1960s'.[56] Strains began to show, and were exacerbated by tensions with Robert Evans, head of Paramount's productions in Los Angeles, leading Ornstein to quit at the beginning of 1969. He was succeeded by Michael Flint, whose own tenure lasted less than a year.

Universal

Universal's profile shares certain similarities with that of Paramount, beginning at a very modest level before expanding markedly after 1966. Up to that point the studio's main involvement in British production was through their association with Hammer Films, a relationship which commenced with *Dracula* (1958) and included films like *The Brides of Dracula* (1960), *Curse of the Werewolf* (1961), *The Phantom of the Opera* (1962), *The Evil of Frankenstein* (1964) and *Kiss of the Vampire* (1964). In addition, Universal made the odd prestige film like *The Grass is Greener* (Stanley Donen, 1961), *Lancelot and Guinevere* (Cornel Wilde, 1962), *The Chalk Garden* (Ronald Neame, 1963) and *The Truth about Spring* (Richard Thorpe, 1964). Then at the end of 1965 the studio announced a bold new British production programme headed by Jay Kanter, another former MCA agent.[57] Alexander Walker notes that 'Kanter was a trusted intimate of Lew Wasserman ... a man who delegated authority either totally or not at all. [He] came to Britain with an enviable freedom probably not matched by the European production chief of any other comparable Hollywood company.'[58] Over the next three years Universal financed more than a dozen films at a total cost of around $30 million (£12.5 million). In an interview with John Russell Taylor in *Sight and Sound*, Kanter confirmed the level of autonomy, noting that the films he has backed reflect his own tastes and were conceived very much as a programme.[59]

But on closer inspection this is another diverse slate of films by experienced veterans including Stanley Donen's *Arabesque* (1966), Charlie Chaplin's swansong *A Countess from Hong Kong* (1966), Guy Green's *Pretty Polly* (1967), Joseph Losey's *Boom!* (1968) and *Secret Ceremony* (1968), and Hal B. Wallis' *Anne of a Thousand Days* (Charles Jarrott, 1969). But these sit alongside work from a younger generation including Michael Winner's *The Jokers* (1966) and *I'll Never Forget What's 'is Name* (1967), Peter Hall's *Work is a Four-Letter Word* (1967) and *Three Into Two Won't Go* (1968), Karel Reisz's *Isadora* (1968), and *Fahrenheit 451* (1966), Francois Truffaut's first English-language film produced by Lewis M. Allen. Kanter also backed the big-screen directing debuts of Albert Finney with *Charlie Bubbles* (1967), Peter Watkins with *Privilege* (1967), John McGrath with *The Bofors Gun* (1968) and Anthony Newley with *Can Heironymus Merkin Ever Forget Mercy Humppe and Find True Happiness?* (1969). Despite many impressive ingredients, Universal's programme proved to be, in Alexander Walker's words, 'a failure of unanticipated and unparalleled proportion',[60] serving to confirm 'the British label and the "swinging" look were not the wonder ingredients that had been supposed'.[61] In February 1969 Kanter announced that he was leaving Universal to pursue his own independent productions.

Warner Bros.

While one of their final British productions of the 1950s had been *Look Back in Anger*, the film that launched Woodfall Films and the British New Wave, Warner Bros. had assumed a very low profile in the early part of the following decade. In addition to selling a third of its 37.5 per cent holding in ABPC[62], the studio made just three British qualifying features between 1960 and 1965: the Australian 'western', *The Sundowners* (Fred Zinnemann, 1960) and two Italian-set dramas, the Seven Arts production of *The Roman Spring of Mrs Stone* (Jose Quintero, 1961) and *The Battle of the Villa Fiorita* (Delmer Daves, 1965). Then at the beginning of 1966 Martin Jurrow was appointed the studio's new production head in London,[63] and a relationship with the young American producers Elliott Kastner and Jerry Gershwin subsequently delivered *Kaleidoscope* (Jack Smight, 1966) and *The Bobo* (Robert Parish, 1967). But it was the connection with Seven Arts that proved the most significant factor in the development of the company's production activities. In 1967 Jack Warner sold his studio to Eliot Hyman, creating a new company, Warner–Seven Arts, with Eliot's son Kenneth installed as head of production. A key source of product following the reorganisation was to come from Seven Arts' long association with Hammer Films, including a slate of eighteen films made for Warner Pathé and 20th Century Fox. Warner Bros. had their own a track record with Hammer dating back to 1957, and the new arrangement resulted in films like *Dracula Has Risen From the Grave* (1968), *When Dinosaurs Ruled the Earth* (1969), *Moon Zero Two* (1969) and *Frankenstein Must Be Destroyed* (1969).

Other Warner projects during the period include contemporary subjects like the spy thriller *The Naked Runner* (Sidney J. Furie, 1967), Richard Lester's San Francisco-set drama, *Petulia* (1968), Donald Cammell and Nicolas Roeg's *Performance*, produced in 1968 but delayed for two years before being released, and Kevin Billington's satire, *The Rise and Rise of Michael Rimmer* (1970); alongside adaptations from famous plays such as Sidney Lumet's *The Seagull* (1968), the Frank Dunlop–Peter Snell version of *The Winter's Tale* (1968) and Bryan Forbes' *The Madwoman of Challiot* (1969). In August 1969 Warner–Seven Arts was bought by Kinney National Services, headed by Steven J. Ross. John Calley became the new executive in charge of production with George Ornstein also joining as vice president in charge of foreign production, although he was to remain in post for just one year.[64]

Walt Disney and others

Compared with their rivals, Disney had a smaller production profile in Britain during the 1960s. Moreover, their films were all family-oriented adventures. As noted above, the company had moved beyond animation in their British runaway productions of the early 1950s including *Treasure Island* (1950), *The Story of Robin Hood and His Merrie Men* (1952), *The Sword and the Rose* (1953) and *Rob Roy the Highland Rogue* (1954). Production was subsequently confined to the United States until *Kidnapped* (Robert Stevenson, 1960) rekindled a new British programme which included features and episodes for the company's NBC television series 'Walt Disney's Wonderful World of Colour' that were also given a UK theatrical release. Films included *Swiss Family Robinson* (Ken Annakin, 1960), *Greyfriars Bobby* (Don Chaffey, 1961), *In Search of the Castaways* (Stevenson, 1962), featuring the studio's big juvenile star of the period, Hayley Mills, *Dr. Syn Alias the Scarecrow* (James Neilson, 1963), *The Three Lives of Thomasina* (Chaffey, 1963), *The Moonspinners* (Neilson, 1964), the latter also with Mills, and *The Fighting Prince of Donegal* (Michael O'Herlihy, 1966). The TV dramas included *The Horsemasters* (1961), *The Prince and the Pauper* (1962), *The Horse Without a Head* (1963), *The Legend of Young Dick Turpin* (1965) and *Guns in the Heather* (1968). While Walt Disney personally oversaw his company's production programme until his death in 1966, the British films were produced either by Bill Anderson or his UK associate, Hugh Attwooll, and made by a group of contract artists and technicians. The studio concentrated the bulk of their sixties production in Burbank and refused to participate in the clamour to make British films in the latter half of the decade. Perhaps tellingly, Disney was one of the few majors to end the decade with healthy finances.

A number of smaller American companies also became involved in British production during the 1960s. In 1956 Joseph E. Levine set up Embassy Pictures, a small producer/distributor specialising in exploitation genres such as horror and Italian peplums. In 1963 Levine signed a major production deal with Paramount and set up a British subsidiary, Anglo-Embassy, which under managing director Ken Hargreaves would supervise his growing interests in Europe.[65] A relationship with Cy Endfield and Stanley Baker led to Embassy financing the features *Zulu* and *The Sands of the Kalahari* in partnership with Paramount. In February 1965 Levine also acquired the worldwide distribution rights to Jo Janni and John Schlesinger's *Darling*, for $1 million.[66] Subsequent Embassy-backed films ranged from low-budget exploitation such as Amicus film's *The Terrornauts* (1967) and Michael Klinger's *Baby Love* (1968), to the prestige historical drama *The Lion in Winter* (1968), produced by Levine and Martin Poll, and the swinging comedy by Roy Millichip and Desmond Davis, *A Nice Girl Like Me* (1969). These films were all distributed in the UK by Avco–Embassy, formed by the 1967 takeover of Levine's company by the Avco Corporation.

The significance of Seven Arts has already been noted in relation to their long association with Hammer Films and brief control of Warner Bros. But the company's participation in British cinema during the sixties is even broader, beginning with an involvement in both Fox's *The World of Suzie Wong* and MGM's *Lolita*. In 1961 James Pattinson was poached from Paramount to become the Seven Arts executive in charge of European production[67] and in March 1962 *Kine Weekly* announced that Seven Arts had formed a British production unit which went on to make a series of films for MGM beginning with *The Main Attraction*, directed by Daniel Petrie,[68] and followed by *Of Human Bondage* (1964), *The Hill* (1965) and *The Dirty Dozen* (1967), the last two produced by Kenneth Hyman. The relationship with Paramount resulted in the US-set *Promise Her Everything* (1965) and the espionage comedy, *The Spy With a Cold Nose* (1966); while the connection with Warners began with *The Roman Spring of Mrs Stone* (1961) followed by *The Shuttered Room* (1966), *The Double Man* (1967) and a host of low-budget films including Harry Allan Towers' *Ten Little Indians* (1965) and Herbert Leder's *The Frozen Dead* (1966) and *It!* (1966). Prior to this, in addition to being co-producer with ABPC on *Tamahine* (1963), Seven Arts had a brief association with Bryanston on *Sammy Going South* (1963), *The Small World of Sammy Lee* (1963) and *The Wild Affair* (1964), before embarking on a more substantial slate of films with Hammer, beginning with in 1965 with *The Nanny* and *She*,[69] which led to a multi picture deal involving Warner Pathé and 20th Century Fox that commenced the following year.

Also noteworthy is James H. Nicholson and Samuel Z. Arkoff's American Independent Pictures (AIP), whose association with Anglo-Amalgamated led to a series of low-budget co-productions beginning with *Circus of Horrors* (1960) and followed by *Konga* (1961), two Edgar Allan Poe adaptations directed by Roger Corman, *The Masque of the Red Death* (1964) and *The Tomb of Ligeia* (1965), *City Under the Sea* (1965), the last directorial outing for Jacques Tourneur, and Daniel Haller's *Monster of Terror* (1965). In the late 1960s a new AIP European production programme was announced under the supervision of Louis M. Heyward,[70] the fruits of which included Tigon's *Witchfinder General* (Michael Reeves, 1968), *The Oblong Box* (1969), *Scream and Scream Again* (1970) and *Cry of the Banshee* (1970), all three directed by Gordon Hessler, and *The Vampire Lovers* (Roy Ward Baker, 1970) which began an association with Hammer Films.

The Financial Impact: An Insight from Film Finances

The files of the completion guarantee company Film Finances provide an invaluable insight into otherwise opaque film-funding arrangements, as well as illuminating many other elements of the film-production process. Film Finances was established in 1950 to provide completion bonds to independent producers, effectively an insurance arrangement against a production exceeding its budget. While aimed primarily at UK-financed films, Charles Drazin points out that the company's involvement with American runaway productions had begun in 1951 when it provided a completion guarantee to United Artists for *The African Queen*, produced by Sam Spiegel.⁷¹ Another significant relationship was established when the company issued a guarantee to Columbia for *The Red Berets* (1953), the first of a series of films by Irving Allen and Cubby Broccoli's Warwick Productions. As Drazin notes, the value of a completion guarantee for a Hollywood studio was that it 'provided the means of asserting control over a production that, made far from Hollywood, it could not supervise itself.'⁷² While the setting up of London-based production offices in the 1960s made this external supervision less necessary, Film Finances continued to be involved in the 'Hollywood, England' phenomenon.

Files for thirty features, wholly or partly financed by American companies and involving all of the majors with the exception of Walt Disney and Avco Embassy, were examined, including six productions backed by United Artists between 1960 and 1963 and seven by Universal, all but one made between 1966 and 1969. These serve to confirm the impact that Hollywood funding had on British production budgets in that while the vast majority of British-financed films supported by Film Finances during the early 1960s cost less than £200,000, the budgets for several of the American-backed films are already substantially higher. Thus the guarantee provided to Cornel Wilde's 1962 production of *Lancelot and Guinevere* for Universal was in respect of a budget of £449,000;⁷³ in the same year the agreement with Woodfall and United Artists for *Tom Jones* was for a production costing £412,374;⁷⁴ while the budget for *Zulu*, backed by Embassy and Paramount, was £666,554.⁷⁵ As the decade progressed budgets continued to rise with completion guarantees offered to Paramount for *The Sands of the Kalahari* costing £746,450 and to Universal for *Isadora* and *Boom!* on budgets of £1,283,942 and £1,531,324 respectively. In the case of the latter film, £769,000 – or almost 50 per cent – went on the fee for the two leads, Richard Burton and Elizabeth Taylor, an indication of star power only matched by Peter Sellers' £267,000 fee for Warners' *The Bobo*.⁷⁶ This new emphasis on 'above the line' talent had been indicated earlier in the decade when Film Finances agreed to provide a completion guarantee for the MGM British production, *The VIPs* (1963), produced by Anatole de Grunwald, directed by Anthony Asquith and featuring an all-star cast headed by Taylor and Burton. The budget was a hefty $3 million of which only $800,000 represented the 'below the line' production costs (i.e. everything apart from the fees to the stars, director, producer and writer).⁷⁷ Elizabeth Taylor's fee alone was $1 million (£280,000) while her husband and co-star was on $280,000. Film finances' concerns about the couple's reputation led them to insist in the agreement that 'Miss Elizabeth Taylor or her company will not be paid any of her salary until after completion of her part. Mr Richard Burton will receive $100,000 and only become entitled to the balance of his salary if Miss Taylor completes her part', and that the living expenses of Burton and Taylor and their travel were limited to the budget allowance and (point 6) that any additional facilities required by Taylor were MGM's responsibility.[78]

But however substantial, the budgets of the above-noted films fall well short of super productions such as Columbia's *Lawrence of Arabia* which cost $13.8 million (£4.93 million), MGM's *Doctor Zhivago,* $11 million (£3.9 million) and *2001: a Space Odyssey,* $10.5 million (£4,375,000) or United Artists' *The Battle of Britain,* $12 million (£5 million) and *You Only Live Twice,* $9.5 million (£3.96 million). Moreover, it should be noted that Film Finances also guaranteed several modestly budgeted films distributed by the Hollywood majors including Columbia's *Naked Evil* (1965) at £37,400, MGM's *Battle Beneath the Earth* (1967) at £116,110, Paramount's *The Skull* (1965) at £80,161 and *The Deadly Bees* (1967) at £106,083, United Artists' *Follow that Man* (1961) at £79,527, and Universal's *The Bofors Gun* (1968) at £165,000.

The completion guarantor's connections with United Artists provide some interesting insights into Hollywood's involvement in British production. A 1960 internal Film Finances memorandum refers to United Artists as 'a very impersonal distribution company' and indicates concern at the number of their films that had gone over budget, including *Mark of the Phoenix* (1958), *The Horse's Mouth* (1958) and *Tunes of Glory* (1960)[79] and the apparent reluctance on the studio's part to accept any liability, regardless of the reasons for these overages.[80] A separate memo from 1963, prompted by apparent criticism of Film Finances by a United Artists representative in Paris, expands on dealings with the studio by clarifying the situation on a number of productions.[81] The (un-identified) author refers to

> a lack of that co-operation which we have from other distributors and financiers in that United Artists representatives, both here and in New York, have allowed themselves to be 'got round' by certain producers. In this regard I need not point out that a guarantor of completion is always a handy scapegoat and no producer, whatever lip service he may pay, would not rather do without a guarantor.

The implication that Hollywood backing may have encouraged producers to exercise less stringent financial control appears to arise with notable regularity within the Film Finances files. It is worth noting that completion guarantees were introduced to help instil greater fiscal discipline on an industry that had been brought to its knees by reckless spending in the late 1940s.

The first film discussed in the memo is Eon Productions' *Dr No*, which despite having taken its place in history as a highly successful start to one of the most lucrative franchises in film history, was actually a problematic production. Charles Drazin indicates that while United Artists hadn't worked with either Harry Saltzman or Cubby Broccoli, Film Finances had a significant track record with both producers, making the deal between Film Finances, United Artists and Eon crucial:

> [t]he whole system, with its balance between producer, guarantor and distributor as well as any other financiers, was geared towards producing not cheap films, but carefully planned ones that made the most of the agreed funds. It may not have suited the European-style auteur, but it was a proven method of control in the mainstream industry where so often huge sums were involved.[82]

Guaranteed on a budget of £322,069[83] *Dr No* subsequently exceeded this by almost £70,000, due largely to a lack of control over production costs both on location in Jamaica and at Pinewood,[84] resulting in Film Finances taking the production over with the support of United Artists. The blame was initially laid on Saltzman, whose tendency to profligacy had been noted by Film Finances on previous occasions.[85] However, following a rousing trade show the studio appeared to change its stance towards Saltzman, as the Film Finances memo indicates: 'since *Dr No* was clearly a success the producer's standing with United Artists was very different to what it had been in the early days.'[86] The implication is that this unfairly cast Film Finances in a rather negative light as 'penny pinching' or over-zealous in its instance on fiscal discipline. This was to be the last time Film Finances was involved with the Bond series, but by the end of 1963 the company had recovered their contribution to *Dr No* from the film's profits.[87]

In the same year, Film Finances was also forced to take over the production of *Tom Jones*, another ostensible success story.[88] While a certain amount of time had been lost early on during the extensive location shoot, it was only towards the end that the true financial situation became clear when the projected overspend rose from £16,000 to nearly £50,000. Once again a rift opened up with United Artists, who had initially supported Film Finances' position, that the situation was largely a consequence of reckless decisions taken by the producers who should accept responsibility for a substantial part of the overspend; they subsequently sided with Tony Richardson and insisted that Film Finances cover the cost. Ultimately a compromise was reached by which the no-claims bonus was increased to £13,500 in exchange for Film Finances receiving indemnity against the overage. But the damage had been done and this was to be the last time a Woodfall production would be guaranteed by the company.[89]

These well-documented difficulties came on the back of previous claims by United Artists productions against a completion guarantee, including two other occasions where Film Finances exercised its right to take over the film.

Jerome Epstein's low-budget comedy *Follow that Man* went over by £13,879 or almost 20 per cent of its projected costs, largely as a result of inexperience on the part of a first-time director who also happened to be the producer.[90] A year later, the World War Two naval drama *The Valiant* exceeded its £181,000 budget by a substantial £60,943 – a situation severe enough for Film Finances boss Robert Garrett to note in an internal memo that 'this would appear to be the worst case of irresponsibility and mis-representation on the part of a producer that we have yet encountered and I suggest that for the first time in our history we may have to consider the possibility of taking legal action against him'.[91] At one stage Garrett also suggested to George Ornstein that the individual in question, Jon Pennington, be replaced by Jack Hanbury.[92] While Pennington survived, this time Ornstein appears to have worked closely with Film Finances to salvage the situation. Unfortunately for all concerned, *The Valiant* fared poorly at the box office, leaving both Film Finances and United Artists out of pocket.

The tendency for productions to exceed budget when American finance is present is further supported by the fact that of the twenty-nine productions surveyed for this chapter, eighteen went over budget, with Film Finances exercising their right to take over eight of these films. Yet as Charles Drazin indicates, Film Finances had only taken over a production on two occasions during its first twelve years of operations.[93] The third production that required such intervention in 1962 alone (alongside *Dr No* and *Tom Jones*) was Cornel Wilde's *Lancelot and Guinevere*, financed by Universal. Shot largely on location in Yugoslavia, the film ran into serious difficulties and ended up costing £691,000 or £142,000 more than the original budget.[94] This shift in risk – and arguably greater recklessness on the part of producers – is striking. Film Finances' consultant John Croydon, who provided the initial assessment of projects, referred to the bad experience with *Lancelot and Guinevere* in his report on *Zulu*,[95] and it is telling that the guarantee subsequently offered to Diamond Films included a number of conditions, notably deferrals of £27,500 against the fees for producers Stanley Baker and Cy Endfield (who were also the film's star and director respectively), a contingency of £82,241 and the appointment of Colin Lesslie as an (uncredited) associate producer.[96] These measures proved to be justified, as while the production exceeded its budget by £34,563, this was comfortably absorbed by the contingency.[97]

Three further Hollywood-financed productions were taken over by the completion guarantor during the decade. Universal's *Isadora* exceeded its budget of £1,284,000 by £200,000, with only half of this being covered by the contingency;[98] MGM's low-budget fantasy *Battle Beneath the Earth* went more than £40,000 – or 35 per cent – over, while Warners' *The Bobo* overspent its £1 million budget by more than £140,000. In the case of *Battle Beneath the Earth*, part of the problem stemmed from the labour costs charged to the production by MGM studios Borehamwood, prompting producer Charles Reynolds to complain to Arvid Griffen that at £26,604 these were twice what had been budgeted for on a film costing only £116,110.[99] In a letter alerting Reynolds to Film Finances concerns, Garrett noted, 'If Metro wish to unload all their studio staff onto a picture, they should at least be prepared to finance the picture accordingly.'[100] The situation on *The Bobo* was more problematic. A key factor here was the erratic behaviour of the film's star, Peter Sellers, who had even been mooted as director before Robert Parrish was hired. Film Finances were wary from the outset, well aware of Sellers' reputation for profligacy despite his undoubted box-office popularity. Consequently, Film Finances' initial offer to provide a completion guarantee for the film on a budget of $2,980,794 (£1,064,569) stipulated conditions that Sellers' contract be limited to twelve weeks, that any subsequent additions to this should be treated as deferrals and that Warners accept responsibility for any loss or cost incurred due to any breach of contract by Sellers.[101] Correspondence indicates that these conditions prompted producer Elliott Kastner to propose that Warners dispense with Film Finances' services, a request which the studio rejected.[102] But the production began to fall behind early on, and Garrett's letter to Kastner informing him that Film Finances were taking over the production noted 'the delays on this film and the consequent considerable over cost are almost wholly due to Peter Sellers becoming involved in the direction of the film'.[103] This was the beginning of an increasingly recriminating correspondence over various costs – including problems with insurance, excesses on publicity or accountancy costs, trips that Kastner had taken between Rome, London and the United States that had been charged to the production, and large phone bills from the producer's flat in Rome. The final cost of the production was $3,397,309, some $185,401 over budget, which led to a protracted argument between Film Finances and Warners' solicitors over ultimate liability.[104]

Other files provide additional examples of friction. In the case of the 1966 low-budget horror film, *Naked Evil,* produced by Steven Pallos for Columbia, a letter from Robert Garrett to Ken Maidment, managing director of the studio's British distribution company, indicates displeasure at Columbia's insistence on receiving 40 per cent of the profits from the home territory immediately after its advance has been recovered. Garrett points out that in the case of an overage, Film Finances would normally recover their contribution before any parties became entitled to profits and that this should apply in any future deals.[105] The production was another problematic one, leading director Stanley Goulder to write to Garrett complaining about the American co-producer, Michael Johnson: 'It soon became apparent to me that Johnson's first and only loyalty was to Columbia, for whom he wanted to make a first-feature film on a second-feature budget.'[106] On *Lock Up Your Daughters*, Robert Garrett wrote to producer David Deutsch indicating surprise at the suggestion Film Finances should be prepared to reduce the contingency; a cover note from Garrett to his colleague Bernard Smith indicates that this letter was 'really intended for Columbia who are up to their usual tricks'.[107] Mistrust re-emerged after the production exceeded its £793,194 budget by £64,304, with (by now familiar) disagreements over responsibilities for additional expenses. While the studio ultimately paid for the film to be re-scored, they refused to cover the costs of a matte shot of a sailing ship which they insisted had been included in the script and initial budget.[108]

The case of *Joanna*, produced by Michael Laughlin and directed by Mike Sarne, indicated how the split between 20th Century Fox's offices in London and Los Angeles could create a further layer of confusion and difficulty. Offered a completion guarantee for a budget of £330,331,[109] the production came off the floor under schedule and £31,000 under budget, providing all concerned with apparently justified confidence in the film-makers' fiscal competence. However during post production the financial situation began to spin rapidly out of control. Garrett's initial concerns were expressed in correspondence with Fox's Stuart Lyons in which he indicated that Laughlin's living expenses were still being charged to the production, while the cost of music was in excess of the budget.[110] Lyons responded, accepting responsibility for the music but not the producer's living costs and some additional shooting which had also come to light.[111] As the projected overage continued to rise from £21,000 to £46,000, Garrett complained to Lyons about how little existed on paper regarding the post-production work and that 'so many of the arrangements seem to have been made by Hollywood'.[112] The unresolved issue appears to be the extent to which Richard Zanuck had personally instructed the film-makers to embark on significantly increased expenditure. While strongly denied by Lyons, Laughlin explained to Garrett that 'since the rough cut stage all of our efforts on JOANNA have been made to please the studio and, in particular, Richard Zanuck,' explaining that the studio's demands led to various changes, expensive scoring, trips to California, overtime work and other costs.[113] A stand-off between Film Finances and Fox subsequently ensued, exacerbated by the producer's refusal to deliver the finished film to the studio until his outstanding expenses were paid, something Film Finances had blocked.[114] In the end, the matter appears to have been resolved with Film Finances paying Fox £13,760,[115] suggesting a compromise had been reached given that the final overspend on *Joanna* was some £34,500.[116]

Conclusion: 1969 and After

American finance continued to dominate British film production to the end of the decade, with even the devaluation of sterling in November 1967 – which reduced the pound's value against the US dollar from $2.80 to $2.40 – and

President Johnson's curbs on US overseas investment and lending announced at the beginning of 1968, having no discernible effect.[117] But by 1969 the underlying confidence was beginning to fray. In the previous year Warner Bros. had sold their remaining 25 per cent holdings in ABPC to the British company EMI, paving the way for a subsequent takeover of Associate British. *Kine Weekly* maintained a notably positive outlook,[118] and in June a front-page headline proclaimed 'British production stays steady', with the accompanying article noting no drop-off in the first half of the year.[119] Yet the evidence of a bleaker picture was mounting. Several departures by key production heads, notably George Ornstein from Paramount and Jay Kanter from Universal, indicated growing anxiety within the studios over their poor financial performance. By September *Kine Weekly's* tone had changed markedly, with columnist Bill Altria citing the continuing battle for control at MGM – leading to the announcement that their British studio would close in 1970,[120] the radical reorientation of 20th Century Fox following the report of heavy losses and the disclosure of a big cutback in studio personnel at Paramount.[121] While in the (usually upbeat) end of year production review, Rod Cooper disclosed no new product lists had been provided by MGM, Paramount, 20th Century Fox, Universal or Warner Bros.[122] Finally an article originally published in *The Economist* but reprinted in the December issue of the ACTT's journal, *Film and TV Technician*, confirmed that four of the Hollywood majors – MGM, Fox, Paramount and Universal – had posted losses, Columbia's profits were down 40 per cent and Warner–Seven Arts had cancelled nineteen projects.[123]

Alexander Walker argues that Hollywood pulled out of British production because several studios were on the verge of going bust and inflated costs of UK production had played a key part in this. Among the conspicuous big-budget British-made flops were 20th Century Fox's *Doctor Doolittle*, United Artists' *The Battle of Britain*, MGM's *Alfred the Great* and *Goodbye Mr Chips* and Columbia's *Cromwell*. Walker cites an interview with United Artist's David Picker who had suggested that the Americans had transferred their vices as well as their virtues to Britain:

> As competition starts, the profit percentages paid to film-makers rise, so does the price of the picture. There was a slow escalation at first of the rising price-scale: we simply weren't alone any more. Then it gets to be a case of aggravated bidding between companies for properties, directors, stars, writers, photographers, designers ... That's when the cost kills you.[124]

Walker also explains that from 1967 there had been a shift in American filmmaking towards a new emphasis on youth and experimentation, heralded by lower-budget productions like *Bonnie and Clyde* (1967), *The Graduate* (1968) and *Easy Rider* (1969). British films no longer had the appeal to US audiences that they had enjoyed in the period from 1963 to 1967, with only the Bond films, *Oliver!* and *2001: A Space Odyssey* managing to compete.

While Hollywood retrenchment had an undeniable impact on British cinema in the early 1970s, this was far from the end of the story. Not only were emblematic films of the early decade such as *Get Carter*, *A Clockwork Orange*, *The Devils* and *O Lucky Man* financed by Hollywood, in 1976 the young American director George Lucas began shooting a science fiction adventure called *Star Wars* at Elstree for 20th Century Fox. Thus Hollywood's investment in British film production during the 1960s was to prove a preview of things to come, as wider shifts in the structures and operations of an increasingly globalised motion-picture entertainment industry began to replace what had been a narrowly transatlantic relationship with one that was much more transnational.

NOTES

1. Alexander Walker, *Hollywood, England: The British Film Industry in the Sixties* (London: Michael Joseph, 1974), p. 16.
2. Terence Kelly, Graham Norton and George Perry, *A Competitive Cinema* (London: Institute of Economic Affairs, 1966), p. 86.
3. *Time*, 15 April 1966.
4. Penelope Houston, 'England, Their England', *Sight and Sound*, 35: 2, Spring 1966, p. 55.
5. Terence Kelly et al., *A Competitive Cinema*, p. 89.
6. *NFFC Annual Report* to 31 March 1969, p. 4.
7. Thomas Guback, 'Hollywood's International Market', in Tino Balio (ed.), *The American Film Industry*, revised edition (Madison: University of Wisconsin Press, 1985), p. 474.
8. Jonathan Stubbs, '"Blocked" currency, runaway production in Britain and *Captain Horatio Hornblower* (1951)', *Historical Journal of Film, Radio and Television*, 28: 3, 2008.
9. Jonathan Stubbs, 'The Eady Levy: A Runaway Bribe? Hollywood Production and British Subsidy in the Early 1960s', *Journal of British Cinema and Television*, 6: 1, 2009, p. 6.
10. Sue Harper and Vincent Porter, *British Cinema of the 1950s: The Decline of Deference* (Oxford: Oxford University Press, 2003), p. 245.
11. Vincent Porter, 'All Change at Elstree: Warner Bros., ABPC and British Film Policy 1945–61', *Historical Journal of Film, Radio and Television*, 21: 1, 2001.
12. Denis Meikle, *A History of Horrors: The Rise and Fall of the House of Hammer* (Lanham, MD and London: Scarecrow Press, 1996).
13. V. L. Barnett, 'Hammering out a Deal: The Contractual and Commercial Contexts of The Curse of Frankenstein (1957) and Dracula (1958)', *Historical Journal of Radio, Film and Television*, 34: 2, 2014. The deals for both films had also involved Eliot Hyman acting as a broker between Carreras and the Hollywood majors, the beginning of another important relationship that would develop in the subsequent decade through Hyman's company Seven Arts.

14. Tino Balio, *United Artists: The Company that Changed the Film Industry* (Madison: University of Wisconsin Press, 1987).
15. Significantly, one of their first successes was the British runaway, *The African Queen*, which Sam Spiegel brought to the company having secured finance from Romulus for the Eastern Hemisphere rights.
16. Douglas Gomery, *The Hollywood Studio System: A History* (London: BFI/Palgrave, 2005).
17. *Kine Weekly*, 4 February 1960, p. 6.
18. *Variety*, 26 January 1966, p. 1.
19. Jonathan Stubbs, 'The Eady Levy: A Runaway Bribe?', p. 7.
20. *Kine Weekly*, 7 January 1967.
21. Figures derived from project database.
22. The reasons may be that our database includes a wider range of productions, including films of less the 72 minutes. Moreover, the NFFC may be including films with a minority American stake in the funding whereas we are counting these as British.
23. Robert Murphy, *Sixties British Cinema* (London: BFI, 1992).
24. In 1967 BLC became a wholly owned subsidiary of Columbia.
25. 'Longshots', *Kine Weekly*, 12 April, 1962, p. 4.
26. Setton produced *Footsteps in the Fog* (1955), *Thunderstorm* (1956), *Wicked as They Come* (1956) for Frankovich's production company and two further films, *Town on Trial* (1957) and *The Long Haul* (1957) for Columbia.
27. *Kine Weekly*, 18 October 1962, p. 3.
28. *Kine Weekly*, 2 January 1964.
29. Bernard F. Dick, 'From the Brothers Cohn to Sony Corp', in Dick (ed.), *Columbia Pictures: Portrait of a Studio* (Lexington: University Press of Kentucky, 1992), p. 21.
30. *Kine Weekly*, 11 August 1966.
31. Terence Kelly et al., *A Competitive Cinema*, p. 88.
32. Neal M. Rosendorf, 'Hollywood in Madrid': American Film Producers and the Franco Regime, 1950–1970', *Historical Journal of Film, Radio and Television*, 27: 1, 2007.
33. Tino Balio, *United Artists: The Company that Changed the Film Industry*.
34. Alexander Walker, *Hollywood, England*, p. 137.
35. Tino Balio, *United Artists: The Company that Changed the Film Industry*, p. 230.
36. Robert Murphy, *Sixties British Cinema*, p. 265.
37. *Kine Weekly*, 5 October 1961, p. 5.
38. *Kine Weekly*, 17 May 1963, p. 3.
39. Written by Emlyn Williams and directed by Richard Thorpe.
40. *Kine Weekly* reported the film will cost in the region of $8.3 million, 13 July 1968.
41. *Kine Weekly*, 27 September 1969.
42. Alexander Walker, *Hollywood, England*, p. 273.
43. *The Daily Cinema*, 29 June 1960.
44. *Kine Weekly*, 30 June 1960, p. 3.
45. James F. Pattinson, 'I Believe in British Films for Britain', *Kine Weekly*, supplement on 20th Century Fox Productions in Britain, 28 September, 1960, p. 6.
46. *Kine Weekly*, 26 July 1962, p. 11.
47. Derek Todd, *Kine Weekly*, 27 August 1964, p. 12.
48. *Kine Weekly*, 5 May 1966.
49. Lyons joined Fox in 1961 as a casting executive, two years later he joined the staff full time and in 1967 became director of the British company. *The Daily Cinema*, 31 July 1968.

50. Advert for 20th Century Fox with the tagline 'Think Young! Think 20th Century Fox!' and images of actors Genevieve Waite and Calvin Lockhart from *Joanna*; Esther Anderson, Marilyn Rickard, Kathy Simmonds and Judy Huxtable from *The Touchables*; Judy Geeson, David Dundas and Irina Demick from *Prudence and the Pill*; Peter Cook and Dudley Moore from *Bedazzled*; Candice Bergen from *The Magus*; Patricia Gozzi from *Mischief*; Isla Blair from *A Flea in Her Ear*; Robin Philips from *Decline and Fall*; directors Robert Freeman and Mike Sarne and executive vice-president Richard D. Zanuck. *The Daily Cinema*, 1 November 1967.
51. John Russell Taylor, 'Backing Britain', *Sight and Sound*, 38: 3, Summer 1969, p. 113.
52. *Kine Weekly*, 18 May 1961
53. *Kine Weekly*, 19 November 1966, p. 3.
54. Baker and Deeley's production company, Oakhurst, also made *Sleep Is Lovely*, directed by David Hart, for Paramount but it was never released.
55. Alexander Walker, *Hollywood, England*, pp. 406–10.
56. Ibid. p. 397.
57. *Kine Weekly*, 9 December 1965.
58. Alexander Walker, *Hollywood, England*, p. 344.
59. John Russell Taylor, 'Backing Britain', p. 113.
60. Alexander Walker, *Hollywood, England*, p. 343.
61. Ibid. pp. 348–9.
62. *Kine Weekly*, 23 March 1961. This reported that Warners had sold one million ordinary shares in ABPC for £2.4 million. It still holds two million of the eight million ordinary shares in the corporation.
63. *Kine Weekly*, 6 January 1966.
64. *Kine Weekly*, 9 August 1969.
65. *Kine Weekly*, 28 February 1963.
66. *Kine Weekly*, 25 February 1965.
67. *Kine Weekly*, 18 May 1961.
68. *Kine Weekly*, 1 March 1962.
69. Although it was reported that Seven Arts had previously provided Hammer with advances of $500,000 for *The Evil of Frankenstein* and *The Secret of Blood Island* (both 1964). *Kine Weekly*, 4 March 1965.
70. *Kine Weekly*, 20 January 1968.
71. Charles Drazin, 'Film Finances: The First Years', *Historical Journal of Film, Radio and Television*, 34: 1, 2014.
72. Ibid. p. 17.
73. 6 November 1961, letter to Emblem Productions Ltd from Film Finances, Film Finances file for *Lancelot and Guinevere*.
74. 16 July 1962, agreement between Woodfall Film Productions Ltd and Film Finances.
75. 2 March 1963, completion guarantee between Diamond Films and Film Finances, Film Finances file for *Zulu*.
76. 22 December 1967, production cost statement, Film Finances file for *Boom!*
77. 7 November 1962, internal Film Finances memo from Robert Garrett to A. H. P. Hope and D. McKelvie referring to a meeting with Red Silverstein, Anatole de Grunwald and Maurice Foster (then working for MGM British). Film Finances file on *The VIPs*.
78. 6 December 1962, letter from Film Finances to MGM British Studios, points 5 and 6. Film Finances file on *The VIPs*.
79. The file for *Tunes of Glory* indicates that a projected overage of £17,251 ended up being false and that the film came in slightly under budget at £267,731. Various correspondence, Film Finances file for *Tunes of Glory*.

80. Film Finances, internal memo, 'Outstanding American Business', 12 July 1960.
81. Film Finances, internal memo, 23 January 1963
82. Charles Drazin, *A Bond for Bond: Film Finances and Dr No* (London: Film Finances, 2011), p. 82.
83. 10 April 1962, agreement between Eon–Nanjaq and Film Finances, Film Finances file for *Dr No*.
84. This included a combination of bad weather and slowness on the part of director Terence Young which extended the Jamaican shoot by almost two weeks, and the cost of Ken Adam's sets, something which apparently Saltzman knew about but withheld from United Artists. The final production cost was £392,022, which included additional contributions of £10,063 from United Artists and £59,890 from Film Finances. Drazin, *A Bond for Bond*, p. 105.
85. James Chapman, 'The Trouble with Harry: The Difficult Relationship of Harry Saltzman and Film Finances', *Historical Journal of Film, Radio and Television*, 34: 1, 2014.
86. Film Finances, internal memo, 23 January 1963
87. 9 October 1963, United Artists letter to Film Finances enclosing a cheque for £39,482 4s 5d, Film Finances file for *Dr No*.
88. Sue Harper, 'The Price of Oysters: Tom Jones (1963) and Film Finances', *Historical Journal of Film, Radio and Television*, 34: 1, 2014.
89. The final cost statement for Tom Jones indicates a total spend of £466,626 – an overage of £54,252. 30 November 1962, Film Finances file for *Tom Jones*.
90. Film Finances file for *Follow That Man*.
91. 8 June 1961, report by Robert Garrett, Film Finances file for *The Valiant*.
92. 9 June 1961, letter from Robert Garrett to George Ornstein, Film Finances file for *The Valiant*.
93. Charles Drazin, *A Bond for Bond*, p.107.
94. Cost report, 31 July 1963, Film Finances file for *Lancelot and Guinevere*.
95. John Croydon, supplementary report to Robert Garrett, 16 March 1963, Film Finances file for *Zulu*.
96. 2 March 1963, completion guarantee between Diamond Films and Film Finances, Film Finances file for *Zulu*. The deferrals were £18,125 against Baker's fees and £9,375 against Endfield's.
97. 18 October 1963, production cost statement, Film Finances file for *Zulu*.
98. 18 February 1968, statement of production costs, Film Finances file for *Isadora*.
99. 6 January 1967, letter from Charles Reynolds to Arvid Griffen at MGM British Studios, Film Finances file for *Battle Beneath the Earth*.
100. 10 January 1967, letter from Robert Garrett to Charles Reynolds, Film Finances file for *Battle Beneath the Earth*.
101. 5 October 1966, letter from Film Finances to Gina Productions, Film Finances file for *The Bobo*. Sellers had experienced a near-fatal heart attack on *Kiss Me Stupid* (1964) and had to be replaced by Ray Walston, which may have made people cautious.
102. 10 October 1966, letter from Robert Garrett to Gerry Blattner at Warners; 28 October 1966, letter from Elliott Kastner to Film Finances. Film Finances file for *The Bobo*.
103. 25 January 1967, letter from Garrett to Kastner, Film Finances file for *The Bobo*.
104. Correspondence, Film Finances file for *The Bobo*.
105. 8 July 1965, letter from Robert Garrett to K. L. Maidment at Columbia Pictures in Wardour Street.
106. 12 January 1966, letter from director Stanley Goulder to Robert Garrett, Film Finances file on *Naked Evil/The Obi*.

107. 12 February 1968, letter from Robert Garrett to David Deutsch, Film Finances file for *Lock Up Your Daughters*.
108. Various correspondence, Film Finances file for *Lock Up Your Daughters*.
109. 4 August 1967, letter from Film Finances to Laughlin Films Ltd, Film Finances file for *Joanna*.
110. 19 January 1968 – letter from Robert Garrett to Stuart Lyons, Film Finances file for *Joanna*.
111. 21 February 1968, Lyons to Garrett.
112. 24 April 1968, Garrett to Lyons.
113. 21 August 1968, letter from Michael Laughlin to Robert Garrett.
114. 11 September 1968, letter from Garrett to Charles Levison.
115. 11 June 1969, letter from Film Finances to Fox in the USA.
116. 17 March 1968, costs statement number 26.
117. *Kine Weekly*, 6 January 1968, p. 4.
118. Bill Altria's column in *Kine Weekly* dismissed the growing pessimism about the outlook for the continuation of American investment. 15 February 1969, p. 4.
119. *Kine Weekly*, 21 June 1969, p. 3.
120. *The Daily Cinema*, 17 November 1969.
121. *Kine Weekly*, 13 September 1969, p. 4.
122. *Kine Weekly*, 20 December 1969, p. 136.
123. 'Hollywood and Bust', *Film and TV Technician*, December 1969, vol. 35, pp. 8–9.
124. David Picker, quoted by Walker, *Hollywood, England*, p. 444.

3. PUBLIC SUPPORT IN A CHANGING CLIMATE

Duncan Petrie

INTRODUCTION

British film policy during the 1960s continued to be primarily directed towards the support and protection of indigenous production. There were three distinct strands to this. The longest-standing measure was the quota, initially introduced in 1927, which ensured that a minimum of 30 per cent of the features booked annually by the major cinema circuits were British.[1] The other two measures provided direct financial support to producers and were both introduced as responses to the immanent collapse of indigenous film production in the aftermath of World War Two. First, the National Film Finance Corporation (NFFC) was effectively a specialised bank established in 1949 with a revolving fund of £6 million to provide loans to producers. In the majority of cases these loans amounted to around 25–30 per cent of a film's production budget. Second, the British Film Production Fund was generated via a levy on cinema tickets and subsequently paid out to producers as a proportion of their box-office receipts. Introduced in 1950 as a voluntary measure, the Eady Levy[2] became mandatory in 1957 and it has been estimated that it was worth on average an additional 44.3 per cent on top of a film's box-office earnings.[3] Eady payments also directly benefitted the NFFC by boosting the chances that films they had invested in were able to turn a profit and thus pay back the loans received from the Corporation.[4] During the 1960s all three measures were subject to scrutiny and debate, sometimes setting different sections of the industry against one another. For example, while producers'

Figure 3.1　Carol White in the NFFC-supported box-office success *Poor Cow* (Ken Loach, 1967).

associations such as the Federation of British Film Makers (FBFM) advocated rises in both quota and levy, many exhibitors, particularly smaller independent cinemas operating on tight margins in a context of declining admissions, lobbied to have these reduced.

However, the National Film Finance Corporation was to face more serious challenges during the 1960s, despite continuing to play a key role in supporting British films. Between 1960 and 1969 the Corporation contributed to 227 feature films (including both first and second features), representing around a quarter of total productions.[5] The range of films backed was broad and diverse and included *Carry On Constable* (1960), *The Angry Silence* (1960), *The League of Gentlemen* (1960), *Peeping Tom* (Michael Powell, 1960), *The Entertainer* (1960), *Saturday Night and Sunday Morning* (1960), *Summer Holiday* (1963), *The Servant* (1963), *The Leather Boys* (1964), *The Gorgon* (1964), *Nothing But the Best* (1964), *Darling* (John Schlesinger, 1965), *Morgan, A Suitable Case for Treatment* (1966), *The Great St Trinian's Train Robbery* (1966), *Cul-de-sac* (1966), *The Family Way* (1966), *Don't Lose Your Head* (1966), *Accident* (1967), *Poor Cow* (1967), *Ulysses* (1967), *Girl on a Motorcycle* (1968) and *Till Death Us Do Part* (1969). Therefore, on the face of things, the NFFC was indisputably a contributor to the commercial and critical success – to say nothing of the cultural importance – of British cinema during the decade.

Table 3.1 provides a breakdown of the key metrics and a more detailed summary of this contribution.[6] This indicates a substantial reduction in the number of projects supported over the period, including a drop of two thirds between 1963 and 1965 and a very low level of activity during the final two years. The first of these is a consequence of the drastic cut in film production from 1963 onwards that was the inevitable outcome of declining admissions. The increasing involvement of Hollywood in the financing of British films had by the end of the decade had become a situation of almost total domination, resulting in fewer projects seeking support from the NFFC. The volatility in lending patterns from 1964 also reflects a rise in production costs and the rather precarious state of the Corporation's underlying finances. Indeed, the NFFC made a loss in all but three years during the decade, which in turn further depleted the Corporation's revolving fund from which they supported producers. This suggests an organisation in crisis and a closer consideration of the fortunes of the NFFC during the 1960s sheds light on the wider context of shifting industrial and policy developments and attitudes towards state support for British cinema.

INTO THE 1960S: OPPORTUNITIES AND CHALLENGES

The NFFC began its second decade in a rather ambiguous position. While it had undoubtedly fulfilled its primary objective in rescuing British film production, this had come at considerable cost. During its first ten years, the Corporation had lost almost £4 million of its revolving fund, three quarters of which had gone to bail out Alexander Korda's British Lion Film Corporation. In 1955 that debt was called in and the NFFC became the principal shareholder of a reconstituted and effectively nationalised British Lion.[7] Yet the Corporation had also supported 53 per cent of all British first features produced between 1950 and 1959, allowing the expenditure to be reinterpreted much more positively as a modest subsidy of just over £3,000 per film.[8] Consequently, the 1957 Films Act extended the life of the NFFC for a further ten years. The following year managing director David Kingsley departed to head British Lion and was succeeded by John Terry who had been the Corporation's in-house solicitor from 1949 to 1956 and then company secretary. Terry was to lead the NFFC for the next two decades, guiding it through some of its most difficult challenges and becoming a powerful figure in the industry and a valued advisor to government in the process.[9]

Terry's major challenge was how to address the steady depletion of the NFFC's revolving fund. The Corporation typically provided 'end money', which was the last to be recouped from box-office earnings and therefore carried more risk than the 'front money' usually provided by a distribution guarantee. The 1957 legislation had allowed the NFFC to make some deals on a more favourable *pari passu* basis, facilitating a very productive relation-

Table 3.1 Projects supported by the National Film Finance Corporation by year

Year (to 31 March)	Projects supported	Funds advanced	Profit (Loss)
1960	46 features, 21 shorts, 17 television films[1]	£1,575,515	(£194,095)
1961	27 features, 8 shorts, 39 television films	£927,504	£18,441
1962	48 features, 5 shorts, 8 television films	£1,034,396	£49,564
1963	36 features, 11 shorts	£1,687,964	(£219,867)
1964	18 features, 2 shorts	£473,149	£72,864
1965	12 features, 3 shorts	£464,102	(£149,855)
1966	17 features, 6 shorts, 78 television films[2]	£1,083,592	(£203,717)
1967	12 features, 5 shorts	£936,161	(£369,699)
1968	6 features, 3 shorts, 6 television films	£258,851	(£159,098)
1969	6 features, 2 shorts, 1 television film	£778,208	(£66,206)

[1] Short films were those with a running time of less than 33 minutes. The figure for TV productions includes every single episode in a series – so for example in 1961 the Corporation supported thirty-nine 30-minute episodes of *The Pursuers*, made by Crestview Productions for ABC Television.
[2] This was an investment in the Hallas and Batcher animated children's series, *Dodo the Kid From Outer Space*, which comprised seventy-eight 5-minute episodes.

ship with Hammer Films, with the Corporation providing loans for thirteen modest productions, co-financed with American distributors Columbia or Universal. The NFFC also began to exert greater control and influence over the projects it supported. Terry was keen to encourage fiscal responsibility and efficiency by insisting that producers share the risk by investing their own money in productions, amounting to around 5 per cent of the budget. He also proposed that the high fees being paid to 'above the line' talent be replaced by a mixture of deferments and profit participation. Thus by 1960 the NFFC were able to cite examples of progress including *The Angry Silence*, produced by Richard Attenborough and Bryan Forbes' Beaver Films, and *The League of Gentlemen*, made by the team of Michael Relph and Basil Dearden.[10] According to Alexander Walker, the budget for the former film was pruned back to £97,000 with Forbes deferring his producer's fee and Attenborough his producer's and actor's fees for shares of 7 per cent and 9 per cent of the net profits respectively.[11] Information on *The League of Gentlemen* held by completion guarantor Film Finances indicates that deferrals provided some £30,000 of the £180,000 budget, a sum in excess of the NFFC's loan of £22,500.[12] In the case of *The Entertainer*, made by Tony Richardson and John Osborne's Woodfall films, £35,000 of the initial budget of £188,000 was made up of deferments including £20,000 of Laurence Olivier's fee for 17 per cent of the profits.[13]

Unfortunately the NFFC's more assertive approach to financial control created tensions with producers. The FBFM criticised the Corporation for interpreting its mandate too rigidly, failing in many cases to recognise the full cost of a film which included development and overheads incurred by the producers (including expenditure on unmade and abandoned subjects), lending on terms that were unnecessarily harsh, and interfering too frequently in decisions which should rest with the producer.[14] Terry responded by insisting that 'producers who are unable to make any investment in their films whether by way of cash or deferments should not engage in independent film-making' and 'a consistently unsuccessful producer cannot expect the same facilities as one with a successful record'.[15] The serious mistrust in some quarters is revealed in correspondence between Michael Balcon (who had recently established the distribution company Bryanston Films with Maxwell Setton and a group of experienced film-makers) and FBFM secretary Andrew Filson, in which Balcon suggests that the NFFC chairman, the City financier, Sir Nutcombe Hume, 'obviously has a poor opinion of film producers ...'[16] In a subsequent letter Filson writes: 'I do agree that the central problem is the attitude of mind of the NFFC Directors. I think it was George (Archibald) who once said that it was like the Captain of a ship not liking the sea: indeed, the Captain doesn't seem to like the sailors either.'[17]

Despite these difficulties, the early 1960s saw an improvement in the NFFC's underlying stability, with modest profits being reported in 1961 and 1962. The Corporation's annual report for the year to March 1962 also noted a record level of income of £323,952, due to the strong commercial performance of a range of previous films including *The Colditz Story* (1955), *Happy is the Bride* (1958), *Carry On Nurse* (1959), *Expresso Bongo* (1959), *I'm Alright Jack* (1959), *Sapphire* (1959), *Tiger Bay* (1959), *Dentist in the Chair* (1960), *The League of Gentlemen* (1960) and *Saturday Night and Sunday Morning* (1960).[18] Relations with key critics also began to improve following the NFFC's decision to fully fund the £27,451 budget for the ACT Films production of Arnold Wesker's *The Kitchen* (1961), while producers were encouraged by the decision that from January 1962 budgets could include fixed overheads of 3 per cent on the first £100,000 of production costs and 2 per cent on the balance up to a maximum overhead of £10,000 – a major increase on the previous £2,000 limit.[19] In the same year the NFFC also provided 50 per cent of the £225,000 budget for Peter Rogers' comedy, *The Iron Maiden*, a decision justified by the Corporation having made profits on the previous five loans advanced to the producer.[20]

Adapting to a Changing Environment

But it wasn't long before new problems emerged. In 1961 the main film union, the Association of Cinema and Television Technicians (ACTT) – another regular source of critical scrutiny – argued that the Corporation's profit for 1961 had been in part the result of a significant reduction in the number of films being supported.[21] This trend became more marked by 1963 and the NFFC claimed that this was largely due to more British films being financed by the Hollywood majors who were also prepared to offer 100 per cent funding deals to producers. Thus in 1963 the NFFC reported that during the previous twelve months nineteen of the forty-four British films exhibited as first features on the Rank and ABC circuits had been backed by American finance, compared to just eleven supported by the NFFC. To underscore a new sense of concern, the Corporation's trading position had also slipped back substantially into the red that year, with loans to seven productions failing to return a single penny.[22]

Hollywood-financed British films tended to have larger budgets, feature major stars and be made in colour, which in turn enhanced their box-office appeal and potential profitability. For example, United Artists invested £322,069 in the first James Bond production, *Dr No* (1962), initiating the most successful British film series of the decade in the process. The same studio also backed Woodfall's *Tom Jones* (1963) to the tune of £412,000, enabling them to poach the project from Bryanston–Seven Arts who were unprepared to risk more than £300,000. The film went on to gross more than $40 million worldwide and win the Oscar for Best Picture. In comparison, more than three quarters of the features supported by the NFFC during the year to March 1963 were budgeted at less than £175,000 and this kind of film was struggling to find an audience in an increasingly competitive market.[23] This in turn exacerbated the Corporation's underlying financial problems and concerns were raised in an internal Board of Trade memo from January 1963, noting that the NFFC's funds had fallen to such a low level that it was being forced to refuse even deserving cases for support.[24]

The situation continued to deteriorate, culminating in the production crisis of 1963 which forced many independents, including all eight of the British Lion satellites – Albion, Britannia, Bryanston, Bryanston–Seven Arts, Garrick, Magna, Pax and Wessex – out of business, and led to a drastic reduction in overall feature-film production. This impacted directly on the NFFC, which reported losses of over £200,000 in respect of six films involving these companies.[25] Rejecting the argument that the crisis was a consequence of overproduction, the Corporation argued that the films being made by British Lion's satellites did not meet the needs and expectations of a changing market. This is partially supported by Kelly et al. who point to a 'temporary glut of films, not all of them as estimable as the hyperboles of the market-place might suggest, indeed few of them good box office'.[26] Whatever the reasons, the seriousness of the crisis was immediately reflected in the Corporation's trading results, with the annual report to March 1964 indicating a loss on investments of £701,129. However, this otherwise catastrophic result was offset by the controversial sale of British Lion, allowing the NFFC to post a modest profit of £72,664.

The Corporation had been eager to divest itself of its responsibilities for British Lion for some time, but had been prevented in doing so by the widely held view that public ownership provided necessary stability to the distributor most closely aligned with the interests of independent producers. Writing in the ACTT's monthly publication, Ralph Bond criticised the NFFC's apparent support for the idea that British Lion should ultimately be privatised, an aspiration which could 'only be regarded as the beginning of the dismantling of the public sector in British films'.[27] However, since 1960 British Lion had begun making modest but encouraging profits,[28] suggesting that they could survive and even flourish as a private enterprise and in 1963 the NFFC reported that £591,000 of the £600,000 invested in the company when British Lion was nationalised in 1955 had been repaid to the Treasury. At this point British Lion was valued at £1.59 million and on 9 December in a preliminary move towards a sale, the Corporation announced that it was to exercise its legal right to acquire the deferred shares held by the five directors of the company and each was paid £158,735.[29] As these had been acquired six years previously for £1,800, this otherwise enforced sale represented a handsome return for the individuals concerned. But the British Lion directors were furious and on 18 December David Kingsley wrote to Nutcombe Hume urging that British Lion be retained in public ownership to prevent total domination by Rank and ABPC, noting that

> competition within the film industry has been steadily declining over the years and has now been almost eliminated. A strong and healthy British Lion – an independent third force to sustain and stimulate independents – has made important efforts over the last four or five years to maintain some form of competitive trading, and we believe should be permitted to continue to do so.[30]

Just before Christmas the NFFC reported it had found a buyer in the veteran producer Sydney Box. But this apparent *fait accompli* was immediately met with protests from the Federation of British Film Makers, the Federation of Film Unions and several members of parliament. John Terry urged that the sale proceed on the grounds that the NFFC had run out of funds and desperately needed an injection of cash, and the controversy rumbled on into January 1964. However, the government was determined to press ahead and, ignoring a narrow vote by advisory body the Cinematographic Films Council against any outright sale,[31] Edward Heath, president of the Board of Trade, instigated a wider formal bidding process. Heath also announced that the NFFC would retain a single share in British Lion, allowing it to veto any future voluntary liquidation or the sale of Shepperton studios. While seven interested parties initially expressed interest,[32] only three official bids were subsequently made: by Sydney Box Associates, a consortium led by Michael Balcon, and the libertarian 'Freedom Group' headed by former politician Edward Martell. After Box's proposal was deemed unsuitable on the grounds that he refused to provide guarantees concerning future operations at Shepperton, Heath accepted the advice of John Terry and the NFFC board[33] and on 17 March 1964 formally announced Balcon's consortium as the new owner of British Lion.[34] Contracts were exchanged a fortnight later for a sale price of £1.6 million. After lobbying by the NFFC and the FBFM[35], the proceeds of the sale were re-advanced to the Corporation, providing a much-needed boost to its funds.

But a new approach to lending was desperately needed if the NFFC was to successfully adapt to the changing circumstances. During the height of the production crisis John Terry had called for an additional £2 million in funding, noting that rising costs were making it increasingly difficult for the NFFC to maintain previous levels of activity.[36] The widening of the gap between what he described as 'the successful and unsuccessful type of film' was also used to make the case for supporting larger-budget productions in the £300,000–£600,000 bracket. While this carried greater risk, the rewards could also be substantial as the success of several American-backed films demonstrated. But this could only be achieved by establishing new joint funding schemes with key partners to provide 100 per cent deals to producers and which would allow the NFFC to share more equitably in the recoupment of investments.

By May 1964 Terry had begun discussions over a joint funding scheme with British Lion. Then two months later came the surprise announcement came that the Rank Organisation had agreed to collaborate with the NFFC on such an initiative with a £500,000 commitment from each of the two partners allowing the National Provincial Bank to provide budget finance of up to £1.5 million. The deal would also give the NFFC control over the management of the scheme, including selection of projects, with Rank providing studio facilities at Pinewood and distribution for the completed films. But the NFFC required the agreement of government which had already proved sluggish over the issue of whether the NFFC could benefit from the profits of the British Lion sale. John Terry informed the Board of Trade in August 1964 of the proposed Backing Funds scheme with Rank and an official submission was subsequently made on 17 November to move forward.[37] However, the Treasury had long harboured scepticism about the necessity of the NFFC[38] and sought to delay any decision until the completion of a general review of film financing initiated in the aftermath of the British Lion sale. By December the NFFC's new chairman, Hilary Scott,[39] wrote to the Board of Trade to protest the lack of progress. But his position was not helped by concerns being raised by both the FBFM and the ACTT, with the union's Ralph Bond suggesting the proposed scheme 'might be interpreted as an admission of complete defeat for the original purposes for which the Corporation was established, and a final admission that the duopoly position is impregnable'.[40]

Behind-the-scenes arguments between the Board of Trade and the Treasury rumbled on, before the issue was finally resolved by Board of Trade president Douglas Jay,[41] and the NFFC–Rank funding scheme was officially announced in the press on 21 January 1965. John Terry made much of the NFFC being granted decision-making powers, noting that 'the withdrawal of the distributor-financier from any control over selection and administration is in the Corporation's experience without precedent.'[42] For their part, Rank was mindful of the Monopolies Commission investigation which had been launched in August 1964 and this initiative provided an ideal opportunity to demonstrate a commitment to independent producers.[43]

The first three productions to be supported under the scheme were the realist drama, *I Was Happy Here*, produced by Roy Millichip and directed by Desmond Davis (both of whom had previous associations with Woodfall) from a story by Edna O'Brien; *Romeo and Juliet*, a film version of the acclaimed Royal Ballet production featuring Margot Fonteyn and Rudolph Nureyev, directed and produced by the veteran émigré Paul Czinner; and *The Sandwich*

Man, a slapstick comedy shot entirely on location in London by the director/producer team of Robert Hartford-David and Peter Newbrook and featuring the fourth Goon, Michael Bentine at the head of an ensemble cast of familiar comic talent. A further three films were subsequently announced the following year: *They're a Weird Mob*, a comedy made in Australia by veteran film-maker Michael Powell, directly addressing the NFFC's aim to promote international co-productions with Commonwealth partners;[44] *Maroc 7*, a crime caper featuring extensive location shooting in Morocco, directed by Gerry O'Hara and starring Americans Gene Barry and Cyd Charisse alongside Leslie Phillips, who also co-produced with John Gale; and *Two Weeks in September*, an Anglo-French co-production directed by Serge Bourguignon and billed as Brigitte Bardot's first starring role in English. While questioning the apparent lack of any clear policy of exactly what the initiative wanted to encourage as 'independent', Robin Bean writing in *Films and Filming* nevertheless acknowledged, 'at the moment it remains the one bright hope [for British cinema], and a very important one.'[45]

Beyond the scheme with Rank, the NFFC had increased its lending substantially during 1965–6 and in a letter to the Board of Trade John Terry outlined a slate of fifteen films in which the Corporation had a £811,000 investment.[46] Significantly only four involved the provision of end money: *The Daleks Invade Earth* (subsequently title *Daleks: Invasion Earth 2150*), *The Great St Trinian's Train Robbery*, *Morgan: A Suitable Case for Treatment* and *Up Jumped a Swagman*. Eight of the productions featured a more favourable *pari passu* deal: *Dr Who and the Daleks*, *The Projected Man*, *A Study in Terror*, *Cul-de-sac*, *Theatre of Death*, *The Night Caller*, *The Trap* and *The Yellow Hat*, while in three cases of more experimental or risky projects – *We're Wrestling Tonight*, *Four in the Morning* and *He Who Rides a Tiger* – the Corporation was the sole or major investor.

Unfortunately, the Rank initiative failed to live up to expectations.[47] The NFFC's report to March 1967 noted that *Romeo and Juliet* had been an artistic success and commercial results were considered promising, *They're a Weird Mob* had broken box-office records in Australasia but unfortunately had failed to do good business elsewhere, both *I Was Happy Here* and *The Sandwich Man* had been judged commercial failures, and the situation with *Maroc 7* was still to be clarified. This latter film proved the most problematic, running £85,000 over its budget of £316,000 and forcing completion guarantor Film Finances to assume direct control of the production.[48] The scheme was already being branded a failure before the final two films had even been released. In January 1967 Robin Bean described it as the saddest event of the year: 'Artistically, the majority of their productions were highly questionable and had the appearance of being projects where the producers had been unable to raise money from commercial resources.'[49] Rank chairman John Davis noted diplomatically that while arrangements with the NFFC had worked smoothly, his company had nevertheless been forced to provide in excess of £200,000 against anticipated losses on the venture.[50]

Around the same time the NFFC suffered yet another blow. In July 1966, just three months after being re-elected with a substantially increased parliamentary majority, the Labour government was forced to introduce a harsh austerity package in a desperate attempt to address the balance-of-payments crisis currently affecting the wider British economy. The subsequent credit squeeze had two direct negative consequences on the NFFC. Firstly, it could now only borrow £750,000 of the £2 million it was legally authorised to obtain from non-government sources. Then Lloyds Bank tightened the screws further by reducing the NFFC's overdraft from £750,000 to £500,000, citing the stringency of the financial situation and the need to prioritise the export trade.[51] By now the Corporation had effectively run out of money and on 20 October a press statement announced that the NFFC was suspending its lending activities until further notice. Unsurprisingly, a record loss was reported for the year to March 1967.

On 31 July the NFFC announced that limited lending activities were to be resumed, but emphasised 'that the fund available is strictly limited and that applications will have to be considered on an extremely selective basis'.[52] This recovery was in part facilitated by the strong box-office performance of Launder and Gilliat's *The Great St Trinian's Train Robbery* and the Boulting brothers' *The Family Way*, which proved the fourth highest-earning film at the British box office in 1967. Consequently, around £500,000 became available for the NFFC to lend over the subsequent twelve months, prolonging what was becoming an increasingly hand-to-mouth existence.[53]

PUBLIC SUPPORT FOR FILM: A LEGITIMACY CRISIS

The tensions between the NFFC and the government apparent in relation to both the joint funding scheme with Rank and the credit squeeze indicate a more serious legitimacy crisis threatening the Corporation's survival. In his study of the British film industry in the 1960s, Alexander Walker described public funding for film as 'an indulgence akin to that of eighteenth-century English gentlemen who built romantic follies on their private estates. It is a pleasant pursuit, provided one can afford it.'[54] Yet this opinion appears to have been shared by some directly involved in the provision of state support, including Nutcombe Hume who unsuccessfully attempted in 1960 and 1962 to persuade the government to allow the NFFC to be taken over by a consortium of banks.[55] In his memoirs, Michael Balcon confirms that Hume 'was a strong advocate of getting the Government out of the film business; in his view it was a business for unrestricted private enterprise'.[56] That he also chaired the Corporation between 1955 and 1964 seems little short of astonishing.

Meanwhile disagreement within Whitehall dating back to the earliest days of the NFFC continued to fester.[57] In the summer of 1964 the Board of Trade launched two separate inquiries into the film industry. The first was the long-demanded investigation by the Monopolies Commission into the supply of films to exhibitors.[58] The second was a major review of film financing in Britain, prompted by disagreements between the president of the Board of Trade and the Treasury about the future of the NFFC following the sale of British Lion. While Edward Heath was keen to allow the Corporation to resume its normal lending activities, the Treasury demanded that a review into the actual financial needs of the industry be conducted first.[59] A Film Finance Review working group, chaired by C. M. P. Brown, a civil servant from the Board of Trade, was established and began its work in September. However, it quickly encountered problems in gaining a reliable and accurate picture of the notoriously opaque financial workings of the film industry. Such problems were starkly illustrated by the unwillingness of the British Film Fund Agency, a body which had been established by government, to provide information concerning the eligible earnings of films receiving payments from the Eady Levy, citing commercial confidentiality.[60] The decision was subsequently taken to refocus the review on the case for continued state involvement in film production in the light of changing industrial circumstances including the increasing involvement of American companies in the funding of British films.

The working party delivered its final report on 15 July 1965. Despite receiving submissions from the Federation of Film Unions[61] and the Federation of British Film Makers[62] that were strongly supportive of the NFFC, the report tended to paint a rather less favourable picture. Increasing costs had made film funding a much riskier and speculative undertaking and thus less appropriate for state financing. While the Eady Levy remained a powerful stimulus to production, the circumstances that had led to the setting up of the NFFC no longer pertained and thus the Corporation was no longer able to play a significant role in maintaining independent production. Moreover, the NFFC's track record showed cumulative losses of nearly £4.5 million of public investment. Claims that state involvement in film financing had a beneficial effect on export earnings could be countered by the fact that US investment made a bigger contribution to the balance of payments than overseas earnings of British films. The main recommendation consequently stated:

> We have come to the conclusion that in present circumstances there is no need to continue Government financial assistance in order to maintain a desirable level of British film production. We therefore recommend that the National Film Finance Corporation be wound up on the expiry of their current statutory powers in March 1967.'[63]

The depth of the Treasury's antipathy to the NFFC is illustrated in a letter from L. Pliatzky (a member of the working party) to G. J. MacMahon of the finance division of the Board of Trade urging the following sentence be added to the report:

> The fact is that most of the films with whose financing the NFFC have been associated have been both artistic and commercial failures; whatever the reasons for this result – and it is arguable that the NFFC were in a situation which made it inevitable – there is no positive evidence to suggest that they have the commercial and artistic judgement which would give a reasonable prospect of a better result in the future, whatever the resources that might be made available to the corporation.[64]

On 3 August the chief secretary to the Treasury, John Diamond, wrote to Douglas Jay, president of the Board of Trade, expressing hope that he would agree to wind up the NFFC and suggesting that any consultations with industry should 'take place on the basis that it is the Government's clear intentions to discontinue existing arrangements'.[65]

However, the ongoing Monopolies Commission investigation into the supply of films to exhibitors threw the Corporation a lifeline when a Board of Trade official raised the possibility that this might recommend a role for the NFFC in ensuring an independent supply of films to exhibitors beyond the main two circuits.[66] After sitting on the working-party report for more than seven months, Jay informed Diamond on 23 February 1966 that a holding operation prolonging the life of the Corporation, along with the quota and levy, until 1970 would be enacted.[67] This decision was subsequently enshrined in law by the 1966 Cinematographic Films Act. During the second reading of the Bill in the House of Lords, unequivocal support was expressed for the Corporation by Lord Moynihan who argued, 'under the leadership of men such as Mr David Kingsley and Mr John Terry ... the NFFC have shown that they have creative and adventuresome traits as well as being trained men of commerce protecting the Government's and the taxpayer's interests.'[68] Moynihan went further, citing the generous support provided by other governments to their film industries to argue that more finance be made available to the NFFC once the present credit squeeze had been lifted.

'HOLLYWOOD, ENGLAND' AND A NEW CRISIS

Despite the reprieve, the wider fortunes of the British film industry continued to fuel debate over the NFFC's future. The increasing Hollywood presence was beginning to have particularly serious ramifications as American finance became inextricably associated with an apparently buoyant local production industry whose films were performing well in the international marketplace and winning prestigious awards. But concerns remained about the wider implications of ceding control of the industry to non-British sources. John Terry had already begun to sound the alarm in 1964, pointing out that American companies were not only appropriating the bulk of the British Film Production Fund but were also scooping up the cream of British directing talent. Terry also argued that there was no guarantee American interest would be maintained in the future, casting doubt on the sustainability of this state of affairs.[69] He returned to the theme in the Corporation's report for the year to May 1965, noting that while 'welcome within limits, this growing involvement in the financing of British films by US distributors, if allowed to expand unchecked, represents a threat to the continuance of a truly British production industry'.[70]

Hollywood's gain also continued to be the NFFC's loss. Between 1962 and 1965 American companies supported 107 of the 200 films qualifying for the British quota, with the NFFC involved in just 46. The trend intensified as the decade progressed and by 1967 the NFFC turned their attention to the proportion of the total finance provided by the Americans, providing an even more vivid illustration of the underlying situation:

> It is estimated that US sources provided approximately 75 per cent of the aggregate finance used to produce the first feature and co-feature films registered as British in each of the calendar years 1965 (69 films) and 1966 (70 films). The corresponding proportions for 1967 and 1968 may exceed 90 per cent.[71]

By 1969 the Americans were supporting 88 per cent of British first features and co-features exhibited on the two major circuits. By this point the NFFC's share had dwindled to just 4 per cent, a decline from 16 per cent the previous year. The Corporation appeared to be heading for oblivion.

Meanwhile the government had embarked on yet another review of film policy, the 1966 Films Act being a short-term measure pending a more sustainable solution. A Films Legislation and Policy Working Group chaired by H. Bailey of the Board of Trade subsequently was set up in early 1967. The NFFC's own submission argued that they be reconstituted to perform a revised and more effective role in supporting production:

> namely the financing on a _pari passu_ recovery basis with British distributors and others, of, say, twelve major feature films a year at average budgets of about £350,000, with the object of actively fostering selected groups of talented film-makers to form the nucleus of a viable and independent British film production industry.[72]

Table 3.2 Details of budgets, NFFC loan and overseas earnings supplied by the National Film Finance Corporation to the Board of Trade in 1967

Film	Budget	NFFC loan[1]	Overseas earnings
Darling	£363,625	£95,000	£455,866
Cul-de-sac	£182,511	£67,548	£111,099
Morgan	£211,557	£41,228	£285,664
They're a Weird Mob	£227,584	£82,700	£207,821
Accident	£280,000	£140,000	£250,000
Maroc 7	£400,186	£165,000	£214,494
The Family Way	£460,641	£190,499	£506,216
Poor Cow	£230,000	£115,000	£312,500
Ulysses	£203,349	£29,500	£300,000
Theatre of Death	£125,000	£62,500	£100,000

[1] These figures do not always tally with the sums listed in the Film Finances files.

This would also require the NFFC's revolving fund to be re-established at a level of £6 million. The call for a rejuvenated Corporation was supported by the new Film Producers Association of Great Britain[73] (formed in January 1967 by a merger of the Federation of British Film Producers and the British Film Producers Association), and the British Film Institute, a chief advocate of the cultural and educational value of film, which had also expressed concern about the industry's over-reliance on American finance.[74]

All of this coincided with the credit crunch which prompted the NFFC to advance the argument that films could make an important contribution to the nation's balance of payments, provided revenues were coming back to British investors. International demand for British films was high and could be capitalised on by locally financed films, not only those supported by the Hollywood majors. To support their case the Corporation cited a range of films they had supported in which a very healthy relationship could be demonstrated between levels of public investment and overseas earnings.[75] Moreover, this applied to both films that had made a healthy profit and those that posted a loss, as shown on Table 3.2.

This information is slightly misleading in that overseas earnings are subject to substantial deductions by exhibitors and distributors before any returns flow back to Britain. Moreover, depending on the specific financing deals the primary beneficiary from overseas receipts may not be British. In the case of *They're a Weird Mob* for example, £68,000 of the production budget was provided upfront by the Australian exhibition and distribution company Williamson for exploitation rights in Australasia, the territories where the bulk of the film's earnings were generated.[76]

Despite their travails, the NFFC continued to enjoy strong support from various quarters within and beyond the industry. In January 1968 the Cinematographic Films Council sent a report to Anthony Crosland, the new president of the Board of Trade,[77] recommending that all three state support measures be retained.[78] In April *Kine Weekly* reported on a cross-party campaign in Parliament to retain the NFFC-led by the Conservative MP F. J. Silvester and his Labour colleague Hugh Jenkins, and by June MPs were starting to link the case for retaining the Corporation to fears of any future cutback in American finance.[79] This was supported by *Kine Weekly*'s columnist Bill Altria who identified the need for 'a much more broadly based British film finance corporation to provide the substantial financial resources, and encouragement of private investment in British film production ... if the British industry is to compete more effectively in the world markets'.[80]

Within the Board of Trade there were significant differences of opinion. An internal memorandum from February 1968 from the Films Branch concluded that the balance of the argument tilted towards the reconstitution and refinancing of the NFFC for a period of ten years.[81] But a report by the Board of Trade's Economic Services Division delivered in June argued that in the presence of the British Film Fund, the quota and the high level of American participation in British film production, the NFFC could not be justified in terms of making a significant contribution to either employment or prosperity in the industry. Moreover, the losses incurred by the Corporation could not be alleviated by any appeal to the level of overseas earnings.[82]

A submission to ministers by the Films Branch of 12 July 1968 sets out the key areas of contention.[83] While endorsing the recommendation by the Cinematographic Films Council that the industry continue to receive protection after 1970, this presented arguments both for and against the retention of the NFFC. The case for closure was familiar: there was no longer the shortage of film finance that had led to the NFFC being established, film was increasingly international and speculative and therefore less appropriate for public finance, the prospect of overseas earnings were too uncertain, the British Film Fund remained the main inducement to production and the Corporation's financial record discouraged hopes of any improved future performance. Moreover, refinancing of the NFFC could not be a priority during a time of restrictions on public expenditure. Arguments for retention on the other hand highlighted anxieties surrounding the industry's dependence on American finance and the dire consequences that would follow should this support be withdrawn, but also pointed to the value of British-funded films in the UK's balance of payments, comparative levels of support for production in European countries, and the potential economic benefits of a shift to *pari passu* lending at the NFFC. The submission also noted that while the Treasury continued to cast doubt on the desirability of refinancing the NFFC, the Department of Education and Science and the Foreign Office/Commonwealth Office were strongly supportive of its continuing operations.[84]

While acknowledging the economic arguments for keeping the NFFC were 'more plausible than persuasive', the submission concluded that there were nevertheless clear political grounds for preserving a body that had been created by a Labour government and which commanded significant support from within the industry. Moreover, if the Corporation were abolished, great pressure would be exerted to introduce new measures of support for film production which in the judgement of the Films Branch would probably be less acceptable than the current arrangements. In addition to urging continued support, the submission recommended that the NFFC's existing debt be written off, thus saving the Corporation the crippling annual repayments of interest on lost loans which had been another bone of contention for some time.[85] It was also recommended that the Corporation's ability to borrow £2 million from non-government sources be reaffirmed. These conclusions were endorsed by Gwyneth Dunwoody, parliamentary secretary to the Board of Trade, who argued that the continuation of the NFFC was 'now vital to an industry almost wholly dependent on American money'. And if this source were to be withdrawn 'there would be no industry in Britain except for the NFFC. This is a very real threat.' Dunwoody therefore strongly urged a 'continuance of the main recommendations of the quota, the levy and most of all the NFFC'.[86] This coincided with the welcome news that British films had increased their surplus of overseas receipts from £9 million in 1966 to £24 million in 1967, with earnings in North America alone rising from £6 million to £15 million.[87]

But Crosland – described by the ACTT-affiliated MP Hugh Jenkins as 'a confirmed marketeer'[88] – needed more persuasion and so engaged the Board of Trade's Industrial Reorganisation Committee (IRC) to provide additional advice on the relevant financial and commercial considerations. Particular attention was paid to three key issues: the basis on which the Corporation made its loans, the prospects should it start with a clean slate, and the possibility of the NFFC raising private capital. In the subsequent report delivered in January 1969, the IRC provided a glowing endorsement of the Corporation's future potential as a key source of public support. They recommended that the NFFC play a more active role in the industry, back only established producers and be able to invest up to £500,000 in pre-production. Loans should be targeted at films in the £250,000–£750,000 budget range, be no more that 40 per cent of budget and be recoupable on a *pari passu* basis. It was also advised that the Corporation should seek deferrals on payments to key talents, obtain a share of the producer's ultimate profit, avoid films with little chance of financial success, and consider lending to a production company against a slate of films rather than in respect of a single production. Moreover, the NFFC should be able to issue completion guarantees, contribute to the creation of a consortium of British distributors, and be able to buy shares in British production companies. Finally, the IRC recommended the Corporation be given a new injection of funds to the tune of £5 million.[89]

The case for retention was strengthened by an article in *The Times* on 10 February 1969 ominously (or helpfully) entitled 'US film-makers in Britain may start a dollar drain'[90] which suggested that the threat of American withdrawal was now credible. Several factors were cited: most of the American studios had been acquired by huge industrial conglomerates looking to reduce costs, US unions had been campaigning against the growing spate of 'runaway' productions and their adverse impact on home production, several big-budget films had been financial failures, and the British Film Fund was to be reduced by around £700,000 in response to complaints that most of the Eady Levy was going to American companies.[91] John Terry also went on the offensive, arguing that it was wrong for a film industry to be wholly dependent on foreign finance: 'We can imagine the outcry that would be heard if it were proposed to sell the BBC to Fox or Columbia. I think the principle is not dissimilar.'[92] Holding firm in the face of continuing Treasury pressure,[93] Crosland issued a press statement on 5 August 1969 announcing that the NFFC's future was safe. By the end of year a new Films Bill had been published which refinanced the NFFC to the tune of £5 million, extended its life and lending powers to 1980, waived the payment of interests on lost loans, and granted new powers such as the ability to provide distribution guarantees.[94] All of these measures were enshrined in law with the passing of the 1970 Films Act – by which time the industry was indeed suffering from the effects of a substantial retrenchment by the American majors.

Into the 1970s

The 1960s provided the National Film Finance Corporation with some serious challenges and arguably its major achievement was that it survived the decade intact. The combination of an ever-reducing fund, the rising costs of film production, and the increasing dominance of American finance which monopolised the higher budget – and therefore more profitable – end of the production spectrum, reduced the NFFC from a key investor in independent production to a relative bystander. This in turn called into question its ongoing purpose and legitimacy, leading to serious attempts within government to close the Corporation down. An ironic twist is that the most concerted efforts to wind up the NFFC came from a Labour administration led by Harold Wilson, who as a young president of the Board of Trade in the Attlee government had been instrumental in establishing the Corporation in 1949.

While the decade witnessed a sharp decline in the NFFC's revolving fund and thus the number of projects it was able to support, even during the lean years it still contributed to domestic hits like *Poor Cow* and *Till Death Us Do*

Part and award-winners such as *Accident*. But over the period the Corporation sustained a cumulative loss of £1,221,668 on a total investment of £9,219,442. The impact of the production crisis is particularly striking, resulting in a 50 per cent drop in the number of features supported and a corresponding reduction of more than £1.2 million in loans made. The increase in lending during 1966 and 1967, set against the relatively low number of projects supported (including the six films made under the joint funding scheme with Rank, with £693,128 committed to the first four films in the year to March 1966), further demonstrates the rising cost of production. Meanwhile the sparse number of features supported in the final two years of the decade indicates just how critical the situation had become before the 1970 Films Act provided a much-needed rescue plan.

But even this apparent resurrection was to carry a sting in the tail. Following the general election in 1970 the new Conservative government, led by former Board of Trade president, Edward Heath, was only prepared to advance an additional £1 million from public funds, leaving the NFFC to seek private investment. This latest development only acted as a confirmation of the lukewarm attitude of the British government to supporting local film production displayed throughout the 1960s and their clear preference for the risky business of production finance to be left to the marketplace. Significantly, this attitude appears to have been shared by both Conservative and Labour administrations.

APPENDIX: BUDGET DETAILS FOR TWENTY-EIGHT PRODUCTIONS INVOLVING THE NFFC AND FILM FINANCES[95]

Table 3.A.1 Budget details for selected British films supported by the NFFC (from Film Finances archive)

Year	Title	Budget	Details of investors
1960	Beat Girl	£80,000	distributor: £56,000, NFFC: £21,000, producer: £3,000
1960	City of the Dead	£45,000	distributor: £16,000, NFFC: £4,500, producer: £24,500
1960	Cone of Silence	£139,000	distributor: £96,000, NFFC: £27,000, producer: £16,000
1960	The Entertainer	£188,000 + deferrals	distributor: £75,000, US distributor: £56,500, NFFC: £56,500, deferrals: £35,000
1960	Peeping Tom	£131,000	distributor: £101,000, NFFC: £15,000, private investment: £15,000
1960	Saturday Night and Sunday Morning	£117,000	distributor: £82,000, NFFC: £28,000, Twickenham Studios: £6,000, Tony Richardson: £1,000 deferral
1961	The Day the Earth Caught Fire	£190,000	distributor: £133,500, NFFC: £41,500, producer: £15,000
1962	Double Bunk	£106,000	distributor: £74,000, NFFC: £26,500 deferrals: £5,500
1962	Two and Two Make Six	£128,000	distributor: £90,000, NFFC: £38,000
1963	Ladies Who Do	£134,500	distributor: £94,000, NFFC: £32,500, deferrals: £8,000
1963	The Servant	£141,500	distributor: £99,000, NFFC: £35,000 deferrals: £7,500
1963	Sparrows Can't Sing	£101,000	distributor: £71,000, NFFC: £20,000 producer: £10,000
1964	French Dressing	£179,000	distributor: £139,000, US distributor: £12,500, NFFC: £25,000, producers: £2,500
1964	The Mind Benders	£200,000	distributor: £140,000, NFFC: £50,000, deferrals: £10,000
1964	The Leather Boys	£106,000	distributor: £74,000, NFFC: £27,500, deferrals: £4,500
1964	Nothing But the Best	£176,500	distributor: £129,500, NFFC: £41,000, producer: £6,000
1965	Darling	£348,000	distributor: £215,000, NFFC: £95,000, Film Finances: £38,000 (over budget costs)
1965	Dr Terror's House of Horrors	£107,000	distributor: £25,000, US distributor: £50,000, NFFC: £25,000, deferrals: £7,000
1965	I Was Happy Here	£169,000	NFFC–Rank joint fund: £169,000
1965	The Sandwich Man	£214,000	NFFC–Rank joint fund: £214,000
1966	Cul-de-sac	£130,000	distributor: £65,000, NFFC: £65,000

Year	Title	Budget	Details of investors
1966	He Who Rides a Tiger	£65,000	NFFC: £65,000
1966	Maroc 7	£316,000	NFFC–Rank joint fund: £316,000
1966	They're a Weird Mob	£235,000	NFFC–Rank joint fund: £167,000, Australian distributor: £68,000
1966	The Trap	£355,000	distributor: £170,000, Canadian investor: £85,000, NFFC: £85,000, deferrals: £15,000
1967	Accident	£300,000	distributor: £150,000, NFFC: £150,000
1967	Press For Time	£272,500	distributor: £175,000, NFFC: £75,000, deferrals: £22,500
1967	Ulysses	£215,000	distributor: £150,500, NFFC: £29,500, deferrals: £35,000

NOTES

1. Until 1948 there were separate quotas for renters and exhibitors.
2. The levy was named after Sir Wilfred Eady, a distinguished Treasury official who had been part of the British delegation at the Bretton Woods conference in 1944.
3. Jonathan Stubbs, 'The Eady Levy: A Runaway Bribe? Hollywood Production and British Subsidy in the Early 1960s', *Journal of British Cinema and Television*, 6: 1, 2009.
4. This was directly acknowledged in the NFFC's annual report to 31 March 1960 which called for the levy to be increased in light of the abolition of entertainment tax, pp. 4–5.
5. Figures derived from NFFC annual reports and Screen Digest/BFI. In the period 1950–9, 1,243 feature films were produced and the NFFC contributed to 483, for 1960–9 the corresponding figures were 999 and 227.
6. Figures derived from NFFC annual reports.
7. In return for writing off the £3 million debt, the NFFC became the principal shareholder in a new company, British Lion Films, to which it advanced a further £569,000 in return for 60 per cent of its share capital.
8. NFFC Annual Report to 31 March 1960, p. 2.
9. One civil servant at the Board of Trade, R. B. Tippets, noted in an internal memo dated 13 January 1965: 'As the managing director of the NFFC he considers his loyalty is to his Board and the Government but being in and of the industry, and wielding as he does much influence within it, he can generally give us an informed inside view.' BT 64/5294 NFFC Proposals to Amend and Enforce Legislation 1964–5.
10. NFFC Annual Report to 31 March 1960, p. 3.
11. Alexander Walker, *Hollywood, England: The British Film Industry in the Sixties* (London: Michael Joseph, 1974), p. 97–8.
12. Film Finances file on *The League of Gentlemen*. The deferrals included £2,500 of fee for the rights in the work, £3,750 each from director and producer Basil Dearden and Michael Relph, £2,500 from writer and actor Bryan Forbes, £2,200 from Jack Hawkins, £3,000 from Nigel Patrick and £3,600 from Richard Attenborough.
13. Film Finances file on *The Entertainer*. The film ended up costing £247,483. The NFFC's loan was £58,500.

14. Report in *The Daily Cinema* 11 July 1960.
15. NFFC report, 18 June 1959, p. 4. Michael Balcon Special Collection British Film Institute. MEB 1956 I/235.
16. Letter from Michael Balcon to Andrew Filson, 7 December 1959, BFI Special Collections, Michael Balcon Collection, MEB 1878 I/266.
17. Letter, Andrew Filson to Michael Balcon, 16 August 1960, BFI Special Collections, Michael Balcon Collection, MEB 1878 I/266.
18. NFFC Annual Report to March 1962, p. 1. This list of films indicates the long commercial life that some titles enjoyed, including overseas releases.
19. *Kine Weekly*, 28 December 1961.
20. 28 February 1962 – letter from John Terry to Peter Rogers. Gerald Thomas Papers, BFI Special Collections.
21. Editorial, *Film and TV Technician*, July 1961, p. 119.
22. *Kine Weekly*, 4 July 1963. American finance was also pushing up production costs and this helps to explain the 50 per cent increase in the amount of money loaned by the NFFC in the year to March 1963 despite the 25 per cent reduction in the number of features being supported during the same period.
23. NFFC Annual Report to March 1963, p. 12.
24. 10 January 1963 – National Film Finance Corporation, Memorandum Regarding Future Financial Needs. BT 258/1573 Application by National Film Finance Corporation for Increase in Borrowing Powers.
25. NFFC Annual Report to March 1964, p. 5. While the films are not listed, the NFFC backed no less than nine of the thirteen titles identified by Kelly et al. in *A Competitive Cinema*: *The Leather Boys*, *A Place to Go*, *Ladies Who Do*, *Hide and Seek*, *Two Left Feet*, *Station Six Sahara*, *The Party's Over* and the 'B' films *The Lunch Hour* and *Dilemma*.
26. Terence Kelly, Graham Norton and George Perry, *A Competitive Cinema* (London: Institute of Economic Affairs, 1966), p. 36.
27. Ralph Bond, 'Whither the NFFC?', *Film and TV Technician*, April 1963, p. 76.
28. These profits were £228,662 in 1960, £634,895 in 1961, £426,098 in 1962 and £468,910 in 1963. Figures from *Kine Weekly*.
29. Bernard Husra, 'Patterns of Power', *Films and Filming*, April 1964.
30. *Kine Weekly*, 9 January 1964, p. 21.
31. *Kine Weekly*, 23 January 1964, p. 3.
32. The identified bidders were: Sydney Box, Michael Balcon, Woolf–Spiegel–Grade, the Freedom Group, the Bloom–Goldstein–Hylton group, the Stanley Gubens Group and the Federation of Film Unions, *Kine Weekly*, 6 February 1964.
33. BT 64/5285 NFFC Sir Michael Balcon's Bid for British Lion 1964.
34. Ibid.
35. Reported in *Kine Weekly*, 25 June 1964.
36. *Kine Weekly*, 24 October 1963.
37. BT 279/261 NFFC and Backing Funds 1965.
38. The opposition of HM Treasury to the initial establishment of the NFFC is examined by Harper and Porter 2003.
39. C. H. Scott replaced Sir Nutcombe Hume as chairman of NFFC on 21 July 1964. He had been deputy chair since 1959.
40. Ralph Bond, *Film and TV Technician,* November 1965, p. 216.
41. Jay communicated his decision in a letter to chief secretary to the Treasury, John Diamond, on 7 January BT 279/261 NFFC and Backing Funds 1965.
42. NFFC Annual Report to 31 March 1965, p. 5.
43. John Davis did not waste the opportunity to make this point at a sales conference, *Kine Weekly*, 9 September 1965.

44. Another example being *The Trap*, a feature made in Canada which was announced in the trade press as being part of the co-financing scheme but was never officially included in the NFFC's reports. *Kine Weekly*, 16 September 1965.
45. Robin Bean, 'Stalemate', *Films and Filming*, November 1965, p. 50.
46. 28 April 1966, letter from John Terry to G. J. MacMahon, Board of Trade, BT 258/2408.
47. See Duncan Petrie, 'Resisting Hollywood Dominance in Sixties British Cinema: The NFFC/Rank Joint Financing Initiative', *Historical Journal of Film, Radio and Television*, 36: 4, 2016.
48. Film Finances file on *Maroc 7*.
49. Robin Bean, 'Trapped in a Sandwich', *Films and Filming*, January 1967, p. 60.
50. Reported in *Kine Weekly*, 30 September 1967.
51. The bank indicated that a letter from the Treasury requesting a relaxation in lending for the NFFC might enable them to raise the overdraft limit. Government documents indicate that while officials and ministers at the Board of Trade were sympathetic to Terry's requests, the Treasury held firm in their refusal. BT 258/2408 National Film Finance Corporation. The Effect of the Credit Squeeze (1966) on the Corporation's Borrowing from Private Sources.
52. 31 July 1967 – press release from the NFFC, BT 258/2408 National Film Finance Corporation. The Effect of the Credit Squeeze (1966) on the Corporation's Borrowing from Private Sources.
53. Note on meeting between John Terry and the secretary of the Board of Trade on 3 August 1967, BT 258/2408 National Film Finance Corporation. The Effect of the Credit Squeeze (1966) on the Corporation's Borrowing from Private Sources.
54. Alexander Walker, *Hollywood, England*, p. 252.
55. Memo raising the possibility of the NFFC being disposed to a consortium of banks, 17 July 1962, BT 279/113 1962.
56. Michael Balcon, *Michael Balcon Presents ... A Lifetime of Films* (London: Hutchison, 1969) p. 204.
57. Sue Harper and Vincent Porter, *British Cinema of the 1950s: The Decline of Deference* (Oxford: Oxford University Press, 2003).
58. *Kine Weekly*, 6 August 1964.
59. FV 81/475, FV 81/175, NFFC; Meetings and report of Board of Trade's Film Finance Review 1964/5.
60. 30 October 1964, memo indicating the unwillingness of the Film Fund agency to provide information of the eligible earnings of films making a claim on the levy. BT 258/2036. Film Industry Finance Official Review.
61. Letter from Alan Sapper to the review panel, 21 December 1964, BT 258/2036 Film Industry Finance Official Review.
62. Letter from FBFP to Board of Trade, 16 June 1965, FV 81/175, NFFC; Meetings and report of Board of Trade's Film Finance Review 1964.
63. Final Report of Working Party, 15 July 1965, BT 528/2037, Film Industry Finance Review (2).
64. 16 July 1965 – letter from L. Pliatzky to G. J. MacMahon, BT 258/2037 Film Industry Finance Review (2).
65. BT 258/2038, BT 258/2038 Film Industry Review (3).
66. Memo from G. J. MacMahon, Board of Trade Finance Division, 21 October 1965. BT 258/2038 Film Industry Review (3).
67. BT 258/2038, BT 258/2038 Film Industry Review (3).
68. Hansard, House of Lords, 6 December 1966, vol. 278, col. 1134.
69. John Terry, 'Where Have all the Young Men Gone?', *Kine Weekly*, 17 December 1964.

70. National Film Finance Corporation, Annual Report to 31st March 1965, p. 4.
71. National Film Finance Corporation, Annual Report to 31st March 1967, p. 4.
72. BT 279/283.
73. *Kine Weekly*, 5 August 1967, p. 3.
74. *Kine Weekly*, 14 January 1967, p. 3.
75. NFFC memorandum to the Board of Trade, 14 December 1967, BT 279/283 Review of Film Support Policy and Legislation 1967/1968.
76. Film Finances file on *They're a Weird Mob*.
77. Crosland had succeeded Douglas Jay in September 1967.
78. BT 279/283 Review of Film Support Policy and Legislation 1967/1968.
79. *Kine Weekly*, 13 April 1968, p. 3, and 1 June 1968, p. 3.
80. Bill Altira, 'Long Shots, *Kine Weekly*, 1 June 1968, p. 4.
81. BT 279/283 Review of Film Support Policy and Legislation 1967/1968.
82. Report by the Economic Services Division of the Board of Trade, June 1968, BT 335/23, Review of Screen: British Film Production Fund, NFFC: Submission to Ministers 1969. This report generated considerable alarm with the NFFC, as indicated in a letter from Hilary Scott to Gwyneth Dunwoody, parliamentary secretary to the Board of Trade on 19 June 1968, BT 279/283 Review of Film Support Policy and Legislation 1967/1968.
83. Submission to ministers by the Board of Trade Films Branch dated 12 July 1968, BT 279/283 Review of Film Support Policy and Legislation 1967/1968.
84. The arts minister, Jennie Lee, was identified as being strongly in favour. Submission to ministers by the Board of Trade Films Branch dated 12 July 1968, BT 279/283 Review of Film Support Policy and Legislation 1967/1968.
85. The NFFC almost achieved break even for the year to 31 March 1968 but a deficit on the interest account of £183,709 meant that it recorded a loss of £199,098. *Kine Weekly*, 3 August 1968.
86. 31 July 1968 Memo on Films Legislation by Gwyneth Dunwoody, Parliamentary Secretary to the Board of Trade, BT 279/283 Review of Film Support Policy and Legislation 1967/1968.
87. *The Daily Cinema*, 9 December 1968.
88. Hugh Jenkins, *Film & TV Technician*, September 1967, p. 242.
89. BT 335/23 Review of Screen: British Film Production Fund, NFFC: Submission to Ministers 1969.
90. David Davis, 'US film-makers in Britain may start a dollar drain', *The Times*, 10 February 10 1969. BT 335/23 Review of Screen: British Film Production Fund, NFFC: Submission to Ministers 1969.
91. David Davis, 'US film-makers in Britain may start dollar drain', republished in *Film and TV Technician*, February, 35: 285, 1969.
92. John Terry, 'Time Right for British Finance', *Kine Weekly*, 15 March 1969, p. 8.
93. A letter from L. Pliatzky at the Treasury to Harold Bailey at the Board of Trade, 1 April 1969, notes that while content with plans regarding the levy and quota, 'we see considerable objection to writing off the NFFC's losses and giving it a new lease of life with replenished resources'. Pliatzky urges the Board of Trade to reconsider this. BT 335/23 Review of Screen: British Film Production Fund, NFFC: Submission to Ministers 1969.
94. *Kine Weekly*, 27 December 1969, p. 3.
95. Source: Film Finances files.

4. THE VERTICALLY INTEGRATED INDEPENDENT

Laura Mayne

Introduction

Concern about monopoly control of the film industry was a major issue during the 1960s. By 1964 the two main UK exhibitors, Rank and ABC, owned around 43 per cent of UK cinema seats between them.[1] Moreover, as the minor chains – including Essoldo, Star, Shipman & King, Granada, Caledonian and A. B. King – tended to follow the pattern set by the two major circuits in their choice of programming, this increased the influence of the duopoly on the British exhibition sector. But there also existed some smaller players who sought to negotiate a changing industry landscape by screening low-budget exploitation films or Continental imports with a sensational flavour, thus differentiating their product from the more family-friendly and mainstream fare offered by the 'majors'. This product was supplied by a group of independent distributors, some of who were sister companies to the specialist exhibitors. The changes experienced by the exhibition and distribution sectors in the British film industry during the 1960s not only led to the demise of many smaller players, as discussed in previous chapters, they also created opportunities for some enterprising companies to adapt to or create a niche in the new landscape from which they were able to survive and even thrive. Some were able to combine exhibition, distribution and even production interests, creating an alternative form of vertical integration in the process, albeit on a micro scale compared to the UK duopoly and the Hollywood majors.

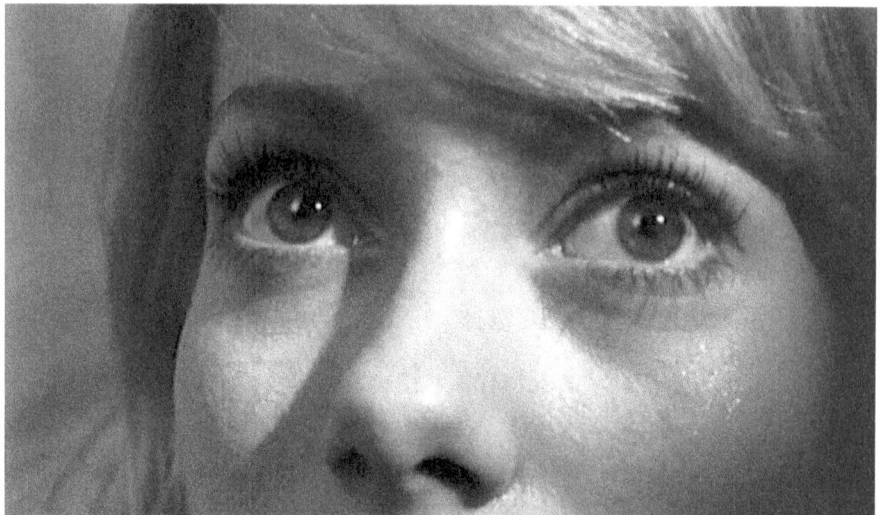

Figure 4.1 The eyes of Catherine Deneuve in the Compton horror production *Repulsion* (Roman Polanski, 1965).

There were three main factors which impacted the industry during the decade. The first was the breakdown of the studio system and the consolidation of monopoly power. The second was a changing censorship climate driven by the expansion in social liberalism and a culture of permissiveness and the role played in this by the BBFC, which was passing an increasing number of films with an X or adults-only certificate. The third was the emergence of a small number of independent exhibitors and distributors who, through an entrepreneurial, creative and at times opportunistic approach to business, were able to weather the changes that ended up putting so many other smaller exhibitors and distributors out of business. These companies tended to operate in the low-budget sector and concentrated on specialised product and markets. While some limited their operations to either exhibition or distribution, other more ambitious players adopted a vertically integrated approach, among them Kenneth Rive's Gala Films and Michael Klinger and Tony Tenser's Compton group of companies.

A Changing Film Market

The general pattern of distribution and exhibition in the 1960s was as follows. Films would have 'first runs' in the biggest cinemas located in city centres (notably those run by Rank and ABC), followed by 'second runs' in the smaller suburban cinemas, before moving on down the chain to more minor and rural theatres (however, sometimes if a non-circuit cinema was bigger than the local Rank-owned Odeon or ABC it would be included in the 'first run' at the expense of those cinemas).[2] In 1966, of the 1,953 cinemas operating in Britain, 330 were owned by Rank and 247 by ABPC, which left 1,376 'independents'.[3] While the duopoly's share combined represented only 30 per cent of the total number, these were the biggest and the best-equipped halls and were often located in major metropolitan centres. As a result, they enjoyed a privileged position and tended to set the release pattern for the entire country. Ongoing distribution deals with the American majors also meant that Rank and ABC cinemas were able to access the newest Hollywood product, while the independents had to wait in line. And while cinemas continued to close at a steady rate throughout the 1960s, it is important to note that these were rarely combine-owned.

The distribution sector was similarly dominated by a small number of big companies. These included the four largest UK companies: Rank, Warner–Pathé, British Lion and Anglo-Amalgamated, and the Hollywood majors, and between them they handled around 80 per cent of British features in the home market. And as we have seen, the smaller independent distribution companies were hit hard by the changes in the market for British films that culminated in the winter production crisis of 1963/4. Among those forced to cease trading were Bryanston Films – which had been a major player at the beginning of the decade – and the other British Lion satellites. Indeed, of the seventy distribution companies active at some point during the decade, almost a third had gone out of business by 1965.[4]

However, the picture is more complex than this summary indicates. During the 1950s a healthy section of the distribution industry developed, led by companies like Anglo-Amalgamated and New Realm, which built their businesses on repackaging older American films with new but cheaply made British and American 'B' movies to smaller independent exhibition circuits and halls.[5] The 1950s had seen the rise of a new breed of US independent producer specialising in low-budget exploitation films aimed at the new teenage market in America. This approach proved successful elsewhere, including in Britain. But by the early 1960s this variant of the long-established 'double bill' was being undermined by other new trends. Old films were being increasingly sold to television, while the great British second feature, that offspring of the 'Quota Quickies', had become another casualty of changing audience taste.

The small independent distributors who survived into the 1960s did so by turning their attention to a different kind of product, including 'Continental' art cinema and increasingly risqué and lurid genre films. Companies like Miracle, Mondial, Planet, S. F. Films and Gala aimed to cater to adults-only audiences with imported films which, as Adrian Smith notes, were treated far more leniently by the British censor than the homegrown variety.[6] Thus, while the major distributors were concerned with differentiating cinema from television through an emphasis on scale and spectacle, some small independents sought to offer products which differed significantly from the mainstream market and from the kind of films being broadcast on television. As Robert Murphy argues:

> the growing disenchantment of the smaller circuits and independents manifested itself in an increasing tendency to break away from the standard release pattern and programme their cinemas with popular classics, foreign sex and art films, and the 'X' films which the circuits were reluctant to show.[7]

Increasing Permissiveness: Changes in Censorship

In terms of censorship controversies, a handful of notorious films bookend the 1960s, beginning with *Room at the Top* (1959) and *Peeping Tom* (1960) and ending with *Performance* (1970), *The Devils* (1971) and *A Clockwork Orange* (1971). During the intervening decade the perception of what was acceptable in cinema changed radically in tune with wider cultural shifts towards greater permissiveness around sex and sexuality. This included the introduction of the birth-control pill, greater rates of cohabitation, the easing of divorce laws, the legalisation of abortion and decriminalisation of homosexuality. A landmark legal reform was the 1959 Obscene Publications Act which paved the way for the famous *Lady Chatterley* trial the following year. The Act coincided with the release of *Room at the Top*, which inaugurated the New Wave that rejuvenated British cinema at the start of the 1960s, a film that had also helped pave the way for a greater range of adult themes and representations. But this was only the beginning and as former secretary of the British Board of Film Censors (BBFC) John Trevelyan wrote in his 1973 autobiography: 'at the time its sex scenes were regarded as sensational . . . Ten years later these scenes seemed very mild and unsensational.'[8]

From its earliest days, the BBFC had established rules about what was and was not acceptable and for a long time these rules had been detailed and proscriptive. For example, films could be automatically rejected for showing 'white men in a state of degradation amid foreign surroundings', 'workhouse officials . . . in an offensive light' and 'irreverent quotations of religious texts'.[9] But by the 1960s such hard and fast regulations had given way to vague evaluations of acceptability encapsulated in expressions like 'you just get the feel of the thing'.[10] This allowed the BBFC the flexibility to keep pace with rapidly changing public tastes and the boundaries of what was deemed acceptable. However, it also left the BBFC open to criticism from both campaigners for public morality and film-makers ever keen to push at the boundaries.

Unusually for secretaries of the BBFC, Trevelyan sought to cultivate a public persona that was eloquent, charismatic and gregarious and to stress his desire to work with film-makers in negotiating the shifting moral climate. But the BBFC's influence on the industry remained considerable. On a practical level, the censor did not just exert final say on the certification of a film; it was common practice for scripts to be sent to the BBFC for approval before a film went into production and so Trevelyan and his colleagues had the power to influence a film's development. Despite this power, Trevelyan often tried to work with rather than against producers, helping them negotiate a shifting terrain of acceptability with celebrated examples that tested the boundaries including another New Wave production, *Saturday Night and Sunday Morning* (1960); the 'social problem' film *Victim* (1961) which starred Dirk Bogarde as a barrister with a secret homosexual life; the 'swinging London' film *Alfie* (1966) and Lindsay Anderson's political satire *If....* (1968).

The growing market for X-certificated material created opportunities for smaller companies, particularly those handling horror films or Continental European product which by the 1950s had gained a reputation for a franker portrayal of sex than British films. As Trevelyan (in many ways a progressive liberal in his personal views on sex) writes:

> We used at this time to be more generous to sex scenes in films with foreign-language dialogue than to films with English dialogue since the former usually had more limited distribution normally only to art theatres, and were less likely to produce criticism, but I used to ask for a 'gentleman's agreement' giving us the opportunity of reviewing a film if it should get a wider distribution.[11]

Such a policy favoured those specialist distributors who supplied more risqué material to independent halls, while working against those who sought certificates for more explicit films for general release. This inconsistent application of rules of acceptability to British and imported films generated controversy. In a 1958 BBC broadcast, the director J. Lee Thompson had criticised the BBFC for being more likely to pass a foreign film with adult themes than a British one, and not without some merit.[12] This apparently continued into the new decade when Guy Hamilton's 1963 beatnik film, *The Party's Over*, faced delays and cuts by the BBFC. While the main issue was a scene in which a man is implied to be having intimate relations with the corpse of a young woman, Trevelyan also cited the Chelsea setting as another problem, suggesting that if the film had been set in Paris, for example, there might have been fewer issues in passing it. As one *Observer* critic noted, 'portrayal of *British* depravity is thought to set a more dangerous example to British audiences.'[13] Thus in *Room at the Top* Joe Lampton (Lawrence Harvey) is permitted to have illicit sexual liaisons with

Table 4.1 Films of smaller distributors (British) by BBFC certification, 1960–9

Distributor	Rating			Total
	X	A	U	
Tigon	8	2	1	11
Regal	2	4	2	8
Planet	4	4	4	12
Grand National	1	6	5	12
Golden Era	1	3	2	6
Gala	3	4	1	8
Eros	1	2	3	6
Compton	10	1	0	11
Britannia	1	4	2	7
Total	31	30	20	81

an older woman played by French star Simone Signoret rather than an English actress. And it is significant that when Lynne Reid Banks's novel *The L-Shaped Room* was adapted by writer/director Bryan Forbes in 1962, the nationality of the unmarried, pregnant young woman at the centre of the drama was changed from English to French.

Censorship restrictions directly affected the sale and distribution of films in the UK, and this also affected patterns of exhibition. While specialist distributors imported Continental films, when it came to British productions there was a clear preference for U- or A-rated films rather than X-rated films (see Table 4.1). In fact, there were the only three companies who funded and distributed British X films in any significant numbers in the 1960s. In the case of Universal International, many of these were horror films produced by Hammer Films, who had been granted the rights to remake the classic Hollywood monster movies of the 1930s and 1940s. But the other two companies were the small independents Compton and Tigon. The rest distributed a mixture of X-, A- and U-rated films, while Grand National, Golden Era, Eros and Britannia distributed just one British X film each over the decade as a whole.

If we cast the net beyond British product, by the beginning of the 1960s the market for Continental films was growing, not just in London but also in the provinces. Kenneth Rive's company Gala was at the forefront of specialist Continental film distribution in the UK. They had made an impact by the late 1950s, introducing French New Wave films to Britain alongside films by high-profile European arthouse directors like Federico Fellini, Ingmar Bergman and Luis Buñuel.[14] Rive had begun his career in exhibition, taking over two cinemas in London's Tottenham Court Road in 1946, the Majestic and the Carlton, and by the early 1960s he was running a number of specialist cinemas across the country.[15] But the slates of specialist distributors like Gala varied from culturally prestigious releases to more sensationalist X films, and this created, in the words of one *Sight and Sound* reviewer, 'an unholy alliance, a policy which results in the optimistic selling of *Une Femme Mariée* as '24 Hours in the Life of an Adulteress'.[16] But Rive's success indicated that the market for Continental films in Britain had clearly expanded beyond specialist film clubs and the UK-wide film-society networks co-ordinated by the British Film Institute.

Specialist distributors and mainstream distributors handled marketing and promotion very differently. In his book *Shepperton Babylon*, Matthew Sweet questions whether a smaller distributor than Anglo-Amalgamated might have sold Michael Powell's *Peeping Tom* differently, given its status as a film that treads a very fine line between exploitation and artistic respectability, exploiting the controversy around the film to their advantage, rather than, as Anglo did, pulling the film from the Plaza Cinema following visceral reactions of disgust among critics.[17] (On a somewhat ironic note, Anglo had begun in the 1950s as a purveyor of 'B' movies and cheap exploitation fare.) Kenneth Rive was one exhibitor who actually *did* decide to turn the bad press to the film's advantage, and with characteristic flair he advertised it at one of his own cinemas using quotes from hostile press articles: 'the nastiest film I have ever seen'; 'it's a long time since a film has disgusted me as much as *Peeping Tom*'.[18] Rive seemed genuinely wounded when his company was (by his own account) subjected to criticism by the wider trade for this initiative. He saw this as a resounding indictment of the lack of entrepreneurial flair among the industry, and in an angry article penned for *The Daily Cinema* he demanded:

> What has happened to the old brand of showmanship which in our business means full houses and a thriving industry? If members of the associations and committees spent more time shouting 'roll up' 'roll up' than sitting on their bottoms and devising methods to curb showmanship ... their services would no longer be required.[19]

Rive's complaint is indicative of the fact that by the early 1960s the 'Wardour Street establishment' was growing increasingly out of touch with the realities facing independent cinema owners around the country, and this had fostered a kind of resentment among the latter group.

The early 1960s also saw the creation of a number of members-only film clubs which, due to a loophole in censorship law, were able to screen films which had been refused a certificate provided these screenings were for members only (the same premise on which the BFI's National Film Theatre operated). In addition to Rive's Gala clubs, these included Derek Hill's New Cinema Club and the Compton Cinema Club, established by Michael Klinger and Tony Tenser, which all opened in London in 1960. Membership was age-restricted and could cost anywhere from a few shillings to one guinea. It was in these newly established clubs that art and exploitation would meet in interesting new ways. There may have been more than a few raised eyebrows when the secretary of the BBFC became a founding member of both the Gala and Compton clubs, but for Trevelyan there was no real conflict of interest, given the limited, adults-only audiences for their programmes. However, in his autobiography Trevelyan admits that he was likely to judge scenes in low-budget exploitation material far more harshly than the same scenes in something with clear artistic motivation. Ever the unapologetic elitist, he wrote that he was 'glad to support the work of Derek Hill, a film critic, campaigner and amateur film-maker, who started the New Cinema Club for intelligent people who were keenly interested in films', believing that such an operation was a valuable 'safety-valve for censorship'.[20]

Membership of the Gala Film Club cost one guinea and was available to those aged 18 or over. Though film societies had long shown films which had failed to obtain official certification, Gala adopted the rather more original policy of screening uncut versions of films which had already been given a release.[21] According to Derek Hill, the National Film Theatre dropped a mooted programme of 'uncut' films because there was a fear that it would be associated with the Gala clubs.[22] Hill's New Cinema Club also screened Continental arthouse films (and this included sensationalist fare) and was thought to be somewhat more highbrow but became an important part of the conversation around censorship towards the end of the decade. In 1967, the club ran a 'Forbidden Film' festival which included the screening of *Danish Blue*, a film about the Scandinavian country's sex industry which advocated the legalisation of pornography. An article in *Other Scenes* noted that the furore over the screening was evidence that Hill was 'winning his fight to make the cinema as free as the stage', while the backlash aggravated the critic Dilys Powell who wrote that the film would 'harm no one' while 'the stupidity around censorship is becoming evident to all'.[23]

A New Kind of Vertically Integrated Independent

If Derek Hill's New Cinema film club was culturally and ideologically motivated, Michael Klinger and Tony Tenser's agenda in starting the Compton Cinema Club was unabashedly commercial. Tenser's background was in cinema management, film distribution and marketing. In the late 1950s he was head of publicity for Miracle Films, a small distribution company which sold European art films – perhaps most notably *And God Created Woman* (1956) starring Brigitte Bardot in one of her most sexually provocative roles – to small independent circuits. Tenser was already proving to be someone who understood the power of showmanship. After bringing Bardot to London to promote her film, he commissioned a naked waxwork of her to stand outside the Cameo cinema in London and then arranged to have it stolen to generate further publicity.[24] It was as a result of such stunts that Tenser met Klinger, who in 1958 was managing a strip club called The Gargoyle when Tenser hired some of his strippers to stage a mock protest outside a screening of Pierre Foucaud's comedy *En Effeuillant La Margeruite* (1956), rebranded *Mademoiselle Strip Tease*.[25] For his part, Klinger was fascinated by film production, and was, according to Andrew Spicer and A. T. McKenna, more interested in the cultural legitimacy and accolades that well-received product could confer.[26] Tenser's chief interest, on the other hand, was profit and his foremost talent lay in marketing and exploitation, although it is well worth noting that he later gained a reputation for creating opportunities for innovative young and emerging directors including Michael Reeves and Peter Sasdy.

In 1960 Klinger and Tenser joined forces by forming the Compton Cinema Club, situated in a 170-seat cinema in Soho's Old Compton Street. The club opened with a US independent crime drama, *Private Property* (1960), screened with a French short, *The Crimson Curtain*, and *The Ring*, a cartoon made in Yugoslavia.[27] Though entrenched in the Soho sex industry, the Compton Cinema Club also had links to the wider film society movement and exhibited a mixture of arthouse fare and exploitation films in the vein of *Mondo Cane* (1962). The club also screened uncut versions of films that had been previously censored by the BBFC and banned films with some cultural cachet, like the American motorcycle-gang film, The *Wild One* (1953). According to Tenser, 'I knew quite a lot of films didn't get a certificate, or else they were heavily cut, not because of sex or violence, but for political or religious reasons ... We knew we could establish our legitimacy by showing those films.'[28] The club also screened nudist films (some of which were produced by Compton), although the genre's heyday had been in the 1950s and by the early 1960s its popularity was beginning to wane.

The club was extremely profitable for Compton and by 1966 boasted around 50,000 members.[29] Indeed, it proved so successful that Klinger and Tenser were able to quickly expand their operations: first into distribution with the formation of Compton–Cameo Pictures, initially to ensure a steady stream of product for the club, and subsequently into production with the naturist documentary *Naked as Nature Intended* (1961), directed by Harrison Marks and starring Pamela Green, who had appeared as a pin-up model in Michael Powell's *Peeping Tom*. Compton was growing fast, and the company regularly took out full-page advertisements in *Kine Weekly* to advertise that fact. A series of business decisions signalled Klinger and Tenser's ambitions towards respectability: their confidence in erecting a super-cinema in Birmingham at a time when halls were closing, their acquisition of the Windmill Theatre, and even their attempt to put in a bid for British Lion when it went up for sale. However, the company's reputation and association with the Soho sex industry often undermined these ambitions.

As a distributor, Compton specialised in Continental arthouse films and released material onto the larger circuits, commonly as double bills.[30] Vertical integration also meant that Tenser and Klinger could benefit from keeping both distributors' and exhibitors' share of the profits. Being an exhibitor also gave them a deeper understanding of their customers and of their changing tastes. According to the producer Milton Subotsky, who ran his own successful independent company, Amicus, with Max Rosenberg, 'Producers and distributors must not only be in touch with their audiences, but two years ahead of them, as it takes as long as that – or more – between the time the idea for a film is conceived and the finished film is released'.[31]

Compton's production activities expanded from 1963 onwards, initially with a series of features that effectively updated the 'social problem' film to the new permissive era. *That Kind of Girl* (1963), directed by Gerry O'Hara concerns the dangers of pre-marital sex and is described by Spicer and McKenna as Compton's first 'hybrid exploitation film'; merging as it does important social issues with a sensationalist approach to marketing.[32] This was followed by the similarly themed *The Yellow Teddy Bears* (1963), *Saturday Night Out* (1964), featuring the adventures of a trio of merchant seamen in London, both directed by Robert Hartford-Davis who had produced *That Kind of Girl,* and O'Hara's *The Pleasure Girls* (1965), which was the company's contribution to the 'swinging London' genre. But Compton began to branch out into other types of production including rather lurid documentaries such as Arnold L. Miller and Norman Cohen's *London in the Raw* (1965) and *Primitive London* (1965), which sought to capitalise on the success of the explicit Italian documentary film *Mondo Cane*. And inspired by the ongoing success of Hammer films, they also made a series of low-budget horror films like Hartford-Davis's *The Black Torment* (1964), a gothic horror in the Hammer tradition, James Hill's *A Study in Terror* (1965), a Sherlock Holmes horror mystery in which Holmes and Watson investigate the crimes of Jack the Ripper (featuring Barbara Windsor as one of the infamous mass murderer's victims) and Compton's first UK film to achieve a full-circuit booking,[33] and the 'mad scientist' vehicle, *The Projected Man* (1966), directed by Ian Curteis.

Michael Klinger's desire for greater cultural legitimacy was given a boost by the arrival in 1964 of the Polish director Roman Polanski, whose first feature *Knife in the Water* (1962) had been nominated for Best Foreign Language Film at the 1963 Academy Awards. Polanski was touring London with his producer Gene Gutowski in the hope of securing finance for his second film. Following several rejections, the pair found themselves in Compton's offices.[34] Polanski could not persuade Klinger and Tenser to fund the film he actually wanted to make, the black comedy *Katelbach*, but Compton was willing to finance Polanski to the amount of £45,000 to direct a horror/psychological thriller with exploitation value. This was *Repulsion*, which featured the French star Catherine Deneuve as a sexually repressed and psychotic young woman who confines herself to the London apartment where she kills a suitor and her landlord. The film proved to be highly exploitable indeed and was an international success both critically and commercially. John Trevelyan was, unsurprisingly, kindly disposed toward the film, given Polanski's status as a highly respected European arthouse director.[35] This allowed Polanski and Gutowski to bring back their original idea to the table and this was subsequently made by Compton under the title of *Cul-de-sac* (1966). Made on location on the island of Lindisfarne in Northumbria with a cast including Lionel Stander, Donald Pleasance and Françoise Dorléac, this odd tale of a couple of eccentrics who are held hostage by an American gangster in their remote castle was also a critical success and won the Golden Bear at the Berlin Film Festival. But the film ran into problems during production and went £30,000 over its initial budget of £130,000, leading to protracted legal wrangling and a souring of the relationship between Compton and the completion guarantors Film Finances that would have significant consequences for Klinger.[36]

Compton's ambitions had magnified at an astonishing rate, creating a new kind of vertically integrated independent in the process. By 1964, Tenser and Klinger were announcing the building of a new state-of-the-art Birmingham cinema, the Superama. It was around this time that the pair became involved with Laurie Marsh, a millionaire with interests in the property business who fronted the cash for Compton to buy the famous (and by this point, flagging) Windmill Theatre in 1964. But the company's most significant strength was their approach to the distribution, marketing and exploitation of their product and how this in turn related to their awareness of their audience. It helped that both Tony Tenser and Compton's publicity manager, Graham Whitfield, had been cinema managers.[37] Klinger and Tenser's marketing of their films was characteristically colourful, but it was also shrewd and designed to appeal to the needs of independent exhibitors; this demonstrated an awareness of how their interests were bound up with that of the cinema managers who booked their films.[38] Compton also relied heavily on an international and regional network of contacts with other independents and they established offices in Belfast, Dublin, London, Cardiff, Glasgow Leeds, Paris, Rome, New York and Tokyo. The international offices enabled Compton to be first in line in obtaining UK distribution rights to foreign films, while the company staffed its UK offices with people who were skilled at maintaining close relationships with cinema exhibitors.[39] This level of organisation also further demonstrates the value of vertical integration within the independent sphere.

Compton often ran campaigns and stunts with the sole purpose of making cinema exhibitors feel involved. This included running competitions for cinema managers in order to find those managers who displayed the most showmanship (or 'Comptonship').⁴⁰ So rather than wasting their energies competing with Rank and ABC, who were giants by comparison, Compton sought to offer something different to the public instead. Klinger elaborated on the company's strategy in *The Daily Cinema*:

> we are not going out in opposition to existing cinemas. We are quite certain we have the product and are trying to set a new pattern. But we think they will be supplementary to other cinemas and will either pull in people not usually going or get other patrons going again.⁴¹

Klinger and Tenser ultimately directed their energies into seeking out niche outlets for their product, and, having identified those outlets, marketing their films in the most effective way possible.

The company also used the apparatuses of censorship to their advantage. Indeed, Spicer and McKenna go as far as to call Compton's films 'something of a test case' for the X certificate.⁴² With *Naked as Nature Intended*, Tenser and Klinger played the censor off against local authorities by submitting the film to London councils, some of which decided to pass it after the BBFC had banned it outright. This forced John Trevelyan to sheepishly capitulate and give the film an A certificate. But this tactic worked both ways: Birmingham City Council banned *Naked as Nature Intended* even though the BBFC had passed it. However, the nearby town of Walsall had not, so Compton sold it there and advertised it as 'the film you can only see in Walsall!' with the result that instead of the originally scheduled three days, it played in Walsall for 6–7 weeks.⁴³ The company sought to balance sensationalism and social relevance in their marketing strategies, and this involved adaptability and the skill to respond to the demands of the bigger circuits and smaller independent chains alike.

Details of Compton's promotional stunts have been well-documented elsewhere, notably by Andrew Spicer, Anthony McKenna and John Hamilton,⁴⁴ but it is worth considering the ways in which the company was able to turn censorship to their advantage by packaging their productions as films which explored important social issues. In the case of *The Yellow Teddy Bears*, a group of schoolgirls wear badges shaped like teddy bears to signal their lost virginity – not exactly a subject designed to appeal to the censor. However, Compton used the production to initiate a conversation about sex education in the UK and held a well-publicised theatrical screening at which medical professionals and school-age girls were invited to discuss the issues explored in the film. *That Kind of Girl* was one of the first commercial British fiction films to deal with the issue of venereal disease which could also be packaged as a 'social problem'. The film follows the sexual adventures of an au pair who engages in unprotected, pre-marital sex only to later discover that she must now live with the shame of having contracted syphilis. Significantly, it also featured the German Margaret Rose Keil, whose deviant actions were therefore easier to pass the censor because she was considered 'exotic'. Prior to the film's release, Compton sought the endorsement of the Royal Medical Association (this appears in large letters in the opening shot of the film) as a means of conferring legitimacy and branding their production as important and educational. Another way of making a film dealing with sexual themes slightly more attractive to the censor was to frame that activity as morally undesirable within the text. In *That Kind of Girl*, the desire to inform as well as educate is a key feature of the film's highly moralistic 'it could happen to you' narrative.

On the other hand, some of Compton's films were rather tame in content, but their promotional materials and publicity strategy often sought to suggest otherwise. For example, the poster for *The Pleasure Girls* features a young woman leapfrogging over a bollard and is overtly phallic in its connotations. But the film is ultimately an innocuous exploration of the lives and loves of a group of young people cohabiting in a London townhouse, although it is notable for the inclusion of a scene depicting a kiss between two men. The *Daily Worker* called *The Yellow Teddy Bears* '[a] film that sets out to be daring but is curiously old fashioned'.[45]

Compton negotiated a fine line between sensationalism and respectability, and some of the cleverly orchestrated publicity fanfares around their films signalled the company's drive towards legitimacy, particularly in terms of how it wanted to be perceived by the trade, the critics and the censors. Seeking the endorsement of professionals in the medical and educational establishments for *That Kind of Girl* and *The Yellow Teddy Bears* may have been an expedient way of mollifying the censor, but this was not the only reason. These films also pushed boundaries of acceptability in their candid representations of sex, love and marriage, and as such they sought to titillate audiences whilst also encouraging them to engage with important social issues.

By the middle of the decade, Michael Klinger's desire to become an important and above all *respected* player in the mainstream industry was increasingly at odds with Tony Tenser's commitment to low-budget horror films. These differing ambitions led Tenser, who would 'rather be ashamed of a film that was making money than proud of one that wasn't', to leave the company in 1966.[46] He sold his shares and immediately started a new venture, Tigon, with the aim of continuing to produce and distribute low-budget horror films. Tigon quickly became an important player in this sector, making over twenty productions between 1967 and 1973. These include two features directed by Michael Reeves, one of the most exciting young directors to emerge in the 1960s and who died tragically at the age of twenty-five – *The Sorcerers* (1967) and *Witchfinder General* (1968); two by the veteran Vernon Sewell – *The Blood Beast Terror* (1968) and *The Curse of the Crimson Altar* (1969); *Blood on Satan's Claw* (1971) and *Doomwatch* (1972), directed Piers Haggard and Peter Sasdy respectively.

Back at Compton, Leslie Elliot had joined the company as a circuit manager in 1965 and had subsequently taken over Tony Tenser's 16 per cent stake.[47] In 1967 Elliot began a campaign to oust Klinger from Compton's board of directors by alleging 'improper dealings'[48] over *The Penthouse* (Peter Collinson, 1967), a strange masochistic thriller/fantasy in which a married man and his young lover are held hostage in a hotel by two sadistic young men. Exactly what constituted these 'improper dealings' is unclear, but in April 1968 Elliot brought a petition to remove Klinger from the board of directors, a move which was backed up with the support of Compton's creditors, which included the NFFC and Film Finances, who were still attempting to recover the bond that rescued *Cul-de-sac*. Klinger penned a desperate letter to Robert Garrett of Film Finances on 28 April 1968, imploring the company not to support the petition and arguing that Elliot was 'abusing the law' in order to 'bring the Compton group of companies to its knees' and would most certainly not pay off any creditors once he gained control.[49] This was to no avail, as Elliot succeeded in his coup, successfully removing Klinger from the board of the company that he had helped to create.

A CHANGING EXHIBITION SECTOR: FROM SINGLE SCREENS TO MULTI-SCREENS

The British cinema ended the 1960s in a state of renewed crisis and turmoil. The mass retrenchment on the part of the Hollywood majors removed much of the finance that had fuelled many medium- and high-budget productions.[50] At the same time, cinema attendances continued their steady decline. By the early part of the new decade both Compton and Tigon found themselves under new management. Tony Tenser had started Tigon with £10,000, a Wardour Street office and a secretary. But he also received support from Laurie Marsh, who had previously been an investor in Compton's expansion, and this enabled Tigon to grow quickly and diversify through acquiring new business interests which led to a stock-market floatation in 1971. By March of the following year Tigon had gone from an annual turnover of £225,000 to a serious business boasting an annual profit of £1.4 million.[51] The company continued to be involved in all sectors of the industry, through Tigon British Film Productions, which was focused on a slate that included horror films as well as more family-friendly fare with wider appeal such as *Black Beauty* (1971), and Tigon Pictures, the company's distribution arm.[52] The Tigon group also branched out into new areas through subsidiaries in music publishing, talent agencies and property development.

But the wider changes in the industry created a new opportunity. As John Hamilton notes:

> With the company's film production plans looking promising, in the autumn of 1971 Tenser took the opportunity to promote Tigon's latest venture: opening cinemas with smaller screens, giving greater choice to the public by screening more films – predicting the idea of multiplexes.[53]

With investment from Laurie Marsh, the company acquired the Classic chain of cinemas for £7 million, and this was shortly followed up by the acquisition of the Essoldo chain in 1972, which added a further fifty-four cinemas to the company's books and effectively made Tigon the third-largest exhibition force in the UK with an asset value of £15 million.[54] According to *The Guardian*, the company was opening one new cinema every eight days by converting old auditoriums into new multi-screen complexes.[55] Marsh rebranded the group the 'Laurie Marsh Group' as he felt that 'Tigon' did not adequately signal the company's identity or interests.[56] It was around this time that Tenser, whose chief interests lay in production, began to phase himself out of the business.

Following Elliot's takeover, Film Finances was assured 'the new policy at Compton is going to be geared to handling specialised films on a restricted sales policy and will be based, I am informed, on the creation of a high-priced, top executive administration, tailored to maximum efficiency.'[57] The company's policy would also place a new emphasis on the theatrical side of operations, specifically a new venture involving the opening of a series of 'mini-multiplexes' under the name Cinecenta.[58] Elliot stepped down as chairman of Compton in 1969, but before he did he set aside £750,000 to open eight new multi-screen cinema complexes.[59]

This was part of a new development in exhibition practices, notably the growing trend on the part of the major circuits towards renovating old city-centre cinemas and essentially dividing them up into smaller cinemas. The Rank and ABC/EMI circuits were ploughing money into renovating their cinemas: by 1969 Rank was opening a new cinema screen every three-and-a-half weeks, while ABPC was opening one new unit every seven weeks.[60] *The Times* reported that the licensing of multiple screens under one roof would allow Rank and ABC to provide audiences with 'two forms of specialised cinemagoing': the premiere and the 'smaller descendant of the continuous performance cinema, where you can come and go as you like and stay as long as you like'.[61] For the Classic circuit, converting its old 1,000–2,000-seater cinemas, two or three smaller units also had the benefit of reducing overheads.[62] In 1973 the Board of Trade found that owing to this new trend towards 'twinning, tripling and quadrupling' cinemas, the number of cinema screens in Britain had risen for the first time in twenty-five years.[63] The new 'multi-screen' trend may also have been lengthening the operation of bars, as films jumped from screen 1 to screen 2 before they moved to other cinemas in the area.[64] Furthermore, of around 100 new 'multi-screen' cinemas which were now operational, independents owned only a very small number.[65] Unsurprisingly it was the stronger players who fared better in this process of consolidation as the major independent circuits expanded and smaller cinemas continued to close (see Table 4.2). Thus, Tigon and Compton's new emphasis on exhibition represented a survival strategy to weather the new storms affecting the British film industry.

Table 4.2   Cinemas owned by major circuits in Britain[66]

Company	1966	1972	Total
ABC/EMI	267	256	−11
Rank	330	234	−96
Classic	29	—	—
Star	60	98	+38
Essoldo	51	—	—
Classic/Essoldo/Tigon	—	130	+130
Total	737	718	−19
Other cinemas	1,276	801	−475
Total UK cinemas	2,013	1,519	−494

It is important to note that the concept of the niche that had served Compton so well during the first half of the 1960s continued to be significant. Thus, competing with Rank and EMI was not a key strategy for Tigon/LMG/Classic. Rather, their plan was to differentiate themselves by showing a combination of older reissues and more specialist films. Classic also enjoyed considerably more flexibility and freedom than Rank and ABC in its booking practices, programming 'the Marx Brothers and the French classics for Chelsea and Notting Hill Gate but decidedly more suggestive films for Piccadilly'.[67] If Rank and ABC were forced to show two X films in two cinemas in the same town, the nearby Essoldo or Classic cinema could opt to show a U instead, further differentiating itself from the majors by its product.[68] Thus by 1973, 'specialist' exhibition had begun to take on new meanings.

Conclusion

A 1963 audience survey report funded by the Federation of British Film Makers had argued that there was a case for selling the cinemagoing experience to the public 'as a separate commodity over and above the film itself. At present it is only the film which is sold to the public.'[69] However, the evidence suggested that, to stem the overwhelming fall in cinema admissions, many independent exhibitors *were* already making considerable efforts to attract audiences by relying on publicity, stunts and good old-fashioned showmanship. Independent exhibitors had long been offering experience and variety to ensure their own survival, positioning themselves in the space not catered for by the big circuits. As we have seen, this idea of identifying and exploiting a niche had created the opportunity for a new kind of independent company to weather the transformation in British cinema in the early 1960s that had put so many other small exhibitors, distributors and producers out of business. Making, renting and screening specialist product could prove a lucrative business, particularly if these activities could be combined as demonstrated by Compton and Tigon.

Shrewd operators like Michael Klinger and Tony Tenser also understood the importance of old-fashioned entrepreneurial showmanship. This aligned them more to the values and business practices of a distributor/producer like Anglo-Amalgamated and a producer like James Carreras or Peter Rogers. But they were also prepared to adapt and exploit new opportunities being created by the wider structural shifts that the industry was undergoing as well as a liberalisation of censorship and changing social mores. Compton's success was no accident; its development was clever, strategic and underpinned by an acute understanding of the industry and how it functioned. Tenser and Klinger recognised that making a profitable living had to entail the cultivation of a strong network of regional contacts, a flair for creative marketing, and crucially, a good relationship with the censor. Changes in censorship heavily influenced the output of some independent distributors, particularly given the BBFC's slightly laxer attitude towards risqué content in Continental imports playing on smaller circuits.

Changing patterns of independent exhibition also served to blur the lines between dividing 'art' and 'exploitation' cinema during the 1960s. This allowed a company like Compton to occupy a space between the majors and the small independents, and their strategies were based around an innate understanding of the growing disenchantment of independents with the major circuits. The company recognised that independent cinema owners felt like their needs were being ignored by the Wardour Street establishment, and in light of this they offered a marketing strategy based on old ideas of 'showmanship' to appeal to these exhibitors, prioritising the local over the national, and networking with small exhibitors from offices based in cities around the country. Compton also reflected the importance of reputation in the film industry. The company's aspiration for greater legitimacy was constrained by their roots in and continuing links to the Soho sex industry, but nevertheless by capitalising on the increasingly fragmented nature of the distribution and exhibition sectors they were able to become, in effect, a successful vertically integrated film company, albeit on a small scale. A similar model was adopted by Tigon, whose own move into exhibition in the early 1970s anticipated the rise of the multiplex a decade and a half later.

Notes

1. Monopolies Commission, *A Report on the Supply of Films for Exhibition in Cinemas* (London: House of Commons, 1966), p. 20.
2. Robert Murphy, *Sixties British Cinema* (London: BFI, 1992), p. 104.
3. National Archives (TNA), FV60/66, 'Monopolies Commission: Action Taken on Report on Cinema Films', letter dated 15 August 1973 from Miss K. Mack, PSDI films branch, to Mr D. Potter.
4. Figures derived from the project database.
5. David Ryder, *Making it in Wardour Street* (Leeds: Cinemuseum Publishing, 2007).
6. Adrian Smith, 'Dolls of Vice: Eurotica repackaged for early 1960s British audiences', <https://www.academia.edu/5163095/Dolls_of_Vice_Eurotica_repackaged_for_early_1960s_British_audiences> (accessed 6 March 2017).
7. Murphy, *Sixties British Cinema*, p. 105.
8. Anthony Aldgate, *Censorship and the Permissive Society: British Cinema and Theatre, 1955-1965* (Oxford: Clarendon Press, 1995), p. 33.
9. John Trevelyan, *What the Censor Saw* (London: Michael Joseph, 1973), p. 41.
10. Derek Malcolm, 'Censored, and Why', *The Guardian*, 17 September 1968, p. 6.
11. Trevelyan, *What the Censor Saw*, pp. 108–9.
12. Aldgate, *Censorship and the Permissive Society*, pp. 36–7.
13. John Ardagh, 'Censor to decide if the party is over', p. 1.
14. Alan Howden, 'Kenneth Rive', *The Guardian*, 3 February 2003, p. 22.
15. *The Times*, 12 December 1966.
16. Quoted in Murphy, *Sixties British Cinema*, p. 71.
17. Matthew Sweet, *Shepperton Babylon: The Lost Worlds of British Cinema* (London: Faber, 2006), p. 255.
18. *The Daily Cinema*, 17 June 1960.
19. *The Daily Cinema*, 17 June 1960.
20. Trevelyan, *What the Censor Saw*, p. 122.
21. Derek Hill, 'Censorship and the New Film Clubs', *Observer*, 28 February 1960, p. 19.
22. Ibid.
23. British Film Institute Special Collections (BFI), Derek Hill Collection, press cutting from *Other Scenes*, file *Danish Blue*.
24. Matthew Sweet, *Shepperton Babylon*, p. 265.
25. Ibid.
26. Andrew Spicer and A. T. McKenna, *The Man Who Got Carter: Michael Klinger, Independent Production and the British Film Industry, 1960–1980* (London: I. B. Tauris, 2013).
27. Anon., 'Club Cinema's First Film', *The Times*, 11 November 1960.
28. John Hamilton, *Beasts in the Cellar: The Exploitation Film Career of Tony Tenser* (Surrey: Fab Press, 2005), p. 11.
29. Spicer and McKenna, *The Man Who Got Carter*, p. 17.
30. Ibid., p. 17.
31. Milton Subotsky, 'The Work of the Film Producer', *Screen* 10: 6 (1969), 24–32.
32. Spicer and McKenna, *The Man Who Got Carter*, p. 24.
33. Ibid., p. 30.
34. Hamilton, *Beasts in the Cellar*, p. 45.
35. Spicer and McKenna, *The Man Who Got Carter*, p. 35.
36. Film Finances file on *Cul-de-sac*.
37. Spicer and McKenna, *The Man Who Got Carter*, p. 18.
38. Hamilton, *Beasts in the Cellar*, p. 66.

39. Spicer and McKenna, *The Man Who Got Carter*, p. 18.
40. Ibid.
41. Quoted in Michael Ahmed, 'Reframing British Exploitation Cinema' (University of East Anglia: unpublished PhD thesis, 2013), p. 61.
42. Spicer and McKenna, *The Man Who Got Carter*, p. 27.
43. Hamilton, *Beasts in the Cellar*, p. 13.
44. See Spicer and McKenna, *The Man Who Got Carter*; Hamilton, *Beasts in the Cellar*.
45. Ibid., p. 26.
46. Hamilton, *Beasts in the Cellar*, p. 8.
47. Spicer and McKenna, *The Man Who Got Carter*, pp. 44–5.
48. Ibid.
49. Film Finances file on *Cul-de-sac*, letter from Michael Klinger to Robert Garrett, 28 April 1968.
50. Although overall production levels remained relatively consistent into the early years of the 1970s. See Sue Harper and Justin Smith, *British Film Culture in the 1970s* (Edinburgh: Edinburgh University Press, 2012).
51. Andrew Davenport, 'Risk Involved in Tigon Offer', *The Guardian*, 13 September 1971, p. 12.
52. Hamilton, *Beasts in the Cellar*, p. 213.
53. Ibid., p. 214.
54. Ibid., p. 223.
55. *The Guardian*, 4 March 1972, p. 15.
56. Hamilton, *Beasts in the Cellar*, p. 232.
57. Film Finances file on *The Projected Man*, letter from Gerald A. Fernback Assocs to John Croydon, 1 September 1967.
58. Spicer and McKenna, *The Man Who Got Carter*, p. 45.
59. Anon., 'The money flows into British films', *The Times*, 16 June 1969, p. 23.
60. Ibid.
61. Ibid.
62. Andrew Davenport, 'Risk involved in Tigon offer', p. 12.
63. TNA, FV60/66, Monopolies Commission: Action Taken on Report on Cinema Films.
64. Ibid.
65. Ibid.
66. Ibid.
67. Davenport, 'Risk Involved in Tigon Offer', p. 12.
68. Ibid.
69. Federation of British Film Makers, *Cinema Going in Greater London*, p. 4.

5. LOW-BUDGET INDEPENDENT PRODUCTION

Laura Mayne

INTRODUCTION

It is not difficult to see why Robert Murphy calls the 1960s the most 'dynamic' era of British cinema 'before or since'.[1] The increasing significance of American finance had led to more international 'British' productions featuring top stars, higher production values and a wholesale shift to colour. However, the

Figure 5.1   Colin Campbell and Dudley Sutton in the Garrick production *The Leather Boys* (Sidney J. Furie, 1964): a film that fell victim to the exhibition crisis.

prevailing 'Hollywood, England' narrative has also obscured a consideration of the transformations affecting many of the smaller players in the domestic industry. As noted in the previous chapter many independent companies across exhibition and distribution were forced to close by the wider transformation of the industry. Yet others – such as Compton and Tigon – were able to adapt and thrive. This chapter will extend the consideration beyond vertically integrated independents to consider how a diverse range of smaller production companies negotiated the changing landscape, largely without access to Hollywood support, creating another important and distinctive dimension of sixties British cinema.

The Death of the British 'B' Film

The winter production crisis of 1963/64 explored in the introductory chapter of this book had effectively sounded the death knell for the British 'B' movie that had been a firm staple of the post-war cinema programme. This marked a transition point for British film production as by the early 1960s television was beginning to produce series and serials that were very similar in style and content to the class 'B' movie, rendering it and the whole idea of the double feature increasingly unsustainable. The rapid decline of the second feature between 1963 and 1965 (see Table 5.1) saw formerly prolific producers such as Butchers and the Danziger brothers go bust as domestic exhibition became increasingly dominated by bigger-budget films and the single feature came to replace the old double bill.

Second features had traditionally performed an important function within the cinema programme. They were cheaply made, tightly scripted, shot in two to three weeks (a third to a quarter of the time required for a routine 'A' feature) and sold to exhibitors for a fixed price. But industrially and aesthetically, they were the natural successor of the derided quota quickie of the 1930s,[2] and a 1963 study into cinemagoing habits in the Greater London

Table 5.1 British film production by year[3]

Year	Films released (British)	Film length 55–72 minutes
1960	132	36
1961	113	37
1962	122	39
1963	114	27
1964	82	18
1965	83	8
1966	82	5
1967	87	7
1968	96	8
1969	80	4

area found that many people arrived at the cinema in the middle of the second feature and tended to use them only as a means of making sure that they were in time for the main film.[4] And as one producer argued in *The Times* in 1962, second features could never hope to be seen as quality products so long as they were treated by the industry like 'free vouchers given away with a packet of soap flakes'.[5]

However, as Brian McFarlane rightly argues, we should not ignore the 'B' film, because to do so would result in a 'skewing' of our sense of how the production industry was organised and functioned in the post-war era.[6] Until 1964 second features made up a significant percentage of annual film production in Britain. Moreover, as they were made on a fraction of the budget for a practical purpose it is unfair and inappropriate to make aesthetic judgements about their quality or to hold them to the same standard as 'A' films. Sue Harper and Vincent Porter argue that 'B' films might also offer a reflection of the times precisely because they are so utterly unself-conscious: they captured the 'residual topoi which lie coiled deep in the culture, and which are primarily comforting'.[7]

'B' films were primarily product which adhered to tight visual and narrative constraints. More than any other type of film produced in post-war Britain, they had a particular 'house style' that reflected the *modus operandi* of the companies that produced them. This was dictated by tight budgetary constraints and fast-paced shooting schedules; writers would pen several scripts for one company – Brian Clemens for Danziger and Philip Mackie for Merton Park, for example – and sets would often be reused out of necessity. Second features produced by Danziger, which had operated from a small studio in Elstree since 1956, were routinely among the most critically panned and often serve as a shorthand joke for the worst examples of the genre. One reviewer from *Monthly Film Bulletin* dubbed the company's output 'a grab bag of assorted clichés'.[8] But in truth their films are actually rather diverse and varied in terms of quality. While *Feet of Clay* (1960), a thriller about the murder of a probation officer, is dull and plodding, *Fate Takes a Hand* (1962), a drama about a bag of stolen letters which are delivered to their recipients fifteen years too late, with interesting consequences, is genuinely gripping.

Another prolific producer in the early part of the 1960s was the Merton Park company, closely tied to Anglo-Amalgamated. They concentrated on thrillers, with the *Edgar Wallace Mysteries* series (loosely adapted from the crime novels of the esteemed writer) produced by between 1960 and 1965 by Jack Greenwood representing the pinnacle of their output and arguably of the British 'B' movie. These films benefitted from distribution on the ABC circuit (Anglo being closely tied to the major) and were also sold abroad to France, Italy and Germany. In terms of narrative, performance and visual style they were technically accomplished and remarkably consistent, but they were also apparently so interchangeable in content that occasionally two Edgar Wallace thrillers could be linked together to make one single feature with top billing.[9] Merton Park made forty-seven of these films over a period of four years, holding out even after rivals like Danziger and Butchers had pulled out of the market. A second crime series, *Scales of Justice*, fronted by the author and criminologist Edgar Lustgarten, was introduced in 1962 and thirteen half-hour films were made over the next five years, the first nine in black and white and the final four in colour. But despite the superior quality of their product, even Merton Park could not resist the direction of change and the company gradually reduced their output of second features after 1964, though the *Edgar Wallace* anthology continued to play in cinemas and subsequently on television.

The decline and death of the 'B' movie was clearly related to wider trends in British cinema. In effect, the circuits were moving their attention away from small-scale, low-budget black-and-white dramas which were increasingly becoming available on television. Running times increased as Hollywood brought the trend towards bigger budget, more 'epic' productions. In 1960 there were four British films released with running times of over 120 minutes, but by 1968 this had risen to fifteen – an increase from 3 per cent to 15 per cent of all productions. But the most pressing reason for the abrupt death of the British second feature was that these films had ceased to be commercially viable. It was becoming increasingly impossible to make a 'B' movie for less than around £20,000, and producers were unlikely to make a profit on any film budgeted higher than this figure, even with payments from the British Film Production Fund and international sales to television. The only way a producer could realistically make a profit was by gaining distribution on one of the major circuits, and this was becoming increasingly difficult as the 1960s progressed. As David Kingsley, managing director of distributor British Lion, wrote to director Francis Searle in 1961: 'I must repeat that there are a number of second features available at the moment, and that it is not always easy to secure a circuit deal unless the film is of above average merit.' The following year Kingsley wrote, 'In our view there have been too many of these robbery stories.'[10] This suggests that the formula was becoming tired as new kinds of stories, themes and styles were beginning to emerge in British cinema.

Diversification in a Changing Market: A Case Study of Independent Artists

One company busy producing second features in the early 1960s was Independent Artists. Formed in the late 1940s by Julian Wintle and Leslie Parkyn, Independent Artists had its most active years in production between 1958 and 1963. While overall a minor industry player, the company is nevertheless notable for its comprehensive approach to business. In addition to a long-standing relationship with the Rank Organisation which meant that ten of Independent Artists' features were released by Rank Film Distributors, they also developed a connection with Anglo-Amalgamated, ensuring access to the rival ABC circuit for a further eleven films. Wintle and Parkyn were also founder members of the Bryanston independent production/distribution consortium which operated as a satellite of British Lion. However, this relationship was the least significant of the three: Bryanston distributed just two of Independent Artists' films and by 1961 Wintle and Parkyn's share in the consortium had been sold to Woodfall Films.[11]

In 1958 Independent Artists had acquired Beaconsfield studios from the Crown Film Unit. This provided a base from which a more ambitious and diverse production programme could be developed, including feature films, one-hour supporting features and ultimately television dramas. Independent Artists now had the necessary floor space, a pool of contract technicians and a steady stream of scripts, allowing them to cultivate a wide and varied slate of low-budget product aimed at both domestic and, on occasion, international markets. They initially gained a reputation for making 'B' movies of superior quality with experienced and emerging directors like Pat Jackson, Sidney Hayers and Don Sharp, produced on budgets of around £22,500 – higher than the average £15,000–£20,000.

Independent Artists' offerings were fairly high-calibre compared to the often formulaic 'whodunnits' made by rivals. For example, *October Moth* (1960) is an atmospheric thriller which follows a mentally disturbed young farmer as he holds a badly injured woman hostage, believing her to be his dead mother. Cinematographer Michael Reed (who would later shoot the James Bond production *On Her Majesty's Secret Service*) uses striking low-key high contrast lighting, which, in conjunction with handheld camerawork in confined spaces, effectively conveys a young man's state of mind. *Snowball* (1960), directed by former Ealing stalwart Pat Jackson, is a family drama in which Denis Waterman plays a young boy who blames an innocent bus driver for his lateness in coming home from school, believing that no one will discover his truancy. The tight script (penned by Anne Wintle, wife of Julian) brings some life to an otherwise unexciting concept. According to Julian Wintle: 'We didn't call them 'B' pictures, because we didn't like the connotation ... They were made by the same technicians who worked on our major pictures, but they enabled us every so often to try out new talent among directors and writers.'[12] Though these productions did not really fulfil their mooted function as a proving ground for new talent (second features rarely did, as the need for efficiency in working to tight schedules favoured the experience of old hands rather than the new) they did provide a training ground for the company as it moved into television production.

By the early 1960s, Wintle and Parkyn were extending their ambitions with first features made by experienced directors, technicians and actors. They included comedies like *Very Important Person* (1962), *The Fast Lady* (1963), both directed by Ken Annakin, and *Father Came Too!* (1963); horror films such as Sidney Hayers' *Circus of Horrors* (1960) and *Night of the Eagle* (1962); the science-fiction film *Earthly Stranger* (1963), directed by John Krish; and Lindsay Anderson's New Wave classic *This Sporting Life* (1963), Independent Artists's most culturally and critically prestigious production.

Unusually for an independent company, only two of Independent Artists' fifteen first features were produced with finance from the NFFC, which indicates the importance of the ongoing ties with Rank and Anglo-Amalgamated. Independent Artists' films for the latter tended to be horror and sci-fi such as *Night of The Eagle*, *The Unearthly Stranger* and *Circus of Horrors*. The latter is notable for being part of a loose trilogy of Sadeian films which also included Michael Powell's *Peeping Tom* (1960) and Arthur Crabtree's *Horrors of the Black Museum* (1959).[13] Shot in lurid colour by former Ealing cinematographer Douglas Slocombe, the film follows the sadistic experiments of a plastic surgeon as he remakes disfigured women into the beautiful stars of his circus show and qualifies as an early example of British exploitation cinema. Independent Artists' films for Rank, on the other hand, tended to be what *Carry On* producer Peter Rogers identified as 'typical Rank comedies', shot in colour on budgets of over £125,000 and featuring familiar domestic stars like Stanley Baxter, James Robertson Justice and Leslie Phillips.[14] *The Fast Lady* and its loose sequel *Father Came Too!* are of the classic British comedy-of-manners school, occasionally veering toward (but avoiding) outright bawdiness. Both films deal with a young man and his strained relationship with his overbearing father-in-law, though Julie Christie (appearing in her second film) lends an air of playfulness to *The Fast Lady* which is perhaps absent in its sequel, although critics were almost united in disparaging its tame, rather old-fashioned style of humour. *Waltz of the Toreadors* (1962), directed by John Guillermin, capitalises on the stardom of Peter Sellers as a womanising general who attempts to contain the damage wreaked by his seedy private life.

Within Independent Artists' diverse production slate, *This Sporting Life* stands out in terms of its artistic and critical aspirations. However, the socially conscious art film was not a comfortable place for Julian Wintle, whose son Christopher recalls that his father 'was, at heart, a popular entertainer, and to be dragged into social realism and to these left-wing film makers was not his natural habitat.'[15] Nevertheless, high hopes were riding on *This Sporting Life*, given the fact that New Wave films like *Saturday Night and Sunday Morning* (1960) and *A Taste of Honey* (1961) had performed well at the box office. The film follows a typical 'angry young man', Frank Machin (Richard Harris), in his career trajectory from miner to Rugby League star – though his happiness is marred by the fact that the object of his affections, his landlady Margaret (Rachel Roberts), regards him as a boorish 'great ape'. But despite being critically acclaimed, the film – which cost £230,000, at the top end for an Independent Artists production – was a box-office failure and retrospectively marked the end of the New Wave cycle. As Christopher Wintle suggests, while technically brilliant, *This Sporting Life* was simply 'too downbeat, and that doesn't make for popular cinema.' [16] Much like the 'B' movie, by 1963 it seemed that the 'kitchen sink' drama and 'social problem' films were fast becoming a relic of an outmoded kind of British cinema.

In 1984 Anne Wintle wrote:

> Professional criticism levelled at Julian and Leslie was that they were incredibly inconsistent in their choice of subjects at Beaconsfield, a verdict Julian contended. Independent Artists, he pointed out, were making a *whole* programme of films, not a few art ones, or solely of the commercial variety. They were trying to have a balanced schedule; and of course, they had to pay their way. The fact that *Circus of Horrors*, for instance, had taken a fortune, enabled them to make pictures of the quality of *This Sporting Life*.[17]

This balance between varieties of genres was arguably a way of mitigating risk. And the success of *The Fast Lady* did partly offset the failure of *This Sporting Life*, though in the end this was not enough.[18] Unable to absorb the financial loss of the latter film, Wintle and Parkyn began to focus exclusively on the growing opportunities presented by television. This began in 1963 with the drama series *The Human Jungle*, featuring a psychoanalyst played by Herbert Lom. Produced for the ITV company ABC (part of the ABPC conglomerate) Independent Artists produced twenty-six episodes over two years. Christopher Wintle recalled *The Human Jungle* 'took up, really, where the 'B' movie left off, I would say, because the experience of working at those very tight scripts for these one-hour films knocked back into working on these 52-minute films'.[19] In 1964 Julian began work on the modish fantasy spy-drama series, *The Avengers*, also for ABC, which stylistically and thematically was far removed from anything that Independent Artists had produced. Previously recorded on black-and-white videotape, production was moving to 35mm film following a major $2 million sale to the American Broadcasting Company, and Wintle had the necessary experience and skill to oversee this transition. He subsequently played a key part in bringing *The Avengers* to a worldwide audience within two years, with 30 million viewers in forty countries.

LOW-BUDGET INDEPENDENT PRODUCTION

The Failure to Adapt: Garrick Film Distributors

International Artists' withdrawal from film production occurred just before the winter crisis of 1963 decimated the independent sector, particularly at the level of low-budget film-making. Douglas Collins, a successful perfumer who served as chairman of British Lion 1958–61, wrote in his memoirs: 'I lost over a stone in weight before I realised that the film industry thrives on crises ... Later I realised that last week's was soon forgotten and that it was promptly replaced by a new one.'[20] Indeed, crisis has been endemic to the industry from its beginnings, but 1963 proved rather more serious for struggling independents, as a number of productions which were due to be released on the major circuits suffered severe delays of anywhere from six months to a year. Negotiations around the sale of British Lion in 1963 was the most publicised aspect of the crisis, but the situation had been brought to a head by the long-standing difficulties faced by the industry throughout the 1950s. The effects had been felt in declining cinema admissions, while the failure of a third-release circuit option for independent films and the monopoly stronghold of Rank and APBC also compounded the misery of the independent producer.

Many smaller companies were badly affected by the winter crisis. One such operation was Garrick, formed in 1960 by producer Raymond Stross, in partnership with the completion guarantor, Film Finances and Ardmore Studios in Ireland, with the aim of producing an initial slate of three movies on modest budgets of between £100,000 and £150,000. The company sought Continental rather than American partnerships, and following its inception entered into a four-picture deal with German company CCC under the aegis of Artur Brauner. However, only two productions materialised: *The Very Edge* (1963) a thriller in which a young woman (played by Stross's wife, Anne Heywood) fights off the attentions of an obsessive, knife-wielding maniac (Jeremy Brett), and *The Brain* (1962), a straightforward black-and-white horror/thriller which documents the story of a scientist possessed by the murderous brain of a deceased businessman. In addition to the psycho-thriller cycle, which had seen some recent successes, Stross was particularly keen to capitalise on the trend for 'kitchen sink' realism, which by 1962 was doing big business at the box office.

With this in mind he persuaded the company's directors to back *The Leather Boys*, a social-realist melodrama based on a novel by Gillian Freeman about the awkward relationship between a young, newly married couple living in the suburbs of South London. The film was directed by Canadian Sidney J. Furie, whose credits included Cliff Richard hit *The Young Ones* (1961), and featured Rita Tushingham who had made her debut in the Woodfall New Wave drama *A Taste of Honey* (1961). Stross clearly felt *The Leather Boys* could be Garrick's headline production. He wrote to Robert Garrett of Film Finances in 1962:

> With every respect in the world to both yourself and John, I believe that 'you are not with it'! If you do not like this script you must have equally disliked the three big winners of recent time, 'Saturday Night and Sunday Morning', 'A Kind of Loving', and 'A Taste of Honey', the profits from which will substantially exceed one million pounds ... the world is crying out for teenage stories.[21]

John Croydon, production consultant to Film Finances, seemed to agree in his report on the film:

> I cannot say I like the story; it seems to carry some odd implications of the effect of fast motor cycling on the morale of the young men who ride them! Be that as it may, I suppose it follows the present tradition of 'kitchen sink' stories as well as any other I have read, but which have turned out to be box office successes.[22]

Film Finances subsequently agreed to bond the film on a budget of £106,000 which comprised a £70,000 distribution guarantee from Garrick, around £26,000 from the NFFC and the remainder in deferments.[23]

But the winter crisis was to directly affect the fortunes of this film. While producers were understandably keen to keep the titles of delayed films out of the press (lest the public should link the delay to assumptions about quality), *The Leather Boys* was identified by British Lion's David Kingsley (along with *Ladies Who Do*) as one of the ten films directly affected.[24] Delays to release also meant that a producer was left to pay interest on the bank loan received to finance the film against the security of the distribution guarantee without any compensating revenue from box-office receipts. The National Provincial Bank had advanced £223,870 for Garrick's first three films but refused to advance any more until the company began to recoup, placing them in an impossible financial situation.[25] Stross stated that the delay in obtaining a release date for *The Leather Boys* had led to £6,000–£7,000 in additional interest charges by November 1963,[26] and these continued to mount beyond that date. The producer wrote to Victor Hoare of British Lion, complaining that 'not only do the circuits seem incapable of keeping their word, but it seems that they are completely contemptuous of their undertakings to British Lion'.[27] While *The Leather Boys* did eventually recoup £97,975 after finally being released in 1964, this did not take the film into profit. In addition, the loss on the bank guarantee for *The Very Edge* was £40,000, giving Stross little option but to wind up his company.

Overall, the Garrick venture was, as Charles Drazin argues, 'a costly, time-consuming struggle that served to illustrate the precarious nature of British financing.'[28] Moreover, by the time *The Leather Boys* was finally released, it was far too late to capitalise on the 'kitchen sink' trend. By 1964 motorcycle rock-and-roll vibe central to *The Leather Boys* might also have seemed old-fashioned, while the implicit themes of homosexuality, though still controversial, had already been done by other 'social problem' films, most notably *Victim* (1961).[29] Given that a film could take two years from pre-production to theatrical release, it's not difficult to see why some producers had trouble keeping up. John Gillett, in his spring 1964 round-up of the industry for *Sight and Sound*, stated that the British film seemed to be moving into a new era:

> The mood is changing; the news from the studios is of Tony Richardson's plans to film *The Charge of the Light Brigade*, of Peter O Toole's forthcoming *Lord Jim*, the casting of Honor Blackman as Pussy Galore . . . Meanwhile, the two most exciting films to have come out of British studios in recent months have been the work of American directors: Stanley Kubrick's *Dr Strangelove* and Joseph Losey's *The Servant*.'[30]

As Terence Kelly et al. point out, the winter crisis of 1963/4 may have been serious, but it was also short-lived and the following winter was a busy one overall on the domestic production front.[31] Rank's chairman John Davis denied that there had been a crisis at all, and argued that the industry was undergoing a period of change and contraction.[32] Behind complaints about 'overproduction' on the part of Rank and ABC lie criticisms of certain *kinds* of film that were no longer of interest to audiences, and it is clear that some British producers were not keeping pace with these changes in taste. It is telling for example that *Sammy Going South* (1963), directed by Alexander MacKendrick, may have been the first (and only) film in the Bryanston catalogue to be made in colour, yet in terms of style and content this adventure yarn featuring a young boy attempting to make his way across Africa could have been made ten years earlier.[33]

The Economics of the *Carry On* Films

Writing on the comedy genre in the 1960s, Robert Murphy identifies a general shift from a kind of realist comedy which dominated in the early part of the decade to more colourful and permissive comedies which seemed more in tune with the phenomenon of 'swinging London'. The exception however was 'the Carry On films, which had a peculiar momentum of their own'[34]. Indeed, what is remarkable about this famous series is the level of continuity in terms of style, theme and sense of humour, achieved through only minor adaption and modification. Beginning with *Carry On Sergeant* in 1958, the series as a whole can broadly be split into three distinct eras. Those written by Norman Hudis (1958–63) which initially defined the cycle were often set against institutional backdrops: national-service recruits in *Carry On Sergeant* (1958), the National Health Service in *Carry On Nurse* (1959), school is *Carry On Teacher* (1959) and the police in *Carry On Constable* (1960). These early instalments were filmed in black and white and were close cousins of the popular *Doctor* series of the 1950s and seemed much in the vein of the 'realist' type of comedy identified by Murphy and indeed, as James Chapman notes, the last Hudis-penned film was *Carry On Cruising*, released in 1963, the same year as the last New Wave production. [35]

When Talbot Rothwell took over as principal writer, the series took a more parodic or satirical turn, with *Carry On Cleo* (1964), *Carry On Spying* (1964), *Carry On Cowboy* (1965) and *Carry On Screaming* (1966) sending up the Hollywood biopic, the spy film, the western and the English Gothic horror respectively. Richard Webber characterises Hudis' writing style as one which attempts to balance the humour of stock situations with pathos, while Rothwell's work is full of bawdy slapstick, double entendres and little in the way of emotional character development.[36] The latter also tended to subvert authority to a greater extent than Hudis, while many of his scripts draw on a more anarchic form of humour and are far more apt to veer into fantasy. Thus, the *Carry On* films of the mid-to-late 1960s belonged more to the 'swinging sixties' than the post-war world of the black-and-white comedy. The series continued to evolve in line with popular tastes and by the early 1970s had begun to take on a more overtly permissive flavour. Chapman argues that the cycle split into two very different directions with bawdy historical efforts such as *Carry On Henry* (1971) and *Carry On Dick* (1974) produced alongside films were more in tune with contemporary events such as union strikes in *Carry On At Your Convenience* (1971) and birth-control pills in *Carry On Matron*, which, at time of filming in 1972, had just become available on the NHS.[37]

Interviewed by *The Times* in 1959, series producer Peter Rogers argued that the success of the films lay in their reliance on familiar tropes as well as 'a regular team of character actors and fairly traditional humour'.[38] The roots of *Carry On* humour in the seaside postcard and the music hall are well established and the series plays on caricatures, stereotypes and stock situations which can be traced back to both traditions. Marion Jordan notes the hard lines drawn between male and female; young and saucy, old and prudish; educated and impotent, working class and virile – these juxtapositions were the mainstays of *Carry On*.[39] But if the series had its roots in traditional British comedy, it also seemed to keep pace with changing social trends. As Penelope Gilliat noted, the films seemed to visually change with the times and yet they were never quite fashionable:

> Thank heaven, no one working on the films seems to have decided whether they are supposed to be 'with-it' or not. This makes them strangely time-

less, a dream-mixture of periods, like the language of Wodehouse; they incorporate without difficulty a lot of the pre-war flavour of beach-postcard humour, but they are also full of sixties camp.[40]

With the exception of Gilliat, most British film critics despaired of the series. But as Rogers often stated in interviews, the films were made not for the critics but rather the audiences, who kept coming back for each instalment. The balance between recycling old gags and keeping up with new trends proved important to the longevity of the series.

Producer Peter Rogers and director Gerald Thomas were responsible for all thirty-one films in the series, demonstrating the value of sticking to one specific formula over a period of twenty years. But this does not fully convey Rogers' shrewd approach to the business of film producing. Firstly, he was connected to an important British film-making dynasty: he had worked for producer Sydney Box at Gainsborough and was married to Box's sister Betty, who became a successful producer in her own right in partnership with director Ralph Thomas, whose brother Gerald became Rogers' regular collaborator. Secondly, he benefitted from long-term deals with major distributors: the *Carry On* series was initially financed and distributed by Anglo-Amalgamated before moving to Rank in 1966 – Rogers had maintained a production base at Pinewood since the early 1950s. During the period at Anglo, in addition to the *Carry On* films Rogers produced the Tommy Steele music films *The Tommy Steele Story* and *The Duke Wore Jeans* and a number of other comedies directed by Thomas, beginning with *Please Turn Over* (1959). He quickly became very important to the company's bosses, Nat Cohen and Stuart Levy, producing on average three films a year, and in 1960 it was announced that Rogers had joined the Anglo board.[41] By the end of 1962, Rogers had expanded his production capability by creating a second unit comprising associate producer Jack Hanbury and director Sidney Hayers.[42]

But Rogers' profile and success was primarily due to the *Carry On* series. The films were made on tight budgets and could typically expect to recoup production costs within a few months and ultimately take around £500,000 at the box office.[43] While average budgets of *Carry On* films fluctuated throughout the 1960s, they remained low in comparison to average production costs, particularly towards the end of the decade.

Rogers apparently never planned for American deals, leaving it to Anglo-Amalgamated to negotiate these as he 'would not like to work on a precarious balance by which some of the cost and all the profit had to be sought from doubtful international markets'.[44] The producer saw himself as negotiating a space in the market somewhere between second features and the kinds of small-to-medium-budgeted comedies that Independent Artists had produced for Rank:

Table 5.2 Carry On budgets, 1958–69[45]

Title (Carry On ...)	Year	Budget (£)
Sergeant	1958	74,000
Nurse	1958	71,000
Teacher	1959	78,000
Constable	1959	82,500
Regardless	1960	100,000
Cruising	1962	140,000
Cabby	1963	149,986
Jack	1963	152,000
Spying	1964	148,000
Cleo	1964	194,323
Cowboy	1965	195,000
Screaming	1966	197,500
Don't Lose Your Head	1966	200,000
Follow That Camel	1967	288,366
Doctor	1967	214,000
Up the Khyber	1968	260,000
Camping	1968	208,354
Again Doctor	1969	219,000
Up The Jungle	1969	210,000

> Throughout the trade one hears people saying that you can't make a film which will show a profit for under £500,000 – which is supposed to automatically make it a super production which will be able to break into world markets. I did not believe this, and I think I have proved my point.[46]

Rogers criticised an industry which often seemed extravagant, in which confidence tricks were routinely deployed, and in which publicists 'built on beating the big drum and high-pressure salesmanship'.[47] He was also suspicious of what he identified as a view among exhibitors that they should pay half the rental for a £100,000 film (even if it was likely to take twice as much at the box office): 'So if you do make a cheap film you have to keep it quiet and pretend it cost more than it did.'[48] Rogers was successful with the *Carry On* series because of his shrewd commercial instincts, but also because his *modus operandi* went against the grain of common industry practice.

Relying on a regular cast and crew undoubtedly helped to keep costs down, while Rogers' and Thomas' working relationship had also evolved to the point where they were able to work together with ruthless efficiency. On average it took six weeks to film a *Carry On*, with the French Revolution spoof *Don't Lose Your Head* taking slightly longer at around seven weeks. The films were rarely shot on locations far from the studio – indeed, as James Chapman notes, *Carry On Camping* appears to have been filmed in the fields around

Pinewood.⁴⁹ The furthest location from Pinewood used for location shooting was Snowdonia, North Wales, for *Carry On Up The Khyber*.⁵⁰ Consequently, Rogers gained a reputation for being a thrifty producer who always delivered on time and under budget. *The Iron Maiden* (1963), a comedy quite unlike its *Carry On* stablemates, the NFFC offered Rogers and his team 'special consideration' given that they had made five profitable films with Anglo which had drawn on additional NFFC funds. The Corporation agreed to put up 50 per cent of the budget, but to treat this as 'end money' (usually, the NFFC would only offer 30 per cent).⁵¹ In addition to ensuring a steady stream of finance and guaranteed distribution, Rogers' deal with Anglo-Amalgamated saved time on legal paperwork as the same distribution agreements were drawn up for each film.⁵² When the series moved to Rank in 1966 the rate of production and the key elements remained much the same. In February 1970 *The Guardian* announced that Rank had negotiated a further deal with Rogers for a programme of five pictures costing around £250,000 each.

By the end of the 1950s the main production groups were moulding their films for international markets, using international locations and stars to appeal to international audiences. However, between 1958 and 1978 Rogers and Thomas concentrated on making a specific kind of product for a domestic audience. While the series was also successful in Commonwealth countries like Australia, Canada and South Africa, Rogers regarded this as a 'bonus', and rather than capitalising on international popularity by raising budgets, tackling international subjects and including recognisable stars (with the exception of Phil Silvers in *Follow That Camel*), he continued to use the same methods of production and personnel including regular performers such as Kenneth Williams, Hattie Jacques, Charles Hawtrey, Joan Sims, Sid James and Kenneth Connor.

Writing to the NFFC as early as 1958, the year of the first *Carry On* film, Rogers noted: 'it has become increasingly evident that the "Carry Ons" will depend more and more for their success upon a handful of feature artistes.'⁵³ This played on the same sense of familiarity common to radio and television comedies. At the same time, it was Rogers' belief that no members of the regular team should become indispensable.⁵⁴ There were no big 'stars' in the way a producer might understand that term in the 1960s (in the sense that there was no one actor who could hold the success of the project hostage) and costs were kept down by paying the returning cast members modestly, regardless of the financial success of the series. According to Joan Sims:

> I got paid the same salary for my first film, Carry On Sergeant, in 1958 as I got for my last, Carry On Emmanuelle, in 1978. The women were paid $2,500 and the men were paid $5,000. I don't think the producer, Peter Rogers, was joking when he said: 'I'd do anything for my actors . . . except pay them.'⁵⁵

Charles Hawtrey was unceremoniously dropped from *Carry On Cruising* (1963) for demanding more money, and was replaced by Lance Percival (who was paid £600).[56] The wage bill for *Carry On Cabby* (1963) was £21,400, and indeed the wage bill hovered around the £20,000 mark for much of the 1960s (with the exception of the bill for *Follow That Camel* (1967), which was £50,350). The wage bill for the penultimate film, *Emmanuelle* (1978) was £20,750.[57] That Rogers managed to keep wages so low over a ten-to-twenty-year period is nothing short of astonishing.

Despite the profitability of the series, Rogers nevertheless felt the need to justify each penny to his financiers. Moreover, as shooting schedules and meagre budgets could throw up unforeseen difficulties, Rogers and Thomas were consistently prepared to reduce their producer/director fees. For example, on *Don't Lose Your Head*, the first film made for Rank, Thomas and Rogers deferred £15,000 of their combined £30,000 fees to push the budget down from £250,000.[58] While in pre-production for *Carry on Regardless*, Rogers wrote an apologetic letter to Anglo-Amalgamated boss Stuart Levy regarding a slight budgetary increase, explaining that extra sets, speaking parts and increased union rates meant that costs had inflated slightly.[59] And in 1969, during pre-production for *Carry On Camping* Rogers wrote to Graham Dowson of Rank to explain why the film could not possibly be budgeted under £208,000 – the reasons included a shooting schedule of seven weeks, the costs of basic production staff rising to £265 a week, and artists fees being £4,000 higher as they were required for longer. Rogers' tone in these letters is one of exasperation – he feels he is doing his best despite being 'neither a producer or a mathematician or a company secretary'.[60] In the same letter Rogers also points out that by this stage Rank had had five pictures from Rogers for less than £1 million, and he ends by writing 'whilst pleading and cajoling somewhat in this letter, you must know that I intend to be a slave to nothing but my work and an admirer of nothing but merit and whatever success I may have had in the past I hope to have deserved so that I may in future command it'.[61]

'A Studio Without Walls': The Amicus House of Horror

Another independent producer that negotiated the volatility of the British film industry during the 1960s was Amicus. Established in 1961 by the Americans Milton Subotsky and Max Rosenberg, the company became associated with portmanteau horror films like *Dr Terror's House of Horrors* (1965), *Tales from the Crypt* (1972) and *From Beyond the Grave* (1974) and became a potential rival to Hammer, although Amicus lacked the infrastructure of that famous studio. But while Amicus may have specialised in horror after 1965, the company's earlier catalogue represents a broad spectrum of genres: from the pop musical film – *It's Trad, Dad!* (1962) and *Just for Fun* (1963), to science fiction – *Dr Who and the Daleks* (1965) and *Daleks Invasion Earth 2150 AD* (1966), produced under the company name 'Aaru'), and even social realism with *A Touch of Love* (1969). Subotsky and Rosenberg navigated the various crises which besieged the industry largely by staying abreast of popular trends and by ensuring that their own company was flexible enough to change with the times.

Rosenberg and Subotsky had been collaborating, mainly on teen musicals, since the 1950s before Subotsky came to the UK to make the horror film *City of the Dead* (1960) on a budget of £45,000[62] and starring Hammer regular Christopher Lee. The relationship between the two men was complementary: Rosenberg was the 'money man', while Subotsky concentrated on script development and devoted a significant amount of time to finding, optioning and reading potential material. Indeed, so highly did he prize the script and editing on a picture above all else that he opined: 'I don't really think it's all that important who directs a picture. That's one of the reasons we've given so many people their first picture to direct.'[63] Subotsky also devoted some effort to ensuring that the company's productions remained in tune with the times. For example, one of Amicus's first productions, *It's Trad, Dad!*, aimed to capitalise on the short-lived vogue, in the early 1960s for so-called 'Trad Jazz'. *It's Trad, Dad!* is a typical pop music film where the plot functions as an excuse to showcase a range of musical acts (Chubby Checker, Del Shannon, John Leyton, and The Brook Brothers, among others). It transcends a dull narrative structure by dint of Richard Lester's kinetic directing, while a postmodern approach to narrative structure imbues the film with a kind of satirical wryness and youthful energy. The company didn't always get it right however; the follow-up, *Just for Fun*, was a 'dismal failure' according to Subotsky because it was in production just as the 'Liverpool sound was coming in' and therefore the music was rather dated by the time the film was released. Likewise, Amicus's first and only foray into the spy genre, *Danger Route* (1967), was released at the tail end of the popular spy-film cycle and suffered as a result.

Horror proved more successful with the anthology film *Dr Terror's House of Horrors*, which was made on a more generous budget of £107,000[64] (though still low by industry standards), putting Amicus on the map. *The Skull* (1965), whose budget of £84,000 was guaranteed by Paramount who also supported *The Deadly Bees*,[65] subsequently confirmed an emerging reputation for gothic horrors in the same vein as Hammer, albeit with a slightly different tone and aesthetic. Subotsky was vocally dismissive of his larger rivals, arguing, 'Their films sometimes have a shock value which I feel may be missing from some of our films. Perhaps we are restrained by good taste. I think our films are more intellectual than Hammer's and have much better plots and scripts.'[66] It is true that when it came to horror Amicus tended to 'suggest rather than show' which distanced them further from Hammer.[67] Amicus's films also featured more contemporary settings and often a more vibrant use of colour in *The Skull*, as well as the candy-coloured, retina-burning sets used in *The Terrornauts* (1967). Peter Hutchings also notes that although Amicus's films were directed by British horror auteurs – notably Freddie Francis – and featured familiar actors like Peter Cushing and Christopher Lee, there was something 'suspiciously foreign' about the company. He suggests this related mainly to the way they tended to adapt horror films from material from the American writer Robert Bloch (*Psycho*) and the 1950s EC Comics. This, according to Hutchings, 'appeared to align [Amicus films] more with 1950s American horror fiction'.[68]

Max Rosenberg boasted that Amicus was 'a studio without walls' because the company relied on a mixture of private investment, 'modest amounts' of money from the Hollywood majors and the completion guarantor company Film Finances.[69] In an interview with the fanzine *Little Shoppe of Horrors*, Subotsky explained that this ad hoc, patchwork financing set-up allowed Amicus to make better distribution deals than they would if they had obtained funding from distribution companies at the pre-production stage, and although they still worked in this fashion, obtaining deals with Columbia, Paramount and Embassy, Subotsky and Rosenberg had found merchant banks and private investors far more flexible.[70] The fact that the company did not have a London head office also meant that they could keep overheads low.[71] Fee deferrals also helped, as Subotsky noted; 'The reason we keep going even in times of recession – so called recessions in the films business – because we put back a great deal of the money that comes into us as producers' fees, into scripts.'[72]

Amicus also worked hard to ensure that their films came in on time and under budget, although with varying degrees of success. John Croydon of Film Finances deemed *Dr Terror* ... 'a good commercial proposition': the stories were claimed from stories of horror authors which were in the public domain, the film was to be made in colour, and the five-act narrative structure would ensure that audiences be held 'spellbound' by 'stories they have seen and read, time and again.'[73] *The Deadly Bees* (1967), a horror in which a young pop star takes a holiday on an island only to find herself surrounded by a swarm of killer bees, was less successful. The original budget was £106,083, but the production went over by more than £19,000, partly due to an extra two days' location shooting that incurred overtime costs. Film Finances were forced to step in, with an irate Bernard Smith writing to Rosenberg, 'I must say I am completely horrified the way the end of this film has been handled.'[74] But in general, Amicus productions tended to come in on budget and the company survived into the 1970s in relatively rude health.[75]

Concluding Remarks

The fortunes of many independent film producers in 1960s British cinema were strongly bound up with the presence of American finance. The typical example of success is represented by a company like Woodfall, which developed its reputation making black-and-white New Wave dramas with support from Bryanston–British Lion and the NFFC before moving to the more lucrative patronage of United Artists, beginning with the Oscar-winning *Tom Jones* in 1963. But as this chapter has attempted to show, the independent production sector and responses to a changing industry and domestic film market were complex and diverse. Diversification was a strategy adopted by some – this might be via vertical integration as demonstrated in the case of Compton in the previous, or in terms of adopting a range of different kind of production, the method favoured by Independent Artists. IA's Julian Wintle and Leslie Parkyn had also read the runes and moved their focus into television production rather than attempt to jump on the 'swinging London' or exploitation film bandwagon. This proved particularly successful for Wintle, who found himself producing one of the most iconic examples of pop-culture television with *The Avengers*. By contrast, Raymond Stross and Garrick suffered the same kind of fate as many others in the low-budget sector and despite attempting to capitalise on the success of the New Wave and its focus on youth with *The Leather Boys*, the ultimate failure of the film demonstrated just how quickly the market was changing and how quickly a subject or style could appear dated. That it was also the highest-profile casualty of the winter crisis simply rubbed salt into the wound.

In stark contrast, the success of Peter Rogers and the *Carry On* cycle demonstrated that it was possible for a genre formula, clearly rooted in the past, to survive with minimal modifications. But this was due to a range of factors including a strong nose for popular taste rather than current fads, solid and ongoing financial commitment from a major distributor, and the careful control of production budgets and schedules. The result was one of the most durable film series in British cinema history that created a recognisable generic brand which during the 1960s was only really on a par with Hammer Horror. The popularity of horror inspired other producers including Tony Tenser, who broke from Compton to establish Tigon Films in order to exploit this niche. But it also inspired Max Rosenberg and Milton Subotsky's Amicus Films, which found its most profitable focus on a particular variant of horror cinema that dated back to the Ealing compendium film, *Dead of Night* (1945), and gave the company a point of differentiation from Hammer. While the *Carry On* comedies were resolutely English in their style and appeal, the Amicus horror films embodied a cosmopolitanism that came from the American sensibilities of their producers as well as the literary and visual sources of their films. So even as the Hollywood studios were scaling back their investment in UK production at the end of 1960s, the US influence on British independent cinema proved more tenacious.

NOTES

1. Robert Murphy, *Sixties British Cinema* (London: BFI, 1992), p. 278.
2. See Steve Chibnall and Brian McFarlane, *Quota Quickies: The Birth of the British 'B' Film* (London: BFI, 2007).
3. Denis Gifford, *The British Film Catalogue*, 1895–1994, 3rd edn (London: Fitzroy Dearborn Publishers, 2000).
4. This was based on a sample of 660 respondents from the Greater London area. See Federation of British Film Makers, *Cinema Going in Greater London, 1963: A survey of attitudes* (FBFM, 1963).
5. Ralph Bond, 'Second Features', *The Times*, 15 November 1962, p. 13.
6. Brian McFarlane, 'Pulp Fictions: The British 'B' Film and the Field of Cultural Production', *Film Criticism*, vol. 21, no. 1 (Fall 1996), pp. 48–70, p. 48.
7. Sue Harper and Vincent Porter, *British Cinema of the 1950s: The Decline of Deference* (Oxford: Oxford University Press, 2003) p. 139.
8. Quoted in David Mann, 'An Industrial and Cultural History of Selected British Crime Supporting Features and Filmed Television Series, 1946–1964' (University of the West of England: unpublished doctoral thesis, 2007), p. 194.
9. Jack Greenwood, 'Two and Two do Make Four', *Kine Weekly*, 25 January 1962, p. 9.
10. Cinema and Television History Research Centre (CATH), Francis Searle collection, letter from David Kingsley of British Lion to Francis Searle, 17 October 1961; CATH, Francis Searle collection, letter from David Kingsley to Francis Searle, 24 August 1962.
11. Christopher Wintle, email communication with author, 19 October 2015.
12. Steve Chibnall and Brian McFarlane, *The British 'B' Film* (London: British Film Institute, 2009) p. 131.
13. See David Pirie, *A Heritage of Horror: The English Gothic Cinema 1946–72* (London: Gordon Fraser, 1973).
14. Anon., 'Successful Film-making on a Small Budget', *The Times*, 5 November 1959.
15. Christopher Wintle, personal communication with author, 1 September 2015.
16. Ibid.
17. Anne Francis, *Julian Wintle: A Memoir* (London: Dukeswood, 1986), p. 70.
18. Christopher Wintle, personal communication with author, 1 September 2015.
19. Ibid.
20. Douglas Collins, *A Nose for Money: How to Make a Million* (London: Michael Joseph, 1963), p. 238.
21. Film Finances Archive on *The Leather Boys*, letter from John Croydon to Robert Garrett, 15 September 1962.
22. Ibid.
23. Ibid.
24. *Kine Weekly*, 7 November 1963, p. 6.
25. Charles Drazin, 'Film Finances: The First Years', *Historical Journal of Film, Radio and Television*, 34: 1, pp. 2–22, p. 18.
26. *Kine Weekly*, 7 November 1963.
27. Film Finances archive, file labelled 'Garrick', letter from Raymond Stross to Victor Hoare of BLC, 18 November 1965.

28. Charles Drazin, 'Film Finances: The first years', p. 18.
29. Similar delays affected the fortunes of other films. In *The Wild Affair*, directed by John Krish for Bryanston, Nancy Kwan's bob haircut may have been à la mode when the film went into production in 1963, but on its release in 1965 the cut was already commonplace.
30. John Gillett, 'State of the studios', *Sight and Sound*, vol. 33, no. 2, Spring 1964, p. 55.
31. Terence Kelly, Graham Norton and George Perry, *A Competitive Cinema* (London: Institute of Economic Affairs, 1966).
32. *Kine Weekly*, 19 December 1963.
33. Duncan Petrie, 'Bryanston Films: An Experiment in Cooperative Independent Film Production and Distribution', *Historical Journal of Film, Radio and Television*, 38: 1, 2018, pp. 95–115.
34. Robert Murphy, *Sixties British Cinema*, p. 252.
35. James Chapman, 'A short history of the Carry On films', in I. Q. Hunter and Laraine Porter (eds), *British Comedy Cinema* (Abingdon and New York: Routledge, 2012), p. 100.
36. Richard Webber, *50 Years of Carry On* (London: Century, 2008), pp. 73–5.
37. Chapman, 'A short history of the Carry On films', p. 111.
38. Anon., 'Successful Film-making on a Small Budget', *The Guardian*, 5 November 1959, p. 16.
39. Marion Jordan, 'Carry On . . . follow that stereotype', in James Curran and Vincent Porter (eds), *British Cinema History* (London: Weidenfeld and Nicolson, 1983), p. 312.
40. Penelope Gilliat, 'In praise of Carrying On', *Observer*, 9 August 1962, p. 20.
41. *Kine Weekly*, 1 December 1960.
42. Announced in *Kine Weekly*, 6 December 1962. In the end, only two were made by Hanbury and Hayers for Anglo – the realist drama *This is My Street* (1963) and the musical *Three Hats for Lisa* (1965).
43. Anon., 'Carry On Cashing In . . .', *The Guardian*, 18 October 1970, p. 17.
44. Anon., 'Successful Film-making on a Small Budget', *The Guardian*, 5 November 1959, p. 16.
45. Figures taken from Kevin Snelgrove, *The Official Carry On Facts, Figures and Statistics: A Complete Statistical Analysis of the Carry Ons* (Clacton on Sea: Apex Publishing, 2008). Accurate film budgets are notoriously difficult to come by, but accuracy of these figures is reinforced by final production figures stated in Gerald Thomas papers at the BFI. Peter Rogers, unlike many film producers, did not seem to care about whether people were aware of the cost of *Carry On*s. In interviews, in fact, he appears to see the low cost as something of a badge of honour.
46. Ibid.
47. Ibid.
48. Ibid.
49. Chapman, 'A short history of the Carry On films', p. 108.
50. Snelgrove, *The Official Carry On Facts, Figures and Statistics*.
51. BFI: Gerald Thomas collection, *The Iron Maiden*, letter from John Terry of NFFC to Peter Rogers, 28 February 1962.
52. BFI: Gerald Thomas collection, letter from Grime to Rogers, 6 January 1961.
53. Quoted in Chapman, 'A short history of the Carry On films', p. 104.
54. Anon., 'Carry On Cashing In . . .', *The Guardian*, 18 October, 1970, p. 16.
55. *Daily Mail*, 20 December 1998, p. 22.
56. Webber, *50 Years of Carry On*, p. 66.
57. Snelgrove, *The Official Carry On Facts, Figures and Statistics*.

58. BFI: Gerald Thomas collection, *Don't Lose Your Head*, letter from John Terry of NFFC to F. Thomas of Rank, 8 September 1966.
59. BFI: Gerald Thomas collection, *Carry On Regardless*, letter from Peter Rogers to Stuart Levy re. budget, 8 November 1960.
60. BFI: Gerald Thomas collection, *Carry On Camping*, letter from Peter Rogers to Graham Dowson of Rank, 23 September 1968.
61. Ibid.
62. Film Finances file on *City of the Dead*.
63. Alan Bryce, *Amicus: The Studio That Dripped Blood* (Plymouth: Stray Cat Publishing, 2000), p. 11.
64. Film Finances file on *Dr Terror's House of Horrors*. This was made of up a £50,000 investment from executive producer Joseph Vegoda, £25,000 from Paramount and £25,000 from the NFFC with the remainder comprising deferments. Film Finances internal memo, 17 April 1964.
65. Film Finances file on *The Skull*, Cost Statement, 4 June 1965.
66. 'Amicus: Two's A Company', *Little Shoppe of Horrors*, 1973, Issue 2, p. 25.
67. Ibid., p. 21.
68. Peter Hutchings, 'The Amicus House of Horror' Steve Chibnall and Julian Petley (eds), *British Horror Cinema* (London: Routledge, 2001), p. 133.
69. Bryce, *Amicus: The Studio That Dripped Blood*, p. 11.
70. 'Amicus: Two's A Company', *Little Shoppe of Horrors*, 1973, Issue 2, p. 25.
71. Ibid., p. 25.
72. Ibid., p. 19.
73. Film Finances file on *Dr Terror's House of Horrors*, box 381.
74. Film Finances file on *The Deadly Bees*, box 407. Letter from Bernard Smith to Max Rosenberg, 8 March 1966.
75. Film Finances file on *Dr Who and the Daleks*, box 393.

PART TWO

CREATIVE AGENCY

6. SCREENWRITING

Melanie Williams

INTRODUCTION

Right from the outset of the 1960s, the professional status of screenwriters was changing. In 1958 Wolf Mankowitz had described his fellow writers as 'very much at the bottom of the so-called creative pyramid', but only two years later, critic Derek Hill claimed that they were now 'enjoying a respect' the industry had 'not extended' to them before, and 'working in unhampered conditions which a few years ago would have been thought impossible'.[1] This transformation marked 'the first real attempt by the industry to make use of native literary talent on any really considerable scale', heralding what Hill called 'a British "new wave"' (one of the first uses of the phrase).[2] Members of that early cohort, followed by subsequent 'writers' waves' throughout 1960s British cinema, effected major shifts in what screenwriters could write about, and how, and redefined their profession's status, both in Britain and internationally. This chapter will survey these developments, concluding with a case study of key sixties screenwriter Frederic Raphael, whose screenplay for *Darling* (1965) won him an Oscar.

AWARDS AND ACHIEVEMENTS IN THE EARLY 1960S

The British Film Academy Awards (voted for by the members of the Society of Film and Television Arts, the forerunner of BAFTA) provide a useful barometer of what the domestic industry itself prized as important. By the

Figure 6.1   Smart repartee and incisive class commentary: Frederic Raphael's dialogue for Alan Bates and Denholm Elliott in *Nothing but the Best* (Clive Donner, 1964).

early 1960s its dominant screenwriter was writer/director/producer Bryan Forbes, BFA-nominated in the screenplay category for both *The League of Gentlemen* (1960) and *The Angry Silence* (1960), which won the award.[3] He was later nominated for his Kingsley Amis adaptation *Only Two Can Play* (1962) and *Séance on a Wet Afternoon* (1964), both of which also won Writers' Guild awards – *Only Two Can Play* the Best British Comedy Screenplay and *Séance on a Wet Afternoon* the Best British Dramatic Screenplay, indicating not only Forbes's range as a writer, encompassing sex comedy and psychological thriller, but also his respected position among his peers. Forbes's background as an actor helped him, he felt, 'to understand what is speakable dialogue', and he was especially proud of his (non-award-nominated) dialogue between Leslie Caron and Tom Bell as they explain their romantic pasts in *The L-Shaped Room* (1962), where he 'wanted to write a love scene that was different and that said something' rather than replicating romantic cliché.[4] Being a writer/director was 'a great advantage' for Forbes when it came to script development, because he could 'still go on writing and re-writing on the studio floor'.[5]

Other all-rounders who enjoyed British Film Academy acclaim during the early 1960s include veteran Val Guest, who was nominated for his screenplay for *Hell is a City* (1960) and co-won the following year (along with Wolf Mankowitz) for *The Day the Earth Caught Fire* (1961); Ken Hughes, who was nominated for *The Trials of Oscar Wilde* (1960); and Peter Ustinov, who was nominated for *Billy Budd* (1962). All three also habitually scripted, directed and produced their film projects.[6] The creative advantages this offered were set out by a different kind of aspiring writer/director, experimental novelist B. S. Johnson: 'Why should a writer want to direct films? In my case, it was for the very basic reason that I could increase by several thousand per cent the chances of seeing what I actually wrote get on to the screen.'[7]

Alongside recognising the work of established figures, screenwriting awards in the early 1960s also began to register the presence of newer voices. These included a group of writers who emerged from the sphere of 'kitchen sink' drama and literature. Nigel Kneale and John Osborne's adaptations of the latter's era-defining Royal Court productions *Look Back in Anger* (1959) and *The Entertainer* (1960) for Woodfall Films earned BFA nominations (with Kneale's experience undoubtedly a key factor in their successful transition to film). Alan Sillitoe was nominated for his film adaptation of his own book *Saturday Night and Sunday Morning* (1960), also for Woodfall. His only preparation for this new foray having been a read-through of *Look Back in Anger*'s script as a template; the kind of thing that Derek Hill suggested had unravelled 'the mystique of writing for films' and revealed 'the industry's cherished insistence that the technique takes years of apprenticeship' to be 'completely groundless'.[8] Woodfall's first BFA-award-winning screenplay, and the inaugural winner of the Writers' Guild award for Best British Screenplay, *A Taste of Honey* (1961), was created in similarly loose fashion by Shelagh Delaney and Tony Richardson. But the apotheosis of this newly liberated approach (in terms of permissive content as well as freewheeling technique) was John Osborne's adaptation of Henry Fielding's eighteenth-century picaresque classic *Tom Jones* (1963), which not only swept the board at British awards for screenwriting but went on to win one of the film's four Oscars. Clearly, Britain's 'writers' wave' was beginning to break on foreign shores as well.

In tracking developments in screenwriting during the 1960s, it is imperative to take into account the influence of television, which functioned both as 'laboratory' and 'creative refuge' for numerous writers.[9] The BBC's Donald Wilson claimed that in the cinema, writers' work was 'progressively emasculated by the fearful, pored over by the ignorant, altered out of recognition by the incompetent, and finally re-written by a committee of accountants calling themselves producers' (unlike television).[10] By contrast, the newer medium already had a strong tradition of prioritising the writer's authorship, borne out in the US by well-known television dramatists such as Paddy Chayefsky and Reginald Rose. In Britain this was emulated by emergent figures like Alun Owen and Clive Exton. Owen, who had written the celebrated Armchair Theatre television plays *No Trams to Lime Street* (1959) and *Lena, O My Lena* (1960), was nonetheless tempted into doing some work for cinema, firstly on Joseph

Losey's underworld film *The Criminal* (1960) and then more prominently on the Beatles' first feature *A Hard Day's Night* (1964), the screenplay for which earned him an Oscar nomination. Immersing himself in the experience of Beatlemania by travelling with the band as they toured, Owen observed how 'they are always being jostled and pushed about by the press and others. I know – I've got a bruise, from one reporter, to prove it!'[11] Cinema's capacity to 'capture bigger images on a bigger screen' initially enthused the writer, but when he realised that the 'complete freedom' he had enjoyed in crafting the screenplay for *A Hard Day's Night* was unusual, Owen returned to working primarily for television.[12]

The award-winning screenwriting duo of Keith Waterhouse and Willis Hall moved between film, television and theatre with greater apparent ease. They were BFA-nominated in successive years for *Whistle Down the Wind* (1961), *A Kind of Loving* (1962), and *Billy Liar* (1963), and continued to undertake screenwriting work throughout the 1960s, including script-doctoring Hitchcock's *Torn Curtain* (1966), alongside various TV single dramas, sitcoms and satirical sketches for *That Was the Week That Was* (1962–3) and *The Frost Report* (1966–7). So prolific were Waterhouse and Hall that *The Times* observed in 1961 that they seemed responsible 'for practically every second or third British film announced for production.'[13] Interestingly, the duo were also positioned as conspicuously in Anglo-Amalgamated's early-sixties publicity material as director John Schlesinger, sharing equal status as harbingers of the company's modernity.[14]

Getting public recognition for the screenwriter in this way was one of the chief aims of the Television and Screen Writers' Guild, formed in 1959 as a more professionalised development of the original Screenwriters' Association.[15] In 1963, the Guild agitated for industry compliance with the Screen Credits Agreement of 1953 which stipulated 'that all paid-for advertising in the United Kingdom must include a writer's credit', particularly after they discovered from a quick trawl of adverts in *Kine Weekly* and *Daily Cinema* that every single company was in breach of it, and took issue with the promulgation of 'the director as the all-talking, all-thinking genius solely responsible for the creation of a motion picture. The Guild insists that the writer is a fundamental contributor to the success of a film, and as entitled to recognition for his work as anyone else.'[16] They made further moves to close loopholes and ensure proper enforcement of the credit agreement in advertising, with a new, tighter, agreement reached in 1964.[17]

Initiatives like this were important in ensuring the creative work of screenwriters was properly acknowledged and celebrated, alongside the Guild's creation of its own awards ceremony in 1961 to fulfil a similar symbolic and social function. But they were clear that 'the most basic question for both its cinema and TV writers' remained 'that of fees', and in this area they achieved important breakthroughs during the 1960s.[18] In 1961 the Guild brokered an agreement with producers that its members would 'receive a minimum of £2,000 for a first feature screenplay', £450 for a second feature, and equivalent rates for TV work.[19] There may have been ongoing problems with rates of remuneration, residual monies, and prompt payment throughout the 1960s and beyond, but the improved situation of film and TV writers during the decade owed much to the growing strength of their guild.

Growing Internationalism and Experimentation

Towards the mid-decade, two new significant figures emerged within the domain of British screenwriting, both of whom had theatrical provenance. The first was Robert Bolt, writer of *Lawrence of Arabia* (1962), Oscar-nominated and winner of the BFA Best British Screenplay award and the Writers' Guild Best Dramatic British Screenplay. Three years later, Bolt won the Oscar in the Best Adapted Screenplay category for *Doctor Zhivago* (1965) – an adaptation he likened to 'straightening cobwebs', such was the delicacy and intricacy of Boris Pasternak's original novel – and again the following year for adapting his own play *A Man for All Seasons* (1966), which also had the BFA Best British Screenplay and Writers' Guild screenplay awards conferred upon it.[20] Initially brought in to do some minor rewrites on *Lawrence*, Bolt's work so impressed David Lean he asked him to completely rework Michael Wilson's initial screenplay. Where Wilson's T. E. Lawrence had been predominantly a man of action, Bolt made him more introspective, painfully aware of the divisions within his character. But in spite of Oscar success and enviable industry acclaim, Bolt's agent Peggy Ramsay would cite him as a cautionary tale (while profiting from her percentage of the sizeable earnings Bolt's film work accrued), as did theatre director Frith Banbury: 'Bob Bolt was a terrible disappointment to me. I thought he was going to be a really important dramatist but he preferred Sam Spiegel's yacht.'[21]

Bolt's travels made him representative of the burgeoning transnationalism of a group of screenwriters who were associated with major productions. They included formerly blacklisted Americans Carl Foreman, Howard Koch and Ben Barzman, who had worked respectively on the epic war films *The Guns of Navarone* (1961), *633 Squadron* (1964), and *The Heroes of Telemark* (1965) and *The Blue Max* (1966). But the trend for runaway production was equally indebted to the fad for 'swinging London' which had made Britain into a global film-making centre. The career of American screenwriter Terry Southern is exemplary in this respect, taking in such paradigmatic 1960s films as *Dr Strangelove* (1964), *The Loved One* (1965), *The Collector* (1965), *Casino Royale* (1967), *Barbarella* (1968), and *The Magic Christian* (1969). He recalled going regularly 'back and forth on these over-the-pole flights, where you would go from LA to London' and 'wrote a lot during those flights'.²²

The other highly prominent British playwright winning multiple screenwriting awards in the mid-1960s was Harold Pinter, who was regarded as successfully balancing his film and stage commitments without detriment to either.²³ Pinter's most important creative relationship in the 1960s was with director Joseph Losey, for whom he scripted *The Servant* (1963), BFA-nominated and winner of the Writers' Guild Award Best British Dramatic Screenplay award (Pinter also won in the Best British Original Teleplay category the same year for *The Lover*, an indication of his facility across different media), and *Accident* (1967), BFA-nominated and winner of a Writers' Guild merit scroll. The protean Pinter would also win the BFA screenplay award for his adaptation of Penelope Mortimer's proto-feminist novel *The Pumpkin Eater* (1964) and be nominated for Cold War thriller *The Quiller Memorandum* (1966), directed by Jack Clayton and Michael Anderson respectively.

Accident's 'barbed, indirect conversation' and suppressed violence 'breaking through the brittle surface of civilisation' was the apotheosis of the Pinteresque rather than a digression from his theatrical vocation.²⁴ Here Pinter strived to create a new kind of film narrative, less focused on causation and clarity, but without drifting into what he felt were the obfuscations of *Last Year in Marienbad* (1961). Trying to find a 'free-association, stream-of-consciousness style' for film proved challenging:

> when one's mind wanders and associates things it's perfectly unself-conscious. Do exactly the same thing on film and the result is precious, self-conscious, over-elaborate [. . .] In this film, everything is buried, it is implicit. There is really very little dialogue, and that is mostly trivial, meaningless. The drama goes on inside the characters, and by looking hard at the smooth surface we come to see something of what is going on underneath.²⁵

Pinter's spare, gnomic approach suggested how more formally innovative screenwriting styles had gained acceptance in the 1960s, also observable in the recognition for Edward Bond, along with Tonino Guerra and Michelangelo Antonioni, Oscar-nominated for the opaquely mysterious screenplay for *Blow Up* (1966); David Mercer, who won a BFA award for *Morgan – A Suitable Case for Treatment* (1966); and David Sherwin, winning the Writers' Guild award for Best British Original Screenplay for the enigmatic *If ....* (1968). Charles Wood won a Writers' Guild award and was BFA-nominated for *The Knack ... and How to Get It* (1965), where his verbal absurdities made a good match with director Richard Lester's syncopated visual style, and a productive partnership ensued through *Help!* (1965), *How I Won the War* (1967), *Petulia*

(1968), and *The Bed Sitting Room* (1969).²⁶ Wood's screenplay for Tony Richardson's *The Charge of the Light Brigade* (1968), full of the oddities of Victorian military expression, authentic to period but strange to modern ears, supplanted the original one written by Woodfall co-founder John Osborne. Thus, the old guard of the New Wave found themselves superseded by the next new wave of writers.

Gender, Credit, Popular Genres and Package Deals

Shelagh Delaney's late return in the award stakes, with a Writers' Guild Best British Screenplay award for her local-boy-done-good story *Charlie Bubbles* (1967), only her second film since her previous award-winner *A Taste of Honey*, was noteworthy partly because she remained one of very few recognised women writers working in British cinema during the 1960s.²⁷ Janet Green, whose credits include the pioneering *Victim* (1961), was clear in her commitment to 'writing movie stories' which offered 'a huge canvas for anyone who wants to have a go'.²⁸ In the same article in *The Screenwriter* (the Writers' Guild in-house magazine) other women screenwriters spoke of problems they had experienced with gender stereotyping. Bridget Boland, later Oscar-nominated for *Anne of the Thousand Days* (1969), recalled being 'teamed with a male writer [. . .] to write the "home", and the man the "away" sequences' when actually its 'technically complicated action sequences were right up Miss Boland's alley'.²⁹ Dail Ambler, writer of the exploitation films *Beat Girl* (1959), *Take Me Over* (1963), and *Night After Night After Night* (1969), had 'a sneaky advantage on the rest of the girls': an androgynous name. ³⁰ She recalled 'working very happily by correspondence' with one director who changed as soon as he met her 'and promptly began demanding re-writes [and] making life difficult'.³¹

The major route by which women entered screenwriting in the 1960s was by adapting their own novels and plays for the screen, the pathway taken by Delaney, Edna O'Brien, Nell Dunn, Gillian Freeman, Margaret Drabble, and others (although many of the resultant films ended up being one-off forays).³² Women writers were also brought in to help 'feminise' dialogue, with O'Brien working uncredited on *Darling*, Drabble contributing additional dialogue to the biopic *Isadora* (1968), and Freeman writing Marianne Faithfull's 'thought sequences' for *Girl on a Motorcycle* (1968), prompting critic Raymond Durgnat to comment, 'English film-makers – even the younger generation, or people like Osborne or Pinter – aren't interested in either the structure or the finer points of feminine characters. Already this had to be half a French film with a female scriptwriter.'³³

The issue of credit, and who gets it, is of course a highly pertinent one in relation to all aspects of screenwriting, whether the politically necessary subterfuge of adopting pseudonyms by blacklisted writers or the more quotidian matter of not every contributor being credited on screen. However, questions of attribution were often inflected in gendered ways, and the input of Johanna Harwood into the genesis of the James Bond films provides an interesting example of this. Terence Young, the director of *Dr No* (1962) and *From Russia With Love* (1963), referred to Harwood as his former 'continuity girl' who had assisted him on *Dr No* but never had any major creative input: 'We gave her script credit, and she became a fairly well-known writer for about one year until they found out she was not really a writer.'[34] Unsurprisingly, her account differed from Young's. An employee of producer Harry Saltzman, she had written the first speculative screenplay of *Dr No* which helped to secure United Artists' financial backing. When Richard Maibaum and Wolf Mankowitz were brought in to co-write a new screenplay, they decided to take a parodic approach to Ian Fleming's work, even changing the megalomaniac super-villain Dr No from a man to 'an intelligent monkey', a decision that appalled the producers.[35] After emergency script conferences and extensive rewriting by numerous writers, the script had become, in Harwood's words, 'chewed around the edges [. . .] everything has been changed'.[36] With only eight days to go until filming began, Harwood 'did what I could with all the scripts lying around, pasting and cutting and rewriting', and this was the version of the script that went before the cameras, resulting in a film that became an outstanding box-office success.[37] Maibaum's account of how its follow-up, *From Russia With Love*, 'crystallised the kind of thing that the Bond movies should be' contrasts with Harwood's invocation of a 'panic-stricken' team who 'didn't know why *Dr No* was such a success'.[38] Shortly afterwards, Harwood left Saltzman's employ and became a freelance script-doctor, doing uncredited work on the producer's subsequent films including the BFA-award-winning *The Ipcress File* (1965).[39]

Despite a discouraging start with the simian high concept for *Dr No*, Richard Maibaum became a key formative influence on the development of the Bond films, recognising what worked and what didn't, and humour's necessity to offer the audience 'safety valves: moments for them to relax before the next dramatic incident'.[40] He upped Hitchcock's number of required 'bumps' per picture (his label for a narrative's 'shocks, high points, thrills') from thirteen to thirty-nine per Bond film, aiming 'to make every foot of film pay off in terms of excitement, comedy or drama. Nothing must drag.'[41] The success of the series bears out the validity of this approach. But Johanna Harwood's alternative account of the birthing of Bond provides a salutary counter-narrative, complicating the notion that any single individual was its primary author (suggested by the title of Maibaum's 1965 article 'How I write the Bond films') and revealing the chaos behind their creation. The fact that Harwood worked on several highly successful thrillers, but only occasionally received on-screen credit for her work, also acts as a reminder of the invisibility of much script development work (including women's), a realm in which official filmographies can only tell us so much.

Neither Harwood nor Maibaum were recognised for their work on two of the most commercially successful films of the early 1960s, indicating that while awards can be useful for tracking certain trends, they often miss out the work that attains the highest levels of commercial popularity. Similarly, neither Wolf Mankowitz, nor Paul Dehn – co-author with Maibaum of the screenplay for *Goldfinger* (1964) – received awards for their work connected to Bond: Dehn received his BFA nomination for his John le Carré adaptation *The Deadly Affair* (1967) instead.[42] Other screenwriters had brief moments of acclaim while the majority of their projects resided within the un-garlanded commercial cinema. Jack Davies for example received an Oscar nomination for his work alongside Ken Annakin on *Those Magnificent Men in Their Flying Machines* (1965) but spent much of the 1960s crafting British comedy staples including Norman Wisdom vehicles *A Stitch in Time* (1963) and *The Early Bird* (1965), and *Doctor in Clover* (1966).[43]

Other important 1960s screenwriters were entirely absent from award listings, often because they worked in less prestigious genres such as horror or lowbrow comedy. One of the most prolific was Jimmy Sangster, Hammer's standout writer (having provided them with fifteen screenplays including 'two Draculas, two Frankensteins, and a Mummy' in just five years, reported *Kine Weekly* in 1963).[44] Sangster maintained a Stakhanovite work-rate throughout the decade but was particularly pleased with his psychological horrors *Taste of Fear* (1961), *Paranoiac* (1963), *Maniac* (1963) and *Nightmare* (1964), which he felt were an astute product diversification for Hammer:

> The introduction of the thriller element into them is a good thing. Whatever the current vogue in audience tastes – for horror or comedy or what-have-you – a good thriller will always do well. This is the sort of thing I think I'm best at.[45]

But arguably Sangster's finest achievement within the subgenre was *The Nanny* (1965), which brought backstreet abortion and its consequences into mainstream cinema ahead of *Alfie* and offered as telling a critique of the psychology of servitude as the more celebrated *The Servant*.[46]

In the realms of comedy, *Carry On* writers Norman Hudis and Talbot Rothwell, were never likely to win awards but made crucial contributions to popular British cinema nonetheless. Hudis had been responsible for establishing the series and setting its institutional imprimatur, while Rothwell shepherded the series towards more genre parody and even saltier innuendo.[47] In her study of British screenwriters, Jill Nelmes examines Hudis and Rothwell alongside their more prestigious contemporaries Janet Green, Robert Bolt and John McGrath, acknowledging their equally important 'place in the history of British cinema', along with the likes of Mark Grantham, writer for Danzigers, turning around screenplays in under two weeks and still displaying a modicum of 'verve and flair'.[48] A shrewd critic might occasionally spot the skill displayed by a writer on a more routine assignment, as with Richard Whitehall noting 'Lyn Fairhurst's splendid ear for the flavour of contemporary teenage dialogue, and the charm and strength with which he has drawn the character relationships' on pop musical *Live It Up* (1963), but generally this echelon of writers had to console themselves with industry respect rather than critical acclaim.[49]

During the 1960s some high-profile screenwriters undoubtedly managed to gain recognition and earn money on a scale that evaded their predecessors, but the majority continued to toil in obscurity. In spite of the Guild's advances, general secretary Alan Sapper wrote in May 1968 that screenwriters remained 'vulnerable', earning a fee which 'frequently constitutes no more than one-thousandth of the profits earned by a successful feature film'.[50] The growing prevalence of package deals 'assembled by agents' presented great opportunities for a chosen few, but their 'closed world' was difficult for aspiring writers to penetrate, thereby confining prosperity 'a small and exclusive group'.[51] The increasing emphasis on inequality within the Guild's membership, as well as the political temper of the times, may have motivated the decision to pare back the lavishness of the Guild's award ceremony by the end of the 1960s. Whereas the first award dinner at the Dorchester Hotel ballroom, 'christened "Night of the Golden Pens"', had been large and lavish, by 1969 'serious rifts' had developed between members 'who favoured the high profile, grande soirée' and 'those who wanted something simpler and cheaper'.[52] By the early 1970s, given the increasingly penurious situation of the British film industry, they decided to cease holding a ceremony and scaled back to a single award presented at their AGM; a rather sad coda to a decade of British cinema which had begun so optimistically and had, on the whole, offered new opportunities to the screenwriter, resulting in many remarkable success stories.

WORKING ON A 22-CARAT TYPEWRITER: FREDERIC RAPHAEL (1931–)

At the height of his success in 1967, Frederic Raphael found himself placed in some very impressive company by *Photoplay*'s reporter:

> In many ways they are alike, writer Frederic Raphael and that earlier Renaissance Raphael, who painted such splendid-hued, imaginative canvasses. Our 20th Century Raphael paints too, but he is far more likely to be remembered for the artistry he has conveyed to the broader canvas of the silver screen.[53]

This was, of course, partly showbiz hyperbole but it also provides a powerful indication of the high esteem in which Raphael was held as a writer of screenplays around this time. His most notable moment of acclaim had come with his Oscar win for *Darling*, the film for which he also won the BFA Best British Screenplay award and a Writers' Guild award. Raphael's previous film *Nothing but the Best* (1964) had also won a Writers' Guild award, while his next, *Two for the Road* (1967), would be Oscar nominated. This level of recognition was all the more remarkable given Raphael's limited output as a screenwriter, with only six film credits to his name throughout the decade, including the lavish Thomas Hardy adaptation *Far From the Madding Crowd* (1967), while he continued his parallel literary career. The films Raphael worked on were generally commercially successful, earning him the title of the 'writer with the 22-carat typewriter'.[54] But in 1968, in the private space of his notebook, he asked searching questions about the way his career had developed: 'Before 1961, my work was almost all fiction. Since then I have written films, and made money. Before I was indifferent to the prospect of riches. [. . .] Have I become smarter or much, much more foolish?'[55]

American-born but British-educated (Charterhouse and Cambridge), Raphael entered film after the successful stage musical he co-wrote with his university friend Leslie Bricusse brought them to the Rank Organisation's attention, and they were signed up on a two-year contract in the late 1950s. Raphael saw this as 'an ideal arrangement' for cross-subsidising what he felt to be his true vocation of literary fiction, and when no one from Rank 'suggested a movie that Leslie and I should write; nor did they look to us to volunteer any ideas', but his monthly cheques still arrived, he was delighted.[56] In undertaking scriptwriting work at this time, Raphael 'had no creative or critical standards', by his own admission, and instead 'accepted, with a kind of masochistic relish that one entered the business by working on the sort of film one would never dream of going to see.'[57]

Post-Rank, after doing dialogue rewrites for the mildly saucy ABPC comedy *Don't Bother to Knock* (1961) and being approached to revise a 'trite, witless and overlong' script for *Damon and Pythias* (1962), Raphael resolved to 'throw away my long spoons and sup no more with the devil'.[58] But around this time he saw Antonioni's *L'Avventura* (1960) in a Rome cinema, which he said hit him 'with stunning and liberating force', and became 'a talisman of a kind of creative cinema in which John Paddy Carstairs and his Pinewood peers had no place'.[59] Its style would later inspire *Darling* but for now the offers Raphael was getting were hardly Antonioni-esque: meeting producers Leslie Parkyn and Julian Wintle, he 'hoped that they wanted to do a realistic movie based on [his 1960 novel] *The Limits of Love*', but 'the project for which they thought me suitable was to be a vehicle for Cliff Richard, about a Butlin's camp'.[60]

Raphael turned to television instead, commissioned by drama producer Stella Richman to provide single plays for ATV, including an adaptation of Stanley Ellin's short story *The Best of Everything,* televised 20 August 1961. This became the basis of *Nothing But the Best,* directed by Clive Donner and produced by David Deutsch. The story of Jimmy Brewster (Alan Bates), a social parvenu willing to resort to murder in pursuit of what Raphael described as 'Power and Prestige, upthereness', *Nothing but the Best*'s most obvious British antecedents were *Room at the Top* (1959) and *Kind Hearts and Coronets* (1949).[61] But it was also a highly personal project for Raphael:

> I think the tone came out of my sense of insecurity about England. I'd arrived in England as a seven-year-old American kid, and I very quickly realised [...] you either learned how to be like the English, or you weren't going to get anywhere. And as most seven-year-olds can, and as Jews traditionally are supposedly able to do, I did manage to do it successfully.[62]

The film's progression would be mostly smooth, although a slight spanner would be put in the works by Anglo-Amalgamated bosses Nat Cohen and Stuart Levy, who after seeing the first cut felt it was in danger of sailing over the audience's heads unless some key plot points and character motivations were clarified. The solution arrived at was an intermittent voice-over from Jimmy, detailing his inner thoughts but also assisting with further exposition. But the narration would have to be deftly deployed, as Deutsch acknowledges in his correspondence with Raphael: 'the commentary should issue direct from Jimmy's subconscious, but if it fails to be comprehensible to the average audience then we will not have achieved part of our reason for using the device.'[63]

In the end, an effective balance between clarification and complexity was reached. Raphael had devised some characteristically smart repartee for Charlie (Denholm Elliott), Jimmy's mentor: 'If you've been to a redbrick university you have to remember what you've learnt but if you've been to a bluebrick you've not only got to forget what you've learnt but if possible what subject you read as well.' Although *The Guardian*'s critic suggested that the film's 'generally bright dialogue occasionally falls flat on its supercilious face', Dilys Powell pronounced Raphael a significant new discovery for British cinema whose 'gifts as novelist and critic are well known; with excitement one now recognises in him the qualities of first-rate scriptwriter.'[64]

While *Nothing but the Best* was in production, the long-running project eventually entitled *Darling* was also underway. Producer Jo Janni's highly discursive script development process would prove challenging for Raphael, who was keen for 'artistic privacy' and doubted the value of 'creation by committee'.⁶⁵ The lack of creative autonomy troubled him, particularly in relation to John Schlesinger's competing authorship as director: 'He doesn't want to know what my imagination can supply [. . .] His attitude is determined by concern for his own credit.'⁶⁶ Although Raphael's correspondence with the director was cordial, praising Schlesinger as 'the first person I've ever met who actually understands how my lines are meant to sound', he expressed concern about the 'mania for cuts' leading to 'terrible truncations which end by destroying a scene's power. Better cut one whole scene than keep two halves.'⁶⁷Raphael was also very perturbed by Edna O'Brien being brought in to do rewrites (in spite of Janni's earlier assurances to the contrary) judging them largely 'incoherent; where coherent, it could be bought by the yard at Woolworth's.'⁶⁸ In retrospect, Raphael felt *Darling* had 'suffered badly from the pace imposed on it by the race to make it entertaining' and would have preferred it to be 'a great deal longer and a great deal duller' than the 'giddy roundabout of contemporary delights' it ended up becoming.⁶⁹

For his next script idea, which occurred to him while driving down to the French Riviera with his wife ('how odd it would be to overtake ourselves as we were in the days when we were penniless hitchhikers on the same road'), Raphael was keen to keep the creative control he felt he'd lost on *Darling*.⁷⁰ When approached by director Stanley Donen, he held firm on not 'conferencing' the script while it was in development, 'justifying every idea that I have, because the connections in any fictional narrative between one scene and another are subconscious [and] we will never get to the end. And what's more you will kill in me any kind of ferment that's going on.'⁷¹ Donen agreed to Raphael's terms and stuck very closely to his original script for *Two for the Road*, tracking the relationship of Joanna (Audrey Hepburn) and Mark (Albert Finney) from the couple's first 'meet cute' to their potential break-up, offering 'some sort of wry testimonial for marriage' in the process.⁷²

Two for the Road became freighted with extra significance by a preface Raphael wrote to accompany the screenplay's publication which accused contemporary film culture as being rife with 'treachery, impatience, superstition, sycophancy and fatty degeneration of the moral fibre'.⁷³ Venal producers, directors, and distributors were partly to blame but so too were writers who abandoned all scruples 'at the mention of a film company'.⁷⁴ But rather than avoiding films, which Raphael argued would be 'preserving a chastity of increasingly suspect value', the modern writer should 'advance a great deal more boldly into them'.⁷⁵ In this, they would require supportive sympathetic film critics rather than 'insular toadies who promote certain directors, often on the thinnest of justifications, to the status of masters'.⁷⁶ It was both ironic and valedictory that many of the reviews for *Two for the Road* clearly regarded the film as primarily Donen's achievement, exemplified by *Films and Filming* only mentioning the writer once (suggesting his dialogue was 'difficult to say') while crediting the director with the film's innovative chronological structure and its overall wit and elegance.[77]

Although Raphael's preface had proposed that 'free composition directly for the screen should become the normal style' instead of 'the laborious and often only half-baked reheating of literary matter' his next film project was to be an adaptation.[78] But he was willing to be honest about his motivations for undertaking *Far From the Madding Crowd*:

> The question of what to do after *Darling* came up, and also 'What are we going to do with Julie?' – because we'd just made her a star, and although it may not be artistically terribly laudable, it was perhaps humanly quite understandable – and we thought 'Well, we'll make a movie quickly.' [T]hinking up originals to a tight time schedule is difficult.[79]

Thomas Hardy had not been adapted for film since the silent period, but Raphael felt his novels were particularly germane to screen adaptation, full of 'just the kind of "ideas" expected of film writers', like Bathsheba's dress getting caught on Troy's spur when they first meet.[80] Hardy also fitted in perfectly with the burgeoning enthusiasm for nineteenth-century pastoralism in the late 1960s. But for all its visual dash (its ad campaign boasting of 'cinematic grandeur') and apposite star casting, Raphael would ultimately conclude that the film 'fell back on taxidermy'.[81]

Future collaborations with John Schlesinger on 'a film biography of Lord Byron and, possibly, a cinema version of *A Severed Head* by Iris Murdoch' were slated in 1967.[82] The latter project materialised in 1970 but through the auspices of Dick Clement and Ian La Frenais, who in Raphael's view botched his screenplay, mainly through miscasting.[83] But the Byron biopic, a long-cherished idea of Raphael's, never reached the screen, and he privately vented his frustrations about Schlesinger's reluctance to direct:

> He does not want to spend 'several years' on Byron [. . .] He prefers, he says, to do smaller films; he has a couple lined up. Modesty? He would sooner take regular curtain calls, and cull regular cuttings, than risk obscurity for a long time in order to produce something monumental.[84]

Raphael became increasingly interested in directing his own projects, keen to 'take the decisions and impose, rightly or wrongly, a more personal stand on the work'.[85] An original idea, *Guilt*, was greenlit by 20th Century Fox, with Faye Dunaway to star, but when Raphael went out to Hollywood in 1969, he found 'a desert' rather than a thriving production hub, and was therefore unsurprised by the project's cancellation shortly thereafter, feeling 'like some berserk infantryman who continues to charge forward while warier companions fall' when 'the wonder was that I had survived so long'.[86] Having begun the decade seeing screenwriting solely as a convenient means of cross-subsidy, Frederic Raphael ended it with (stymied) ambitions to direct. But somewhere in the compromised middle, he had also been responsible for writing a small but highly impactful body of work that epitomised its era.

NOTES

1. Derek Hill, 'A Writers' Wave?', *Sight and Sound*, vol. 29, no. 2, Spring 1960, p. 56.
2. Ibid., p. 57.
3. Following on from *I'm All Right Jack*'s win the previous year, it looked like BFA voters were particularly drawn to stories querying the abuse of trade union power at this time.
4. Bryan Forbes, 'How I write a film script', *Showtime*, March 1964, p. 24.
5. Ibid., p. 25.
6. Likewise, at the end of the decade, the Writers' Guild awards in the screenplay category went to the writer/directors Dick Clement (with Ian La Frenais) for *Otley* (1969) and Anthony Newley for *Can Hieronymous Merkin Ever Forget Mercy Humppe and Find True Happiness?* (1969).
7. B. S. Johnson, 'Why should a writer direct?', *Film and Television Technician*, February 1969, p. 6.
8. Hill, 'A Writers' Wave?', p. 59. Sillitoe provides a fascinating account of his process for adapting *Saturday Night and Sunday Morning* 're-read[ing] it about six times, until every scene fell down into my hands. I wrote scenes on cards, and I sort of shuffled them, just like a pack of cards, in order to rearrange them for atmosphere' in Gordon Gow, 'Novel into film', *Films and Filming*, May 1966, p. 21.
9. Pat McGilligan, 'Introduction', *Backstory 3: Interviews with Screenwriters of the 60s* (Berkeley: University of California press, 1997), p. 2.
10. Quoted in Tony Gruner, 'Television', *Kine Weekly*, 10 November 1960, p. 27.
11. Alun Owen, 'What it is like working with the Beatles', *Showtime*, June 1964, p. 4.
12. Alun Owen, 'Why I wrote a script for the Beatles', *Photoplay*, May 1964, p. 12. Owen, 'What it is like working with the Beatles', p. 5.
13. Anon., 'Playwrights for British films', *The Times*, 29 December 1961, p. 11.
14. See, for instance, the trade press announcement of production on *Billy Liar*, *Kine Weekly*, 10 August 1962, p. 13.
15. The Guild affiliated to the TUC in 1964 (which enabled it to join the Federation of Film Unions). Anon., 'We're in the TUC – and it's strictly non-political', *The Screenwriter*, no. 15, Spring 1964, p. 3. In 1966 it would broaden its range and alter its name accordingly to become the Writers' Guild of Great Britain.
16. 'Guildman', 'You'd hardly credit it', *The Screenwriter*, no. 12, Spring 1963, p. 21. Anon., 'Film credits – we demand a better deal', *The Screenwriter*, no. 14, Winter 1963, p. 3.
17. A sign of its practical usage appears in the publicity guidance for *Morgan – A Suitable Case for Treatment*: 'David Mercer: Credit to be given as the author of the play (naming the play if its title differs from that of the film) and as the scriptwriter in accordance with the BFPA/Screenwriters Association Agreement dated 1 July 1964 which provides that screenplay writers must receive credit in all advertising where the director's name is used and must be similar in size.' Karel Reisz special collection, National Film and Television Archive, KRS/1/7/13.
18. 'Guildman', 'You'd hardly credit it', p. 21. As underlined elsewhere, 'nothing in the Guild's programme at this moment is more important than the all-out fight to

get script fees increased, quickly and substantially.' Allan Prior, 'The economics of screenwriting', *The Screenwriter*, no. 13, Summer 1963, p. 10.' Guild chair Ted Willis stated the value of their awards 'as a practical recognition of the status of the writer', and noted how ' every important television and film company was represented, together with scores of leading personalities from both sides of the camera' at their ceremony. Ted Willis, 'The 1962 awards', *The Screenwriter*, no. 12, Spring 1963, p. 3.
19. Anon., 'Producers and screenwriters sign two-year agreement', *Kine Weekly*, 16 November 1961, p. 6.
20. Quoted in Melanie Williams, *David Lean* (Manchester: Manchester University Press, 2014), p. 29.
21. Quoted in Adrian Turner, *Robert Bolt: Scenes from Two Lives* (London: Vintage, 1999), p. 179.
22. Quoted in Lee Hill, 'Terry Southern: ultrahip', in Patrick McGilligan (ed.), *Backstory 3: Interviews with Screenwriters of the 60s* (Berkeley: University of California Press, 1997), pp. 382–3.
23. Pinter shrugged off queries about the difficulties of working across different media, saying 'I just write about characters; after all, they don't know what medium they're appearing in, do they?' Quoted in John Russell Taylor, 'The Servant and The Caretaker', *Sight and Sound*, Winter 1963, p. 39. The other screenwriter with whom Losey had an especially productive alliance in the 1960s was Evan Jones, the Jamaican-born writer who contributed to the screenplays for *Eve* (1962), *The Damned* (1962), *King and Country* (1964) and *Modesty Blaise* (1966). Jones also wrote the race-relations satire *Two Gentlemen Sharing* (1969) and is one of very few writers of mixed ethnic heritage in the overwhelmingly white British production landscape of the time. See Colin Gardner, 'From mimicry to mockery: Cold War hybridity in Evan Jones's *The Damned, Modesty Blaise* and *Funeral in Berlin*', *Media History*, vol. 12, no. 2 (2006), pp. 177–91. Although *The Times* reported that 'Mr Barry Reckord, the West Indian dramatist' was 'working on a screen version of Mr Colin McInnes's novel *City of Spades*' for Woodfall in 1961, this project failed to materialise. See 'Playwrights for British films', *The Times*, 29 December 1961, p. 11.
24. John Russell Taylor, 'Accident', *Sight and Sound*, Autumn 1966, p. 182.
25. Pinter quoted in John Russell Taylor, 'Accident', *Sight and Sound*, Autumn 1966, pp. 183–4.
26. Wood's work on *Petulia* was uncredited. For more on his 1960s work, see David Cairns, 'Woodery-pokery', *Shadowplay*, <https://dcairns.wordpress.com/2017/09/12/woodery-pokery-in-york/> (accessed 1 August 2018).
27. Lavinia Brydon offers a useful overview of Delaney's screenwriting career in Jill Nelmes and Julie Selbo (eds), *Women Screenwriters: An International Guide* (London: Palgrave Macmillan, 2015), pp. 654–62.
28. Quoted in Jean McConnell, 'Girls of the Guild', *The Screenwriter*, no. 12, Spring 1963, p. 19.
29. Ibid., p. 19.
30. Ibid., p. 29.
31. Ibid.
32. Reflecting on this, producer Roy Millichip cited 'a crying need for good scripts featuring female artists. But the strange thing is that although there's a whole battery of good woman writers nowadays, they're primarily novelists and they just aren't writing for the cinema.' Desmond Davis and Roy Millichip, 'Take two nice guys like them', *Films and Filming*, December 1969, p. 51. Ruth Prawer Jhabvala also began her long-running association with Merchant Ivory in the 1960s, starting off adapting her own novel for *The Householder* (1963).

33. Raymond Durgnat, 'Girl on a Motorcycle', *Films and Filming*, October 1968, p. 37.
34. Young quoted in Matthew Field, 'The girl with the golden pen', *Cinema Retro: Movie Classics*, no. 4, 2012, p. 136.
35. Ibid.
36. Ibid.
37. Ibid. Even Young concedes that she came up with one of its wittiest moments, when the recently stolen Goya portrait of Wellington turns up in the mise en scène of Dr No's lair, a story confirmed by Ken Adam.
38. Maibaum in McGilligan, 'Richard Maibaum: a pretence of seriousness' in Patrick McGilligan (ed.), *Backstory: Interviews with Screenwriters of Hollywood's Golden Age* (Berkeley: University of California Press, 1986), p. 284. Harwood in Field, 'The girl with the golden pen', p. 139.
39. Daniel Kremer, *Sidney J. Furie: Life and Films* (Lexington: University Press of Kentucky, 2015), p. 79.
40. Richard Maibaum, 'How I write the Bond films', *Showtime*, April 1965, p. 28.
41. Ibid. The concept provided a title for Richard Maibaum's article 'James Bond's 39 bumps', *New York Times*, 13 December 1964, p. 9.
42. For more on Dehn's screenwriting career, see David Kipen, 'Tinker Tailor Soldier Schreiber', *Virginia Quarterly Review*, vol. 89, no. 1, Winter 2013, pp. 224–31.
43. Similarly, veteran British journeyman Vernon Harris suddenly found himself Oscar-nominated late in his career for translating Lionel Bart's *Oliver!* (1968) to the screen.
44. Derek Todd, 'Production', *Kine Weekly*, 3 January 1963, p. 13. Sangster also wrote for Tempean Films as well as contributing to Anglo-Amalgamated's *Edgar Wallace Mystery Theatre* film series under the pseudonym John Samson.
45. Derek Todd, 'Production', *Kine Weekly*, 5 July 1962, p. 13. Derek Todd, 'Production', *Kine Weekly*, 3 January 1963, p. 13.
46. Discussed in Jimmy Sangster BECTU interview, <https://historyproject.org.uk/interview/jimmy-sangster> (accessed 1 August 2018).
47. Hudis saw himself as an 'all-round writer' who would 'tackle a blank-verse drama about a Polynesian shepherd as blithely as I hope to sail into the subsequent Carry Ons', and ended up flourishing as a writer for American television from the mid-1960s onwards. Norman Hudis, 'It just happened', *Kine Weekly (Studio Review)*, 28 January 1960, p. 32.
48. Jill Nelmes, *The Screenwriter in British Cinema* (London: BFI, 2014), p. 183, p. 146.
49. Richard Whitehall, 'Live It Up', *Films and Filming*, January 1964, p. 28.
50. Alan Sapper, 'The writer: isolation or interdependence?', *Film and TV Technician*, May 1968, p. 20.
51. Ibid.
52. Nick Yapp, '*The Write Stuff*: A History of the Writers' Guild of Great Britain 1959–2009', Writers' Guild of Great Britain, <https://writersguild.org.uk/history-writers-guild-awards/> (accessed 18 June 2018).
53. Peter Howell, 'The trials and tribulations of being a movie screenwriter', *Photoplay*, December 1967, p. 18.
54. Ibid, p. 19.
55. Frederic Raphael, *Personal Terms: The 1950s and 1960s* (Manchester: Carcanet, 2001), p. 149.
56. Frederic Raphael, *Going Up: To Cambridge and Beyond* (London: Biteback, 2015), p. 256–7. The only completed project to emerge from this period was the Cambridge-set comedy *Bachelor of Hearts* (1958), which Raphael described as 'a

square-wheeled vehicle' for German actor Hardy Krüger, who showed 'remarkable steadiness under a remorseless fire of old jokes'. Frederic Raphael, 'Preface', *Two For the Road* (London: Jonathan Cape, 1967), p. 12.
57. Ibid., pp. 8–9.
58. Ibid., p. 17.
59. Ibid., p. 18. Raphael, *Going Up*, p. 378.
60. Ibid., p. 373.
61. Letter from Frederic Raphael to Clive Donner dated 25 March 1963. Clive Donner special collection, National Film and Television Archive, CSD 6/32.
62. Raphael in John Baxter, 'Frederic Raphael: Renaissance man', in McGilligan (ed.), *Backstory 4: Interviews with Screenwriters of the 1970s and 1980s* (Berkeley: University of California Press, 2006), p. 323. Fleshing out such a character also offered him the vicarious pleasure 'of impersonating the kind of heartless, double-dealing bounder whom I have always been, in practice, too squeamish to emulate.' Raphael, *Going Up*, p. 397.
63. Letter from David Deutsch to Frederic Raphael, dated 2 September 1963. Clive Donner special collection, CSD 6/16.
64. Richard Roud, 'New films in London', *The Guardian*, 28 February 1964, p. 18. Dilys Powell, 'Climber with a knife', *The Sunday Times*, 1 March 1964, p. 20. Raphael's growing literary eminence was also exploited in the film's publicity material generated for the film describing him as 'one of the country's top novelists'. *Nothing but the Best* pressbook, BFI Library.
65. Interview with Frederic Raphael, *Web of Stories*, <www.webofstories.com/playAll/frederic.raphael?sId=55701> (accessed 1 August 2018). Raphael, 'Preface', p. 9. In his semi-autobiographical novel *The Glittering Prizes*, Raphael would send up Janni's insistence that the 'only one way to make a good film [. . .] is to work and work for weeks and weeks, all in the same room, looking for the right image [. . .] there must be many conferences and research and interviews – and conferences.' Frederic Raphael, *The Glittering Prizes* (London: Penguin, 1976), p. 156. Nonetheless, Raphael also admired Janni's instinctive script knowledge, when 'he would ring you up and say, "You are the writer but I feel that in this scene – something is missing." I'd say, "Fine. What do you think it is?" And he'd say, "I don't know." But after a bit, you'd find he was right.' Quoted in Baxter, 'Frederic Raphael: Renaissance man', p. 341.
66. Raphael, *Personal Terms*, p. 95.
67. Letter from Frederic Raphael to John Schlesinger dated 13 August 1964. John Schlesinger special collection, National Film and Television Archive, JRS 4/8. Raphael adds a sardonic mention of Janni, and the fact that he is working on the script unpaid at that point: 'How is our producer? You might remind him that I'm doing all this for love and that it wouldn't hurt him to send me a kiss or two.' Raphael would later state that he was only ever paid £3,500 for two years' work on it. Baxter, 'Frederic Raphael: Renaissance man', p. 329.
68. Letter from Frederic Raphael to John Schlesinger, dated 6 November 1964. John Schlesinger special collection, National Film and Television Archive, JRS 4/8. Raphael, *Personal Terms*, p. 114.
69. Raphael, 'Preface', pp. 28–9.
70. Ibid., p. 32.
71. Quoted in Howell, 'The trials and tribulations of being a movie screenwriter', p. 19.
72. Raphael, 'Preface', p. 33.
73. Ibid., p. 7.
74. Ibid.
75. Ibid., p. 22, p. 18.

76. Ibid., p. 24. Unsurprisingly, Raphael's preface angered many people, including Michael Balcon who took issue with his depiction of Ealing as 'complacently and self-admiringly parochial' and also queried his controversial suggestion that American investment had been the best thing for British film's creative development. Responding to a truncated version of the preface published in *The Sunday Times*, 21 May 1967 (under the title 'Frederic Raphael, author of Darling, writes off the movie Napoleons and their coteries – and sees a vision of a new private cinema'), Balcon wrote to express his irritation at what he felt to be Raphael's ignorant rewriting of history and his self-contradictions: 'was not the solitary memorable film with which he has been associated – "Darling" – sponsored entirely by a British company?' Letter from Michael Balcon, *The Sunday Times*, 28 May 1967. Raphael then counter-responded the following week, saying 'when a man is as zealous a curator of his own laurels as Sir Michael Balcon, he hardly needs praise from anyone else' (*The Sunday Times*, 4 June 1967). This rather unedifying media spat added to the feeling, expressed by David Robinson, that Raphael had indulged in 'the crabbed enthusiasm of a proper old bitching' in his preface and 'destroy[ed] his argument by over-protesting it', showing a 'lack of balance and proportion all the more frustrating when so much of the anger is justified'. David Robinson, untitled article, *Financial Times*, 1 September 1967. BFI Library press cuttings file.
77. Mike Sarne, 'Two for the Road', *Films and Filming*, September 1967, p. 20.
78. Raphael, 'Preface', p. 35.
79. Benedict Shephard, 'Cinema – Frederic Raphael John Schlesinger talk to Cover', *Cover*, 27 December 1967, p. 25. Cuttings scrapbook, John Schlesinger special collection, National Film and Television Archive, JRS/ 68.
80. *Far From the Madding Crowd* pressbook. Bill Douglas Cinema Museum collection.
81. Interview with Frederic Raphael, *Web of Stories*, <www.webofstories.com/playAll/frederic.raphael?sId=55701> (accessed 1 August 2018).
82. Anon., 'Vivid Victoriana', *Time*, 27 October 1967, p. 58.
83. Originally been commissioned by the Woolf brothers as a vehicle for Laurence Harvey, its screenplay represented the first time Raphael 'was offered real money for a script', the impressive sum of $75,000. Baxter, 'Frederic Raphael: Renaissance man', p. 333.
84. Raphael, *Personal Terms*, p. 194.
85. Howell, 'The trials and tribulations of being a movie screenwriter', p. 47.
86. Raphael interview, *Web of Stories*. Baxter, 'Frederic Raphael: Renaissance man', p. 333. A Fox production manager slightly desperately tried to persuade him to write in a fly-past by Zero Fighters, recently acquired for *Tora! Tora! Tora!* (1970): 'I could let you have them for, like, nothing. In fact you would be doing me a service.'

7. DIRECTING

Melanie Williams

Introduction: The Critical Context

Even more so than the screenwriter, the profession of director underwent dramatic changes in status during the 1960s. New ideas about directorial work were facilitated by the era's burgeoning auteurism, which in Britain was spearheaded by the new film periodical *Movie*, launched in June 1962. *Movie*'s credo was that 'the director is the author of a film, the person who gives it any distinctive quality it may have', and its writers would passionately advocate for the work of Hollywood directors such as Otto Preminger and Howard Hawks.[1] But it was evident from its first issue that British cinema was anathema by comparison, and its infamous opening salvo, 'The British cinema' by V. F. Perkins, made clear that in *Movie*'s view any supposed 'renaissance' or 'New Wave' was entirely illusory; 'British cinema is as dead as before. Perhaps it was never alive.'[2]

Perkins railed against 'the British concept of The Good Film' which he found sadly limited in its horizons: 'a "cinematic" treatment' of 'an important and if possible controversial subject' with 'a fair representation of all points of view', exemplified by the 'social problem' oeuvre of Basil Dearden, deemed by Perkins to have a 'total lack of feeling for cinema'.[3] Bigger cinematic guns did not fare any better: it counted for nothing that David Lean's *The Bridge on the River Kwai* (1957) had won multiple Oscars; indeed, this could be taken as a sign of its middlebrow mediocrity.[4] But pivotal too was the belief that the new young film-makers making headway around that time offered no positive alter-

Figure 7.1   Clive Donner directs Barry Evans directing the participants in his teenage fantasies in *Here We Go Round the Mulberry Bush* (Clive Donner, 1968).

native; their leading light Tony Richardson was judged to have a 'conspicuous lack of talent'.[5] Perkins polemically insisted that there was 'as much genuine personality in *Room at the Top*, method in *A Kind of Loving*, and style in *A Taste of Honey* as there is wit in *An Alligator Named Daisy*, intelligence in *Above us the Waves* and ambition in *Ramsbottom Rides Again*', damning the New Wave by association with lowest-common-denominator product from the 1950s British studio system.[6]

Perkins' diagnosis/jeremiad on the inadequacies of British cinema was followed by a 'talent histogram' comparing the merits of British and American directors which, as Peter Hutchings and Charles Barr both noted, underlined the sense that British cinema was 'authorially impoverished' offering an 'eloquent and polemically very effective asymmetry' of thirty-four US-based directors deemed either great, brilliant or very talented, while only two British-based directors were deemed to have made the same grade – the US émigré Joseph Losey and Argentinian visitor Hugo Fregonese.[7] A few more were categorised as talented – Karel Reisz, Seth Holt, Robert Hamer – but the majority of British directors were either damned with the faint praise of being 'competent or ambitious' or simply homogenously categorised as 'the rest'.[8] Thus, the ability of any British director to occupy the status of auteur was comprehensively undermined, creating a disjuncture with remarkable staying power. And while it would be hard today to find ready acceptance of Perkins' blithe dismissal of Jack Clayton's *The Innocents* (1961) as merely 'a pseudo-ambitious project', and while many of the directors derogated have since found retrospective champions, the value judgements of *Movie* nonetheless cast a long shadow over numerous critical reputations, of both old-guard and new-wave directors.[9]

However, *Movie* was not totally monolithic in its opinions and it permitted space occasionally for more appreciative accounts of directors working within the British cinema (besides Joseph Losey), such as Richard Lester and Clive Donner (the latter this chapter's concluding case study), and Michael Powell, subject of an early auteurist reappraisal by Raymond Durgnat (writing under the pseudonym O. O. Green).[10] Nor was *Movie* the only influential organ of film criticism at the time. The BFI-supported *Sight and Sound* was a key site of debate too, and although *Movie* defined itself against it, in many respects the two publications had a lot in common: V. F. Perkins slated Jack Clayton for his pseudo-seriousness, Penelope Houston for his attempts at 'keeping up with the Antonionis'; either way, his work was (unfairly) deemed meretricious and stylistically deficient.[11] Elsewhere, the more populist magazine *Films and Filming* took an admirably non-partisan approach to assessing the achievements of a wider range of British directors, including such infra dig figures as Peter Glenville, Guy Green, Cyril Frankel, Terence Fisher, Ken Hughes and Val Guest (who defensively pre-empted *Movie*'s critique with a 1960 article entitled 'British films were never bad').[12] *Movie* may have published Raymond Durgnat's reappraisal of Michael Powell, but they would probably have drawn the line at his eight-page analysis of the work of Basil Dearden and producing partner Michael Relph, which appeared in *Films and Filming* in 1966, in which he claimed provocatively that the Relph–Dearden partnership:

> constitutes an auteur, in every sense as distinctive and interesting as many of the American directors currently enjoying rediscovery. [. . .] If Hawks is critically popular, it's because his attitudes are American, and spreading, while if R–D remain unexamined, it's because theirs are upper-middle-class English, and, even in England, contracting. But since there's a Hawks cult there'd be no harm in having a Relph–Dearden one too, as a moral balance to it.[13]

Auteurism may have begun in Britain as a cult of rather fixed preoccupations and prohibitions, but critics like Durgnat also suggested how its ideas could be appropriated to explore a wider range of directorial achievements, stealthily bringing British cinema back into the fold of acceptability.

Auteurs, Journeymen, Veterans, Neophytes: The Directorial Landscape of the 1960s

In spite of *Movie*'s animus against both David Lean and Tony Richardson, the Oscar success of these two film-makers over successive years, winning the Best Director awards for *Lawrence of Arabia* (1962) and *Tom Jones* (1963) respectively, forcefully confirmed the growing international renown of the British director. Lean's perfectionism and single-minded obsessive vision, as reflected in the mise en scène and the lead character of *Lawrence of Arabia*, gave way to a looser model of how to make a film, with plenty of improvisation and treating a location shoot like 'a holiday' (which is how Richardson sold the assignment to his cast and crew), conveyed via the picaresque style and happy-go-lucky eponymous lead character of *Tom Jones*.[14] But despite their differences, both directors espoused ideas of authorship which corresponded perfectly with the auteur theory: 'A film is essentially a creative art form and MUST be under the control of one man', Richardson announced in the publicity material for *A Taste of Honey*, while Lean had stated in previous interviews that the best films inevitably had 'the stamp of one man's personality'.[15] However, this desire for personal creative autonomy was more often than not blocked by an industry where, Joseph Losey regretfully observed, 'people so cavalierly hire specialists at vast prices only to devote themselves to hampering the work of the specialist they've hired.'[16]

In the early 1960s there was sustained debate in the British film press about how best to overcome the major obstacles to directorial freedom, as summarised by writer/producer Carl Foreman in 1961: 'Production costs are too high, the unions are concerned only with working conditions, the archaic and monopolistic British distribution system wants only what it considers safe, and the national film subsidy pays a premium only on proved success.'[17] In this context, the arrival of Woodfall Films was welcomed as a very important and much-needed shot in the arm for a moribund industry. As *Kine Weekly* put it in 1960, 'while producers have for some 20 years now been repeating that hoary old battle-cry "We must have new blood in the industry"', Woodfall went ahead and 'administered the injection', not only creating opportunities for Free Cinema compatriots Tony Richardson and Karel Reisz, but also nurturing the directorial careers of talented film-makers like former cameraman Desmond Davis on *Girl with Green Eyes* (1964), Peter Yates on *One Way Pendulum* (1965), and Richard Lester on *The Knack . . . and How to Get It* (1965).[18]

The 1960s pop-music boom also 'had a very healthy effect on British cinema' in enabling new directorial talent to percolate through, according to one of its beneficiaries, Michael Winner:

> You had these young pop stars who the older directors knew nothing about. [. . .] They called them spotty-faced messenger boys. Nevertheless

these spotty-faced messenger boys were able to maintain a motion picture and bring in the public enough to make it viable. Because the record industry was run by young people, the producers reluctantly turned to young people to direct these pictures. They turned to Sidney Furie to do Cliff Richard, to Dick Lester to do *It's Trad, Dad* and to me to do *Play It Cool*.[19]

If one adds Peter Yates directing *Summer Holiday* (1963), Richard Lester's subsequent films with The Beatles, *A Hard Day's Night* (1964) and *Help!* (1965), and John Boorman making his feature debut on *Catch Us If You Can* (1965), Winner's case becomes even more compelling. These directors used pop films as a way into or leg up in the industry, going on to make more adult-orientated films as their individual careers developed. The origins of the cool aesthetics of Furie's *The Ipcress File* (1965), Boorman's *Point Blank* (1967) and Yates' *Bullitt* (1968) lay, at least in some part, with the earlier popularity of Cliff Richard and the Dave Clark Five. Winner's own later films *The System* (1964), *The Jokers* (1967), and *I'll Never Forget What's 'is Name* (1967) also have their origins in that earlier engagement with pop which had helped him to defy the previous received wisdom that 'you can't direct until you're fifty'.[20] Winner had been given his chance by producer David Deutsch, who firmly believed that 'using a new young director is a risk well worth taking. Far too much importance is given to directors who are tried and known [. . .] we tend to stultify ourselves by playing safe all the time.'[21] Winner's identification of a generation gap opening up between a younger cohort of pop-friendly film-makers and an older group resistant to its charms also reverberates in Richard Lester's comments on his own identifications and allegiances as a director. 'I prefer the social attitudes of the young people to the disapproval of their parents . . . you have to take sides somewhere so I've chosen the side which I have most sympathy for.'[22]

Meanwhile, more seasoned directors brought up through the British studio system continued to prosper in the 1960s. Among the highest-profile examples of this lineage are the Oscar-winners Lean and Carol Reed, as well as other senior figures such as Anthony Asquith and former Rank and ABPC contract directors Roy Baker, Ken Annakin, Ralph Thomas, J. Lee Thompson and Michael Anderson. Almost without exception, these individuals graduated from modest parochial productions into bigger internationalised films, usually filmed in widescreen colour. Basil Dearden, for instance, had begun the decade with the black-and-white comedy *The League of Gentlemen* (1960) and 'social problem' film *Victim* (1961) before progressing to the lavish international-ism of *Woman of Straw* (1964), *Masquerade* (1965) and *Khartoum* (1966). The directors of the James Bond films – Terence Young, Guy Hamilton and Lewis Gilbert – perhaps best exemplified the flourishing of British post-war journeymen in the new big-budget world of the 1960s.[23] Terence Young's work in international co-production in the 1950s for Irving Allen and Albert 'Cubby' Broccoli's Warwick Films made him the natural choice to direct the first Bond film, *Dr No* (1962) for Broccoli and Saltzman's newly formed company Eon. As far as Young was concerned, the production's timing was crucial to its success, arriving 'not only in the right year but the right week of the right month of the right year' just as audiences 'were getting tired of the realistic school, the kitchen sinks and all those abortions. When I made *Dr No* I was conscious of this. I was trying to make a picture in the mood of the vintage period of the thirties cinema.' [24] Young's subsequent Bond films also benefitted from this combination of old-fashioned panache infused with the more modern elements provided by casting, music, design and editing, as did Guy Hamilton's *Goldfinger* (1964) and Lewis Gilbert's *You Only Live Twice* (1967).[25] Gilbert's career perhaps demonstrated best of all how certain canny established film-makers were able to keep pace with the changing times. In the 1950s, he had excelled in the black-and-white British war film, directing box-office hits such as *The Sea Shall Not Have Them* (1954), *Reach for the Sky* (1956) and *Carve Her Name with Pride* (1958) but in the 1960s, he successfully changed tack, shifting to colour, and to permissive rather than restrained heroes, not only James Bond but also Michael Caine as *Alfie* (1966). Based on Bill Naughton's play about a Cockney Casanova, *Alfie* was not only daring in its content but also technically up to date, using hidden cameras and radio mikes for its location filming, and was formally bold in its use of direct address to camera by the lead character.[26]

Interestingly, it was also to Naughton that the veteran film-making team of the Boulting brothers turned when they wanted to show they were keeping pace with the times, adapting his northern marital comedy 'All in Good Time' as *The Family Way* (1966). John Boulting offered a thoughtful consideration of the position of more seasoned film-makers, like himself, in the 1960s and how they might best respond to changing audience tastes:

> What the public wants next week we cannot say, and our friends in Wardour Street can only know what it went for yesterday and the day before that. So we rely upon our own instincts and inclinations [...] Our awareness of the world around us, of the trends and tendencies to change, is the factor that determines our choice of subject and its treatment. But this is not something that happens consciously. We are part of the changing world and therefore ourselves changing. All the time.[27]

While the Boultings chose to adapt, other directors of a similar vintage prospered with more traditional modes of practice. Frank Launder and Sidney Gilliat maintained a presence during the 1960s mainly through their intermittent *St Trinian's* films – the 1966 effort *The Great St Trinian's Train Robbery* managing to become one of the biggest box-office successes of its year in spite of the joke wearing quite thin by that point. Brothers Ralph and Gerald Thomas continued to helm the highly successful *Doctor* and *Carry On* comedy series respectively throughout the 1960s, although Ralph Thomas interspersed his output with more diverse directorial assignments including *No Love for Johnnie* (1961) and *The High Bright Sun* (1964). By contrast, Gerald's occasional forays beyond *Carry On* stuck to very similar generic territory and his efficient niche professionalism made him one of the decade's most prolific directors, averaging two films a year.

Other established directors similarly developed and honed generic specialisms, as with Terence Fisher, John Gilling, Freddie Francis and Don Chaffey's work predominantly in horror and fantasy. Fisher argued for the cinema as a site of timeless elemental entertainment: 'the moment you put out the light, man reverts to the primitive. What is the cinema? It's the place where the lights are put out', going 'for very basic things in drama. Fire is a pictorially very exciting thing, isn't it?'[28] Meanwhile, directors such as Montgomery Tully and Robert Hartford-Davis successfully ploughed their own furrows of second feature and exploitation production, generally unheralded like their screenwriting colleagues in those sectors although a piece by 'Arkadin' in *Sight and Sound* in 1962 highlighted the work of Robert Day, John Moxey, Sidney Hayers, and Vernon Sewell as 'very enjoyable, full of imaginative touches, and well out of the British second-feature rut; but of course nobody except *The Monthly Film Bulletin* bothered to write about them'.[29] But this arena of production would contract over the course of the decade, forcing its exponents – like many others in the film industry of the 1960s – to adapt or die.

SMALL SCREEN OR SWINGING CAPITAL: NEW ROUTES INTO DIRECTING

Among the younger emergent directors of the 1960s, a previous career in television proved an effective route into cinema. Major newcomers such as John Schlesinger and Ken Russell had first built their directorial reputations in BBC arts programming and while making his debut feature *A Kind of Loving* (1962), Schlesinger advocated the vocational grounding it offered him, arguing that 'you could learn far more working on say *Tonight* or *Monitor* where you are handling film and people in all sorts of situations. It is a far better training than being a teaboy or an assistant.'[30] Other beneficiaries of the opportunities offered by the BBC, in drama as well as documentary, included Ken Loach, Jack Gold, Kevin Billington, Waris Hussein and Anthony Page, all of whom were identified by *Sight and Sound* in 1968 as rising stars representative of British cinema's 'next renascence'.[31]

Commercial television proved an equally important source of directorial talent as public-service broadcasting, nurturing Richard Lester, Joe McGrath (the 'new Dick Lester' according to *Showtime* in 1967), and Peter Collinson among others.[32] Collinson, who became one of the most talked-about young directors of the late 1960s, had directed episodes of numerous popular ATV series, including *The Plane Makers* (1963–5) and its sequel *The Power Game* (1965–9), before making his film debut with the claustrophobic thriller *The Penthouse* (1967). He went on to enjoy a creative purple patch in the late 1960s, with the box-office success of his Nell Dunn adaptation *Up the Junction* (1968), followed by the Charles Wood-scripted Cannes entry *The Long Day's Dying* (1968), and the ingenious heist film, *The Italian Job* (1969). Collinson was a typical sixties success story, going from an orphanage childhood to a Rolls Royce and a 'five-picture contract with Paramount', which Collinson felt 'sums things up in a way: I came from nowhere – and I might be going somewhere...'[33]

Equally vital to the establishment of commercial TV in the UK were Canadian directors Ted Kotcheff and Silvio Narizzano, brought over in the 1950s, the latter recalled, because 'the only experienced people, of course, were at the BBC, and they [ITV] had a kind of agreement not to raid them, and so they had scouts out searching around for likely prospects'.[34] They also moved into cinema, with Narizzano's hugely successful feature *Georgy Girl* (1966) acting as the 'harbinger of a new television-bred wave of directors'.[35] This included the influence of television advertising on film-making, with directors like Narizzano feeling equally at home in the commercial world, and enjoying 'the problem of telling the story about a product or whatever the message was that had to be conveyed into something like thirty seconds'.[36] Kotcheff, who directed *Tiara Tahiti* (1962), *Life at the Top* (1965) and *Two Gentlemen Sharing* (1969) in between his television work, also felt that as an outsider he could offer fresh insights into its society: 'in a very detached way you can see what's funny, idiosyncratic, eccentric, interesting about the way a country and its people live in a way they can't do themselves, because they're not conscious of these things.'[37]

The same kind of exilic insight is often attributed to Joseph Losey, better able to see the workings of the British class system through not being implicated in it from birth, and might also be applied to fellow blacklist fugitive Cy Endfield, US expats Richard Lester and Stanley Kubrick, and perhaps Karel Reisz and Peter Medak too, who had arrived as teenage refugees from Czechoslovakia and Hungary respectively.[38] It also resonates within the British-based work of a host of other directors who came to make films in Britain as the country became a global production hub: Hollywood directors Sidney Lumet, Martin Ritt, Stanley Donen, Otto Preminger, Fred Zinnemann and Robert Aldrich, and European auteurs Roman Polanski, François Truffaut, Michelangelo

Antonioni, Jean-Luc Godard, and Jerzy Skolimowski. Each deepened and enriched British cinema's growing cosmopolitanism while offering new and surprising takes on elements of British society, encompassing its public affairs and private obsessions, the ancestral past and swinging present.

The influx of overseas investment, and a thirst for innovative projects that would most effectively monetise the buzz of 'swinging London', enabled diverse new talents to be entrusted with surprisingly large budgets, regardless of whether they had extensive experience in film-making. Perhaps still flush from the record-breaking success of *The Sound of Music* (1965), 20th Century Fox enabled former pop star Mike Sarne, who had hitherto directed some short films, to make his elaborate 'swinging London' fantasia *Joanna* (1968) and also supported photographer Robert Freeman's debut feature *The Touchables* (1968), described (rather ominously) by the director as not 'a story too much, more an atmosphere or a vague modern environment'.[39] According to Sarne, both films were greenlit by Fox's young executive Richard Zanuck in the most impromptu of circumstances: 'all of this happened on a street corner, outside Zanuck's hotel, in a matter of seconds. Zanuck just looked at me, looked at Bob, and said, "I'm going to give each of you a million to do your pictures" and that was that.'[40]

This was the period in which Hollywood studio investment in British production reached its peak. Universal took a chance on stars better known for their acting or singing talents, supporting the directorial debuts (both idiosyncratic male midlife-crisis films and both one-offs as it turned out) of Albert Finney with *Charlie Bubbles* (1967) and Anthony Newley with *Can Hieronymus Merkin Ever Forget Mercy Humppe and Find True Happiness?* (1969). Warner Brothers was persuaded to let first-time directing team Donald Cammell and Nicolas Roeg make *Performance* (1970) but would subsequently regret their decision, demand re-edits and delay release for several years. Paramount financed 25-year-old film-maker David Hart, with only one featurette and some amateur films under his belt, to make the feature *Sleep Is Lovely* (a.k.a. *The Other People* or *I Love You, I Hate You*), completed in 1968 but never shown.[41]

However, amidst the allocation of funds to directors of more outlandish or self-consciously modish projects, there was also a return to classicism in the work of some of the new entrants into British cinema towards the very end of the decade. Editor-turned-director Anthony Harvey got himself noticed with his confrontational two-hander *Dutchman* (1966), made in six days on a single set for $60,000, but then moved into a more sober style of period drama for Avco–Embassy's *The Lion in Winter* (1968), starring Katharine Hepburn and Peter O'Toole, receiving an Oscar nomination for Best Director as well as the Director's Guild of America's Director of the Year award for 1968 (despite not being a member at the time). Harvey was characterised in the film's publicity material as a director whose 'preoccupation tends to be more with people rather than with visual tricks. He also has a great respect for his actors at all times', and he himself stated that he valued 'austerity' and 'professionalism' in film-making: 'it is not enough to throw a lot of beautiful images on the screen and make it up as you go along.'[42] With *The Lion in Winter* and Kevin Billington's contemporaneous feature debut *Interlude* (1968), a *Brief Encounter*-esque modern romance between a married symphony conductor and a young reporter, critic David Robinson detected a new-found 'strong preference for the "well-made film" in contrast to the informality of construction and writing until recently in vogue'.[43] Even Ken Russell's latent excess was still kept in check by the strictures of literary fidelity on *Women in Love* (1969), awaiting its fuller expression in the subsequent decade.

But in spite of a late return to classicism, the extent to which practices and personnel within British film direction had changed over the course of the 1960s was incontrovertible. How far things had been transformed is notable from a comparison between *Sight and Sound*'s 1958 audit of British film directors and the situation in 1968, the peak year of US investment in British production.[44] Many of the directors in the original list had died, retired, or left film-making for other fields by then, while those still working had shifted gear dramatically and were now engaged in zeitgeist-infused projects such as Guy Green's unsettling fantasy *The Magus* (1968), the Boulting brothers' study of psychopathy *Twisted Nerve* (1968), or Basil Dearden's hip heist film, *Only When I Larf* (1968), co-produced by sixties luminaries Len Deighton and Brian Duffy.[45] Clive Donner, the youngest director in the 1958 list, had become an established figure by the late 1960s, while Joseph Losey had likewise moved on from the taut black and white of *The Criminal* (1960) to the eccentricities of his lavish colour vehicle for Richard Burton and Elizabeth Taylor's talents, *Boom!* (1968). Meanwhile the directors associated with the British New Wave, who had debuted between 1959 and 1963, had also moved on significantly from their social-realist origins: Tony Richardson to *Charge of the Light Brigade* (1968), Karel Reisz to *Isadora* (1968), Lindsay Anderson to *If ....* (1968), while John Schlesinger was working towards his first US film, *Midnight Cowboy* (1969), which would later win the Best Picture Oscar and the newly created British Film Academy award for Best Director.[46] Using the critical lens of auteurism, *Films and Filming*'s Gordon Gow was able to intuit 'a basic similarity between Joe Buck, the *Midnight Cowboy* of John Schlesinger's latest film, and the lost little boy who stood crying on Waterloo Station in *Terminus*, a documentary Schlesinger made in 1960' but this interpretation of Schlesinger's work had to traverse the vast stylistic and thematic distances opened up during the 1960s, navigated not only by Schlesinger but by most of his sixties contemporaries.[47]

'MAN OF THE MOMENT': CLIVE DONNER (1926–2010)

In 1966 American critic Charles Champlin hailed Clive Donner as 'one of the best and most consistently exciting of a very exciting generation of film-makers who have emerged in Britain in the last decade or so', carving out a niche for himself in his exploration of 'the curious, kooky, alienated, talky, midway times we live in' with their 'swift shifting and questioning of values'.[48] Donner would be consistently identified with the prevailing mood of the times, both to his benefit and detriment, and, like his peer Richard Lester, would become a director firmly associated with 'inventive, forward-looking' sixties film-making in spite of an industry background that was, as Gordon Gow noted, 'fairly trad'.[49]

Donner started out as a teenage apprentice in the cutting rooms of Denham and Pinewood (with a break for wartime army service) before developing a distinguished career as an editor of notable British films of the 1950s including *Scrooge* (1951), *Genevieve* (1953) and *I Am a Camera* (1955).[50] On the strength of this, he was given a chance to direct by the Rank Organisation, with his debut feature, the realist thriller *The Secret Place* (1957), marking him out as 'a man to watch for'.[51] Donner was thoroughly embedded in the mixed production economy of the period and alongside directing a final feature for Rank, *Heart of a Child* (1958), and two well-handled hour-long Edgar Wallace mysteries, *Marriage of Convenience* (1960) and *The Sinister Man* (1961), he also directed episodes of ITC TV series *Danger Man* and *Sir Francis Drake* and a documentary series on India, *The Mighty and the Mystical*, for Granada in the early 1960s.[52] This was further interspersed with extensive work for the advertising agency J. Walter Thompson on television commercials, including successful campaigns for Ribena and Aero. Donner found directing commercials 'both relaxing and stimulating', and the work acted 'like five-finger exercises' in maintaining and honing his skills.[53] He argued that directing an advert 'should be thought out with as much attention to detail as is normally given to the script of a full-length feature film', and advocated for the form's cultural significance:

> Better commercials that do not insult the viewer or further help to lower standards of taste are worth a special effort. The satisfaction of doing that is worth the amount of effort and energy that any piece of film-making demands if it is to be done well.[54]

This experience would prove particularly useful for his next feature, *Some People* (1962), which came about as an offshoot of this work in advertising. James M. Archibald, director in charge of film and television at J. Walter Thompson, and former senior employee at Rank, had been approached to make a promotional documentary encouraging recruitment to the Duke of Edinburgh's Award Scheme. Archibald engaged Donner to work on it and they then undertook extensive market research among a range of different teenage communities across the country, talking to 'approximately 300 boys and girls', and through this process came to the conclusion that the 'soft sell' of a narrative feature film (with full theatrical distribution) would work far better than something in more instructional mode.[55] Obvious proselytising for the scheme would be avoided, taking into account that among contemporary youth 'there exists a deep-rooted suspicion against attempts to impose organisation on them'.[56] Originally titled 'Johnnie', reflecting its focus on the central character played by Ray Brooks, the film tracks this young man and his mates as they become involved in a youth club offering the scheme among its activities. It was important to its makers that the characters came first, rather than the scheme: 'If this were primarily a film about the Award scheme [...] then any character that dropped out half way through would cease to be of interest to us. But this film isn't that – it is a story about Johnnie, mainly, and Bill and Bert and Terry and Anne' (and in order to build the camaraderie of its group of friends, Donner arranged for extensive rehearsal and preparation time ahead of shooting to inculcate the right sense of unforced familiarity).[57] As *Television Mail* recounted, 'the National Film Finance Corporation (which usually provides about 30 per cent of a film's cost) took the unusual step of completely financing the project', with all profits to be ploughed back into the Award Scheme.[58]

Given its difficult brief, it was small wonder that V. F. Perkins had expected 'a monstrous mating of *Reach for the Sky* and *The Young Ones*', but instead was very pleasantly surprised by an 'intelligent, honest and enjoyable picture' which had 'a less self-conscious, and therefore more genuine, freedom than any of the films of the so-called British new wave'.[59] Perkins admired 'Donner's refusal to force the pace, to make the connections too obvious', avoiding overemphasis or hysteria in favour of a more gently observational approach to depicting teenage life.[60] This assessment was shared by *The Daily Cinema*, which also praised how *Some People* 'skilfully avoids any preaching or patronising. A genuine effort is made to understand the winkle-picker-and-leather-jacket set and they're presented, not as monsters and mugs, but roundly believable people.'[61] The unusual choice of Bristol as the setting bucked the prevailing New Wave trend, reminding the film industry that 'real people exist in all parts of England and are not just a phenomenon observable in cities to the north of Birmingham.'[62] The decision to make the film in colour was also unusual for its genre and, according to Donner, 'partly done for the entertainment value, but also because to me the convention that reality is better in black and white is just a convention, and there's no reason why you shouldn't adopt another one.'[63]

Donner returned to black and white with *The Caretaker* (1963), which although very different in subject and tone from its predecessor would be equally unorthodox in its financing methods. But whereas *Some People* had been NFFC-funded in service of a public good, *The Caretaker* would draw on individual subscriptions – from Richard Burton, Elizabeth Taylor, Noel Coward, Peter Hall, Leslie Caron, Harry Saltzman and Peter Sellers, amongst others – to raise the necessary £30,000 to cover costs, making it 'historically the first British feature film capitalised to the full extent by private individuals alone'.[64] Harold Pinter's original play was not opened out but tightly compressed for the purposes of filming, a sense of claustrophobia further underlined by filming taking place in the cramped, cluttered rooms of a real house in Hackney.[65] Donner argued that the lengthy confessional speech by Aston (Robert Shaw) was just 'as cinematic as a herd of buffaloes roaming across the plain. [. . .] A sequence like that where one man talks non-stop for, I think it's about eight or nine minutes altogether, the whole speech, to me is cinematic. Words are cinematic.'[66] Its high-profile premiere at the Edinburgh Film Festival, and the awarding of a Silver Bear at the Berlin Film Festival, helped assure subsequent British and international distribution for the film. Back in 1959, Donner had spoken up in *Sight and Sound* in favour of a wider range of films being made possible within the British film industry: 'If film makers are given the opportunity to demonstrate their faith that audiences are interested in unusual subjects, then they will be freed from the need to create films to a narrow, obsolete and evidently unprofitable pattern.'[67] Enabled by producer Michael Birkett and various illustrious investors, he had been able to follow through on this objective, and hoped to set a precedent for other film-makers, who 'could successfully adopt the methods we used to do *The Caretaker*'.[68]

While *The Caretaker* was moving towards distribution, Donner had begun work on *Nothing but the Best* (1964), financed along more orthodox lines courtesy of Anglo-Amalgamated. Working with producer David Deutsch and writer Frederic Raphael, Donner crafted a film he felt was poised between the categories of 'thriller', 'serious social study' and 'comedy-noir', centred on a character 'caught up in an ever-increasing cyclone of his own feverishly insatiable immorality'.[69] As Alexander Walker suggests, the film continually plays visually with the trustworthiness of images:

> The close-up opening shot of a stately home is revealed by the camera pulling back to be simply a picture on a cheap biscuit-tin; and the 'mood' sequence of the hero and his girl apparently dancing the night away in some plush club, like those that were opening almost monthly in London, adjusts its focus to let us discover that they are actually moving to the music of a car radio on a dilapidated old Thames barge.[70]

Appearing in London cinemas in 1964 around the same time as *The Caretaker* (and during the West End run of a modern play he also directed, *The Formation Dancers*), *Nothing but the Best* consolidated Donner's status as 'a "key" British director' and 'man of the moment', according to *The Guardian*'s M. G. McNay.[71] McNay also suggested, slightly prophetically, that '"swinging" is a good word for a lot of Donner's work'.[72] The director would later describe 'the notion of swinging London' as 'anathema' to him, but he was already beginning to be associated with its emergence.[73] His next film, *What's New Pussycat?* (1965), may have been set in swinging Paris rather than London, but it still participated in what the director felt was the new transnational lingua franca of permissiveness: 'this, without being idiotic about it, is a mod film. It's a film about people who, wherever they are in Europe, have come under the cultural influence of the mid-1960s.'[74] Its 'intensely decorative, erotic' art-nouveau aesthetic, carried through from its Parisian interiors and exteriors and certain costumes to Richard Williams's ornate credits and intertitles, suggested the 'reaction against restriction' of all kinds in the high 1960s, including sexual.[75] The film found some high-profile critical friends. Andrew Sarris declared it 'the best picture of the year thus far' in the *Village Voice*, finding 'new nuances in the direction' each time he watched it.[76] The Cinémathèque Française's Henri Langlois, was head of the jury which awarded *What's New Pussycat?* the prestigious 'Prix Jean-George Auriol – Paul Gibson', and Donner wrote him a personal letter of thanks, delighted that 'a film made in Paris, about Paris, yet directed by an Englishman should be taken so well'.[77] These kinds of accolades spoke of the nascent cult following Donner was developing among cineastes, but the film was far from being a minority taste and came fifth on *Variety*'s list of 'Big rental pictures of 1965'.[78]

Following another neurotic rom-com, *Luv* (1967), this time set and filmed in the US as well as financed by American money, Donner's third comedy in swinging mode, *Here We Go Round the Mulberry Bush* (1968), returned him to a very British setting – Stevenage new town – and to the teenage milieu he had previously explored in *Some People* but now enmeshed within sixties sexual liberation. The film follows the misadventures of another young male protagonist, A-Level student Jamie (Barry Evans), as he tries to lose his virginity and understand the brave new world of adult relationships. Described by one critic as 'surface-light but sad deep down', Donner claimed – perhaps slightly disingenuously – that his film was 'of high moral standing' and queried rather than celebrated teenage promiscuity.[79] However, BBFC's John Trevelyan expressed his doubts about this in correspondence with the director:

> I am afraid that I cannot see in it clearly the social purpose that you claimed that your film would have [. . .] It is true that Jamie reacts against the over-sexed girls whom he encounters but this is mixed up with

some crazy comedy, and I have the feeling that the point may not come through quite clearly.[80]

Kine Weekly described *Here We Go Round the Mulberry Bush* as typical of 'a Clive Donner film, full of tricks and twists and ideas, using colour strangely and motion jerkily to represent interpolated dream sequences'.[81] If its look was up-to-the-minute, so too was its soundtrack provided primarily by Steve Winwood's newly formed band Traffic. The director was very aware of the film's contemporaneity ('very much a film of the moment – a film that is trying to say something and capture something about "now" [. . .] in its outlook, in its music, in its fashion') being a core part of its appeal and wrote to United Artists' Arnold Picker to request a rapid release 'to somehow capitalise on all this as soon as possible and to certainly prevent holding it over for a long period during which some of these few points might change'.[82] It was launched with a star-studded premiere attended by sixties celebrities Paul McCartney, Michael Caine, Patti Boyd, the Animals, the Who, Manfred Mann, and the members of Traffic, but more sedate mature figures such as Valerie Singleton, Alan Whicker and Vera Lynn were also in attendance, suggesting a rather broader appeal for the film than its primary teenage market.[83]

Donner's final feature of the 1960s marked quite a departure from his preceding work, indicating his desire 'to have a break from modern, with-it movies' and avoid 'the danger of being typed'.[84] The historical biopic *Alfred the Great* (1969) presented an opportunity to work in period and on an epic scale courtesy of MGM, still at that stage investing in big-budget runaway production prior to its impending contraction.[85] But as its advance publicity announced, the film would be 'distinguished by a modern approach to historical characters'; an intent also signalled by the casting of David Hemmings as the legendary English monarch and Michael York as his Viking antagonist Guthrum.[86] The latter was described by Donner as 'not unlike that of some of today's outspoken, uninhibited young men' whereas Alfred himself, the 'rebel king' of twenty-two, was 'a mixed-up young man, to use modern parlance', suggesting this was actually another of Donner's stories of male maturation, albeit in historical dress, and emphasising the contemporary relevance of this ninth-century story, which Donner himself suggested could 'be viewed in terms of current circumstances and events'.[87] This did not wash with film critic Margaret Hinxman who shrewdly suggested that Alfred 'resembles anyone today as much as the buns he apocryphally burnt (not shown here) resemble a packaged cake mix.'[88] She identified the film's underlying problem as one of split personality in its aims – 'it wants to have it both ways: to be admired for its narrow integrity and loved for its rousing popular appeal' – a situation in part created by a confused marketing campaign, unsure whether to sell the film as a 'boy's own' heritage blockbuster, as suggested by its royal gala performance to benefit the Scouting Association, educational tie-ins, associated children's books and model-making kits, or as a dark investigation into a young man's psychological tensions.[89]

Donner's preference was for the latter and he declared himself 'absolutely horrified to discover a totally disastrous advertising campaign' being used by MGM to promote the film, and tried to counter it with screenings to students who showed 'a hostility to anything smacking of establishment thinking', who he felt would enjoy the film more.[90] There was some defence of *Alfred the Great* from *Movie* critic Ian Cameron who felt the film was accomplished and 'uniquely good, too, in its use of the weather as a dramatic element'.[91] Fledgling director Peter Bogdanovich wrote Donner an appreciative letter, quotations from which were then used in press advertising to try to re-orientate audience perspectives towards the film: '[. . .] deserves to be an out-and-out award-winning blockbuster. The characters live and breathe with a rare immediacy. A beautiful almost classical movement, filmed without one anachronistic shot. The best directed historical film I've seen in years.'[92] But the initial campaign, described in *Variety* as 'unfortunately over-centred on swinging sword and other graphic depictions of Anglo-Saxon warfare' and 'geared to attracting a family type of roadshow audience' with 'broad action selling', had made its mark, with the result that *Alfred the Great* was generally judged a 'stilted pageant'.[93]

Clive Donner ended the 1960s at something of a career hiatus, although this appears to have been a strategic choice. He wrote to a friend in November 1969:

> I am now sitting quietly in London, reading a great deal, thinking a great deal and generally having a winter hibernation and lying fallow. I don't expect to be in production before next summer, and as yet I have made no final decision as to what it will be. Both United Artists and MGM are very willing to make deals with me [. . . But] for the past 8 or 9 years, I have gone continuously from picture, overlapping scripts, and I think this is a good time to take a breather.[94]

Although he 'hope[d] in the New Year to come out into the world', Donner also acknowledged the film business was in a far less healthy state than just a year before, and his retreat from film-making lasted longer than he originally seemed to have planned.[95] He diversified into theatre, directing a production of *Twelfth Night* at the Nottingham Playhouse in early 1970, while a full-page advertisement in *Television Mail* announced in the autumn of 1970, 'Clive Donner joins Film Contracts', indicating a return to directing commercials.[96] Television directing was another outlet for his talents. But while there would be numerous subsequent achievements, Donner never quite recovered the status of 'man of the moment' beyond the 1960s, when his expressive style and his ease with dealing with the age's twinned fascinations – youth and sex – made him one of the decade's key directors.

NOTES

1. Ian Cameron, 'Films, directors and critics', *Movie*, no. 2, September 1962, p. 5.
2. V. F. Perkins, 'The British cinema', *Movie*, no. 1, June 1962, p. 3.
3. Ibid., p. 4.
4. It was later compared to Don Siegel's 'less respected' war film *Hell Is for Heroes* (1962) and found wanting in vigour and style. Cameron, 'Films, directors and critics', p. 7. When Lean's Oscar-winning epic *Lawrence of Arabia* (1962) was released not long after the magazine's launch, Philip French recalled how its editorial board 'huffily announced they were off to see a truly serious film in the NFT's first Howard Hawks season'. Philip French, 'Not just desert', *Observer*, 28 May 1989, p. 44.
5. Perkins, 'The British cinema', p. 5.
6. Ibid., p. 3.
7. Peter Hutchings, 'The histogram and the list: the director in British film criticism', *Journal of Popular British Cinema*, no. 4, 2001, p. 31. Charles Barr, 'Introduction: amnesia and schizophrenia', in Barr (ed.), *All Our Yesterdays: 90 Years of British Cinema* (London: BFI, 1986), p. 4.
8. Perkins, 'The British cinema', p. 9.
9. See Neil Sinyard, *Jack Clayton* (Manchester: Manchester University Press, 2000), and also the prestigious DVD and Blu Ray editions of the film from BFI and Criterion. The British Film Makers series in which Sinyard's book appeared has also offered reappraisals of the work of Lean, Richardson, Fisher, and other British directors working in the period. The work of Dearden and Relph was examined in detail in Alan Burton, Tim O'Sullivan, and Paul Wells (eds), *Liberal Directions: Basil Dearden and Post-war British Film Culture* (Trowbridge: Flicks Books, 1997) and Alan Burton and Tim O'Sullivan, *The Cinema of Basil Dearden and Michael Relph* (Edinburgh: Edinburgh University Press, 2009). B. F. Taylor, *The British New Wave: A Certain Tendency?* (Manchester: Manchester University Press, 2006) takes the critical apparatus of the *Movie* critics and deftly uses it to argue for the stylistic complexity of the cycle of films they had originally dismissed.
10. Richard Lester was interviewed twice, in issue no. 14 (Autumn 1965) and issue no. 16 (Winter 1968/69), and Clive Donner profiled in issue no. 3 (October 1962) and interviewed in issue no. 14 alongside Lester. O. O. Green, 'Michael Powell', *Movie*, no. 14 (Autumn 1965), pp. 17–20. A dialectical debate on the merits of Lindsay Anderson's *This Sporting Life* (1963) was also set up in its pages: Gavin Millar, 'This Sporting Life', *Movie*, no. 7 (Spring 1963), p. 33, and Anon., 'Against *This Sporting Life*', *Movie*, no. 10 (June 1963), pp. 21–2.
11. Penelope Houston, 'Keeping up with the Antonionis', *Sight and Sound*, vol. 33, no. 4, Autumn 1964, pp. 163–8. One important distinction between them initially was *Sight and Sound*'s scepticism about *Cahiers*-style auteurism (expressed in Richard Roud, 'The French line', *Sight and Sound*, vol. 29, no. 4, Autumn 1960, pp. 166–71) while *Movie* embraced their methods, but their approach towards assessing directorial achievement converged as the decade progressed.
12. Val Guest, 'British films were never bad', *Films and Filming*, October 1960, p. 34.
13. Raymond Durgnat, 'Dearden and Relph: two on a tandem', *Films and Filming*, July 1966, pp. 26–7.

14. See Robert Shail, *Tony Richardson* (Manchester: Manchester University Press, 2012), p. 52.
15. *A Taste of Honey* pressbook, BFI Library, David Lean, 'The film director', in Oswald Blakeston (ed.), *Working for the Films* (London: Focal, 1947), p. 36.
16. Joseph Losey, 'The monkey on my back', *Films and Filming*, October 1963, p. 11.
17. Quoted in 'The cost of independence: an enquiry', *Sight and Sound*, vol. 30, no. 3, Summer 1961, p. 112, which also included comments from Tony Richardson and Bryan Forbes amongst others. Further examples of discussions on how to reinvigorate British film and bring in new personnel around this time include: 'How to get into films', *Films and Filming*, May 1961, pp. 7–9, 37–8, with comments from Michael Balcon, the Boulting brothers, Leslie Norman, and Peter Sellers; *Journal of the Society of Film and Television Arts* special issue on 'the individual approach in film and television', no. 7, Spring 1962; 'How to get into films by those who have done it', *Films and Filming*, July 1962, pp. 11–14, with input from Forbes again and fellow directors Karel Reisz, John Schlesinger, Don Sharp, and Peter Yates. Problem with restrictive practices from the ACTT around new talent getting union accreditation, minimum crewing requirements, and the lack of opportunities for financial support and distribution of lower-budget films, of the kind emergent directors might hone their skills on, were all identified as the primary problems in developing a new talent base. There was also a robust exchange of views between Karel Reisz and the editor of *Films and Filming* on the subject of the BFI's experimental film fund (of which he had been a beneficiary and was now on the committee for dispensing), with Reisz defending its short film output as good value for money 'achieved for less than it costs to make one cheap British second feature. To talk of waste in these circumstances becomes a little churlish.' The editor countered, 'Is money spent on haphazard experiment more useful than money spent on planned study, training and practical experience?' 'Karel Reisz and the experimenters', *Films and Filming*, December 1961, p. 41.
18. Bill Edwards, 'Production', *Kine Weekly*, 24 March 1960, p. 16. Although, as the Boulting brothers quipped, 'one Reisz does not make a Renaissance!' In 'How to get into films', *Films and Filming*, May 1961, p. 8. Woodfall also gave chances later in the decade to Anthony Page, on *Inadmissible Evidence* (1968), and to Ken Loach, on *Kes* (1969). Desmond Davis would write thoughtfully about the challenges of trying to build a career and remain prolific while also trying to maintain control over his output: 'It takes a director one year to make a film, so how many chances have you in life of making films? And that year is a grinding one of working non-stop and tremendously long hours. And if you can keep up one film a year that you want to do, you're lucky. Of course if you do commercial films you make more films and more money, because you can come in a few weeks before shooting when most things are cast, scripted and organised, dive onto the floor for an average of ten weeks, and kiss it goodbye when it hits the cutting rooms. But you can't do that with a film if you try to make it one that is individual. You must start it with the writer and end it when you hand over the final print from the laboratory, and that takes a year of your life if it's a fairly medium budget.' Quoted in Robin Bean, 'Passage of love', *Films and Filming*, September 1965, p. 46.
19. Winner in Robin Bean, 'The importance of being what's 'isname?', *Films and Filming*, February 1968, pp. 9–10.
20. Ibid., p. 6. There was another rather interesting suggestion of a British documentary movement gerontocracy in the Boulting brothers' comments that 'Grierson's young crusaders stormed the citadel a very long time ago. Now, grizzled veterans, they sit in the centre of the banqueting hall, feeding off their own carcasses, and

like all the aged, inclined to talk to themselves.' The Boulting brothers in 'How to get into films', *Films and Filming*, May 1961, p. 8.
21. Deutsch in John Champ, 'Production', *Kine Weekly*, 15 February 1962, p. 16.
22. Lester in Philip French, 'Richard Lester', *Movie*, no. 14 (Autumn 1965), p. 9.
23. Although, as Penelope Houston suggested, 'one can think of few films in which the director's contribution seems so subordinate to a total production strategy'. Penelope Houston, '007', *Sight and Sound*, Winter 1964, p. 16. However, working for Harry Saltzman on a non-Bond production, *Battle of Britain* (1969), Guy Hamilton seems to have directed in a manner commensurate with auteurist understandings of the profession: 'he had, of necessity, to be extremely subjective in his attitude to directing the picture. With five units to control, with all the facets of the story to polish and keep sharp, he was always aware during the making of the film that his was the only will that had to come through in the telling of such a remarkable story.' 'The director: Guy Hamilton' in *Battle of Britain* pressbook, Bill Douglas Cinema Museum collection.
24. John Francis Lane, 'Young romantic', *Films and Filming*, February 1967, p. 58.
25. Both were to return to the Bond series in subsequent decades.
26. Derek Todd, 'Alfie – strictly for the birds', *Kine Weekly*, 1 July 1965, p. 16. As well as being a major international box-office hit, *Alfie* also went on to win the jury prize at Cannes.
27. John Boulting in 'The individual approach: film', *Journal of the Society of Film and Television Arts (the individual approach in film and television)*, no. 7, Spring 1962, p. 5.
28. Terence Fisher, 'Horror is my business', *Films and Filming*, July 1964, pp. 7–8. Fisher also noted how 'Continental film critics acknowledge the English as the world experts in horror. It's because we're timid. Shyness breeds shadows and shadows breed vampires.' (p. 7). For more on Fisher's pre-eminence in Hammer horror, see Peter Hutchings, *Terence Fisher* (Manchester: Manchester University Press, 2002). Lower-budget horror production also offered valuable opportunities for younger directors such as Michael Reeves: Benjamin Halligan, *Michael Reeves* (Manchester: Manchester University Press, 2003) provides a good account of his sadly truncated career.
29. 'Arkadin', 'Film clips', *Sight and Sound*, Summer 1962, p. 140. See Steve Chibnall and Brian McFarlane, *The British B Film* (London: BFI Palgrave, 2009) for more on this production sector.
30. Schlesinger in John Champ, 'Production', *Kine Weekly*, 7 December 1961, p. 16.
31. David Robinson, 'Case histories of the next renascence', *Sight and Sound*, vol. 37, no. 1, Winter 1968, pp. 36–40. Peter Watkins, who had moved from ambitious award-winning amateur film to ground-breaking dramatised history for the BBC with *Culloden* (1964), was another remarkable entrant into cinema via the television route. His terrifying post-nuclear holocaust docudrama *The War Game* (1965) ended up being shown theatrically after its banning from television, but his first film intended for cinema, *Privilege* (1967), met with critical bafflement; a young director biting the pop hand from which he was feeding.
32. 'Casino Royale . . . and the stars you don't see', *Showtime*, June 1967, p. 20.
33. Derek Todd, 'Ex-orphanage kid now of Paramount importance', *Kine Weekly*, 9 September 1967, p. 14. Collinson featured frequently in popular film magazines, prime representative of a new generation of film-making talent. See for instance 'All change! Now meet the man who changed it . . .' *Showtime*, December 1967, p. 15 and 'From panto horse to top director', *ABC Film Review*, February 1968, p. 4.

34. David Austen, 'Blue', *Films and Filming*, August 1968, p. 6. Sidney J. Furie, another important Canadian director working in Britain at this time, was not a television émigré.
35. 'Arkadin', 'Film clips', *Sight and Sound*, vol. 36, no. 2, Spring 1967, p. 99. Another US-television veteran who then made an impact in 1960s British cinema was David Greene, a British actor who had enjoyed substantial success directing US television but returned to the UK to build a feature-film career, starting with the sinister *The Shuttered Room* (1967). See Rod Cooper, 'David Greene and the changing scene', *Kine Weekly*, 3 May 1968, p. 12. Raymond Durgnat judged him 'a formidable stylist' in 'TV's young turks: part two', *Films and Filming*, April 1969, p. 29.
36. David Austen, 'Blue', *Films and Filming*, August 1968, p. 6.
37. Koetcheff in Vincent Porter and Chris Wicking, 'The making of *Life at the Top*', *Film and Television Technician*, December 1965, p. 230.
38. Colin Gardner suggests that 'displacement is the ideal state of aesthetic engagement with British culture' in *Joseph Losey* (Manchester: Manchester University Press, 2004), p. 1, echoing previous critical accounts of the director's work.
39. Robert Freeman, 'Touch of Eros', *Films and Filming*, May 1968, p. 21.
40. 'Pop star, director, actor: an interview with Michael Sarne' in Wheeler Winston Dixon, *Cinema at the Margins* (London: Anthem Press, 2013), p. 199. Sarne also discussed why he had gone with US money (which was generous) for his project rather than British money (which was not forthcoming) in Mike Sarne, 'It need not cost a ton', *Today's Cinema*, 29 January 1968, p. 6. John Krish, described by Durgnat as a notable 'zig-zagger between TV and cinema', had also been launched into big-budget film-making through the auspices of Fox at the same time, on *Decline and Fall . . . of a Birdwatcher* (1968).
41. For more on Hart, see Melanie Williams, 'No Scruggs, or my truncated journey into the mysterious film career of David Hart', *Transformation and Tradition in Sixties British Cinema*, <https://60sbritishcinema.wordpress.com/2017/05/24/no-scruggs-or-my-truncated-journey-into-the-mysterious-film-career-of-david-hart/>. Paramount's Charles Bluhdorn and Bud Ornstein prided themselves on being supporters of 'new young talent that is forcing its way to the forefront of the British production scene' including Peter Collinson and Peter Medak. John Ware, 'Production-wise', *Daily Cinema*, 10 April 1968, p. 9. Among all the young talent invited to make films, women were conspicuous by their absence, and in fact this goldrush era was worst for women getting a chance to direct than other more supposedly staid periods. The formerly active Wendy Toye and Muriel Box were no longer making feature films by the mid-1960s while Joan Littlewood's debut *Sparrows Can't Sing* (1963) had turned out to be a one-off in spite of being acclaimed as someone with 'all the qualities of a great filmmaker' by her experienced editor Oswald Hafenricher. Reg Williams, 'Joan Littlewood: the perfectionist from East Stratford', *Film and Television Technician*, March 1963, p. 56. This view was echoed by journalist Barrie Pattison: 'Watching her carefully change the emphasis and interpretation of a scene to get exactly what she wanted made it possible to believe' her work could 'have as great an effect on British film making as it has on the theatre.' Barrie Pattison, 'Ladies day', *Films and Filming*, September 1962, p. 15. For more on barriers to women directing in 1960s British cinema, see Sue Harper, *Women in British Cinema* (London: Continuum, 2000), pp. 199–200.
42. 'Anthony Harvey: director' in *The Lion in Winter* pressbook, Bill Douglas Cinema Museum. Harvey in Philip K. Scheuer, 'Anthony Harvey, Director's Guild Award winner', *Action!*, May/June 1969, p. 12.

43. Robinson, 'Case histories of the next renascence', p. 40.
44. 'British feature directors: an index to their work', *Sight and Sound*, vol. 27, no. 4, Autumn, 1958, pp. 289–304.
45. Perhaps the ultimate example of a veteran director moving with the times was Gainsborough stalwart Bernard Knowles, born 1900, being engaged to direct sequences (uncredited) for the Beatles' television movie *Magical Mystery Tour* (1967). Mark Lewisohn, *The Complete Beatles Chronicle* (London: Pyramid Books, 1992).
46. This award was created in 1968 and its scope was international. The first winner was Mike Nichols for *The Graduate* (1967). Schlesinger won in 1969, beating Richard Attenborough, Ken Russell and Peter Yates.
47. Gordon Gow, 'A buck for Joe', *Films and Filming*, November 1969, p. 5.
48. Charles Champlin, 'Donner: sociology on a wide screen', *Los Angeles Times*, 7 September 1966, p. 12.
49. Gordon Gow, 'The urge of some people', *Films and Filming*, July 1969, p. 4.
50. He gave advice on good editing, using a scene from *I am a Camera* as an example, to the readers of *Amateur Movie Maker*, August 1960, pp. 994–6.
51. 'Take a bow, Pinewood', *Picturegoer*, 7 March 1957, p. 16. In the *Sight and Sound* 1958 listing of British directors, Donner, the youngest man on the list, was judged 'one of the most promising newcomers for some years'. 'British feature directors', p. 293.
52. Donner also did some work for the BBC, including three hour-long films with Woodrow Wyatt, each profiling a British institution: Sandhurst, Somerset House and the Football Association.
53. Rod Allen, 'Profile: Clive Donner', *Television Mail*, 20 September 1963, p. 18. 'In the picture', *Observer*, 23 February 1964, p. 24.
54. Clive Donner, 'Live action commercials', *Journal of the Society of Film and Television Arts (television commercials)*, no. 4, Winter 1960–1, pp. 6–7.
55. 'Proposed film for Duke of Edinburgh's Award Scheme', undated document, Clive Donner special collection, National Film and Television Archive, CSD 13/12, p. 9. Making the promotional message 'concealed and subsidiary in the film', Donner argued, would 'show how the Duke of Edinburgh Award Scheme fits into the normal nature of life, and is not something separate.' p. 4
56. Ibid.
57. 'Johnnie: story outline', September 1961, Clive Donner special collection, National Film and Television Archive, CSD 12/2, p. 14.
58. 'Proposed film for Duke of Edinburgh's Award Scheme', p. 2. Allen, 'Profile: Clive Donner', p. 18.
59. V. F. Perkins, 'Clive Donner and *Some People*', *Movie*, no. 3, October 1962, pp. 23–4.
60. Ibid.
61. 'Film review: Some People', *The Daily Cinema*, 20 July 1962, p. 6. *Some People* received a mild ribbing from *Private Eye*: 'The National Federation of Youth Clubs in Association with the Duke of Edinburgh's rock-climbing and playing fields award scheme invite you to a gala premiere of *The Outward Bounders*'. *Private Eye*, July 1962, p. 12. Although Penelope Gilliatt sent it up in her review for the *Observer*, Dilys Powell of *The Sunday Times* praised it for its freshness and naturalism, given its very difficult brief of lacing fiction with propaganda.
62. Perkins, 'Clive Donner and *Some People*', p. 23. Donner said of the choice of setting, that it was 'visually exciting' and he 'could go back to Bristol and make four more pictures without feeling that I was repeating myself'.
63. Ibid.

64. Donner in 'Ten questions to nine directors', *Sight and Sound*, vol. 33, no. 2, Spring 1964, p. 64.
65. Here the production design of Reece Pemberton working in tandem with Nicolas Roeg's cinematography was vital to its disquieting atmosphere, as was Ron Grainer's minimalist soundtrack.
66. Gow, 'The urge of some people', p. 7.
67. Donner in 'A free hand', *Sight and Sound*, Spring 1959, p. 61. A range of directors, including Jack Clayton, Robert Hamer, Seth Holt, John Krish and Tony Richardson, were asked what film they would make 'assuming they enjoyed a completely free hand – ignoring the complexities of securing finance, distribution guarantees, and so on'. (p. 60).
68. In John Gillett, 'The state of the studios', *Sight and Sound*, vol. 33, no. 2, Spring 1964, p. 60.
69. Letter from Clive Donner to David Deutsch, undated, Clive Donner special collection, National Film and Television Archive, CSD 6/29.
70. Alexander Walker, *Hollywood England* (London: Orion, 2005), p. 277. Donner preferred to work on location wherever possible, stating 'I feel that studios, with their bare walls and familiar doors and signs, tend to destroy atmosphere and concentration', and was keen to facilitate it by using 'TV innovations like neck microphones and flexible lighting equipment'. In Gillett, 'The state of the studios', p. 60.
71. M. G. McNay, 'Clive Donner director', *The Guardian*, 18 March 1964, p. 9.
72. Ibid.
73. Gow, 'The urge of some people', p. 7. In 1964, Donner was set to direct a Woodfall project entitled *Let's Get Steamed Up* from original screenplay by John Osborne and Penelope Gilliatt and mooted to direct *Fanny Hill* with Jane Fonda to star, both in 1964. Derek Todd, 'Production', *Kine Weekly*, 16 January 1964, p. 16, and 4 June 1964, p. 15. The following year, there was also the possibility of a film shot in Russia with a script by John and Penelope Mortimer, and a short film written by Pinter 'for inclusion in "Project One", the three-part film-of-the-absurd' with contributions from Samuel Beckett (starring Buster Keaton – the only section which was actually completed) and Eugène Ionesco. 'Clive Donner film with Soviet pends', *Variety*, 23 June 1965, p. 5.
74. Donner in Ian Cameron and Mark Shivas, 'Clive Donner interview', *Movie*, no. 14, Autumn 1965, p. 15.
75. Ibid. Richard Williams described his work in more detail in an interview with Jonathan Gili and Misha Donat, 'Titles for Pussycat', *Isis*, 17 November 1965, p. 11. In its examination of sexual neurosis, it was also of course a founding work in writer and star Woody Allen's career, and is written about mainly as an Allen text in Ronald Bryden, 'Pussycat gets the cream', *Observer Magazine*, 28 February 1965.
76. Andrew Sarris review from *Village Voice*, 5 August 1965, reproduced in *New Statesman*, 29 August 1965, p. 263.
77. Letter from Clive Donner to Henri Langlois, dated 19 January 1966. Its producer Charles K. Feldman also assembled some impressive endorsements from veteran US vaudevillians to boost the film, from Jack Benny's 'One of the funniest, craziest pictures I've ever seen! I loved it!' to Milton Berle's 'A classic movie which is wild, swinging and just plain marvellous.' Memo from Warren Cowan to Charles K. Feldman, dated 20 June 1965. Clive Donner special collection, National Film and Television Archive, CSD 30/18.
78. 'Big rental pictures of 1965', *Variety*, 5 January 1966, p. 8. It was just down from the mega-hits *Mary Poppins*, *The Sound of Music*, *My Fair Lady* and *Goldfinger*.

79. Gow, 'The urge of some people', p. 7.
80. Letter from John Trevelyan to Clive Donner, dated 2 January 1967, Clive Donner special collection, National Film and Television Archive, CSD 18/6 (he also took issue with lots of the script's innuendo, pleading 'This is not a "Carry On" film!')
81. 'Here We Go Round the Mulberry Bush', *Kine Weekly*, 6 January 1968, p. 12.
82. Draft of letter from Clive Donner to Arnold Picker, undated, Clive Donner special collection, National Film and Television Archive, CSD 18/9. Clive Donner wrote to the band's manager Chris Blackwell encouraging them to come to the premiere 'dressed in their most dashing gear' and sent them a congratulatory telegram after they'd appeared on *Top of the Pops* singing the film's theme song. Letter from Clive Donner to Chris Blackwell, dated 31 October 1967, and telegram from Clive Donner to Steve Winwood and Traffic dated 24 November 1967. CSD 18/6.
83. 'Something for everyone at UA's "Mulberry Bush" premiere', *Kine Weekly*, 13 January 1968, pp. 6–9.
84. Donner in 'Between battles', *ABC Film Review*, September 1969, p. 11. Donner in Gow, 'The urge of some people', p. 5.
85. Moving to this larger scale of production presented new logistic challenges, as Donner noted: 'providing tea for a thousand extras is maddeningly time-consuming.' In 'Between battles', p. 11.
86. Full-page advertisement in *Kine Weekly*, 9 December 1967, p. 9.
87. Donner in 'Between battles', p. 11. Tie-ins with contemporary fashion also emphasised the historical story's modern parallels.
88. Margaret Hinxman, 'Out of season', *Sunday Telegraph*, 20 July 1969, press cuttings file, BFI Library.
89. Ibid.
90. Letter from Clive Donner to Mike Kaplan, dated 10 July 1969, Clive Donner special collection, National Film and Television Archive, CSD 3/15.
91. Ian Cameron, 'Films', *Queen*, 6 August 1969.
92. Quoted in teaser ad, *New York Times*, 28 October 1969.
93. 'As to "Alfred the Great", Clive Donner muses on hazards of "campy" critics', *Variety*, 10 September 1969, p. 8. Derek Prouse, 'Multiple divisions', *The Sunday Times*, 20 July 1969, p. 48.
94. Letter from Clive Donner to Everett Aison, dated 24 November 1969, Clive Donner special collection, National Film and Television Archive, CSD 3/15. Donner had also recently married Jocelyn Rickards, the costume designer who had worked on *Alfred the Great*, and so the wish for a break may have been personal as much as professional.
95. Letter from Clive Donner to Howard Hausman, dated 21 November 1969, Clive Donner special collection, National Film and Television Archive, CSD 3/15.
96. Advertisement in *Television Mail*, 25 September 1970, p. 14.

8. PRODUCTION DESIGN

Melanie Williams

INTRODUCTION

Art historian Lesley Jackson suggests that the 1960s were 'a particularly exciting and creative time' for British visual and material culture, constituting a design boom.¹ The British 'look' became internationally influential to an unprecedented degree as 'art, design, and popular culture all intertwined. Mary Quant was part of it, as were the Beatles, Bridget Riley, David Hockney, David Bailey and Twiggy, demonstrating that Britain was at the centre of things.'² Innovative 'youthful designer-entrepreneurs' such as Habitat's Terence Conran and Biba's Barbara Hulanicki 'united design and popular culture' while the new style gospel was vigorously espoused by the colour supplements in Britain's weekend newspapers from 1962 onwards, bringing 'what had hitherto been seen as a design/style-led elite taste to a mass audience'.³ Exhilarating for some, for others the new emphasis on image epitomised the nation's slide into rapacious consumerism and mindless 'neophilia'.⁴

In the diverse mix of influences on British design's reinvention in the sixties, film and television played an integral role. Michael Wolff (of advertising consultancy Wolff Olins) noted in 1965 that the 'sort of designers who have really given people a bang in the past two years' were 'Ken Adam, as Art Director of the James Bond films, Frederick Starke, with his clothes for Cathy Gale [in *The Avengers*]; and Ray Cusick, with his Daleks'.⁵ British film (and television) therefore participated in and responded to a growing sense of excitement around design. As well as designing the iconic 'war room'

Figure 8.1   Michael Crawford, Rita Tushingham, Ray Brooks and Donal Donnelly in the whitewashed art deco interior created by production designer Assheton Gorton for *The Knack ... and How to Get It* (Richard Lester, 1965).

for Kubrick's *Dr Strangelove* (1964), Ken Adam created the 'grandiloquent inner sanctums' of numerous Bond villains.[6] His spectacular Bond sets had what he called a 'tongue-in-cheek, slightly ahead-of-contemporary concept', only minimal extrapolations of the increasingly grand architectural visions of the time.[7] The decor of the villains' lairs blends modernist and traditional elements in the style of ultra-fashionable British interior designer David Hicks, who featured in David Bailey's infamous *Box of Pin Ups*.[8] Hicks demonstrates clearly the interplay between on- and off-screen design in the 1960s: creating Vidal Sassoon's hair salons and the nightclub for the QE2, as well as Richard Lester's dining room, then acting as 'design consultant' on the director's film *Petulia* (1968).[9] Similarly, Christopher Gibbs, stylist and *éminence grise* of 'swinging London', provided his own Chelsea apartment to stage the decadent marijuana-fuelled party in *Blow Up* (1966) as well as contributing to the louche look and feel of *Performance* (1970) to an extent that transcended his on-screen credit as merely 'Turner's house design consultant'.[10]

In the 1960s, British production design returned to the levels of international acclaim it had enjoyed twenty years earlier.[11] John Box won Oscars for a series of large-scale productions: *Lawrence of Arabia* (1962) with John Stoll as his assistant, *Doctor Zhivago* (1965) and *Oliver!* (1968) both with Terence Marsh. Tom Morahan and Lionel Couch on *Sons and Lovers* (1960), Ralph

Brinton, Ted Marshall and Jocelyn Herbert on *Tom Jones* (1963), John Bryan and Maurice Carter on *Becket* (1964), Tony Masters and Ernest Archer among the team for *2001: A Space Odyssey* (1968), and Maurice Carter and Lionel Couch for *Anne of the Thousand Days* (1969) were all Oscar-nominated, testifying to the high esteem in which British film design was held during the decade. When the Guild of Film Art Directors was relaunched in June 1963 (revitalising the previous Society of British Film Directors and Designers, established in 1946), its chief boast was a membership made up 'of those artists who have worked on the productions that have already made British and international films famous throughout the world'.[12] Its chair was Ken Adam, who suggested in a 1964 interview that art directors might now be 'as indispensable to a film as the star or the director'.[13]

Design had certainly become pivotal within the conception of many films. Art directors might be 'cast', like actors, for their ability to incarnate a certain look. For instance, Clive Donner hired Brian Eatwell on *Here We Go Round the Mulberry Bush* (1968) for his 'experience in television doing teenage shows'.[14] Ken Adam didn't just flesh out a pre-existing script on the Bond films but increasingly 'came up with ideas that were incorporated into a screenplay'.[15] He appreciated this new centrality in the film-making process, but was also aware of the 'immense responsibility' it entailed, 'conscious of the fact that we had to keep up the spectacle of the visual effects'.[16] 'Keeping up' became a key concern, for fundamental logistic reasons centred on longer production timescales which made it harder for film to be at the cutting edge of fashion, unlike the more swiftly turned-around media of television or print journalism. As critic John Russell Taylor observed:

> A new vogue is born, and actuality television is reporting it to us within hours. A month or so, and the colour supplements are onto it. But by the time a film has gone through all the processes from script to screen the big new thing is likely to be thoroughly old hat.[17]

This meant that film now either had to try to set trends, or hedge its bets and take a more knowingly eclectic approach, 'throw[ing] in a bit of everything which is on the scene [. . .] a constant dazzle of stylistic reference, half-straight, half-ironic, full of get-out clauses if anyone asks awkward questions.'[18] This is the perfect description of Michael Stringer's designs for the Bond send-up *Casino Royale* (1967), characterised by the art director as full of 'mad extravagant Pop Art ideas':

> we devised a number of design gags such as having the top of Nelson's column outside Ursula Andress's bedroom, fish-tanks one could shoot through; miniature baccarat tables in a recess; a sofa well and

about fifty feet of Elgin marbles down one wall [. . .] In her dressing room we put a multitude of mirrors as a pastiche of early Jean Harlow films with the deliberate contrast of Hieronymous Bosch wardrobe cupboards.'[19]

This density of wildly diverse clashing styles encapsulates the stylistic excess of many late 1960s films, with a bold eclecticism that could be aesthetically dazzling, but equally visually cacophonous at times, relegating to history previous notions of British restraint.

It was symptomatic of developments that the professional title of 'production designer' rather than 'art director', gained increasing currency during the decade. Coined by David O. Selznick to describe William Cameron Menzies, production designer 'elevated technicians to the category of contributing artists' and had been 'adopted in Britain by the star designers' like Alfred Junge and John Bryan.[20] Although art director still continued to be the default title for the person heading up the design department on most 1960s films, it began to be used more interchangeably with production designer, and by the end of the decade the latter term had increasingly taken over. During this period, individuals were given different titles while doing the same work: while Adam took his first credit as production designer on *The Rough and the Smooth* (1959), the equally authoritative Assheton Gorton was only described as such from 1968 onwards. Further complications follow from the convention that when the title of production designer is used, the term art director then designates the person who would previously have been called deputy art director, thus implicitly querying the older term's status.

LOCATION VERSUS STUDIO

Ian Christie refers to an 'endless debate between authenticity and stylisation' in the way that film production-design work is conceptualised, which certainly rings true of British cinema in the 1960s.[21] Initially, the defining issue was whether to embrace wholly location filming or to cleave to the control afforded by studio environments. Technological developments made it more feasible than before to move beyond the confines of the purpose-built set for entire productions and for some directors this became a personal crusade, exemplified by Tony Richardson's proclamation: 'For me studios are death, they are anathema, they are everything I hate.'[22] Despite being schooled in more traditional modes, Richardson's veteran art director Ralph Brinton proved himself highly adept at location work on *The Entertainer* (1960), the entirely location-shot *A Taste of Honey* (1961), *The Loneliness of the Long Distance Runner* (1962), and *Tom Jones*, earning him the title 'premier designer of the kitchen sink'.[23] In 1963 Brinton explained why he felt 'location is the better bet' for filming, giving 'a feeling of spontaneity which is difficult to create consciously in the studio' and helping to 'produce the true realism which we are seeking'.[24] As his colleague Ted Marshall suggested, you could 'look out of the windows and see something immediately outside', as when the heroine of *Girl with Green Eyes* (1964) 'came down into this dark staircase into the hall and then opened the front door, and suddenly [. . .] there was a Sunday in Dublin with the church bells ringing and people going to church on a sunny day. You can't do that in the studio.'[25] But it was still important to exercise what Ken Adam called the 'designer's eye' on location: 'one has to have taste; and one has to be able to improvise and adapt the locations to the subject matter.'[26] One famous example of this is John Box's laying of a line of pebbles on the sand in *Lawrence of Arabia* to subtly draw the eye towards the distant figure on the horizon, of which David Lean said to Box 'you'll never do a better bit of designing in films, ever!'[27]

Others questioned the new credo of location filming being preferable. Although not a neutral voice in this debate, Kip Herren, the general manager of Pinewood studios, nonetheless made a pertinent critique of certain idiosyncrasies in its adoption:

> If we want to depict an incident in Djakarta we send a unit of 30, 40, 60 or 100 people to Djakarta, for we have become slaves to the cause of realism. And we also send a construction unit to build sets in Djakarta to make Djakarta look as we imagine Djakarta ought to look. Our business is make-believe. We have the finest craftsmen in any industry anywhere with specialised skills, whose job it is, whose pride it is, to reproduce anything anywhere. I firmly believe that Tahiti would look far better and be infinitely cheaper by the addition of some fibre glass palm trees to the shores of Frensham Ponds than Tahiti itself does, with its present mass of cigarette and cola advertisements.[28]

Moreover, as Ken Adam argued, lots of the rooms used for location filming were 'just square boxes and don't give good pictures and interesting angles' whereas 'on a set you can often give the director a better picture by getting away from architectural principles'.[29] For Joseph Losey's frequent collaborator Richard MacDonald, bespoke rather than adapted design was crucial in order to fully realise the concept for *The Servant* (1963) based on 'circular movements [. . .] round and down into the basement, round and up into the bedrooms.'[30] Rather than use a pre-existing location, MacDonald needed to 'invent a plan of a house', enabling complete control over 'where they needed doorways, where the characters would have to get to, what sort of doorways they had to come out of'.[31] Working exclusively on location could be professionally frustrating too: Peggy Gick recalled her experienced colleague Edward

Carrick complaining in the 1960s: 'I don't want to work on location. I'm an art director, I want to build things!'[32]

But there were still ample opportunities to build things, resulting in some remarkable achievements in studio production design, including John Bryan's recreation of Canterbury Cathedral at Shepperton for *Becket*, Ken Adam's visualisation of the secret inner workings of the US gold repository Fort Knox in *Goldfinger* (1964), 'the Aladdin's cave of Western capitalism', and John Box's eloquent Dickensian London for *Oliver!* which ended up becoming 'one of Shepperton's enduring assets, endlessly refurbished and re-dressed for dozens of later films'.[33] On a far more transitory basis, the enormous inflatable dome that functioned as the main setting for *The Touchables* (1968), produced by John Bryan, was a *folie de grandeur* that spoke to the emphasis on visual spectacle within British films of the time.

Less high-concept productions could still boast inventive design using traditional art-director techniques. Alan Withy, later to work on *This Sporting Life* (1963), did some remarkable *trompe-l'oeil* work on the comedy *Go to Blazes* (1962), designing its fire station set 'to have the feeling of being large – far larger than I could afford to build', artificially 'perspectivis[ing] the set [...] until the back wall in fact only came to one foot six inches in height'.[34] Likewise, Robert Jones created 'a remarkable "perspective street"' for *Crooks in Cloisters* (1964), 'which, though only a few feet long, seems to stretch for hundreds of yards'.[35] Examples such as these drew on the ingenious trickery of model work, false perspective, scenic art and mattes creating plausible but totally unreal spaces, upholding Syd Cain's contention that their work was 'the business of creating illusions'.[36]

Stock materials were also vital to studio production design. Maurice Carter recalled Pinewood's 'excellent stock bay [which] made the building of sets very economical'.[37] The most outstanding recyclers were Hammer's art department, headed by Bernard Robinson, able to maintain high production values even when the sets 'cost buttons'.[38] Although by the early 1970s many companies were 'tending to do away with scene docks as an unnecessary expense (on the premise that it is cheaper to build inexpensive sets for low-budget productions rather than employ expensive labour to look after scene docks that take up valuable space)', this was not the case for companies specialising in 'one genre'.[39] Hence the castle hall for *Dracula* (1958) was used for many subsequent Hammer films as was the village square originally for *The Brides of Dracula* (1960), while 1965's production slate of *Dracula, Prince of Darkness, Rasputin, the Mad Monk, The Plague of the Zombies* and *The Reptile* was specifically intended to re-use the same sets.[40] Hammer also made smart use of real locations, most notably the ornate gothic mansion Oakley Court in Bray, and Black Park in Buckinghamshire, 530 acres of woodland, heath and grassland with a large lake which stood in, surprisingly plausibly, for everything from Transylvania to the Far East.[41]

This low-budget, high-impact approach was mirrored in the production design of the *Carry On* comedies which used white-stuccoed Heatherden Hall at Pinewood as frequently and variously as Hammer used Oakley Court. And they too appreciated a bargain: *Carry On Cleo* (1964) famously benefitted from being able to use leftover sets from *Cleopatra* (1963). Numerous art directors worked on the series during the 1960s, including Lionel Couch, Bert Davey, Cedric Dawe, and Carmen Dillon, but the most important was Alex Vetchinsky. He designed *Carry On Sergeant* (1958) which inaugurated the cycle, having by that point already amassed more art-director credits than anyone else in British films in a career stretching back to the 1920s. Vetchinsky's work on these low-budget genre productions may seem a world away from the high-profile lavish designs of Ken Adam and John Box, but there were some intriguing similarities. For example, Box's strategy to use Snowdonia to stand in for China on *The Inn of the Sixth Happiness* (1958) was echoed in his former mentor Vetchinsky's use of the same countryside to represent the Afghan–Indian border in *Carry On Up the Khyber* (1968).[42]

Lower-budget enterprises took great care to maximise efficiency in their use of sets. Compton–Tekli proudly announced 'meticulous planning of schedules and filming logistics', integrating all thirteen sets for *Saturday Night Out* (1964) into 'one vast complex', so actors could be moved 'from set to set with a minimum loss of time', saving 'one full week of shooting'.[43] But similar efficiency-drives extended beyond second features. *A Man for All Seasons* (1966) suffered 'loss of studio space' as Columbia's contemporaneous production *Casino Royale* spread out but John Box knew how to put every penny of his tight budget up on screen, relying on his team's 'illusionistic skills' (and careful framing) to achieve 'a credible Hampton Court Palace out of painted flats'.[44] Indeed, he made a virtue of necessity, focusing far more on the interior spaces and inward lives of its characters, taking an appropriately austere approach to invoking historical period with just 'key images and elements to anchor the film in the Tudor era'.[45] Box's frugal but effective designs for *A Man for All Seasons* ended up winning 1967's British Film Academy award for Production Design, triumphing over strong fellow contenders Carmen Dillon for *Accident* (1967), Assheton Gorton for *Blow Up*, and even Ken Adam for *You Only Live Twice* (1967), which boasted a bespoke hollowed-out volcano, 460 feet in diameter and 120 feet high.

The work of these four individuals perfectly encapsulated the diversity of British film design at this time. Box's spare, allusive approach to history differed equally from Adam's fantastic visions, Gorton's surreal twist on modern London, and Dillon's bourgeois donnish Oxford. Dillon herself described the look of *Accident* as 'that of not having a look, of avoiding any obtrusive visual stylisation':

we have concentrated on making everything look used, lived in, believable as a background for them: in real life no one ever has six matching coffee-cups because two have got broken and they have to use something else that doesn't match.[46]

Dirk Bogarde described its house set as 'quite uncanny, it matches the exterior so exactly, with no cheating at all [and] so meticulously detailed according to the way people like this actually live that it aids the actor enormously when he is playing in it.'[47]

In some respects, Dillon's designs for *Accident* epitomised the emerging model by combining sets and real locations seamlessly, hybridising 'realism in the raw and realism reconstructed.'[48] Although some directors embraced the all-location shoot, the number of productions which adhered to that ethos absolutely remained small. From poverty-row productions to Hollywood-backed mega-budget film-making, the design philosophy remained the same: to do what veteran art director Peter Proud had done for Compton–Tekli's unpretentious thrillers and 'create settings in which people live, rather than backings against which actors posture'.[49]

Intuition, Character and Colour

Despite being a creative occupation, the practical dimensions of film-design work cannot be overemphasised, as Michael Stringer made clear:

> the Art of Art Direction is to make the imagination soar to seemingly impossible heights within a practical and economic framework [. . .] the hard and fascinating task of making all things physically possible for filming [and] the dreams of the film-makers a splendid reality.[50]

The production designer's relationship with the director was vital to achieving success in these endeavours. Despite his strong claim to authorial status, Ken Adam believed that 'only if you understand what the story of the film is about, what the director is trying to say with it, can you function to the best of your ability', and talked about developing 'almost a platonic love relationship' with the director 'to be able to give of one's best'.[51] As Stringer reiterated: 'If the designer allows himself to be carried away by beautiful set sketches that do not relate to the action then it will be impossible for the director to develop his characters within the prepared set.'[52] Design may be important but it behoves the designer not to become too hubristic, no matter how expansive or expensive the worlds they create. As designer Jonathan Barry wittily observed, for all its sumptuous Egyptian spectacle, 'the most interesting scenes in *Cleopatra* take place in front of two square yards of wallpaper.'[53]

But while being functional and self-effacing, good production design had to be imaginative too, dependent on the designer's 'intuitive ability to grasp almost indefinable subtleties'.[54] It was this kind of creative alchemy that led John Box to blend the image of an onion-domed dacha that he saw on a postage stamp with a photograph taken inside a frozen hut from a book about Antarctic expeditions in order to envisage the Varykino 'ice palace' from *Doctor Zhivago*.[55] Characters often determined a design scheme, and when preparing *The Pumpkin Eater* (1964) with Jack Clayton, Ted Marshall recounted how they 'discussed the characters mostly. I find this is the only way to design sets, to know who you're designing the sets for.'[56] Marshall's character-led production design, with attention paid to the tiniest details of decor, continued into *Charlie Bubbles* (1967), where for the protagonist's ex-wife's house in the country:

> we put a few decorative tiles near the window in the kitchen because we felt that the woman in the story would bring some of the city culture to her country cottage when she moved in. She was after all an exile [. . .] We didn't do a finished job with the tiles because we felt she would most likely start the job herself and leave the work unfinished.[57]

That tiny bit of kitchen tiling – anomalously cheerful, slightly bodged – may not even be consciously registered by the viewer but nonetheless, along with all the other little telling details, plays a vital role in creating a believable and expressive dramatic world.

The production designer's need to pay attention to the tiniest details inevitably took on a new significance as films shifted increasingly to being shot in colour as the decade progressed. A tiny dot of misplaced red or yellow could easily unbalance the most careful composition in a way that could not occur to quite the same extent in black and white. Colour generated new concerns for production designers, with Michael Stringer advising, for instance, that they should 'always co-operate closely with the costume designer' to avoid unpleasant unintended clashes of decor and dress, aiming instead to achieve 'a total harmony of colour on the screen'.[58] The increasing ubiquity of colour presented certain challenges but also generated excitement at the vastly enlarged chromatic palette at their disposal. In the later years of the decade, with US finance facilitating ever-larger budgets and strenuous efforts to exploit the colourful visual excitements associated with 'swinging London', vivid production design often figured as the primary source of cinematic spectacle (and a primary means of distinguishing cinema from television, at least in the UK). But Ken Adam cautioned that 'every tin of colour paint should be printed with "Danger – Handle with Care"' because colour could 'be a monster. It can bring places to life, but it can also kill them.'[59] Adam used 'a documentary approach' on *The Ipcress File* (1965), presenting London as overwhelmingly 'grey and brown' but punctuated with the occasional pop of colour like the red buses and telephone boxes, or the surprising single pink rose on Colonel Ross's desk; an overall chromatic reduction that made the impact of the multi-coloured lightshow used to brainwash secret agent Harry Palmer (Michael Caine) all the greater.[60]

Films that aimed to have realist credentials faced particular challenges with colour, as suggested by one review of Ken Loach's *Poor Cow* (1967) which found its downbeat setting, overseen by art director Bernard Sarron, 'romanticised in a way probably never intended – never did dustbins look so picturesque or washing on a line so resemble a display of flags'.[61] Yet, colour production presented dilemmas which were met with remarkably similar solutions across the range of genres: films as diverse as *Blow Up* and *Carry On Camping* (1969) resorted to painting the grass green to obtain sufficiently strong colour values on screen. Their common practice pointed to an underlying ethos in British production design, striving to make the most of the newly colourful world of the 1960s.

'Design Auteur': Assheton Gorton (1930–2014)

Reviewer Majorie Bilbow said of *Wonderwall* (1968) that she 'knew without looking at the credits' that Assheton Gorton was its designer.[62] A 'design auteur', Gorton's defining characteristic was his 'extreme sensitivity to contemporary style' which meant his films always spoke to the decade's key aesthetic developments, from the monochrome mod look to the more 'self-conscious historical revivalism' of the late 1960s.[63] He worked entirely in contemporary or futuristic feature films throughout the decade, on *The Knack* (1965), *Blow Up*, *Wonderwall*, *The Bliss of Mrs Blossom* (1968), *The Bed Sitting Room* (1969) and *The Magic Christian* (1969), but this didn't stop him from dabbling in styles redolent of the past, with *Wonderwall*, for example, drawing quite deliberately in 'images of the 1880s' which just 'seemed right' for the project.[64] Indeed, all his 1960s films operated in postmodernist mode, artfully blending high and low culture, old and new, with Gorton getting ideas 'from everywhere, from the history of the world'.[65]

After studying architecture at Cambridge, Gorton ended up working as a draftsman in the design department at ABC Television, benefitting from the mentorship of the company's progressive head of design Tim O'Brien, an advocate of 'light and fluent scenery'.[66] Although television, particularly its commercial iteration, was sometimes looked down upon as vulgar, Gorton found it exciting to be 'at the beginning of a new medium. The whole world came through the studios.'[67] He designed sets for the innovative drama strand *Armchair Theatre* from 1958 to 1965, becoming adept at dealing with its diverse demands and rapid turnover of sets, 'one a month, or every five weeks'.⁶⁸ These required contemporary settings (for Alun Owen and Harold Pinter plays, amongst others) but also different historical eras for period dramas, embedding information about wealth and social position in 'very basic little three-walled sets' through details like the height of a skirting board: 'a six-inch skirting is very downmarket, a nine-inch is very middle class, and an eleven-inch skirting is for country houses. [. . .] So there's a whole class system that's expressed in the height of skirtings.'⁶⁹ Gorton also began to crystallise ideas around design's creation of a 'subliminal world':

> The foreground is for the conscious mind – and the design is often for the unconscious mind, which is just as important as the conscious mind. You have to feed that unconscious mind. Whether people recognise what you do or pick up on it or not is immaterial in a way.⁷⁰

Gorton associated with a number of talented directors at ABC, Ted Kotcheff, Philip Saville, Charles Jarrott, Joseph McGrath, and Richard Lester among them, and the latter provided the designer with his entrée into films, recruiting him to work as art director on *The Knack* following their collaboration on some television advertisements.⁷¹ This was typical of a number of other designers who moved from or between one medium and the other, including his ABC colleagues Reece Pemberton, Philip Harrison, Brian Eatwell, and most notably perhaps Robert Fuest, best known for his work as designer and later director on the visually innovative adventure series *The Avengers*, and the person who best 'demonstrated the increased feeling of synergy between film and television' at this time.⁷²

For Gorton, the biggest shock in moving from television to film was the shift to location work. Because 'there were no such thing as location managers then', he spent a lot of time scouting out suitable places for 'the various gags that were being written'.⁷³ This extended to interiors as well as exteriors. The house in which much of *The Knack*'s action takes place was a real three-storey terrace in (then unfashionable) West London and the main problem the unit had to contend with was 'lack of space':

> 'No room!' is the constant cry of the assistant directors. [. . .] Would life be easier, more comfortable, in a studio? It would. But, of course, the Woodfall people much prefer to make their pictures on location. That's why [they] find themselves pinned against the wall at Melrose Terrace, Shepherd's Bush, in tiny rooms piled with junk or in an entrance hall four feet wide.⁷⁴

The style in which the house was decorated would provide an enriching background to the action, in this case the then-unfashionable interwar *moderne* mode, not yet rebranded art deco. Inventing a backstory that Colin (Michael Crawford) had inherited the house from a mad aunt, 'a do-it-yourself home decorator before the war', Gorton devised 'sunset-pattern marquetry', wallpaper and stained glass, dressing the set with further appropriate accoutrements from the Bakelite era, trying to strike a deliberately old-fashioned note.[75] This corresponded perfectly to young protagonist's feeling that he is mired in old outmoded ways while desperately trying to embrace permissive modernity. The moribund look of the house was then modified by monochromatic contrast, with the top-floor room decorated in black while the ground floor was entirely whitewashed; 'the only time I ever had a violent migraine', Gorton later recalled.[76] *The Knack* also underlined how resonant tiny details in the mise en scène could be: having got the crew and passing schoolchildren to deface the hallway with graffiti in as many differing styles of handwriting as possible, Gorton was pleased to see one of these bits of graffiti, 'there is no tomorrow so how about this afternoon?' interpreted by a film critic as 'the central theme of the film': *carpe diem* in the shadow of the H-bomb.[77]

Gorton started work on *Casino Royale* but had the honour of being 'the first person to be fired from that. They didn't understand my designs. And they didn't want to spend any money' (they would later disregard such budgetary restraint).[78] But this enabled him to work on *Blow Up*, on which he 'learned a lot from Antonioni about controlling landscapes' particularly in terms of their colour values.[79] The director's approach to locations was boldly interventionist rather than assimilative: he was not only 'the man who painted Woolwich black' (as the title of one magazine article had it) but also the man who painted shopfronts red, walls white, and grass green when necessary, ordering the tips of distant buildings to be painted crimson in order to obtain the perfect colour composition.[80] *Blow Up* sensed how attitudes to the trappings of the past were changing. The girl who owns the junk shop proclaims herself 'fed up with antiques' but the hip photographer protagonist is entranced with the vintage wooden propeller he finds among their jumbled stock, buying it immediately. He lives and works in trendily repurposed Victorian buildings, which do not carry the association of pre-war fustiness possessed by the house in *The Knack* but instead seem like apt environments for the beautiful people to inhabit, exacerbating their coolness through the piquantly contrasting traditionalism, just as *Life* magazine thought that Mary Quant's miniskirts seemed 'wackier than they are because they come from England, stronghold of the court gown, the sturdy tweed and the furled umbrella'.[81]

After helping Tony Richardson with a mirrored nightclub stage on the short film *Red and Blue* (1967), Gorton's next two assignments, *The Bliss of Mrs Blossom* and *Wonderwall*, would show he was in tune with the stylistic sea-changes taking place, when a 'melt-down of forms' took over from the 'sharp edged, precise' look of the earlier 1960s, and 'people began to rediscover and revel in the richness of Victorian design.'[82] In using retro looks to conjure the contemporary fashion, Gorton's design for both films corresponded with the Beatles' reinvention as psychedelic neo-Edwardians for *Sgt Pepper's Lonely Hearts Club Band*, vintage boutiques such as *Granny Takes a Trip* and *I Was Lord Kitchener's Valet*, and the increasing deployment of Beardsley and Mucha-esque art nouveau across a range of advertising and print culture. Both *Blossom* and *Wonderwall* centre on distinctive domestic interiors, in which adjoining rooms or floors become integral to the action and the characters' personalities are reflected in the architecture of their homes. The former is a benign variation on *The Collector*, with a woman keeping a man shut away, but in an attic rather than a basement and with his full consent rather than against his will. Although some of the action takes place at other visually striking locations – a high-tech aluminium-panelled psychiatrist's treatment room, a massive marketing rally to launch a new inflatable bra – its most important set is undoubtedly the Baillie Scott-influenced house in which Mrs Blossom (Shirley MacLaine) conducts her unorthodox romance. Constructed at Twickenham studios, its 'stunning design', complete with 'railed balconies, specially printed wallpapers, a fascinating collection of *objets d'art* and a vast domed stained-glass conservatory', gave Gorton his 'first chance to build proper sets' and he relished the possibilities it offered: 'It was wonderful, going from television to be able to have real plaster, real cornices, and make your own wallpaper.'[83]

The multi-levelled Blossom house was painstakingly dressed with amassed curios such as a cottage-shaped teapot, a Victorian china doll in a lilac dress and art deco teacups; a mixture of styles and periods that upheld Gorton's statement that historical coherence didn't matter in design 'as long as it's evocative'.[84] Working with Joe McGrath, a director he considered 'appreciative of design', Gorton embraced the opportunity to go all out for spectacle and surprise, throwing in random real-life artefacts like a car in the shape of a Guinness bottle and an eleven-seater bicycle.[85] But there were still limits. Gorton's idea for a 'wonderful Art Deco fibreglass organ that came up shooting stars [. . .] pure Sixties – pure Beatles record cover' did not make it past the planning stages.[86]

The Beatles aesthetic was realised on *Wonderwall*, which featured the clothes, art and furniture of the collective, The Fool, having designed clothes for the Apple boutique as well as the cosmic mural on its exterior wall. But despite The Fool's significant input, it was Gorton's overarching art direction which made the film visually, if not narratively, coherent. *Wonderwall* centres on an eccentric professor who spies on his beautiful young neighbour through the wall. The Fool were responsible for decorating her flat in their distinctive psychedelic style. But the adjacent room inhabited by the professor, with its colour scheme of sage green and mauve (like the Blossom house), Arthurian mural, and text from a Tennyson poem emblazoned in neo-gothic script across the picture rail, was pure Gorton. Ironically perhaps for a film aiming to be 'a way-out winner of the new psychedelic school', the hippy harlequin stylings of The Fool ended up looking less cutting-edge than the professor's room by the time *Wonderwall* came out, its dark sludgy colours and pre-Raphaelite aesthetics corresponding perfectly with the revivalist look of the times.[87]

The continuity of design between *Blossom* and *Wonderwall* presents a solid case for regarding Assheton Gorton as design auteur, although John Russell Taylor felt he was more a talented professional trapped in 'our chic-mad recent swinging British cinema':

> Very splendid a lot of the sets are, as sets, and it is certainly not Mr Gorton's fault that the films they decorate are unable to live up to them. [. . .] *Wonderwall* and *The Bliss of Mrs Blossom* end up looking rather uncomfortable, all dressed up in maximum splendour, but then left with nowhere really to go.[88]

The same could be said of *The Magic Christian*, which reunited Gorton with Joe McGrath but mislaid its clarity of purpose in the overall chaos. More effective satire came in the shape of *The Bed Sitting Room*, Richard Lester's post-apocalyptic comedy about a Britain trying to keep calm and carry on after nuclear decimation. It demanded a far sparser visual environment than Gorton's three previous films. Desolate post-industrial wastelands with 'no natural green' in them became the arena for a surreal display of the fragments these survivors have shored against their ruins, like the cracked dome of St Paul's (which Gorton saw as 'a gutted broken egg'), an escalator that leads nowhere, and a makeshift triumphal arch constructed from scrap washing machines.[89]

The repurposing of old objects and buildings, which had been exhilaratingly fresh and fashionable in *Blow Up*, had now become desperately poignant. Bed-sitting rooms were no longer the site of youthful liberation, as they had been in *The Knack*'s house-share, but a metaphor for humanity's demise instead. In Gorton's progression through 1960s cinema, his designs triumphantly fulfilled his aim of 'speaking to the subconscious' through his work, echoing the decade's dreams, aspirations and sometimes darkest fears.[90]

Notes

1. Lesley Jackson, *The Sixties: Decade of Design Revolution* (London: Phaidon, 1998), p. 7.
2. Ibid.
3. Ibid., p. 145. Penny Sparke, 'At home with modernity: the new domestic scene', in Christopher Breward and Ghislaine Wood (eds), *British Design from 1948: Innovation in the Modern Age* (London: V&A Publishing, 2012), p. 132.

4. The point of origin for these arguments is Booker's *The Neophiliacs*, first published in 1969.
5. Wolff quoted in Christopher Breward, 'Boutiques and beyond: the rise of British fashion', in Breward and Wood (eds), *British Design from 1948*, p. 208.
6. Philip French in David Sylvester (ed.), *Moonraker, Strangelove and Other Celluloid Dreams: The Visionary Art of Ken Adam* (London: Serpentine Gallery, 1999), p. 32. Adam contributed to the escalating gadget-ology of the series, including devising the ingeniously adapted Aston Martin DB5 in *Goldfinger*. Christopher Frayling notes that the car made its debut appearance against a backdrop of other 'classics of British design' in Q's workshop – a Mini-van, a parking meter, an anglepoise lamp – therefore situating Adam's Bond design on a continuum with other key developments in the field. Christopher Frayling, *Ken Adam and the Art of Production Design* (London: Faber, 2005), p. 144.
7. Quoted in James Delson, 'Art Directors: Ken Adam', *Film Comment*, January/February 1982, p. 38.
8. On Hicks, see Christopher Breward and Ghislaine Wood, 'Tradition and modernity 1945–79', in Breward and Wood (eds), *British Design from 1948*, p. 36.
9. Penny Sparke, 'At home with modernity: the new domestic scene', in Breward and Wood (eds), *British Design from 1948*, p. 123. Hicks's geometric carpet design later dominated *The Shining* (1980).
10. This was also the era of eye-catching design for credit sequences, exemplified by Maurice Binder and Robert Brownjohn's work on the Bond films. For more on Brownjohn's credits, see 'Meet the man who gets the Bond films off to a sizzling start', *Showtime*, October 1964, pp. 21–3.
11. When there had been with Oscar wins in 1940, 1947 and 1948 for Vincent Korda, John Bryan, Alfred Junge, Carmen Dillon and Hein Heckroth. For more on this history, see Laurie Ede, *British Film Design: A History* (London: I. B. Tauris, 2010), p. 114.
12. 'Guild of Film Art Directors new service', *Daily Cinema*, 17 April 1964, p. 5. News of the guild's forthcoming second annual dinner, due to be held at Pinewood studios, was reported in *Kine Weekly* on 9 December 1965, p. 10. But as Laurie Ede observes, the low- to medium-budget production that had been a staple of British films for decades, and therefore bread-and-butter for many art directors, began to wane as US-funded production concentrated on 'fewer, but bigger, pictures', and in the process many skilled and experienced craftsmen found it harder to gain regular employment. Ede, *British Film Design*, p. 114.
13. Stanley Price, 'The man who gilded Goldfinger', *Observer Magazine*, 6 September 1964, p. 24.
14. Letter from Clive Donner to Reece Pemberton dated 28 March 1967, Clive Donner special collection, National Film and Television Archive, CSD 18/6.
15. Adam quoted in Terence St John Marnier with Michael Stringer, *Film Design* (London: Tantivy, 1974), p. 30.
16. Adam quoted in Delson, 'Art Directors: Ken Adam', pp. 39–40.
17. John Russell Taylor, 'Larking back', *Sight and Sound*, vol. 37, no. 2, Spring 1968, p. 69.
18. Ibid., pp. 69–70.
19. Stringer in Marnier with Stringer, *Film Design*, p. 43.
20. Mary Corliss and Carlos Clarens, 'Designed for film: the Hollywood art director', *Film Comment*, May/June 1978, p. 32. Ede, *British Film Design*, p. 2.
21. Ian Christie, *The Art of Film: John Box and Production Design* (London: Wallflower, 2009), p. 167.

22. Quoted in Marnier with Stringer, *Film Design*, p. 52. It is important to add that the turn towards location filming was not only motivated by aesthetic end results but also by the greater opportunity it offered to handpick crew members and evade the control of the studio-based union shop.
23. Ede, *British Film Design*, p. 97.
24. Ralph Brinton, 'The New Realism in British Films', *Journal of the Society of Film and Television Arts*, no. 11, Spring 1963, p. 9.
25. Marshall in Roger Hudson, 'Three Designers', *Sight and Sound*, vol. 33, no. 1, Winter 1964, p. 30. Nor was this the exclusive preserve of the New Wave vanguard. Shooting in a Battersea cul-de-sac for the working-class melodrama *This Is My Street* (1964), producer Jack Hanbury enthused: 'We could have built this in the studio but we'd never have got this atmosphere: look at this railway bridge with trains going over every few minutes, that little pub on the corner, those gasometers. And that dog's home!' Derek Todd, 'No end to realism in a Battersea cul-de-sac', *Kine Weekly*, 8 August 1963, p. 11.
26. Quoted in Marnier with Stringer, *Film Design*, p. 50. Although famed for his studio work, Adam also did extensive location work on a number of 1960s films including *The Ipcress File* (1965) and *Goodbye Mr Chips* (1969).
27. Lean quoted in Christie, *The Art of Film*, p. 4.
28. Kip Herren, 'Film production – do or die?', *Kine Weekly* (Production Review supplement), 24 October 1962, p. 15.
29. Hudson, 'Three Designers', p. 27.
30. Ibid., p. 31.
31. Ibid., p. 30.
32. Peggy Gick BECTU interview, <https://historyproject.org.uk/interview/peggy-gick> (accessed 20 July 2018). She herself had queried director Guy Hamilton's assumption, while filming a scene for *The Party's Over* (1965) in 'a long sort of passageway in the Pheasantry down in Chelsea', that 'you could never get this effect in a set': 'I thought, well I could easily have built that as a set.'
33. Philip French in Sylvester (ed.), *Moonraker, Strangelove*, p. 35. Christie, *The Art of Film*, p. 97. To complete the circle, Box's *Oliver!* set was partly inspired by John Bryan's original work for David Lean's 1948 *Oliver Twist*.
34. Withy in Marnier with Stringer, *Film Design*, p. 90. Withy used similar techniques in his work on television commercials.
35. Peter Todd, 'Getting into the comedy habit', *Kine Weekly*, 13 June 1963, p. 14.
36. Cain in Marnier with Stringer, *Film Design*, p. 60. Scenic artist Ben Healey noted 'the crowning irony' that 'the better his work is, the less it must be recognised as painting. [. . .] All the really good stuff is invisible.' Healey, 'The gay bohemians', *Film and Television Technician*, October 1967, p. 257.
37. Maurice Carter BECTU interview, <https://historyproject.org.uk/interview/maurice-carter> (accessed 20 July 2018). The replica House of Commons chamber Carter created for *No Love for Johnnie* (1961) ended up going into the Pinewood stock bay along with other 'stock sets like the central criminal courts, the Old Bailey'.
38. Ede, *British Film Design*, p. 85.
39. Marnier with Stringer, *Film Design*, p. 114.
40. Detailed information on these and other examples from the period 1957–67, see Wayne Kinsey, *Hammer Films: The Bray Studios Years* (Richmond: Reynolds & Hearn, 2002). Hammer's specialisation in gothic helped with their recycling too, as designer Scott McGregor observed, because 'one tends to use lots of plaster and masses of dirt and you can give lots of atmosphere and character to the set' and disguise a re-vamp, whereas with sci-fi 'you have to produce a very polished job.

[. . .] It is possible to get away with a certain amount of bad workmanship in horror films but never on a modern set.' In Marnier with Stringer, *Film Design*, p. 120.
41. Wayne Kinsey and Gordon Thomson, *Hammer Films on Location* (London: Peveril, 2012) provides exhaustive coverage of the studio's range of locations.
42. But whereas Box had the real Arabian desert for *Lawrence of Arabia*, Vetchinsky had to make do with Camber Sands for *Carry On Follow That Camel* (1967).
43. Marcus Harrison, 'Better sets – but at no greater cost', *Kine Weekly* (Production Review supplement), 26 September 1963, p. 28.
44. Christie, *The Art of Film,* pp. 76–8.
45. Ibid., p. 78.
46. In John Russell Taylor, 'Accident', *Sight and Sound*, vol, 35, no. 4, Autumn 1966, p. 179.
47. Ibid., p. 182. Bogarde drew a revealing comparison between Richard MacDonald, 'a marvellous improvisator, an ideas man who throws off dazzling notions every minute of the day and leaves others to work out the prosaic details [. . .] exactly right for a film like *Modesty Blaise*' and Dillon, 'a completely practical designer [and] a professionally trained architect and all her designs are calculated exactly to *work*. In this sort of film, which is meant to have its feet very much on the ground, she is ideal'.
48. Carrie Rickey, 'Theatrical Realism', *Film Comment*, January/February 1982, pp. 32–3.
49. Harrison, 'Better sets – but at no greater cost', p. 28.
50. Stringer in Marnier with Stringer, *Film Design*, pp. 9–10.
51. Hudson, 'Three Designers', p. 27.
52. Stringer in Marnier with Stringer, *Film Design*, p. 35.
53. Ibid., p. 50.
54. Marnier with Stringer, *Film Design*, p. 46. Tellingly, several designers use variations on the words 'instinct' or 'intuition' to describe quintessential aspects of their work. Ted Marshall described dressing sets 'by instinct [. . .] one feels intuitively'. Ibid., p. 131. Ken Adam said he also worked 'on instinct. You digest all the problems and overall aims but the actual designs come mainly instinctively.' Hudson, 'Three Designers', p. 27.
55. Christie, *The Art of Film*, p. 64. Of course it then took the skill, hard work and ingenuity of the entire art department to render what Box had envisaged in practical form, with prop master Eddie Fowlie blasting the set with a mixture of molten wax and sparkling mica dust to create the requisite interior frosting. Ibid., p. 66.
56. Hudson, 'Three Designers', p. 29.
57. Marnier with Stringer, *Film Design*, p. 73.
58. Ibid., p. 27, p. 48.
59. Frayling, *Ken Adam and the Art of Production Design*, p. 164. Richard MacDonald's favourite use of colour was 'to paint [a wall] a cold grey or a cold brown – a sort of raw umber – and then spatter a warm colour over it. The camera can't make up its mind because it can't quite decide what it's going to do with this cool colour and warm colour. So it gives the wall a marvellous sort of feeling and a tremendous intensity.' MacDonald in Vincent LoBrutto, *By Design: Interviews with Film Production Designers* (Westport, CT: Praeger, 1992), p. 66.
60. Quoted in Sylvester (ed.), *Moonraker, Strangelove*, p. 77. Carmen Dillon spoke of 'trying to make a colour film almost in monochrome, with just occasional accents of colour' on *Accident*. Taylor, 'Accident', p. 179. Although she hadn't enjoyed producer Ross Hunter's edicts for a monochromatic look on the melodrama *The Chalk Garden*: 'He doesn't even like creams or pale greens. I must say that I personally like English country houses to look like English country houses. But he has

a passion for white.' Quoted in Derek Todd, 'White Hunter sets his sights on *The Chalk Garden*', *Kine Weekly*, 4 April 1963, p. 11.
61. Patrick Gibbs, 'Poor Cow', *Daily Telegraph*, 8 December 1967 (BFI press cuttings file).
62. Marjorie Bilbow,' Wonderwall', *Today's Cinema*, 10 January 1969, p. 8.
63. Elizabeth-Marie Tuson, 'Consumerism, the Swinging Sixties and Assheton Gorton', *Journal of British Cinema and Television,* vol. 2, no. 1, 2005, p. 107. Ede, *British Film Design*, p. 116. Jackson, *The Sixties*, p. 55.
64. Gorton quoted in Murray Pomerance, 'Assheton Gorton: A Life in Film', *Film International*, no. 71, March/April 2015, p. 68.
65. Assheton Gorton BECTU interview, <https://historyproject.org.uk/interview/assheton-gorton-0> (accessed 20 July 2018).
66. Gorton in Elizabeth-Marie Tuson, 'Creating Space: Production Designer Assheton Gorton', *Journal of British Cinema and Television*, vol. 4, no. 2, November 2007, p. 362.
67. Ibid.
68. Ibid.
69. Assheton Gorton BECTU interview. Pomerance, 'Assheton Gorton: A Life in Film', p. 90.
70. Ibid., pp. 67–8. Given its semiotic richness, Gorton sometimes felt frustrated at his designs being under-exploited by directors even though he had given them 'the ammunition to use [. . .] whether he uses it or not I don't know, but it's there in the background, subliminal or neglected or not seen at all.'
71. Gorton said a designer could 'earn five or six thousand pounds doing a commercial [. . .] and then you could get on with your own work'. BECTU interview.
72. Ede, *British Film Design*, p. 153. Those working for the BBC tended to work more exclusively for them, although Luciana Arrighi worked on BBC's *Monitor* and *Omnibus* before entering film through the auspices of her former BBC colleague Ken Russell, as set designer on *Women in Love* (1969), a similar trajectory to BBC designer Natasha Kroll who, having worked with Russell on *Monitor*, was then production designer on *The Music Lovers* (1970). Julia Trevelyan Oman, better known for her BBC work in the 1960s, was also associate art director on *The Charge of the Light Brigade* and art director for *Laughter in the Dark* (1969).
73. Tuson, 'Creating Space', p. 363.
74. Derek Todd, 'Woodfall shoots it out in a very tight corner', *Kine Weekly*, 3 December 1964, p. 10.
75. Tuson, 'Creating Space', p. 362. Pomerance, 'Assheton Gorton: A Life in Film', p. 62.
76. BECTU interview.
77. Ibid.
78. Pomerance, 'Assheton Gorton: A Life in Film', p. 62.
79. Ibid.
80. Anthony Haden-Guest, 'Than Man Who Painted Woolwich Black' *Weekend Telegraph Magazine*, 23 September 1967, p. 114. Not everyone appreciated this approach to colour control in production design. Ted Marshall, perhaps unsurprisingly given his more realist proclivities, disliked 'the extremes of Antonioni painting streets red or black. That is falsifying colour.' In Marnier with Stringer, *Film Design*, p. 85.
81. Quoted in Dominic Sandbrook, *The Great British Dream Factory: The Strange History of our National Imagination* (London: Penguin, 2015), p. 65.
82. Jackson, *The Sixties*, pp. 206–7

83. Derek Todd, 'How to "Blossom" into a Fun Film', *Kine Weekly*, 26 August 1967, p. 10. Pomerance, 'Assheton Gorton: A Life in Film', p. 68.
84. John Ware, 'Production-Wise', *Daily Cinema*, 1 November 1967, p. 8.
85. Tuson, 'Creating Space', p. 365.
86. Ibid.
87. John Ware, 'Production-Wise', *Daily Cinema*, 1 November 1967, p. 8. A further irony around film and fashionability around this time, as noted by John Russell Taylor: in 1967 the Odeon Leicester Square was refurbished and stripped 'of all its thirties splendours of veneer and chrome to make – the Rank Organisation thought – a bright, modern cinema', just as what it was obliterating came back into fashion. Taylor, 'Larking back', p. 70.
88. John Russell Taylor, 'Background to the Fore', *The Times*, 22 March 1969, p. 19.
89. BECTU interview. Gorton recalls creating the haunting image of a pile of (real) artificial limbs for the film, finding one leg stuffed with Scottish banknotes.
90. Tuson, 'Creating Space', p. 369.

9. COSTUME DESIGN

Melanie Williams

INTRODUCTION

The most significant aspect of the 1960s design boom was arguably the new international prominence for British fashion. London in particular became 'perceived by many as chief amongst fashion capitals, prime dictator of style and taste', and the 'British invasion' of pop music was paralleled, and indeed pre-empted, by an incursion of fashion into overseas markets, including

Figure 9.1 A diverse array of feminine fashions created by costume designer Julie Harris for *Casino Royale* (Val Guest, Ken Hughes, John Huston, Joseph McGrath, Robert Parrish, 1967).

America.[1] A crucial figure in this was Mary Quant, who signed a deal with J. C. Penney for a mass-market range as early as 1962, and featured in *Life* magazine's 1963 celebration of the 'brash new breed of British designers' alongside peers Jean Muir, James Wedge, Kiki Byrne, Marion Foale and Sally Tuffin, all said to be 'catching on with young Americans'.[2]

Given her popularity, it was hardly surprising that Quant was approached to provide film costumes, a practice that had a long heritage. She had supplied some dresses for minor British pop films *Live It Up* (1963) and *Ferry Cross the Mersey* (1964) but the first concerted effort to utilise Quant's clothes as a major attraction, on the comedy *The Wild Affair* (1963), was stymied by its release being held up until late 1965, by which time its innovative fashions no longer looked fresh.[3] Another significant tie-up came with *Georgy Girl* (1966), for which Quant 'supplied advance models of her spring Ginger Group collection' for Charlotte Rampling to wear as Meredith, 'an ultra-modern playgirl who copes with life, lovers and a marriage with cool detachment'.[4] A press release suggested how Quant's 'avant-garde look' was 'exactly right for ex-model Rampling [who] wears thigh-length shifts and op-art day dresses with great dash'. But, as Pamela Church Gibson points out, Meredith is really the film's 'flinty-hearted semi-villainess' who compares very unfavourably to Lynn Redgrave's empathetic heroine Georgy, generally clad in shapeless separates.[5] Ironically, the most successful feature film showcase for Quant's fashions probably came with Claire Bloom's wardrobe for the supernatural thriller *The Haunting* (1963), nicely characterised by critic John Coleman as 'black and cryptic schoolgirlery'.[6] But Quant's input remained marginal to the film and had no presence in its marketing. So ultimately the iconic designer's forays into cinema failed to capitalise on her fashionable 'British invasion' cachet and seem symptomatic of a larger impasse between cinema and fashion around this time.

Nonetheless, the new dominance of London as 1960s fashion capital provided a crucial context for the creation of screen costumes. Films aimed to capitalise on the densely intermedial phenomenon of 'swinging London' of which fashion was such an important component part. Numerous films featured the paradigmatic sixties retail environment, the boutique, from enthusiastic shopping sequences in Biba in *I'll Never Forget What's 'is Name* (1967) and Countdown in *Sebastian* (1968), to more satirical send-ups in *The Knack* (1965) and *Smashing Time* (1967). Photographers and models became key protagonists in films, ranging from the enigmatic *Blow Up* (1966) starring David Hemmings as its David Bailey-inspired protagonist alongside real supermodels of the period Peggy Moffatt, Jill Kennington and Verushka, to the more routine thriller *Maroc 7* (1967) which had to make do with Leslie Phillips as its 'Beatle-cut, Cockney-genius school of photography'.[7] Film costuming developed a far closer, but occasionally ambivalent or tense, relationship with contemporary fashion, its 'whole function' changing, one commentator wrote, 'from an under-financed production blind-spot' to an 'integral expression of character'.[8] Its promotional value was also considerable because 'to work up a fashion interest is by no means the only way of getting people talking about a film that is coming, and writing about it, but it is one of the very best ways.'[9]

HIDEOUS DISTORTIONS: FASHION DESIGNERS AND FILM

As we have seen, one tactic for achieving a fashionably dressed film was to get a fashion designer on board to provide costumes. Beyond Mary Quant's various collaborations cited above, other notable examples of this tactic included Foale and Tuffin designing Susannah York's wardrobe for *Kaleidoscope* (1966), Jean Muir dressing Eleanor Bron on *Bedazzled* (1968); in menswear, Doug Hayward dressing Terence Stamp in *Modesty Blaise* (1966) and Michael Caine in *The Italian Job* (1969), and Mr Fish costuming James Coburn and James Fox (in 'domino-patterned stripes with ruffled shirt and velvet bow tie') for *Duffy* (1968).[10] Sometimes an intermediary or consultant was brought in to broker a deal. One was Marit Allen, former *Vogue* 'Young Idea' editor, later an Oscar-nominated costume designer herself, who persuaded Foale and Tuffin to take on the *Kaleidoscope* job. Another was fashion buyer and ex-model Sandy Moss, credited as 'costume advisor' and 'fashion co-ordinator' on trend-driven films *The Touchables* (1968) and *Here We Go Round the Mulberry Bush* (1968).[11]

Mike Sarne took a chance on two recent graduates of the Royal College of Art, Virginia Hamilton-Kearse and Sue West, to provide a cornucopia of appropriately swinging costumes for his film *Joanna* (1968). The designers explored the heroine's metamorphosis in sumptuary terms, echoing Jane Gaines's observation that costume in films frequently 'tells the woman's story', as the heroine moved 'from kooky immature outfits like a spotted mini-coat to mid-calf fashion ensembles, with long culottes, wide waistbands of ultra-sophistication'.[12] They also stated their aim to influence real-life fashion and 'get birds to wear all lengths of clothes to suit their moods and surroundings rather than dictating a different length for each season', with copies of their clothes then sold through the US boutique Paraphernalia.[13] The dress code for *Joanna*'s premiere promoted a similarly eclectic aesthetic, encouraging everything from kaftans to kimonos, with its guests rising to the occasion with appropriately outlandish outfits which offered great promotional photo opportunities.[14] *Joanna* was therefore typical in that fashion was crucial both to its on-screen diegesis and its off-screen promotional strategies, both intricately intertwined.[15]

But there remained an ambivalence towards fashion in many British features of the period.[16] *Georgy Girl* had used Quant's cutting-edge miniskirts but dressed the film's most unsympathetic character in them. Likewise, *Kaleidoscope*'s female lead was a trendy boutique owner, with a Foale and Tuffin designer wardrobe, and the film's release was launched with a 'way out' dress competition in ABC cinemas, but its dialogue was still downright snarky about the profession it was ostensibly celebrating. 'I design clothes for baby-faced Chelsea girls who like to show off their pretty knees', Susannah York's character Angel says in the completed film, but an earlier version of the script she had continued along far more critical lines: 'I'm terribly "in" right now, and scandalously pampered, just bounce in with a stack of new drawings every week or so, and everyone sighs blissfully. [. . .] Nonetheless, it's a hideous distortion of values, and quite good fun.'[17] The rest of that speech may have been cut because the script needed to be tighter, but perhaps also because of a recognition that it was unwise to antagonise the real fashion designers they'd got on board to do their costumes.

FOR A CHARACTER, ALWAYS? COSTUME DESIGNERS AT WORK

While some productions sought to ensure their costuming was as close to the cutting edge as possible, others relied on their costume designers to do that work instead. Sometimes this was very successfully accomplished, as with the work of Julie Harris on *Darling* (1965) or Jocelyn Rickards on *Blow Up*, but a great deal hinged on luck in addition to sound judgement. They had to correctly anticipate what would be in fashion as Harris explained in 1967:

> One of the problems facing the designer particularly with modern-day films, is the time lapse between actual preparations of the wardrobe and the time when the public finally sees the film which in many cases can be a year, or even two years, after the initial planning stages. Yet the wardrobe must still look excitingly new. So you see we are continually having to look ahead.[18]

Although this problem had always existed in costuming, Harris felt that it had escalated and become 'more noticeable in the sixties' due to the increasingly rapid turnover in fashions.[19]

But even when their work managed to capture the fashionable zeitgeist with impeccable timing, costume designers took pains to distinguish their work from fashion design, as with Rickards' insistence that: 'Fashion is totally different from theatricality [. . .] Verushka's clothes in *Blow Up,* even though she's meant to be a model, aren't fashionable; they help define her extraordinary character.'[20] She later elaborated that costume design was 'not a self-serving device to make the audience stop and wonder at the beauty of your invention', but 'rather a means of conveying by a visual signpost the background of each character. [. . .] All this saves valuable minutes of screen time by getting points across through the eyes rather than verbally.'[21] This was why Rickards and her peers paid attention to the tiniest details if they felt it could shed light on a character. In the case of *Blow Up*, this meant tie-dyeing the junk-shop owner's skirt to make it 'fragmented like a sapphire' (likening her to a jewel in a rough setting), or getting the multicoloured minidresses for aspiring models Gillian Hills and Jane Birkin deliberately badly sewn so they would look homemade.[22] As fellow costume designer Anthony Mendleson summarised the credo of their profession: 'it was design for a character, always.'[23] Costume designs could overlap with contemporary fashion, if that happened to fit the character in question, but it should never be pre-eminent or lead the design process.[24] This fits with the recurrent tension Stella Bruzzi identifies in how screen costumes work: as 'functionaries of the narrative', helping with characterisation, but with the potential to become 'spectacular interventions that interfere with the scenes in which they appear', noticeable in their own right.[25] She summarises this as the quandary of 'whether to look *at* or *through* the clothes', and it reverberates through the work of many costume designers of the period, in which fashionable forms of dress become more outlandish, physically revealing, vibrantly colourful, and therefore more likely to be distractingly spectacular, than ever before.[26]

But invoking fashionable modernity was in many respects a secondary concern for most costume design of the period. In terms of award nominations and wins during the 1960s, British designers' work in contemporary dress was greatly outnumbered by their historical assignments, corresponding to an older vision of British cultural capital owing more to Merrie England than 'swinging London'. Although Harris won the black-and-white costume design Oscar for *Darling,* and Rickards was nominated in the same category the following year for *Morgan – A Suitable Case for Treatment* (1966), all the other British nominees and winners of costume Oscars in the 1960s were recognised for period drama of various kinds. They include Cecil Beaton who won in the colour category for *My Fair Lady* in 1964 with Margaret Furse and Tony Walton nominated for *Becket* and *Mary Poppins* respectively; in 1965 Phyllis Dalton won in the colour category for *Doctor Zhivago*, a triumph repeated by Elizabeth Haffenden and Joan Bridge with *A Man for All Seasons* the following year; in 1968 Margaret Furse and Phyllis Dalton were nominated for their work on *The Lion in Winter* and *Oliver!* respectively, with Furse then winning for *Anne of the Thousand Days* in 1969.

It was a slightly more complicated picture on the domestic front, with British Film Academy awards for costume design (instigated in 1964) conferred upon modern-dress costumes designed by sister design team Motley for *The Pumpkin Eater* (1964) and Rickards for *Mademoiselle* (1966), in addition to nominations received by Julie Harris for *Psyche 59* (1964), *Help!* (1965), and *Casino Royale* (1967), Beatrice Dawson for *Woman of Straw* (1964), Margaret Furse for *A Shot in the Dark* (1965), and Rickards again for *The Sailor from Gibraltar* (1967). But generally, it was historical design that swept the board of nominations and winners at the BFA awards throughout the decade, and exclusively in the years 1968–70. Julie Harris may have got her Oscar for *Darling* but won her only BFA award for her Victorian costumes for *The Wrong Box* (1966).

Designers themselves were often relieved to escape the pressures of keeping up to date and enjoyed throwing themselves into historical research, with Rickards, Harris, Mendleson, and Dalton all citing the V&A and Bath Museum of Costume collections as important sources for their work.[27] Publicity materials for films often took pride in their costume designer's efforts to recreate an authentic sense of historical period, often on an epic scale. The pressbooks for *The Lion in Winter* and *Anne of the Thousand Days* boasted of Margaret Furse being 'responsible for the nearly 800 medieval costumes' worn in the former, while on the latter she 'personally designed some 120 costumes' and oversaw 'over 100 "stock" costumes worn by extras in crowd scenes'.[28]

The designer herself took out an advertisement in *Kine Weekly* after *Becket* had won the British Film Academy award for costume 'to thank all those whose invaluable help to her on the production of "BECKET" made it possible', including 'her friends and co-workers at Bermans and at Nathans, the studio wardrobe department [. . .] and particularly DINAH GREET who was her assistant and whose name did not appear on the film's screen credits – as it ought to have!'[29] Furse's heartfelt thanks in the trade press acknowledges the large workforce behind each film's wardrobe, of which the costume designer was merely the visible tip. Costumiers like Bermans and Nathans not only made up specific designs – and were able to rise to all manner of challenges, including a gorilla suit installed with smoke packs for *Morgan* – but also provided access to their vast collections of stock costumes, an essential resource especially for large-scale period films.[30]

The wardrobe department itself could be an extensive team; Phyllis Dalton recalled having 'as many as 15 or 20' on location with her for *Doctor Zhivago*, and felt that 'when you've got a good army you can be quite proud of it'.[31] In marshalling her them on various productions, Dalton felt that 'diplomacy' was 'a great part of [her] job' of costume designer, recognising how its intense demands could often 'bring out the harridan in you'.[32] Jocelyn Rickards had likewise realised the importance of good communication back when she'd worked on *The Prince and the Showgirl* (1957) and there was an unforeseen colour clash between Roger Furse's red male costumes and Beatrice Dawson's pink female costumes for a key scene: the lesson Rickards took away was 'don't keep your hand over your work'.[33]

But while working collaboratively, the costume designer bore ultimate responsibility for conceiving, budgeting, and delivering everything required within a film's 'dress plot', which Julie Harris called the 'Bible' for 'what each character wears in each scene', a potentially enormous workload on large-scale productions.[34] Sketches for bespoke costumes were an important part of this process but in practice did not always predominate in the costuming process. Dalton described her work as 'partly doing sketches and having things made specially but after that sometimes it's adapting things, a lot of it is just shopping, getting the appropriate things, you know, dyeing and adapting'.[35] However the costumes were acquired, they then had to be fitted: 'the moment of truth' for Rickards, proving 'whether it succeeds in itself and whether the artist feels right and can work in it'.[36] The process of fittings could also entail complex interpersonal negotiations, especially if an actor had particular ideas about what they would and wouldn't wear, further complicated if a star got to keep their costumes as part of their contract, and you would be, Harris remembered, 'fighting their own taste the whole time, which may not be your idea of what the character should wear'.[37]

Once shooting began, Harris, like many of her peers, regarded being on location or 'being on the studio floor right through shooting' as 'essential' because 'every day brings unforeseen problems'.[38] A schedule might be drawn up but 'changes constantly. Something supposedly not wanted for two weeks is wanted yesterday.'[39] Or a previously agreed costume might be rejected by a director, as happened to Harris when dressing Eunice Gayson for the casino scene of *Dr No* (1962), so she had to improvise something else at short notice, adapting a red dress from Pinewood's stock costume rails to dazzling effect.[40]

A Gendered Profession

As will be clear from most of the recurrent designer names mentioned above, 1960s British costume design was distinctive in being an area of film production work dominated by women, unlike the other male-dominated creative domains.[41] Alongside the award-nominated and award-winning female costumiers already mentioned – Harris, Rickards, Furse, Dalton, Beatrice 'Bumble' Dawson, the Harris sisters of Motley, Elizabeth Haffenden – there were other female designers and costume supervisors less garlanded but still putting in strong work, such as Cynthia Tingey, former in-house designer at Berman's (who felt she worked 'much better if given four days to complete a job than four months'), Yvonne Caffin, Joan Ellacott, and Hammer costume stalwart Rosemary Burrows.[42] Younger female designers starting out in the 1960s who were to make more of an impact in later decades, included Ruth Myers, Emma Porteous, Yvonne Blake and Shirley Russell.

The gendering of the profession as female may be one reason why its professional skillset has been 'misinterpret[ed] as shopping or fashion', cultural realms generally coded as feminine.[43] This is in evidence in one male journalist's slightly patronising description of Phyllis Dalton costuming *Lawrence of Arabia* (1962):

> It is only when she sees the traders beginning to pull down their shutters that she realises the day's shopping must come to an end. By that time she has ordered clothes and materials running into many hundreds of pounds, and done it as coolly as a girl going out to buy three yards for a skirt and a new blouse for Spring.[44]

But while feminised, the profession was not exclusively female and there were also some notable men in evidence during the period, from occasional costume contributors like artistic polymath Cecil Beaton to experienced designers such as Ealing veteran Anthony Mendleson, as well as younger exponents such as Carl Toms, described in 1967 as 'a most talked about designer' whose 'set designs, dressings and artistic work have become internationally known'.[45] His best-known film costumes were the 'skins of leopard, wolf and bear which are specially cut and stitched by hand for the large cast, every single one made to measure' for Hammer's *One Million Years BC* (1966), 'cost[ing] more than the normal "costume" picture' despite their skimpiness.[46] Another notable male designer 'making his presence felt on the movie scene' around the same time was John Furniss, award-nominated for his work on the First World War film *The Blue Max* (1966) but pulling out all the stops on another Hammer production, *The Viking Queen* (1967) for which he was 'commissioned to create an array of abbreviated battle gear for the ladies. His creations consist of the briefest and most alluring ensembles yet devised for the screen – chain, bauble and gauze costumes'.[47]

History's Hummingbirds

All film costume designers, whether male or female, working in period dress or with the most swinging contemporary fashions, had to satisfy competing demands: character *and* spectacle, authenticity *and* visual interest, costumes to be looked *through* and looked *at*. These tensions played out in particular ways in films with historical settings and entailed a tricky balancing act. Phyllis Dalton was committed to realism in her approach, getting people to wear in their costumes because 'you don't know where the creases will come', but broke with strict verisimilitude for effect, making T. E. Lawrence's white robes from progressively thinner fabric as the character become more mentally exhausted and 'washed out'.[48] Jocelyn Rickards was presented with 'a period never before filmed' on *Alfred the Great* (1969) which meant 'designs had to be evolved without the benefit of earlier research or the usual quantities of "stock" costumes'.[49] Yet Anglo-Saxon accuracy was not Rickards's only consideration when designing and despite spending 'weeks reading, making notes' she 'put all the books on one side' when she began sketching, trying to create costumes 'which should appeal to the eyes of the 20th century while remaining true to the spirit of the 9th'.[50] Rickards hoped to inspire 'the young and imaginative' in her own time: 'in the end the film is about young people who, although they lived in the dark ages, glittered like hummingbirds'.[51] *Alfred the Great*'s promotional campaign went on to try to exploit the connections between glittering youth, ancient and modern, with 'David Hemmings personality coathangers' offered for use in male fashion boutiques, and strained connections made between modern male fashions from Cardin and Cerutti and King Alfred's capes and tunics.[52]

The promotional campaign for *Alfred the Great* shows how the entanglement of screen costume and real-life fashions was by no means restricted to films with contemporary settings, and period costumes from all eras could equally be mobilised as stylistic influences. This could be glimpsed back when Dior designer Marc Bohan created a low-cut 'Tom Jones' dress named after 1963's hit film.[53] But perhaps the most formative film in relation to this trend was *Doctor Zhivago* in spite of Phyllis Dalton's protestation that she 'never thought of myself as influencing fashion'.[54] According to *Sunday Times* fashion editor Ernestine Carter, Dalton was surely 'the only person amazed by the Zhivago craze' which by 1966 had 'spread like an epidemic of pink eye through the High Fashion salons of Italy and Paris'.[55] Carter concluded by noting how 'an Englishwoman, once a little girl from the Ealing College of Art, can change the course of international fashion'.[56] But this apparently spontaneous 'Zhivago craze' was actually underpinned by extensive promotional strategising on MGM's part, and numerous carefully orchestrated commercial tie-ins, as the film's hefty exhibitor's manuals make clear. It also helped enormously, in terms of the female fashion influence, that Julie Christie played the female lead since, as *Time* magazine suggested, what she wore on screen had 'more real impact on fashion than all of the clothes of the ten best-dressed women combined', whether modern or period dress.[57]

In the later part of the decade, the climate seemed especially germane for period-influenced fashions to catch on as nostalgia-chic increasingly began to predominate across popular culture. British Film Academy-nominated costumes for *Far From the Madding Crowd* (1967) and *The Charge of the Light Brigade* (1968), by Alan Barrett and David Walker respectively, proved timely in their showcasing of Victoriana, their military uniforms for the men and 'long, demure dresses' with 'milkmaid sleeves' for the women corresponding perfectly to styles sold in retro boutiques.[58] 'The Isadora look' was promoted in advance of the biopic *Isadora* (1968), which included a specially commissioned new hairstyle by Vidal Sassoon, a perfume by Yardley, and a fashion range including long floaty scarves (somewhat ironically).[59] Younger costume designers like Shirley Russell preferred to use the real thing whenever possible, and drew on her large personal collection of vintage clothing, particularly from the 1920s (sourced from 'old ladies with great secret mounds of clothes in distant garages') for her husband Ken Russell's period films *Women in Love* (1969) and *The Boy Friend* (1971).[60] All this chimed with what film producer Judd Bernard observed happening in fashionable late 1960s London, which was 'present-day people masquerading as people in the past. If you go up and down the Kings Road you see people with gear-type outfits and I think it's a desire not only to be trendy and with-it but to escape.'[61]

From hand-crafting fur bikinis to rummaging in garages, dressing Charlotte Rampling in an op-art dress or Peter O'Toole in worn-out muslin, costume design for British films in the 1960s encompassed a range of practices, but in each case the designers regarded their primary responsibility as creating on-screen character through clothes. In the meantime, the relationship between film and fashion had moments when it sprang vividly into mutually beneficial life. But they remained in a minority, demonstrating how hard it was to predict what might or might not work when attempting to harness the power of costume to get a film in the public eye and sometimes even into the public's wardrobe.

The Full Fig of Glamour: Julie Harris (1921–2015)

Despite Julie Harris's reputation as a designer being inextricably linked to the 1960s, with Brian McFarlane pointing out that 'she not only got an Oscar for *Darling* but also dressed the Beatles twice', she herself drew inspiration from a much earlier era, having been 'brought up in the film fan era of Carole Lombard and Joan Crawford', whose glamour had made a 'tremendous impression' on her as a girl.[62] Harris claimed to 'belong to my own period, the 30s, when there was an elegance in dress'.[63] By comparison, she felt that 1960s fashions were generally 'funny, ugly clothes' which could 'only be worn by the very young' (unlike Jocelyn Rickards who embraced sixties mod style despite being of similar age to Harris).[64] Harris's favourite star to dress was Deborah Kerr because she 'liked her kind of clothes – and the way she wore them', indicating her attachment to more residual forms of feminine elegance.[65]

Having studied at the Chelsea School of Art before the war with the initial idea of becoming a fashion illustrator, Harris joined Gainsborough in 1945 as an assistant to Elizabeth Haffenden, 'the queen of dress designers then', and the woman behind the studio's flamboyant period costumes.[66] During the 1950s, Harris rose to become the Rank Organisation's lead designer, not only making film costumes but also clothes for stars' personal appearances; most infamously a faux-mink bikini for Diana Dors which garnered huge amounts of publicity at the 1955 Venice Film Festival.

The 1960s marked an important career watershed for Harris, as she began working on a freelance basis, a mode of employment which she claimed to prefer: although it meant the loss of guaranteed regular work (and automatic usage of Pinewood's well-stocked wardrobe facility). [67] Harris contributed to some twenty-five films across the decade, a sign not only of her personal pre-eminence but also the vitality of British production during the period. She participated fully in its range, characterised by Anthony Mendleson as doing 'a great big multi-million budget film and then [. . .] one of these little domestic British comedies!' [68] Her forays in the latter genre included *The Fast Lady* (1962), *We Joined the Navy* (1962), *The Cracksman* (1963), *Father Came Too!* (1964), and *Carry On Cleo* (1964), whereas among the more internationally inclined productions she worked on in the first part of the decade were Disney's *Swiss Family Robinson* (1960), Columbia's *The War Lover* (1962), and Universal's *The Chalk Garden* (1964). Later in the decade she would work on the big-budget runaways *Casino Royale*, *Prudence and the Pill* (1968), and the musical *Goodbye, Mr Chips* (1969).

Psyche 59, Troy–Schenck's British-set thriller with a transnational cast and American director, would earn Harris her first BFA award nomination, but another film of 1964, *A Hard Day's Night*, had the greater impact on her future career trajectory. Even though the Beatles' tailor Dougie Millings designed their suits while Harris took responsibility for dressing everyone else, she still benefitted from association with the paramount sixties pop phenomenon. She worked with them a second time on their first colour film *Help!*, providing a selection of ready-to-wear casuals for their scenes in the Bahamas.[69] But Harris's other film of 1965 proved even more crucial in consolidating her growing reputation as a costume designer adept at invoking 'swinging London': *Darling*, for which she would win an Oscar. Harris had come to it just ten days before shooting was due to begin and 'no one had a costume to wear!' [70] A 'quick shop with Julie Christie in the High Street' ensued, 'just to get a few things so we could get by'.[71] These off-the-peg acquisitions included a pinstripe trouser suit from Biba, a pivotal sixties retailer, recognised with delight by designer Barbara Hulanicki when she saw it on screen.[72] Diana's casual outfits of trousers, miniskirts, skinny-rib polo neck and knee-high boots, would prove powerfully influential on contemporary fashion, particularly in the US.[73] Christie's input into *Darling*'s costuming, especially the miniskirts, had played a crucial role in its fashionability, as Harris acknowledged: 'it was Julie Christie who said keep it short and she was so right'.[74]

Harris said *Darling* 'wasn't exactly Cinderella but she went from an ordinary model girl to the Italian princess' therefore ending up wearing 'the clothes that I felt I understood and loved more than the early ones which were King's Road sixties'.[75] But ironically when Diana adopts Harris's preferred costumes it is when her character is at her unhappiest, as the lonely, neglected *principessa*, a sign perhaps of Harris swimming against the general tide of sixties fashion. Her primary recollection of working on the film was the labour it entailed: 'The work that went into those clothes was amazing [. . .] There were a tremendous amount of clothes in that film!', and not only for Diana but for the entire cast.[76] The apparently effortless final result belied the 'sheer physical slog' involved in its creation, comprising both frantic shopping and bespoke designing.[77]

Forced to work in collaboration, Harris hints that within production hierarchies, the person 'who least got their way was the costume designer because you had to please so many different people'.[78] It was typical of Richard Lester to specify 'a dark suit and a beige shirt and a brown tie with a pin', while Harris had to adhere to producer Ross Hunter's overall colour concept for *The Chalk Garden* encompassing all decor and costumes, and her work on *Goodbye, Mr Chips* meant fitting in with Ken Adam's overall design vision, like his stipulation that all the extras for the large prize-giving scene be dressed solely in 'cream, beige and grey'.[79] Sometimes there was scope for more active exchange between different personnel, working to common goals: on *The Wrong Box*, Harris planned 'a water-colour effect with the clothes to complement the stylised colour photography' by Gerry Turpin.[80] She certainly valued the mutual trust she built up with Turpin, the film's art director Ray Simm and its director Bryan Forbes, each of whom she worked with on several projects, observing, 'it's nice working with the same people because you learn how their thinking goes, and they have confidence in you.'[81]

Like many of her peers, Harris benefitted from the escalation of production values and budget for costume design that came courtesy of large-scale American investment, albeit in quite chaotic ways: with *Casino Royale*, its producers 'always wanted something "yesterday" so it was a case of "Pay anything, just get it"'.[82] But the extravagance, along with the production's emphasis on dazzling visual spectacle, as well as an absence of singular directorial vision on how costumes should look, gave rise to unprecedented levels of creative agency for Harris. She later described working on *Casino Royale* as 'wholly satisfactory', in spite of its disordered production history and the incoherence of the final product: 'Some of it is very bad,' she conceded, 'but there was lots for me.'[83] Her extensive sketch portfolio for the film reveals a designer responding to a huge and crazily diverse brief with brio and wit, creating wild flamboyant costumes which demanded to be looked at, as visual spectacles in their own right.

Markedly different however was Harris's contemporaneous work on Bryan Forbes's film *The Whisperers* (1967), starring Edith Evans as an impoverished and delusional elderly woman. Here, character totally determined costuming, and beauteous visual spectacle was antithetical to the film's aims. Harris recalled the difficulty of making Evans look suitably abject when the actress gave even the shabbiest flea market finds an air of unintended elegance, but finally achieved her objective.[84] But in a later interview, the designer seemed more ambivalent about her work, gently querying the inevitable privileging of realistic characterisation over flamboyant spectacle:

> Character is harder than dressing someone up in the full fig of glamour, but it's not always more rewarding. It's an achievement if you make someone look right in character, like Edith Evans in *The Whisperers*, which was really quite difficult, and therefore very satisfying. However, no one is going to say you are a great designer for having done that.[85]

The effort required to create plausible characters through costuming is fully acknowledged, but Harris raises some interesting questions about this representing a costume designer's supreme achievement, suggesting some of the concomitant problems around status and respect that come with successfully undertaking that kind of invisible labour. The 'full fig of glamour' had considerable appeal for Julie Harris, which had as much to do with it providing a space for a fuller recognition of her creative achievements as it did with her intrinsic love of 'really glamorous clothes'.[86]

Her sketches show her evident enjoyment in creating costumes in exotic/erotic vein, from Balinese-influenced nightclub dancers for *The Cracksman*, to witty pastiches of Irene Sharaff's designs for Elizabeth Taylor's *Cleopatra* on *Carry On Cleo*, to spangled showgirl outfits for both *We Joined the Navy* and *A Hard Day's Night*. Following the 'fancy dress' aspects of *Casino Royale*, Harris also showed great relish in designing for masked ball scenes in Bryan Forbes's *Deadfall* (1968) – with designs including Medusa, Scheherazade, and Nell Gwynn – and John Krish's mangled *Decline and Fall . . . of a Birdwatcher* (1968), for which she devised an outrageously callous peasant costume for the character of Margot Beste-Chetwynde (Genevieve Page), sadly unused in the film.[87] This spirit of inventive delight had also infused her costuming for Eleanor Bron as Ahme in *Help!* where there was 'no guidance in the script as to how she should be dressed', so Harris was able to fill the sartorial blank as she saw fit, doing so with costumes which cleverly blended Courrèges's space-age look with traditional Indian dress.[88] Harris's *Help!* costumes also made striking use of vivid colour, the increasing dominance of which allowed her to explore more fully its possibilities in costume design (with her favoured shade of fuchsia, used for numerous costumes, eventually becoming known in the trade as 'Harris Pink').[89] Pink was the colour she chose for conducting an intriguing experiment in *Casino Royale*, making four identical gowns, each one a darker pink, to be worn sequentially by Ursula Andress so that her costume would appear to deepen in shade as the scene progressed; although unfortunately the effect was then mangled in the editing.[90]

Harris was associated far more in the trade press with female costuming than male, described as an 'elegant lady who knows all about elegant fashions'.[91] Women's costumes vastly outnumber men's in her sketch archive, and whereas male costuming often just entailed 'going to the tailor and choosing fabrics, ensuring the fittings were done and having the shirts made and choosing the ties [. . .] all administration really', female costume seemed to offer greater potential for creative expression.[92] Period costume also offered greater creative control than contemporary costuming, which is one reason why Harris preferred it: 'with modern things it's different because the director can look at them and might say, 'Oh, my wife doesn't like that.' [. . .] But with period clothes, people know less so they accept the pretty drawing that I give them.'[93]

But Harris's best-laid costuming plans could still easily be foiled during production or post-production, as happened with her deepening pink gowns on *Casino Royale*. A beautiful feathered gown with gradations of colour from brown to orange designed for Petula Clarke on Harris's final film of the 1960s *Goodbye, Mr Chips* was eventually shot only in head-and-shoulder close-up so, as the designer put it, 'you just saw the top bit, the ugly bit'.[94] She found it 'frustrating when a scene in the film has to be cut and perhaps one of my favourite dresses doesn't get used', suggesting that if someone has gone to the bother of creating a beautiful costume then the director should 'show it!'[95] For Harris, it seems, narrative coherence and characterisation were important but so too was spectacle, and proper respect being accorded to a showstopping costume, which made her very much a costume designer suited to the spectacular terrain of the 1960s, despite her ambivalence about the decade's more outré fashions.

NOTES

1. Pamela Church Gibson, 'Myths of the Swinging City: The Media in the Sixties', in Christopher Breward, David Gilbert and Jenny Lister (eds), *Swinging Sixties: Fashion in London and Beyond, 1955–1970* (London: V&A, 2006), p. 96.
2. Sally Kirkland, 'Brash new breed of British designers', *Life*, 18 October 1963, p. 79. For more on this period of her career, see Mary Quant, *Quant by Quant* (London: V&A, 2012), originally published in 1966, the same year she was awarded the OBE in recognition of her services to British exports.
3. See Melanie Williams, 'Making the cut: *The Wild Affair*', *Transformation and Tradition in Sixties British Cinema*, November 2015, <https://60sbritishcinema.wordpress.com/2015/11/05/making-the-cut-the-wild-affair/>.
4. Jean Osborne, 'For the trades: *Georgy Girl*', press release from Shepperton Studios, 31 January 1966. BFI press cuttings file for *Georgy Girl*.
5. Ibid. Church Gibson, 'Myths of the Swinging City', p. 95.

6. John Coleman, 'The Haunting', *New Statesman*, 10 January 1964, BFI press cuttings file.
7. *Maroc 7* script, Film Finances archive, box 418b, p. 11.
8. Shelia More, 'Women behind the scenes of success', *The Times*, 19 July 1967, p. 9.
9. Alison Adburgham, 'The charge of the rag brigade', *The Guardian*, 21 March 1968, p. 9.
10. Geoffrey Aquilina Ross, *The Day of the Peacock: Style for Men 1963–1973* (London: V&A, 2011), p. 77. Michael Fish, 'the tailor who brought colour to Saville Row', judged a line-up of 'young people garbed in way-out gear that had even the most swinging of Londoners goggling' at the film's premiere. 'Top gear for Duffy first night at the Warner', *Kine Weekly*, 12 October 1968, p. 20. An equally important sartorial influence on male fashions in the 1960s was the suave, sharp James Bond look. Terence Young took Sean Connery to his own tailor Anthony Sinclair and encouraged him to sleep in his suits in order to feel 'more at ease' in them. Bronwyn Cosgrove, *Designing 007: Fifty years of Bond Style* (London: Barbican, 2012), p. 11.
11. Clare Rendlesham, former *Vogue* and *Queen* fashion editor, acted as wardrobe supervisor for a number of Stanley Donen's London-based films, including *Two for the Road* which not only put Audrey Hepburn in Mary Quant but also put Albert Finney in Hardy Amies.
12. Jane Gaines 'Costume and Narrative: how dress tells the woman's story', in *Fabrications: Costume and the Female Body* (London: Routledge, 1990), pp. 180–211. 'Revelations of a Film Fox', *Kine Weekly*, 15 June 1968, p. 5.
13. For more on Paraphernalia boutique, see Jonathan Walford, *Sixties Fashion* (London: Thames and Hudson, 2013), pp. 47–51. It is not known how well the clothes sold but since the film was not a success, probably not well. Even tie-in fashions for more successful films didn't guarantee huge sales: Mia Fonssagrives and Vicki Tiel's womenswear tie-ins or *What's New Pussycat?* were judged a costly flop by Adburgham, 'The charge of the rag brigade', p. 9.
14. 'Joanna premiere will be for "beautiful people"', *Kine Weekly*, 25 January 1969, p. 11.
15. Another studio, Paramount, created the new position of 'fashion co-ordinator responsible for supervising all fashion promotions for the company's pictures' that same year to address these needs. 'Fashion post', *Kine Weekly*, 9 November 1968, p. 9.
16. Fashion was represented in more celebratory ways in non-fiction films, from Pathé Pictoral and Rank's Look at Life shorts on the subject, to supporting features like 20th Century Fox's 23-min factual film *World of Fashion* (1968), directed by Robert Freeman and starring model Genevieve Gilles, which 'portrays 60 years of fashion' including latest clothes from YSL, Apple and Top Gear. Trade press coverage suggested 'the fashion content will interest and amuse most women ... men will be too busy looking at Miss Gilles to notice what she's wearing'. 'Just look at what Genevieve's got!', *Today's Cinema*, 1 January 1969, p. 9.
17. Undated shooting script for *Kaleidoscope*, Film Finances archive, box 408, p. 41. Discussed in more detail in Melanie Williams, 'A kaleidoscope of costume: putting swinging London's fashions on screen', *Transformation and Tradition in Sixties British Cinema*, <https://60sbritishcinema.wordpress.com/2016/10/20/a-kaleidoscope-of-costume-putting-swinging-londons-fashions-on-screen/>.
18. Quoted in 'Way Out in the Fashion Field', in *Star TV and Film Annual 1968* (London: Odhams, 1967), p. 42.
19. In Brian McFarlane, *Autobiography of British Cinema* (London: Methuen/BFI, 1997), p. 284.

20. Quoted in More, 'Women behind the scenes of success', p. 9. This was no slighting of couture though: Rickards found 'the lure of high fashion quite irresistible. My interest in it wasn't frivolous, it was passionate.' Jocelyn Rickards, *The Painted Banquet* (London: Weidenfeld and Nicolson, 1987), p. 40.
21. Ibid., p. 58.
22. Jocelyn Rickards BECTU interview, <https://historyproject.org.uk/interview/jocelyn-rickards> (accessed 30 July 2018).
23. Quoted in Catherine A. Surowiec, 'Anthony Mendleson: Ealing's wardrobe wizard', in Mark Duguid, Lee Freeman, Keith M. Johnston and Melanie Williams (eds), *Ealing Revisited* (London: BFI, 2012), 111.
24. Jane Gaines observes how costume designers have always 'dissociated themselves from trend-setting' in order to boost their status as creative artists untainted by consumerist concerns. Gaines, 'Costume and Narrative', p. 198. But some were able to bridge the gap between costume and fashion more deftly. While characterisation determined Rickards' design decisions on *Blow Up*, she was still willing to act as an ambassador for mod fashion while promoting the film in the US, dressed in her own 'tweed miniskirt' and 'high suede boots', undertaking extensive promotional interviews for TV, radio and press about the hip new (bra-less) London look, helping to sell *Blow Up* and British fashion simultaneously. Rickards, *The Painted Banquet*, pp. 102–3.
25. Stella Bruzzi, *Undressing Cinema: Clothing and Identity in the Movies* (London: Routledge, 1997), p. xv.
26. Ibid., p. 36.
27. In BECTU interviews, <https://historyproject.org.uk/interview/jocelyn-rickards>, <https://historyproject.org.uk/interview/julie-harris-0>, <https://historyproject.org.uk/interview/anthony-mendleson>, <https://historyproject.org.uk/interview/phylis-dalton> (all accessed 30 July 2018).
28. Pressbook for *The Lion in Winter*. Bill Douglas Cinema Museum collection. Pressbook for *Anne of the Thousand Days*, BFI Library. Furse's hard work on *Anne of the Thousand Days* got at least one more acknowledged airing before it entered the stock costume rails: the Tudor parody *Carry On Henry* (1971) re-used her lavish creations for Richard Burton to clothe their own Henry VIII, Sid James.
29. *Kine Weekly*, 9 April 1965, p. 13.
30. BECTU interview with Jocelyn Rickards. Historical advisors also had a vital role to play on that genre of film, typified by the input of brothers Andrew and John Mollo in ensuring the accuracy of military dress on *Doctor Zhivago* and *The Charge of the Light Brigade*.
31. Phyllis Dalton BECTU interview.
32. Ibid.
33. Jocelyn Rickards BECTU interview. She aimed to work as collaboratively as possible, and spoke very highly of her assistants Ruth Myers and Evangeline Harris, as Furse had of Dinah Greet. Rickards, *The Painted Banquet*, p. 88, p. 104.
34. McFarlane, *Autobiography of British Cinema*, 287.
35. Phyllis Dalton BECTU interview. Anthony Mendleson confirms that most of them 'didn't sit and draw and draw and draw, of course not! They used to go out and go around the shops and buy things' as well as 'going to the costumiers, going through the rails'. BECTU interview.
36. More, 'Women behind the scenes of success', p. 9.
37. David Castell, 'More by accident than design', *Films Illustrated*, October 1976, p. 69. She added, 'a designer doesn't necessarily get her own way because, when it comes to a showdown, the director will always side with the star'.

38. Iain F. McAsh, 'The Shape of Clothes to Come', *Film Review*, November 1975, p. 11.
39. Unattributed newspaper article *c.*1967, BFI Library press cuttings file on Julie Harris.
40. Although she went without credit. Cosgrove, *Designing 007*, p. 9.
41. Indeed, Sue Harper describes the 1960s being the period in British cinema when 'women's dominance of costume design was complete'. Sue Harper, *Women in British Cinema* (London: Continuum, 2000), p. 216.
42. Barry Ward, 'Keeping the funny men in stitches', *Daily Express*, 7 May 1980, no page number.
43. Miranda J. Banks, 'Gender below the line: defining feminist production studies', in Mayer, Banks and Caldwell (eds), *Production Studies*, p. 95.
44. Howard Kent, *Single Bed for Three: A Lawrence of Arabia Notebook* (London: Hutchinson, 1963), p. 132.
45. 'Way Out in the Fashion Field', p. 44.
46. Ibid.
47. Ibid. Furniss's *piéce-de-résistance* was the Viking queen's bronze breastplate, intended to look striking even in the outlandish environment of 'swinging London': 'I just don't see metal bras, even with all that Carnaby Street PVC around'.
48. See Adrian Turner, *The Making of David Lean's Lawrence of Arabia* (London: Dragon's World, 1994), p. 140. Production designer John Box also seems to have some imaginative input into this idea, demonstrating the interplay between design departments in creating a film's overall look on many productions.
49. Pressbook for *Alfred the Great*, BFI Library. Rickards also drew inspiration from a tract in praise of virginity from the period which mentioned 'satin underclothing, blue and violet, scarlet tunics with hoods, sleeves with silk stripes, shoes edged with red fur, hair carefully arrayed on forehead and temples with the curling iron'. Rickards, *The Painted Banquet*, p. 114.
50. Jocelyn Rickards BECTU interview.
51. Undated MGM press release for *Alfred the Great*. BFI Library press cuttings file.
52. Pressbook for *Alfred the Great*.
53. Walford, *Sixties Fashion*, p. 76.
54. Ernestine Carter, 'A Winter of Zhivago', *The Sunday Times*, 28 August 1966, no page number (BFI press cuttings file).
55. Ibid.
56. Ibid.
57. Paula Reed, *Fifty Looks That Changed the 1960s* (London: Conran Octopus, 2012), p. 42. Christie's stardom anchored an intriguing tie-up for *Petulia*: a series of sewing patterns from McCall's enabling home dressmakers to copy Christie's fashionable outfits from the film. The distributors Warner–Pathé supplied stills 'illustrating three widely different roles portrayed by Julie Christie – from Billy Liar, Darling, and Far From the Madding Crowd' to promote it in department stores. Rod Cooper, 'Petulia tie-ups', *Kine Weekly*, 12 October 1968, p. 30. For more on Christie and sixties fashion, see Pamela Church Gibson, 'New stars, new fashions and the female audience: cinema, consumption and cities 1953–66', in Christopher Breward and David Gilbert (eds), *Fashion's World Cities* (Oxford: Berg, 2006), and 'The Fashioning of Julie Christie and the Mythologizing of "Swinging London": Changing Images in Sixties Britain', in Eugenia Paulicelli, Drake Stutesman and Louise Wallenberg (eds), *Film, Fashion, and the 1960s* Bloomington: Indiana University Press, 2017), p. 135–48.
58. Reed, *Fifty Looks That Changed the 1960s*, p. 46.
59. 'Fashion world takes to the Isadora look', *Kine Weekly*, 18 January 1969, p. 20. Valerie Gilbert, 'It's Isadora!', *Today's Cinema*, 20 January 1969, p. 12.

60. David Lewin, 'Shirley and the Petticoat Line', *Daily Mail*, 26 January 1971, no page number (BFI press cuttings file).
61. Derek Todd, 'Negatives Explores the Youthquake', *Kine Weekly*, 23 March 1968, p. 19.
62. McFarlane, *Autobiography of British Cinema*, p. 284. Castell, 'More by accident than design', p. 66.
63. Julie Harris BECTU interview.
64. Harris quoted in More, 'Women behind the scenes of success', p. 9.
65. McFarlane, *Autobiography of British Cinema*, p. 286. Harris costumed Kerr five times in the 1960s on *The Naked Edge* (1961), *The Chalk Garden*, *Casino Royale*, and *Prudence and the Pill* (1968), and she was specifically brought in to design Kerr's gowns on *Eye of the Devil* (1966). For more on Harris, see Melanie Williams, 'The girl you don't see: Julie Harris and the costume designer in British cinema', *Feminist Media Histories*, vol. 2, no. 2, 2016, pp. 71–106.
66. Julie Harris BECTU interview.
67. Anne Hooper, 'So you want to be a movie fashion designer?', *Photoplay*, September 1966, p. 61. In her later interview with Jo Botting, Harris said she'd actually preferred the stability of the studio era. NFT interview with Julie Harris by Jo Botting, 2002. Transcription available, <http://old.bfi.org.uk/features/interviews/harris.html> (accessed 24 February 2018).
68. Anthony Mendleson BECTU interview.
69. Harris recalled: 'In those days it was easy to get things on approval from the big shops and I got lots of casual stuff to show them so that they could choose. Harvey Nichols had a very good men's department and I took a lot from there to show them.' Frances Tempest, 'Interview with Julie Harris', on *Costume on Screen*, <https://costumeonscreen.wordpress.com/2011/06/25/julie-harris-darling-1965/> (accessed 24 February 2018).
70. Ibid.
71. Ibid.
72. Barbara Hulanicki and Martin Pel, *The Biba Years, 1963–1975* (London, V&A, 2014), p. 40.
73. Felicity Green observed *Darling*'s influence stateside (alongside *The Knack*) in 1966: 'Two British hit films have given New York its latest "in" words. Now everything is either "Darling" or "Knacky"', with Julie Christie enshrined as the new look's 'no. 1 exponent [. . .] from her wild blonde mane to her little girl shoes'. Felicity Green, 'What isn't knacky is just darling', *Daily Mirror*, 31 March 1966, p. 9.
74. Vincent William Gagliostro, 'A Darling Party', on Diane Pernet, *A Shaded View on Fashion Film*, <http://ashadedviewonfashion.com/blog/rip-julie-harris-sweet-memory-tea-iconic-costume-designer-and-short-doc-darling-party-vincent> (accessed 20 June 2018).
75. Julie Harris BECTU interview.
76. Harris was particularly pleased with the 'suede jacket, very Bohemian' she got for Dirk Bogarde to wear. She 'very seldom went shopping with the men, I may have taken them to Simpsons for some things because they had a very good men's department [. . .] I knew the buyer there and they would always look after you and put things out for you.' Tempest, 'Interview with Julie Harris'.
77. Julie Harris BECTU interview.
78. Ibid.
79. Botting NFT interview. Others like Billy Wilder on *The Private Life of Sherlock Holmes* (1970) made no firm recommendations at all, although Harris found this disengagement with costume slightly disappointing.

80. 'Production-wise', *The Daily Cinema*, 15 October 1965, p. 8.
81. McFarlane, *Autobiography of British Cinema*, p. 285.
82. Ibid., p. 286.
83. McFarlane, 288. Harris also said it was her most enjoyable film in McAsh,'The shape of clothes to come', p. 12.
84. Hooper, 'So you want to be a movie fashion designer?', p. 61. Jocelyn Rickards noticed the attention Evans paid to costuming while working with her on *Look Back in Anger*: 'I'll have my charlady's bag and the same kind of stockings she has', Evans said, and she bought earrings, 'little crystals on the end of a chain' from Woolworths, which she felt would have been a gift from Jimmy Porter. BECTU interview.
85. McFarlane, *Autobiography of British Cinema*, 288.
86. Hooper, 'So you want to be a movie fashion designer?', p. 61.
87. Harris notes in her annotations, the design represents 'Margot's idea of "the poor"': 'very "couture" rags. Twigs by Constance Spry. Fabulous long wig. Becoming smudges of "dirt" on face.'
88. Tempest, 'Interview with Julie Harris'.
89. McAsh, 'The shape of clothes to come', p. 11.
90. Julie Harris BECTU interview.
91. 'Think 20th Century-Fox: The Look Ahead', *The Daily Cinema*, 18 October 1967, p. 5.
92. McFarlane, *Autobiography of British Cinema*, p. 286. Harris confessed that men were not her forte: 'I can't draw them very well. My males still tend to look rather feminine.' McAsh, 'The Shape of Clothes to Come', pp. 11–12.
93. Botting NFT interview.
94. Ibid.
95. McAsh, 'The Shape of Clothes to Come', p. 11. Gagliostro, 'A Darling Party'.

10. CINEMATOGRAPHY

Duncan Petrie and Melanie Williams

INTRODUCTION

Among the numerous stylistic transformations taking place in 1960s British films, one of the most striking was the shift in cinematography: from the predominance of black and white to the ubiquity of colour; from hard edged, high-contrast lighting to softer, more diffused illumination; from carefully composed images and minimal camera movement to a freer and more spontaneous visual register; from the aesthetics of classicism to a much more self-conscious use of form appropriate for a decade associated with a new emphasis on spectacle and sensation. These changes were driven by a number of factors, including developments in technology and film-making practice, changing patterns of production and employment within the industry, and influences from other creative spheres including television, advertising, fashion and art. Prior to the 1960s, the British studio system had been characterised by rigid working practices, and career progression in the camera department was a lengthy process with individuals beginning as a clapper/loader and gradually progressing to focus puller, operator, and finally director of photography (DoP), usually in their late thirties. But with the studio system's demise came new (faster) career pathways. The increased movement of personnel between different spheres of production including documentary, television and advertising, further fuelled a breaking down of old hierarchies and moribund convention.[1]

More than 150 individuals are credited as cinematographers on the nearly

Figure 10.1 James Fox and Dirk Bogarde clash on the staircase, with Sarah Miles silhouetted in the middle, in *The Servant* (Joseph Losey, 1963), photographed by Douglas Slocombe.

1,000 British feature films released between 1960 and 1969, and despite their individual differences, they can be categorised in three distinct generations. The first was veterans whose careers stretched back to silent cinema, among them Desmond Dickinson, Basil Emmott, Geoffrey Faithfull, Otto Heller and Freddie Young. The second comprised the celebrated cohort who advanced the craft in the post-war years including Christopher Challis, Freddie Francis, Jack Hildyard, Erwin Hillier, Robert Krasker, Ted Moore, Oswald Morris, Douglas Slocombe, Gilbert Taylor and Geoffrey Unsworth.[2] The third was a younger generation whose diverse backgrounds embraced traditional studio training alongside formations in other fields like documentaries and advertising, such as Walter Lassally, Arthur Ibbetson, Nicolas Roeg, Ken Higgins, David Watkin, Billy Williams, Gerry Fisher and Alex Thomson.[3]

Work by British cinematographers achieved new levels of international recognition during the 1960s, with five Oscars in that category over the decade, equalling the total from the previous twenty years.[4] The winners were Freddie Francis for *Sons and Lovers* (1960) and Walter Lassally for *Zorba the Greek* (1964), both in the black-and-white category, alongside colour awards for Freddie Young for *Lawrence of Arabia* (1962) and *Doctor Zhivago* (1965), and Ted Moore for *A Man for All Seasons* (1966).[5] In addition, nominations were also received by Geoffrey Unsworth for *Becket* (1964), Ken Higgins for *Georgy Girl* (1966), Oswald Morris for *Oliver!* (1968) and Arthur Ibbetson for *Anne of the Thousand Days* (1969). Period subjects rendered in a largely unobtrusive, pictorial and ultimately traditional visual style tended to predominate, reflecting the preferences of Academy voters. The British Film Academy awards, by comparison, suggested the broader range of cinematographic achievement occurring in British films of the period, with wins for *The Servant* (1963), photographed by Douglas Slocombe, *The Ipcress File* (1965), shot by Otto Heller, and *The Pumpkin Eater* (1964), *The Hill* (1965) and *The Spy Who Came in from the Cold* (1966), all photographed by Oswald Morris, as well as multiple nominations for emergent talents such as Denys Coop, Gerry Turpin, Nicolas Roeg, David Watkin and Billy Williams.

Although certain cinematographers were recognised in high-profile award ceremonies, the individuals who amassed the largest number of credits during the 1960s tended to be specialise in less heralded low-budget productions. The most prolific individual during the decade is Jimmy Wilson, who photographed forty-two films at Merton Park studios between 1960 and 1966, including several of the successful series of thrillers adapted from the writings of Edgar Wallace.[6] Arthur Grant amassed thirty-one credits, the vast majority of which were horror films and action adventures made for Hammer Films, and had a reputation for combining speed with style, which made him a valuable asset to a company with keen commercial instincts.[7] Other highly prolific cinematographers of the decade included Alan Hume and Ernest Steward, both of whom worked on the *Carry On* series alongside other popular genre assignments. In addition to their twenty-nine film credits each, Hume and Steward also worked in television, with the medium's increasing use of 35mm film for drama creating openings for cinematographers who were prepared to diversify, serving emerging talents as well as providing a refuge for veterans like Lionel Baines, Walter J. Harvey, and Gerald Gibbs, who finished their careers working exclusively in television.

THE NEW NATURALISM

Several models of film camera had become smaller, lighter and more portable since World War Two, but their usage had largely been confined to documentary. However, by the late 1950s the French Éclair Cameflex and German Arriflex 35 started to be used on feature films, facilitating greater spontaneity, improvisation and intimacy in film-making. The introduction in 1963 of the zoom lens by the French engineer, Pierre Angénieux, which had a range of 10 to 1, afforded new cinematographic possibilities.[8] Improvements in the speed of film stocks were also crucial, with Eastman Kodak's black-and-white TRI X stock, which had a ground-breaking rating of 200 ASA for daylight exposure when it was launched back in 1954, then being doubled to 400 ASA with its 4X film launched a decade later. But this was preceded by the English manufacturer Ilford's HPS stock which first became available in 1960 and was enthusiastically taken up by numerous British cinematographers.[9] The greater light sensitivity of these stocks allowed much greater latitude when using natural light sources on location and would be crucial to the development of a new naturalistic style in British cinematography exemplified by the work of Walter Lassally.

The initial group of New Wave films had been shot by established cinematographers, usually at the insistence of financiers, thus Oswald Morris photographed Woodfall's *Look Back in Anger* (1959) and *The Entertainer* (1960) and his former operator Freddie Francis was responsible for *Saturday Night and Sunday Morning* (1960). While location shooting featured strongly in these films, conventional high-contrast lighting and solid camerawork still predominated, particularly in the interiors: Lassally describes them as 'basically studio films'.[10] He had photographed many of the Free Cinema documentaries of the 1950s, and his formative years in low-budget independent film-making predisposed him to innovation and improvisation. Tony Richardson was finally able to hire Lassally for *A Taste of Honey* (1961), and they worked closely together to create what remains stylistically the most significant film of the New Wave. Unlike its predecessors, *A Taste of Honey* was made entirely on location and filmed entirely on an Arriflex. Lassally used Ilford's new high-speed stock, allowing him to shoot with natural lighting sources throughout, even in a cave illuminated only by candle light in one sequence:

> I found that by making use of this extra film speed and by accepting the grainy look as part of the atmosphere, I could shoot in quite small rooms, using just a few small lights, often reflecting off the ceiling, and still giving the director the chance to use most of the space for deploying his actors.[11]

Whereas traditional studio cinematography had placed a high premium on seamless visual continuity, Lassally deployed three different Ilford stocks for different types of location and lighting condition:

> The first, very shabby flat that the heroine, played by Rita Tushingham, lives in with her mother (Dora Bryan) was shot on grainy HPS stock, but when she gets a flat of her own, which she takes some pride in fixing up nicely, this location was shot on a finer grain film, Ilford HP3. All the exteriors were shot on the slower Ilford FP3, as the higher speed of the other films gave one no advantage outdoors. There was considerable opposition from the laboratory to my approach, but it proved entirely successful ...[12]

Tom Jones (1963), Lassally's third feature with Richardson, was the film that decisively marked the transition between the poetic austerity of the New Wave and the emergence of a more colourful and exuberant cinema of 'swinging London'. Oswald Morris had originally been hired but disagreed with Richardson's planned visual approach, and so the director turned to Lassally instead, who enthusiastically adapted the techniques he had pioneered with Richardson on their preceding films for a period drama in colour. A verité approach is in evidence throughout, including the extended hunt sequence, beginning with the preparations, shot wild in documentary style with three handheld cameras, before moving into the chase which combines low-angle travelling shots, including material filmed from the back of a pick-up truck, with helicopter material providing an aerial overview of the horses and hounds.

Tom Jones was shot in colour, which was considerably slower in comparison to black-and-white stocks: Eastmancolor 5251, introduced in 1962, rated at just 50 ASA (this remained standard until the appearance of Eastmancolor 5254 in 1968 doubled the speed to 100 ASA). While this did not rule out flexible location shooting, much more lighting was required to achieve a suitable exposure, particularly in the interiors. Ever the innovator, Lassally manipulated the colour to lower the contrast and create a softer and more pastel look by shooting everything through a net placed over the lens. This entailed a major risk however, as the cinematographer acknowledges:

> The piece we obtained was very small, just big enough to fill two small frames, which we used on short and long focus lenses respectively. It was a considerable risk as the net was not replaceable, and the entire look of the film more-or-less depended on it, and United Artists, who backed the film, would have had a fit if they had known.[13]

The muted effect ensured that the colour did not detract from the overall aesthetic of naturalism, a significant shift from colour's prevailing use at the time for exotic spectacle and non-realist genres such as musicals and action adventures. For the day-for-night sequences, Lassally used filters that gave a monochromatic rather than the usual blue effect. All of this served to give *Tom Jones* a very different look from other colour productions of the time, including those that were also regarded as in tune with the cultural zeitgeist. For example, on the James Bond series of films, beginning with *Dr No* (1962), Ted Moore continued to favour the traditional and rather garish use of high contrast, hard-edged lighting combined with unobtrusive camera movement, leaving the leading players, exotic locations and Ken Adam's sets to provide the necessary aura of cosmopolitan glamour and modernity.

Developments in Colour and Light

A younger cinematographer who became closely associated in the 1960s with innovative uses of colour was Nicolas Roeg, despite his conventional training at MGM Elstree during the 1950s where he worked as operator for Freddie Young, Jack Hildyard and Ted Moore. Roeg graduated to director of photography in the early 1960s, initially making his mark with black-and-white features like *The Caretaker* (1963) and *The System* (1964) before becoming a leading exponent in colour. Here he eschewed the muted naturalism favoured by many of his contemporaries in favour of a more expressionist approach reminiscent of the earlier Technicolor achievements of the 1940s and 1950s. On Roger Corman's *The Masque of the Red Death* (1964) he created a lurid world of primary colours, notably in the masked-ball sequence and in the long tracking shot of a young Jane Asher wandering through a series of different coloured rooms in Prince Prospero's castle. The film was made on a three-week schedule, with Roeg responding enthusiastically to Corman's speed and energy.[14]

For the adaptation of Ray Bradbury's futuristic drama, *Fahrenheit 451* (1966), Roeg's creative imagination was fuelled by François Truffaut's vision of a colour scheme that rejected the vogue for a soft muted palate in favour of more garish tones. As the cinematographer recalled:

> Truffaut said 'It should be big bright 'orrible colours . . . like Technicolor!' The old three-strip process was very lush looking, artificial and glossy [. . .] I knew what he meant and so we had things like the shiny red fire engine, then perhaps a drab street.[15]

The high-contrast photography emphasised both the brightness of colours and the solidity of the blacks, which were set against an otherwise colourless environment. In the interiors, Roeg used a translucent wall gently lit from behind, the illumination provided by the light spillage producing a suitably other-worldly effect for this dystopian vision of the future.

While Roeg's poetic rendering of the Dorset coast and countryside across the four seasons in John Schlesinger's *Far From the Madding Crowd* (1967) owed much to pastoral pictorialism, this was punctuated by the improvised scene in which Terence Stamp's Sergeant Troy displays his swordsmanship to Julie Christie's Bathsheba, rendered via an impressionistic melange of handheld camera movements, zooms and lens flare, emphasising the spontaneous, the unplanned and the accidental. These aesthetic impulses were further developed by Roeg on Richard Lester's dark relationship drama *Petulia* (1968), and further still on *Performance* (1970), where the cinematographer also co-directed with Donald Cammell, in which the photographic design is used to deconstruct the solidity and certainty of the world, in the same way James Fox's Chas has his identity gradually broken down by Mick Jagger's reclusive Turner and his female companions. The restless visuals, encompassing zooms, forced angles, off-kilter compositions, slow motion and some degraded 16mm images, renders space and time as essentially shifting, unstable and random, while occasional expressionistic interruptions of red suggest the violence of the gangster's realm.

Another key element in 1960s cinematography was the shift away from predominantly hard and direct light sources to the use of more diffused lighting. This moved the texture of both black-and-white and colour cinematography away from classical, glossy, high-contrast images towards a softer hazier look. Innovations in soft lighting were often transplanted from other media, with the important pioneer David Watkin working for British Transport Films in the 1950s before he moved into the new burgeoning sphere of television commercials in 1960 where he developed an inclination for a particular style of illumination:

> Partly as boredom relief, I thought an interesting way to light interiors was to use reflected light. I decided on one scene in a documentary with a housewife in Welwyn Garden City to aim a brute through the window and light the scene with reflected light, which looks better and is more natural if you know what you are doing. People poured shit on that for about five years and then started copying it![16]

Having worked with Richard Lester on a commercial for Shredded Wheat, Watkin imported the advert's whited-out aesthetic into the director's feature film, *The Knack* (1965). Watkin's artistic preferences dovetailed with his technical ingenuity on Peter Brook's film *Marat/Sade* (1966) where his solution to its tight shooting schedule and limited space was to create a single lighting set-up comprising a translucent wall through which twenty-six 10-kilowatt lamps were diffused. The soft illumination proved not only conducive to fast and efficient production, but the distortion of the outline of figures when backlit added to the unsettling intensity of the drama's setting in a lunatic asylum.

For *The Charge of the Light Brigade* (1968), Watkin found other ways of creating a diffused look. The slowness of colour film stock meant that backgrounds and windows burned out (through overexposure) to ensure correct exposure for the foreground action, which then created a dreamlike quality in the romantic scenes featuring lovers Captain Nolan (David Hemmings) and Clarissa Morris (Vanessa Redgrave). When the action switched from England to the Crimea, Watkin utilised a greater depth of field which enhanced the harsh realities of this notorious military catastrophe. But what also gave the film its distinctive look was the use of old Ross Express lenses, which Watkin encountered when he first started his career in documentary production:

> They had been around since the early 1930s [. . .] and had a very beautiful and gentle quality to them. Also, they carried no coating or blooming, so that there would occur light refraction within the elements of the lens itself. When you put a net, a diffuser, or a fog filter in front of a lens it is an overall dead thing you are seeing through – whereas, inside the Ross lenses were constantly alive, giving rise sometimes to the most wonderful accidents. And accidents (of the right sort) are always the best things in photography.[17]

Eschewing the properties of current technology equipment in favour of a retro or antiquated effect, renders Watkin's cinematography on *The Charge of the Light Brigade* a fascinating blend of modernity and nostalgia.

The soft light revolution continued apace through the 1960s, suffusing the work of Ken Higgins, Larry Pizer, Gerry Fisher, Peter Suschitzky, Brian Probyn, Chris Menges and Billy Williams. The popularity of this style of illumination led the Coltran lighting company to manufacture a unit called a 'soft' light or 'north light', comprising quartz-iodine lamp tubes within a metal box which produced a non-directional glow. While as Barry Salt notes these tended to be used for fill lighting, which corrected the contrast created by a strong key light, some cinematographers used them as principal light sources, notably Freddie Young on *Ryan's Daughter* (1970).[18]

Old Guys, New Tricks

New techniques were not the exclusive proclivity of younger cinematographers, and veterans also had a role to play in the changing look of British films of the period. As well as adopting new soft lights, Freddie Young developed a technique for manipulating colour for *The Deadly Affair* (1966), a film that hitherto would have been considered more suitable in black and white (as with the previous Le Carré adaptation, *The Spy Who Came in from the Cold*). Young's technique involved pre-exposing the Eastman colour negative to create a more muted or subdued range of tones, a process later known as 'flashing' and associated with Vilmos Zsigmond who first used it on the Robert Altman western, *McCabe and Mrs Miller* (1971). Young found that a pre-exposure of 30 per cent gave the best effect and the British Technicolor lab subsequently pre-exposed negative in batches of 30,000 feet for the production. With no loss in definition, film speed was increased from 50 to 75 ASA and very little filler light was required.[19]

Other older cameramen besides Young displayed experimental leanings in their 1960s work. Gilbert Taylor had been shooting features since the late forties but enthusiastically embraced the improvisational approach that Richard Lester wanted on *A Hard Day's Night* (1964), capturing the action documentary-style with five operators shooting on handheld Arriflex cameras fitted with 10:1 zoom lenses. The film also incorporated a series of set piece 'performances' of some of the Beatles' songs which use a variety of modern techniques including variable speeds, freeze-frames, as well as shaky aerial photography in 'Can't Buy me Love', and an early instance of lens flare in 'And I Love Her', all anticipating the postmodern visual language of the music video. Taylor experimented further on his next assignment, Roman Polanski's psychological horror *Repulsion* (1965), simultaneously modern in its look while borrowing from the rich expressionist traditions of late 1940s British cinematography, using external physical elements to simultaneously convey and explore psychic states and internal conflicts. The film makes liberal use of camera movement, from the intrusive hand-held close shots of Catherine Deneuve wandering the London streets, to the long takes that relentlessly follow her as she paces around the apartment. Taylor reverted to a hard-edged, high-contrast look with extreme and forced angles and a gradual lowering of the overall lighting level to convey the protagonist's steadily deteriorating state. Various lenses, from a 50mm to a wide angle 18mm, were used to produce distortion in the interior close-ups.

One particularly serendipitous paring of youth and experience came with cinematographer Otto Heller work on *The Ipcress File*, directed by Sidney J. Furie. Heller's affinity with expressionism had been demonstrated in *Peeping Tom* (1960), where his grubby Eastmancolor palate evocatively captured the drab London streets, the tawdry British film studio, and the sleazy environs of the Soho porn industry. He lent a similarly drab look to both the interiors and exteriors of *The Ipcress File*, a decision that communicated the film's conception as a kind of anti-Bond. One of its most striking stylistic aspects was its inventive approach to widescreen composition, using low angles, blocked framing, and audacious 45-degree Dutch tilts to create an unsettling mise en scène, exemplified by the scene in which Harry Palmer fights off assailants shot from inside the phone box he has recently vacated. The obscured perspective echoes Palmer's interiority as he finds himself caught up in events which evade understanding. Given his strikingly expressive style on *The Ipcress File*, it is surprising to see Heller arguing elsewhere against too much overt expressionism in cinematography:

> I know I'm talking against myself, but the drama is in the story and does not have to be stressed in the lighting. After all, when people are unhappy in real life they don't turn the light out – they carry on with it just the same as when they were happy.[20]

But the narrative of *The Ipcress File* clearly necessitated an especially expressionistic approach, and Heller responded to the brief with consummate versatility.

While the overarching narrative of 1960s cinematography was clearly one of innovation and experimentation, this co-existed alongside the continuation of traditional styles and techniques. There may be some truth in Walter Lassally's observation that 'cameramen are a very conservative lot, they like to stick with the film stock and the lighting units they know, and usually when the speed goes up, they just stop the lens down another stop and go on using the same large lighting units as before'.[21] But this clearly didn't apply to him or David Watkin or Nicolas Roeg as their respective innovations demonstrate, and neither did it restrict considerably older practitioners like Freddie Young or Otto Heller. In the 1960s, British cinematographers of all generations began to 'let in a little more sunlight, a little more realism and a sense of scope more defined by imagination than by an anamorphic lens' and like their compatriots in other film industries at this time began 'embracing rather than avoiding accentuated style', often doing so to magnificent effect.[22]

Controlling Light and Shade: Douglas Slocombe (1913–2016)

As the 1960s began, Douglas Slocombe was already a well-established figure. He had been 'the pre-eminent cinematographer at Ealing' during the studio's post-war peak, pulling off remarkable feats like multiple versions of Alec Guinness in the same shot in *Kind Hearts and Coronets* (1949) and the eerie glow of the same actor's titular outfit in *The Man in the White Suit* (1951).[23] Slocombe also undertook Ealing's first foray into colour with *Saraband for Dead Lovers* (1948), crafting shadowy images which flew in the face of accepted practices around the use of Technicolor at the time (although he was in good company there, alongside the likes of Jack Cardiff and Christopher Challis who similarly chafed against the process's self-imposed restrictions). In many ways, Slocombe's talent for 'sophisticated and expressive cinematography' ran counter to Ealing's reputation for realism.[24] But his background as a cameraman was impeccably grounded in documentary. He began his professional life as a freelance photojournalist and cameraman in the 1930s, and he spent the war shooting documentary footage for Ministry of Information propaganda purposes, mostly 'on destroyers escorting Atlantic convoys'.[25] Ealing, which produced many of these propaganda films, took him on post-war as a regular employee and he thus avoided the usual career progression of working up through the camera department's hierarchy and moved straight into a DoP role; a product of the shake-up caused by wartime exigencies.

Slocombe's association with Ealing lasted seventeen years but with the demise of the company in the late 1950s, the cinematographer found himself, like many of his industry peers, moving into freelance work. Some of his early sixties assignments felt very Ealing-esque, especially Charles Crichton's *The Boy Who Stole a Million* (1960), highly reminiscent of *Hue and Cry* (1947) in its location filming and focus on the antics of a young boy coming up against the criminal underworld.[26] But the most significant working relationship Slocombe carried over from Ealing was with his camera operator Chic Waterson who worked with him on all but three of the twenty-one assignments he undertook during the 1960s.[27] Eventually working together for nearly forty years, Slocombe described how he and Waterson developed so intuitive a partnership that 'just a few words between us would be enough to line things up without any misunderstandings'.[28] Their division of labour enabled Slocombe to devote himself fully to perfecting his craft as a lighting cameraman as he explained: 'if one had to stand around checking up on the dolly tracks and trying out camera rehearsal, one would waste a lot of time that could be better spent lighting the set with more precision.'[29]

Despite his documentary provenance, Slocombe had developed a taste for studio filming at Ealing, enjoying the control it offered him, where 'every single thing depended on me, the cameraman. Any bit of light or shade I wanted was in my own control.'[30] The stylistically adventurous climate of 1960s filmmaking would offer Slocombe new opportunities and he would be 'embarking on one of the most innovative periods in his career'.[31] His early-sixties assignments varied wildly in style and genre: from the sadistic horror *Circus of Horrors* (1960), to the ebullient widescreen pop musical *The Young Ones* (1961), to the atmospheric black-and-white realist drama of *The L-Shaped Room* (1962), all very different but all tackled equally effectively.[32] Indeed, Slocombe's career has often been defined in terms of its incredible versatility, as a cinematographer of 'extraordinary range' who could 'seemingly switch styles as easily as he could change lenses'.[33] Slocombe himself said 'I don't keep a style going. I treat each picture on its own merits. I respond to what it asks.'[34] He described himself variously as 'an instinctive cinematographer', 'very much a mood person [. . .] inclined to do a thing as I see it, almost on the spur of the moment', who 'personally fought slightly shy' of too much forward planning because 'invention on the floor was often more creative and less inhibited than the preconceptions fostered while gazing at a model or a batch of set drawings'.[35] By the end of the 1960s, Slocombe had even stopped relying on a light meter and instead used his perception of how the light was hitting the back of his hand as his guide, with no loss of accuracy (much to the amazement of other crew members).[36]

Although versatility could signal compliance with the wishes of a director, this was not the way Slocombe envisaged his own work. Indeed, he was emphatic about his own claims to authorship, claiming to have 'always brought entirely my own look to any picture I made. I like to be my own auteur in terms of the photography.'[37] Slocombe made a compelling case for the primacy of the DoP in defining the look of a film in a 1965 *Sight and Sound* article on cinematography symptomatically entitled 'The Secret Profession', in which he was interviewed alongside his younger colleague Walter Lassally. Interestingly, Lassally's more auteurist views – that the ideal cinematographer is 'the perfect servant to the master' – contrasts with Slocombe's rather less submissive statements of the cinematographer's centrality and agency within film-making, which are worth quoting at length:

> To me the director's most important function is to get the actors working along the level of the story. [...] But I've always felt that this is where a director's credits should cease, unless they do in fact prove that he did more than that, and that beyond that point other people (the art director; the lighting cameraman; to some extent the editor) function as individuals.
>
> I often wonder whether the public realises that if ten different cameramen photographed the same situations on the same sets in the same pictures, they could give ten completely different results. The modern title 'Director of Photography' is an attempt to recognise that the cameraman doesn't just photograph what already exists; but I prefer the credit the French used to give – 'Images de . . .' In the end the visual image is the lighting cameraman's.[38]

For Slocombe, it was the DoP far more than the director who created the look of a film and had most control over what appeared on screen, flying in the face of auteurism. It is all the more fascinating that the cinematographer developed this hypothesis having recently worked with two directors with such strong authorial identities: John Huston on the butchered biopic *Freud* (1962) and Joseph Losey on the class-conflict psychodrama *The Servant*.

Slocombe undertook experiments with film stock on *Freud*, likening his choices to a draughtsman's selection of 'his grade of paper and his drawing medium – with grain in mind and overall contrast'.[39] This film required distinctively different visual styles for its various components, as he recalled:

> very sharp photography for the main part of the film, to give the clarity of steel etchings and help the period feeling. For flashbacks I shot through a glass plate, treated to fuzz out all details except those most clearly recalled by the patient. For the dream sequences I aimed for a very contrasty, grainy effect of extreme black and white, in which chalky faces and relevant details would stand out like luminous figures in tunnels of blackness [...] I shot on positive stock instead of negative.[40]

Freud ended up being 'a visually brilliant film sadly reduced by studio pressure from its original three and a half hours of screen time to only two', with much of Slocombe's work disappearing in the edit.⁴¹ But he would gain greater recognition for *The Servant*, winning both the BFA and British Society of Cinematographers awards. He would bring to the project techniques he'd developed on previous films, bringing from *The L-Shaped Room* the idea of 'develop[ing] the stock contrary to the Kodak set instructions [. . .] which gave me twice the approved film speed and a very interesting contrast', as well as the capacity for 'very deep focus' which worked well for *The Servant*'s long takes of 'four minutes or more, with the actors moving about from foreground to background', keeping everyone in focus throughout because of this technical adjustment to increase the film's speed.⁴²

As he had in *Freud*, Slocombe needed to distinguish between different narrative phases in *The Servant* by applying different visual styles to each:

> One had to convey the feeling of this house that was empty but nevertheless had possibilities. I shot the opening scenes in an overall grey tone that showed the bare bones of the building and its intrinsic coldness. Then we wanted to make things look exciting with new furniture, new belongings, so I shot it with a certain glossy contrast. Then, as the servant takes over, we wanted some things to show meaningfully for their own sake, wanted to find sinister meanings in objects that before seemed merely pretty and inoffensive, I used the lighting to rub out a number of things that had to be forgotten, and bring forward new elements that had to be given sinister implications.'⁴³

In this latter respect, Slocombe was returning to the chiaroscuro painterly technique of the Dutch old masters that had inspired him back in the 1940s, in which selected details were illuminated but 'the rest of the picture area was allowed to shade off into monochromatic darkness. The result is that the observer's eye goes immediately to the focal point the painter desired.'⁴⁴ This visual schema came into its own in *The Servant*'s 'final orgy and degradation' on which, according to Slocombe, Losey was not only 'at great pains not to emulate anyone else's orgies' but also wanted 'to suggest that more was going on than actually was. Just an eye, a hand, pools of blackness'; invoking decadence but not enervating the censor.⁴⁵

Slocombe also deployed particular lenses to create effects, including using 'a 14mm lens, the widest there is, to shoot the scenes in the home of the fiancée's parents [. . .] to over-accentuate the formality'.⁴⁶ But the most notable stylistic feature of *The Servant*'s cinematography was its combination of long takes with a highly mobile camera, sometimes making 360-degree turns while filming fluidly throughout. Slocombe recalled how:

> [Losey] liked to shoot a scene as continuously as he possibly could. If he could get you to move through the scene in one long take, room to room, upstairs and through corridors even, he enjoyed it. Of course, that makes it very difficult for the cameraman, because the moment you move around, one or two lights that you might have hidden somewhere to your advantage become impossible to use because they come into the shot.[47]

But the sense of the camera seamlessly insinuating itself into all levels of the house, just as Dirk Bogarde's Barrett does, was well worth the extra effort it entailed, and Slocombe enjoyed working with Losey who he felt 'went to great pains to feel that I was in sympathy with what he had in mind', fostering a genuine collaboration in which 'the camera movement was all his own, and the actors' positioning and movement, but he left me alone to work out my own patterns beyond that'.[48]

Shortly afterwards, Slocombe was signed up by 20th Century Fox producer Elmo Williams on a three-year contract.[49] The cinematographer did remarkable work on his first assignment, *Guns at Batasi* (1964), which its star Richard Attenborough felt perfectly invoked 'the image of the end of empire' in spite of being filmed entirely on the Pinewood backlot rather than on location in Africa.[50] Slocombe 'had to somehow turn grey skies and very dark grey light outside [into] simmering hot African sunshine', rising to this challenge by creating high contrast through hard lighting.[51] In Attenborough's estimation, this 'created an atmosphere on the set which helped me as an actor tremendously because he really did make you believe that that light was Africa, sweating hot'.[52]

Guns at Batasi was Slocombe's final film in black and white as mainstream production shifted predominantly into colour. Thereafter, the cinematographer's muted, washed-out, softly lit tones on the nautical tale *A High Wind in Jamaica* (1965), with occasional moments of dramatic chiaroscuro below decks, were one of the glories of this 'truncated but underrated' tale of lost innocence.[53] On loan to Paramount, Slocombe turned in suitable rom-com visuals for *Promise Her Anything* (1966), and beautifully presented Leslie Caron once again, who 'thought she had never looked better' than in *The L-Shaped Room* and was keen for Slocombe to photograph her again.[54] Despite his 'dislike [of] artificial glamour', he presented key sixties pin-ups Ursula Andress and Raquel Welch at the height of their allure, on *The Blue Max* (1966) and *Fathom* (1967) respectively, giving both women an earthier, sensual quality perhaps because he was 'careful about not entirely blanking out all traces of character in the face'.[55] Andress's semi-nude scenes in *The Blue Max* make effective use of low-key lighting which pick out twinned golden highlights on a brass bedstead and the tiny rivulets of water on the actress's back, fresh from the bath. But the woozily mobile tilted camera which captures her liaison with the film's ambitious anti-hero George Peppard suggests the instability and untrustworthy nature of their affair. Of *Fathom*, John Russell Taylor said that 'credit must go as much to photographer Douglas Slocombe as to director Leslie Martinson' for the fact that it was 'very pretty to look at'; a proper acknowledgement of his significant contribution.[56]

Slocombe's preference for complete control of the filming environment, where 'you walk into a dark stage and suddenly have to create everything yourself' (whereas 'with documentary photography, you're shooting what exists, naturally') was given full expression in the artificial Transylvanian environments created for the horror comedy *Dance of the Vampires/The Fearless Vampire Killers* (1967).[57] Its 'wonderful sets, huge sets' spread across numerous studios (Elstree, MGM Borehamwood, Shepperton and Pinewood) were filmed in the manner of folktale illustrations, deep red and blue jewel tones standing out against the snowy surroundings. Slocombe's extensive experience of filming with mirrors for Losey probably helped him to orchestrate the clever revelation where the protagonists are reflected in a large mirror while their vampire pursuers immediately behind them are not.

The cinematographer's reunion with Losey on *Boom!* (1968) moved away from the interiority of *The Servant* to invoke instead 'intense, almost mesmerising sunshine, sunlit whites which daze the senses'.[58] By comparison, *The Lion in Winter* (1968) demanded 'very much a feeling of dreary, if you like, damp, dirty, unlit castle. One threw most of the sets into dark relief.'[59] The key inspirations for its visual style were medieval tapestry and a photograph of 'a nun in a cell' which director Anthony Harvey showed him, which 'had a cold atmosphere which he loved.'[60] Slocombe particularly enjoyed working with Katharine Hepburn, playing Eleanor of Aquitaine in the film, finding the 'wonderful bonework' of Hepburn's face 'lovely to light'.[61]

Slocombe took the documentary-inflected aesthetic of another film, *Robbery* (1967), and cross-pollinated it with patriotic playfulness for another Oakhurst heist film, *The Italian Job* (1969). He described as the 'greatest commercial for cars the world had ever known', not only for its nifty Minis but also for the orange Lamborghini gliding gracefully along a winding mountain road to the accompaniment of Matt Monro during the opening credits: a glamorous streamlined spectacle presented as enticingly as Raquel Welch in her *Fathom* bikini.[62]

The cinematographer ended the 1960s displaying the same wide range with which he had commenced the decade. His sunlight-dappled romantic style on *The Buttercup Chain* (1970) exemplified the 'delicate and sensitive use of soft light' associated with Billy Williams and David Watkin but also drew on 'the style of the French Impressionists who, together with the Dutch masters, are the painters with light he most admires'.[63] Meanwhile, his work on Ken Russell's *The Music Lovers* (1970) demanded everything from nineteenth-century tsarist elegance to the gothic gloom of the lunatic asylum.[64] In working through the rapidly changing mainstream British cinema of the 1960s, Douglas Slocombe had managed to navigate the distance between Cliff Richard perkily singing at the youth club and Glenda Jackson writhing naked on the floor, finding the appropriate style for both scenes. This is an indication of the consummate versatility that had come to distinguish his career.

NOTES

1. This chapter reworks material from Duncan Petrie, 'A changing visual landscape: British cinematography in the 1960s', *Journal of British Cinema and Television*, vol. 15, no. 2, 2018, pp. 204–27.
2. Duncan Petrie, *The British Cinematographer* (London: BFI, 1996), pp. 32–6. Other key figures of this generation, notably Jack Cardiff and Guy Green, had graduated to directing by the 1960s.
3. The second half of the 1960s also saw film-school graduates earning their first DoP credits, notably Peter Suschitzky, who studied at the French Institute des Hautes Études Cinématographiques (IDHEC) and Ian Wilson, who attended the London Film School. But even while the profession was changing, in one key respect it remained unchanged: unlike production design, costume design, editing, screenwriting, and even direction, cinematography was an all-male citadel throughout the 1960s, and is still a craft area in which women are drastically underrepresented.
4. Petrie, *The British Cinematographer*, pp. 1–2.
5. The Academy moved to a single award for cinematography in 1967.
6. Dave Mann, *Britain's First TV/Film Crime Series and the Industrialisation of its Film Industry 1946–1964* (Lampeter: Edwin Mellen Press, 2009).
7. The significance of his work for Hammer and director Val Guest is acknowledged by Robert Murphy, *Sixties British Cinema* (London: BFI, 1992), p. 7.
8. Barry Salt identifies its use on *Billy Liar* and *Darling*, shot respectively by Denys Coop and Ken Higgins. Salt, *Film Style and Technology* (London: Starword, 1992), p. 258.
9. Nicolas Roeg, Walter Lassally, and Gilbert Taylor, amongst others, took part in a publicity campaign for Ilford running across the industry press in the early 1960s, in which they extolled the virtue of the company's film stocks. For instance, Roeg recounted how for *Nothing but the Best* he 'wanted a stock with the fullest range of mid-tones. To use a contrasty stock and lighting would have been a too obvious and easy treatment of the subject. We tested five or six different materials with various lighting techniques and in each case Ilford HP3 came out best.' 'Ilford interviews Nicolas Roeg', *Film and Television Technician*, April 1963, p. 78.
10. B. White, 'Lassally on British Cinematography', *Journal of the University Film Association*, vol. 26, no. 4, 1974, p. 62.
11. Walter Lassally, *Itinerant Cameraman* (London: John Murray, 1987), p. 86.
12. Ibid., pp. 64–5.
13. Ibid., p. 68.
14. Gordon Gow, 'Identity: Nicolas Roeg', *Films and Filming*, January 1972, pp. 20–4. Low-budget horror also provided a platform for John Coquillon, whose striking images of East Anglian landscapes in Michael Reeves' *Witchfinder General* (1968) paved the way for a close association with Sam Peckinpah.
15. Petrie, *The British Cinematographer*, p. 136.
16. Ibid., p. 151.
17. Donald Chase, 'David Watkin', *American Cinematographer*, vol. 65, no. 3, 1984, pp. 42–6.

18. Salt, *Film Style and Technology*, p. 254.
19. Freddie Young, 'A method of pre-exposing color negative for subtle effect', *American Cinematographer*, vol. 47, no. 8, 1966, p. 537.
20. Quoted in Derek Ware, 'Production', *Kine Weekly*, 6 December 1962, p. 21.
21. Lassally, *Itinerant Cameraman*, p. 68.
22. Armond White, 'Illuminations', *Film Comment*, September 1989, p. 58.
23. Petrie, *The British Cinematographer*, p. 33.
24. Ibid., p. 36.
25. Roger Hudson, 'The secret profession', *Sight and Sound*, Summer 1965, p. 112.
26. Throughout the 1960s Slocombe would work with former Ealing colleagues on numerous projects: with editor-turned-director Seth Holt on *Taste of Fear*, with Crichton again on *The Third Secret* (1964), and with Alexander Mackendrick on *A High Wind in Jamaica* (1965), although the latter infuriated the usually mild-mannered Slocombe so much that Slocombe threw his light meter at Mackendrick after one argument too many. Douglas Slocombe BECTU interview, <https://historyproject.org.uk/interview/douglas-slocombe> (accessed 1 August 2018).
27. Desmond Davis operated on *Taste of Fear* (1961) and *Freud* (1962) and Gerry Fisher on *Guns at Batasi* (1964).
28. John Pavlus, 'A versatile legacy', *American Cinematographer*, March 2002, p. 91.
29. Ibid.
30. Ibid., p. 90.
31. Pertie, *The British Cinematographer*, p. 139.
32. Slocombe also photographed the Hammer psychological thriller *Taste of Fear* and the noir-inflected social-issue drama *The Mark* (1961) during this same period.
33. Alan Parker in 'Behind the Camera: Douglas Slocombe', BBC2, tx 18 December 1999. Viewed via, <http://www.vimeo.com/22208399> (accessed 1 August 2018). Geoffrey Macnab, 'Douglas Slocombe: Obituary', *Independent*, 23 February 2016, <https://www.independent.co.uk/news/obituaries/douglas-slocombe-cinematographer-whose-six-decade-career-took-in-newsreels-ealing-films-and-the-a6891996.html> (accessed 1 August 2018). The obituary quotes Steven Spielberg's assessment of Slocombe when they worked together: 'I thought he could do anything.'
34. Peter Evans, 'An eye for a picture', *The Guardian*, 5 March 1983, p. 8.
35. Slocombe quoted in 'The five films nominated for Best Cinematography of 1981', *American Cinematographer*, May 1982, p. 483. Hudson, 'The secret profession', p. 114. Douglas Slocombe, 'Through a glass not-so-darkly', *American Cinematographer*, November 1981, p. 1104.
36. Douglas Slocombe BECTU interview.
37. Pavlus, 'A versatile legacy?', p. 91.
38. In Hudson, 'The secret profession', pp. 112–14. He also added: 'Years ago, I was terribly amused to read one of the newspaper critics referring to "Mr Hitchcock's use of long shadows". They're not Mr Hitchcock's shadows at all. Actually when he was on the set, with a hundred arc lamps all glowing out, he probably wouldn't even notice that there was a shadow out there.'
39. Ibid., p. 117.
40. Ibid., p. 114. Slocombe's fuzzing out of certain elements of the frame, to suggest something beyond comprehension or memory, was paralleled by Freddie Francis's work on *The Innocents* where he used 'special optical glass camera filters which have an effect of making a vignette of the most important part of the frame', especially useful for films 'shot in a widescreen process', and used by cameraman Arthur Grant for the film Francis directed shortly afterwards, *Paranoic*. Derek Todd, 'Production', *Kine Weekly*, 23 August 1962, p. 16.
41. Evans, 'An eye for a picture', p. 8.

42. Hudson, 'The secret profession', p. 117.
43. Ibid.
44. Douglas Slocombe, 'Colour through the camera', in *Saraband for Dead Lovers: The Film and Its Production at Ealing Studios* (London: Convoy Publications, 1948), p. 87.
45. BECTU interview. Hudson, 'The secret profession', p. 117.
46. Ibid.
47. Pavlus, 'A versatile legacy', p. 92.
48. Hudson, 'The secret profession', p. 117.
49. Partly on the strength of *The Third Secret* which he had photographed for them. BECTU interview.
50. Quoted in 'Behind the Camera: Douglas Slocombe'.
51. Ibid.
52. Ibid. Slocombe felt that *Guns at Batasi* had 'a documentary aspect [...] which did take me back to my war days with a roving camera. I probably instinctively gave the film some of the feeling that I had in some of the documentary footage that I shot.'
53. Petrie, *The British Cinematographer*, p. 140. The film was truncated not only in its eventual running time but also in its mise en scène, with Elmo Williams 'almost crying when he told us how little money he had to do the picture'. A tight budget meant that they were only able to construct 'two tiers instead of four' of the pirate ship that was the film's central setting, so 'you never see top of the ship'; a lack very artfully elided by Slocombe's photography. BECTU interview.
54. 'Behind the Camera: Douglas Slocombe'.
55. Evans, 'An eye for a picture', p. 8. However, Elizabeth Taylor on *Boom!* still took issue with Slocombe's lighting, asking him 'do I have to have that frigging thing in my eyes?' BECTU interview.
56. John Russell Taylor, '*Fathom*', *The Times*, 24 August 1967, p. 4. Both films complemented their feminine attractions with spectacular aerial photography (some of it undertaken by specialist photographers Jacques Dubourg and Skeets Kelly), with Welch playing a stunt parachutist in *Fathom* and *The Blue Max* being set within the milieu of German aviation during the First World War. But the impulse to capture *The Blue Max*'s aerobatic exploits with the greatest possible immediacy led to serious injury for Slocombe while filming. A plane was ordered to swoop extra low to the ground by director John Guillermin so that it could 'fill the screen' but it was, Slocombe recalled, 'too damn low'. Its wheel hit him on the back and knocked him fifty feet across the airfield and had 'just missed the centre of my spinal column by about half an inch', he later learned. BECTU interview.
57. Pavlus, 'A versatile legacy', p. 90.
58. PHS, '*Times* diary: Kind Hearts to Boom', *The Times*, 16 January 1969, p. 8.
59. Ibid.
60. Ibid.
61. 'Behind the Camera: Douglas Slocombe'.
62. BECTU interview.
63. Petrie, *The British Cinematographer*, p. 140. Evans, 'An eye for a picture', p. 8.
64. Slocombe stated his admiration for Glenda Jackson's professionalism while giving such a fearless performance: the pair had an unexpectedly close encounter when filming the challenging train-carriage scene of orgasmic frenzy. Philip French recounted how 'after a brutal third take, he dropped on top of her from the luggage rack, and said, in his charming stammer: "I'm a m-married m-man."' 'Douglas Slocombe: A Tribute', *Observer*, 13 December 2009.

11. EDITING

Melanie Williams

INTRODUCTION

Patterns of editing in feature films, not only in Britain but across Europe and America, underwent significant transformation during the 1960s. Barry Salt suggests that 'the general cutting rate speeded up as the sixties wore on' with a film's Average Shot Length (ASL) coming down from 11 seconds to 9.3 seconds over the period 1958–63, and then reducing further between 1964 and 1970 to 7.7 seconds, 'its lowest value since the silent period' according to his calculations.[1] Likewise David Bordwell describes the 1960s as the era of accelerated cutting, when ASLs 'between six and eight seconds' increasingly predominated, marking the beginning of a new dominant style of 'intensified continuity' in mainstream cinema.[2] This was partly the result of technological developments, most notably the introduction of the Italian CIR joiner in 1964. The new equipment created new possibilities, as Peter Tanner relates:

> we used to have what was called the hot splicer, a rather cumbersome thing [...] and you used to cement and scrape the film, it was an overlap join. When the new joiner came in, which was not an overlap joiner but a butted joiner, it immediately did away with having to put in black frames.[3]

Editors now had far greater flexibility because 'splices made with it could be undone and then remade, without having lost any frames if the editing of a scene had to be changed'.[4] Tony Lawson saw it as the main progeni-

Figure 11.1 Albert Finney as the titular hero of *Tom Jones* (Tony Richardson, 1963) in the film's bravura seduction sequence edited by Antony Gibbs.

tor of the 'experimental editing' on films such as *Bonnie and Clyde* (1967) and *Performance* (1970), both with montages so rapid they recalled the eye-assaulting dazzle of sixties op art.[5] But since the overall lowering of ASL in the 1960s predated the joiner's introduction, technological determinism alone cannot explain the changes in editing styles across the decade. Rather, a series of more complex industrial and aesthetic factors were contributory, with television and advertising often cited as key populshowers of a more compressed style of editing. Tanner described television commercials as the apotheosis of editing, because 'time is precious and they have to project the product being advertised in the best and most effective way possible in the shortest possible time'.[6] Lessons learned from advertising were then exported into feature films (sometimes by the same editors), for an audience that was newly receptive to abbreviated cutting through their regular consumption of commercial television which had normalised 'rapid change on the screen'.[7] Some editors, like Reginald Mills, decried what they saw as the craft's 'steep decline' because of 'the bad influence of instant television editing'. But others were only too pleased to dispense with some of the languor and long-windedness that had accompanied classical editing style.

The French *Nouvelle Vague* had a similarly galvanising effect in this respect, their rejection of traditional editing conventions suggesting ways in which the craft's more laborious elements could be foreshortened or simply elided. It meant, as John Victor-Smith put it, 'people no longer had to walk in and out of doors', one small loosening of convention that represented a whole new credo of liberation in editing.[8] Furthermore, cuts no longer had to be self-effacing, they could be deliberately visible instead, exemplified by the jump cut, exposing the film-making (and film-joining) process: 'Movies are a world of fragments', Jean-Luc Godard stated, 'so why pretend smoothness?'[9] This attitude lay behind the increasing abandonment of dissolves and fades, previously deemed good practice for showing the passage of time or a change of location between scenes, but now replaced by straight cuts. One landmark example is the direct cut from an extinguished match straight to the desert sunrise in *Lawrence of Arabia* (1962). This was originally conceived as a dissolve but when seen as a straight jump by editor Anne Coates and director David Lean in the rough cut (before the opticals were added) was kept that way for its startling visual impact. Coates had been emboldened by the *Nouvelle Vague*, whose audacious approach to cutting tallied with her own instincts that 'too much time was lost in matching, opening and closing doors. I always thought there was room for much sharper cutting.'[10] On her next film, *Becket* (1964), Coates' decision to move between locations in a similarly snappy way met with opposition from veteran Hollywood producer Hal Wallis ('You can't do a direct cut. You've got to do a dissolve in there. He's fifty miles away.') but her approach prevailed, indicating how more liberated editing styles had begun to reach beyond the confines of European art cinema.[11] This was seen by some commentators as a necessary reflection of the pace of 'modern life itself': 'We don't live a life of slow dissolves but of straight, hard cuts. There are no fade-ins and fade-outs in our situations: without wasting time, bang, we are right in the middle of them.'[12]

But while slower transitional devices like dissolves lost their former commonplace function, they simultaneously gained a new cachet and accrued new meanings, potentially becoming more poetic or mysterious. This is certainly in evidence in Jim Clark's use of dissolves in the supernatural drama *The Innocents* (1961) which went beyond the standard 4-foot mix of images to extend the overlap to 15 to 20 feet of film, and, according to Clark, 'often there would be a third image in there too, so these mixes were like mini montages'.[13] Indeed, alongside the shortening ASLs and abrupt transitions which represented the most visible signs of change to editing styles, there was an equal and opposite tendency towards slower transitions and longer takes, the latter often influenced by the naturalistic approach of *cinéma vérité*, in which 'the dull bits weren't left out, but kept in proudly, gloriously', as Robert Vas put it.[14]

Vas wrote in 1966 that he was living through 'perhaps the most exciting years in the cutting room since the Great Russian Revolution', as 'cinema became editing-conscious again, whether in the dramaturgy of quick cuts or endless takes, jump cuts for staccato or slow fusions for floating effect, frantic involvement or alienating distanciation', and triumphantly concluded:

'The editor's art, in fact, is "in" again.'[15] Britain was an integral player in the renewed sense of excitement around editing, with Salt suggesting how 'British films of the middle sixties' were crucial in popularising non-classical cutting styles.[16] Bernard Gribble identified Antony Gibbs's 'very loose fast cutting' on *Tom Jones* (1963) as particularly influential, and the thing that 'turned Hollywood upside down' and 'influenced the whole industry': 'Up until then everything was very cut and dried and pedantic, predictable I should say, and then suddenly it was all freeform from then on.'[17] Gibbs's earlier editing on *The Loneliness of the Long Distance Runner* (1962) had exerted 'more direct influence on me than anything' for American editor Dede Allen cutting *Bonnie and Clyde*.[18]

As with other technical areas, British editors began to receive greater international recognition in the 1960s and were in contention for Oscars with increasing frequency. Alan Osbiston, Anne Coates, Norman Savage and Ralph Kemplen were nominated for their work on the big-budget runaway productions *The Guns of Navarone* (1961), *Becket*, *Doctor Zhivago* (1965), and *Oliver!* (1968) respectively, with Coates then winning the Oscar for *Lawrence of Arabia*.[19] The decade also saw the men and women of the cutting room forge a stronger sense of their professional identity, founding the Guild of British Film Editors (GBFE) in 1966, chaired by Freddie Wilson and boasting a membership of sixty practitioners.[20] The Guild was then approached by the Society of Film and Television Arts to propose nominations for a British Film Academy Editing award, inaugurated in 1968; Sam O'Steen for *The Graduate* (1967) ended up pipping native editors Kevin Brownlow, Ralph Kemplen and Reginald Mills for *The Charge of the Light Brigade* (1968), *Oliver!* and *Romeo and Juliet* (1968) respectively. Thus, the GBFE played an important role in making more visible the achievements of a frequently self-effacing profession.[21]

Usually predicated on constructing 'a flow of images that tell a story without *reminding* the audience they are watching a motion picture', editing's habitual invisibility sometimes 'obscured understanding of the editor's role', as Roy Perkins and Martin Stollery suggest.[22] They cite the example of the famously eroticised eating scene from *Tom Jones*, which hinges on the 'metronome sensitivity and precision' of its shot/reverse shot pattern, finding 'an editing rhythm which traces the eating gestures of Finney and Redman, who start and complete each other's actions in alternating cuts' which is more often credited to the skills of director Tony Richardson, or actors Albert Finney and Joyce Redman (all Oscar-nominated), than it is to Gibbs as editor (un-nominated).[23] Yet his contribution to that iconic scene is vital and exemplifies what Reginald Mills offered as answers to the questions 'What is film editing? Good film editing? Great film editing?': 'a) Timing b) Good timing c) Perfect timing.'[24] Anne Coates described editing as an instinctive, 'intuitive' process: 'When I sit down to make an editorial choice, it's a gut feeling [. . .] not an intellectual choice.'[25] Jim Clark argued in similarly visceral terms that 'the precise moment you expose the nerve is something you can't determine beforehand, and that *is* a matter of the cutting'.[26] The 'matter of the cutting', crucial to all cinema, was particularly pertinent in 1960s British cinema: a moment of intense innovation that would have a lasting effect on editing styles worldwide for decades to come.

AGE, GENDER, AUTONOMY AND COLLABORATION: BRITISH EDITING IN THE SIXTIES

Some of the era's most prolific editors had begun their careers many decades earlier, and the longevity of someone like Oswald Hafenrichter, born in 1899, could connect the past and present of film history in startling ways. An attendee of Pudovkin's lectures who edited *Mädchen in Uniform* (1931), he then brought that experience to bear on *Sparrows Can't Sing* (1963), *Ladies Who Do* (1963) and *The Skull* (1965). Likewise, Reginald Beck, born in 1902, who supplied the quintessence of sixties modernism in his cutting on *Accident* (1967), had started out at Gainsborough in the late 1920s.[27] But there was also an influx of younger editors, born in the 1930s, making a name for themselves: Jim Clark, Anthony Harvey, Tom Priestley and John Bloom among them. But for all the stylistic brio on display in some British cinema, whether by veterans or newcomers, most film editing continued to operate along traditional lines, particularly at the outset of the decade. A good example is Alfred Roome, born in 1908, who started out on Aldwych farces and Will Hay comedies in the 1930s, continuing to work in comedy right through to the 1960s. He edited the major box-office hits *Doctor in Love* (1960), *Doctor in Distress* (1963), and *Doctor in Clover* (1966), turning his hand to the *Carry On* series after its relocation from Anglo-Amalgamated to Rank in 1966. Although the *Carry Ons* involved more editorial labour than some of Roome's previous films, with lots of cutaways 'getting reactions', he still found them 'very easy to do once you got the formula right' and his speed in turning them round delighted the famously parsimonious producer Peter Rogers.[28] Apart from occasionally having to do some 'nifty cutting' to get around a problem like Phil Silvers fluffing his lines on *Follow That Camel* (1967), Roome's work on the series generally went, in his words, 'like clockwork'.[29] He was a prime exponent of a deep-seated tradition of British film editing, still flourishing in the 1960s, founded on joining together the component parts of the film for coherence and continuity above all else and guided by a strong instinct for maximising its generic appeal.[30]

Although no longer on a studio contract by the sixties, Roome benefitted from the long-standing professional associations he built up while working at Gainsborough and Pinewood, with his strong working relationships with Ralph Thomas, Betty Box, and Gerald Thomas, helping to guarantee him regular work as a freelance. This was helpful when there was competition between peers for work, as Teddy Darvas recounts, with 'four or five of your mates [. . .] up for the same film'.[31] But due to the limited labour pool created by the ACTT's operation of a closed shop, and the boom in British production facilitated by American finance, the 1960s were generally a good time to be a freelance editor. The increase in US runaway productions in the 1960s not only boosted employment but also gave editors access to top-of-the-range equipment that was, as editor Stuart Baird points out, 'better, more modern, more up-to-date than Hollywood because Hollywood still had the residues of the studio system [. . .] and they weren't renewing like in England'.[32] However, others like Richard Best found the 'remote control' exercised from Hollywood creatively inhibiting and therefore felt he could 'give much more input to indigenous films'.[33] Others found studio control less of a problem than directorial diktats: Frank Clarke had worked harmoniously on numerous MGM British productions but ended up refusing the editor credit for *Blow Up* (1966) because of director Michelangelo Antonioni 'interfering all the time' and 'controlling far too much'.[34]

This question of this key relationship became an increasingly complex and at times fraught one as the decade progressed. On the one hand, hitching your wagon to a particular director could be a useful way of acquiring regular work, as well as often being very creatively rewarding. Many of the editors who enjoyed notable careers during the 1960s enjoyed creative rapport of this kind, including Jim Clark with Jack Clayton and then John Schlesinger, Antony Gibbs with Tony Richardson and then Richard Lester, Bernard Gribble with Michael Winner, John Trumper with Peter Collinson, Fergus McDonell with Clive Donner, and Reginald Mills then Reginald Beck with Joseph Losey. Beck cannily nurtured his relationship with Losey and made a point of directly stating his admiration from the outset, which the director clearly valued:

> I said I hope he didn't mind my saying how much I appreciated working with him, which I'd never done with anybody else, and that secured my future because when Reggie Mills finally decided he was going to direct rather than edit he came back to me.[35]

However, Beck still maintained his critical independence while they were working together. He recalled having 'a lot of arguments' and 'terrible scenes' with Losey during *Accident* about 'timing and the pace of a shot in a scene', although Beck added that his 'relationship with Joe was good enough that you could have a disagreement and still be friends at the end of it'.[36] But a different version of the director–editor relationship seemed to be in operation for Jim

Clark and Jack Clayton while making *The Innocents*; initially very intimate, resulting in a remarkable evocation of the supernatural on screen but then, according to Clark, suddenly soured over a minor misunderstanding:

> I had become too close to Jack and had, perhaps, transcended the boundary that should exist between director and editor. This is in some ways a master and slave relationship, and although I had never tried to impose my own will on the material, perhaps he felt he had, in some way, lost his own picture.[37]

The pair worked together once more but with a certain mutual wariness, by Clark's account, and were never to collaborate again.[38]

The interlinked personal and professional dynamics between editor and director was of crucial importance to their collaboration, and often hinged on questions of power and control. Richard Best described often feeling caught between producer and director 'like a nut in the crackers, with the pressure *not* lightly applied', although when the balance of power was less dysfunctional, he felt more like 'the pivot of a see-saw'.[39] But this period also saw old divisions of labour begin to break down with directors increasingly making their presence felt in the previously cloistered space of the cutting room. Technology once again played an important part in facilitating new kinds of working practices; the director's greater involvement was made significantly easier by the popularisation of flat-bed editing technology with larger viewing screens, notably the Steenbeck which became available in Europe from 1965 onwards.[40] These machines differed from the Moviola and its ilk which only permitted only a single viewer to easily see the sequence being cut, thus offering a privacy relished by many editors, like Anne Coates: 'A Moviola is almost impossible to share with anybody, which is what I loved about it, in that you could cut quietly by yourself.'[41] However Coates's contemporary John Bloom felt that flat-bed equipment was useful precisely 'because of the ability to sit with the director without the clackety-clack of the Moviola, or having to go into the theatre to see reels' which 'discouraged joint working'.[42]

The editor's need to exercise autonomous creative expression, exemplified by their desire to work alone on their Moviola, reverberates through numerous practitioner accounts. John Trumper, one of the most prolific British editors of the sixties, asserted that he 'wouldn't work with a director who dictated every frame. I'd rather work with one who trusted the editor to contribute something creative.'[43] Likewise, Teddy Darvas spoke of his frustration at receiving hardly any coverage to work with beyond the strictly necessary from Basil Dearden on *The Assassination Bureau* (1968) leaving him no scope for editorial lassitude: this turned out to be a deliberate tactic from Dearden who told Darvas that 'every editor' he'd worked with had 'directed me from behind so I have evolved a system of directing whereby no editor can muck me up'.⁴⁴ Directors with different stylistic and ideological leanings could behave in similarly restrictive ways. David Gladwell recalled how, after signing up to work on *If....* (1968), Lindsay Anderson 'made it clear that it would be he and not I who would be editing the picture and that my job would be to organise the cutting room and to "prevent all the sound-tracks from getting tangled up"', although they eventually arrived at a more positive working arrangement.⁴⁵

Bill Lenny suffered from the opposite problem, that of trying to orchestrate meaning from chaos, in cutting together the five different directors' contributions to *Casino Royale* (1967), attempting to construct a coherent narrative from them while maintaining continuity as far as possible: a task *Kine Weekly* likened to completing a 'twenty-reel jigsaw'.⁴⁶ By comparison, Coates had a much happier experience with the 'thousands and thousands of feet' she had to work with on *Lawrence of Arabia* because 'it was much better to have a lot of choices in the editing room, to give yourself the opportunity to change things'.⁴⁷

Coates was described in the trade press as 'one of the few women in Britain doing the job' of editing, although there were other notable female exponents of the craft at the time, including Thelma Connell, described by her former apprentice Peter Honess as 'a quite extraordinary woman' who 'cut very, very fast', Noreen Ackland, and Ann Chegwidden.⁴⁸ These women built solid careers but their progress was not unimpeded. Jim Clark candidly admits stipulating 'a man who spoke tolerable English would be preferable to a woman' when recruiting an assistant for *Charade* (1963).⁴⁹ Similarly Anne Coates recalls Ronald Neame not wanting to engage a female editor on *The Horse's Mouth* (1959) because 'he thought women were too into their homes and their boyfriends, and he particularly didn't want a married woman'.⁵⁰ Coates took off her wedding ring and concealed her marital status until she had proved that it had no impact on the quality of her work. Neame was sufficiently impressed to then offer her the job of editing *Tunes of Glory* (1960).

Gendered self-perceptions affected the career development of Noreen Ackland, who did the (superb) editing on *Peeping Tom* (1960) for a lower rate of pay than she could have requested because she 'didn't feel she deserved top whack for it', and later regretted not having 'more confidence' or being 'a little more pushy' in her career.⁵¹ But in the view of some female editors, it was precisely this feminised tendency towards being conciliatory and non-confrontational that made women well suited to the job, with Anne Coates even suggesting that 'so many women have been such good editors [...] because they're mothers, and directors are like children!'⁵² The idea of the editor as self-effacing, patient and calm, a sounding board (David Gladwell's idea of being 'an ear to think aloud into') all map very conveniently onto certain ideas around gendered labour.⁵³

Coates showed considerable confidence in putting herself forward to edit the screen tests for *Lawrence of Arabia*, after hearing about a possible opening from a friend. Her initial nerves were assuaged when David Lean described her first sequence as 'the first time I've ever seen a piece of work cut exactly as I would have done it'.[54] The tone was set for a working relationship which seems to have been demanding but deeply *simpatico*. During the three-month period in which Coates had to assemble the final cut of the film in time for its royal premiere, working through an estimated 35 miles of footage, she worked seven-day weeks, with plenty of late nights, thriving on 'working against the clock, with your adrenaline going', but admitted that this had its personal costs too: 'during that time I hardly saw my husband or my little boy, who used to have to come to the cutting room to see me!'[55]

More Inner World, Less Outer World: Changing Styles

Gavin Millar, in his contribution to the 1968 update of the key textbook *The Technique of Film Editing*, suggested that contemporary cinema had become 'less concerned with the outer world, a good deal more with the inner: with thought processes, with our experience of memory, of time passing', and had developed new kinds of editing to match these new preoccupations.[56] As we have already seen, these new aesthetic practices were admired (and emulated) by some while being repudiated by others for flagrantly disregarding the established rules for good editing. Indeed, this fundamental disagreement about what editing should do, and moreover how films should work, may have contributed to Frank Clark's disagreement with Antonioni on *Blow Up* as much as what he felt to be infringement of his professional autonomy. A more classically inclined editor like Richard Best expressed his disapproval of the 'absolutely ridiculous' jumping of David Warner across a room in *Morgan – A Suitable Case for Treatment* (1966).[57] But *Morgan*'s editor Tom Priestley – sixteen years Best's junior – exemplified a new attitude to editing technique and a rejection of what appeared to be outdated, restrictive conventions, stating: 'I don't believe in continuity. I don't think it's important. I think the only continuity is the continuity of emotion. If it feels right, then it is right.'[58] In that way, Priestley and other editors of his ilk not only represented a new approach to film editing but were also absolutely of a piece with the broader sixties repudiation of old ways perceived as irrelevant, embracing affect as a guiding principle instead.

This emphasis on the importance of emotional rather than the locational or temporal coherence of a sequence resonates in the comments of many British editors of the 1960s. Anthony Harvey, who became a director himself after editing films such as *Dr Strangelove* (1964) and *The Spy Who Came in from the Cold* (1966), stated that 'the most important thing in editing is truthfulness in the use of the performances [. . .] If I do have a rule at all, it is to look at the actor's eyes. They give you a good guide to the emotion that is going into the performance and sometimes a guide as to where to cut.'[59] Antony Gibbs also saw himself as 'an actor's editor' whose selection of shots was determined by finding the most truthful performances: 'you will never be able to look at any of my movies and say, yes, well he's cut this in the classical manner, and it's graceful, and we're moving to the right size of shot, because I don't do that, I'm looking for the acting all the time.'[60]

While Tom Priestley was 'jumping' David Warner across rooms in a cartoon style in *Morgan*, the master of abbreviated editing in the 1960s was Peter Hunt on the Bond films. Hunt pioneered an action-packed style he called 'crash cutting', done in 'broad strokes' with 'almost a comic strip feel to it', according to Hunt's protégé John Glen.[61] Its philosophy was 'if it's boring, cut it out', and Hunt therefore happily 'eliminated a lot of the pedestrian movement that bogged down so many films of the era. Sean Connery would be seen looking towards a door and it would cut to the corridor outside and him emerging from the doorway' in 'abbreviated, almost impressionistic' style.[62] As the series advanced, the cutting got even tighter: *Goldfinger* (1964) reached an ASL of just 4 seconds according to David Bordwell's calculations.[63] *Thunderball* (1965) presented particular problems for keeping up the same breakneck pace as its predecessors since its extensive underwater sequences slowed down the action significantly: Peter Hunt's solution was to run those scenes 'at double speed, removing alternate frames', a risky exercise in 'damage limitation' which paid off and prevented the film from 'grinding to a virtual standstill'; indeed it became one of the highest-grossing of the Bond films.[64] When Hunt took on the role of director for *On Her Majesty's Secret Service* (1969), John Glen became chief editor in his place, and tried to maintain his mentor's 'golden rule' for editing Bond, which was 'never to show anything unless it's going to hit the audience right between the eyes'.[65] Bond films of the 1960s still used fades and dissolves and had moments of languor but these largely functioned to offset the crash-cut dynamism of their action sequences, which soon became the industry standard for an attention-grabbing modern thriller.

Across a range of genres, editing became much less bound by classical conventions around matching, transitions, or self-effacing invisibility, and experimentation of various kinds became much easier, and indeed desirable, in mainstream as well as experimental films. Anthony Harvey was able to use jump cuts in *The L-Shaped Room* (1962), 'cutting erratically instead of dissolving so that, watching, you kept going in and out, closer and away again' to suggest the protagonist's enervation in one particular sequence.[66] Jim Clark's idea that the tedious raw footage they had of the heroine's second marriage in *Darling* (1965) could be made to work by converting it into a mock newsreel sequence was enthusiastically taken up by John Schlesinger.[67] John Bloom was encouraged to 'try anything', even 'outrageous ideas', by director Silvio Narizzano on *Georgy Girl* (1966), resulting in a bold slow-motion jump-cut dance sequence which intercuts Georgy dancing with the children she teaches and dancing alone later.[68] Such techniques would have been the preserve of arthouse cinema even a few years before; now they were recognisable and *normal* in a more mainstream production, another way for a film to signal its youthful verve.

IMAGE MIXER: ANTONY GIBBS (1925–2016)

Antony Gibbs entered the film industry after being demobbed from the Royal Marines, beginning as props assistant before moving into the cutting rooms, and spent four years acting as an assistant to the 'great dialogue editor' Ralph Kemplen.[69] Gibbs then assisted Alan Osbiston, who proved an important mentor and recommended Gibbs for 'movies that Alan couldn't do', like the biopic *Oscar Wilde* (1960).[70] By the early 1960s, Gibbs was beginning to notch up editor credits on low-budget productions, including several with young director Sidney J. Furie: *During One Night* (1960), and *Doctor Blood's Coffin* and *The Snake Woman* (both 1961). Gibbs also cut the thrillers *Offbeat* and *The Unstoppable Man* (both 1961) and several episodes of the filmed BBC television series *The Third Man*. But his major break came through assisting Osbiston on the editing of the Woodfall production *The Entertainer* (1960), which paved the way for further work with Tony Richardson on the subsequent Woodfall films *A Taste of Honey* (1961), *The Loneliness of the Long Distance Runner* and *Tom Jones* and membership of what Richardson described as Woodfall's 'repertory group of technicians' or 'guerrilla' army.[71] Richardson believed in surrounding himself with fresh talent and enabling them to do their thing while reaping the benefits of their experimentation, a hands-off stewardship that emboldened Gibbs to break 'farther away from convention than I would have dared go alone'.[72] The editor experimented with very long dissolves in *A Taste of Honey*, accelerated montage and sudden flashbacks in *The Loneliness of the Long Distance Runner*, and developed what would become the British New Wave trademark of playing intimate dialogue over long shots.[73]

Gibbs recalled thinking that with *Loneliness* he had achieved a stylistic breakthrough, not yet aware of parallel developments taking place across the channel:

> I was feeling pretty proud and arrogant about the whole thing, you know 'this is the way we're going to go, kids'. Then I went and saw *Breathless* and there was this sequence with Belmondo and Seberg in the car and it

was jump-cut, jump-cut. I went 'Oh God', because I'd thought in some silly way that I'd thought of something new and here was someone who's done it six months earlier, and much better.[74]

Nonetheless, Gibbs persisted in his experimental vein on his next film with Richardson, *Tom Jones*, a highly influential film in shifting mainstream aesthetics. Aside from the eating scene – of which Gibbs said that 'of all the things I've ever done, that has given millions of people so much pleasure that I'm very happy with it' – *Tom Jones* has numerous other glories in its editing: from the decision to edit the opening sequence, in which the foundling Tom is discovered, in the style of a silent movie (an brainwave from Vanessa Redgrave) to its energetic stag-hunt scene which creates a sense of hot pursuit by intercutting Walter Lassally's 'helicopter stuff', 'crane stuff', and 'moving ground stuff' at a galloping pace.[75] The playfully confident tone of *Tom Jones* which proved so beguiling to audiences internationally had a lot to do with the dash, rather than stentorian respectfulness, that Gibbs brought to his editing of literary adaptation, reviving old techniques like the wipe and the iris rarely used since silent film as well as using more modernist devices such as freeze frames. As Tom and Sophie pursue their rural romance, there is a scene that totally breaks continuity as they appear to follow themselves on horseback in the farmyard but the rule-breaking technique tallies perfectly with the youthful rebellion and exuberance embodied by its hero.

Gibbs returned to Woodfall as (uncredited) supervisory editor on *Girl with Green Eyes* (1964), edited by his former assistant Bryan Smedley-Aston, and would continue his association with Richardson by editing the first of his two films with Jeanne Moreau, *Mademoiselle* (1966), and supervising editing on the second, *The Sailor from Gibraltar* (1967).[76] But by this point, Gibbs had been put together with Richard Lester on another Woodfall film, *The Knack* (1965), thus forging another important working partnership. Gibbs later suggested that if Richardson had freed him up to try new ideas, then 'Richard Lester lost me my final inhibitions'.[77] What both directors had in common was that they let Gibbs get on with the cutting without undue interference. *The Knack* took some of the freewheeling *Nouvelle Vague*-inflected elements of *Tom Jones* but pushed even further into outright experimentation, making more use of repetition and jarring cuts as well as speeded-up motion. Don Fairservice cites Gibbs's use of repeated action punctuated with jump cuts during the scene where Colin discovers his bathroom is crammed full of nubile young women as an apt way to 'convey the character's excitement and the repetition his need to sustain it'.[78] The moment in which Colin and Nancy's eyes first meet is presented through very rapid intercutting between their mutually rapt expressions, an incisive way of suggesting love, or lust, at first sight.

On their next collaboration *Petulia* (1968), Lester told Gibbs that 'he felt that its strength would be in the editing': '*Petulia* was a mosaic; it had to be'.[79] Gibbs recalled:

> He said something to me that has never been said before or since: 'I don't want to see this film until it's in the form you feel it should be. I don't want to see your rough cut or assembly. When you've arrived at a presentation you like, show it to me and we'll see where we are.'[80]

The solution he finally arrived at was to use flash-forwards as well as the flashbacks already written into the script.[81] This provided the kind of narrational complexity desired by the director as well as supplying an underlying structural symmetry 'where you have flash-forwards at the beginning, which naturally enough decrease as the film goes on. And you also have flashbacks that start late in the film and increase as the film proceeds. So you have these two curves.'[82]

Editing was not only crucial to the narrative architecture of *Petulia* but also gave the film its very specific textural qualities. One sequence blends television images of conflict in Vietnam, a globular psychedelic oil-and-water projection, and a pulsing red lightshow at a rock gig, which then merges into the medical imagery of movement of cells seen through a microscope, and an X-ray being perused by the doctor protagonist. The sheer density of this very brief moment's aural and visual combinations and juxtapositions and its shifts from inner visions to outer realities, memories and mental associations, and the confusions between all of those cognitive categories, is truly dazzling. *Petulia* even inspired David Lean to write Richard Lester a fan letter in which he said: 'I used to think I was a bit of a dab hand as a cutter but I'm not in your league as an image mixer.'[83] But perhaps his praise should have been directed as much at Gibbs as Lester.

Gibbs favoured working on the Moviola because it was the 'most precise editing tool that's ever been invented [...] the only machine that will stop on a frame. It will stop on *that* frame.'[84] This exactitude would be essential for Gibbs's next assignment, Donald Cammell and Nicolas Roeg's *Performance*, which represented the apex of Gibbs's editorial ambitions during the 'beautiful madness' of the 1960s:

> we were, I like to think, leading the world in where film could go [...] I wanted to do strange things with film. I wanted to see if it would work, laying images and images upon images to convey an emotion. [...] It was all part of the Sixties, when we felt confident that we could do things with film that had not been done – at least in professional theatrical movies.[85]

Although the version that we see of *Performance* is not Gibbs and Smedley-Aston's original cut, but rather one further revised by Frank Mazzolo under Donald Cammell's supervision, there is still ample evidence for Gibbs's imprint upon the film in its creation of a richly textured dramatic milieu, with 'some lovely, marvellous opticals' including the infamous shattering image of Jorge Luis Borges at the centre of Turner's brain on the point of his death, that made the blending identities of Chas and Turner not only plausible but inevitable.[86]

The idea of being able to discern an editor's authorial presence goes against the grain of how many editors conceptualised their work: for Reginald Mills, for instance, good editing was when 'one is never aware of cutting from one shot to another'.[87] But Gibbs was unusual in proposing the idea of individual editorial style or 'handwriting' and felt his own was defined by:

> use of extreme long shot with dialogue over. Breaking up the rhythm of a long dialogue scene, bringing it almost to a halt and then starting the rhythm again. The deliberate use of unrhythmic cuts to create nervousness [. . .][88]

But style could develop and 'mature as the years go by', and Gibbs could track his progress from project to project:

> I think I couldn't have done *Performance*, in particular, and *Walkabout*, if I hadn't done *Petulia*. And I couldn't have done *Petulia* if I hadn't already done *Tom Jones* for Tony Richardson and *The Knack* with Richard. It's all a progression from one to the other. On most of my movies at this time, I can see a thread for myself as a film editor.[89]

Tony Gibbs's input into numerous key British films of the 1960s was indispensable, bearing out his own distinction between merely good and great film editing:

> Good editing is the total interpretation of the director's and writer's intentions. Great film editing is taking their intentions even farther and showing them a dimension to their project which even they may not have imagined to be there.[90]

Coda: The Party's Over

Antony Gibbs, along with many other highly innovative and creative British editors, faced an impasse in advancing his career further within the British-based film industry as US investment in British production began to be withdrawn in the 1970s. Indeed, many creative professionals across a range of specialisms who had benefitted from the 1960s production boom decided to migrate to where the work was, which was increasingly in a newly reinvigorated Hollywood rather than in a no-longer-swinging Britain. Gibbs followed up the intense Roeg-directed Australian drama *Walkabout* (1970) with an apparently unlikely assignment, the big-screen version of the hit Broadway musical *Fiddler on the Roof* (1971), but it instigated another mutually beneficial editor–director partnership, this time with Norman Jewison who Gibbs would work with on several subsequent productions.[91] His editing peer Jim Clark followed John Schlesinger to act as 'creative consultant' on the director's debut American film *Midnight Cowboy* (1969) and eventually went on to become a respected Hollywood 'film doctor' (or 'dream repairman' in Clark's own evocative phrase).

Some who stayed in the UK moved into advertising, such as Gerry Hambling who, after his sixties work on Norman Wisdom and Morecambe and Wise films, spent the 1970s building a profile in television commercials before returning to film editing with his advertising colleague, director Alan Parker. But others, who did not move sideways into television drama or commercials, found the territory increasingly challenging. A poem entitled 'Waiting for a picture', published anonymously in the August 1970 issue of the Guild of British Film Editors newsletter, provides a vivid sense of the growing anguish experienced by an increasingly precarious freelance workforce:

> The alarm bell doesn't ring any more at 6.45 a.m.
> There is no need to spring or to drag oneself from
> a warm bed at the crack of dawn.
> [. . .]
> This wonderful film industry of ours is like an errant mistress
> For whom we have a love hate relationship.
> At these times we wonder why she spurns us. We are hurt.
> She only has to beckon and we go running back.[92]

An editorial in the newsletter later that year continued in the same spirit of anguished insecurity as the end of the boom and the withdrawal of American finance from a British film industry which had now become heavily reliant upon it really began to take effect, leading to some serious soul-searching:

> When we're busy we tend to be complacent about the industry and overlook its shortcomings, but when we sit by the phone for weeks on end between pictures we begin to see the facts as they really are. We see only too clearly the hazards, the uncertainties, and the frightening fact that we're past the point of no return and there's little else outside the cutting rooms that we could (or would like to) do. We finish a film and start to

look around and often to our horror we find that there's nothing about anywhere and we get frightened . . . until the next job turns up. But even when the next job comes these days we realise that the whole cycle will come round again and we start to ask ourselves what it's really all about. [. . .] Maybe the fact that our futures aren't monotonously mapped out for us acts as an attraction when times are good and as an incentive when times are bad. Who really knows any more?[93]

Some editors took more decisive action in controlling their fate: Norman Wanstall, the Oscar-winning sound editor of *Goldfinger* and other Bond films, and editor of *Joanna* (1968) and *Twinky* (1970), even retrained as a plumber and heating engineer in the 1970s due to the paucity of UK-based film work.[94]

Far from being the exclusive preserve of editors, this sense of growing anxiety and uncertainty applied to a whole cohort of highly trained and often highly talented technicians who had survived, or triumphantly ridden, the changes of the 1960s but who now found themselves facing unemployment, emigration, retraining in an entirely new profession, or just hoping that the cycle would come round again as soon as possible and that British film production might recapture some of the swing it had seemed to possess in the 1960s. Runaway production would continue to employ numerous British technicians in the 1970s, albeit on a more modest scale than before and on productions (James Bond aside) that tended to hide their British provenance rather than it being a core part of the marketing, exemplified by later blockbusters such as *Star Wars* (1977) and *Superman* (1978). British cinema may not have recaptured the same buoyancy it had in the sixties but the reputation for craftsmanship and innovation that British technicians developed during that time would endure.

Notes

1. Barry Salt, *Film Style and Technology*, p. 265. Salt focuses mainly on Hollywood but encompasses transatlantic production within that.
2. David Bordwell, 'Intensified continuity: visual style in contemporary American film', *Film Quarterly*, vol. 55, no. 3 (Spring 2002), pp. 16–17.
3. Peter Tanner BECTU interview, <https://historyproject.org.uk/interview/peter-tanner> (accessed 1 August 2018).
4. Salt, *Film Style and Technology*, p. 265.
5. In Roy Perkins and Martin Stollery, *British Film Editors: The Heart of the Movie* (London: BFI, 2004), p. 164.
6. Peter Tanner, 'Editing: theory and practice', *Photographic Journal*, vol. 102, no. 11, November 1962, p. 296.
7. Geoffrey Foot BECTU interview, <https://historyproject.org.uk/intervew/geoffrey-foot> (accessed 1 August 2018). Richard Best, who worked across both media, discussed the difference in his approaches to them: 'In the case of television cutting, one does *not* linger on so many nuances, reactions or "pregnant moments" as one does in a feature, and where one does they are cut much tighter.' Quoted in 'Editing

– the beginning of the end', *Journal of the Society of Film and Television Arts*, no. 26, Winter 1966/67, p. 5.
8. In 'Film editors forum', *Film Comment*, March/April 1977, p. 25.
9. Quoted in Robert Vas, 'Meditation at 24 F.P.S.', *Sight and Sound*, Summer 1966, p. 122.
10. Anne V. Coates BECTU interview, <https://historyproject.org.uk/interview/anne-v-coates> (accessed 1 August 2018).
11. Coates quoted in Gabriella Oldham, *First Cut: Conversations with Film Editors* (Berkeley: University of California Press, 1995), p. 156.
12. Vas, 'Meditation at 24 F.P.S.', p. 122.
13. Jim Clark, *Dream Repairman: Adventures in Film Editing* (London: PDC, 2011), p. 46.
14. Vas, 'Meditation at 24 F.P.S.', p. 121.
15. Ibid., p. 120.
16. Barry Salt, *Film Style and Technology*, p. 251. Even those who disliked the new approaches to editing still felt that its provenance was British, with Ralph Rosenblum laying the blame for what he saw as a triumph of style over substance squarely at the Beatles pop musicals *A Hard Day's Night* and *Help!*, cut by John Jympson and John Victor-Smith respectively, in whose wake, he felt, 'technique has taken over. Editing has become flamboyant solely for its own sake.' Quoted in 'Film editors forum', *Film Comment*, March/April 1977, p. 25.
17. Bernard Gribble BECTU interview, <https://historyproject.org.uk/interview/bernard-gribble> (accessed 1 August 2018).
18. Quoted in *Vincent LoBrutto, Selected Takes: Film Editors on Editing (Westport: Praeger, 1991), p. 78*.
19. Their slightly more sporadic forerunners (as British editors nominated for Oscars) were Fergus McDonell for *Odd Man Out* in 1947, Reginald Mills for *The Red Shoes* in 1948, Oswald Hafenrichter in 1950 for *The Third Man*, and Peter Taylor who won for his work on another David Lean film, *The Bridge on the River Kwai* in 1957.
20. 'Editors' guild', *Kine Weekly*, 25 August 1966, p. 4.
21. Bill Altria, 'None better', *Kine* Weekly, 26 April 1969, p. 4.
22. Perkins and Stollery, *British Film Editors*, p. 12. Invisibility as the keynote of classical continuity editing is emphasised in David Bordwell, Janet Staiger, and Kristin Thompson, *The Classical Hollywood Cinema* (London: Routledge, 1985) and in Don Fairservice, *Film Editing: History, Theory and Practice* (Manchester: Manchester University Press, 2001).
23. Paul Falkenberg, 'The editor's role in film making', *Cinema Journal*, vol. 7, Winter 1967/68, p. 28. Perkins and Stollery, *British Film Editors*, p. 19.
24. Mills' response is part of 'Film editors forum', *Film Comment*, March/April 1977, p. 24. Jim Clark's responses to the same questions are even more telling on the unsung nature of much editing work: 'a) Taking a pile of uncut rushes and sticking them together in a manner which reflects the director b) . . . which goes unnoticed c) . . . which goes unnoticed even by other film editors.'
25. Coates quoted in 'The art and craft of film editing: a critical symposium', *Cineaste*, Spring 2009, p. 58.
26. Quoted in Roger Hudson, 'Putting the magic in it: two editors, James Clark and Anthony Harvey, discuss their work', *Sight and Sound*, Spring 1966, p. 83.
27. Allen Eyles, 'Cutting remarks', *Stills*, May 1985, p. 12.
28. Alfred Roome BECTU interview, <https://historyproject.org.uk/interview/alfred-roome> (accessed 1 August 2018). Rogers queried Roome's meagre expenditure on essential equipment like pencils and rubber bands, asking him 'why can't you use

ones from the last picture?' The tight turnaround was not limited to the cheaper end of the film production sector; it also affected those working on prestige big-budget productions too, like dubbing editor Don Sharpe: The Guild of British Film Editors newsletter from August 1969 (issue no. 25) made a joke about *Anne of the Thousand Days* being retitled 'Don of the 28 Nights' because he 'only had 4 weeks' to complete his work. (p. 8).
29. Alfred Roome BECTU interview.
30. Peter Tanner felt that comedies were 'among the most difficult to edit. Not only has the timing to be exact and allowance made for the audience's laughter, but the editor must manage to keep an objective viewpoint all through. A "gag" which has everyone roaring with laughter in the rushes may not seem at all funny after repeated runnings in the cutting room. The editor must try to look at such scenes as though he were a member of the audience seeing it for the first time, and not fall for the fatal mistake of over-cutting and getting stale on a picture.' Tanner, 'Editing: theory and practice', p. 296.
31. Teddy Darvas BECTU interview, <https://historyproject.org.uk/interview/teddy-darvas> (accessed 1 August 2018).
32. Quoted in Perkins and Stollery, *British Film Editors*, p. 96.
33. Ibid., p. 95.
34. Ibid., p. 195.
35. Reginald Beck BECTU interview, <https://historyproject.org.uk/interview/reginald-reggie-beck> (accessed 1 August 2018).
36. Ibid.
37. Clark, *Dream Repairman*, p. 47.
38. Clark's subsequent partnership with John Schlesinger resulted in some equally strong work but seems to have remained at a more jocular level.
39. Best quoted in 'Editing – the beginning of the end', p. 2.
40. Salt, *Film Style and Technology*, p. 265.
41. Quoted in Perkins and Stollery, *British Film Editors*, p. 148.
42. Ibid. pp. 146–7.
43. Trumper quoted in Colin Vaines, 'Man of mystery', *Screen International*, 18 February 1978, p. 17.
44. Teddy Darvas BECTU interview.
45. David Gladwell, 'Editing Anderson's *If . . .*', *Screen*, vol. 10, no. 1, January 1969, p. 25.
46. Derek Todd, 'Casino Royale – the twenty-reel jigsaw', *Kine Weekly*, 29 September 1966, p. 9.
47. Coates quoted in 'The art and craft of film editing', p. 61. She faced the opposite challenge when she took over cutting on *Those Magnificent Men in Their Flying Machines* and had to create the impression of a close-run race in the skies in when there was no coverage of planes overtaking each other. BECTU interview.
48. John Champ, 'Production', 31 August 1961, p. 12. Honess quoted in Perkins and Stollery, *British Film Editors*, p. 166. Interestingly, both Connell and Ackland were married to fellow editors, Douglas Myers and Richard Best respectively, and perhaps were able to get on better due to having partners who understood many of the professional challenges they faced, having encountered the same. For more on women's general pre-eminence in editing, see Mark Cousins, 'Scissor sisters', *Sight and Sound*, August 2015, p. 6.
49. Jim Clark, *Dream Repairman*, p. 48. Ironically his assistant Laurence Mery *was* female, and they ended up marrying shortly after working together.
50. Gary Crowdus, 'The editing of *Lawrence of Arabia*: an interview with Anne V. Coates', *Cineaste*, Spring 2009, p. 49.

51. BECTU interview, <https://historyproject.org.uk/interview/noreen-ackland-best> (accessed 1 August 2018). Perkins and Stollery include a nice anecdote about Ackland's assistant Alma Godfrey encouraging her bold cutting on *Peeping Tom*: 'I could talk to her and she would give me confidence: "Go on, Nor. Do it!" she would say.' Perkins and Stollery, *British Film Editors*, p. 179.
52. Coates in 'The art and craft of film editing', p. 57.
53. Gladwell, 'Editing Anderson's *If . . .*', p. 33,
54. Crowdus, 'Editing of *Lawrence of Arabia*', p. 49.
55. Ibid., p. 50. Family commitments predetermined many of Coates' subsequent career choices, since her desire to spend lots of time with her children would not easily combine with jobs that required her to work on rushes and rough cuts in foreign locations: the reason she declined both *Doctor Zhivago* and *The Comedians*; 'I had three small children, I couldn't fly out to Haiti!' (BECTU interview). It does seem that post-production was a slightly more 'family-friendly' area of film labour than others, with Thelma Connell described by Teddy Darvas as 'pregnant yet again' while she was working on the first *St Trinian's* film in the early 1950s, implying her continuance of a career through motherhood. However, the family-friendliness of editing also proved attractive to some male exponents like Jonathan Morris: 'I valued being able to read the kids a story at seven o'clock when you got home. Almost any other grade in film-making you can't rely on that. The only time you're home is when you're out of work.' Roger Crittenden, *Fine Cuts: The Art of European Film Editing* (London: Focal, 2005), p. 27. Coates's initial ambitions to move into directing, as her previous colleagues Clive Donner and John Krish had done, seemed incompatible with motherhood so she stuck to the professional area which generally offered more flexibility around childcare ('If they were ill it was easier to take time off') and 'really concentrated' on the development of her husband Douglas Hickox's directorial career instead.
56. Karel Reisz and Gavin Millar, *The Technique of Film Editing, Second Edition* (London: Focal Press, 2009 [1968]), p. 274.
57. Quoted in Perkins and Stollery, *British Film Editors*, p. 109.
58. Ibid., p. 38.
59. Harvey quoted in Hudson, 'Putting the magic in it', p. 81.
60. Perkins and Stollery, *British Film Editors*, p. 201.
61. Ray Zone, 'Wrap shot: *Dr. No*', *American Cinematographer*, November 2002, p. 112. John Glen, *For My Eyes Only: My Life with James Bond* (London: Batsford, 2001), p. 45, p. 37.
62. Ibid.
63. Bordwell, 'Intensified continuity', p. 17.
64. Glen, *For My Eyes Only*, p. 44. As Glen notes, this technique had to be used with caution: 'if you frame-cut footage of someone running, you end up making them look like Charlie Chaplin.'
65. Ibid., p. 45.
66. Quoted in Hudson, 'Putting the magic into it', p. 79.
67. Clark, *Dream Repairman*, p. 64.
68. Perkins and Stollery, *British Film Editors*, p. 109.
69. Lesley Gibbs and Tessa Lumley, 'Tony Gibbs obituary', *The Guardian*, 16 May 2016, <https://www.theguardian.com/film/2016/may/16/tony-gibbs-obituary> (accessed 1 August 2018).
70. Perkins and Stollery, *British Film Editors*, p. 210.
71. Ibid., p. 104.
72. Gibbs in 'Film editors forum', *Film Comment*, March/April 1977, p. 25.
73. Perkins and Stollery, *British Film Editors*, p. 106

74. Ibid., p. 141.
75. Ibid., p. 107.
76. Gibbs also supervised editing on Richardson's Hollywood black comedy *The Loved One* (1965)
77. Gibbs in 'Film editors forum', *Film Comment*, March/April 1977, p. 25.
78. Fairservice, *Film Editing*, p. 305.
79. In Richard Combs, '*Petulia*: blood, glass, and feathers', *Film Comment*, vol. 35, no. 1 (January/February 1999), p. 62.
80. Ibid.
81. Flash-forwards have been identified as 'unthinkable in the classical narrative cinema'. Bordwell, Staiger, and Thompson, *The Classical Hollywood Cinema*, p. 374.
82. Gibbs quoted in Combs, '*Petulia*: blood, glass, and feathers', p. 62.
83. Reproduced in Neil Sinyard, *Richard Lester* (Manchester: Manchester University Press, 2010), p. 176.
84. Quoted in Perkins and Stollery, *British Film Editors*, p. 153.
85. Gibbs in 'Film editors forum', *Film Comment*, March/April 1977, p. 24.
86. Quoted in Combs, '*Petulia*: blood, glass, and feathers', p. 62.
87. Gibbs in 'Film editors forum', *Film Comment*, March/April 1977, p. 24. Jim Clark described how an editor 'alters style according to subject and director, becoming the director's "alter ego"'.
88. Ibid.
89. Gibbs quoted in Combs, '*Petulia*: blood, glass, and feathers', p. 62.
90. Gibbs in 'Film editors forum', *Film Comment*, March/April 1977, p. 24.
91. Jewison's *Rollerball* (1975) also made use of the talents of numerous British film personnel, including cinematographer Douglas Slocombe, production designer John Box and costume designer Julie Harris.
92. Guild of British Film Editors newsletter, August 1970, p. 10.
93. Bernard Gribble, 'Editorial', Guild of British Film Editors newsletter, no. 36, April 1971, pp. 2–3.
94. Matthew Field, 'Sounding out Norman Wanstall', *Cinema Retro: Movie Classics*, no. 4, 2012, p. 119.

PART THREE

MEDIA CONVERGENCE

12. FILM AND TELEVISION

Richard Farmer

INTRODUCTION

Television in Britain expanded as a consequence of the increasing prosperity enjoyed by many sections of post-war British society and became symbolic of the nation's shift from austerity to affluence.[1] By January 1956, almost 37 per cent of British homes had a television, and this trend intensified over the subsequent decade: by the start of the 1960s it was 67 per cent, and 92 per cent by 1970, a state of near-saturation.[2] Cinema risked becoming yesterday's medium, but the British film industry's response was never one of simple resignation to this new state of affairs. Rather, it made strenuous efforts to reposition itself in a changed media landscape. Moreover, the film and television industries were never entirely adversarial: although the two media were often posited as rivals, many recognised that there was scope for mutually beneficial co-existence. Britons could be both cinemagoers and television viewers; the specificities of the two media created room for both. Television could provide a sense of the immediate, whereas the cinema was able to utilise the different technologies at its disposal to showcase the spectacular.[3] One was domestic, with all the convenience and privacy that entailed; the other public, affording a greater sense of occasion and communality.

Problems initially arose when cinema felt television was trespassing on its territory. Sections of the British film industry were concerned that broadcasting films on TV would reduce ticket sales, and so attempted to prevent films being sold to television companies. But there was also an understanding

Figure 12.1 Aspirational artist: radio and television star Tony Hancock makes his film debut in *The Rebel* (Robert Day, 1961).

that television offered a new medium by which the film industry might communicate with the nation's consumers and maximise the earnings of existing and future product. Feature films being shown on TV was the most obvious expression of this, but film-review programmes and the screening of film trailers on commercial stations also provide evidence of the ways in which the film industry used television to sell films and promote itself. The various initiatives that emerged from the British film industry's response to and engagement with television should caution us against understanding that industry as being in any sense monolithic: exhibitors, distributors and producers reacted differently to the advent of mass television ownership, and within each of these three sectors, there were disagreements and discrepancies, especially between large and small businesses. Although there were some individuals, groups or companies who regarded television as a threat to the future of the cinema, others recognised that TV would alter established business practices and income streams and sought to adjust accordingly. Furthermore, there was scope for both content and talent to move between these two media. Television became the primary workplace for many former film personnel in the 1960s, while some of those who initially forged careers in television moved into cinema; others criss-crossed between the two media. Likewise, television and film borrowed ideas and products from each other, albeit with variable end results. Each of these elements of interaction between the two media in the 1960s will be explored in this chapter, ranging from the outright conflict of the Film Industry Defence Organisation (FIDO) to the warm embrace of the sitcom spin-off film.

Diversification and FIDO

The growth of television pre-dated the arrival of ITV in September 1955, but the BBC's publicly financed monopoly prevented large film and cinema organisations from muscling into the industry. However, with the advent of commercial television, and as part of a wider process of diversification, a number of larger British film companies joined other media organisations in the scramble for ITV franchises (commercial television was run as a network, with different stations serving different parts of the country, or offering programming at different times of the week). Rank took a stake in Southern Television, whilst Sidney Bernstein brought the name of his Granada cinema chain to the station he owned and operated in the north of England. Associated British's ABC franchise, which broadcast to the Midlands and north of England at weekends, also shared a title with its parent company's chain of cinemas. In 1960, more than 60 per cent of ABPC's trading profit was derived from its television interests, seemingly demonstrating that these companies were, to quote another franchisee, 'a license to print money'.[4] In 1968, ABC lost its franchise, but ABPC gained a majority stake in the newly formed Thames Television. Both Rank and ABPC used (or rented out) their studio facilities for the production of television programming, whilst ABC television's global sales were handled by Associated British–Pathé distributors. Elsewhere, John Woolf, of Romulus Films and Independent Film Distributors, was a key figure in the formation of Anglia Television and became head of drama at the station, John Baxter became executive controller of Television Wales and the West, and Sydney Box – whose Beaconsfield studio was home to television series *Ivanhoe* – played a central role in the creation of Tyne Tees Television. Michael Balcon, meanwhile, became a director of Border Television having contributed to that company's successful franchise application.[5]

However, others in the British cinema industry believed television to be a key factor in the rapid decline in cinema attendances and in an attempt to prevent the sale of films to television, the Film Industry Defence Organisation was established in 1958 by five trade bodies, including the Cinema Exhibitors' Association and the Federation of British Film Makers. When FIDO was founded, feature films were not a major component of television schedules – only sixty-four were transmitted between January and June 1957. There were, though, justifiable concerns that this number would grow: despite FIDO's best efforts, more than 300 films were broadcast in 1959,[6] and by late 1964 television viewers in Britain were presented with an average of ten films each week spread across two BBC channels, and the local ITV station(s).[7]

FIDO focused primarily on more recently released films, as these were considered most likely to keep potential cinemagoers at home. However, the broadcast of older films was also believed to threaten exhibitors, as FIDO secretary Bill Speakman noted in 1964:

> Some of the [older] films may have been great – at the time they were made. But, show them now and they are awful [. . . A]fter seeing them on TV, they'll think – the younger people especially – 'Heavens, is that the best that films can do?' And they'll go to the cinema even less than they do now.[8]

Exhibitors might also have worried that broadcasting films, of any age, might bring about a loss of control over medium-specific selling points. Martin McLoone notes that the transition from live to pre-recorded television was 'very slow' in Britain compared to the USA.[9] Live broadcasts privileged performance and script, providing a space for intimate, discursive drama. As screenwriter Alun Owen recognised, 'Television can make a virtue of words. You can sustain a ten-minute duologue on television, but concentrated dialogue is far more difficult in the cinema.'[10] Cinema, by contrast, offered scope for visual spectacle and editing. The desire to keep films off television might, therefore, have stemmed in part from a desire to keep what television did separate from what films did.

This situation changed as the 1960s progressed and more television was shot on film, creating what Troy Kennedy Martin called 'the drama of our age. It is fast, quick, compact. It has urgency, and immediacy.'[11] Filmed television could foreground sound and vision editing, in contrast to multi-camera, studio-bound productions, where lengthy sections of a play were shot with editing taking place between cameras in real time. Kennedy Martin complained that live television afforded 'editing . . . the comparative clumsiness of a steam hammer'. He was, though, thrilled by the skilful editing of the filmed *Up the Junction* (BBC TV, 1965): 'four sound-tracks were playing simultaneously . . . and jump cuts took you back and forth till you were lost in time.'[12] As television made greater use of cinematic techniques, the two media began to converge aesthetically, undermining FIDO's rationale.

FIDO paid producers to secure undertakings, known as covenants, that the right to broadcast a film would not be sold to television for a given period (often ten years). FIDO's funds were generated by a farthing-a-seat levy on ticket sales, raising an estimated £500,000 annually by 1960.[13] Exhibitors with smaller incomes did not collect the levy, but as ticket sales declined and more halls closed, fewer cinemas were left to contribute to FIDO. However, the organisation still paid out significant sums: by August 1963, the covenants to 899 films had been purchased for a total of £1,689,396.[14]

While many smaller and medium-sized distributors and exhibitors were committed to FIDO, Rank and ABPC never formally joined, preferring to operate 'a policy of co-operation' which amounted to not selling their own films to television.[15] However, the majors' involvement in television compromised the film industry's ability to unite in response to the challenge posed by the small screen.[16] Though the larger circuits were broadly sympathetic to the smaller exhibitors' plight, their television interests resulted in divided loyalties. ABPC, Granada and Rank found themselves uncomfortably positioned when commercial television companies with no, or less extensive, film or cinema interests adopted a more cavalier approach to buying and broadcasting films, as when in 1964 ATV purchased fifty films from Sam Goldwyn, and the station's managing director, Lew Grade, stated, 'It's my job to give the best in entertainment. If we upset the film industry – well. We just upset them.'[17] If such films were made available for networking (i.e. offered for transmission across all franchises), ABC, Granada and Southern had to decide whether or not to show them, potentially bringing different parts of their businesses into conflict and testing their commitment to their allies on either side of the film–television divide. Additionally, competition for advertising revenue meant that franchises were reluctant to leave themselves at a disadvantage, as *Variety* noted following a conversation with Granada's Cecil Bernstein: 'ABC was in opposition to Granada TV in the north, and anything the former claimed the right to do, [the latter] must put itself in the position to do likewise.'[18]

These tensions were evident from the beginning. In 1958, ABPC upset FIDO by selling ninety-five films made by Ealing Studios and acquired by ABPC through its acquisition of Associated Talking Pictures, to its ABC Television subsidiary. ABPC insisted that its substantial holdings in 'cinema bricks and mortar', and its refusal to let these films be broadcast on other stations, demonstrated its commitment to FIDO and to film exhibition; critics noted that this did not preclude the screening of the Ealing films on ABC television.[19] Furthermore, Rank's interest in exploiting what it hoped would be the profitable pay-TV market antagonised FIDO, which was alarmed by the conglomerate's desire to show films on pay-TV concurrent with their general release.[20]

The Rank–ABPC duopoly's ambivalent attitude to FIDO reflects the various commercial pressures acting on them as diversified businesses. As the most important players in the exhibition sector, they often enjoyed first-run rights to more popular films, thereby insulating themselves against falling ticket sales; as producers, they had extensive film catalogues that generated additional funds should they be sold to television. As investors in television, they appreciated the appeal of films, both because of their popularity with viewers and because of the 'breathing space' they provided – that is, 90 minutes of programming that the television broadcasters did not have to produce themselves.[21] This last point, though, troubled the trade unions, and Tom O'Brien, NATKE general secretary, claimed that television 'had the responsibility to employ part of its profits in building a new TV film industry, instead of buying up old movies'.[22]

But buy them up they did; FIDO was unsuccessful in its attempts to keep films off British television screens. From the outset, the organisation had been limited in its ability to effectively sanction companies that sought to break its embargo. In early 1960, in a move indicative of the swelling coffers of some ITV franchises, Associated–Rediffusion purchased Independent Film Distributors in a deal that gave it control of fifty-five films including *The African Queen* (1951) and *A Kid for Two Farthings* (1955); in 1965, Rediffusion also purchased Bryanston. Although FIDO discussed the possibility of boycotting companies that sold films to television, fears that such actions might breach US anti-trust laws and the British Restrictive Trade Practices Act rendered such threats largely toothless.[23] This created a seller's market, despite FIDO's unwillingness to overpay for unappealing product, such as in 1961 when it refused to pay Stratford Films the 'exaggerated price' of £365,000 for seventy features including *Life in Emergency Ward 10* (1959) and *Inn for Trouble* (1960).[24]

Although FIDO managed to acquire covenants for a good number of 'A' films, it was recognised contemporaneously that there was 'something of the finger-in-the-dyke' about the organisation.[25] Indeed, the BBC had purchased 100 films from RKO prior to FIDO's foundation, although the Corporation agreed not to increase the proportion of time it spent broadcasting films.[26] The budgets commanded by television, especially after the arrival of ITV, made the small screen too important a potential source of revenue for a fragmented and declining film industry to ignore. As it became increasingly evident that feature films were to be a permanent and regular feature of television schedules, FIDO decided in September 1964 not to oppose the sale to television of films older than five years. Exhibitor collections were discontinued from January 1965.

In 1968, British Lion and the BBC concluded a deal for 136 films.[27] Some of these, including *The Third Man* (1949), had previously been included a package of 76 British Lion covenants purchased by FIDO for £410,000 in 1960.[28] The British Lion deal reflected a 'striking increase' in the number of films shown on BBC television during the 1960s, and by 1972 the Corporation noted that there was a 'requirement' for 200 feature film premieres per year across BBC1 and BBC2, although repeats increased the total number of films broadcast. Yet if the television stations had hoped that the demise of FIDO would reduce competition for films and so lower prices, they would be disappointed: the 1968 deal, concluded in the face of stiff competition from the ITV contractors, cost the BBC £1.75 million.[29] For British Lion, as for other distributors, television money provided a very welcome windfall which could be used to sustain production activities; the small screen thus helped to maintain the supply of new product on the big.

TRAILERS AND FILM REVIEW PROGRAMMES

It took time for the British film industry to recognise and exploit television's ability to advertise its wares. The first specially produced film trailer did not appear on ITV until mid-1956,[30] and the following year *Kine Weekly* was still seeking to persuade its readers that they should look upon television as 'a channel of propaganda for our use', declaring: 'It is time that we used television as anyone else does who wants to advertise a product – buy time and use it as a direct advertising platform.'[31] Admittedly, television did not always allow a film to be advertised to its best advantage; screen size was smaller, picture quality lower, and acoustic limitations could make transmissions 'sound like something happening in a bag of wool'.[32] Further, all advertising on British television, even for colour films, was black and white until November 1969.[33] However, these drawbacks subtly reinforced cinema's technological superiority, and were less important than the access television provided to hordes of potential cinemagoers.

Although there was some promotion of the experiential pleasures offered by a night at the pictures, film trailers constituted the majority of cinema advertising on television.[34] Release patterns meant that the major chains, and in some cases particular venues, featured prominently in the marketing of individual films. Geographically appropriate information was added region by region. When *Thunderball* (1965) was advertised in north-east England, the first half of a 30-second television trailer communicated the pleasures of the film – Bond theme, Connery, guns, girls, an underwater shootout – whilst the title card at its conclusion referenced the attractions of the cinematic medium: widescreen, colour, an A certificate. The remainder of the trailer lists cinemas screening *Thunderball*: 'From tomorrow at Odeons Middlesbrough, Stockton, Darlington, Bishop Auckland, West Hartlepool, Gateshead, Byker, Gaumont South Shields, and from Monday, Gaumont North Shields.'

Relatively few made-for-television trailers produced in the 1960s have survived. However, it is possible to get a sense of them from reviews carried in *Television Mail*, a trade paper for the television advertising industry. Trailers made for television did not tend to be positively received, with criticism focused upon their lack of originality, as a review from September 1962 indicates: 'three trailers for three quite different feature films [*The Children's Hour, Tiara Tahiti, Escape from Zahrein*] all with identical selling treatment ... If spliced together they would look like one long, loud trailer for the same film!'[35]

Moves towards novelty and experimentation were hampered by the need to conform to ITCA guidelines. Even after X-certificate cinema trailers were introduced in 1968, television trailers for films targeted at adults had to be suitable for family audiences. Hammer's *Dracula Has Risen from the Grave* (1968) was advertised on television by means of 'a strangely muted U Certificate commercial,' with the trailer's tameness mocked by reference to a then-current Colgate toothpaste slogan: 'even [Dracula's] fangs had a ring of confidence.'[36]

Moreover, trailers looked to advertise a range of attractions to as wide an audience as possible; referencing romance, action, violence, comedy and spectacle produced 'hotch-potches of highlights'.[37] Television trailers also had to give a sense of a film's theme – but not *too* much of its narrative – in less time than was afforded to a cinema trailer: some television spots ran to a minute, but others were thirty or even fifteen seconds long, resulting in swift cutting and a relentless tone. Consequently, creatives bemoaned the trailer-makers' unwillingness to 'borrow something from the style' of film they were promoting, complaining that trailers were more closely aligned with other trailers than the advertised film's genre.[38]

The sense of déjà vu that frustrated the critics might have resulted from so many trailers being produced by the same small group of film-makers working to tight deadlines at a limited number of organisations. National Screen Service was the largest of the companies that specialised in producing television (and cinema) trailers in Britain. The same male voices – Tim Turner, Robert Beattie and David Healy – recited similar lines from the same book of portentous clichés, a situation made more noticeable because the variable quality of the television image placed greater emphasis on a trailer's commentary.[39] Some trailers were, however, more positively received. A television spot for *Carry on Screaming* (1966) provided 'this year's novelty – an out-of-the-ordinary film trailer',[40] whilst one for *Up the Junction* (1968) was praised for the clarity with which it established the film's themes and utilised the slogan 'What's a bird like this doing up there?' to tie it into print and poster publicity campaigns.[41]

Film-review programmes on television provided another way of putting new releases in front of the public, although this was not without its complications.[42] On the one hand, the film industry wanted such programmes 'to advertise films, not evaluate them'.[43] On the other, broadcasters wanted a more questioning tone, not least because this allowed for more arresting television – 'I am tempted to say that if I want to see film trailers I can do it in my local cinema, thank you,' sniffed one viewer of a programme she felt to be insufficiently critical.[44] Distributors therefore had to balance the possibility of a poor review against the free marketing opportunity offered by permitting a clip to be put before the considerable audiences that film-review programmes could command.[45]

Programmes like the BBC's *Picture Parade* were heavily reliant on clips: material from more than 400 films was used during the show's first hundred episodes, constituting approximately 40 per cent of the series' running time.[46] As such, they struggled in instances where distributors retaliated against critical reviews by withholding films.[47] The final edition of *Picture Parade* was broadcast in December 1962, the programme 'starved out of existence' by distributors convinced that the BBC's undertaking 'that the programme should be non-critical' had too often been disregarded during the course of Robert Robinson's '*amer-piquant*' observations on the current releases.[48]

Granada's *Cinema*, first broadcast in July 1964, enjoyed a better relationship with the film industry. Indeed, the time that the show went out, seven o'clock in the evening, reflects this: many distributors had previously refused to licence material for transmission that early, fearful that potential customers might stop in rather than visit a cinema.[49] Key to *Cinema*'s eventual success was its decision to adopt a 'selective [and] flexible' approach to the films it featured. Concentrating on films that were 'sufficiently good, newsworthy or interesting' meant refusing to guarantee screen time to all pictures being premiered or going on general release, a decision that might have alienated distributors eager for free publicity. However, renters were assuaged by *Cinema*'s declaration that it did not intend to operate as 'a "knocking" programme' – if host Bamber Gascoigne and his successors couldn't find something positive to say, they tended to say nothing at all.[50] This did not mean that *Cinema* was toothless, but nor did it always live up to its aim to 'eschew all puffs';[51] early in the programme's run, *Sight and Sound* complained that it was too much 'like a series of commercials for what's on at your local this week'.[52] That *Cinema* remained a feature of ITV schedules until 1975 suggests that it was popular with viewers and able to find a mutually agreeable means of co-existence with the film industry, allowing the cinema to maintain its cultural prominence and sell itself as an entertainment medium that was at once easily accessible and experientially different to television.

Creative Intersections

In the March 1969 edition of *Films and Filming*, Raymond Durgnat noted that such was the creative and industrial interplay between film and television that the two media had been 'revealed as different dialects within a common language – dialects which it's quite possible for one person to use alternately'.[53] Although Durgnat's words minimise the many differences between film and television, his assertion makes clear not only the extent to which during the 1960s these media had found ways to co-exist within the market for moving-image entertainment, but also the frequency with which ideas, properties and talent moved between them.

The arrival of ITV necessitated the swift expansion of the television production sector, creating opportunity for a range of practitioners working in a variety of fields, be they old hands or young Turks. The growth in television-licence sales increased the amount of money that the BBC could spend on programming; the desire to counter the popularity of ITV increased the amount that it felt obliged to.[54] The rival broadcasters' battle for viewers resulted in formal and thematic innovation, with the Pilkington Committee finding that 'the element of competition has, on many occasions, tended to lift the standard of programmes on both channels'.[55] Such innovation made television work more attractive to those who had hitherto worked in film, and made those who worked in television more attractive to film producers.

Television proved to be a wellspring of new talent, and amongst those directors Durgnat identified as having made the move into feature films were Alvin Rakoff, Richard Lester, John Schlesinger, Ken Russell, Silvio Narizzano, Peter Collinson and John Boorman.[56] Elsewhere, *Sight and Sound* noted that *The Wrong Arm of the Law* (1963), a film it feared would be 'one of those dispiriting British comedies', quickly revealed 'the unmistakable hand of a director'; that hand belonged to Cliff Owen, who had cut his teeth at Granada and Associated–Rediffusion.[57] There were, though, concerns that in amongst the 'never ending' flow of practitioners moving from television to film, there were a 'host' who found it much harder to adapt to cinema, a sentiment that spoke to residual snobbery about the aesthetic deficits of a younger medium, and the different techniques required to get the best out of each.[58] To take but one example, Paul Watson's difficulties on *A Fine and Private Place*, one of the films put into production by Bryan Forbes following his appointment as production chief at Elstree, demonstrate that talent in one field did not always easily translate to success in another. Watson's career had begun in television documentaries, but his enthusiasm and vision for A. E. Coppard's short story persuaded Forbes to let him direct *A Fine and Private Place*. The production was a 'fiasco' and Forbes closed it down after discovering that Watson had spent a third of the film's budget on only 10 minutes' screen time.[59] Whilst the director's productivity was not helped by appalling weather,[60] Watson's inexperience and intransigence were the deciding factors.[61] He subsequently returned to TV, enjoying considerable success with the ground-breaking documentary series *The Family* (1974).

Television took from the cinema, just as films took from television. In some instances, these transitions occurred at the level of individual practitioners. Veteran directors Charles Frend, Charles Crichton, Pat Jackson and Roy Ward Baker spent the 1960s moving between film and television production, whereas Brian Clemens and Peter Yeldham also proved adept at writing for both media. Elsewhere, entire formats found a new home: the supporting feature mutated into television series, with the same companies – Danzigers,

Independent Artists and Tempean amongst the most noteworthy – producing both.[62] Small-screen adaptations of feature-film characters were not unknown: Jack Warner resurrected the policeman from *The Blue Lamp* (1955) in the BBC's *Dixon of Dock Green* (1955–76), whilst John Ford's 1958 police drama *Gideon's Day* found its way onto ITV as *Gideon's Way* (1964), with John Gregson replacing Jack Hawkins as the eponymous Scotland Yard detective. Richard Gordon's tales of comic misadventure at St Swithin's medical school were adapted for both film and television: the sequence of seven films initiated by *Doctor in the House* in 1954 ran until *Doctor in Trouble* (1970), by which time LWT's *Doctor in the House* (1969–70) had premiered on commercial television. Each of these programmes sought to build on the popularity of the films that preceded them.

The success of Carol Reed's 1949 feature *The Third Man* inspired a BBC radio adaptation – *The Lives of Harry Lime* (1951–2), with Orson Welles in the lead role – and then a television programme, *The Third Man* (1959–65), in which Lime was played by Michael Rennie. Because the rights to *The Third Man* were owned by British Lion, it was brought on-board as a partner for the television programme, with filming taking place at its Shepperton studios rather than the BBC's Ealing facility.[63] This 'enabled a feature-film degree of technical polish' but made the series more expensive, necessitating foreign sales and the signing of a co-production deal with National Telefilm Associates, which took responsibility for selling the show in America and filming half of the programmes in California.[64] The move to television, as had the radio adaptation, necessitated changes to both characterisation and narrative. The cinematic Harry Lime could be charismatically malevolent, but there were concerns that viewers wouldn't want to follow his adventures on a weekly basis if his venality wasn't toned down. Lime became less unpleasant with each successive iteration; by the time he got to television he was 'a wealthy art dealer and conman with, essentially, a heart of gold.'[65] The link to the 1949 film provided by Lime's presence did not always benefit the television programme. As *Variety* noted of an episode produced in 1963, 'Those with memories of [Reed's] movie might have switched off in despair'.[66] Episodes ran to 25 minutes, leaving little room for the film's rich plotting and subtle characterisation. Although regularly attracting brickbats, *The Third Man* ran for seventy-seven episodes, suggesting that it successfully adapted to the needs and specificities of television.

Despite mutual influence and exchange, there was perhaps a greater flow of personnel from television to film. In addition to the directors Durgnat listed, numerous others made the same journey, including Peter Watkins (whose 1965 film *The War Game* was made for the BBC, who refused to broadcast it, then got a cinema release and won the Academy Award for Best Documentary Feature[67]), Kevin Billington, whose 'immense technical assurance' on *Interlude* (1968) was attributed by *Sight and Sound* to his extensive TV work, and Jack Gold, who had 'high regard' for the training he received working in television: 'you learn to think quickly and react quickly.'[68] Alumni of Granada's long-running current affairs programme *World in Action*, first broadcast in 1963, included cinematographers Brian Probyn and Chris Menges, and directors Mike Hodges and Michael Apted. Amongst the many practitioners who worked in both film and television were screenwriters Troy Kennedy Martin, Joe McGrath and Roger Smith, production designers Assheton Gorton, Reece Pemberton and Brian Eatwell, and editors Michael Bradsell and Richard Best.

Actors, too, worked across both media. The early careers of Sean Connery and Roger Moore included extensive television credits, although Moore was the more famous of the two when taking on the role of James Bond, having found fame in *The Saint* (1962–9), episodes of which were edited together for theatrical release on more than one occasion. Two of the best-known Bond girls of the decade, Honor Blackman and Diana Rigg, who appeared in *Goldfinger* (1964) and *On Her Majesty's Secret Service* (1969), respectively, had both been female leads in *The Avengers* (1961–9). Blackman claimed that the martial artistry she demonstrated during her time as Cathy Gale led to her casting as Pussy Galore: 'I was the only lady as tough as Bond.'[69] The Bond–*Avengers* interplay extended beyond the movement of personnel, and the success of the Bond films stimulated a demand for spy programmes in the American market. Indeed, *The Avengers*' move into colour in 1967 was made 'at the behest' of the US network on which it was shown (ITV stations broadcast in black and white until late 1969).[70] Moreover, the Bond series' increasingly ironic approach to the world of the secret agent seems to have been influenced by television spy shows.

The Avengers had been created by Sydney Newman whilst in post as head of drama at ABC Television between 1958 and 1962. From ABC, Newman moved to the BBC, and then in late 1967 to ABPC, with this latter switch regarded as a coup for the film industry.[71] Newman's popular entertainment series were frequently successful, but he had also been a pivotal figure in the development of the single play in British television, exemplified by his ground-breaking drama strands *Armchair Theatre* (ABC, 1956–74) and *The Wednesday Play* (BBC, 1964–70). Newman brought with him contacts amongst television writers and directors hitherto untapped by the cinema, and ABPC clearly hoped that he might use his connections, and his knowledge of 'what contemporary audiences dig', to generate a profitable 'new revolution in films'.[72]

By his own admission, Newman had 'an awful lot to learn' about the film industry.[73] However, given that his 'first love was the single play', it was hoped that Newman's ability to produce stand-alone dramatic works would translate into film in a relatively straightforward manner.[74] It did not work out that way: Newman was sacked in the summer of 1969 without a single production credit to his name. The restructuring that followed EMI's takeover of ABPC saw Bryan Forbes appointed head of production; Newman's abilities as 'a putter-together of creative people' was deemed surplus to requirements.[75] Newman also found that kudos accrued in television did not allow *carte blanche* in film production. The contraction of budgets in the latter years of the 1960s resulted, he complained, in him having 'to prove to [ABPC/EMI] that I could make money their way before they'd trust me to do the things I really wanted'.[76] The projects that he was asked to develop – 'one about a decadent Scottish family in the Highlands, treated like a Hollywood cowboy film; another about a heart transplant surgeon who kills a woman to get her heart' – did not inspire him; the films that he might have produced in more favourable circumstances remain intriguing 'what-ifs'.[77]

Some of Newman's protégés and television projects had better luck when moving into film. *The Wednesday Play* not only 'changed the face of television drama in Britain' but also had a significant cinema legacy.[78] Although best known for an 'agitational contemporaneity' which provoked campaigners such as Mary Whitehouse, *Wednesday Plays* were individual and diverse, and included comedies, thrillers, sci-fi and literary adaptations.[79] The breadth and scale of its single dramas honed the skills of directors such as Charles Jarrott, Christopher Morahan, Philip Saville, Anthony Page, Waris Hussein, Peter Sasdy, Jack Gold, and John Mackenzie, who would each go on to work in the cinema. But its best-known director was Ken Loach, who directed *Up the Junction* and *Cathy Come Home* (1966).

Loach's cinema debut, *Poor Cow* (1967), was understood by critics as bringing the aesthetics and thematic concerns of his *Wednesday Plays* to the commercial feature. However, Penelope Mortimer noted that many of 'the tricks of [the] trade' for which Loach was being praised had been 'learned from the cinema in the first place'.[80] Loach's television took inspiration from a range of film types, and whilst the documentary influence was important, *In Two Minds* (1967), directed from David Mercer's script, shifted between objectivity and subjectivity in a manner indebted to European 'art cinema'.[81] This interweaving of documentary and drama could be controversial. Anthony Burgess complained that *In Two Minds* was a 'dangerous hybrid'; whereas the BBC's head of documentary worried that viewers would be 'misled' by *Cathy Come Home* into believing that the actors were 'real people'.[82] Loach might have welcomed such concerns: as a 1968 profile noted, the director was 'an incorrigible idealist, and sees the only purpose of film and television as the chance to speak directly to ordinary folk'.[83] Television was probably the medium that spoke to the greatest number of those ordinary folk in the 1960s, although *Poor Cow* was a significant box-office hit.

So familiar-feeling was *Poor Cow* that one critic observed that it was 'perhaps not quite fair to say that anyone who saw *Cathy Come Home* or *Up the Junction* has already seen ... *Poor Cow*, but it's near enough'.[84] Some of this familiarity related to the presence in all three productions of Carol White, an actress described as 'a Battersea Bardot who has cornered the market in portraying working-class girls'.[85] Having started with bit parts, White worked her way up to more substantial roles in films including *Cary on Teacher* (1959) and *Never Let Go* (1960), but it was her work on *The Wednesday Play* that advertised her talent and made her a credible and sought-after lead. More than a lead, in fact; a star: *Variety* said of *Poor Cow* that White was 'almost the entire film' and noted that the two male leads, Terence Stamp and John Bindon, 'play[ed] support to her'.[86] White was subsequently worked in America, making *Daddy's Gone A-Hunting* (1968) and *Something Big* (1971). Despite her increasing international success, White continued to work in Britain, appearing in such films as *I'll Never Forget What's 'is Name* (1967) and *The Fixer* (1968), but not in the 1968 cinematic version of *Up the Junction*, 'because Mr Loach didn't direct it'.[87] Instead, direction was provided by Peter Collinson, another television graduate, and although the film was – like Loach's play – shot largely on location, it was not a remake of the TV play, but rather a fresh adaptation of Nell Dunn's original stories. Without White and Loach, the film lost some of its impact, but its greatest perceived failing, it seems, was its inability to generate the same degree of controversy as its TV precursor.[88] Nonetheless, it joined *Poor Cow* as one of 1968's top box-office hits.

Another of Newman's BBC series, *Doctor Who*, was made into two features, *Dr Who and the Daleks* (1965) and *Daleks – Invasion Earth: 2150 AD* (1966), produced by Aaru Films (an offshoot of Milton Subotsky and Max Rosenberg's Amicus). Subotsky had a talent for exploiting popular trends, and the two films are about the Daleks as much as they are about the Doctor (Peter Cushing). The wave of Dalekmania that swept Britain in 1964 persuaded Subotsky that there was money to be made from the TARDIS, or more accurately from the creatures implacably determined to destroy it. The Daleks became a merchandising phenomenon, swelling BBC coffers and making Terry Nation, who had created the creatures and shared co-copyright with the Corporation, a wealthy man.[89] The BBC had until this time taken very little interest in monetising the properties that it developed, so it is unsurprising that Subotsky was able to make a deal that enabled him to tap a market created by the less commercially minded Corporation, and developed tie-ups with retailers: Selfridges, for instance, re-erected a set from *Dr Who and the Daleks* during 'Dalek Fortnight'.[90]

The Dalek films were made as attempts to cash in on, rather than enrich, the Whoniverse. Originally budgeted at just £135,000, *Dr Who and the Daleks* went over to an extent that Film Finances eventually took control of the shoot.[91] Although the film was positioned squarely in relation to its television predecessor, it also had to offer something distinct: *'splendour'*. 'We intend,' said Subotsky, 'to make full use of the colour, spectacle and action that make the difference between large and small screen entertainment.'[92] Because children were the key market for the film, *Dr Who and the Daleks* was designed to attract them. Educational elements of the television programme were removed (there are no teachers aboard the cinematic TARDIS) and merchandise-friendly elements foregrounded: 'a semi-educational, science fiction TV programme appealing to children and adults alike was reworked ... into two commercial movies explicitly aimed at Dalek-crazed schoolchildren.'[93] The strategy worked: *Dr Who and the Daleks* was one of the ten highest-grossing films of 1965.[94] With a budget of approximately £180,000, *Daleks – Invasion Earth: 2150 AD* cost more to produce, but was less of a draw at the box-office: Subotsky and Vegoda, recognising the moment of Dalekmania had passed, decided not to take up their option for a third film.

The *Dr Who* films were as much attempts to profit from marketable elements of a televisual property as they were films. The same is true of *Thunderbirds Are Go* (1966) and *Thunderbird 6* (1968), two feature-length spin-offs made to exploit the rich merchandising seam of Gerry and Sylvia Anderson's 'Brobdingnagian gold-mine', estimated by some to be worth several million pounds in 1966 alone.[95] Shows such as *Thunderbirds* featured numerous characters and gadgets that could easily become toys. Indeed, *The Times* observed of the absent Mrs Tracey that 'it was thoughtful of her to produce five sons, who can drive five different gorgeous rockets. And that makes five times as many models to sell in the toy shops.'[96] The release of *Thunderbirds Are Go* shortly before Christmas 1966 was timed to coincide with peak sales of *Thunderbird* merchandise, which it was hoped would act as auxiliary publicity for the film (and vice versa). *Thunderbirds Are Go* was not a success. However, United Artists, whose faith in the value of merchandise-friendly franchises had been confirmed by the success of its Bond and Beatles films, saw sufficient potential to agree to the production of *Thunderbird 6* (with similarly disappointing results).[97] Whilst medium-specific technologies (widescreen, colour) were utilised to make the film appear more cinematic, these were held by some critics to have failed – 'no more than the television series writ large,' complained *Monthly Film Bulletin* – and could not overcome the problem of a ponderous and padded narrative; stretching a format that was more used to telling stories over 30 or, later, 60 minutes to feature-length had drained the *Thunderbirds* of their energy.[98]

If many television-to-film transfers were motivated by primarily commercial considerations, kudos and creativity could also be factors. Even working within the constraints of an established television property and the tight budgets afforded by Aaru, Gordon Flemyng, director of both *Dr Who* films, claimed that 'TV people go into films ... because the director has so much more control.' By contrast, Flemyng regarded television as a producer's medium: 'because almost all drama in TV now is series, control lies with the producer and he has the continuity.'[99] Others felt that the cinema was better placed than television to bestow prestige. For a comedian such as Tony Hancock, whose career was based upon the intimacy and parochialism of radio and television, films were also seen as a way to reach a larger international (read 'American') audience.[100] Hancock longed for artistic credibility beyond the sitcom format that had shaped and provided the perfect vehicle for his comic persona, but was wary of undermining the 'Anthony Aloysius St John Hancock' character that audiences adored: 'I'm not being big-headed, but I feel that my position is such that, if I'm offered a film, it should be one written around ME.'[101] Having turned down numerous scripts from producers eager to 'cash in on the popularity of his name', he eventually decided to work with his regular writers Ray Galton and Alan Simpson on *The Rebel* (1961): 'Every word,' director Robert Day noted, 'has been written specially for him.'[102]

The Rebel presented a character that was 'recognisably an *extension* of the Hancock personality', thereby demanding 'a genuine performance'.[103] The combination of familiarity and novelty proved quite a draw and *The Rebel* broke box-office records on the ABC circuit.[104] Yet despite domestic success, the film failed to find an audience in the USA, where it was released as *Call Me Genius* ('no one is likely to,' said Bosley Crowther in a savage *New York Times* review).[105] Subsequently, Hancock redoubled his efforts to create 'a universal comedy that will transcend class and state barriers'.[106] Ahead of his next film, *The Punch and Judy Man* (1963), Hancock, determined to escape his TV image, broke with Galton and Simpson. As *Variety* noted, '[*The Punch and Judy Man*] should prove his real testing time.'[107] It was a test that he failed. In part this was because of the weakness of the material that Hancock wrote with Philip Oakes, but also because for all his dreams of cinematic stardom and artistic credibility, Hancock's style was ideal for television or radio, domestic media that delivered his explorations of, and frustrations with, everyday life straight into people's homes. Such forensic examinations of culture and character did not translate well to film, where too often they appeared slight or inconsequential. Television suited the subdued physicality of much of Hancock's comedy – the close-ups that captured his shifting facial expressions so well on TV did not work in the same way on the big screen, where the subtlety of his best performances could get lost. *The Rebel* did not succeed despite its resemblance to Hancock's television work, but because of it; *The Punch and Judy Man* failed because Hancock feared being seen as *just* a television comedian, rather than accepting that television afforded him the shot at greatness he so desperately desired.

Following their split with Hancock, Galton and Simpson created another hugely successful comedy for the BBC, and later adapted it into two films, *Steptoe and Son* (1972) and *Steptoe and Son Ride Again* (1973). There was, however, an earlier 'unofficial' *Steptoe* film, *The Bargee* (1964), the first of five pictures that Galton–Simpson films agreed to make for Associated British.[108] Featuring Harry H. Corbett, a theatre actor whose fame was bound up with his portrayal of Harold Steptoe, *The Bargee* was a film in which, as *Kine Weekly* put it, 'Steptoe casts off as the Casanova of the canals'.[109] Corbett, Galton and Simpson were also reunited with Duncan Wood, who had produced and directed numerous episodes of *Hancock's Half Hour* and *Steptoe and Son* for television, and who was making his debut as a feature-film director. Although *Kine Weekly* stated that 'it was inevitable and not unwelcome that the central characters have loud echoes of Steptoe',[110] *Variety* complained that an 'overdose of interbreeding' prevented the film from throwing off its televisual associations and functioning as a film.[111]

The success of *Till Death Us Do Part* (1968) – a *Kine Weekly* box-office winner[112] – suggests that there was a market for big-screen adaptations of small screen hits.[113] Johnny Speight, who wrote *Till Death* ... for both film and TV, included sequences in his screenplay that the BBC had made him cut from his television scripts, knowing that the coarser material permitted by the BBFC classification system would constitute an additional point of appeal.[114] Furthermore, the *Till Death* ... film tapped into the continuing popularity of and demand for Alf Garnett (Warren Mitchell) following the decision to end the sitcom in February 1968, a decision that the BBC insisted was taken because the programme was 'exhausted', but one which Speight regarded as the culmination of the Corporation's 'savage censorship' of his work.[115] With Speight no longer constrained by the BBC, Alf could become more transgressive than he had been on television,[116] and posters for *Till Death Us Do Part* stressed this by presenting a naked Alf, his hands covering his genitals, with the tagline 'Yer never saw Alf like this before!'

Conclusion

Before BBC television revived *Till Death Us Do Part* in 1972, shortly after the release of *The Alf Garnett Saga*, Warren Mitchell played the lead in *All the Way Up* (1970), the first feature produced by Granada Films, established in 1967 as a subsidiary of Granada Television. Granada Films offered opportunities to 'television directors who are ready to move into film production'.[117] *All the Way Up* made good on this promise: it was directed by James MacTaggart, an experienced TV producer and director, and produced and written by Philip Mackie, another old television hand, whose Granada series *The Caesars* Granada Films considered adapting for cinema.[118]

Granada's decision to open a films division spoke of its belief that there was still a market for feature films, even as the number of cinemas that it operated shrank. However, the economics of this market changed as film and television became increasingly interconnected and interdependent. Whereas Granada's Cecil Bernstein had insisted in 1952 that the CEA should attempt to use its influence to keep the film and television industries entirely separate – 'a producer or renter cannot be prevented from deciding which of these two markets he desires to serve, but it cannot be both'[119] – by the end of the 1960s Granada was itself looking to use the skills and talent it had acquired as a successful producer for the small screen to make content for the big. Moreover, whereas Cecil Bernstein had been integral to the formation of FIDO, by the end of the 1960s the new films needed to keep cinemas open were produced, by Granada and others, on the understanding that they would subsequently be sold to television, with the value of television rights becoming a determining factor in financing.[120] Yet we should not see this simply as the triumph of television, or the defeat of cinema, but rather as two industries converging in order to adapt to and take mutually beneficial advantage of the opportunities created by new commercial, social and aesthetic realities.

NOTES

1. Roof-mounted aerials made television a conspicuous form of a post-war consumer culture. See *Derby Evening Telegraph*, 29 May 1950, p. 2, which joked, 'Display this rooftop monstrosity and you are in the fashion. The neighbourhood will know you as a man of means.'
2. Ownership statistics taken from John Spraos, *The Decline of the Cinema: An Economist's Report* (London: George Allen & Unwin, 1962), p. 24; <http://www.barb.co.uk/resources/tv-ownership/> (accessed 22 March 2018).
3. Elizabeth II's coronation in June 1953, popularly associated with stimulating television sales, was the subject of *A Queen is Crowned*, the most successful film in Britain that year. *Motion Picture Herald*, 9 January 1954, p. 32.
4. *Spectator*, 2 September 1960, p. 350; *The Economist*, 16 July 1960, p. 318. Roy Thomson used the phrase to describe Scottish Television. Quoted in *Observer*, 13 May 1962, p. 3.
5. Jeremy Potter, *Independent Television in Britain – vol. 4: Companies and Programmes, 1968-80* (London: Macmillan, 1990), p. 140; *Kine Weekly*, 10 November 1960, p. 27; Andrew Spicer, *Sydney Box* (Manchester: Manchester University Press, 2006), pp. 161–6; Michael Balcon, *Michael Balcon presents . . . a lifetime of films* (London: Hutchison, 1969), p. 191.
6. Duncan Crow, 'From screen to screen: cinema films on television', *Sight and Sound*, 27: 2 (1957), p. 62; *The Economist*, 16 January 1960, p. 229.
7. *Variety*, 2 December 1964, p. 41.
8. *Daily Express*, 21 August 1964, p. 6.
9. Martin McLoone, 'Boxed in? The aesthetics of film and television', in John Hill and Martin McLoone (eds), *Big Picture, Small Screen: The Relations Between Film and Television* (Luton: University of Luton Press, 1996), p. 95.
10. Quoted in Derek Hill, 'A Writers' Wave?', *Sight and Sound*, Spring 1960, p. 59.

11. Troy Kennedy Martin, 'Is this the way ahead?', *Screenwriter*, no. 15, Spring 1964, p. 23. This piece was originally published as 'Nats go home' in *Encore*, 11: 2 (1964).
12. Troy Kennedy Martin, '*Up the Junction* and after', *Contrast*, 4: 5/6 (1966), pp. 138, 140. See also Roger Smith, 'The future of the TV play', *Film and Television Technician*, May 1967.
13. *Daily Express*, 22 April 1960, p. 12.
14. *Television Mail*, 8 November 1963, p. 4.
15. Edward Buscombe, 'All bark and no bite: the film industry's response to television', in John Corner (ed.), *Popular Television in Britain: Studies in Cultural History* (London: BFI, 1991), p. 204.
16. John D. Ayers, 'The Two Screens: FIDO, RFDA and Film vs. Television in Post-Second World War Britain', *Journal of British Cinema and Television*, 14: 4 (2017), pp. 509–11.
17. *Daily Express*, 21 August 1964, p. 6. Grade and his brother, Leslie, were involved with Elstree Films, the company established in 1961 to make the Cliff Richard films.
18. *Variety*, 30 July 1958, p. 15.
19. *The Economist*, 25 October 1958, pp. 346, 350.
20. *Television Mail*, 30 August 1963, p. 10. Although there were numerous discussions and experiments, widespread pay-TV did not materialise in Britain until later.
21. Howard Thomas of ABC TV. Quoted in Asa Briggs, *The History of Broadcasting in the United Kingdom – vol. v: Competition* (Oxford: Oxford University Press, 1995), p. 186.
22. *Television Mail*, 15 January 1960, p. 3.
23. *The Economist*, 16 January 1960, pp. 228-9; Buscombe, 'All bark and no bite', p. 204.
24. Stratford subsequently looked to sell the films to ATV, a station linked to the Hyams through their interest in the Independent Television Programme Company. Spraos, *Decline of the Cinema*, p. 59; *Kine Weekly*, 5 October 1961, p. 3; *Variety*, 18 October 1961, p. 13; 29 November 1961, p. 19.
25. *Television Mail*, 8 November 1963, p. 3
26. Briggs, *History of Broadcasting: Competition*, p. 187.
27. *Independent Film Journal*, 23 July 1968, p. 24.
28. *Daily Express*, 22 April 1960, p. 12; *Television Mail*, 19 August 1960, p. 5.
29. Briggs, *History of Broadcasting: Competition*, pp. 953–4.
30. Keith M. Johnston, '"An intelligent and effective use of the rival screen": rediscovering early British television trailers', *Media History*, 17: 4 (2011), p. 380.
31. *Kine Weekly*, 7 November 1957, p. 52.
32. J. B. Priestley, 'The Magic Beanstalk', *Contrast*, Autumn 1961, p. 5.
33. A trailer for *The Gypsy Moths* (1969) was the first to be broadcast in colour. *Television Mail*, 21 November 1969, p. 27.
34. See ABC's 'Don't take your wife for granted – take her out to the pictures' campaign, in which newspaper advertisements were augmented by TV spots produced by Associated British–Pathé's Television and Advertising Films division and shown on the ABC television across a region containing 150 ABC cinemas. *Television Mail*, 4 November 1960, p. 15.
35. *Television Mail*, 7 September 1962, p. 25.
36. *Television Mail*, 6 December 1968, p. 17.
37. *Television Mail*, 7 September 1962, p. 25.
38. *Television Mail*, 2 February 1968, p. 17.
39. Johnston, 'Early British television trailers', p. 386.

40. *Television Mail*, 23 September 1966, p. 18.
41. *Television Mail*, 22 March 1968, p. 21.
42. On early film review programmes, see Su Holmes, '"Designed specially for television purposes and technique": the development of the television cinema programme in Britain in the 1950s', *Historical Journal of Film, Radio and Television*, 25: 3 (2005).
43. The *Daily Cinema*'s Bernard Charman, paraphrased in Boleslaw Sulik, 'Film Criticism on Television', *Contrast*, 2: 2 (Winter 1962), p. 106.
44. *Listener*, 2 June 1960, p. 988.
45. In 1962, the BBC's *Picture Parade* attracted almost 4.5 million viewers – more than half the average weekly cinema attendance – per episode. *Sight and Sound*, 31: 2 (1962), p. 65.
46. *Kine Weekly*, 10 April 1958, p. 34; 25 September 1958, p. 5.
47. *Picture Parade* was forced into a year-long hiatus from late 1958 because 'clips were becoming increasingly difficult to get'. *Variety*, 18 February 1959, p. 36.
48. *Variety*, 22 July 1964, p. 64; *Kine Weekly*, 25 May 1961, p. 5; *Listener*, 7 June 1962, p. 1004.
49. *Picturegoer*, 5 January 1957, p. 9. Distributors licenced material to ABC's *Film Fanfare* (1956–7) for use after 9.45 p.m., whilst *Picture Parade* was rarely transmitted before 9.30 p.m.
50. *Kine Weekly*, 25 June 1964, p. 3; 23 June 1966, p. 16.
51. *Kine Weekly*, 25 June 1964, p. 3.
52. *Sight and Sound*, 33: 4, 1964, p. 206.
53. Raymond Durgnat, 'TV's young Turks – Part 1', *Films and Filming*, March 1969, p. 5.
54. Between 1955 and 1965, television licence sales in Britain almost tripled, whilst BBC operating expenditure on television increased by almost 550 per cent. Briggs, *History of Broadcasting: Competition*, p. 1005, p. 1007, p. 18.
55. The Committee was, however, critical of ITV's populism. *Report of the Committee on Broadcasting, 1960* (London: HMSO, 1962), pp. 877, 34.
56. Durgnat, 'Young Turks', pp. 5–10. Durgnat also notes that film directors such as Sidney Cole and Ralph Keene moved into television in the 1950s.
57. *Sight and Sound*, Spring 1963, p. 94.
58. *Kine Weekly*, 11 January 1969, p. 17.
59. Bryan Forbes, *A Divided Life* (London: Heinemann, 1992), pp. 174–9.
60. *Boxoffice*, 18 May 1970, p. E5.
61. Forbes, *Divided Life*, pp. 174–9; Alexander Walker, *Hollywood England: The British Film Industry in the Sixties* (London: Michael Joseph, 1974), p. 433.
62. See David Mann, *Britain's First TV/Film Crime Series and the Industrialisation of its Film Industry 1946–1964* (London: Edward Mellen Press, 2009). Supporting feature producers such as Monty Berman and Bob Baker also moved from film into television.
63. British Lion's exploitation of its *The Third Man* rights contributed to increased profits in the financial year 1959–60: 'These revenues cannot be expected to continue at a high level, despite the durability of Mr Harry Lime.' *The Economist*, 13 August 1960, p. 672.
64. *Television Mail*, 17 June 1960, p. 7.
65. Richard J. Hand and Andrew Purssell, *Adapting Graham Greene* (London: Palgrave, 2015), pp. 68–9.
66. *Variety*, 17 April 1963, p. 30.
67. See John R. Cook and Patrick Murphy, 'After the Bomb Dropped: The Cinema Half-life of *The War Game*', *Journal of Popular British Cinema*, 3 (2000).

68. David Robinson, 'Case Histories of the next renascence', *Sight and Sound*, Winter 1968, pp. 40, 38.
69. *Life*, 20 May 1966, p. 128.
70. James Chapman, *Saints and Avengers: British Adventure Series of the 1960s* (London: I. B. Tauris, 2002), pp. 31–2, 75. *The Avengers*' move from tape to film was supervised by Julian Wintle, whose previous work in the film industry had seen him involved with Bryanston, Independent Artists and Beaconsfield studios.
71. Newman's stock was high because of the revenues generated by *The Avengers*, which by 1968 had been sold to more than seventy countries, earning $5,000,000 in America alone. *Variety*, 17 January 1968, p. 30.
72. *Daily Express*, 3 October 1967, p. 10; *Variety*, 18 October 1967, p. 24.
73. Quoted in *The Times*, 11 October 1967, p. 8.
74. Shaun Sutton, 'Sydney Newman', in Jonathan Bignell and Stephen Lacey, *British Television Drama: Past, Present and Future* (London: Palgrave Macmillan, 2014, 2nd edn), p. 41.
75. Quoted in *The Times*, 25 July 1969, p. 12.
76. *The Guardian*, 27 July 1969, p. 32.
77. *The Guardian*, 27 July 1969, p. 32.
78. Lez Cooke, *British Television Drama: A History* (London: BFI, 2015, 2nd edn), pp. 71, 72.
79. *The Guardian*, 17 August 1966, p. 2. Whitehouse described *The Big Flame* (February 1969) as 'a blueprint for the communist takeover of the docks'. Quoted in *The Times*, 21 February 1969, p. 2.
80. *Observer*, 10 December 1967, p. 24.
81. John Hill, *Ken Loach: The politics of film and television* (London: BFI/Palgrave Macmillan, 2011), p. 69. *In Two Minds* informed Loach's *Family Life* (1971), with both produced by Tony Garrett. A play that Mercer wrote for the BBC in 1962 was adapted for cinema as *Morgan – A Suitable Case for Treatment* (1966).
82. *Listener*, 9 March 1967, p. 335; quoted in Hill, *Ken Loach*, p. 75.
83. Robinson, 'Case Histories', p. 40.
84. *Observer*, 10 December 1967, p. 24.
85. *Daily Express*, 16 November 1967, p. 5. White was also directed by Loach in *The Coming Out Party*, a *Wednesday Play* from 1965.
86. *Variety*, 7 February 1968, p. 18.
87. Ibid.
88. See Mary Whitehouse's letter to the Minister of Health: 'It would appear that [with *Up the Junction*] the BBC is determined to do everything in its power to present promiscuity as normal.' In Ben Thompson (ed.), *Ban This Filth!: Letters from the Mary Whitehouse Archive* (London: Faber, 2012), p. 119.
89. Alwyn W. Turner, *Terry Nation: The Man who invented the Daleks* (London: Aarum, 2011), pp. 96–7.
90. *Kine Weekly*, 8 April 1965, p. 12.
91. Film Finances Archive – *Dr Who and the Daleks*: 18 February 1965, John Croydon to Robert Garrett; 27 April 1965, Robert Garrett to Aaru Productions Ltd.
92. Quoted in *Kine Weekly*, 8 April 1965, p. 12. Formatting in original.
93. John R. Cook, 'Adapting telefantasy: The *Doctor Who and the Daleks* films', in I. Q. Hunter (ed.), *British Science Fiction Cinema* (London: Routledge, 1999), p. 119.
94. James Chapman, *Inside the Tardis: The Worlds of Doctor Who* (London: I. B. Tauris, 2013, revised edn), p. 48.
95. *The Times*, 14 February 1966, p. 5; *New Society*, 11 May 1967, p. 681.

96. *The Times*, 14 February 1966, p. 5.
97. Ian Fryer, *The Worlds of Gerry and Sylvia Anderson: The Story Behind International Rescue* (Stroud: Fonthill, 2016), pp. 111–12.
98. *Monthly Film Bulletin*, January 1967, p. 31; *The Times*, 17 December 1966, p. 13.
99. *Kine Weekly*, 10 March 1966, p. 16.
100. Julian Upton, *Fallen Stars: Tragic Lives and Lost Careers* (Manchester: Critical Vision, 2004), p. 48; Freddie Hancock and David Nathan, *Hancock* (London: William Kimber, 1969), p. 96.
101. *Picturegoer*, 9 February 1957, p. 21.
102. *Kine Weekly*, 25 August 1960, p. 17. Hancock's agent, Beryl Vertue, noted, '[Galton and Simpson] were him and he was them. They created this character between them.' Hancock and Nathan, *Hancock*, p. 110.
103. *The Times*, 2 March 1961, p. 4; John Fisher, *Tony Hancock* (London: HarperCollins, 2008), pp. 302–9. Emphasis added.
104. *Kine Weekly*, 20 April 1961, p. 4; 13 April 1961, p. 18.
105. *New York Times*, 17 October 1961, p. 47.
106. Fisher, *Tony Hancock*, p. 312.
107. *Variety*, 2 May 1962, p. 89.
108. *Kine Weekly*, 6 September 1962, p. 3.
109. *Kine Weekly*, 19 September 1963, p. 14.
110. *Kine Weekly*, 23 April 1963, p. 13.
111. *Variety*, 29 April 1964, p. 6.
112. *Kine Weekly*, 20 December 1969, p. 8.
113. The sitcom spin-off became a film industry 'staple' in the 1970s: see, amongst many others, *Up Pompeii* (1971), *On the Buses* (1971) and *Dad's Army* (1971). Precursors to this trend include *I Only Arsked!* (1958), based on Granada's *The Army Game*, and *Bottom's Up* (1960), based on the BBC's *Whack-O!* See Peter Waymark, '"From telly laughs to belly laughs": The rise and fall of the sitcom spinoff', in I. Q. Hunter and Laraine Porter, *British Comedy Cinema* (London: Routledge, 2012), pp. 141–3.
114. Waymark, 'Telly laughs', pp. 148-9. The film was awarded an A certificate.
115. *The Times*, 16 February 1968, p. 1.
116. The television version of *Till Death ...* was one of Mary Whitehouse's particular bugbears. However, reflecting the relative cultural importance of film and TV in the second half of the 1960s, the film seems to have passed her by. Mary Whitehouse, *Who does she think she is?* (London: New English Library, 1971), pp. 77–84.
117. *The Times*, 21 March 1967, p. 2.
118. *Variety*, 17 July 1968, p. 28.
119. Quoted in Michael Jackson, 'Cinema versus television', *Sight and Sound*, vol. 39, no. 3, Summer 1980, p. 179.
120. *Kine Weekly*, 25 March 1967, p. 4.

13. FILM AND TV ADVERTISING

Richard Farmer

INTRODUCTION

> I wouldn't go on an advert ... How can one retain one's dignity, blabbing on about frozen peas?

By the time that Tony Hancock delivered these words on the evening of 29 December 1959, during the final episode of the *Hancock's Half Hour* radio show, television commercials had become an established feature of British popular culture.[1] Independent Television (ITV) had begun broadcasting in September 1955 to create competition for the BBC and provide a new outlet through which advertisers might reach British consumers. As Hancock's words suggest, television advertisements did not always enjoy much by way of cultural prestige. But nevertheless, they became a fertile training ground and major revenue stream for British film-industry personnel during the 1960s. Directors, cinematographers, production designers and actors all took advantage of the constant need for new advertisements. There were, claimed Actors' Equity, 300,000 transmissions of commercials across ITV stations each year by 1959–60, although the number of advertisements produced in a given year was, of course, much smaller (between 7,000 and 8,000 by the end of the 1960s).[2] These commercials needed to be written, designed, directed, edited, scored, voiced, and animated and/or acted. Further, the sizable budgets that even short television advertisements commanded allowed those involved in the production of commercials to gain experience and to experiment with

Figure 13.1 The ad man and his product: Orson Welles sells Barley Flakes in London's docklands in *I'll Never Forget What's 'is Name* (Michael Winner, 1967).

form, technique and equipment. One historian of commercial television has even claimed that 'the development of the art of the television commercial in Britain' was 'the British equivalent of the French cinema's *nouvelle vague*,' so formative was its creative input into the visual culture of the 1960s.[3] Weighing up the validity of this bold proposition, this chapter explores the interplay between television advertising and the cinema in the 1960s, both in terms of how cinema practitioners moved between these two fields, and the ways in which the new cultural prominence of advertising in 1960s Britain influenced the look, feel and thematic concerns of its cinema.

Debating Advertising

In 1958, a manual of television advertising felt compelled to explain that 'creative workers' should 'realise that it is no more a betrayal of their art to work for advertisers than it was for the great painters and sculptors of the past to produce "to order"' and understand that 'technical quality and artistic integrity are often most truly combined when given the purpose and direction of a paid assignment'.[4] Such a defence of advertising work indicates the low regard, occasionally bordering on contempt, in which it was held in some quarters.

Even film-industry practitioners who made advertisements were not above criticising them once they had become successful enough to bite the hand that had once fed them. Ken Russell, for example, made a number of television commercials in the mid-1960s, but later would describe advertising as 'immoral', its exponents shaping society 'to their own image, which is a rotting death's head'.[5] His comments are echoed in dramatist Charles Marowitz's tirade:

> Advertising necessitates the prostitution of art-forms in order to induce the public to spend money on items it may not want or does not need but which ad-men are duty-bound to push no matter what their own personal feelings ... they delude themselves that what they are doing is 'necessary', 'useful', 'artistic' and 'dignified' whereas it is really base, conniving, exploiting and selfish.[6]

Some television viewers, initially at least, took a similarly dim view. In April 1959, Gallup found that 15 per cent of those surveyed considered advertisements as one of the bad points of ITV, and 22 per cent disliked the disruption caused by ad breaks.[7]

Resented and disliked advertising may have been, but its results were such that it was deemed increasingly vital to modern consumer culture. Continuing an upward trend first visible in the mid-1950s, between 1960 and 1964, total estimated advertising expenditure in the UK increased by 25 per cent.[8] The advent of ITV was an important but not the sole contributory factor in this increase, since money spent on television commercials was frequently in addition to, rather than a reallocation of, that spent on other media.[9] In 1955, restrictions on newsprint, a legacy of the Second World War, had been eased, meaning that newspapers could carry more pages and thus more advertisements. Radio stations based on the European mainland, popular with British listeners for decades, were joined from 1964 in transmitting advertisements to the United Kingdom by pirate broadcasters such as Radio Caroline and Radio London, at least until their activities were curtailed in 1967.[10]

In February 1962, *The Sunday Times* launched Britain's first weekend colour supplement, which provided readers with an occasionally awkward blend of photojournalism, lifestyle advice and glossy colour advertising. The *Observer* and the *Daily Telegraph* followed suit in September 1964.[11] Alongside trendily rebooted publications such as *Queen*, the colour supplements propagated, and grew in response to, notions of consumerism and the idea that particular lifestyles were available to those able to construct them by buying – and being seen to have bought – the right clothes or furniture or food or car at the right shop. As consumption became an increasingly important factor in the way that identities were formed, advertising offered a template for those seeking to understand the latest trends in a society becoming more comfortable with the notion of fashionable obsolescence and disposability. For the same reasons, it was attacked for seeking to reshape individuals, and society, in a largely superficial manner; the phrase 'colour supplement,' for example, became 'a favourite term of abuse in the Sixties'.[12] Britons in the age of advertising were encouraged to want it all, immediately, or to be dissatisfied with their lot; to *Live Now – Pay Later* (1963), to quote the title of an acid film satire of the consumer society.

The development of the affluent, consumer society changed the status of the advertising industry, with one observer noting how 'advertising men finally succeeded in shaking off that old barker's straw hat and assuming the black homburg to which their central position entitled them. They no longer merely sold an article, but generated an atmosphere, propagated a philosophy and projected a vision of the good life.'[13] Advertising had become ubiquitous, moving 'far beyond mere salesmanship to become one of the chief creators and communicators of social values in our time'.[14] Although its critics presented this ubiquity in apocalyptic terms, it was experienced in far more quotidian ways, as part of the everyday lived experience of 1960s Britain. Jingles written for television commercials by composers such as Johnny Johnston ('the thirty-second Mozart') were designed to stick in the mind, and in some instances endured in schoolchildren's playground rhymes and games, outlasting the campaigns from which they initially emerged.[15] The music from a Kellogg's Corn Flakes commercial lives on in the Beatles' 'Good Morning Good Morning'. John Lennon heard the song whilst watching television and worked it, in amended form, into his own composition, which was then included on the *Sgt Pepper's Lonely Hearts Club Band* (1967) album.[16] To focus too intently on critical attitudes to advertising, then, is to ignore the ways in which television commercials and other forms of advertising functioned as vibrant and highly visible (and audible) elements of British popular culture.

Working in Advertising

In 1980, Jo Gable observed that although few American directors had made advertising films, a great many of their British counterparts had worked on television commercials – almost every director of note with the exception of David Lean, claimed John Schlesinger (who himself made advertisements for Stork margarine and Polo mints, amongst other things).[17] The barriers that had previously 'segregated' American film directors from television advertising began to break down in the 1980s, but until that point, British directors – or, in the case of Richard Lester, Cy Endfield and Joseph Losey, American directors working in Britain – were readier and more willing to sign up to direct television commercials than were their counterparts in the US.[18]

In the earliest days of British commercial television, many – although by no means all – of the directors who made advertisements were drawn from documentary. Indeed, according to James Garrett, who worked for British Transport Films before moving into the production of advertisements, such was 'the antagonism toward television in general and commercials in particular which prevailed in the "establishment" film industry' that, initially at least, personnel working in the established British studios, or for British feature-film production companies, were reluctant to work in advertising. This left the field open for documentarists, a group that

> had existed and evolved through sponsorship, sometimes oblique and obscure in its purpose, [and] who understood and accepted that it was reasonable to receive money in return for producing a message with a commercial purpose.[19]

This might go some way towards explaining why many of the names associated with the Free Cinema group – directors such as Lindsay Anderson, John Schlesinger and Karel Reisz, and cinematographers such as Walter Lassally – all regularly made advertising films, even if they displayed differing levels of ambivalence about such work.[20]

It was quickly established that most television commercials would be filmed, rather than go out live. Filming made it easier to ensure quality, control for mistakes, was cheaper as far as repeat transmissions were concerned, and allowed the same commercial to be shown simultaneously on more than one station.[21] Television commercials therefore offered many a young practitioner a pathway into film production. Richard Lester claimed to have 'learned what I know by making commercials':

> They are an excellent way to learn about filmmaking. The problems are the same, in miniature. Ideally, you should know everybody's job, how to lay in a musical score, what the lab does, how to handle film and cut it.[22]

Ridley Scott, employed by the BBC as an art director and director of live programmes, agreed, and likened his work on television commercials to continuing film school: 'I was working on celluloid, I was actually turning film, and I loved the process of turning film and going to an editing room, editing, cutting, and making up my own little mini-movie'.[23] Scott's enthusiasm impressed Jeremy Bullmore of the J. Walter Thompson (JWT) agency, who in 1965 noted that he was a 'very intelligent and no-nonsense Director who is genuinely interested in making commercials'.[24]

Although many practitioners saw the production of commercials as offering the opportunity for artistic growth, few were shy about admitting that there was another important consideration: money. The preparedness of British filmmakers to seek out advertising work reflects the uncertain nature of employment in the chronically unstable British cinema industry. Not knowing where the next job was going to come from, film-industry personnel accepted work where they could find it. As Richard Lester put it, 'My whole purpose of doing commercials was to learn film. And to eat.'[25] Indeed, making television commercials could prove lucrative: Joseph Losey, who directed hundreds of British advertisements, was earning £210 a day directing advertisements by late 1963, and even found time to make a film for Cossack Vodka whilst in Cannes promoting *Modesty Blaise* in May 1966, thereby pocketing 'some much-needed holiday money'.[26] This money was paid promptly, whereas money earned for directing feature films, especially low-budget feature films, might be deferred for considerable periods.

The prospect of a semi-regular pay cheque was, during the 1960s, appealing to practitioners of all ages. Alexander Mackendrick, who had worked for the J. Walter Thompson agency before moving to Ealing Studios in the 1940s, returned to JWT to direct an advertisement for Horlicks.[27] His former Ealing colleagues also made commercials: Pat Jackson for chocolate bars and cigarettes, and Charles Frend for beer, Brylcreem and Lux soap (this last featuring Jane Fonda).[28] 'Hot' younger directors similarly made television commercials in between working on feature films. Clive Donner, having completed *What's New Pussycat* (1965), contacted JWT to let the agency know that he had a spare couple of months and was 'likely to be free to make commercials' before embarking on his next project.[29]

Cinematographers also proved unable to resist the siren song of cold, hard cash. David Watkin could pocket £35 per day working as a lighting cameraman on commercials, more than he might earn pro rata on a feature film.[30] When Nicolas Roeg unexpectedly found himself at a loose end having been fired from *Doctor Zhivago* (1965), he was quick to find solace – financial, if not artistic – in the arms of the advertising agencies. But there could be bathos in the contrast between those worlds: on a shoot for a PG Tips commercial featuring chimpanzees, Roeg said to himself regretfully, 'It's come to this!'[31]

Looking at the JWT files for 1965, it becomes clear just how many film and television industry practitioners wanted to get in on the act. Henry Mancini's British representatives offered his client's services scoring and conducting music for advertising films,[32] whilst John Barry earned £200 writing the music for a Sunsilk television advertisement that proved so popular that members of the public wrote to television stations asking where they could buy it.[33] When Reece Pemberton completed his assignment as art director on *Arabesque* (1966), he sought to 'renew his association with JWT' and let the agency know that he was available for £30 to £35 per day.[34] Away from JWT, Spike Milligan's work as copywriter for a Pirelli television advertisement in 1965 was featured in the Design and Art Direction (D&AD) annual the following year – an accolade to which many advertising creatives aspired. Milligan also appeared in commercials for products such as Nestlé Dairy Crunch.

By the mid-1960s, some of the reticence shown by well-known actors to appear in commercials had begun to dissipate. However, it was notable that stars with active film careers still tended to steer clear of advertising work, although by the end of the decade Orson Welles, for example, had been heard on British televisions banging the drum for Findus and Texaco.[35] Actors for whom offers of starring roles had dried up, or who made most of their money outside the cinema, were more willing to make commercials. Diana Dors was paid £5,000 – or '£333 6s 8d per second,' observed the *Daily Mirror* incredulously – to film a 15-second spot for Golden Wonder crisps in 1965, whilst Jessie Matthews, then starring in BBC radio's *The Dales*, was paid £5,000 a year to promote Tide washing powder.[36] John Slater, a film actor who was still recognisable from his work on television, signed a contract worth £3,500 a year to make a series of advertisements for Kellogg's Special K.[37] When JWT decided to search for a 'female John Slater', the list of stars who 'would be interested' in making commercials included Margaret Lockwood, Dulcie Gray, and Ann Todd.[38] Hattie Jacques' agents explored the possibility of her doing voice-over work; 'her fee,' noted Bullmore, 'would be a reasonable one'.[39] Bernard Braden, Canadian actor, comedian and presenter of ATV's *On the Braden Beat*, a consumer-affairs programme, advertised Campbell's Soup, and negotiated a contract which would see him earn as much as £25,000 for the financial year 1966–7.[40]

Earning money for making commercials also afforded what David Watkin described as 'some useful independence': 'it wasn't necessary to do a rubbishy [feature] film just because there was nothing else.'[41] This was a widely held sentiment. Joseph Losey stated that:

> Making commercials was a way of not doing the pictures you didn't want to do. An alternative way of making a living, which is something you really must have if you are going to be selective. You have *got* to be able to say 'no'. It's really the only freedom of choice anywhere in the commercial world.[42]

Lindsay Anderson returned to advertising time and again because 'much worse than making commercials is to undertake feature films that you don't respect'.[43] John Carson, a regular on British television and cinema screens in the 1960s, found himself in demand for voice-over work: 'When you've done a few [commercials] and the repeat fees start coming in, there's not the same absolute sweat to accept everything that's offered to you. You can afford to wait for the right role.' The money Carson made in advertising made it possible for him to appear alongside Albert Finney in the 1968 Broadway production of *A Day in the Death of Joe Egg*.[44] As far as animation was concerned, advertising played a crucial role in keeping the sector afloat: the profit that companies such as Richard Williams Animated Films, Halas and Batchelor, TV Cartoons or Biographic could make taking on advertising work supported 'a programme of personal projects' for which it might otherwise have proved difficult to secure funding.⁴⁵

Because so many film-industry practitioners contributed to the production of television commercials, they allowed professional relationships to be established, maintained or occasionally undermined. Partnerships that began in advertising often continued into the production of feature films. Alan Withy, who had been art director on Lindsay Anderson's *This Sporting Life* (1963), worked with the director on an 'adventurous, responsibly risky' commercial for Alcan kitchen foil titled 'Fat Chef', first broadcast in late 1967;⁴⁶ and the pair later renewed their partnership on *O Lucky Man!* (1973).⁴⁷ Richard Lester used television commercials to audition cinematographers and saw enough in David Watkin's ability to light and photograph advertisements to sign him up for *The Knack ... and How to Get It* (1965), *Help!* (1965), *How I Won the War* (1967) and *The Bed Sitting Room* (1969).⁴⁸ Lester also made commercials with Nicolas Roeg and was sufficiently impressed to engage him as cinematographer for *A Funny Thing Happened on the Way to the Forum* (1966) and *Petulia* (1968). Ken Russell and Billy Williams first teamed up to make commercials and continued their partnership into the features *Billion Dollar Brain* (1967), *Women in Love* (1969) and *The Rainbow* (1989).

Some producers used commercials to scout for, or develop, talent. Joseph Janni orchestrated the movement of practitioners between TV advertising and feature films, and in the early 1960s founded Augusta, a television-commercial production company, with Jack Lee, who had previously directed *A Town Like Alice* (1956) for Janni's Vic Films. Lee would make advertisements for, amongst other things, Oxo stock cubes, Players cigarettes and Stork margarine. Augusta gave work to Joseph Losey, and it was partly as a result of this professional connection that Janni asked the American to direct *Modesty Blaise* after Sidney Gilliat left the production.⁴⁹ The most significant relationship that Janni formed through Augusta, though, was with John Schlesinger. Janni was convinced of Schlesinger's future as a feature-film director but was concerned that his background in documentary films and television arts programmes had not afforded him enough experience of working with actors. So before hiring Schlesinger to direct *A Kind of Loving* (1962), Janni 'had him direct some commercials' for Augusta ('several for Polo Mints, a couple for Fray Bentos meats, a quartet for Kellogg's') and only after he passed this test was he finally signed up.⁵⁰

By the start of the 1960s, Leon Clore had built a reputation as a producer of documentary films and patron of documentarians.⁵¹ Film Contracts, established by Clore in 1960, encouraged film-makers to make commercials in between their other projects, thus 'financing more time to plan and prepare feature films and documentaries'.⁵² However, Clore was also a businessman, and any 'charitable intentions [towards directors working for Film Contracts] were tempered by exclusive contracts'.[53] Although Clore did not act as feature film producer for either Anthony Simmons, John Krish or Joseph Losey,[54] all of whom made commercials for him, he twice performed that role for Karel Reisz – *Morgan: A Suitable Case for Treatment* (1966) and *The French Lieutenant's Woman* (1981) – another director with whom he had worked at Film Contracts.

THE BRITISH STYLE

The economics of television advertising in Britain, and the medium's cultural position, worked to develop a specific style of advertising that encouraged production companies to court talent from a variety of creative fields, and made it easier to persuade this talent to sign on.[55] However, the British television commercial did not arrive fully formed; rather, it evolved in response to a specific set of cultural, economic and social factors. With more than 50 million people concentrated in a comparatively small geographical area, Britain constituted a populous, single, national market (as compared to, say, America or Australia, where advertising developed in more regional ways). Consequently, specifically local advertising tended to account for less than 5 per cent of most ITV companies' revenues, although it constituted a slightly higher proportion of screen time.[56] Commercials made to be shown nationally tended to have larger budgets and higher production values; many commercials, either for television or the cinema, cost as much or more per foot than many feature films.[57] Bringing in 'name' directors was a way to both justify the sum being spent, and to persuade advertisers that a project was in safe hands: consumers might not have known who was behind a 30-second spot entreating them to eat Birds Eye fish fingers or drink Mackeson's stout, but for the advertiser, 'who will be spending hundreds of thousands of pounds on this product in air time alone, it is a comfort to know that So-and-So who made So-and-So is now making his commercial'.[58] The same was true of cinematographers: feature cameramen were offered to clients 'like plum catches', their skills essential to a successful commercial – 'unless considerable skill is used a plate of baked beans when photographed will look like cold, unappetising buckshot'.[59]

Whilst not all commercials were made by well-known practitioners, television advertising increasingly came to be known as a creative medium.[60] Production companies able to sign up directors known for making features or commercials (or both) found themselves in advantageous positions when tendering for work. Film Contracts and Augusta, for example, both developed strong reputations as a consequence of always having established and prestigious directors on their books. When James Garrett and Partners was formed in 1963, it brought Richard Lester in as an in-house director: Lester was 'in demand, and [the] new company's business was good from the start', turning over £125,000 in its first year.⁶¹ Later, Garrett would sign directors like Sidney Furie (*The Leather Boys*, 1964; *The Ipcress File*, 1965) to exclusive contracts.

As far as the practitioners were concerned, sizeable budgets were obviously appealing. Money was available for location shooting, the construction of imaginative sets and the recording of lush musical scores. Furthermore, directors or cameramen wanting to use new lenses, stocks, processes or equipment found that television-commercial production companies had the wherewithal to facilitate experimentation. Wolf Rilla, directing a Knorr soup commercial in 1963, was able to make use of a location crane imported from Italy for the occasion,⁶² whilst Lester claimed, 'I used advertising films as a means of trying lab processes, trying to learn about the various new machines that were available, new lenses, new ways of doing anything. It was a free ride.'⁶³

The large sums spent – and occasionally wasted⁶⁴ – on television-commercial production meant that advertisements were not always the best training ground for young directors. Although Clive Donner had several films to his name by the time he was engaged to direct *Nothing But the Best* (1964), Film Finances still considered his work making television advertisements before deciding whether or not to provide a completion guarantee for a feature initially budgeted at a little over £180,000. John Croydon, who assessed the proposal for Film Finances, advised caution:

> there are many elements in it which I do not like. The main one – given confidentially – is the appointment of Clive Donner as the director. He is a 'mixed bag' . . . I have seen him at work on many TV Commercials and this is a truly frightening spectacle!⁶⁵

Croydon's concerns related in large part to Donner's inability to keep to schedule, and therefore to budget. Advertisers and agencies did, of course, keep a tight rein on time and money, but overruns tended to constitute relatively small sums in absolute terms (although they may constitute a large proportion of the budget), and so were easier to accommodate, especially if the work was finished to everybody's satisfaction. Feature films were a different matter. Here, Donner's reputation could count against him. He might have enjoyed the 'very difficult technical exercise' of making commercials, but his desire to find bespoke solutions was not always economical.⁶⁶ By contrast, Richard Lester was known to be much better at sticking to schedules and budgets. On one occasion, Lester was working on a commercial and arrived on set to find that a pair of Mies van der Rohe chairs requested by the art director had been replaced by something less distinctive. Lester waited from 8.30 a.m. until mid-morning for the correct chairs to be sourced, and then began shooting without them, explaining that to wait any longer would almost certainly incur overtime costs that had not been planned for: 'the chairs had been worth waiting until 11 o'clock, but not beyond'.[67]

The political and cultural discourse that attended the launch of independent television created the expectation that advertising was something that *needed* to be controlled.[68] Although few would have agreed with Lord Reith that the introduction of ITV and its commercials was comparable to the introduction of 'smallpox, bubonic plague and the Black Death',[69] there was a strong desire to limit the impact that advertisements might have on programming proper. Recognising that the advertiser was an 'uninvited visitor in people's homes', those responsible for the production of television commercials needed to adopt a mode of advertising that went about its business 'politely, quietly and entertainingly'.[70] This put a premium on practitioners who were able to communicate in this manner.

Furthermore, advertising – especially television advertising – was associated with Americanisation. This catch-all term spoke not only of well-established British cultural chauvinism, but also to uncertainty about Britain's place in the world and the global influences increasingly coming to bear on British culture. In a development that has some parallels with the British feature-film production sector, American companies, and American money, flooded into the British advertising industry in the 1960s,[71] prompting criticism of a situation in which 'what British families should be taught to feel and think in order to persuade them to spend, has more and more become the prerogative of American advertising men or their disciples'.[72] Early British television commercials owed a debt to their American predecessors – many were, indeed, made by Americans temporarily relocated to Britain – but it soon came to be understood that what drove sales on Main Street might not achieve similar results on the High Street. As one advertising executive noted, too many early British television commercials featured 'loud-mouthed salesmen who confused shouting with communication and bullying with persuading'.[73] The 'hard-sell' approach that characterised much American television advertising proved to be poorly suited to the specific conditions of the British market.[74]

What's more, because there was only a single commercial television broadcaster in Britain in the 1960s, and because the amount of time given over to advertising was strictly controlled (an average of 6 minutes per hour, with guidelines concerning where and how often ad breaks might appear), there were fewer commercials and, as a result, less 'competition and clutter'.[75] This, when coupled with distaste for the hard-sell approach, permitted a greater degree of subtlety in advertising techniques and strategies, in turn producing an environment wherein advertisers and advertising agencies saw the advantages offered by creative commercials, and film-industry practitioners wanted to make them.

A native style evolved which adapted elements of American consumerism and advertising practice in order that they might align with British cultural norms and expectations, thereby talking to British consumers in a language that they could understand and accept, and to which (it was hoped) they might respond.[76] It has been noted that British television advertising, from the 1960s to the 1980s, demonstrated 'a passion for the humorous, for satire and parody and spoof, for caricature or farce, for wit and ridicule' to a far greater degree than did American commercials.[77] Richard Lester's 1969 advertisement for L & M cigarettes, parodying Alain Resnais' modernist *Last Year at Marienbad* (1961), is one example of such a trend, the series of 'Milk Tray Man' commercials, which first aired on British television in 1968, and which seemed to owe a debt to the spy mania of the 1960s, not least in their apparent pastiche of John Barry's Bond scores, another. Advertisements made in this British style, noted for the humanism and (relative) subtlety of its approach, were more eager to actively engage the viewer; information is communicated, meaning is constructed, and entertainment facilitated not by strident proclamation, but rather by a process of dialogue in which the viewer might be actively involved. This encouraged acceptance and aided recall.[78]

The skills required to successfully produce television advertisements reliant upon character or narrative were not altogether common, and so practitioners with experience of working in the film industry – where for decades such abilities had been valued, even if not always fully utilised – became highly sought after. 'It's remarkable how 60 or even 30-second commercials can, when expertly devised, pack in a whole dramatic story,' noted one advertising man.[79] Consequently, film-industry personnel come to enjoy a very high status in the world of television-commercial production, with directors becoming, in Anthony Sampson's phrase, 'the aristocracy of advertising'.[80] As television advertising's association with a hard-sell approach began to wane, stars became more willing to appear in front of the camera, recognising both that their talents might be better utilised, and their reputations better protected, by this new approach.[81] Ruth Lipton, a former film publicist who established her own commercials production company, noted, 'the stature of the directors who make commercials has . . . been known to invoke a feeling of awe among the artists appearing in them.'[82]

The development of the British style took time and was not universal. British advertising agencies remained (and remain) more than capable of producing dull, over-earnest, overbearing, cloying or ill-thought-out commercials. However, in the 1960s the shape and structure of the television-advertising market – and the film industry more widely – left a space for the creative artist in the promotion of even the least promising of products. Thus, a reviewer for *Television Mail* was able to observe of the host of instant mashed potato advertisements aired in 1967, 'if a campaign must be singled out for this sort of product it has to be Yeoman, with Ken Loach's sensitively directed "People like us" commercials'.[83] When combined with the money that could be earned, the possibility of blending commerce and creativity within a well-funded environment meant that working in the production of television commercials was not an unappealing prospect.

Formal and Thematic Intersections

With the fields of film-making and television commercials having such porous boundaries, and with the increased visibility and cultural significance of advertising during the 1960s, it is not surprising to find that British cinema produced in the decade often owed a debt to advertising. Indeed, the sense of energy, and the faster pace, visible in at least some 1960s films can be attributed to changes orchestrated within television advertising after 1955. David Bernstein, former director at three front-rank advertising agencies, has observed that the earliest British television commercials were often a minute long, and this, combined with a desire to stick to established methods of rhythm, editing and structure, led to some rather leisurely ads:

> A character could not move from A to B in other than real time unless a dissolve was interposed. You needed an establishing shot to show where you were before moving in (tracking rather than cutting) to a medium close-up … Everything had to be spelled out. And, because this was advertising, much of it had to be repeated.[84]

However, the cost of producing and broadcasting these commercials meant by the start of the 1960s they were trimmed to 45 or, more commonly, 30 seconds.[85] Having to find a way to communicate a message, construct a narrative, create an atmosphere, elicit a particular kind of feeling, or set up a gag, in such a short period of time led to the development of what Bernstein dubbed a 'new grammar' of film in which the viewer was relied upon, and trusted, to do at least some of the work: 'the new breed of writer realised that the commercial communicated far more than what was written. Pictures lead. Words became comments.'[86] There were fewer establishing shots, fewer dissolves, a quicker pace, what Ronald Bryden called 'the shortest possible transition from the image of need to the image of [the advertiser's] product, the image of satisfaction to that of their brand name … the jump-cut from wish to fulfilment'.[87]

Faster-paced editing was one of, but not the only reason that Richard Lester's films were described in terms that equated them to advertising media: *A Hard Day's Night* (1964) was said by Alexander Walker to be 'firmly anchored in the world of the television commercial',[88] whilst *How I Won the War* (1967) was said by the *Spectator* to possess 'the mannerisms of the commercial – eye-catching incongruities of the wrong people in the wrong places, clichés jerked out of alignment'.[89] Comments of this kind may, in part, have resulted from Lester's willingness to talk openly and positively about his experiences of making television commercials, in contrast to someone like Ken Russell, who claimed that the 'minds and values' of the ad men were 'depraved'.[90] Unsurprisingly, Lester was frustrated that his films should be judged as little more than extended television commercials. Refuting the claim that *A Hard Day's Night* had been 'hysterically overcut', he pointed to an academic analysis of films released during 1964 which demonstrated that the Beatles' vehicle had fewer edits than comparable features released that year.[91] Lester insisted that periods of fast cutting in *A Funny Thing Happened on the Way to the Forum* were forced upon him by the inability of particular actors to deliver complete lines of dialogue, rather than being the product of a preconceived cinematic vision.[92] In as much as there were similarities between Lester's television commercials and his feature films, such similarities arose because both were linked by his creative vision and as such might be expected to share certain traits (although, illustrating the contemporary cultural hierarchy, nobody criticised his advertisements for looking like his films).[93] Furthermore, Lester's work emerged from, and was grounded in, the same cultural moment, speaking to, celebrating and satirising the contemporary fascination with advertising, pop music and fashion as interlinking elements of the consumer society.

Techniques developed whilst making commercials were adopted and adapted for feature films. Anthony Simmons replicated the handheld camera aesthetic used in some of his advertising work in *Four in the Morning* (1965), bringing with him a piece of kit, a gyroscope, that allowed the film to be photographed without excessive shaking.[94] The cinematography – by Larry Pizer, a veteran of many commercials who would work with Simmons on ads for Persil shortly after *Four in the Morning* was released – is observational without being intrusive, distanced without being unsympathetic. Whilst the relatively slow pace of *Four in the Morning* and its investigation of small, frustrated lives, clearly sets it apart from the commercials that Simmons' made, there is an exciting and energetic speed-boat ride down the Thames that, accompanied by upbeat music and an aspirational voice-over, could have worked as an advertisement for cognac or chocolates.

Commercials offered scope for innovation and experimentation in terms of lighting. The lighting equipment utilised by David Watkin in shooting an advertisement for Shredded Wheat so impressed Richard Lester that the director brought both cinematographer and equipment on board for *The Knack*. Knowing that one of *The Knack*'s most striking sets was to be a room in which everything had been painted white, and that such a space might prove difficult to light and photograph, Lester and Watkin took advantage of the opportunity afforded by a commercial for Lyons tea to practice filming within just such an environment. Shot on location at Barbara Mullen's house in Dun Laoghaire, the footage of the 'all-white' kitchen came out well, much to Lester and Watkin's satisfaction.[95]

Billy Williams credits his work in advertising with fast-tracking his career – working on commercials allowed him to sidestep the more heavily unionised, and hierarchical feature film industry whilst he was still a junior – and affording him the chance to play around with technique and form.[96] Williams, previously employed at British Transport Films, found that photographing commercials prepared him for photographing feature films, giving him the opportunity 'to work in a studio, work with dialogue . . . with actors . . . do portraiture'.[97] A conversation with a stills photographer on the set of a jelly commercial prompted a Damascene conversion:

> [H]e said, 'Haven't you tried shooting this jelly with softer light?' Well we didn't have any soft lights in those days, so . . . we got some tracing paper, and this provided a very nice diffusion . . . it got rid of these very hard high-lights, and on something like a jelly it looked so much better lighting it with soft light. And then I thought, there's a lot to be said for this soft light, and I really became really interested in developing it.[98]

The outcome of such experimentation can be seen in films like *Billion Dollar Brain* and *Women in Love*, for example in a sequence in the latter film where Alan Bates, seated at a table under a beech tree, eats a fig. Williams was concerned that Bates, who was backlit, would disappear into the gloom, and persuaded Ken Russell to allow him to use diffused lighting to rescue the actor from obscurity without losing what appeared to be natural lighting.[99]

Advertising aesthetics informed films that contained few, if any, overt references to advertising. *The Touchables* (1968) was based on a script by Donald and David Cammell, the latter of whom ran a successful advertising company alongside Hugh Hudson – later to direct *Chariots of Fire* (1981) – and Robert Brownjohn, the American graphic designer whose title sequence for *Goldfinger* (1964) won a D&AD gold award, and whose commercial for the Midland Bank's 'Money Talks' campaign won a prize at Venice. Directed, and based on an original idea by Robert Freeman, a fashion photographer who had who had shot commercials for Cammell, Hudson and Brownjohn, *The Touchables* was conceived as 'an atmosphere or a vague modern environment'.[100] Because so much of this atmosphere and environment was created visually, by means of ultra-contemporary sets and fashions, rather than by the development of character or narrative, Freeman's film 'ends up', as one American reviewer put it, 'as simply a commercial for itself'.[101]

If *The Touchables* was decried as a film that replicated advertising's prioritisation of surface over substance, it was also recognised as being part of a wider international trend. The urtext of such films was perhaps Claude Lelouch's *Un Homme et Une Femme* (1966), which *The Times* lambasted for featuring characters who possessed 'the glamorous, glittering unreality of figures out of a colour supplement advertisement'.[102] Elsewhere, Michael Billington identified *The Thomas Crown Affair* (1968) as belonging to a series of films 'indistinguishable from inflated television commercials', and as 'a classic case of a work starting out with a lot in its favour and then ruining everything through being excessively chic and modish'.[103]

Given firstly the growing visibility of advertising within British popular culture, secondly the influence that it had on the aesthetics of the cinema, and thirdly the widespread cross-employment of British film practitioners in television-commercial production, it comes as no surprise that advertising also became a significant thematic presence in British cinema in the 1960s. However, although the influence of advertising and/or television commercials could inject a film with energy, wit and visual flair, lingering distrust of advertising often affected the way in which the industry and its products were portrayed within films. Advertising was often used to critique societal change. Producer David Deutsch explained that the look and feel of *Nothing But the Best* was determined by the choice to ape the 'lush colour photography you get in glossy magazines, using restricted focus where you get a sharp foreground and everything else tends to melt away'.[104] This homage to the high-end advertising aesthetic was appropriate to the film, given that in order to succeed, this satire on the affluent society needed to create a vision of the good life that was simultaneously appealing and recognisably superficial, which justified the lengths to which Jimmy Brewster (Alan Bates) was prepared to go in order to elevate his status whilst suggesting that his understanding of what constituted 'the best' was the product of a materialistic outlook.[105] Similarly, Peter Whitehead made *Tonite Let's All Make Love in London* (1967) in 'the style of ... a colour supplement.'[106] Although the film was criticised on these very grounds,[107] its structural debt to the colour supplement magazines – 'like a series of articles, but on film' – allows *Tonite* ... to operate as an appraisal and ironic celebration of, and a contribution to, the vacuous glamour and consumerism at the heart of 'swinging London'.[108] Associated British–Pathé's television-commercials division was sufficiently impressed to sign Whitehead to an exclusive contract, although he does not appear to have directed any advertisements for them.[109]

Elsewhere, the structure of an advertising break is incorporated into *The Loneliness of the Long Distance Runner* (1962), in a sequence showing Colin's (Tom Courtenay) memories of the Smith family going on a shopping spree to spend insurance money paid out after his father's death. Brief shots inspired by the 'Adastral' star – used by Associated–Rediffusion at the beginning and end of a commercial break, and between each advertisement – mark the start of the sequence, as well as separating shots of the family buying furs, rugs, mattresses, furniture, toys and food. The sequence is told in flashback, and the transition from present to past is marked by a change in music, from a tune played by the Chris Barber Jazz Band which emphasises the sense of freedom and purpose that Colin feels as he runs through the woods, to an anodyne jingle, complete with whistling and woodblock percussion, that accompanies the Smiths to the shops.

One of their first purchases is a television, and the first thing that they see when they switch it on is a song-and-dance number advertising Roller Roy women's clothes that encapsulates Colin's contempt for the soulless banality of freshly minted working-class consumerism. Hostility towards television commercials as exemplars of the supposed vacuity of modern culture is visible in films made throughout the 1960s. In many instances, such as a spot for Direct Action ('the perfume with the provocative aura') in *Smashing Time* (1967), a film suffused with advertising imagery, these commercials are played for laughs. As the *Monthly Film Bulletin* noted, *Smashing Time* worked best 'when unequivocally parodying the world of the colour supplements', something it might have found easier to achieve given cinematographer Manny Wynn's back-catalogue of television commercials.[110] However, even less explicitly comic examples seem to despair at the amount of money spent on clichéd attempts to influence public opinion, and the seriousness with which commercials are taken by those who helped produce them. In *The Comedy Man* (1964), the success and wealth that Kenneth More's failing actor enjoys through taking on the role of Mr Honeybreath in a television advertising campaign is shown to be unsatisfying and undeserved. In *Darling* (1965), which Penelope Houston claimed had 'all the immediate snap and crackle of the cornflakes advertisement', the shooting of an advertisement for Cupid chocolates ('those fairy tale centres take you out of this world') provides an opportunity to mock both those who take such productions seriously, and also any pleasure that Diana Scott (Julie Christie) might take in her status as the commercial's 'star'.[111] It is, of course, ironic that the directors of these two films, Alvin Rakoff and John Schlesinger, directed numerous advertisements in the 1960s, although, as one character observes in *Darling* of his work making television commercials, 'a lie can be shot with integrity, just like anything else'.

Equally popular were jaundiced takes on advertising as a whole, which was often presented as simultaneously shallow and self-important, and contrasted with the integrity of work requiring *real* creativity or soul. If Gary Fenn (Roger Moore) in *Crossplot* (1969) exemplifies the smug glibness of the advertising executive, *Every Home Should Have One* (1970) and *I'll Never Forget What's 'is Name* (1967) present an unambiguously negative vision of the advertising industry as a site of deceit, manipulation and superficiality. In *Catch Us If You Can* (1965), Dinah (Barbara Ferris), 'the Butcha Girl', and Steve (Dave Clark), a stuntman working with her, become so disillusioned with shooting a commercial at Smithfield Market that they steal a car from the set and flee into the west, an action that is then cynically exploited by the advertising agency that has employed them. Derogatory references to advertising can even be found in a film such as *Mrs Brown, You've Got a Lovely Daughter* (1968), in which the work that Peter Noone's Herman does for an advertising company is shown to be less valuable and satisfying than the working-class Manchester milieu from which he and his fellow Hermits emerge.

Conclusion

For all that advertising was often compared unfavourably to the realist styles of film-making so often privileged within British film criticism and was deemed to have a deleterious effect on 'authentic' working-class lives of the kind that so interested British New Wave film-makers (and many of the reviewers that praised them), television commercials, and advertising more generally, spoke to changes in British culture and economics, and to the aspirational ideals of the consumer society. Whilst it would clearly be naïve to claim that all commercials were well made, or had any measurable influence on consumer behaviour, the advertising industry was central to British creative life in the 1960s, both as it functioned as a site of artistic employment and innovation, and as it was consumed by the public. Opponents sneered that moving-image advertising was little more than cynical manipulation, that the dreams it sold were unrealistic and unrealisable. Similar claims could be, and had often been, made of the narrative feature film, of course, and such a parallel might explain why, for all the occasional tensions between them, the linkages between the film and advertising industries became so well established, and why the products of these connections were so often satisfying for the practitioners involved and the consumers who enjoyed the eventual fruits of their labour.

Notes

1. In the episode, Hancock's theatrical career is undermined by an advertisement's use of a soundalike. This intentionally echoes a 1958 court case actor Alastair Sim instigated against Heinz, following the broadcast of a commercial featuring a voice he believed was an imitation of his own. Sim's lawyers insisted that as he had never deigned 'to prostitute his art by advertising baked beans' the commercial had caused Sim great embarrassment and done 'great harm to [his] reputation'. *Daily Mirror*, 19 December 1958, p. 1; *Daily Express*, 19 December 1958, p. 8; Mark Simpson, *Alastair Sim* (Stroud: History Press, 2008), pp. 150–6. Hancock continued to extract humour from similar situations, and in 1965, starred in a series of egg commercials with Patricia Hayes. In the first, Hancock addresses the

camera: 'Ladies and gentlemen, owing to the present state of the theatrical profession, I have, with great reluctance, been forced to accept a job as a supporting actor to a lady doing a commercial for eggs.'
2. *What Equity is Doing: The Twenty-ninth Annual Report of the Council, 1959–60*, p. 21; *ITV 1970: A guide to Independent Television* (London: ITA, 1970), p. 127.
3. Jeremy Potter, *Independent Television in Britain – vol. 3: Politics and Control, 1968–80* (London: Macmillan, 1989), p. 209.
4. Wallace S. Sharps, *Commercial Television: A Manual of Advertising Production and Techniques* (London: Fountain Press, 1958), p. 2.
5. Quoted in John Baxter, *An Appalling Talent: Ken Russell* (London: Michael Joseph, 1973), p. 131. Russell returned to advertising later in his career.
6. *Campaign*, 11 September 1970, p. 23.
7. *The Gallup International Public Opinion Polls: Great Britain 1937–1975: vol. 1 – 1937–1964* (New York: Random House, 1976), p. 509.
8. David Clayton, 'Advertising Expenditure in 1950s Britain', *Business History*, 52: 4 (2010), p. 658.
9. Walter Taplin, *The Origin of Television Advertising in the United Kingdom* (London: Sir Isaac Pitman & Sons, 1961), pp. 37–9.
10. By 1966, pirate stations were estimated to have generated advertising revenues of approximately £3 million. *Financial Times*, 5 August 1967, p. 8.
11. See Richard Farmer, 'Supplemental income: British newspaper colour supplements in the 1960s', *Media History* <https://www.tandfonline.com/doi/full/10.1080/13688804.2018.1481372> (advanced online access).
12. *Sunday Times Magazine*, 14 December 1969, pp. 27, 29.
13. Harry Hopkins, *The New Look: A Social History of the Forties and Fifties in Britain* (London: Secker & Warburg, 1963), p. 317.
14. Francis Williams, *American Invasion* (London: Anthony Blond, 1962), p. 21.
15. On Johnston's jingles, see Joe Moran, *Armchair Nation: An Intimate History of Britain in Front of the TV* (London: Profile Books, 2013), p. 105. On children's use of advertising jingles, see Christopher Booker, *The Neophiliacs: The Revolution in English Life in the Fifties and Sixties* (London: Pimlico, 1992 [1969]), p. 134; Iona and Peter Opie, *Children's Games With Things* (Oxford: Oxford University Press, 1997), p. 213. The Opies found that a Murray Mints jingle first broadcast in the late 1950s was still used for skipping games in Edinburgh in 1975.
16. See Ian MacDonald, *Revolution in the Head: The Beatles' Records and the Sixties* (London: Fourth Estate, 1994), p. 186.
17. Jo Gable, *The Tuppenny Punch and Judy Show: 25 Years of TV Commercials* (London: Michael Joseph, 1980), p. 32. Tony Richardson was also an advertising refusenik, although David Watkin claims he agreed to direct a commercial in order to pay for a new swimming pool at his French home, but later changed his mind. David Watkin, *Why is there only one word for Thesaurus?* (Brighton: Trouser Press, 1998), pp. 121–2.
18. John Thornton Caldwell, *Televisuality: Style, Crisis, and Authority in American Television* (New Brunswick, NJ: Rutgers University Press, 1995), p. 10.
19. James Garrett, 'Commercial Production', in Brian Henry (ed.), *British Television Advertising: The First 30 Years* (London: Century Benham, 1986), pp. 388–9.
20. Anderson, for example, claimed to 'make commercials in order to subsidise my serious work.' *Financial Times*, 17 July 1969, p. 15. Lassally discusses making commercials – 'I was never able to take them quite as seriously as was often demanded' – in his autobiography. Walter Lassally, *Itinerant Cameraman* (London: John Murray, 1987), pp. 154–6.

21. *Kine Weekly*, 27 January 1955, p. 7.
22. Joseph Gelmis, *The Film Director as Superstar* (London: Secker & Warburg, 1971), pp. 235–6.
23. Ridley Scott, speaking on *The Men from the Agency* (produced and directed by Michael Wadding, Tiger Aspect, 2002; first broadcast BBC4, 8 January 2003). Scott had studied film-making at the Royal College of Art.
24. History of Advertising Trust (HAT): J. Walter Thompson archive (JWT): 50/2/1/1/4/1/4: Jeremy Bullmore to All Producers, 29 December 1965.
25. Quoted in Ian Cameron and Mark Shivas, 'Interview with Richard Lester', *Movie*, 16 (Winter 1968/69), p. 18.
26. David Caute, *Joseph Losey: A Revenge on Life* (London: Faber, 1996), pp. 214–15; *New York Times*, 26 March 1967, p. 89.
27. HAT/JWT: 50/2/1/1/4/1/6: Jeremy Bullmore to Creative Directors, Creative Group Heads and TV Producers, 9 June 1965.
28. For a synopsis of a Jackson Kit Kat commercial, see Henry (ed.), *British Television Advertising*, p. 264.
29. HAT/JWT: 50/2/1/1/4/1/6: Jeremy Bullmore to All Producers, 13 August 1965.
30. David Watkin online archive: David Watkin Account Book, 1962–76.
31. Jim Clark, with John M. Myers, *Dream Repairman: Adventures in Film Editing* (Crockett, Texas: Landmarc Press, 2010), pp. 66–7.
32. HAT/JWT: 50/2/1/1/4/1/4: Henry Howard to Jeremy Bullmore, 19 August 1965. Mancini wrote the music for a Heinz tomato soup commercial.
33. HAT/JWT: 50/1/53/1/2/5/4: Television Production Estimate – Sunsilk Shampoo, 8 April 1965; HAT/JWT 50/1/53/1/2/5/1: B. V. Squires to Mrs Walley, 16 November 1965. Crossover between advertising and pop music went both ways. The artists listed in an October 1969 *Television Mail* supplement as being available to write or record music for commercials included Cat Stevens, Alan Price, Jeff Wayne, Bruce Welsh and Hank Marvin, Manfred Mann and Mike Hugg, and Vivian Stanshall and Neil Innes.
34. HAT/JWT: 50/2/1/1/4/1/4: Denis Singleton to All Producers, 28 October 1965.
35. *Financial Times*, 17 July 1969, p. 15.
36. *Daily Mirror*, 6 February 1965, p. 9.
37. HAT/JWT: 50/1/91/3/23: Ron Wiles to Mr M Vernon, 2 September 1965. Slater also had script approval.
38. HAT/JWT: 50/1/91/3/22: Lulu Lloyd-Jones to Mr D. Michel, 18 May 1965.
39. HAT/JWT: 50/2/1/1/4/1/4: Auriol Moore to Jeremy Bullmore, 15 March 1965.
40. HAT/JWT: 50/2/1/1/4/1/2: P. C. Adams to Jeremy Bullmore, 1 June 1965. To comply with advertising regulations, JWT and Campbell's ensured that Braden's commercials were not broadcast during television shows in which he appeared. Braden's contract with Campbell's did not preclude him from criticising Campbell's products.
41. Watkin, *Why is there only one word for Thesaurus?*, p. 102.
42. Losey quoted in Richard Roud, 'The Reluctant Exile', *Sight and Sound*, 48: 3 (Summer 1979), p. 146. Advertisements shot by Losey between March 1958 and December 1961 are listed in Michel Ciment, *Conversations with Losey* (London and New York: Methuen, 1985), pp. 422–3.
43. Gelmis, *Film Director as Superstar*, pp. 100–1. Anderson was speaking in February 1969.
44. *Financial Times*, 17 July 1969, p. 15.
45. Derek Hill, 'Cartoons and commercials', *Sight and Sound*, Spring 1963, p. 67. Animation had been a key component of moving-image animation in Britain for many years before the arrival of ITV, but declined in importance during the 1960s.

By 1970, animated advertisements formed 'a very small percentage indeed' of commercials made in the UK. *Television Mail*, 29 May 1970, p. 22.
46. *Television Mail*, 15 December 1967, p. 28.
47. The 'Fat Chef' advertisement was described by *Television Mail* as 'the most effective kitchen foil advert ever' and was backed by air time to the tune of £22,428 during its first week of release. *Television Mail*: 3 November 1967, p. 17; 24 November 1967, p. 21.
48. Watkin, *Why is there only one word for Thesaurus?*, pp. 84–5; *Television Mail*, 4 December 1964, p. 15.
49. Colin Gardner, *Joseph Losey* (Manchester: Manchester University Press, 2004), p. 122.
50. William J. Mann, *Edge of Midnight: The Life of John Schlesinger* (London: Arrow, 2005), pp. 175–6. Schlesinger forged relationships in advertising that he took into feature films, for example making a commercial with Billy Williams before working with him on *Sunday, Bloody Sunday* (1971).
51. On Clore's career, see Patrick Russell and James Piers Taylor, *Shadows of Progress: Documentary Film in Post-War Britain* (London: BFI–Palgrave, 2010), pp. 35–8.
52. *Television Mail*, 21 January 1966, p. 12.
53. Russell and Taylor, *Shadows of Progress*, p. 38.
54. Losey's promiscuity as far as advertising work was concerned 'led to acrimony' as varying companies with whom he had signed contracts all demanded his services. In the course of making a commercial for Nimble Bread, Losey attracted the ire of Paddington's borough engineer and surveyor, who wrote to Film Contracts: 'complaints have been received from residents in the vicinity that your activities created a nuisance by completely blocking all passage through Fulton Mews, and leaving the area in a filthy condition.' Caute, *Joseph Losey*, p. 214; BFI Special Collections: Leon Clore Papers: Production File – FC65 – 23 March 1961.
55. This section owes a debt to some of the arguments developed by Terence Nevett in 'Differences between American and British television advertising: Explanations and implications', *Journal of Advertising*, 21: 4 (1992), pp. 61–71.
56. Bernard Sendall, *Independent Television in Britain – vol. 2: Expansion and Change, 1958–62* (London: Macmillan, 1983), p. 319.
57. One cinema advertising film for hair dye had a budget of more than £15,000 and cost more per minute than *Dr No* (1962). See Richard Farmer, 'Cinema advertising and the Sea Witch "Lost Island" film (1965)', *Historical Journal of Film, Radio and Television*, 36: 4 (2016), pp. 573–4.
58. Brien O'Brian, 'Private Lives', *Films and Filming*, 10: 7 (April 1964), p. 57.
59. Lassally, *Itinerant Cameraman*, p. 154; Institute of Practitioners in Advertising, *How a Television Commercial is Made* (IPA Occasional Paper, No. 9, London, 1960), pp. 14–15.
60. In commercials that relied on a 'presentational' approach – i.e. 'the setting in which the stuff is eaten [or used]' – art directors took the lead. Alan Withy, for example, made a number of advertisements for Fry's Turkish Delight. Animated advertisements, of which there were many in the early years of ITV, were produced by specialist companies such as Hallas and Bachelor. O'Brian, 'Private Lives', p. 58.
61. Jeremy Scott, *Fast and Louche: Confessions of a flagrant sinner* (London: Profile, 2003), p. 170; *CampaignLive*, 26 September 2003, <http://www.campaignlive.co.uk/article/lord-jim-james-garrett-one-great-names-british-commercials-gentleman-jim-retiring-40-years-caroline-marshall-reports/191172> (accessed 5 May 2016).

62. *Television Mail*, 16 August 1963, p. 8.
63. Quoted in Joseph McBride, 'Running, jumping and standing still: an interview with Richard Lester', *Sight and Sound*, Spring 1973, p. 76.
64. For an example of an extravagantly profligate location shoot in Italy, see Lassally, *Itinerant Cameraman*, pp. 154–6.
65. Film Finances archive: Realised Film Box 371: *Nothing But the Best*: John Croydon to R. E. F. Garret, 3 April 1963.
66. *Daily Mirror*, 14 April 1964, p. 14.
67. Watkin, *Why is there only one word for Thesaurus?*, p. 88.
68. On the debates about the role of advertising in the development of the consumer society, see Sean Nixon, '"Salesmen of the Will to Want": Advertising and its critics in Britain, 1951–1967', *Contemporary British History*, 24: 2 (2010), pp. 213–33.
69. Lord Reith, 22 May 1952. *Parliamentary Debates: House of Lords*, 5th series, vol. 176, col. 1297.
70. Garrett, 'Commercial Production', p. 397.
71. In 1960, twelve American-based advertising agencies in London accounted for 30 per cent of the total press and television billings in Britain; by 1970, the number of American-based companies had doubled, and their billings accounted for 42 per cent. Douglas West, 'Multinational Competition in the British Advertising Agency Business, 1936–1987', *Business History Review*, 62: 3 (1988), p. 474.
72. Williams, *American Invasion*, p. 22.
73. David Bernstein, 'The Television Commercial: An Essay', in Henry (ed.), *British Television Advertising*, p. 257. On the search for a British television advertising idiom, see Winston Fletcher, *Powers of Persuasion: The Inside Story of British Advertising, 1951–2000* (Oxford: Oxford University Press, 2008), pp. 34–6.
74. Renée Dickason, *British Television Advertising: Cultural Identity and Communication* (Luton: University of Luton Press, 2000), p. 38.
75. Mark F. Toncar, 'The use of humour in television advertising: revisiting the US–UK comparison', *International Journal of Advertising*, 20:4 (2001), p. 534.
76. Frank Mort has shown that businesses and cultures in many European countries sought to 'negotiate' with and accommodate American influence within their own consumer societies. Frank Mort, 'Paths to mass consumption', in Mica Nava, Andrew Blake, Iain MacRury and Barry Richards (eds), *Buy this book: Studies in advertising and consumption* (Abingdon: Routledge, 1997), p. 24. See also Sean Nixon, 'Looking westwards and worshipping: The New York "Creative Revolution" and British advertising, 1956–1960', *Journal of Consumer Culture*, 17: 2 (2017).
77. Paul Rutherford, *The New Icons? The Art of Television Advertising* (Toronto: University of Toronto Press, 1994), pp. 80–1. American commercials are now as likely to use humour as British commercials, although the types of humour used, and the ways in which they are deployed, differs. See Marc G. Weinberger and Harlan E. Spotts, 'Humor in US versus UK TV Commercials: A Comparison', *Journal of Advertising*, 18: 2 (1989), pp. 39–44; Mark F. Toncar, 'The use of humour in television advertising: revisiting the US–UK comparison', *International Journal of Advertising*, 20: 4 (2001), pp. 521–39.
78. Bernstein, 'The Television Commercial', p. 272.
79. Stanhope Shelton, 'Television Advertising: Its Part in Mass Communication', *Journal of the Royal Society of Arts*, 118: 5166 (May 1970), p. 336.
80. Anthony Sampson, *Anatomy of Britain* (London: Hodder & Stoughton, 1962), p. 587. See also Francis Williams, *American Invasion*, p. 21: 'artists and copy writers are the priests and ballad singers of our day.'

81. *Kine Weekly*, 20 May 1965, p. 12.
82. *Kine Weekly – Studio Review Supplement*, 27 July 1961, p. 15.
83. *Television Mail*, 15 December 1967, p. 28. Loach would later turn his back on advertising, calling it 'indefensible' and stating that 'having been publically identified with a socialist point of view, I shouldn't sell my services to advertisers'. Quoted in Graham Fuller (ed.), *Loach on Loach* (London: Faber, 1998), 80–1.
84. Bernstein, 'The Television Commercial', pp. 271–2.
85. Renée Dickason, *British Television Advertising: Cultural Identity and Communication* (Luton: University of Luton Press, 2000), p. 35.
86. Bernstein, 'The Television Commercial', pp. 271–2.
87. Ronald Bryden, *Observer Magazine*, 7 August 1966, p. 6.
88. Alexander Walker, *Hollywood, England: The British Film Industry in the Sixties* (London: Michael Joseph, 1974), p. 242.
89. *Spectator*, 26 October 1967, p. 26. See also Philip French's observation that Lester's films were a celebration 'principally and unashamedly' of 'the ad-man's ... world of youth revolution.' 'The alphaville of admass', *Sight and Sound*, Summer 1966, pp. 106–11. For Lester's reply, see *Sight and Sound*, Autumn 1966, p. 170.
90. On Lester, see *Sunday Times Magazine*, 25 July 1965, p. 27; Ian Cameron and Mark Shivas, 'Interview with Richard Lester', *Movie*, 16 (Winter 1968/69), pp. 17–18. Russell quoted in Baxter, *An Appalling Talent*, p. 131.
91. Lester, quoted in Steven Soderbergh, *Getting Away With It – Or: The Further Adventures of the Luckiest Bastard you Ever Saw* (London: Faber, 1999), p. 4.
92. Ibid.
93. On the contrary, the advertising industry was more complimentary: '[Lester's] features may well be criticised for being a string of commercials ... but what marvellous commercials!' 'A sense of direction' *Round the Square* (JWT magazine), 30 March 1966, p. 6.
94. *Observer*, 28 February 1965, p. 23. When *Four in the Morning* won prizes at the Cannes and Locarno festivals, Film Contracts put out an ad congratulating Simmons and reminding readers that he was 'one of the team of talented filmmakers' under exclusive contract. *Television Mail*, 10 September 1965, p. 1.
95. Not everyone was so pleased, however, as Watkin later recalled: 'knobs were quickly adjusted, the white walls became grey, and Barbara looked like the black Madonna having a brew-up'. Watkin, *Why is there only one word for Thesaurus?*, pp. 84–5.
96. James Garrett recalls that feature film and television directors were sometimes approached to make commercials because they already had union cards, and so could start work straight away. *CampaignLive*, 26 September 2003, <http://www.campaignlive.co.uk/article/lord-jim-james-garrett-one-great-names-british-commercials-gentleman-jim-retiring-40-years-caroline-marshall-reports/191172> (accessed 5 May 2016).
97. Billy Williams, interview with Neil Binney, recorded September 2003, <http://www.webofstories.com/play/billy.williams/24> (accessed 12 April 2016).
98. Ibid.
99. David A. Ellis, *Conversations with Cinematographers* (Plymouth: Scarecrow Press, 2012), p. 7.
100. *Films and Filming*, May 1968, p. 21.
101. *Independent Film Journal*, 12 November 1968, p. 899.
102. *The Times*, 19 January 1967, p. 6.
103. *Illustrated London News*, 8 February 1969, p. 28.
104. *Kine Weekly*, 6 June 1963, p. 17.

105. *Observer*, 1 March 1964, p. 24.
106. Whitehead to Andrew Oldham, 30 July 1966. Peter Whitehead, 'Letters to Andrew Oldham', *Framework*, 52: 1 (2011), p. 207.
107. *Monthly Film Bulletin*, January 1968, p. 30.
108. Whitehead to Andrew Oldham, 30 July 1966. Whitehead, 'Letters to Andrew Oldham', p. 207.
109. *Television Mail*, 15 March 1968, p. 9.
110. *Monthly Film Bulletin*, January 1968, p. 11.
111. *New Statesman*, 17 September 1965, p. 419.

14. FILM AND POP MUSIC

Richard Farmer

INTRODUCTION

In the chapters of *The True Adventures of the Rolling Stones* chronicling the band's rise to fame and fortune, Stanley Booth returns repeatedly to reports that Brian Jones, Mick Jagger, Keith Richards, Charlie Watts and Bill Wyman were set to become film stars.[1] Since they never actually made a feature film, the references to abandoned projects become something of a running joke, one founded on the Stones' reputation first as the bad boys of the 'beat boom' period and, subsequently, as the 'greatest rock and roll band in the world'. For although it seems entirely fitting that the Stones' live shows and almost unreal lifestyles should be captured in concert films or documentaries such as *Teenage Command Performance* (1964), *Charlie is My Darling* (1966), *One Plus One/ Sympathy for the Devil* (1968), *Gimme Shelter* (1970) and *Cocksucker Blues* (1972) – this last a rarely seen film that now exists 'more as myth than reality'[2] – the possibility that the group might have appeared in an exploitation feature like *Gonks Go Beat* (1965) seems a compromise that is almost comically out of character.[3]

However, we can use the Stones' unmade feature-film projects to construct a shadow history of the British pop music film in the 1960s, one that parallels the developments of the genre in the decade whilst leaving few celluloid traces save Jagger's brief career as a leading man in *Performance* and *Ned Kelly* (both 1970) and the documentaries mentioned above. For whilst the precise combination of problems that waylaid the Stones' cinematic ambitions were

Figure 14.1 Pop fans on the dancefloor in the low-budget exploitation film *Gonks Go Beat* (Robert Hartford-Davis, 1964), which very nearly starred the Rolling Stones.

unique, the band's experiences remain broadly representative of the relationship between the pop and film industries in the 1960s. Projects that never came to fruition, and which were perhaps never intended to, still have much to tell us about how pop music and the cinema intersected, about how pop music's cultural status was transformed during the 1960s, and about the types of films that were deemed suitable vehicles for performers whose fame was associated with music rather than acting. Before seeking to bring the Stones' often opaque cinematic ambitions into slightly clearer focus, this chapter will provide an outline of some of the commercial intersections between pop music and cinema, and an overview of the British pop film.

Film Music and Filmusic

By the start of the 1960s, the film and music industries had been collaborating in mutually profitable ways for decades. Elements of film soundtracks had been issued since the coming of the talkies, both as sheet music and on gramophone records.⁴ A combination of increasing affluence and micro-groove technology led to the rapid growth of the record industry after 1950, and between 1955 and 1970 the number of records sold in the UK almost doubled:

1955:   59.9 million (85% singles, 15% albums)
1960:   72.7 million (76% singles, 24% albums)
1965:   93.8 million (66% singles, 34% albums)
1970:   113 million (42% singles, 58% albums)

Furthermore, there was an almost fourfold increase in the value of recorded music sales, from £9.1 million in 1955 to £39.3 million in 1970, with the disproportionate increase in sales of more expensive LPs accounting for much of this faster rate of growth.⁵

Increased spending on recorded music was part of a wider expansion of leisure services that coincided with, and perhaps precipitated, what in 1958 *The Economist* called a 'sickening acceleration of the decline in cinema attendances'.⁶ Companies involved with the cinema diversified in an attempt to tap into the new leisure sector: by the early 1960s, the Rank Organisation was operating bowling alleys, motorway service stations, dance venues and, bringing company founder J. Arthur Rank into conflict with some of his fellow Methodists, bingo halls.⁷ There were parallel moves to exploit the growing market for recorded music, although these were not as widespread and were made more difficult by the established dominance within the sector of EMI and Decca. In 1958 Rank attempted to gain a foothold the music industry by establishing Top Rank records and buying Filmusic, a publishing company.

Although Top Rank also put out straight pop, the label's 'naturally very close' association with the film industry saw it issue music from Rank-distributed features.⁸ This was sensible: until the advent of Beatlemania – and after, as the success of the *Sound of Music* (1965) demonstrated – soundtracks dominated the British album chart, with Hollywood musicals proving particularly popular.⁹ British soundtrack albums were also successful. Although pop albums such as *Summer Holiday* (1963) or *A Hard Day's Night* (1964) might spring to mind when we think of 1960s British film soundtracks, LPs from musicals such as *Oliver!* and *Chitty Chitty Bang Bang* (both 1968) sold in large numbers, whilst those from *Doctor Zhivago* (1965), and *2001: A Space Odyssey* (1968) also did well. Popular film music came in a range of forms.

Film themes could be similarly successful when released as singles, and in April 1961 *Disc* proclaimed, 'What was a trickle in the old days of the "Harry Lime Theme" [from *The Third Man*, 1949] has turned into a flood ... almost every other tune you hear on the radio or in a record shop comes from a film.'¹⁰ Again, many of these songs emerged from American productions, but it was not unusual for British film, or sometimes television themes to become popular. This was a trend that continued throughout the decade, often in association with well-established artists such as Shirley Bassey (*Goldfinger*, 1964), Tom Jones (*Thunderball* and *What's New Pussycat?*, both 1965), the Seekers (*Georgy Girl*, 1966), Lulu (*To Sir With Love*, 1967, in which she also acted), Petula Clark (*Countess from Hong Kong*, 1967) and Manfred Mann (*Up the Junction*, 1968). Such songs could act as very effective marketing.

Despite increasing record sales, and the fact that its discs were played and promoted at Rank-controlled venues, Top Rank did not secure enough hits to prove profitable; the Organisation lost its 'million pound gamble' and sold the label to EMI in 1960.[11] Rank's foray into music publishing, however, lasted longer and was more successful. Helen Shapiro's 1961 single 'Walkin' Back to Happiness' was published by Filmusic as part of an agreement that saw the song promoted in an edition of Rank's *Look at Life* cinemagazine called 'For the Record'. Sales and radio play of the single and its sheet music generated income for Filmusic. Associated British employed a similar form of cross-promotion, with Pathé newsreels in ABC cinemas featuring stories on pop stars such as Cliff Richard or Frank Ifield in advance of the singers' films being released into those same halls.[12]

Although Filmusic published music in a range of styles, its general manager, Harold Shampan, persuaded Rank to produce more contemporary-sounding scores, with an eye to supplying music that was both 'a vital part of the production [and] a good saleable piece'.[13] This provided a boost to the careers of younger, more commercially minded composers such as Ron Goodwin, Norrie Paramor and John Barry, an already successful recording artist whose later work on the Bond films earned him international acclaim and whose music for *Born Free* (1966) won two Oscars. As Shampan noted in 1966, 'British [composers] have the edge in the international market at the moment, it appears to me only logical to use them'.[14]

Filmusic offered a music consultancy, and was commissioned to provide, and publish, music included in films made by producers and distributors such as Sidney Box and Anglo-Amalgamated, whose *Play It Cool* (1962) starred Shapiro and Billy Fury. Shampan also worked with independent producers to develop projects featuring particular acts or music-based narratives. This process resulted in *Band of Thieves* (1962), Filmvale's vehicle for trad-jazz clarinettist Acker Bilk which Shampan claimed to have 'virtually produced',[15] Sevenay's now-lost *Farewell Performance* (1963), featuring Heinz and the Tornadoes, on which Shampan acted as musical advisor, and Three Kings' musical compendium pictures *Live It Up* (1963) and *Be My Guest* (1965), which were from an idea by, and produced in association with Shampan, respectively. This last film featured the Zephyrs, a band Shampan had signed to Filmusic when the company moved into artist management, and which also appeared in 'Sound of a City' (1964), a *Look at Life* film exploring beat music.[16] From these films emerged a slew of records – singles, EPs and albums – containing songs published by Filmusic.

Having purchased Filmusic from Rank in late 1964, Shampan continued to work with Rank-financed independent producers, and contributed the idea that became *Dateline Diamonds* (1965), Viscount Film's collage of pop stars (the Small Faces, Kiki Dee) and then-topical pirate radio references. Shampan, however, became increasingly focused on accumulating the rights to film scores and themes – he took control of some 750 when buying Filmusic[17] – and published John Barry's music for *The Ipcress File* (1965) and Manfred Mann and Mike Hugg's score for *Up the Junction*. He was, therefore, well placed to benefit from the expansion of colour television in Britain. When ITV and BBC1 announced that they would introduce colour services in late 1969, the rights that Filmusic held in seventy colour features were expected to generate a 'healthy increase' in performance fees.[18]

Pop: Music/Film/Culture

As the commercial linkages between popular music and cinema strengthened, successful acts were mooted as potential film stars. Those who sold records, the thinking went, might be relied upon to sell cinema tickets, and often to the same people. The established model of a pop star's career was to build a reputation as a musician before using film and television appearances to cement their status as an artist whose status was not entirely reliant on their musical abilities. As George Melly noted:

> The belief that the only path for a pop artist lay in the direction of general acceptance was to persist well into the 60s. The cliché 'I want to be an all-round entertainer' may have become a joke, but it remained the only answer that most pop artists came up with when questioned as to their ambitions.[19]

Although hindsight allows us to understand pop music in terms of its longevity, until the 1960s, few pop artists survived beyond the first flush of their musical popularity without developing parallel, and frequently predominant, careers as actors or song-and-dance men (or women). This, though, should not necessarily be thought of in terms of compromise. Rather, this was simply the way to prolong a career and gain a measure of professional security away from the churn and relentless neophilia of the pop charts.

Tommy Steele, Britain's first indigenous pop star, quickly moved into variety, television and cinema. While *The Tommy Steele Story* (1957), sought only to exploit his musical popularity, Steele's performance in *The Duke Wore Jeans* (1958), wherein he was 'lured into doing a certain amount of acting',[20] persuaded critics to suggest that he might 'outlast the rock 'n' roll era that fostered him'.[21] The prescience of this observation was demonstrated by Steele's subsequent appearances in the big-budget musicals *Half a Sixpence* (1967), reviving a role he had played in the West End, and Disney's *The Happiest Millionaire* (1967). Cilla Black also parlayed pop stardom into a long-running career as a popular entertainer, mostly in television, although she did appear in *Ferry Cross the Mersey* (1964) and *Work is a Four Letter Word* (1967) – for which she also provided the theme song. By contrast, Petula Clark was both an actor and a singer from childhood. Although the success of her recording career reduced the number of film roles that she took, Clark's popularity as a singer led to her casting, alongside Steele, in *Finian's Rainbow* (1968), and also in a musical version of *Goodbye Mr Chips* (1969).

As John Mundy has noted, rock and roll, and the forms of pop it inspired, was only one of a number of musical genres – alongside calypso, skiffle, trad jazz – that were, for a period, deemed 'equally influential'.[22] And just as there was no single conception of popular music, so there was no single conception of the 'popular music film'. The critical and commercial success of the Beatles' cinematic output has retrospectively marginalised films that cannot easily be positioned in relation to *A Hard Day's Night* or *Help!* (1965), or which are compared and found wanting, but we should be careful to recognise the range of productions contemporaneously recognised as being popular music films. Such films might include: *Beat Girl* (1960) which featured Adam Faith and a Barry score;[23] the Cliff Richard vehicles *The Young Ones* (1961), *Summer Holiday* and *Wonderful Life* (1964); jazz-oriented productions such as *All Night Long*, which featured Gerry Mulligan and Charles Mingus, and *Band of Thieves*; juke-box musicals *It's Trad, Dad!* (1962) or *Just for Fun* (1963); shorts such as *The Johnny Leyton Touch* (1961), *Chris Barber Bandstand* (1963) or *Rhythm 'n' Greens* (1964), the last of which saw the Shadows provide a pop-inflected overview of British history; cinemagazines containing concert footage of the Beatles, the Dave Clark Five and the Rolling Stones, amongst others; and newsreel stories about famous musicians.

Indeed, the fact that *Pop Weekly* felt comfortable describing *A Place to Go* (1964) as a 'major' pop music film, on the strength of it featuring Mike Sarne, suggests that adopting a less-blinkered view about what constitutes a pop film allows for a surer grasp of popular music culture and popular music cinema.[24] Although Sarne might be remembered as a director whose career was all but destroyed by *Myra Breckinridge* (1970), he released a series of singles in 1962 and early 1963, the first of which, 'Come Outside', topped the charts. Similarly generous definitions were still being used in July 1969, when the *New Musical Express* (*NME*) noted that although that year's 'expected pop film blitz' had been reduced to 'no more than a light summer shower' following the cancellation of films starring the Bee Gees, the Rolling Stones and Lulu, readers would 'not . . . find music missing from the screen of your holiday resort cinema'. New films or re-releases that the *NME* thought its readers might enjoy included *The Sound of Music* (recommended by 'no less a rugged character' than the Who's Keith Moon), Barbra Streisand's *Funny Girl* (1968), and *Take a Girl Like You* (1969), featuring Noel Harrison, who had recorded 'The Windmills of Your Mind' for *The Thomas Crown Affair* (1968).[25]

Because popular music was conceptualised as malleable and pluralistic, it could be incorporated into established film styles. Cliff Richard's cinematic career exemplifies the way in which rock and roll, and pop, stardom could be imbricated within the cultural-commercial mainstream. In his first films, the dramas *Serious Charge* (1958) and *Expresso Bongo* (1959), rock and roll was shown as a novelty, and its fans as potential delinquents. Yet in his subsequent musicals, the number of songs performed in a style speaking to Cliff's rock and roll roots is reduced with each successive film; the music is sanitised and merged with pre-existing forms of music and film to create a pop-rock hybrid aimed at youngsters but safe for all to enjoy.[26]

The Young Ones and *Summer Holiday* were, according to the *Motion Picture Herald*, the second most-successful films at British cinemas in 1962 and 1963, respectively.[27] The same surveys also named Cliff as the most-popular film star in Britain. Record sales were equally strong and both soundtracks spent months in the charts. In Britain alone, 'The Young Ones' single sold more than 900,000 copies,[28] whilst 'Summer Holiday' was one of the records that kept the Beatles' 'Please Please Me' from the number-one spot. The tables soon turned, however, and despite *Disc* carrying side-by-side rave reviews of the soundtrack albums of both *Wonderful Life* and *A Hard Day's Night*, only one of these films was commercially successful. *Wonderful Life* lost money (although some of the records associated with it were popular) and Cliff's moment as film star passed.[29] The pop musical moved in a different direction, engaging with pop *qua* pop, whilst Cliff took advantage of pop's increasing stability to continue his career as a singer and TV star.

Cliff's musicals were shot in colour and in widescreen, their higher budgets demonstrating their elevated status. Colour was only granted to the Beatles in their second feature outing, *Help!*, an American poster for which demonstrated that film's determination to promote its polychromatic nature: 'The Colorful Adventures of the Beatles are more colorful than ever . . . in color!' Cinema technology afforded pop acts certain advantages – colour, high-definition images, high-fidelity sound – whilst films' longer running times allowed for the incorporation of numerous songs, making them ideal vehicles for more lucrative LPs.

However, feature films took a long time to produce, a notable disadvantage given that pop traded in the new. They could also struggle to capture the vitality and spontaneity of pop (sometimes because of a pop star's lack of screen presence). Consequently, to boost record and ticket sales, media strategies blended occasional film work with regular television, radio, press and magazine appearances. These were complementary, not competing, media, each of which had its own strengths. Television and radio, for example, had shorter lead-times and a voracious hunger for new content, suiting them to the promotion of a new single.[30]

Before 1960, pop music programming on television and radio tended to be, in Ian Inglis' words, 'intermittent and desultory'.[31] Moreover, it presented popular music in a largely undifferentiated manner, as turns on a variety bill.[32] However, the increasing power of the pop pound brought about the expansion of pop provision across a range of media, an expansion which raised the profile of, and bestowed greater legitimacy upon, the cultural preferences of youth. Magazines that had previously focused on films began to dedicate space to popular music (*Photoplay* made the Stones its Group of the Month in March 1964 and provided an 'ABC of Mick Jagger' in December the same year),[33] whilst cinema circuit magazines such as *ABC Film Review* enthusiastically promoted pop stars.

Alongside publications dedicated to individual acts such as the Beatles and Gerry and the Pacemakers, the music press expanded in 1963 and 1964 with the introduction of a range of glossy magazines such as *Pop Weekly* and *Rave*. Television programmes such as *Ready Steady Go* and *Top of the Pops* generated a 'right-here-right-now buzz' that also re-energised pre-existing shows like *Thank Your Lucky Stars*.[34] A compressed-for-TV version of the Beatles, *The Monkees* was first broadcast in Britain in December 1966 and detailed the lives of an imaginary band (which, ironically, became a hugely successful act in its own right). As importantly, the arrival of the first pirate station, Radio Caroline, in spring 1964, was a sign, according to Christopher Booker's gloomy prognosis, that 'the kingdom of the teenager was at hand'.[35] Although pop became increasingly accessible across a range of media, a process that might possibly have lessened cinema's usefulness to pop acts, films continued to offer unique pleasures: 90-minute features allowed fans more time in the company of their favourite artists than other media.

Stones I: Earlier Unmade Films

From late 1963 onwards, it seems like every other edition of *Melody Maker*, *NME* or *Disc* carried news of planned pop films. One brief article in a January 1964 edition of *Pop Weekly*, for example, mentioned the cinematic ambitions of the Searchers, Freddie and the Dreamers, the Beatles, Billy J. Kramer and Mike Sarne.[36] In such circumstances, it is not surprising to find the Rolling Stones seeking to line up a film appearance. The Stones' co-manager Andrew Oldham understood that it was possible to raise the band's profile simply by presenting the music press with 'waffle' about plans to step before the cameras.[37] It is therefore difficult to tell which of the Stones' purported film projects were real, and which were just ballyhoo. Either way, stories of the Stones and the cinema suggest that films were still considered to matter, both because they continued to enjoy an elevated cultural status in relation to pop music (to anchor a film was to have one's status as star formally recognised), and also because film was a viable commercial medium through which bands might generate income.

In November 1963, just weeks after *Kine Weekly* first carried news of a Beatles film,[38] *Pop Weekly* reported that:

> The Rolling Stones, top R&B group from London, are likely to be filming in the New Year! Co-manager Andrew Oldham could not confirm any of the plans, but hinted at strong possibilities around May/June. The feature film is likely to be shot in colour.[39]

Whilst it is possible that the Stones' management was involved in genuine negotiations, the fact that the readers of *Pop Weekly* had to be reminded (or informed) who the Rolling Stones were suggests that Oldham was seeking to publicise a band which had only recently released its second single and whose first gig outside London had only taken place four months previously. In contrast with pop compendium films such as *Every Day's a Holiday* (1964), which featured John Leyton, Mike Sarne and Freddie and the Dreamers – and which was at one point believed to have a 'good chance' of also featuring the Rolling Stones[40] – the proposed film would have privileged the Stones, alone. This worked to align the Stones' film with the Beatles', the band in whose wake all pop groups trailed and whose success they all hoped to emulate. Oldham's claim that the Stones' film would probably be made in colour, which would have placed it in the minority of British productions in 1964, suggests that the success of the project was more likely to be measured in column inches than footage shot. Also intended to raise the Stones' profile and position the band at the forefront of the coming pop wave were stories about movies being written by Lionel Bart, co-produced by Peter Sellers, directed by Clive Donner or featuring guest appearances by Peter O'Toole.[41]

Other projects appear to have enjoyed a greater grounding in reality, although the vagaries of the production sector meant that many films were never made. In spring 1964, for instance, Michael Winner was informed by renter-turned-producer E. J. Fancey that he'd set up a meeting with the Stones' management to discuss a film.[42] Fancey was an exploitation film-maker who had been involved with *Rock You Sinners* (1957), a primitive British rock film, and his connection with the project, and seeming willingness to pass it on to Winner, a relatively inexperienced director, suggests that this would not have been a prestige production. Even Charlie Watts, who mentioned Fancey's Border Films in relation to the unnamed feature, conceded that the script 'was not marvellous ... it's not going to win us any Academy Awards or anything'.[43]

What's more, Fancey does not seem to have been entirely convinced of the Stones' star potential: 'They're so ugly we'll 'ave to make an 'aunted 'ouse film with 'em! That's all you could do with 'em, 'aunt an 'ouse!'[44] Whilst what some commentators have regarded as the band's lack of conventional photogenicity – 'as various in their ugliness as the Beatles were indistinguishable in prettiness'[45] – appears to have counted against them, the popsploitation film's privileging of music and musicians would likely have rendered this point largely moot.[46] Oldham's decision to position the Stones in opposition to the Beatles was a more difficult problem to overcome. Whereas Beatlemania was reported largely positively by a slightly bewildered press, the Stones became a lightning rod for adults concerned about the younger generation's prospects and attitudes. Even the Stones' hair was compared unfavourably with the Beatles'.[47] The Beatles were seen as professionals who could take direction and behave in front of the cameras; the Stones, whose 'catarrhal grunts' on *Juke Box Jury* in July 1964 failed to win over new fans, were not.[48] The Stones, Oldham and his amanuenses often claimed, were surly, uncooperative and unapologetic, as were those other great, 'loud ... and rebellious' unfilmed bands of the era, the Kinks and the Who.[49] And although the Stones' reputation excited those who bought their records, it led many of those who might be asked to finance feature films to fight shy of the band. As Oldham noted, 'the rebel image that had worked for them in rock worked against them' in the cinema.[50] Would you let your company produce a feature for the Rolling Stones?

Much of the impetus for the Stones' entry into cinema came from Oldham, who claimed to have been 'seduced and hooked ... instantly' by the French *Nouvelle Vague* to the extent that he adopted the clothes and mannerisms of some of its most influential figures and sought to pass these on to the Stones.[51] Oldham did not want his involvement to end with the setting up of a Stones film, and reports concerning many of the band's cinematic projects noted that he – and in some instances Allen Klein, who joined the band's management in 1965 – was also to produce, possibly through his own company.[52] From his earliest days with the Stones, Oldham had carved out a position for himself in relation to the band and the music industry that extended beyond simple management: he produced the band's records (although how much influence he had on their sound remains open to question), shaped their image, and in 1965 founded the Immediate record label.

In attempting to move beyond talent management, Oldham's career paralleled Brian Epstein's, who enjoyed fame as the Beatles' manager and the businessman who ran NEMS Enterprises. Having committed the Beatles to a three-picture deal with United Artists, Epstein recognised that Beatlemania afforded him the power to maintain greater control over films featuring other NEMS acts and to retain a greater proportion of the revenues that they generated. In 1964, as part of a 'major thrust into spheres of the entertainment industry above and beyond artist management', Epstein associated himself with four film companies.[53] It is difficult to ascertain the precise nature and extent of Epstein's involvement in three of these: Long Distance Films, where he joined Tony Richardson, John Osborne, Karel Reisz and Oscar Lewenstein as a director; Woodfall Films, in which he made a 'substantial but not *very* substantial' investment;[54] and Pickfair Films, which he set up with George 'Bud' Ornstein, who had contracted the Beatles whilst head of European production at United Artists.[55] Epstein was, however, more actively involved in Subafilms Ltd, which he established to make *Ferry Cross the Mersey* for United Artists. Epstein produced the film, which featured Gerry and the Pacemakers, Cilla Black and the Fourmost, all Epstein artists, and used his connection with Richardson and Osborne to bring on board producer Michael Holden, who had worked on *Tom Jones* (1963).[56]

Epstein wanted to become an impresario whose reach extended across the popular arts. He leased London's Saville Theatre and put on pop concerts and works by Arnold Wesker;[57] he wanted to publish both film and pop music;[58] he wanted Pickfair to make *Woman on Horseback*, the tale of Eliza Lynch, an 'Irish redhead who became the mistress of [the] dictator of Paraguay during... the War of the Triple Alliance,' and *A Talent For Loving*, a comedy/western that would have fulfilled the Beatles' obligations to United Artists.[59] These wider artistic ambitions remained largely unfulfilled, and Epstein enjoyed his greatest commercial successes through his continued association with pop music in general, and the Beatles in particular. Subafilms was involved in the production of *Help!*, *Yellow Submarine* (1968) and *The Beatles at Shea Stadium* (TV, 1966), and co-secured the rights to film the 1965 National Jazz and Blues Festival. It was also mentioned in connection with a proposal to make a TV pilot that looked to 'develop [the Who] into Britain's answer to *The Monkees*,'[60] and was a pioneer in the field of the pop promo, selling films to American television programmes such as *Where the Action Is*, *Shindig* and *Hullabaloo*.[61]

In their attempts to seek out new opportunities across different media industries, Epstein and Oldham mirror, on a smaller scale, the trend towards diversification in the British leisure sector. Although many companies remained committed to production and distribution of cultural goods or services in a single medium, and so continued to see these media as discrete and competitive, others came to view the leisure industry as a single large market. The Beatles' Apple Corps – which operated a record label, a retail department, an electronics division, a music-publishing company and a film company that produced, amongst others, *Magical Mystery Tour* (TV, 1967), *Yellow Submarine* and *Let It Be* (1970) – stands as perhaps the most hubristic example of this tendency towards multi-media and multi-sector business strategies.

Stones II: Later Unmade Films

Despite increasing media convergence, the differing commercial and cultural rhythms of the film and music industries could still work to stymie a pop group's feature-film career. This was especially true during the winter production crisis of 1963/4, which coincided with the onset of Beatlemania and the unprecedented success of British acts in America; both symptoms of a pop explosion that carried youth-oriented music into the mainstream. Artists who made films saw their releases held up: 'About six companies already have small pop films "on the shelf" but cannot release them.'[62] Emergent acts such as the Rolling Stones found it harder to get film projects off the ground.

The Stones soon found themselves facing other difficulties. As Peter Whitehead, director of *Charlie Is My Darling*, told Oldham, problems with any proposed Stones feature related to the band's increasing prominence: by the end of 1965 they were 'too big to do anything less than a great success Hollywood type picture'. The mistake, Whitehead suggested, was that the band had not made a low-budget, relatively low-risk film 'during and before their [early] success'.[63] In two years, the Stones had gone from groundlessly boasting about their cinematic future, to fearing that appearing in a poorly produced and lukewarmly received film might damage their reputation. This was especially true in the wake of *A Hard Day's Night*, the commercial and critical success of which raised the bar unrealistically high as far as subsequent pop films, including the Beatles' later cinematic efforts, were concerned. Whilst an ostensibly second-tier act such as the Small Faces or the Spencer Davis Group might get away with appearing in a slightly creaky supporting feature such as *Dateline Diamonds* or *The Ghost Goes Gear* (1966), and Herman's Hermits or Freddie and the Dreamers could churn out film after sub-par film, this was not the case for the Rolling Stones. Unlike the Beatles, whose unprecedented popularity allowed them to swat aside middling reviews to ride *Help!* all the way to the bank, the Stones were not, until 1967, too big to fail. Their spot in the limelight had been afforded them through the quality of their music, their rebellious bravado and their swaggering aura of churlish invincibility. Not for the Stones, then, the option of playing 'It's All Over Now' for a crowd of excitable teens in *Gonks Go Beat*.

However, the pop film, like pop music, was not static. Diverging from the exploitation formula that had worked in the early 1960s, working through transitional texts such as the melancholic *Catch Us If You Can* (1965) and the anarchic *Help!*, and working in parallel to the increasingly prevalent pop-rock documentary/concert film, the British pop film arrived at its 'decadent' phase in the later years of the decade.[64] Here, the Stones' image allowed them to toy with stories beyond the range of other bands. As Mick Jagger observed in 1966:

> I can't see, for instance, Ringo [Starr] with a gun in his hand and being nasty in a movie and going to kill somebody. It just wouldn't happen. But I don't think you'd think it was very peculiar if you saw Brian [Jones] do it.[65]

Whilst this observation offers amateur psychologists an intriguing insight into Jagger's deteriorating relationship with Jones, whose increasingly erratic behaviour would prompt his departure from the Stones in 1969, more important is the fact that by this point a pop star could openly discuss making a film in which one of his bandmates might shoot someone. Clearly, the Stones' assiduously cultivated image, previously so difficult to accommodate within a feature film, was becoming less problematic. This is not to say that all pop films suddenly took a turn to the dark – the relentlessly cheerful *Mrs Brown, You've Got a Lovely Daughter*, starring Herman's Hermits and produced, incidentally by Allen Klein, was released in late 1968 – but as the decade progressed, the more adversarial positions adopted by pop music made it easier for pop films to embrace more complex and controversial themes. To this end, we should not be surprised that Michelangelo Antonioni considered engaging the Stones – and their anti-Establishment baggage – for the nightclub scene in *Blow Up* (1966) which eventually featured the Yardbirds.[66]

The move towards more serious material was also linked to changes in the film industry that dramatically reduced the number of low-budget exploitation pictures going into production.[67] The pop musical was one of the casualties; the genre – understood as broadly as possible – had never been integral to the British film industry, the success of the Cliff and Beatles films and a couple of smaller hits notwithstanding. Nevertheless, popular musicians were still worked into film narratives, both to increase appeal to a youthful demographic and to add a contemporary British feel. This had happened earlier, of course: the Zombies had been inserted almost at random into Otto Preminger's *Bunny Lake is Missing* (1965), but the trend continued throughout the decade, with the Pretty Things performing in *What's Good for the Goose* (1969), for example. For the artists concerned, such appearances could be enticingly remunerative: the Spencer Davis Group was paid £1,710 for recording songs for, and briefly appearing in, *Here We Go Round the Mulberry Bush* (1968).[68]

The decline of the popsploitation film created new, potentially more satisfying, opportunities for musicians hankering after film stardom. Now, the films in which they appeared were not necessarily required to revolve around pop music, and their presence no longer automatically signified low-grade material. The musician as extra-textual star was central to such productions: they might contribute music to the soundtrack, but these new productions were understood as films, not opportunities to promote records. Paul Jones' appearance in *Privilege* (1967), set in a dystopian near-future, can be understood as fitting this trend. Formerly the lead singer of Manfred Mann, Jones recorded vocals for three songs on the soundtrack, but despite this, and the fact that he played a pop star in the film, *Privilege*'s jaundiced view of pop music as a sinister vehicle for totalitarianism precludes it being understood as a conventional pop film. Jones admitted that he had passed on the roles offered to him prior to *Privilege*: '[The parts] were lousy. They were pop films, all about groups. *Privilege* is still pop, but oh, what a difference. The story is good'.[69]

John Lennon used Richard Lester's *How I Won the War* (1967) to distance himself from his previous incarnation as mop-topped pop star. Lennon cut his hair and donned 'National Health goggles' for his role as Musketeer Gripweed, a character that *Rave* warned was a 'rotten type who thieves from the bodies of dead soldiers'.[70] Lennon's presence in *How I Won the War* promised to benefit both artist and production. For Lennon, it was an opportunity to participate in a film that did not ask him to play a version of himself; he did not contribute to the soundtrack and used the 'anti-war-film film' to burnish his image as a serious cultural figure.[71] For the film, Lennon was a useful promotional tool; he received second billing, behind Michael Crawford, and a caricature of his face featured on many posters. *Rave* did not like *How I Won the War*, but noted of its readers, 'No doubt you'll be going anyway because it is John Lennon's solo film debut': the film's narrative and politics mattered less than its co-star.[72]

The Rolling Stones' association with two ultimately unrealised film projects, *A Clockwork Orange* and *Only Lovers Left Alive*, indicates the way in which the group and its management wanted to use the cinema to exploit and underline the band's reputation. Oldham had been interested in Anthony Burgess' *A Clockwork Orange* since its publication in 1962, and regarded it as a suitable vehicle for the Stones.[73] He failed to option the book, but lobbied for the Stones' inclusion in any adaptation; this might not have displeased Burgess, who believed that Jagger 'looked the quintessence of delinquency'.[74] Although *A Clockwork Orange* suited the Stones' public profile, it is unclear how serious Oldham's plans were, not least because any screenplay that cleaved to Burgess' story was likely to antagonise the BBFC.[75] Again, associating the band with the book was perhaps as important as actually making the film.

Dave Wallis' 1964 novel *Only Lovers Left Alive* – 'a sort of poor man's ... *Clockwork Orange*'[76] – came closer to entering production. Wallis's book imagined how Britain might develop following the suicide of the entire adult population and was considered an apt choice given the Stones' perceived tendency to 'hit out in rage, almost in blind anger and certainly with overtones of destructiveness, against the adult world'.[77] It was certainly too much for the Dave Clark Five, who passed on the 'horrific' story: 'It just wasn't our image – maybe the Stones are more suited to it.'[78] Keith Waterhouse and Willis Hall – whose *Billy Liar* might have appealed to, or even echoed, the fantasist in Oldham – were engaged to write a screenplay;[79] Nicholas Ray was approached to direct.[80] Reports circulated that *Only Lovers . . .* would have £1 million budget – the band would have enjoyed a handsome payday for the accompanying soundtrack album – and *Rave* claimed that it would be shot in a style influenced by Ingmar Bergman, a Jagger favourite.[81]

Rather than casting the Stones as a band – in what Jagger feared would be 'another pop stars on ice fiasco'[82] – they would appear in *Only Lovers . . .* as 'character actors',[83] as had the musicians appearing in *Catch Us If You Can*, *Privilege* and *How I Won the War*. Oldham was, though, quick to allay fan concerns: the Stones would play 'a basic projection of themselves in the film situation'.[84] Wallis, however, was unhappy about the Stones starring in an adaptation of his work, and his wife stated, 'I don't see it being a serious subject with those people in it, do you?'[85] Jagger diplomatically noted, 'I wouldn't condemn a film as bad until I'd seen it' and insisted that the Stones had 'every intention of treating this film as seriously as the subject demands'.[86]

Again, the project ran into problems. Films are made with an eye to the box office and potential audience engagement needs to be considered. For all that Wallis's work was not as contentious as that of Joe Orton – whose 'dark, sexually ambiguous' screenplay *Up Against It* was written for the Beatles and rejected by Epstein[87] – it was still likely to have been given an X certificate by the BBFC. Restricting entry to over-sixteens meant that many Stones fans would be too young to gain admission; the pop press received letters from readers anxious that having waited patiently for a Stones film, they might not be able to watch it when it was finally released.[88] This was a quandary that many bands were unable to solve: the youthfulness of potential audience members militated against the inclusion of adult themes; as pop mutated into rock – a more self-consciously serious form of music which understood itself as both an artistic and commercial enterprise – its aesthetic pretensions discouraged youth-oriented narratives.

Needless to say, the Stones' did not make *Only Lovers Left Alive*. In November 1966, Brian Jones was photographed wearing a Nazi uniform, prompting public outrage. In January 1967, the band were derided for their point-blank refusal to stand on the revolving stage and wave to the audience following an appearance on the *London Palladium Show*. The following month, the police raided Keith Richards' Redlands property looking for drugs, and the subsequent legal proceedings – in which butterflies were broken upon wheels – put any film project on hold. Moreover, Oldham, the driving force behind the Stones' cinematic endeavours, was becoming progressively less influential, his fragile emotional state and fear of arrest on drugs charges distancing him from a band whose increasing confidence in their status and talent as musicians made them less reliant upon his PR nous.[89]

The Redlands affair and Jones' own drugs bust put the kibosh on *Only Lovers Left Alive*, but were not entirely bad news, cinematically speaking. Uncertain as to whether Jagger and Richards' convictions – soon overturned on appeal – would prevent them from performing their new single on *Top of the Pops*, Oldham engaged Peter Whitehead to direct a promotional short for 'We Love You'. The film, which drew parallels between the treatment meted out to Jagger and Richards and the trial of Oscar Wilde, also featured Marianne Faithfull, a pop star who enjoyed more success as an actor than her then partner Mick Jagger, appearing on the stage and in *I'll Never Forget What's 'is Name* (1967), *Girl on a Motorcycle* (1968) and *Hamlet* (1969). In keeping with the Stones' cinematic travails, the BBC refused to broadcast 'We Love You', although the fact that the film was shot in colour suggests that it was made to be shown elsewhere, too.[90]

Oldham later pronounced that the failure to get *Only Lovers . . .* off the ground left the Stones' film career 'dead'.[91] However, his departure from the band might have obscured from him some subsequent projects that – predictably – came to nought. In December 1967 Jagger authorised the Stones' solicitors to prepare an agreement with an Indian production company to prepare a treatment for a film based upon *Sir Gawain and the Green Knight*[92] – 'Mick and Keith do the Middle Ages! Who was going to cut off whose head was a subject of much discussion, but at least they could both wear tights,' recalled Faithfull.[93] Another unrealised production gloried in the title of *Maxigasm*; made from a '"trippy" science-fiction script' featuring 'a colony of hermaphrodite "sky people"', the film was to be produced by Carlo Ponti and star Mick, Keith and Brian.[94] On the scrapheap of unmade Stones films, it joined *Back, Behind and in Front* – to be shot partially behind the Iron Curtain, and for which was a precise start date was given: 10 or 19 April 1966, depending on who you believed[95] – *The Assassination of Mick Jagger* – supposedly involving David Bailey[96] – and *When the Kissing Had to Stop*, based on Constantine FitzGibbon's novel.[97]

CONCLUSION

Although the Rolling Stones never appeared together in a feature film, Mick Jagger brought elements of the band with him to his first solo role in *Performance*. The singer portrayed the reclusive, creatively frustrated rock star Turner, aping the appearance of one bandmate (Keith Richards) and the manner of another (Brian Jones).[98] Although Jagger's participation was 'the very condition of the film's existence', it is difficult to discern exactly what it was that Warner Bros., which funded *Performance* to the tune of $1.5 million, expected from the movie.[99] True, Jagger was famous as the charismatic frontman of one of the most successful bands in the world. But he was an untried actor, and his involvement was not guaranteed to translate into ticket sales – not least because *Performance* was conceived by writer/co-director Donald Cammell, and producer Sandy Lieberson (who as Jagger's agent for film and television work played an important role in putting the film together), as a troubling, brooding meditation on identity and creativity: the 'antithesis of *Summer Holiday*'.[100] One might expect, then, that Jagger's appeal would be associated with the music he brought to the project. After all, *A Hard Day's Night* had proved more successful at the box office than most people anticipated, but United Artists had financed the film in order to secure the American distribution rights to its soundtrack album – advance sales of which exceeded one million units and so ensured that the film was in profit before it premiered.[101] Further, Decca, the Stones' British label, had been willing to finance mid-1960s Stones movies in return for the soundtrack rights – a first for a British record company.[102] Yet *Performance* guaranteed Warner Bros. Records Jagger's vocals on a single track: Jagger eventually delivered 'Memo From Turner', the tortured genesis of which owed much to the did-they-didn't-they nature of Jagger's sex scenes with Richards' then partner (and Jones' former partner), Anita Pallenberg. Although early reports suggested that Jagger might contribute to the score, music was instead composed by Jack Nitzsche.[103] Indeed, one wonders whether Warner Bros., which did not release *Performance* in the States until July 1970, and even then in a fairly half-hearted manner following a re-edit that provided less violence, less sex, but more Mick, might have promoted the film more enthusiastically had it come attached to a blockbuster soundtrack.[104]

Warner's uncertainty about how to market *Performance*, its lack of clarity about how to maximise its prospects, exemplifies the idea that although the film and music industries recognised the benefits that each offered the other, they were unable to regularly find a way to realise them. As Andy Medhurst observes, these were 'two constituencies never quite speaking the same language but carrying out a conversation nevertheless.'[105] This conversation could occasionally prove harmonious, as the success of the Cliff Richard musicals and *A Hard Day's Night* demonstrate. But these films were unusual: Cliff's movies were traditional musicals repackaged with a pop veneer, whereas the Beatles' first film was a complete outlier in terms of quality and popularity.

Indeed, *A Hard Day's Night* has skewed our understanding of what a pop film might be, obscuring both Cliff's success and the diversity of pop-related films produced in the 1960s. It has come to be seen not as atypical, but as the marker against which other pop music films should be measured; not as an exploitation quickie made to milk the Beatles' possibly transient popularity, but as a document of the excitement surrounding the phenomenon they exemplified; not just as a film, but as a demonstration that pop's vitality can be communicated via the cinema as well as via television, the medium which has probably done more to preserve the sixties pop moment. That the Rolling Stones never made a feature film was not for lack of trying, but this failure did not hold them back. If the pop film exists to market an act, then the feature-length documentaries in which the Stones appeared did that, complementing their appearances on television and in the print media. Pop's cultural and commercial value made it attractive to a film industry looking to maintain its relevance in an increasingly crowded media marketplace. In 1970, George Melly suggested that pop culture in general, and pop music in particular, had 'profoundly affected the way we live now', bringing about and/or responding to social and cultural changes that resonated beyond the bedrooms, discotheques, boutiques and coffee bars of teenage fans.[106] But Melly was confident that pop culture, like pop music, was essentially disposable, meaningful only within the moment of its production and forever destined to be superseded by something new. The sustained interest in sixties pop music, and the films that emerged from it, tells us as much about how subsequent generations remember and venerate 1960s pop music, as it does about the position of pop in that decade. The 'now' that Melly described has passed, but the music remains: pop was the bubble that did not burst.

NOTES

1. Stanley Booth, *The True Adventures of the Rolling Stones* (London: Heinemann, 1985), see e.g. pp. 177, 178.
2. David E. James, *Rock 'n' Film: Cinema's Dance with Popular Music* (Oxford: Oxford University Press, 2016), p. 307.
3. Peter Newbrook on *Gonks Go Beat*: '[The Stones] had just broken through and they wouldn't do it for what we could pay them, and at the eleventh hour they pulled out.' Quoted in Michael Ahmed, 'Corrupted, Tormented and Damned: Reframing British Exploitation Cinema and the Films of Robert Hartford-Davis', PhD thesis, UEA, 2013, p. 145.
4. See Katherine Spring, *Saying It With Songs: Popular Music and the Coming of Sound to Hollywood Cinema* (Oxford: Oxford University Press, 2013).
5. Dave Harker, *One for the Money: Politics and Popular Song* (London: Hutchinson, 1980), p. 99, p. 226.
6. *The Economist*, 20 September 1958, p. 971.
7. Carolyn Downs, 'Mecca and the birth of commercial bingo 1958–70: A case study', *Business History*, 52: 7 (2010), p. 1091.
8. *Kine Weekly*, 28 May 1959, p. 24.
9. Other than 1958, when the Broadway recording of *My Fair Lady* topped the chart, between 1956 and 1962 the best-selling album of the year in Britain was a film soundtrack: 1956 – *Carousel*; 1957 –*The King and I*; 1959 and 1960 – *South Pacific*; 1961: *G. I. Blues*; 1962: *West Side Story*, <http://www.officialcharts.com/galleries/the-biggest-selling-album-of-every-year-since-1956/> (accessed: 24 January 2017).

10. *Disc*, 29 April 1961, p. 13.
11. *Melody Maker*, 13 August 1960, p. 1.
12. See Pathé News: 10 May 1962, for Cliff learning to drive a bus in preparation for *Summer Holiday*; 21 October 1965, for Ifield shooting *Up Jumped a Swagman* (1965).
13. *Variety*, 16 March 1966, p. 57; *Kine Weekly*, 3 December 1959, p. 15.
14. *Variety*, 16 March 1966, p. 57.
15. Quoted in *Variety*, 23 October 1963, p. 47.
16. *NME*, 24 January 1964, p. 8.
17. *Variety*, 11 November 1964, p. 55.
18. *Variety*, 15 January 1969, p. 72. These fees might have amounted to $150,000 over five years.
19. George Melly, *Revolt into Style: The Pop Arts in Britain* (Harmondsworth: Penguin, 1972), p. 50.
20. *Variety*, 2 April 1958, p. 16.
21. *Monthly Film Bulletin*, January 1958, p. 61.
22. John Mundy, *The British Musical Film* (Manchester: Manchester University Press, 2007), p. 172.
23. Adam Faith's role in *Beat Girl* was rewritten after 'What Do You Want?', became a hit. Posters for the film promised 'exciting beat tunes sung by Adam Faith'. Stephen Glynn, *The British Pop Music Film: The Beatles and Beyond* (Basingstoke: Palgrave Macmillan, 2013), p. 39.
24. *Pop Weekly*, w/e 25 January 1964, p. 8.
25. *NME*, 5 July 1969, pp. 28, 30.
26. See K. J. Donnelly, 'The Perpetual Busman's Holiday: Sir Cliff Richard and British Pop Musicals', *Journal of Popular Film and Television*, 25: 4 (1998), pp. 146–7. The Cliff Richard musicals were produced by Elstree Films, an ABPC–Grade Organisation joint venture.
27. Results quoted in *The Times*: 4 January 1963, p. 4; 3 January 1964, p. 4. Within ten months of its premiere, *The Young Ones* had been booked for a total of 1,400 weeks. *Kine Weekly*, 11 October 1962, p. 17.
28. *Billboard*, 21 April 1962, p. 22.
29. *Disc*, 4 July 1964, p. 10; Donnelly, 'Perpetual Busman's Holiday', p. 153. On the problems affecting the production of *Wonderful Life*, see Glynn, *British Pop Music Film*, pp. 65–6.
30. Simon Frith, Matt Brennan, Martin Cloonan and Emma Webster, *The History of Live Music in Britain, vol. 1: 1950–1967 – From Dance Hall to the 100 Club* (Farnham: Ashgate, 2013), p. 161.
31. Ian Inglis, 'Here, There and Everywhere: Introducing the Beatles', in Ian Inglis (ed.), *Popular Music and Television in Britain* (Farnham: Ashgate, 2010), p. 180.
32. This practice is shown in *A Hard Day's Night* (the Beatles play the same television show as a conjurer and the Lionel Blair dancers) and *Farewell Performance*, where pop star Ray Baron (David Kernon) is killed by a chimp trainer whose performing primate appears on the same bill.
33. This continued a trend first visible in the late 1950s.
34. Andy Medhurst, 'It sort of happened here: The strange, brief life of the British pop film', in Jonathan Romney and Adrian Wootton (eds), *Celluloid Jukebox: Popular music and the movies since the 50s* (London: BFI, 1995), p. 61.
35. Christopher Booker, *The Neophiliacs: The Revolution in English Life in the Fifties and Sixties* (London: Pimlico, 1992 [1969]), p. 235. Radios Atlanta and London began broadcasting in May and December 1964, respectively.
36. *Pop Weekly*, w/e 25 January 1964, p. 8.

37. Andrew Oldham, *2Stoned* (London: Vintage, 2003), p. 153.
38. *Kine Weekly*, 31 October 1963, p. 5.
39. *Pop Weekly*, w/e 30 November 1963, p. 9.
40. *Disc*, 21 March 1964, p. 4.
41. Oldham, *2Stoned*, p. 153; *Stage*, 9 July 1964, p. 8; *Disc*, 11 April 1964, p. 2; *Australian Women's Weekly*, 23 September 1964, p. 77.
42. Michael Winner, *Winner Takes All: A Life of Sorts* (London: Robson Books, 2005), p. 103.
43. *Disc*, 11 April 1964, p. 2.
44. Winner, *Winner Takes All*, p. 103.
45. David E. James, *Rock 'n' Film: Cinema's Dance with Popular Music* (Oxford: Oxford University Press, 2016), p. 256.
46. Mundy, *British Musical Film*, p. 196.
47. In Coventry, eleven students with Stones-inspired hairstyles were suspended until they 'cut their hair neatly, like the Beatles'. *Daily Mirror*, 27 May 1964, p. 2.
48. *Daily Sketch*, quoted in John McMillan, *Beatles vs. Stones* (New York: Simon & Schuster, 2013), p. 104. When on *Jury* service the Stones made numerous unflattering comments about the records they were asked to judge, thereby cementing their reputation as monosyllabic and petulant.
49. Andrew Caine, *Interpreting Rock Movies: The Pop Film and Its Critics in Britain* (Manchester: Manchester University Press, 2004), p. 188.
50. Andrew Oldham, *Rolling Stoned* (Syracuse, NY: Gegensatz, 2011), p. 303.
51. Oldham, *Rolling Stoned*, pp. 43–5.
52. See, for example, *Rave*, August 1966, p. 31; *Disc*, 8 December 1966, p. 8.
53. *Variety*, 25 March 1964, p. 7.
54. *Financial Times*, 19 March 1964, p. 15.
55. Ray Coleman, *Brian Epstein: The Man Who Made the Beatles* (London: Viking, 1989), pp. 440–3.
56. Brian Epstein, *A Cellarful of Noise* (London: Souvenir Press, 1964), pp. 71–2.
57. *Financial Times*, 29 August 1967, p. 9.
58. *Variety*, 17 May 1967 p. 1.
59. *Boxoffice*, 8 February 1965, p. E4.
60. *NME*, w/e 28 January 1967, pp. 8–9.
61. Tony Bramwell, *Magical Mystery Tours: My Life with the Beatles* (London: Robson Books, 2005), pp. 133–4.
62. *Pop Weekly*, w/e 25 January 1964, p. 8.
63. Whitehead to Oldham, 26 December 1965. In Peter Whitehead, 'Letters to Andrew Oldham', *Framework: The Journal of Cinema and Media*, 52: 1 (2011), p. 202.
64. Glynn, *British Pop Music Film*, pp. 116–63.
65. Jagger quoted in *Melody Maker*, 4 June 1966, p. 10.
66. Whitehead to Andrew Oldham, 30 July 1966. In Whitehead, 'Letters to Andrew Oldham', p. 208. Antonioni also considered using the Who, before settling on the Yardbirds, whom he persuaded to ape elements of the Who's act. See Andy Neill and Matt Kent, *Anyway Anyhow Anywhere: The Complete Chronicle of the Who, 1958–1978* (London: Virgin, 2002), pp. 66–7; John Platt, Chris Dreja, Jim McCarty, *Yardbirds* (London: Sidgwick & Jackson, 1983), p. 109.
67. Robert Murphy, 'Gonks Go Beat', unpublished paper, <http://www.academia.edu/6660851/Gonks_Go_Beat> (accessed 31 May 2017).
68. The *Mulberry Bush* soundtrack featured the Spencer Davis Group and Traffic, featuring ex-Spencer Davis vocalist and keyboardist Stevie Winwood. There were disagreements about sharing a title card and name order. BFI Special Collections,

Clive Donner Papers: Larry Kramer to Chris Blackwell, 15 December 1967; John Martin to Martin Davis, 23 May 1967; George L. Canham to Michael Rabin, 1 June 1967.
69. *Rave*, October 1966, p. 31. Jones' role had previously been offered to the Animals' Eric Burden. In August 1964, the Animals had been discussed in connection with an MGM-financed musical set to feature Stan Getz and Mary Wells; the following month, reports claimed the Animals were set to sign a three-picture, £170,000 deal with Columbia. The Animals eventually stepped before the cameras in *It's a Bikini World* (1967). Glynn, *British Pop Music Film*, p. 121; *Melody Maker*, 1 August 1964, p. 4; *NME*, 18 September 1964, pp. 8–9.
70. Janne Mäkelä, *John Lennon Imagined: Cultural History of a Rock Star* (New York: Peter Lang, 2004), p. 111; *Rave*, November 1967, pp. 26–7. *Rave*'s discussion of 'THAT haircut' included claims that 'quite a few girls we know definitely seem to have gone off him'. *Rave*, October 1966, p. 53. Formatting in original. The man who cut Lennon's hair became a minor celebrity, and was invited to America to appear on television. *Rave*, November 1967, p. 27.
71. Scriptwriter Charles Wood, quoted in *Observer*, 22 October 1967, p. 9.
72. *Rave*, October 1967, p. 8. The other Beatles also struck out on their own: Paul wrote the score for *The Family Way* (1966); Ringo appeared in *Candy* (1968), *The Magic Christian* (1968), *That'll Be the Day* (1973) and *Lisztomania* (1975); George wrote music for *Wonderwall* (1968), produced *Little Malcolm and His Struggle Against the Eunuchs* (1974), appeared in *The Rutles: All You Need is Cash* (TV, 1978), and in 1978 established HandMade Films.
73. Oldham's sleeve notes for the *Rolling Stones No. 2* LP were inspired by Burgess: 'Cast deep into your pockets for loot to buy this disc of groovies and fancy words. If you don't have bread, see that blind man, knock him on the head, steal his wallet and low and behold you have the loot, if you put in the boot, good, another one sold!'
74. Anthony Burgess, *You've Had Your Time: Being the second part of the confessions of Anthony Burgess* (London: Heinemann, 1990), p. 142.
75. A 1967 screenplay by Terry Southern, at one time linked with the Stones, was rejected. James C. Robertson, *The Hidden Cinema: British Film Censorship in Action, 1913–1972* (London: Routledge, 1989), pp. 143–4.
76. Marianne Faithfull, with David Dalton, *Faithfull: An Autobiography* (New York: Cooper Square Press, 2000), pp. 149–50.
77. Ralph J. Gleason, 'Like a Rolling Stone', *American Scholar*, 36: 4 (Autumn 1967), p. 561. One reviewer noted that title, theme and cover photograph of *Only Lovers Left Alive* meant that the book 'already looks like a Rank product'. *Observer*, 21 June 1964, p. 27.
78. *Disc*, 21 May 1966, p. 4.
79. *Kine Weekly*, 30 June 1966, p. 12.
80. *Variety*, 29 June 1966, p. 4.
81. *Rave*, November 1966, p. 36.
82. *Rave*, November 1967, p. 24.
83. *Rave*, August 1966, p. 31.
84. *Disc*, 14 May 1966, p. 6.
85. *Daily Mail*, 16 May 1966, p. 4.
86. *Disc*, 21 May 1966, p. 9. Jagger's placatory tone was undercut by Keith Richards' assertion that Wallis' book was 'crummily written'. *NME*, 27 May 1966, p. 3.
87. Martin King, *Men, Masculinity and the Beatles* (Abingdon: Ashgate, 2013), p. 85. There were rumours that the Stones would make the film instead.
88. See Carole Charing's letter in *Rave*, October 1966, p. 33. 1964 estimates put the

average age of a Rolling Stones fan club member at ten. This probably increased as the band and its music matured. Booker, *Neophiliacs*, p. 221.
89. Booth, *True Adventures*, p. 242.
90. *Rave*, November 1967, p. 24; Bill Wyman, *Stone Alone: The story of a rock 'n' roll band* (London: Viking, 1990), p. 453.
91. *The Guardian*, 6 April 2001, pp. B10–11.
92. Wyman, *Stone Alone*, pp. 483–4.
93. Faithfull, with Dalton, *Faithfull*, pp. 149–50.
94. Christopher Sandford, *The Rolling Stones: Fifty Years* (London: Simon & Schuster, 2012), p. 179; *NME*, 21 September 1968, p. 8. Wyman (*Stone Alone*, p. 484): 'Charlie and I were obviously regarded as "too straight" and not "hip" enough.'
95. *Melody Maker*, 18 December 1965, p. 4; *Rave*, April 1966, p. 53.
96. *Disc*, 8 December 1966, p. 8; Michael Gross, *Focus: The secret, sexy, sometimes sordid world of fashion photographers* (New York: Atria Books, 2016), p. 123.
97. Bryan Forbes claims that Klein and Oldham approached him to direct the film; Oldham disputes this. Bryan Forbes, *A Divided Life* (London: Heinemann, 1992), pp. 326–7; Oldham, *2Stoned*, p. 160.
98. Philip Norman, *The Stones* (London: Elm Tree, 1984), p. 247. Poor old Bill and Charlie, marginalised again.
99. Colin MacCabe, *Performance* (London: BFI, 1998), p. 34.
100. Caine, *Interpreting Rock Movies*, p. 188.
101. Alexander Walker, *Hollywood, England: The British Film Industry in the Sixties* (London: Michael Joseph, 1974), pp. 230–2, 241; *Variety*, 1 July 1964, p. 1.
102. *Variety*, 1 September 1965, p. 47.
103. *Boxoffice*, 17 June 1968, p. SE2.
104. *Performance* was released in Britain in January 1971, enjoying a better critical reception than it had in the US.
105. Medhurst, 'It sort of happened here', p. 62.
106. Melly, *Revolt into Style*, p. 223.

CONCLUSION

Duncan Petrie and Melanie Williams

A principal consideration underpinning the research project from which this book derives has been the extent to which British cinema in the 1960s was characterised by both transformation and tradition, change and continuity. Perhaps unsurprisingly, there is ample evidence throughout the preceding

Figure C.1 Simultaneously mocking *and* backing Britain towards the end of the sixties: the closing shot of *Carry On Up the Khyber* (Gerald Thomas, 1968).

chapters of transformation and change, closely intertwined with wider developments in British culture of the period. This historical moment of modernity, defined by youth's growing power, greater sexual permissiveness, booming consumerism, and new levels of social and geographical mobility, left an indelible mark on the production, style and content of films made during the decade. Other shifts within the operations of the British film industry at the time were more specific to the cinema, including the escalation of American investment in British production (although it was partly driven by the growing sense of excitement around broader British popular culture, particularly music), the eclipse of black-and-white features by colour production and the demise of the 'B' movie, the intensification of freelance and transmedia work for many of its creative personnel, and a greater sense of connectivity between film and other media and creative industries. Many of these diverse, intersecting developments in British cinema during the 1960s suggested an industry fully participating in the decade's overall milieu of innovation and experimentation.

But, as we have seen, not everything was subject to change, and tradition and continuity exerted a strong pull. The basic structure of the industry remained largely constant throughout, dominated by familiar and long-established companies, mostly led by middle-aged men of predominantly conservative tastes and habits. Despite being challenged from certain quarters, UK film policy continued to support the industry through what had become the familiar mechanisms of the National Film Finance Corporation and the Eady Levy. Some aspects of film technology, production protocol, and creative labour changed dramatically, but others remained essentially the same. And while a new generation of film-makers and stars emerged in the 1960s, many veterans both in front of and behind the camera also continued to flourish.

Sometimes the old and the new co-existed alongside each other in unexpected ways. Asked to name his favourite film star during a press conference at the height of Beatlemania, George Harrison cited Margaret Rutherford, then best known for playing elderly village detective Miss Marple, rather than any of the more obvious youthful choices.[1] The citation is jokey but intriguing and obliquely telling: the Beatles may have been the most culturally prominent exemplars of the 'British invasion' in the sixties, but someone like Rutherford, representing a completely different model of British identity, also enjoyed significant international reach and success both in her role as Agatha Christie's Marple in consecutive MGM British productions as well as in her Oscar-winning turn as a dotty aristocrat in the star-studded *The V.I.P.s* (1963), directed by another British veteran enjoying renewed sixties success, Anthony Asquith. Examples such as these suggest the co-existence, and sometimes mutual admiration, of styles of film-making running the full sixties gamut from charmingly residual to thrillingly emergent.

Ironically, the former has often stood the test of time better than the latter, with many of the most archetypally sixties films, most notably those associated with 'swinging London' or psychedelia, now looking very much like period pieces. But other British productions from the 1960s are much more readily relatable to the style and content of contemporary films, to the extent that the decade could arguably be regarded as the starting point for modern British cinema. The lasting influence of the likes of *A Taste of Honey* and *Kes* on social realism, of *Performance* on the crime film, of *2001: A Space Odyssey* on science fiction, of *A Hard Day's Night* and *Help!* on the pop film, or the original Bond films on the subsequent additions to the series and its broader derivatives are only some of the most outstanding examples.

Beyond this sense of inauguration, several other aspects of 1960s British cinema have proven notably enduring or prophetic. The first of these concerns is the efficacy of the concept of the national. The perennial presence of Hollywood companies, the significance of the Film Europe phenomenon of the inter-war period, and the defining cosmopolitanism of the film-production community have generated a great deal of insightful commentary on how British cinema was connected to or dependent on external developments and activities. But the 1960s witnessed an intensification of this transnationalism that was to have major and lasting consequences. The retrenchment of many of the US studios at the end of the decade may have brought Alexander Walker's concept of 'Hollywood, England' to a close, but the ties remained, and the Americans continued to be attracted to making films in London by the facilities, expertise, and policy incentives such as Eady and from the 1990s various lottery and tax benefits. Consequently, the importance of big-budget 'inward investment' movies made in UK studios today – including the James Bond, *Harry Potter* and *Star Wars* franchises – to the health of the local industry cannot be overemphasised.

The 1960s also saw the beginning of much greater and more habitual mobility on the part of creative personnel. This not only led to many foreign film-makers contributing to British cinema, it also created opportunities for a greater number of British directors, actors, cinematographers and other specialists to begin to take jobs overseas, most notably in the United States. Pathfinders in this respect included Tony Richardson, who directed *Sanctuary* (1961) and *The Loved One* (1965) in Hollywood, John Boorman with *Point Blank* (1967) and *Hell in the Pacific* (1968), Peter Yates with *Bullitt* (1968) and John Schlesinger with *Midnight Cowboy* (1969), subsequently followed in the early 1970s by Karel Reisz, Jack Clayton, Michael Winner, and others. Previously, critic Barrie Day noted in 1969, there had been 'a tradition of an English director being given a job in Hollywood [. . .] and the system would suddenly swamp him' but 'suddenly this is not necessarily true anymore'.[2] Rather, 'internationalisation' of that kind became increasingly commonplace to the point where it defines many high-profile creative careers today. Meanwhile, Richardson's 'British' films made in Europe, such as *Mademoiselle* (1966) and *The Sailor from Gibraltar* (1967), also spoke of the establishment of co-production treaties with France and Italy (although take-up of these new opportunities proved slow), while collaborations with Commonwealth countries such as Canada and Australia, as seen in the production of *The Trap* (1966) and *They're a Weird Mob* (1966) respectively, were also significant harbingers of British cinema's growing internationalism, on a slightly different footing from its previous identity as imperial centre.

Another phenomenon that came to the fore during the decade was the closer inter-connectivity between film and other creative industries, representing a particular type of 'media convergence'. While the use of that term today largely relates to the impact of new digital technologies on the production and consumption of creative content, our contextual study of British cinema of the 1960s has shown just how significant an earlier form of cross-fertilisation between cinema and other media was at this time. While British cinema's long-standing debt to literature and theatre remained vital (as the New Wave demonstrated so forcefully), they were joined in the 1960s by the new(er) fields of television, mass advertising, pop music, fashion and design, each working in increasingly sophisticated and novel ways. Barriers between distinct media, industries, art forms or creative endeavour began to break down as popular culture became more protean and participatory in its production, and London's status as the epicentre of this creative 'melting-pot' – which for a short period also afforded the city an unparalleled global profile – was also vitally important.

For these reasons, the 1960s continue to act as the template and benchmark for all subsequent British cultural renaissances. The celebratory (and self-congratulatory) Britishness of phenomena like 1990s Britpop and 'cool Britannia' echoed that initial moment of 1960s cultural dynamism (and were co-opted by government just as Harold Wilson had done in bestowing MBEs upon the Beatles).[3] Few decades are returned to quite so frequently or enthusiastically as the sixties, the latest example being the documentary *My Generation* (2017), presented by Michael Caine and scripted by Dick Clement and Ian La Frenais, which offers a largely straightforward celebration of class mobility and youthful inspiration during the period, and shows that there is still plenty of capacity for those long-established myths of the sixties to be perpetually retold.[4] And firmly entrenched within those mythologies is the story of British cinema's renaissance during the period and its creation of new kinds of star (exemplified by someone like Caine).

In this study, we have sought to test the existing narratives circulating around this period of British film production – both popular and scholarly, through detailed archival investigation and critical analysis – and have found a British cinema in which transnationalism and media convergence were of crucial importance, injecting new vitality into an industry that in other respects was in crisis, struggling with declining attendances and a moribund infrastructure. Its irrefutable filmic legacy, embodied by films as rich and various as *Saturday Night and Sunday Morning* and *Carry on Up the Khyber*, *The Nanny* and *The Servant*, *Goldfinger* and *If . . .*, *The L-Shaped Room* and *Poor Cow*, *Lawrence of Arabia* and *Witchfinder General*, as well as countless others (including many that deserve to be much better known than they currently are), is a body of work that continues to entertain, provoke and inspire new audiences and creative practitioners in Britain and beyond.

Notes

1. Philip French, 'Screen legends: Margaret Rutherford', *Observer*, 26 July 2009.
2. Barry Day, 'The suggestive experience', *Films and Filming*, August 1969, p. 4.
3. The imprint of the 1960s could also be felt in the opening ceremony of the 2012 London Olympics, another celebration of British national identity, particularly in the significant place allotted to pop music from the period and the presence of a sixties-born film phenomena, James Bond, in one of its main events.
4. Although the context continually changes as the decade passes further into distant memory and many of its key protagonists are dead, which inevitably affects its historicisation. And perspectives on specific cultural artefacts may change too: the Michael Caine star vehicle *The Italian Job* (1969), revived as charmingly laddish and harmlessly jingoistic in the 1990s, now looks more like a retrenchment of bullish British exceptionalism versus a European foe prophetic of Brexit (even more so given the older demographic profile of many of those voting for it – Caine's 'my generation', sixties youth grown old).

APPENDICES

APPENDIX I: UK FILMS AT THE DOMESTIC BOX OFFICE, 1960–9

Reliable figures for box-office earnings are notoriously difficult to access and what follows is an indication of some of the top-grossing British films in the UK during the decade. The data is derived from the trade press, notably *Kine Weekly* and *The Daily Cinema*. The former makes a distinction between films on general release and those given special presentations (usually significantly longer films shown without a second feature).

1960

The top performing general releases of British provenance included:

Table A.I.1960 Top-performing domestic films at the British box office

Title	Producer	Director	Distributor	Genre	Ranking for year
Doctor in Love	Betty Box	Ralph Thomas	Rank	Comedy	1
Carry on Constable	Peter Rogers	Gerald Thomas	Anglo-Amalgamated	Comedy	2
Two Way Stretch	E. M. Smedley Aston	Robert Day	British Lion	Comedy	4
Conspiracy of Hearts	Betty Box	Ralph Thomas	Rank	War	5

The League of Gentlemen	Michael Relph	Basil Dearden	British Lion	Crime	6
Sink the Bismark!	John Brabourne	Lewis Gilbert	20th Century Fox	War	7
Dentist in the Chair	Bertram Ostrer	Don Chaffey	Renown Pictures	Comedy	11
School for Scoundrels	Hal Chester	Robert Hamer Cyril Frankel	ABPC	Comedy	12

A strong performance overall for British product, this demonstrates the popularity of modest domestic comedies. Key stars are also significant, although *Doctor in Love* featured Michael Craig and Leslie Phillips rather than Dirk Bogarde who had played Simon Sparrow in the three previous instalments. *Two Way Stretch* starred Peter Sellers, who was to prove a major box-office draw throughout the decade.

1961

The two top-grossing films on general release were both American – Disney's *Swiss Family Robinson*, directed by Britain's Ken Annakin and starring John Mills, and the western *The Magnificent Seven*. But six British films appeared in the top twelve with the breakthrough New Wave film *Saturday Night and Sunday Morning* coming out as top British film of the year:

Table A.I.1961   Top-performing domestic films at the British box office in 1961

Title	Producer	Director	Distributor	Genre	Ranking for year
Saturday Night and Sunday Morning	Tony Richardson	Karel Reisz	Bryanston British Lion	Drama	3
The Rebel	W. A. Whittaker	Robert Day	Warner Pathé	Comedy	6
The Sundowners	Gerry Blattner	Fred Zinnemann	Warner Pathé	Crime	7
Whistle Down the Wind	Richard Attenborough	Bryan Forbes	British Lion	Drama	8
Carry On Regardless	Peter Rogers	Gerald Thomas	Anglo-Amalgamated	Comedy	10
The Long and the Short and the Tall	Michael Balcon Hal Mason	Leslie Norman	Warner Pathé	War	12

1962

The Guns of Navarone had also topped *Kine Weekly*'s developing 'special presentation' category. While *Dr No* may have been the first outing of the relatively unknown Sean Connery as James Bond, *The Young Ones* featured the popular singer Cliff Richard, and *Only Two Can Play* served to confirm Peter Sellers power as a box-office draw.

Table A.I.1962 Top-performing domestic films at the British box office in 1962

Title	Producer	Director	Distributor	Genre	Ranking for year
The Guns of Navarone	Carl Forman	J. Lee Thompson	Columbia	War	1
The Young Ones	Kenneth Harper	Sidney J. Furie	Warner Pathé	Musical	2
Dr No	Albert Broccoli Harry Saltzman	Terence Young	United Artists	Crime (Bond)	3
Only Two Can Play	Leslie Gilliat	Sidney Gilliat	British Lion	Comedy	4
The Road to Hong Kong	Melvin Frank	Norman Panama	United Artists	Comedy	5
HMS Defiant	John Brabourne	Lewis Gilbert	Columbia	Adventure	9
The Pirates of Blood River	Michael Carreras	John Gilling	Columbia	Adventure	10

1963

David Lean's epic, *Lawrence of Arabia*, produced by Sam Spiegel for Columbia achieved third place in the US-dominated special presentations category. But British films also performed strongly once again in the general-release tables. Here we begin to see the Bond brand being established, with the second film out-performing its predecessor. The pulling power of a number of new British male stars was being consolidated; with Sean Connery's appeal confirmed in *From Russia with Love* along with Albert Finney's in *Tom Jones* (having been introduced to audiences two years previously in *Saturday Night and Sunday Morning*) and Cliff Richard's in *Summer Holiday*:

Table A.I.1963a   Top-performing domestic films at the British box office in 1963

Title	Producer	Director	Distributor	Genre	Ranking for year
From Russia With Love	Albert Broccoli Harry Saltzman	Terence Young	United Artists	Crime (Bond)	1
Summer Holiday	Kenneth Harper	Peter Yates	Warner Pathé	Musical	2
Tom Jones	Tony Richardson	Tony Richardson	United Artists	Adventure	4

Seven of the next twelve biggest-grossers for the year were also British; with domestic parochial comedies featuring strongly in this list (the trade press did not provide their individual rankings):

Table A.I.1963b   Other top-performing domestic films in 1963 (unranked)

Title	Producer	Director	Distributor	Genre
Doctor in Distress	Betty Box	Ralph Thomas	Rank	Comedy
The Fast Lady	Julian Wintle Leslie Parkyn	Ken Annakin	Rank	Comedy
Heaven's Above	John Boulting	Roy Boulting	British Lion	Comedy
Jason and the Argonauts	Charles H. Schneer	Don Chaffey	Columbia	Fantasy
On the Beat	Hugh Stewart	Robert Asher	Rank	Comedy
The VIPs	Anatole de Grunwald	Anthony Asquith	MGM	Drama
The Wrong Arm of the Law	Aubrey Baring	Cliff Owen	British Lion	Comedy

1964

The third Bond film took the popularity of the series to even greater heights, *A Hard Day's Night* capitalised on Beatlemania, while *Wonderful Life* starred the still-popular Cliff Richard. More residual attractions still attained high levels of popularity, with *A Stitch in Time* featuring Norman Wisdom who had been a box-office draw since the early 1950s, doing excellent business.

Table A.I.1964 Top-performing domestic films at the British box office in 1964

Title	Producer	Director	Distributor	Genre	Ranking for year
Goldfinger	Albert Broccoli Harry Saltzman	Guy Hamilton	United Artists	Crime (Bond)	1
A Hard Day's Night	Walter Shenson	Richard Lester	United Artists	Musical	2
Zulu	Cy Endfield Stanley Baker	Cy Endfield	Paramount	Adventure	3
A Stitch in Time	Hugh Stewart	Robert Asher	Rank	Comedy	4
Wonderful Life	Kenneth Harper	Sidney Furie	Warner Pathé	Musical	5
633 Squadron	Lewis Rachmil	Walter Grauman	United Artists	War	9

1965

The domestic box office was dominated by American features led by *Mary Poppins* (albeit set in London with a British director, star, and source material) and followed by two features starring Peter Sellers: *What's New Pussycat?* and *A Shot in the Dark* (the second of the *Pink Panther* series). The only three British films to make the top ten were:

Table A.I.1965 Top-performing domestic films at the British box office in 1965

Title	Producer	Director	Distributor	Genre	Ranking for year
Help!	Walter Shenson	Richard Lester	United Artists	Musical	2
Operation Crossbow	Carlo Ponti	Michael Anderson	MGM	War	9
Carry on Cleo	Peter Rogers	Gerald Thomas	Anglo-Amalgamated	Comedy	10

The highest-ranking British production, the second big-screen outing for the Beatles, demonstrated their ongoing multimedia success.

1966

The overall box-office winner in the UK was the American musical *The Sound of Music*, which again starred the very English Julie Andrews. But British films held their own in the general-release top ten:

Table A.I.1966 Top-performing domestic films at the British box office in 1966

Title	Producer	Director	Distributor	Genre	Ranking for year
Thunderball	Albert Broccoli Harry Saltzman	Terence Young	United Artists	Crime (Bond)	1
Alfie	Lewis Gilbert	Lewis Gilbert	Paramount	Drama	2
Born Free	Sam Jaffe Paul Raddin	James Hill	Columbia	Drama	3
Those Magnificent Men in Their Flying Machines	Stan Marguiles	Ken Annakin	20th Century Fox	Comedy	5
The Early Bird	Hugh Stewart	Robert Asher	Rank	Comedy	6
The Great St Trinian's Train Robbery	Sidney Gilliat Frank Launder	Sidney Gilliat Frank Launder	British Lion	Comedy	8

The most successful film once more featured Sean Connery as 007, *The Early Bird* was another Norman Wisdom comedy, while Launder and Gilliat's film was the fourth instalment in the comedy series featuring a school of wayward girls that had begun in 1954. The inclusion of *Alfie* in second place provides an indication of the growing star appeal of Michael Caine.

1967

The two biggest overall money-makers of the year were special presentations, reflecting the more general move towards big-budget 'event' films. While *The Sound of Music* was American, David Lean's epic, *Doctor Zhivago,* produced by Carlo Ponti for MGM was British. The film had initially been released in April 1966 as a roadshow presentation.[1] Fred Zinnemann's *A Man for All Seasons*, distributed by Columbia was the second highest-grosser in the category. UK films in the top-ten general releases were:

Table A.I.1967 Top-performing domestic films at the British box office in 1967

Title	Producer	Director	Distributor	Genre	Ranking for year
You Only Live Twice	Albert Broccoli Harry Saltzman	Lewis Gilbert	United Artists	Crime (Bond)	1
The Family Way	John Boulting	Roy Boulting	British Lion	Comedy	4
The Blue Max	Christian Ferry	John Guillermin	20th Century Fox	War	6
Casino Royale	Charles Feldman	Various	Columbia	Crime (Bond)	9
One Million Years BC	Michael Carreras	Don Chaffey	Warner Pathé	Fantasy	10

This time there are two Bond films: *You Only Live Twice,* and *Casino Royale,* Charles Feldman's self-indulgent pastiche featuring several 007s played by David Niven, Peter Sellers and Woody Allen among others. The Boultings' *The Family Way* marks the return of a more intimate and domestic comedy, while *One Million Years BC* represented Hammer Films' most expensive – and successful – production of the decade.

1968

The increasing propensity of big-budget films to dominate the box office was confirmed with the biggest money-makers again being *Doctor Zhivago* and *The Sound of Music,* the latter for the third year running. The top-grossing general release was Disney's *The Jungle Book.* But further down the list contemporary British realist drama and comedy featured strongly, taking advantage of the increasing permissiveness of the British censor.

Table A.I.1968a Top-performing domestic films at the British box office in 1968 (general release)

Title	Producer	Director	Distributor	Genre	Ranking for year
Up the Junction	John Brabourne	Peter Collinson	Paramount	Drama	2
Poor Cow	Joseph Janni	Ken Loach	Anglo-Amalgamated	Drama	5

| Here We Go Round the Mulberry Bush | Larry Kramer | Clive Donner | United Artists | Comedy | 6 |
| Carry On Doctor | Peter Rogers | Gerald Thomas | Rank | Comedy | 10 |

American-backed British films also performed strongly in the special presentation category for 1968, including some of the most audacious and aesthetically radical mainstream productions of the decade directed by Kubrick, Schlesinger and Richardson:

Table A.I.1968b Top-performing domestic films at the British box office in 1968 (special presentations)

Title	Producer	Director	Distributor	Genre	Ranking for year
Half a Sixpence	Charles Schneer	George Sidney	Paramount	Musical	2
A Man for All Seasons	Fred Zinnemann	Fred Zinnemann	Columbia	Historical drama	5
Far From the Madding Crowd	Joseph Janni	John Schlesinger	MGM	Drama	7
Charge of the Light Brigade	Neil Hartley	Tony Richardson	United Artists	Historical drama	9
2001: A Space Odyssey	Stanley Kubrick	Stanley Kubrick	MGM	Fantasy	11

1969

British films again enjoyed a particularly strong showing in the special presentation category with epic spectacle and special effects increasingly to the fore in several productions:

Table A.I.1969a Top-performing domestic films at the British box office in 1969 (special presentations)

Title	Producer	Director	Distributor	Genre	Ranking for year
Oliver!	John Woolf	Carol Reed	Columbia	Musical	1
Chitty Chitty Bang Bang	Albert Broccoli	Ken Hughes	United Artists	Musical	3
Where Eagles Dare	Elliot Kastner	Brian Hutton	MGM	War	4
Doctor Zhivago	Carlo Ponti	David Lean	MGM	Drama	5
The Battle of Britain	Harry Saltzman	Guy Hamilton	United Artists	War	6
The Lion in Winter	Joseph Levine	Anthony Harvey	Avco–Embassy	Historical drama	8
2001: A Space Odyssey	Stanley Kubrick	Stanley Kubrick	MGM	Fantasy	9
Romeo and Juliet	John Brabourne	Franco Zefirelli	Paramount	Romance	10

The general-release category looked strikingly different meanwhile. Once again modest domestic comedies proved popular, with *Till Death Us Do Part* capitalising on the popularity of the television series. The reprise of *Half a Sixpence* indicates the potential for films crossing over profitably from one category to the other.

Table A.I.1969b Top-performing domestic films at the British box office in 1969 (general release)

Title	Producer	Director	Distributor	Genre	Ranking for year
Till Death Us Do Part	John Pennington	Norman Cohen	British Lion	Comedy	1
Carry On Camping	Peter Rogers	Gerald Thomas	Rank	Comedy	2
Carry On Up the Khyber	Peter Rogers	Gerald Thomas	Rank	Comedy	5
The Virgin Soldiers	Leslie Gilliat	John Dexter	Columbia	War	6
Shalako	Euan Lloyd	Edward Dymytryk	Anglo-Amalgamated	Western	7
Oh! What a Lovely War	Len Deighton Brian Duffy	Richard Attenborough	Paramount	Musical	8
Half a Sixpence	Charles Schneer	George Sidney	Paramount	Musical	9

APPENDIX II: BRITISH FILMS AT THE US BOX OFFICE

Sarah Street's book *Transatlantic Crossings* provides a list of the top British earners in the American market with figures up to 1990.[2] The top twenty overlap significantly with the productions which enjoyed success at the UK box-office but with some interesting exceptions (*To Sir With Love* and *Blow Up*):

Table A.II Top-performing British films at the US box office 1960–9

Film title (date, company)	Ranking for year	Rentals ($ millions)
Thunderball (1965, UA)	2	28.6
2001: A Space Odyssey (1968, MGM)	1	25.5
Goldfinger (1964, UA)	1	22.9
The Dirty Dozen (1967, MGM)	1	20.4
Lawrence of Arabia (1962, Columbia)	1	20.2
You Only Live Twice (1967, UA)	7	19.3
To Sir With Love (1967, Columbia)	8	19.1
Romeo and Juliet (1968, Paramount)	6	17.5
Tom Jones (1963, UA)	4	17.0
Oliver! (1968, Columbia)	7	16.8
The Guns of Navarone (1961, Columbia)	2	13.0
A Man for All Seasons (1966, Columbia)	5	12.8
Casino Royale (1967, Columbia)	13	10.2
The Lion in Winter (1968, Embassy)	14	10.0
From Russia with Love (1964, UA)	5	9.9
On Her Majesty's Secret Service (1969, UA)	10	9.1
Dr No (1962, UA)	9	6.4
Blow Up (1966, MGM)	10	6.3
A Hard Day's Night (1964, UA)	9	6.2
Help! (1965, UA)	15	5.4

NOTES

1. There is no reference to it in the box office for 1966 in either *Kine Weekly* or *The Daily Cinema* but given its overall popularity it is very likely that it also featured strongly in the special presentations for that year.
2. Sarah Street, *Transatlantic Crossing*, p. 170. It is interesting to note that all of these films are American-financed. The relatively stronger performance of *2001*, *The Dirty Dozen* and *Blow Up* in the United States may also reflect the strong American subject matter of the first two (the Dirty Dozen was also a US–UK co-production), while the third arguably captures the moment of 'swinging London' that had been coined by American journalists.

BIBLIOGRAPHY

Anon. (1961), 'How to get into films', *Films and Filming*, May, 7–9, 37–8.
Anon. (1961), 'Playwrights for British films', *The Times*, 29 December, 11.
Anon. (1962), 'How to get into films by those who have done it', *Films and Filming*, July, 11–14.
Anon. (1963), Ilford interviews Nicolas Roeg', *Film and Television Technician*, April, 78.
Anon. (1963), 'Film credits – we demand a better deal', *The Screenwriter*, 14, Winter, 3.
Anon. (1964), 'We're in the TUC – and it's strictly non-political', *The Screenwriter*, 15, Spring, 3.
Anon. (1964), 'Meet the man who gets the Bond films off to a sizzling start', *Showtime*, October, 21–3.
Anon. (1969), 'Hollywood and Bust', *Film and TV Technician*, December, 35, 8–9.
Anon. (1970), 'Carry On Cashing In . . .', *The Guardian*, 18 October, 16.
Adburgham, A. (1968), 'The charge of the rag brigade', *The Guardian*, 21 March, 9.
Agajanian, R. (1998), '"Just for Kids?" Saturday Morning Cinema and Britain's Children's Film Foundation in the 1960s', *Historical Journal of Film, Radio and Television*, 18: 3, 395–409.
Ahmed, M. (2013), 'Corrupted, Tormented and Damned: Reframing British Exploitation Cinema and the Films of Robert Hartford-Davis', University of East Anglia, unpublished doctoral thesis.
Aldgate, A. (1995), *Censorship and the Permissive Society: British Cinema and Theatre, 1955–1965*, Oxford: Clarendon Press.
Aquilina Ross, G. (2011), *The Day of the Peacock: Style for Men 1963–1973*, London: V&A Publishing.
Ardagh, J. (1963), 'Censor to decide if the party is over', *Observer*, 27 October, 1.
Armes, R. (1978), *A Critical History of British Cinema*, London: Secker & Warburg.
Austen, D. (1968), 'Blue', *Films and Filming*, August, 6.

Ayers, J. D. (2017), 'The Two Screens: FIDO, RFDA and Film vs. Television in Post-Second World War Britain', *Journal of British Cinema and Television*, 14: 4, 504–21.
Bailey, D. and P. Evans (1969), *Goodbye Baby & Amen: A Saraband for the Sixties*, New York: Coward–McCann.
Balcon, M. (1969), *Michael Balcon Presents . . . A Lifetime of Films*, London: Hutchison.
Balio, T. (1987), *United Artists: The Company that Changed the Film Industry*, Madison: University of Wisconsin Press.
Barber, S. (2013), *The British Cinema in the 1970s: Capital, Culture and Creativity*, Basingstoke: Palgrave Macmillan.
Barnett V. L. (2014), 'Hammering out a Deal: The Contractual and Commercial Contexts of *The Curse of Frankenstein* (1957) and *Dracula* (1958)', *Historical Journal of Radio, Film and Television*, 34: 2, 231–52.
Barr, C. (1986), 'Introduction: amnesia and schizophrenia', in C. Barr (ed.), *All Our Yesterdays: 90 Years of British Cinema*, London: BFI, 1–26.
Baxter, J. (1973), *An Appalling Talent: Ken Russell*, London: Michael Joseph.
Baxter, J. (2006), 'Frederic Raphael: Renaissance man', in P. McGilligan (ed.), *Backstory 4: Interviews with Screenwriters of the 1970s and 1980s*, Berkeley: University of California Press, 317–41.
Bean, R. (1965), 'Passage of love', *Films and Filming*, September, 46.
Bean, R. (1965), 'Stalemate', *Films and Filming*, November, 49–51.
Bean, R. (1967), 'Trapped in a Sandwich', *Films and Filming*, January, 60.
Bean, R. (1968), 'The importance of being what's 'isname?', *Films and Filming*, February, 9–10.
Bernstein, D. (1986), 'The Television Commercial: An Essay', in B. Henry (ed.), *British Television Advertising: The First 30 Years*, London: Century Benham, 251–86.
Best, R. (1966/7), 'Editing – the beginning of the end', *Journal of the Society of Film and Television Arts*, no. 26, Winter, 5.
Bond, R. (1962), 'Second Features', *The Times*, 15 November, 13
Bond, R. (1963), 'Whither the NFFC?', *Film and TV Technician*, April, 76.
Booker, C. (1969), *The Neophiliacs: A Study of the Revolution in English Life in the Fifties and Sixties*, London: HarperCollins.
Booth, S. (1985), *The True Adventures of the Rolling Stones*, London: Heinemann.
Bordwell, D. (2002), 'Intensified continuity: visual style in contemporary American film', *Film Quarterly*, 55: 3, Spring, 16–28.
Bramwell, T. (2005), *Magical Mystery Tours: My Life with the Beatles*, London: Robson Books.
Breward, C. (2012), 'Boutiques and beyond: the rise of British fashion', in C. Breward and G. Wood (eds), *British Design from 1948: Innovation in the Modern Age*, London: V&A Publishing, 202–27.
Breward, C. and G. Wood (2012), 'Tradition and modernity 1945–79', in C. Breward and G. Wood (eds), British Design from 1948: *Innovation in the Modern Age*, London: V&A Publishing, 30–9.
Briggs, A. (1995), *The History of Broadcasting in the United Kingdom – vol. v: Competition*, Oxford: Oxford University Press.
Bright, M. and Ross, R. (2000), *The Life and Work of Peter Rogers*, London: BBC.
Brinton, R. (1963), 'The New Realism in British Films', *Journal of the Society of Film and Television Arts*, no. 11, Spring, 9.
Bruzzi, S. (1997), *Undressing Cinema: Clothing and Identity in the Movies*, London: Routledge.
Bryce, A. (2000), *Amicus: The Studio That Dripped Blood*, Plymouth: Stray Cat Publishing.

Burgess, A. (1990), *You've Had Your Time: Being the second part of the confessions of Anthony Burgess*, London: Heinemann.
Burke, A. (2001), *Laughter in the Dark: The Plays of Joe Orton*, London: Greenwich Exchange.
Burton, A., T. O'Sullivan and P. Wells (eds) (1997), *Liberal Directions: Basil Dearden and Post-war British Film Culture*, Trowbridge: Flicks Books.
Burton, A., and T. O'Sullivan (2009), *The Cinema of Basil Dearden and Michael Relph*, Edinburgh: Edinburgh University Press.
Buscombe, E. (1991), 'All Bark and No Bite: The Film Industry's Response to Television' in J. Corner (ed.), *Popular Television in Britain: Studies in Cultural History*, London: BFI, 197–209.
Caine, A. (2004), *Interpreting Rock Movies: The Pop Film and Its Critics in Britain*, Manchester: Manchester University Press.
Cairns, D. (n.d.), 'Woodery-pokery', *Shadowplay*, <https://dcairns.wordpress.com/2017/09/12/woodery-pokery-in-york/> (accessed 1 August 2018).
Caldwell, J. T. (1995), *Televisuality: Style, Crisis, and Authority in American Television*, New Brunswick, NJ: Rutgers University Press.
Caldwell, J. T. (2008), *Production Culture: Industrial Reflexivity and Critical Practice in Film and Television*, Durham, NC, and London: Duke University Press.
Cameron, I. (1962), 'Films, directors and critics', *Movie*, 2, 5.
Cameron, I., and M. Shivas (1965), 'Clive Donner interview', *Movie*, 14, 12–16.
Cameron, I., and M. Shivas (1968–69), 'Interview with Richard Lester', *Movie*, 16, Winter, 8–13.
Carter, E. (1966), 'A Winter of Zhivago', *The Sunday Times*, 28 August, no page number.
Castell, D. (1976), 'More by accident than design', *Films Illustrated*, October, 69.
Caute, D. (1996), *Joseph Losey: A Revenge on Life*, London: Faber.
Chapman, J. (2000), *License to Thrill: A Cultural History of the James Bond Films*, New York: Columbia University Press.
Chapman, J. (2012), 'A short history of the Carry On films', in I. Q. Hunter and L. Porter (eds), *British Comedy Cinema*, Abingdon and New York: Routledge, 100–15.
Chapman, J. (2013), *Inside the Tardis: The Worlds of Doctor Who*, revised ed., London: I. B. Tauris.
Chapman, J. (2014), 'The Trouble with Harry: The Difficult Relationship of Harry Saltzman and Film Finances', *The Historical Journal of Film, Radio and Television*, 34: 1, 43–71.
Chapman, J., M. Glancy and S. Harper (eds) (2007), *The New Film History: Sources, Methods, Approaches*, Basingstoke: Palgrave Macmillan.
Chase, D. (1984), 'David Watkin', *American Cinematographer*, 65: 3, 42–6.
Chibnall, S. and B. McFarlane (2007), *Quota Quickies: The Birth of the British B Film*, London: BFI.
Chibnall, S. and B. McFarlane (eds) (2009), *The British 'B' Film*, Basingstoke: Palgrave Macmillan/BFI.
Christie, I. (2009), *The Art of Film: John Box and Production Design*, London: Wallflower.
Church Gibson, P. (2006), 'Myths of the Swinging City: The Media in the Sixties', in C. Breward, D. Gilbert and J. Lister (eds), *Swinging Sixties: Fashion in London and Beyond, 1955–1970*, London: V&A Publishing, 80–100.
Church Gibson, P. (2006), 'New stars, new fashions and the female audience: cinema, consumption and cities 1953–1966', in C. Breward and D. Gilbert (eds), *Fashion's World Cities*, Oxford: Berg, 89–108.

Church Gibson, P. (2017), 'The Fashioning of Julie Christie and the Mythologizing of "Swinging London": Changing Images in Sixties Britain', in E. Paulicelli, D. Stutesman and L. Wallenberg (eds), *Film, Fashion, and the 1960s*, Bloomington: Indiana University Press, 135–48.
Ciment, M. (1985), *Conversations with Losey*, London and New York: Methuen.
Clark, J. with J. M. Myers (2010), *Dream Repairman: Adventures in Film Editing*, Crockett, Texas: Landmarc Press.
Clayton, D. (2010), 'Advertising Expenditure in 1950s Britain', *Business History*, 52: 4, 651–65.
Coleman, R. (1989), *Brian Epstein: The Man Who Made the Beatles*, London: Viking.
Collins, D. (1963), *A Nose for Money: How to Make a Million*, London: Michael Joseph.
Combs, R. (1999), 'Petulia: blood, glass, and feathers', *Film Comment*, 35: 1, January/February, 54–63.
Cook, J. R. (1999), 'Adapting telefantasy: The Doctor Who and the Daleks films', in I. Q. Hunter (ed.), *British Science Fiction Cinema*, London: Routledge, 113–27.
Cook, J. R. and P. Murphy (2000), 'After the Bomb Dropped: The Cinema Half-life of The War Game', *Journal of Popular British Cinema*, 3, 129–32.
Cooke, L. (2015), *British Television Drama: A History, 2nd edn*, London: BFI.
Cooper, R. (1968), 'Petulia tie-ups', *Kine Weekly*, 12 October, 30.
Corliss, M. and C. Clarens (1978), 'Designed for film: the Hollywood art director', *Film Comment*, May/June, 27–58.
Cosgrove, B. (2012), *Designing 007: Fifty years of Bond Style*, London: Barbican.
Cousins, M. (2015), 'Scissor sisters', *Sight and Sound*, 25: 8, 13.
Crittenden, R. (2005), *Fine Cuts: The Art of European Film Editing*, London: Focal Press.
Crow, D. (1957), 'From screen to screen: cinema films on television', *Sight and Sound*, 27: 2, 62.
Crowdus, G. (2009), 'The editing of Lawrence of Arabia: an interview with Anne V. Coates', *Cineaste*, 34: 2, 48–53.
Davenport, A. (1971), 'Risk involved in Tigon offer', *The Guardian*, 13 September, 12.
Davis, D. (1969), 'US film-makers in Britain may start dollar drain', republished in *Film and TV Technician*, February, 35: 285, 8–9.
Davis, D. and R. Millichip (1969), 'Take two nice guys like them', *Films and Filming*, December, 51.
Delson, J. (1982), 'Art Directors: Ken Adam', *Film Comment*, 18: 1, 38.
Denisoff, R. S. and W. D. Romanowski (1991), *Risky Business: Rock in Film*, New Brunswick, NJ: Transaction.
Dick, B. F. (1992), 'From the Brothers Cohn to Sony Corp', in B. F. Dick (ed.), *Columbia Pictures: Portrait of a Studio*, Lexington: University Press of Kentucky, 2–69.
Dickason, R. (2000), *British Television Advertising: Cultural Identity and Communication*, Luton: University of Luton Press.
Dickinson, M. (ed.) (1999), *Rogue Reels: Oppositional Film Making in Britain 1945–90*, London: BFI.
Dixon, W.W. (2013), 'Pop star, director, actor: an interview with Michael Sarne', *Cinema at the Margins*, London: Anthem Press, 195–204.
Docherty, D., Morrison, D. and Tracey, M. (1987), *The Last Picture Show: Britain's Changing Film Audience*, London: BFI.
Donnelly, K. J. (1998), 'The Perpetual Busman's Holiday: Sir Cliff Richard and British Pop Musicals', *Journal of Popular Film and Television*, 25: 4, 146–54.
Donnelly, M. (2005), *Sixties Britain*, Harlow: Pearson Education.

Donner, C. (1960–1), 'Live action commercials', *The Journal of the Society of Film and Television Arts (television commercials)*, 4, Winter, 6–7.
Downs, C. (2010), 'Mecca and the birth of commercial bingo 1958–70: A case study', *Business History*, 52: 7, 1086–106.
Drazin, C. (2011), *A Bond for Bond: Film Finances and Dr No*, London: Film Finances.
Drazin, C. (2014), 'Film Finances: The First Years', *The Historical Journal of Film, Radio and Television*, 34: 1, 2–22.
Dupin, C. (2012), 'The BFI and Film Production: Half a Century of Innovative Independent Film-Making' in G. Nowell-Smith and C. Dupin (eds), *The British Film Institute, the Government and Film Culture, 1933–2000*, Manchester: Manchester University Press, 197–218.
Durgnat, R. (1966), 'Dearden and Relph: two on a tandem', *Films and Filming*, July, 26–7.
Durgnat, R. (1968), 'Girl on a Motorcycle', *Films and Filming*, October, 37.
Durgnat, R. (1969), 'TV's young Turks – Part 1', *Films and Filming*, March, 5.
Durgnat, R. (1969), 'TV's young turks – Part 2', *Films and Filming*, April, 29.
Dux, S. (2012), 'Allied Film Makers: Crime, Comedy and Social Concern', *Journal of British Cinema and Television*, 9: 2, 198–213.
Ede, L. (2010), *British Film Design: A History*, London: I. B. Tauris.
Ellis, D. A. (2012), *Conversations with Cinematographers*, Plymouth: Scarecrow Press.
Epstein, B. (1964), *Cellarful of Noise*, London: Souvenir Press.
Evans, P. (1983), 'An eye for a picture', *The Guardian*, 5 March, 8.
Eyles, A. (1985), 'Cutting remarks', *Stills*, May, 12.
Fairservice, D. (2001), *Film Editing: History, Theory and Practice*, Manchester: Manchester University Press.
Faithfull, M. with D. Dalton (2000), *Faithfull: An Autobiography*, New York: Cooper Square Press.
Falkenberg, P. (1967–8), 'The editor's role in film making', *Cinema Journal*, 7, Winter.
Farmer, R. (2016), 'Cinema advertising and the Sea Witch "Lost Island" film (1965)', *Historical Journal of Film, Radio and Television*, 36: 4, 569–86.
Farmer, R. (2017), 'Supplemental income: British newspaper colour supplements in the 1960s', *Media History* <https://www.tandfonline.com/doi/full/10.1080/13688804.2018.1481372> (advanced online access).
Field, M. (2012), 'Sounding out Norman Wanstall' and 'The girl with the golden pen', *Cinema Retro: Movie Classics*, no. 4, 119, 136.
Fisher, J. (2008), *Tony Hancock*, London: HarperCollins.
Fisher, T. (1964), 'Horror is my business', *Films and Filming*, July, 7–8.
Fletcher, W. (2008), *Powers of Persuasion: The Inside Story of British Advertising, 1951–2000*, Oxford: Oxford University Press.
Forbes, B. (1964), 'How I write a film script', *Showtime*, March, 24.
Forbes, B. (1993), *A Divided Life*, London: Mandarin.
Foreman, C. (1963), 'The Revolution in the Film Industry', *The Daily Cinema*, Preview of 1963, January, 13.
Foster, L. and S. Harper (eds) (2010), *British Culture and Society in the 1970s: The Lost Decade*, Newcastle: Cambridge Scholars Press.
Francis, A. (1986), *Julian Wintle: A Memoir*, London: Dukeswood.
Frayling, C. (2005), *Ken Adam and the Art of Production Design*, London: Faber.
Freeman, R. (1968), 'Touch of Eros', *Films and Filming*, May, 21.
French, P. (1965), 'Richard Lester', *Movie*, 14, 5–11.
French, P. (1966), 'The alphaville of admass', *Sight and Sound*, 35: 3, 106–11.
French, P. (1989), 'Not just desert', *Observer*, 28 May, 44.
French, P. (2009), 'Douglas Slocombe: A Tribute', *Observer*, 13 December.

Frith, S., M. Brennan, M. Cloonan and E. Webster (2013), *The History of Live Music in Britain, vol. 1: 1950–1967 – From Dance Hall to the 100 Club*, Farnham: Ashgate.
Fryer, I. (2016), *The Worlds of Gerry and Sylvia Anderson: The Story Behind International Rescue*, Stroud: Fonthill.
Fuller G. (ed.) (1998), *Loach on Loach*, London: Faber.
Gable, J. (1980), *The Tuppenny Punch and Judy Show: 25 Years of TV Commercials*, London: Michael Joseph.
Gaines, J. (1990), *Fabrications: Costume and the Female Body*, London: Routledge.
Gagliostro, V. W. (n.d.), 'A Darling Party', on Diane Pernet, A Shaded View on Fashion Film, <http://ashadedviewonfashion.com/blog/rip-julie-harris-sweet-memory-tea-iconic-costume-designer-and-short-doc-darling-party-vincent> (accessed 20 June 2018).
Gardner, C. (2004), *Joseph Losey*, Manchester: Manchester University Press.
Gardner, C. (2006), 'From mimicry to mockery: Cold War hybridity in Evan Jones's *The Damned, Modesty Blaise* and *Funeral in Berlin*', *Media History*, 12: 2, 177–91.
Garrett, J. (1986), 'Commercial Production', in B. Henry (ed.), *British Television Advertising: The First 30 Years*, London: Century Benham, 383–402.
Gelmis, J. (1971), *The Film Director as Superstar*, London: Secker & Warburg.
Geraghty, C. (2000), *British Cinema in the Fifties: Gender, Genre and 'the New Look'*, London: Routledge.
Gifford, D. (2000), *The British Film Catalogue*, 3rd edition, London: Routledge.
Gillett, J. (1964), 'The state of the studios', *Sight and Sound*, 33: 2, 55–61.
Gladwell, D. (1969), 'Editing Anderson's If . . .', *Screen*, 10: 1, 24–33.
Gleason, R. J. (1967), 'Like a Rolling Stone', *American Scholar*, 36: 4, 557.
Glen, J. (2001), *For My Eyes Only: My Life with James Bond*, London: Batsford.
Glynn, S. (2013), *The British Pop Music Film: The Beatles and Beyond*, Basingstoke: Palgrave Macmillan.
Gomery, D. (2005), *The Hollywood Studio System: A History*, London: BFI/Palgrave.
Gow, G. (1966), 'Novel into film', *Films and Filming*, May, 21.
Gow, G. (1969), 'The urge of some people', *Films and Filming*, July, 4.
Gow, G. (1972), 'Identity: Nicolas Roeg', *Films and Filming*, January, 20–4.
Green, F. (1966), 'What isn't knacky is just darling', *Daily Mirror*, 31 March, 9.
Green, J. (1999), *All Dressed Up: The Sixties and the Couterculture*, London: Pimlico.
Green, O. O. (1965), 'Michael Powell', *Movie*, 14, 17–20.
Greenwood, J. (1962), 'Two and Two Do Make Four' *Kine Weekly*, Studio Review Supplement, 25 January, 3, 9.
Gross, M. (2016), *Focus: The Secret, Sexy, Sometimes Sordid World of Fashion Photographers*, New York: Atria Books.
Guback, T. (1985) 'Hollywood's International Market', in T. Balio (ed.), *The American Film Industry*, revised edition, Madison: University of Wisconsin Press, 463–86.
Guest, V. (1960), 'British films were never bad', *Films and Filming*, October, 34.
Halligan, B. (2003), *Michael Reeves*, Manchester: Manchester University Press.
Hamilton, J. (2005), *Beasts in the Cellar: The Exploitation Film Career of Tony Tenser*, London: FAB Press.
Hancock, F. and D. Nathan (1969), *Hancock*, London: William Kimber.
Hand, R. J. and A. Purssell (2015), *Adapting Graham Greene*, London: Palgrave.
Hanson, S. (2007), *From Silent Screen to Multi Screen: A History of Cinema Exhibition in Britain Since 1896*, Manchester: Manchester University Press.
Harker, D. (1980), *One for the Money: Politics and Popular Song*, London: Hutchinson.
Harker, D. (1992), 'Still crazy after all these years: what was popular music in the 1960s?', in B. Moore-Gilbert and J. Seed (eds), *Cultural Revolution? The Challenge of the Arts in the 1960s*, London: Routledge, 236–54.

Harper, S. (2000), *Women in British Cinema*, London: Continuum.
Harper, S. (2014), 'The Price of Oysters: *Tom Jones* (1963) and Film Finances', *Historical Journal of Film, Radio and Television*, 34: 1, 72–84.
Harper S. and Porter V. (2003), *British Cinema of the 1950s: The Decline of Deference*, Oxford: Oxford University Press.
Harper, S. and Smith J. (eds) (2012), *British Film Culture in the 1970s*, Edinburgh: Edinburgh University Press.
Harrison, M. (1963), 'Better sets – but at no greater cost', *Kine Weekly* (Production Review supplement), 26 September, 28.
Healey, B. (1967), 'The gay bohemians', *Film and Television Technician*, October, 257.
Herren, K. (1962), 'Film production – do or die?', *Kine Weekly* (Production Review supplement), 24 October, 15.
Hewison, R. (1986), *Too Much: Art and Society in the Sixties*, London: Methuen.
Hill, D. (1960), 'A Writers' Wave?', *Sight and Sound*, 29: 2, 56–60.
Hill, D. (1960), 'Censorship and the New Film Clubs', *Observer*, 28 February, 19.
Hill, J. (1986), *Sex, Class and Realism: British Cinema 1956–1963*, London: BFI.
Hill, J. (2011), *Ken Loach: The politics of film and television*, London: BFI/Palgrave Macmillan.
Hill, L. (1997), 'Terry Southern: ultrahip', in P. McGilligan (ed.), *Backstory 3: Interviews with Screenwriters of the 60s*, Berkeley: University of California Press, 382–3.
Hobson, H., P. Knightley and L. Russell (1972), *The Pearl of Days: An Intimate Memoir of The Sunday Times, 1822–1972*, London: Hamish Hamilton.
Hooper, A. (1966), 'So you want to be a movie fashion designer?', *Photoplay*, September, 61.
Hopkins, H. (1963), *The New Look: A Social History of the Forties and Fifties in Britain*, London: Secker & Warburg.
Houston, P. (1963), *The Contemporary Cinema*, Harmondsworth: Penguin.
Houston, P. (1964), '007', *Sight and Sound*, 33: 1, 16.
Houston, P. (1964), 'Keeping up with the Antonionis', *Sight and Sound*, 33: 4, 163–8.
Houston, P. (1966), 'England, Their England', *Sight and Sound*, 35: 2, 54–6.
Howell, P. (1967), 'The trials and tribulations of being a movie screenwriter', *Photoplay*, December, 18–9.
Hudis, N. (1960), 'It just happened', *Kine Weekly* (Studio Review), 28 January, 32.
Hudson, R. (1965), 'Three Designers', *Sight and Sound*, 34: 1, 26–31.
Hudson, R. (1965), 'The secret profession', *Sight and Sound*, 34: 3, 112–17.
Hudson, R. (1966), 'Putting the magic in it: two editors, James Clark and Anthony Harvey, discuss their work', *Sight and Sound*, 35: 2, 78–83.
Hulanicki, B. and M. Pel (2014), *The Biba Years, 1963–1975*, London: V&A Publishing.
Hunt, L. (1998), *British Low Culture: From Safari Suits to Sexploitation*, Abingdon: Routledge.
Hunter, I. Q., L. Porter and J. Smith (eds) (2017), *The Routledge Companion to British Cinema History*, London: Routledge.
Husra, B. (1964), 'Patterns of Power', *Films and Filming*, April, 49–56.
Hutchings, P. (2001) 'The Amicus House of Horror', in S. Chibnall and J. Petley (eds) British Horror Cinema, London: Routledge, 131–42.
Hutchings, P. (2001), 'The histogram and the list: the director in British film criticism', *Journal of Popular British Cinema*, 4, 30–6.
Hutchings, P. (2002), *Terence Fisher*, Manchester: Manchester University Press.
Inglis, I. (2010), 'Here, There and Everywhere: Introducing the Beatles', in I. Inglis (ed.), *Popular Music and Television in Britain*, Farnham: Ashgate, 179–95.

Institute of Practitioners in Advertising (1960), *How a Television Commercial is Made*, London: IPA Occasional Paper, 9.
Izod, J., K. McGee, K. Hannan and I. Gourdin-Sangouard (2012), *Lindsay Anderson: Cinema Authorship*, Manchester: Manchester University Press.
Jackson, L. (1998), *The Sixties: Decade of Design Revolution*, London: Phaidon.
Jackson, M. (1980), 'Cinema versus television', *Sight and Sound*, 49: 3, 179.
James, D. E. (2016), *Rock 'n' Film: Cinema's Dance with Popular Music*, Oxford: Oxford University Press.
Johnson, B. S. (1969), 'Why should a writer direct?', *Film and Television Technician*, February, 6.
Johnston, K. M. (2011), '"An intelligent and effective use of the rival screen": rediscovering early British television trailers', *Media History*, 17: 4, 377–88.
Jordan, M. (1983), 'Carry On . . . follow that stereotype', in J. Curran and V. Porter (eds), British Cinema History, London: Weidenfeld and Nicholson, 312–27.
Kelly, T., G. Norton and G. Perry (1966), *A Competitive Cinema*, London: Institute of Economic Affairs.
Kemp, P. (1991), *Lethal Innocence: The Cinema of Alexander Mackendrick*, London: Methuen.
Kennedy Martin, T. (1964), 'Nats go home', *Encore*, 11: 2, 21–33.
Kennedy Martin, T. (1966), 'Up the Junction and after', *Contrast*, 4: 5/6, 138–40.
Kent, H. (1963), *Single Bed for Three: A Lawrence of Arabia Notebook*, London: Hutchinson.
King, M. (2013), *Men, Masculinity and the Beatles*, Abingdon: Ashgate.
Kinsey, W. (2002), *Hammer Films: The Bray Studios Years*, Richmond: Reynolds & Hearn.
Kinsey, W. and G. Thomson (2012), *Hammer Films on Location*, London: Peveril.
Kipen, D. (2013), 'Tinker Tailor Soldier Schreiber', *Virginia Quarterly Review*, 89: 1, 224–31.
Kremer, D. (2015), *Sidney J. Furie: Life and Films*, Lexington: University Press of Kentucky.
Lahr, J. (ed.) (1988), *The Joe Orton Diaries: including the correspondence of Edna Welthorpe and others*, New York: Harper & Row.
Lane, J. F. (1967), 'Young romantic', *Films and Filming*, February, 58.
Lassally, W. (1987), *Itinerant Cameraman*, London: John Murray.
Levin, B. (1970), *The Pendulum Years*, London: Jonathan Cape.
Levy, S. (2002), *Swinging London and the Invention of Cool*, London: Fourth Estate.
Lewin, D. (1971), 'Shirley and the Petticoat Line', *Daily Mail*, 26 January, no page number.
Lewis, B. (1964), 'What is a freelance?', *Film and Television Technician*, March, 54.
Lewisohn, M. (1992), *The Complete Beatles Chronicle*, London: Pyramid Books.
LoBrutto, V. (1992), *By Design: Interviews with Film Production Designers*, Westport, CT: Praeger.
McAsh, I. F. (1975), "The Shape of Clothes to Come", *Film Review*, November, 11.
McBride, J. (1973), 'Running, jumping and standing still: an interview with Richard Lester', *Sight and Sound*, 42: 2, 75–9.
MacCabe, C. (1998), *Performance*, London: BFI.
McConnell, J. (1963), 'Girls of the Guild', *The Screenwriter*, no. 12, Spring, 16–19, 29.
MacDonald, I. (1994), *Revolution in the Head: The Beatles' Records and the Sixties*, London: Fourth Estate.
McFarlane, B. (1996), 'Pulp Fictions: The British B Film and the Field of Cultural Production', *Film Criticism*, 21: 1, 48–70.
McFarlane, B. (1997), *Autobiography of British Cinema*, London: Methuen/BFI.

McGilligan, P. (1986), 'Richard Maibaum: a pretence of seriousness' in P. McGilligan (ed.), *Backstory: Interviews with Screenwriters of Hollywood's Golden Age*, Berkeley: University of California Press, 266–89.
McGilligan, P. (1997), 'Introduction', *Backstory 3: Interviews with Screenwriters of the 60s*, Berkeley: University of California Press.
Mackillop, I. and Sinyard N. (eds) (2003) *British Cinema of the 1950s: A Celebration*, Manchester: Manchester University Press.
McLoone, M. (1996), 'Boxed in? The aesthetics of film and television', in J. Hill and M. McLoone (eds), *Big Picture, Small Screen: The Relations Between Film and Television*, Luton: University of Luton Press.
Macnab, G. (1993), *J. Arthur Rank and the British Film Industry*, London: Routledge.
McNay, M.G. (1964), 'Clive Donner, director', *The Guardian*, 18 March, 9.
Maibaum, R. (1965), 'How I write the Bond films', *Showtime*, April, 28.
Mäkelä, J. (2004), *John Lennon Imagined: Cultural History of a Rock Star*, New York: Peter Lang.
Malcolm, D. (1968), 'Censored, and Why', *The Guardian*, 17 September, 6.
Mann, D. (2007), 'An Industrial and Cultural History of Selected British Crime Supporting Features and Filmed Television Series, 1946–1964', University of the West of England: unpublished doctoral thesis.
Mann, D. (2009), *Britain's First TV/Film Crime Series and the Industrialisation of its Film Industry 1946–1964*, London: Edward Mellen Press.
Mann, D. (2014), *Harry Alan Towers: The Transnational Career of a Cinematic Contrarian*, Jefferson, NC: McFarland & Co.
Mann, W. J. (2005), *Edge of Midnight: The Life of John Schlesinger*, London: Arrow.
Marnier, T. St. J. with M. Stringer (1974), *Film Design*, London: Tantivy.
Marwick, A. (2012), *The Sixties*, London: Bloomsbury Reader.
Masters, B. (1985), *The Swinging 60s*, London: Constable.
Matthews, S. (2016), *Psychedelic Celluloid: British Pop Music in Film and TV, 1965–1974*, Harpenden: Oldcastle Books.
Mayer, V., M. J. Banks and J. T. Caldwell (eds) (2009), *Production Studies: Cultural Studies of Media Industries*, New York and London: Routledge.
Mayne, L. (2017), 'Whatever happened to the British 'B' movie? Micro-budget film-making and the death of the one-hour supporting feature in the early 1960s', *Historical Journal of Film, Radio and Television*, 37: 3, 559–76.
Medhurst, A. (1995), 'It sort of happened here: The strange, brief life of the British pop film,' in J. Romney and A. Wootton (eds), *Celluloid Jukebox: Popular music and the movies since the 50s*, London: BFI, 60–71.
Medhurst, A. (2007), *A National Joke: Popular Comedy and English Identities*, London: Routledge.
Meikle, D. (1996), *A History of Horrors: The Rise and Fall of the House of Hammer*, Lanham, MD and London: Scarecrow Press.
Melly, G. (1970, 2012), *Revolt into Style: The Pop Arts*, London: Faber.
Monopolies and Mergers Commission (1966), *A Report on the Supply of Films for Exhibition in Cinemas in the UK*, London: HMSO.
Moore-Gilbert, B. and J. Seed (eds) (1992), *Cultural Revolution: The Challenge of the Arts in the 1970s*, London: Routledge.
Moran, J. (2013), *Armchair Nation: An Intimate History of Britain in Front of the TV*, London: Profile Books.
More, S. (1967), 'Women behind the scenes of success', *The Times*, 19 July, 9.
Mundy, J. (2007), *The British Musical Film*, Manchester: Manchester University Press.
Murphy, R. (1992), Sixties British Cinema, London: BFI.

Murphy, R. 'Gonks Go Beat', unpublished paper, <http://www.academia.edu/6660851/Gonks_Go_Beat> (accessed 31 May 2017).
Nava, M., A. Blake, I. MacRury and B. Richards (eds) (1997), *Buy This Book: Studies in advertising and consumption*, Abingdon: Routledge.
Nelmes, J. (2014), *The Screenwriter in British Cinema*, London: BFI.
Nelmes, J. and J. Selbo (eds) (2015), *Women Screenwriters: An International Guide*, London: Palgrave Macmillan.
Nevett, T. (1992), 'Differences between American and British television advertising: Explanations and implications', *Journal of Advertising*, 21: 4, 61–71.
Newland, P. (ed.) (2010), *Don't Look Now: British Cinema in the 1970s*, Bristol: Intellect.
Newland, P. (2013), *British Films of the 1970s*, Manchester: Manchester University Press.
Nixon, S. (2010), '"Salesmen of the Will to Want": Advertising and its critics in Britain, 1951–1967', *Contemporary British History*, 24: 2, 213–33.
Nixon, S. (2017), 'Looking westwards and worshipping: The New York "Creative Revolution" and British advertising, 1956–1960', *Journal of Consumer Culture*, 17: 2, 147–66.
Norman, P. (1984), *The Stones*, London: Elm Tree.
Nowell-Smith, G. and C. Dupin (eds) (2012), *The British Film Institute, the Government and Film Culture, 1933–2000*, Manchester: Manchester University Press.
Nuttall, J. (1970), *Bomb Culture*, London: Palladin.
O'Brian, B. (1964), 'Private Lives', *Films and Filming*, 10: 7, 57.
Oldham, A. (2003), *2Stoned*, London: Vintage.
Oldham, A. (2011), *Rolling Stoned*, Syracuse, NY: Gegensatz.
Oldham, G. (1995), *First Cut: Conversations with Film Editors*, Berkeley: University of California Press.
Opie, I. and P. Opie (1997), *Children's Games with Things*, Oxford: Oxford University Press.
Owen, A. (1964), 'Why I wrote a script for the Beatles', *Photoplay*, May, 12.
Owen, A. (1964), 'What it is like working with the Beatles', *Showtime*, June, 4.
Pattinson, J. F. (1960), 'I Believe in British Films for Britain', *Kine Weekly*, supplement on 20th Century Fox productions in Britain, 28 September, 6.
Pattison, B. (1962), 'Ladies day', *Films and Filming*, September, 15.
Pavlus, J. (2002), 'A versatile legacy: Douglas Slocombe, BSC, recipient of the 2001 ASC International Achievement Award, surveys a career that began with Ealing comedies and ended with Indiana Jones', *American Cinematographer*, 83: 3, 86–94.
Perkins, R. and M. Stollery, *British Film Editors: The Heart of the Movie*, London: BFI.
Perkins, V. F. (1962), 'The British cinema', *Movie*, 1, 2–9.
Perkins, V. F. (1962), 'Clive Donner and Some People', *Movie*, 3, 23–4.
Perry, G. (1985), *The Great British Picture Show*, London: Pavilion.
Petrie, D. (1996), *The British Cinematographer*, London: BFI.
Petrie, D. (2016), 'Resisting Hollywood Dominance in Sixties British Cinema: The NFFC/Rank Joint Financing Initiative', *Historical Journal of Film, Radio and Television*, 36: 4, 548–68.
Petrie, D. (2018), 'Bryanston Films: An Experiment in Cooperative Independent Production and Distribution', *Historical Journal of Film, Radio and Television*, 38: 1, 95–115.
Pierce-Jones, R. (2011), 'The men who played Bond,' in R. G. Weiner, B. L. Whitfield and J. Becker, *James Bond in World and Popular Culture: The Films are Not Enough*, Newcastle: Cambridge Scholars Publishing, 359–73.

Pirie, D. (1973), *A Heritage of Horror: The English Gothic Cinema 1946–72*, London: Gordon Fraser.
Pomerance, M. (2015), 'Assheton Gorton: A Life in Film', *Film International*, no. 71, March/April, 68.
Porter, V. and C. Wicking (1965), 'The making of Life at the Top', *Film and Television Technician*, December, 230.
Porter, V. (2001), 'All Change at Elstree: Warner Bros., ABPC and British Film Policy 1945–61', *Historical Journal of Film, Radio and Television*, 21: 1, 5–35.
Porter, V. (2012), 'Making and Meaning: The Role of the Producer in British Films', *The Journal of British Cinema and Television*, 9: 1, 7–25.
Potter, J. (1989), *Independent Television in Britain – vol. 3: Politics and Control, 1968–80*, London: Macmillan.
Potter, J. (1990), *Independent Television in Britain – vol. 4: Companies and Programmes, 1968–80*, London: Macmillan.
Powell, D. (1964), 'Climber with a knife', *The Sunday Times*, 1 March, 20.
Priestley, J. B. (1961), 'The Magic Beanstalk', *Contrast*, Autumn, 5.
Price, S. (1964), 'The man who gilded Goldfinger', *Observer Magazine*, 6 September, 24.
Prior, A. (1963), 'The economics of screenwriting', *The Screenwriter*, 13, Summer, 10.
Rees, A. (2011), *A History of Experimental Film and Video*, London: BFI/Palgrave Macmillan.
Quant, M. (2012), *Quant by Quant*, London: V&A Publishing.
Reid, I. (2017), 'Trade Unions and the British Film Industry: 1930s–1980s, in I. Q. Hunter, L. Porter and J. Smith (eds), *The Routledge Companion to British Cinema History*, London: Routledge, 251–61.
Raphael, F. (1967), 'Preface', *Two For the Road*, London: Jonathan Cape.
Raphael, F. (2001), *Personal Terms: The 1950s and 1960s*, Manchester: Carcanet.
Raphael, F. (2015), *Going Up: To Cambridge and Beyond*, London: Biteback.
Reed, P. (2012), *Fifty Looks That Changed the 1960s*, London: Conran Octopus.
Reisz, K. and G. Millar (2009), *The Technique of Film Editing, Second Edition*, London: Focal Press.
Richards, J. (1992), 'New Waves and Old Myths: British Cinema in the 1960s' in B. Moore-Gilbert and J. Seed (eds), *Cultural Revolution: The Challenge of the Arts in the 1970s*, London: Routledge, 171–85.
Rickards, J. (1987), *The Painted Banquet*, London: Weidenfeld and Nicolson.
Rickey, C. (1982), 'Theatrical Realism', *Film Comment*, 18: 1, 32–3.
Robertson, J. C. (1989), *The Hidden Cinema: British Film Censorship in Action, 1913–1972*, London: Routledge.
Robinson, D. (1968), 'Case Histories of the next renascence', *Sight and Sound*, 37: 1, 38–40.
Rosendorf, N. M. (2007), '"Hollywood in Madrid": American Film Producers and the Franco Regime, 1950–1970', *Historical Journal of Film, Radio and Television*, 27: 1, 77–109.
Roud, R. (1960), 'The French Line', *Sight and Sound*, 29: 4, 166–71.
Roud, R. (1979), 'The Reluctant Exile', *Sight and Sound*, 48: 3 145–7.
Russell, P. (2007), *100 British Documentaries*, London: BFI/Palgrave.
Russell, P. and Taylor, J. P. (eds) (2011), *Shadows of Progress: Documentary Film in Post War Britain*, London: BFI/Palgrave Macmillan.
Russell Taylor, J. (1963), 'The Servant and The Caretaker', *Sight and Sound*, 32: 1, 39.
Russell Taylor, J. (1966), 'Accident', *Sight and Sound*, 35: 4, 179–84.
Russell Taylor, J. (1968), 'Larking back', *Sight and Sound*, 37: 2, 68–71.

Russell Taylor, J. (1969), 'Backing Britain', *Sight and Sound*, 38: 3, 112–5.
Rutherford, P. (1994), *The New Icons? The Art of Television Advertising*, Toronto: University of Toronto Press.
Ryder, D. (2007), *Making it on Wardour Street*, Leeds: Cinemuseum Publishing.
Salt, B. (1992), *Film Style and Technology*, London: Starword.
Sampson, A. (1965), *Anatomy of Britain Today*, London: Hodder & Stoughton.
Sandbrook, D. (2005), *Never Had It So Good: A History of Britain from Suez to the Beatles*, London: Little, Brown.
Sandbrook, D. (2006), *White Heat: A History of Britain in the Swinging Sixties*, London: Little, Brown.
Sandbrook, D. (2015), *The Great British Dream Factory: The Strange History of our National Imagination*, London: Penguin.
Sandford, C. (2012), *The Rolling Stones: Fifty Years*, London: Simon & Schuster.
Sapper, A. (1968), 'The writer: isolation or interdependence?', *Film and TV Technician*, May, 20.
Sarne, M. (1967), 'Two for the Road', *Films and Filming*, September, 20.
Schroeder, J. (2016), *All For the Love of Music*, Kibworth Beauchamp: Matador.
Scott, J. (2003), *Fast and Louche: Confessions of a flagrant sinner*, London: Profile.
Self, M. (2012), 'The View From Outside London' in G. Nowell-Smith and C. Dupin (eds), *The British Film Institute, the Government and Film Culture, 1933–2000*, Manchester: Manchester University Press, 116–32.
Sendall, B. (1983), *Independent Television in Britain – vol. 2: Expansion and Change, 1958–62*, London: Macmillan.
Shail, R. (ed.) (2008), *Seventies British Cinema*, London: BFI/Palgrave Macmillan.
Shail, R. (2012), *Tony Richardson*, Manchester: Manchester University Press.
Sharples, W. (ed.) (1977), 'Film editors forum', *Film Comment*, 13: 2, 6–29.
Sharps, W. S. (1958), *Commercial Television: A Manual of Advertising Production and Techniques*, London: Fountain Press.
Scheuer, P. K. (1969), 'Anthony Harvey, Director's Guild Award winner', *Action!*, May/June, 12.
Shelton, S. (1970), 'Television Advertising: Its Part in Mass Communication', *Journal of the Royal Society of Arts*, 118: 5166, 332–43.
Simpson, M. (2008), *Alastair Sim*, Stroud: History Press.
Sinyard, N. (2000), *Jack Clayton*, Manchester: Manchester University Press.
Sinyard, N. (2010), *Richard Lester*, Manchester: Manchester University Press.
Slocombe, D. (1948), 'Colour through the camera', in *Saraband for Dead Lovers: The Film and Its Production at Ealing Studios*, London: Convoy Publications, 87.
Slocombe, D. (1981), 'Through a glass not-so-darkly', *American Cinematographer*, 62: 11, 1104–5, 1123.
Smith, A. 'Dolls of Vice: Eurotica repackaged for early 1960s British audiences', <https://www.academia.edu/5163095/Dolls_of_Vice_Eurotica_repackaged_for_early_1960s_British_audiences> (accessed 06 March 2017).
Smith, A. (2017), '"As long as indifferent sexy films are box office they will abound!", the Jacey cinema chain and independent distribution and exhibition in 1960s Britain', in I. Q. Hunter, L. Porter and J. Smith (eds), *The Routledge Companion to British Cinema History*, London: Routledge, 209–19.
Smith, R. (1967) 'The future of the TV play', *Film and Television Technician*, May, 134–5.
Snelgrove, K. (2008), *The Official Carry On Facts, Figures and Statistics: A Complete Statistical Analysis of the Carry Ons*, Clacton on Sea: Apex Publishing.
Soderbergh, S. (1999), *Getting Away With It – Or: The Further Adventures of the Luckiest Bastard you Ever Saw*, London: Faber.

Sparke, P. (2012), 'At home with modernity: the new domestic scene', in C. Breward and G. Wood (eds), *British Design from 1948: Innovation in the Modern Age*, London: V&A Publishing, 118–37.
Spicer, A. (2006), *Sydney Box*, Manchester: Manchester University Press.
Spicer A. and McKenna, A.T. (2013), *The Man Who Got Carter: Michael Klinger, Independent Production and the British Film Industry, 1960–1980*, London: I. B. Tauris.
Spicer, A. (2017), 'Producers and Moguls' in I. Q. Hunter, L. Porter and J. Smith (eds), *The Routledge Companion to British Cinema History*, London: Routledge, 139–50.
Spraos, J. (1962), *The Decline of the Cinema: An Economist's Report*, London: George Allen & Unwin.
Spring, K. (2013), *Saying It With Songs: Popular Music and the Coming of Sound to Hollywood Cinema*, Oxford: Oxford University Press.
Street, S. (2002), *Transatlantic Crossings: British Feature Films in the United States*, London: Continuum.
Stubbs. J. (2008), '"Blocked" currency, runaway production in Britain and Captain Horatio Hornblower (1951)', *Historical Journal of Film, Radio and Television*, 28: 3, 335–51.
Stubbs, J. (2009), 'The Eady Levy: A Runaway Bribe? Hollywood Production and British Subsidy in the Early 1960s', *Journal of British Cinema and Television*, 6: 1, 1–20.
Surowiec, C. A. (2012), 'Anthony Mendleson: Ealing's wardrobe wizard', in M. Duguid, L. Freeman, K. M. Johnston and M. Williams (eds), *Ealing Revisited*, London: BFI, 111–24.
Sutton, S. (2014), 'Sydney Newman', in J. Bignell and S. Lacey (eds), *British Television Drama: Past, Present and Future* 2nd edn, London: Palgrave Macmillan, 40–4.
Subotsky, M. (1969), 'The Work of the Film Producer', *Screen*, 10: 6, 24–32.
Sulik, B. (1962), 'Film Criticism on Television', *Contrast*, 2: 2, 106.
Sweet, M. (2006), *Shepperton Babylon: The Lost Worlds of British Cinema*, London: Faber.
Sylvester, D. (ed.) (1999), *Moonraker, Strangelove and Other Celluloid Dreams: The Visionary Art of Ken Adam*, London: Serpentine Gallery.
Tanner, P. (1962), 'Editing: theory and practice', *Photographic Journal*, 102: 11, November, 296.
Taplin, W. (1961), *The Origin of Television Advertising in the United Kingdom*, London: Sir Isaac Pitman & Sons.
Taylor, B. F. (2006), *The British New Wave: A Certain Tendency?* Manchester: Manchester University Press.
Tempest, F. (n.d.), "Interview with Julie Harris", on Costume on Screen, <https://costumeonscreen.wordpress.com/2011/06/25/julie-harris-darling-1965/> (accessed 24 February 2018).
Terry, J. (1964), 'Where Have all the Young Men Gone?', *Kine Weekly*, 17 December, 139.
Terry, J. (1969) 'Time Right for British Finance', *Kine Weekly*, 15 March, 8.
Thompson, B. (ed.) (2012), *Ban This Filth!: Letters from the Mary Whitehouse Archive*, London: Faber.
Threadgall, D. (1994), *Shepperton Studios: An Independent View*, London: BFI.
Todd, D. (1963), 'The Boulting Brothers Find Pegs on Which to Hang the World', *Kine Weekly*, 30 May, 66.
Todd, D. (1963), 'White Hunter sets his sights on The Chalk Garden', *Kine Weekly*, 4 April, 11.
Todd, D. (1963), 'Getting into the comedy habit', *Kine Weekly*, 13 June, 14.

Todd, D. (1963), 'No end to realism in a Battersea cul-de-sac', *Kine Weekly*, 8 August, 11.
Todd, D. (1966), 'Casino Royale – the twenty-reel jigsaw', *Kine Weekly*, 29 September, 9.
Todd, D. (1967), 'How to "Blossom" into a Fun Film', *Kine Weekly*, 26 August, 10.
Todd, D. (1967), 'Ex-orphanage kid now of Paramount importance', *Kine Weekly*, 9 September, 14.
Todd, D. (1968), 'Negatives Explores the Youthquake', *Kine Weekly*, 23 March, 19.
Todd, D. (1969), 'The Stable Door: after the (US) horse has gone', *Kine Weekly*, 6 December, 6.
Toncar, M. F. (2001), 'The use of humour in television advertising: revisiting the US–UK comparison', *International Journal of Advertising*, 20: 4, 521–39.
Trevelyan, J. (1973), *What the Censor Saw*, London: Michael Joseph.
Turner, A. (1994), *The Making of David Lean's Lawrence of Arabia*, London: Dragon's World.
Turner, A. (1999), *Robert Bolt: Scenes from Two Lives*, London: Vintage.
Turner, A. W. (2011), *Terry Nation: The Man who invented the Daleks*, London: Aarum.
Tuson, E. M. (2005), 'Consumerism, the Swinging Sixties and Assheton Gorton', *Journal of British Cinema and Television*, 2: 1, 100–16.
Upton, J. (2004), *Fallen Stars: Tragic Lives and Lost Careers*, Manchester: Critical Vision.
Various (1973), 'Amicus: Two's A Company', *Little Shoppe of Horrors*, Issue 2.
Various (2009), 'The art and craft of film editing: a critical symposium', *Cineaste*, 34: 2, 54 (11).
Vas, R. (1966), 'Meditation at 24 F.P.S.', *Sight and Sound*, Summer, 35: 3, 122.
Wakely, M. (1970), 'Situation hopeless but not serious', *Films and Filming*, May, 9.
Walford, J. (2013), *Sixties Fashion*, London: Thames and Hudson.
Walker, A. (1974) *Hollywood, England: The British Film Industry in the Sixties*, London: Michael Joseph.
Ward, B. (1980), 'Keeping the funny men in stitches', *Daily Express*, 7 May, no page number.
Ware, J. (1967), 'Production-Wise', *Daily Cinema*, 1 November, 8.
Watkin, D. (1998), *Why is there only one word for Thesaurus?* Brighton: Trouser Press.
Waymark, P. (2012), '"From telly laughs to belly laughs": The rise and fall of the sitcom spinoff', in I. Q. Hunter and L. Porter (eds), *British Comedy Cinema*, London: Routledge, 141–53.
Webber, R. (2008), *50 Years of Carry On*, London: Century.
Weinberger, M. G. and H. E. Spotts (1989), 'Humor in US versus UK TV Commercials: A Comparison', *Journal of Advertising*, 18: 2, 39–44.
West, D. (1988), 'Multinational Competition in the British Advertising Agency Business, 1936–1987', *Business History Review*, 62: 3, 467.
White, A. (1989), 'Illuminations', *Film Comment*, 25: 5, 58.
White, B. (1974), 'Lassally on British Cinematography', *Journal of the University Film Association*, 26: 4, 61.
Whitehall, R. (1964), 'Live It Up', *Films and Filming*, January, 28.
Whitehead, P. (2011), 'Letters to Andrew Oldham', *Framework: The Journal of Cinema and Media*, 52: 1, 196–208.
Whitehouse, M. (1971), *Who does she think she is?* London: New English Library.
Williams, F. (1962), *American Invasion*, London: Anthony Blond.
Williams, M. (2014), *David Lean*, Manchester: Manchester University Press.

Williams, M. (2015), 'Making the cut: *The Wild Affair*', *Transformation and Tradition in Sixties British Cinema*, November 2015, <https://60sbritishcinema.wordpress.com/2015/11/05/making-the-cut-the-wild-affair/>.
Williams, M. (2016), 'The girl you don't see: Julie Harris and the costume designer in British cinema', *Feminist Media Histories*, 2: 2, 71–106.
Williams, M. (2016), 'A kaleidoscope of costume: putting swinging London's fashions on screen', *Transformation and Tradition in Sixties British Cinema*, <https://60sbritishcinema.wordpress.com/2016/10/20/a-kaleidoscope-of-costume-putting-swinging-londons-fashions-on-screen/>.
Williams, M. (2017), 'No Scruggs, or my truncated journey into the mysterious film career of David Hart', *Transformation and Tradition in Sixties British Cinema*, <https://60sbritishcinema.wordpress.com/2017/05/24/no-scruggs-or-my-truncated-journey-into-the-mysterious-film-career-of-david-hart/>.
Williams, R. (1963), 'Joan Littlewood: the perfectionist from East Stratford', *Film and Television Technician*, March, 56.
Willis, T. (1963), 'The 1962 awards', *The Screenwriter*, 12, Spring, 3.
Winner, M. (2005), *Winner Takes All: A Life of Sorts*, London: Robson Books.
Wood, L. (1980), *British Film Industry: Information Guide, No. 1*, London: BFI.
Wyman, B. (1990), *Stone Alone: The story of a rock 'n' roll band*, London: Viking.
Yapp, N. (n.d.), 'The Write Stuff: A History of the Writers' Guild of Great Britain 1959–2009', Writers' Guild of Great Britain, <https://writersguild.org.uk/history-writers-guild-awards/> (accessed 18 June 2018).
Young, F. (1966), 'A method of pre-exposing color negative for subtle effect', *American Cinematographer*, 47: 8, 537.
Zone, R. (2002), 'Wrap shot: Dr. No', *American Cinematographer*, 83: 11, 112.

INDEX

20th Century Fox, 11, 14, 41, 44, 53, 65, 66, 67, 68, 69, 75–7, 80, 82, 88, 89, 112, 174, 188, 254, 355, 359, 360
24 Hours to Kill (1965), 44
30 is a Dangerous Age Cynthia (1967), 71
55 Days at Peking (1963), 40
633 Squadron (1964), 73, 165, 358
2001: A Space Odyssey (1968), 74, 84, 90, 205, 329, 351, 361, 362, 363
80,000 Suspects (1963), 38

A. B. King Cinemas, 12, 119
Aaru, 154, 294, 296
ABC Cinemas, 11, 12, 100, 119, 121, 130, 133, 142, 147, 225, 296, 330
ABC Film Review, 10, 334
ABC TV, 44, 144, 212, 283, 285, 292
Above us the Waves (1955), 181
Accident (1967), 3, 20, 96, 109, 113, 115, 166, 209–10, 263, 264
Ackland, Noreen, 266
ACT Films, 50, 100
Adam, Ken, 203, 204, 205, 206, 207, 208, 209, 210, 211–12, 233, 245
African Queen, The (1951), 83, 286
Albion (Distributors), 50, 101
Aldrich, Robert, 75, 187
Alf Garnett Saga, The (1972), 297
Alfie (1966), 3, 78, 123, 169, 185, 359

Alfred the Great (1969), 75, 89, 194–5, 229
All Neat in Black Stockings (1969), 49, 57
All Night Long (1961), 39, 332
All the Way Up (1970), 297
Allen, Dede, 262
Allen, Irving, 66, 70, 83, 185
Allen, Lewis M., 79
Allen, Marit, 224
Allen, Woody, 360
Allied Artists, 39
Allied Film Makers, 15, 38–9, 51, 54, 58
Alphabet Murders, The (1965), 74
Altria, Bill, 89, 110
Ambler, Dail, 167
American International Pictures, 47, 54, 82
Amicus, 15, 71, 78, 81, 128, 152–4, 155, 294
Amis, Kingsley, 162
Amorous Adventures of Moll Flanders, The (1965), 77
Amorous Prawn, The (1962), 51
And God Created Woman (1956), 126
An Alligator Named Daisy (1955), 181
Anderson, Bill, 81
Anderson, Gerry, 73, 295
Anderson, Lindsay, 15, 17, 38, 78, 123, 143, 189, 266, 307, 309, 310

380

Anderson, Michael, 41, 74, 166, 184, 358
Anderson, Sylvia, 73, 295
Andress, Ursula, 205, 235, 254–5
Andrews, Julie, 359
Angel, Danny, 43, 57
Angenieux, Pierre, 243
Anglia Television, 283
Anglo-Amalgamated, 11, 13, 14, 15, 20, 22, 33, 34, 35, 37, 43–4, 45–9, 50, 54, 55, 57, 82, 121, 125, 135, 140, 141, 143, 149–51, 152, 164, 172, 192, 263, 354, 355, 358, 360, 362
Anglo-American Film Agreement, 1948, 65, 67
Anglo-Embassy, 67, 81
Angry Silence, The (1960), 51, 96, 99, 162
Animals, the, 194
Annakin, Ken, 38, 41, 70, 76, 81, 143, 169, 184, 355, 357, 359
Anne of a Thousand Days (1969), 79, 167, 205, 226, 227, 242
Anstey, Edgar, 17
Antonioni, Michelangelo, 63, 74, 166, 171, 187–8, 214, 264, 267, 339
Apple boutique, 215
Apple Corps, 337
Apted, Michael, 292
Arabesque (1966), 79, 308
Arbeid, Ben, 74
Archer, Ernest, 205
Archibald, George, 99
Ardmore Studios, 14, 145
Arkoff, Samuel Z., 82
Armchair Theatre, 163, 212–13, 292
Arriflex Cameras, 243, 244, 249
Asher, Robert, 34, 37, 47, 357, 358, 359
Asquith, Anthony, 6, 43, 74, 83, 184, 350, 357
Assassination Bureau, The (1968), 78, 265
Assassination of Mick Jagger, The (unmade film) 342
Associated British Picture Corporation (ABPC), 6, 10, 11, 12, 21, 24, 33, 42–4, 47, 54, 55, 66, 80, 82, 89, 121, 133, 145, 171, 184, 283, 285, 292–3, 297, 318, 330, 355
Associated–Rediffusion, 45, 286, 290, 319
Associated Talking Pictures, 285
Association of Cinema and Television Technicians (ACTT), 16, 22, 24, 41, 89, 100, 101, 103, 264
ATV, 172, 187, 193, 285, 309
Attack on the Iron Coast (1968), 73

Attenborough, Richard, 15, 38–9, 51, 78, 96, 355, 362
Atwooll, Hugh, 81
Augusta, 310, 311
Avco Corporation, 81
Avco–Embassy, 13, 81, 83, 188, 362
Avengers, The (1961–9), 6, 44, 144, 155, 213, 292
Avventura, L' (1960), 171

Baby Love (1968), 81
Bachmann, Laurence P., 74
BAFTA, 16, 161
Bailey, David, 203, 204, 223, 342
Bailey, H., 108
Baines, Lionel, 243
Baird, Stuart, 264
Baker, Robert, 38
Baker, Roy Ward, 38, 45, 51, 82, 184, 290
Baker, Stanley, 15, 47, 48, 77, 78, 81, 86, 358
Balcon, Michael, 17, 43, 50, 52, 53, 65, 99, 102, 105, 283, 355
Balio, Tino, 66, 72, 73
Banbury, Frith, 165
Band of Thieves (1962), 330, 332
Barbarella (1968), 165
Barber, Sian, 8
Bardot, Brigitte, 104, 126
Bargee, The (1964), 42, 297
Baring, Aubrey, 51, 357
Barr, Charles, 181
Barrett, Alan, 230
Barry, Gene, 104
Barry, John, 308, 314, 330, 331, 332
Barry, Jonathan, 210
Bart, Lionel, 335
Barzman, Ben, 165
Bassey, Shirley, 330
Bates, Alan, 2, 3, 39, 48, 162, 172, 317, 318
Battle beneath the Earth (1967), 84, 86–7
Battle of Britain, The (1969), 73, 84, 89, 362
Battle of the Sexes, The (1960), 51, 56
Battle of the Villa Fiorita, The (1965), 80
Baxter, John, 283
Baxter, Stanley, 143
BBC, 5, 7, 18, 53, 112, 123, 163, 186, 187, 269, 283–4, 286, 289, 290, 291, 292, 293, 297, 303, 307, 331, 342
Be My Guest (1965), 330

381

Beaconsfield Studios, 14, 22, 142, 144, 283
Bean, Robin, 104
Beat Girl (1960), 114, 167, 332
Beatles, the, 3, 6, 9, 15, 52, 72, 73, 74, 164, 184, 203, 215, 231, 232, 295, 306, 316, 329, 332–8, 339, 341, 343, 350, 352, 357, 358
  Sgt Pepper's Lonely Hearts Club Band, 7, 215, 306
Beatles at Shea Stadium, The (1966), 337
Beaton, Cecil, 226, 229
Beattie, Robert, 288
Beaver Films, 99
Beauty Jungle, The (1964), 38
BECTU, 10
Bedazzled (1967), 77, 224
Beck, Reginald, 263, 264
Becket (1964), 77, 208, 226, 227, 242, 261, 262
Bed Sitting Room, The (1969), 73, 166, 212, 216, 310
Bee Gees, the, 332
Bell, Tom, 162
Benedek, Laslo, 42
Benjamin, Robert, 66–7
Bennett, Hywel, 51
Bentine, Michael, 104
Beresford, Bruce, 17–18
Bergman, Ingmar, 124, 341
Berlin Film Festival, 3, 48, 129, 192
Berman, Monty, 38
Berman, Padro S., 74
Bermans (costumiers), 227, 228
Bernard, Judd, 231
Bernstein, Cecil, 285, 298
Bernstein, David, 315
Bernstein, Sidney, 283
Best of Everything, The (1961), 172
Best, Richard, 264, 265, 267, 292
Bezencenet, Peter, 39
Biba, 203, 223, 232
Big Job, The (1965), 46
Bilbow, Margery, 212
Bilk, Acker, 330
Bill Douglas Cinema Museum, University of Exeter, 10
Billington, Kevin, 71, 80, 186, 189, 291–2
Billington, Michael, 318
Billion Dollar Brain (1967), 73, 310, 317
Billy Budd (1962), 39, 163
Billy Liar (1963), 20, 48, 57, 164, 341

Bindon, John, 294
Biographic (Production Company), 309
Birkett, Michael, 192
Birkin, Jane, 226
Black Beauty (1971), 132
Black, Cilla, 332, 337
Black Torment, The (1964), 128
Blackman, Honor, 6, 147, 292
Blake, Yvonne, 228
Blattner, Gerry, 355
BLC Films, 50, 54, 70
Bliss of Mrs Blossom, The (1968), 212, 214–16
Bloch, Robert, 154
Blood Beast Terror, The (1968), 132
Blood of Fu Manchu, The (1968), 49
Blood on Satan's Claw (1971), 132
Bloom, Claire, 223
Bloom, John, 263, 265, 269
Blow Up (1966), 3, 74, 166, 204, 209, 212, 214, 216, 223, 225–6, 264, 267, 339, 363
Blue Max, The (1966), 76, 165, 229, 254–5, 360
Bluhdorn, Charles, 78
Board of Trade (HM Government), 102, 103, 104, 106, 107, 110, 111, 112, 113
Bobo, The (1967), 80, 83, 86, 87
Bofors Gun, The (1968), 79, 84
Bogarde, Dirk, 36, 37, 38, 39, 43, 48, 123, 210, 242, 254, 355
Bogdanovich, Peter, 195
Bohan, Marc, 230
Boland, Bridget, 167
Bolt, Robert, 165, 170
Bond, Edward, 166
Bond, Ralph, 101, 103
Bonnie and Clyde (1967), 89, 260, 262
Booker, Christopher, 5, 334
Boom! (1968), 20, 79, 83, 189, 255
Boorman, John, 47, 184, 290, 351
Booth, Stanley, 327
Border Television, 52, 283
Bordwell, David, 259, 268
Borges, Jorge Luis, 272
Born Free (1966), 70, 330, 359
Bottoms Up! (1960), 43
Boulting Brothers, 6, 13, 14, 49, 50–1, 52, 54, 105, 185, 189, 360
Boulting, John, 53, 54, 55, 185, 357, 360
Boulting, Roy, 357, 360
Bourguignon, Serge, 104

Box, Betty, 15, 36–7, 40, 149, 263, 354, 357
Box, John, 204, 207, 208, 209, 211
Box, Muriel, 43
Box, Sydney, 14, 37, 58, 102, 149, 283, 330
Boy and Bicycle (1965), 18
Boy Friend, The (1971), 231
Boy Who Stole a Million, The (1960), 51, 56, 77, 251
Boyd, Patti, 194
Brabourne, Lord (John), 17, 76, 78, 355, 356, 360, 362
Bradbury, Ray, 246
Braden, Bernard, 309
Bradsell, Michael, 292
Brain, The (1962), 145
Brauner, Artur, 145
Brett, Jeremy, 145
Bricusse, Leslie, 171
Bridge, Joan, 226
Brides of Dracula, The (1960), 79, 208
Brides of Fu Manchu, The (1966), 49
Bridge on the River Kwai, The (1957), 66, 180
Brigand of Kandahar, The (1965), 44
Bright, Morris, 48
Brinton, Ralph, 204–5, 206–7
Britannia (Distributors), 50, 52, 56, 101, 124
British Board of Film Classification (BBFC), 10, 18, 19, 39, 120, 121, 122–4, 126, 127, 130, 135, 193, 340, 341
British Film Academy Awards, 161–9, 171, 189, 209, 226–7, 230, 232, 243, 253
British Film Institute (BFI), 10, 12, 15, 109, 125, 182
  Experimental Film Fund, 17
  BFI Production Board, 17–18
British Film Producers Association, 16, 22, 45, 67, 109
British Film Production Fund, 17, 65–6, 95, 106, 108, 110, 112
British Lion, 10, 12, 13, 14, 21, 22, 24, 33, 34, 35, 49–53, 54, 55, 70, 97, 101–2, 103, 106, 121, 127, 141, 142, 145, 146, 155, 286–7, 291, 354, 355, 356, 357, 359, 360, 362
British Society of Cinematographers, 253
British Transport Films, 247, 306, 317
Broccoli, Albert 'Cubby', 13, 14, 18, 38, 66, 72, 73, 83, 85, 185, 356, 357, 358, 359, 360, 362

Bromily, Alan, 43
Bron, Eleanor, 224, 234
Bronston, Samuel, 40
Brook, Peter, 51, 73, 247
Brooks, Ray, 191, 204
Brooks, Richard, 71
Brown, C. M. P., 106
Brown, George H., 15, 40, 51, 76
Brownjohn, Robert, 317
Brownlow, Kevin, 262
Bruzzi, Stella, 226
Bryan, Dora, 244
Bryan, John, 72, 77, 206, 208
Bryanston Films, 12, 13, 14, 20, 22, 50, 51–2, 54, 56, 70, 77, 82, 99, 101, 121, 142, 147, 155, 286, 355
Bryanston–Seven Arts, 53, 56, 72, 82, 101
Bryden, Ronald, 315
Brynner, Yul, 41
Bulldog Breed, The (1960), 37
Bullitt (1968), 184, 351
Bullmore, Jeremy, 307, 309
Bunny Lake is Missing (1965), 71, 339
Bunuel, Luis, 124
Burgess, Anthony, 293, 340
Burning, The (1968), 15, 18
Burrows, Rosemary, 228
Burton, Richard, 3, 20, 83–4, 189, 191
Butcher (Distributor), 12, 13, 139, 141
Buttercup Chain, The (1970), 255
Byrne, Kiki, 223

Cacoyannis, Michael, 77
Caesars, The (1968), 297
Cain, Syd, 208
Caine, Michael, 3, 40, 78, 185, 194, 212, 224, 352, 359
Cairo (1963), 74
Caffin, Yvonne, 228
Caledonian Cinemas, 12, 119
Call Me Bwana (1963), 38
Calley, John, 80
Cameron, Ian, 195
Cameron Menzies, William, 206
Cammell, David, 317
Cammell, Donald, 80, 188, 246, 271–2, 317, 343
Campbell, Colin, 138
Can Heironymus Merkin Ever Forget Mercy Humppe and Find True Happiness? (1969), 79, 188
Canadians, The (1961), 76

383

Cannes Film Festival, 3, 75, 76, 187, 308
  Palme D'Or, 3, 72, 67, 78
Cardiff, Jack, 53, 70, 74, 75, 250
Caretaker, The (1963), 51, 192, 193, 246
Caron, Leslie, 51, 162, 192, 254
Carreras, James, 14, 22, 66
Carreras, Michael, 15, 356, 360
Carrick, Edward, 207–8
Carry On (Series), 6, 13, 15, 37, 46–7, 48, 143, 147–52, 155, 169, 186, 209, 243, 263
  At Your Convenience (1971), 148
  Cabby (1963), 46, 152
  Camping (1969), 20, 38, 150, 152, 212, 362
  Cleo (1964), 46, 148, 209, 232, 234, 358
  Constable (1960), 46, 96, 148, 209, 354
  Cowboy (1965), 46, 148
  Cruising (1962), 46, 148, 152
  Dick (1974), 148
  Doctor (1968), 38, 361
  Don't Lose Your Head (1967), 37, 96, 150, 152
  Emmanuelle (1978), 151, 152
  Follow that Camel (1967), 20, 37, 151, 152, 263
  Henry (1971), 148
  Jack (1964), 46
  Matron (1972), 148
  Nurse (1959), 46, 100, 148
  Regardless (1961), 20, 46, 152, 355
  Screaming (1966), 46, 148, 288
  Sergeant (1958), 20, 46, 147, 148, 151, 209
  Spying (1964), 46, 148
  Teacher (1959), 148, 294
  Up the Khyber (1968), 38, 151, 209, 349, 353, 362
Carson, John, 309
Carstairs, John Paddy, 42, 171
Carter, Ernestine, 230
Carter, Maurice, 205, 208
Carve Her Name with Pride (1958), 185
Casino Royale (1967), 71, 165, 205, 209, 214, 222, 227, 232, 233, 234–5, 266, 360, 363
Castle of Fu Manchu, The (1969), 49
Castle, William, 121
Catch Us If You Can (1965), 47, 184, 320, 338, 341
Cathy Come Home (1966), 293–4
CCC Distributors, 145

Chaffey, Don, 71, 81, 186, 355, 357, 360
Chalk Garden, The (1963), 79, 232, 233
Challis, Christopher, 242, 250
Champlin, Charles, 190
Chaplin, Charlie, 63, 79
Chapman, James, 148, 150
Charade (1963), 266
Charge of the Light Brigade, The (1968), 73, 147, 167, 189, 230, 247–8, 262, 361
Chariots of Fire (1981), 317
Charise, Cyd, 104
Charlie Bubbles (1967), 15, 41, 79, 167, 188, 211
Charlie is My Darling (1966), 327, 338
Chasman, David, 67, 73
Chayefsky, Paddy, 163
Cheaters, The(1960–2), 14
Chegwidden, Ann, 266
Chester, Hal, 355
Children of the Damned (1963), 74
Children's Film Foundation, 12
Children's Hour, The (1961), 287
Chitty Chitty Bang Bang (1968), 73, 329, 362
Chris Barber Bandstand (1963), 332
Chris Barber Jazz Band, 319
Christie, Agatha, 74, 350
Christie, Ian, 206
Christie, Julie, 3, 48, 143, 230, 232, 246, 319
Church Gibson, Pamela, 223
Cinecenta, 133
Cinema (TV Show), 289
Cinema Exhibitors Association (CEA), 16, 283, 297
CinemaScope, 75
Cinematograph Films Act 1966, 107
Cinematograph Films Act 1970, 112
Cinematograph Films Council, 102, 109, 110
Cinerama (Distributors), 41
Circus of Horrors (1960), 46, 82, 143, 144, 251
City of the Dead (1960), 52, 56, 114, 153
City under the Sea (1965), 47, 82
Clark, Dave, 320
Clark, Jim, 261, 263, 264–5, 266, 268, 273
Clark, Petula, 235, 330, 332
Clark, Robert, 42, 45, 55
Clarke, Frank, 264, 267
Classic Cinema Chain, 11, 133

Clavell, James, 71
Clayton, Jack, 71, 75, 76, 166, 181–2, 211, 264–5, 351
Clemens, Brian, 140, 290
Clement, Dick, 174, 352
Cleopatra (1963), 76, 209, 210, 234
Clockwork Orange, A (1971), 90, 122, 340
Clore, Leon, 49, 53, 310–11
Clue of the Twisted Candle, The (1960), 47
Clyde, Thomas, 42
Coates, Anne V., 261, 262, 265, 266, 267
Coburn, James, 224
Cocksucker Blues (1972), 327
Coe, Peter, 71
Cohen, Herman, 47
Cohen, Nat, 13, 14, 22, 45–6, 48, 49, 149, 172
Cohen, Norman, 53, 128, 362
Colditz Story, The (1955), 100
Cole, Sid, 41
Coleman, John, 223
Collector, The (1965), 165, 215
Collins, Douglas, 50, 145
Collinson, Peter, 78, 132, 187, 264, 290, 294, 360
Columbia, 11, 40, 50, 54, 66, 67, 68, 69, 70–1, 72, 83, 84, 87, 88, 89, 99, 112, 154, 209, 232, 356, 357, 359, 360, 361, 362, 363
Come Fly with Me (1962), 74
Comedy Man, The (1964), 319
Comfort, Lance, 39
Commonwealth United Entertainment, 41
Compton, 13, 14, 55, 120, 124, 126–32, 133, 134, 135, 138, 155
Compton Cameo Cinema, 127
Compton Cameo Pictures, 127
Compton Cinema Club, 125–6, 127
Compton-Tekli, 209, 210
Connell, Thelma, 266
Connery, Sean, 268, 287, 292, 356, 359
Connor, Kenneth, 151
Cone of Silence (1960), 56, 114
Conran, Terence, 203
Conspiracy of Hearts (1960), 36, 354
Constant Husband, The (1955), 50
Continental Distributors, 20, 56
Cooke, Fielder, 77
Coop, Denys, 243
Cooper, Rod, 89
Coppard, A. E., 290

Corbett, Harry H., 42, 43, 54, 297
Corman, Roger, 47, 82, 121, 246
Couch, Lionel, 204, 205, 209
Countdown Boutique, 223
Countess from Hong Kong, A (1966), 79, 330
Courtenay, Tom, 51, 318
Coward, Noel, 192
Crabtree, Arthur, 46, 143
Cracksman, The (1963), 42, 232, 234
Craig, Michael, 355
Craigie, Jill, 17
Crawford, Joan, 231
Crawford, Michael, 204, 214, 340
Crichton, Charles, 51, 76, 77, 251, 290
Criminal, The (1960), 47, 163, 189
Cromwell (1970), 89
Crosland, Anthony, 109–10, 111, 112
Crooks in Cloisters (1964), 42, 208
Crossplot (1969), 319
Crown Film Unit, 142
Crowther, Bosley, 296
Croydon, John, 86, 146, 154, 312
Cry of the Banshee (1968), 82
Cusick, Ray, 203
Cul-De-Sac (1966), 3, 96, 104, 109, 114, 129, 132
Curse of the Fly (1965), 76
Curse of the Crimson Altar, The (1969), 132
Curse of the Werewolf (1961), 79
Curteis, Ian, 128
Cushing, Peter, 154, 294
Czinner, Paul, 103

Daddy's Gone A-Hunting (1969), 49, 294
Dad's Army (1968–77), 7
Daily Cinema, The, 10, 41, 125, 130, 164, 191
Daily Mirror, 309
Daily Telegraph, 305
Daleks: Invasion Earth 2150 (1966), 104, 153, 294–6
Dales, The, 309
Dalton, Phyllis, 226, 227, 228, 229, 230
Daly, John, 15
Damned, The (1961), 71
Damon and Pythias (1962), 171
Dance of Death, The (1968), 78
Dance of the Vampires (1967), 75, 255
Danger Man (1960–2), 190
Danger Route (1967), 153
Danischewsky, Monja, 51

Danziger, Edward and Harry, 14, 15, 43, 71, 72, 74, 77, 139, 140, 141, 170, 290
Darling (1965), 20, 48, 57, 81, 96, 109, 114, 161, 167, 171, 172–3, 174, 225, 226, 227, 231, 232–3, 268, 319
Darvas, Teddy, 264, 265
Dateline Diamonds (1965), 331, 338
Dave Clark Five, the, 47, 184, 332, 341
Daves Delmer, 80
Davey, Bert, 209
Davies, Allan, 47
Davies, Jack, 169
Davis, Desmond, 72, 81, 103, 183
Davis, John, 23, 34–6, 39, 40, 41, 49, 55, 104, 147
Dawe, Cedric, 209
Dawson, Beatrice, 227, 228
Dawson, Graham, 152
Day, Barrie, 351
Day, John, 186
Day the Earth Caught Fire, The (1961), 52, 56, 114, 162
Day the Fish Came Out, The (1967), 77
Day in the Death of Joe Egg, A (play), 309
Day of the Triffids (1962), 39
Day, Robert, 42, 44, 51, 282, 296, 354, 355
De Grunwald, Anatole, 41, 74, 83, 357
De Grunwald, Dimitri, 76
De Saigny, Peter, 38
Dead of Night (1945), 155
Deadfall (1967), 77, 234
Deadly Affair, The (1967), 71, 169, 248
Deadly Bees, The (1967), 78, 84, 153–4
Deadlier Than the Male (1966), 37, 40, 58
Dearden, Basil, 15, 38–9, 48, 51, 72, 78, 99, 180, 182, 184, 189, 265, 355
Death is a Woman (1965), 44
Decca, 329, 343
Decline and Fall . . . of a Birdwatcher (1968), 77, 234
Dee, Kiki, 331
Deeley, Michael, 15, 55, 78
Dehn, Paul, 169
Deighton, Len, 40, 189, 362
Delaney, Shelagh, 163, 167
Delfont, Bernard, 43, 45
Delon, Alain, 53
Deneuve, Catherine, 120, 129, 249
Denham Studios, 65, 190
Dentist in the Chair (1960), 100, 355

Dentist on the Job (1961), 47
Deutsch, David, 47, 48, 71, 87, 172, 184, 192, 318
Devil Rides Out, The (1968), 45
Devil Ship Pirates, The (1963), 44
Devils, The (1971), 90, 122
Devil's Daffodil, The (1961), 52
Dexter, John, 362
Diamond Films, 86
Diamond, John, 107
Dick, Bernard F., 70
Dickinson, Desmond, 242
Dickinson, Margaret, 8
Dillon, Carmen, 209–10
Dirty Dozen, The (1967), 75, 82, 363
Disc Magazine, 329, 333, 334
Dixon of Dock Green (1955–76), 291
Doctor Blood's Coffin (1961), 269
Doctor in Clover (1966), 36, 169, 263
Doctor in Distress (1963), 36, 263, 357
Doctor in Love (1960), 36, 263, 354–5
Doctor in the House (1954), 36, 291
Doctor in the House (1969–70), 291
Doctor in Trouble (1970), 291
Doctor Who (1963–), 294
Doctor Zhivago (1965), 74, 84, 165, 204, 211, 226, 227, 230, 242, 262, 308, 329, 359, 360, 362
Donat, Robert, 75
Donnelly, Mark, 7
Donen, Stanley, 15, 77, 79, 172, 187
Donnelly, Donal, 204
Donner, Clive, 48, 51, 75, 162, 172, 181–2, 189, 190–6, 205, 264, 308, 312, 335, 361
Don't Bother to Knock (1961), 171
Don't Raise the Bridge, Lower the River (1968), 71
Doomwatch (1972), 132
Dorleac, Francoise, 129
Dors, Diana, 232, 309
Double Bunk (1961), 51, 56, 114
Double Man, The (1967), 82
Douglas, Gordon, 38
Douglas, Kirk, 40
Dr Doolittle (1967), 77, 89
Dr No (1962), 3, 18, 72, 84–5, 86, 100, 168, 185, 228, 245, 356, 363
Dr Strangelove (1964), 71, 147, 165, 204, 267
Dr Syn Alias the Scarecrow (1963), 81
Dr Terror's House of Horrors (1965), 114, 152, 153, 154

Dr Who and the Daleks (1965), 104, 153, 294–6
Drabble, Margaret, 167
Dracula (1958), 79, 208
Dracula Has Risen From the Grave (1968), 80, 288
Dracula, Prince of Darkness (1965), 44–5
Drake, Charlie, 42, 54
Drazin, Charles, 82–3, 84–5, 86, 146
Drop Dead Darling (1966), 78
Duffy (1968), 224
Duffy, Brian, 189, 362
Duke Wore Jeans, The (1957), 46, 149, 331
Dunaway, Faye, 174
Dunlop, Frank, 80
Dunn, Nell, 167, 187, 294
Dunwoody, Gwyneth, 111
Durgnat, Raymond, 1, 167, 182, 289, 291
During One Night (1960), 269
Dutchman (1966), 188
Dux, Sally, 39
Dymytryk, Edward, 362

Eady Levy, 17, 65–6, 67, 95, 106, 112, 149, 152, 350, 351
Eagle Lion (Distributors), 67
Ealing Films, 38, 51, 142, 143, 155, 229, 250–1, 285, 308
Early Bird, The (1965), 34, 37, 169, 359
Earth Dies Screaming, The (1964), 76
Earthly Stranger (1963), 143
Eastmancolor, 245, 248, 249
Eastman Kodak, 243, 253
Easy Rider (1969), 90
Eatwell, Brian, 205, 213, 292
Economist, The, 329
Edgar Wallace Mysteries, 140–1, 190
Edinburgh Film Festival, 192
Edwards, Blake, 73
Eggar, Samantha, 3, 37
El Cid (1961), 40
Ellacott, Joan, 228
Elliot, Denholm, 162, 172
Elliot, Leslie, 132–3
Ellin, Stanley, 172
Elstree Distributors, 12, 13, 20, 43, 54, 55, 57
Elstree Studios (ABPC), 11, 22, 24, 33, 42, 44, 45, 57, 66, 75, 102, 255, 290
Elton, Arthur, 17
Embassy Pictures, 20, 48, 77, 78, 81, 83, 154, 363

EMI, 24, 45, 49, 75, 89, 134, 293, 329, 330
Emmott, Basil, 242
Endfield, Cy, 15, 48, 71, 77, 81, 86, 187, 306, 358
Enterprise Distributors, 56
Entertainer, The (1960), 51, 52, 56, 96, 99, 114, 163, 206, 244, 269
Eon Productions, 13, 72, 84–5
Epstein, Brian, 52, 72, 336–7, 341
Epstein, Jerome, 86
Equity, 16, 303
Eros (Distributor), 124
Escape from Zahrein (1962), 287
Essoldo Cinemas, 12, 119, 133, 134
Evans, Edith, 3, 233–4
Evans, Barry, 181, 193
Evans, Peter, 9–10
Evans, Robert, 78
Every Day's a Holiday (1964), 335
Every Home Should Have One (1970), 319
Evil of Frankenstein, The (1964), 79
Expresso Bongo (1959), 100, 333
Exton, Clive, 163
Eye of the Devil (1966), 74

Face of Eve, The (1968), 49
Face of Fu Manchu, The (1965), 44
Faces in the Dark (1960), 58
Fahrenheit 451 (1966), 79, 246
Fairhurst, Lyn, 170
Fairservice, Don, 270
Faith, Adam, 332
Faithfull, Geoffrey, 242
Faithfull, Marianne, 53, 167, 342
Fall of the Roman Empire, The (1964), 40
Family, The (1974), 290
Family Way, The (1966), 50, 96, 105, 109, 185, 360
Fancey, E. J., 335–6
Far From the Madding Crowd (1967), 48, 74, 171, 174, 230, 246, 361
Farewell Performance (1963), 330
Fast Lady, The (1963), 38, 143, 232, 357
Fate Takes a Hand (1962), 140
Father Came Too (1963), 38, 143, 232
Fathom (1967), 254–5
Federation of British Film Makers (FBFM), 16, 21, 22, 45, 67, 99, 102, 103, 106, 109, 134, 283
Federation of Film Unions (FFU), 16, 22, 102, 106

387

Feet of Clay (1960), 140
Feldman, Charles K., 71, 360
Fellini, Federico, 124
Ferris, Barbara, 320
Ferry, Christian, 360
Ferry Cross the Mersey (1964), 223, 332, 337
Fiddler on the Roof (1971), 273
Field, Harry, 44
Fielding, Henry, 163
Fighting Prince of Donegal, The (1966), 81
Film Contracts, 310–11, 311
Film Finances, 10, 56–8, 82–8, 99, 114–15, 129, 132, 133, 145–6, 154, 295, 312
Film Industry Defence Organisation (FIDO), 283–7, 298
Film Production Association of Great Britain, 45, 67, 109
Filmusic, 329, 330–1
Filmvale, 330
Films and Filming, 10, 104, 173, 182, 189, 289
Film and Television Technician, 10, 24
Filmways, 74
Filson, Andrew, 99
Finch, Peter, 3, 48
Fine and Private Place, A, 290
Finian's Rainbow (1968), 332
Finney, Albert, 3, 15, 41, 51, 74, 79, 173, 188, 260, 262, 309, 356
First Men on the Moon, The (1964), 71
Fisher, Gerry, 242, 248
Fisher, Terence, 45, 76, 182, 186
FitzGibbon, Constantine, 342
Five Golden Dragons (1967), 49
Fixer, The (1968), 294
Flame in the Streets (1961), 38
Fleming, Ian, 168
Flemyng, Gordon, 296
Flesh and the Fiends, The (1960), 38
Flint, Michael, 78
Foale and Tuffin, 224, 225
Foale, Marion, 223
Follow that Horse (1960), 43
Follow that Man (1961), 84, 86
Fonda, Jane, 308
Fonteyn, Margot, 103
Fool, the (Art Collective), 215
Forbes, Bryan, 15, 17, 24, 38–9, 45, 51, 71, 77, 80, 99, 124, 162, 233, 234, 290, 293, 355

Ford, John, 74, 291
Foreman, Carl, 15, 17, 23, 70, 165, 183, 356
Forsyte Saga, The (1967–8), 7
Foster, Laurel, 8
Foster, Maurice, 74
Foucaud, Pierre, 127
Four in the Morning (1965), 104, 316
Fourmost, the, 337
Fowler, George, 72
Fowles, John, 77
Fox, James, 43, 224, 242, 247
Foxhole in Cairo (1960), 52
Foxwell, Ivan, 15, 38, 41, 77
Francis, Freddie, 51, 154, 186, 242, 244
Franco, Jess, 49
Francovich, Mike, 70
Frank, Melvin, 356
Frankel, Cyril, 45, 47, 182, 355
Frankenstein Created Woman (1967), 45
Frankenstein Must be Destroyed (1969), 80
Fraser, Ronald, 42
Frears, Stephen, 18
Freddie and the Dreamers, 334, 335, 338
Free Cinema, 17, 183, 244, 307
Freed, Arthur, 74
Freeman, Gillian, 145, 167
Freeman, Robert, 77, 188, 317
Fregonese, Hugo, 181
French Dressing (1964), 43, 57, 114
French Lieutenant's Woman, The (1981), 311
French Mistress, A (1960), 51
French, Philip, 2
Frend, Charles, 290, 308
Freud (1962), 252–3
From Beyond the Grave (1974), 152
From Russia with Love (1963), 18, 72, 168, 356–7, 363
Frost Report, The (1966–7), 164
Frozen Dead, The (1966), 82
Fuest, Robert, 213
Funeral in Berlin (1966), 78
Funny Girl (1968), 333
Funny Thing Happened on the Way to the Forum, A (1966), 73, 310, 316
Furie, Sidney J., 40, 43, 52, 72, 80, 138, 145, 184, 249, 269, 312, 356, 358
Furniss, John, 229
Furse, Margaret, 226, 227, 228
Furse, Roger, 227
Fury, Billy, 330

Gable, Jo, 306
Gaines, Jane, 224
Gainsborough Pictures, 37, 149, 231, 263, 264
Gala Distributors, 13, 120, 121, 124–5, 126
Gale, John, 104
Gallup, 305
Galton, Ray, 296–7
Garnett, Tony, 73
Garrett, James, 306, 311–12
Garrett, Robert, 86, 87, 88, 132, 145
Garrick Films, 22, 50, 52, 56, 101, 138, 145-7, 155
Gascoigne, Bamber, 289
Gaumont Cinemas, 21, 287
Gayson, Eunice, 228
Genevieve (1953), 190
Genghis Khan (1965), 70
Geordie (1955), 50
Georgy Girl (1966), 71, 187, 223, 225, 242, 269, 330
Geraghty, Christine, 8
Gerry and the Pacemakers, 334, 337
Gershwin, Jerry, 80
Get Carter (1971), 90
Ghost Goes Gear, The (1966), 338
Gibbs, Antony, 260, 262, 264, 268, 269–73
Gibbs, Christopher, 204
Gibbs, Gerald, 243
Gilbert, Lewis, 51, 76, 78, 184–5, 355, 356, 359, 360
Gick, Peggy, 207
Gideon's Day (1958), 291
Gideon's Way (1964), 291
Gilliat, Leslie, 51, 356, 362
Gilliat, Penelope, 148–9
Gilliat, Sidney, 6, 13, 14, 49–50, 51, 52, 105, 185, 310, 356, 359
Gillet, John, 147
Gilling, John, 44, 45, 186, 356
Gimme Shelter (1970), 327
Girl in the Headlines (1963), 51
Girl on a Motorcycle (1968), 53, 96, 167, 342
Girl on the Boat (1962), 72
Girl with Green Eyes (1964), 72, 183, 207, 270
Gladwell, David, 266
Glen, John, 268
Glenville, Peter, 43, 77, 182
Go to Blazes (1962), 43, 208

Godard, Jean-Luc, 188, 261
Gold, Jack, 186, 292, 293
Golden Era (Distributor), 124
Goldfinger (1964), 18, 20, 72, 169, 185, 208, 268, 274, 292, 317, 330, 353, 358, 363
Goldstone, John, 71
Goldwyn, Sam, 285
Gonks Go Beat (1965), 47, 327, 328, 338
Goodbye Mr Chips (1969), 75, 89, 232, 233, 235, 332
Goode, Frederic, 44
Goodman, Lord (Arnold), 53
Goodwin, Ron, 330
Gordon, Richard, 291
Gorgon, The (1964), 96
Gorton, Assheton, 204, 206, 209, 212–16, 292
Goulder, Stanley, 87
Gow, Gordon, 189, 190
Grade, Leslie, 43
Grade, Lew, 285
Graduate, The (1967), 89, 262
Granada Cinemas, 11, 119, 283, 285
Granada Films, 297–8
Granada TV, 190, 283, 285, 289, 290, 292, 297–8
Grand National (Distributor), 13, 124
Granny Takes a Trip (boutique), 215
Grant, Arthur, 243
Grantham, Mark, 170
Grass is Greener, The (1961), 79
Grauman, Walter, 358
Gray, Dulcie, 309
Great St Trinian's Train Robbery, The (1966), 50, 96, 104, 105, 186, 359
Green, Guy, 15, 38, 75, 77, 79, 182, 189
Green, Janet, 167, 170
Green Man, The (1958), 50
Green, Pamela, 127
Greene, David, 78
Greenwood, Jack, 15, 46, 47, 140
Greet, Dinah, 227
Gregson, John, 291
Greyfriars Bobby (1961), 81
Gribble, Bernard, 262, 264
Griffen, Arvid, 67, 74, 87
Guardian, The, 133, 151, 172, 193
Guback, Thomas, 65
Guerra, Tonino, 166
Guest, Val, 38, 44, 45, 52, 162, 182, 222
Guild of British Film Editors, 262, 273
Guild of Film Art Directors 205

389

Guillermin, John, 38, 76, 143, 360
Guinness, Alec, 250
Gulf + Western, 69, 78
Guns at Batasi (1964), 76, 254
Guns in the Heather (1968), 81
Guns of Darkness (1962), 43
Guns of Navarone, The (1961), 70, 165, 262, 356, 363
Gutowsi, Gene, 128-9

Haffenden, Elizabeth, 226, 228, 231
Haggard, Piers, 132
Hafenrichter, Oswald, 263
Hakim, Andre, 76
Half a Sixpence (1967), 78, 332, 361, 362
Halas and Batchelor, 309
Hall, Peter, 79, 192
Hall, Willis, 43, 164, 341
Haller, Daniel, 47, 82
Hambling, Gerry, 273
Hamer, Robert, 181, 355
Hamilton, Guy, 39, 73, 76, 123, 184-5, 358, 362
Hamilton, John, 130, 133
Hamilton-Kearse, Virginia, 224
Hamlet (1969), 342
Hammer Films, 14, 15, 22, 41, 44-5, 46, 55, 66, 71, 76, 79, 80, 81, 82, 99, 124, 128, 135, 152, 153-4, 155, 169, 208, 209, 228, 229, 243, 288, 360
Hancock, Tony, 42, 54, 282, 296-7, 303
Hancock's Half Hour (1956-60), 297, 303
Hand of Night (1965), 44
Hanbury, Jack, 46, 86, 149
Hands of Orlac (1960), 52
Happiest Millionaire, The (1967), 332
Happy is the Bride (1958), 100
Hard Day's Night, A (1964), 3, 72, 164, 184, 232, 234, 249, 315, 316, 329, 332, 333, 338, 343, 351, 357-8, 363
Hardy, Thomas, 48, 74, 171, 174
Hargreaves, Ken, 50, 67, 81
Harlow, Jean, 206
Harper, Kenneth, 14, 43, 356, 357, 358
Harper, Sue, 8, 36, 42, 46, 49, 66, 140
Harris, Julie, 222, 225, 226, 227, 228, 231-5
Harris, Richard, 3, 38, 40, 143
Harrison, George, 350
Harrison, Harvey, 67
Harrison, Howard, 77
Harrison, Noel, 333

Harrison, Philip, 213
Harrison, Rex, 3
Harry Potter, 351
Hart, David, 188
Hartley, Neil, 361
Harvey, Anthony, 188-9, 255, 263, 267, 268, 362
Harvey, Walter J., 243
Harwood, Johanna, 168-9
Harryhausen, Ray, 45, 70-1
Hartford Davis, Robert, 37, 47, 104, 128, 186, 328
Harvey, Lawrence, 123
Haunting, The (1963), 74, 223
Havelock-Allan, Anthony, 17
Hawkins, Jack, 15, 38, 291
Hawks, Howard, 180, 182
Hawtrey, Charles, 46, 151, 152
Hay, Will, 263
Hayers, Sidney, 40, 46, 142, 143, 149, 186
Hayward, Doug, 224
He Who Rides a Tiger (1965), 56, 104, 115
Healy, David, 288
Heart of a Child (1958), 190
Heath, Edward, 23, 102, 106, 113
Heaven's Above (1963), 50, 357
Heinz and the Tornadoes, 330
Hell in the Pacific (1968), 351
Hell is a City (1960), 44
Heller, Otto, 242, 243, 249-50
Hellions, The (1961), 70
Hellman, Marcel, 77
Help! (1965), 72, 166, 184, 227, 232, 234, 310, 332, 333, 337, 338, 351, 358, 363
Hemmings, David, 15, 75, 194, 223, 230, 247
Hepburn, Audrey, 173
Hepburn, Katharine, 188, 255
Herbert, Jocelyn, 205
Here We Go Round the Mulberry Bush (1968), 181, 193-4, 205, 224, 339, 361
Herman's Hermits, 74, 338, 339
Heroes of Telemark, The (1965), 40, 71, 165
Herostratus (1968), 18
Herren, Kip, 207
Hessler, Gordon, 82
Hewison, Robert, 5-6
Heyward, Louis M., 82

Heywood, Anne, 145
Hicks, David, 204
Hildyard, Jack, 242, 246
Higgins, Ken, 242, 248
High Bright Sun, The (1965), 37, 186
High Wind in Jamaica, A (1965), 76, 254
Hill, Derek, 125, 126, 161, 163
Hill, James, 70, 359
Hill, John, 8
Hill, The (1965), 74, 75, 82, 243
Hillier, Erwin, 242
Hills, Gillian, 226
Hinds, Anthony, 15
Hinxman, Margaret, 194
History of Advertising Trust, 10
Hitchcock, Alfred, 164, 168
HMS Defiant (1962), 356
Hoare, Victor, 146
Hockney, David, 203
Hodges, Mike, 292
Holden, Michael, 337
Holt, Seth, 44, 181
Honess, Peter, 266
Hope, Bob, 38
Horror of it All, The (1964), 76
Horrors of the Black Museum (1959), 46, 143
Horse Without a Head, The (1963), 81
Horse's Mouth, The (1958), 84, 266
Horsemasters, The (1961), 81
Hot Enough for June (1964), 36
Houston, Penelope, 1, 25, 63, 182, 319
How I Won the War (1967), 73, 166, 310, 315–16, 340, 341
Howard, Trevor, 3, 41
Hudis, Norman, 147–8, 169
Hudson, Hugh, 317
Hue and Cry (1947), 251
Hugg, Mike, 331
Hughes, Ken, 52, 73, 78, 162, 182, 222, 362
Hulanicki, Barbara, 203, 232
Human Jungle, The (1963), 38, 44, 144
Hume, Alan, 243
Hume, Nutcombe, 99, 102, 105
Humphries Labs, 52
Hunt, Leon, 8
Hunt, Peter, 268
Hunter, Ross, 233
Huntingdon, Lawrence, 39
Hurt, John, 37
Hussein, Waris, 186, 293

Huston, John, 73, 222, 252
Hutchings, Peter, 154, 181
Hutton, Brian, 75, 362
Hyman, Elliot, 80
Hyman, Kenneth, 74, 75, 80, 82

I Am a Camera (1955), 190
I Thank a Fool (1962), 74
I Was Happy Here (1965), 40, 58, 103, 104, 114
I Was Lord Kitchener's Valet (boutique), 215
Ibbetson, Arthur, 242
Idol, The (1966), 78
If . . . . (1968), 3, 15, 78, 123, 166, 189, 266, 353
Ifield, Frank, 43, 330
Ilford Film Stock, 244
I'll Never Forget What's 'is Name (1967), 79, 184, 223, 294, 304, 319, 342
I'm Alright Jack (1959), 100
In Search of the Castaways (1962), 81
In the Doghouse (1961), 37
In Two Minds (1968), 293
Inadmissible Evidence (1968), 18, 78
Independent Artists, 14, 38, 39, 47, 141–4, 145, 149, 155, 291
Independent Film Distributors, 283, 286
Informers, The (1963), 38
Inglis, Ian, 334
Inn for Trouble (1960), 286
Inn of the Sixth Happiness, The (1958), 209
Innocents, The (1961), 76, 181, 261
Inspector Clouseau (1968), 73
Intelligence Men, The (1965), 37
Interlude (1968), 71, 189, 292
Intimate Stranger, The (1956), 45
Invasion Quartet (1961), 74
Ipcress File, The (1965), 40, 58, 169, 184, 212, 243, 249–50, 312, 331
Iron Maiden, The (1962), 46, 100, 151
Isadora (1968), 79, 83, 86, 167, 189, 230–1
Isherwood, James, 52
It! (1966), 82
Italian Job, The (1969), 15, 78, 187, 224, 255
ITC, 190
It's Trad Dad! (1962), 71, 153, 184, 332
ITV, 42, 144, 283–4, 286, 289, 290, 303, 305, 311, 313, 331
Ivanhoe (1958–9), 283

J. Walter Thompson (JWT), 307, 308, 309
Jacey Cinemas, 12
Jackson, Glenda, 3, 256
Jackson, Lesley, 203
Jackson, Pat, 142, 290, 308
Jacques, Hattie, 46, 151, 309
Jaffe, Sam, 359
Jagger, Mick, 247, 327, 334, 339, 341–2, 343
James Bond, 3, 6, 13, 16, 18, 20, 37, 38, 67, 71, 72, 90, 100, 168, 184, 203, 204, 205, 245, 268, 274, 287, 292, 295, 314, 330, 351, 356, 357
James, C., 67
James, Sid, 46, 54, 151
Janni, Joseph, 13, 14, 20, 48, 52, 74, 77, 81, 172–3, 310, 360, 361
Jarrott, Charles, 79, 213, 293
Jason and the Argonauts (1963), 71, 357
Jay, Douglas, 103, 107
Jenkins, Hugh, 110, 111
Jewison, Norman, 273
Jigsaw (1962), 52
Joanna (1968), 77, 88, 188, 224, 274
Johnson, B. S., 163
Johnson, Johnny, 306
Johnson, Michael, 87
Johnson, Richard, 37
Joey Boy (1965), 51
Jones, Brian, 327, 339, 341–2
Jones, Paul, 340
Jones, Robert, 208
Jones, Tom, 330
Johnny Leyton Touch, The (1961), 332
Jokers, The (1966), 79, 184
Jordan, Marion, 148
Josephine and Men (1955), 49
Journal for the Society of Film and Television Arts, 10
Juke Box Jury (1959–67), 336
Junge, Alfred, 206
Jungle Book, The (1967), 360
Juran, Nathan, 71
Jurrow, Martin, 80
Just for Fun! (1963), 71, 153, 332

Kaleidoscope (1966), 80, 224, 225
Kanter, Jay, 79, 89
Karloff, Boris, 47
Kastner, Elliot, 75, 80, 87, 362
Katz, Norman, 67

Keil, Margaret Rose, 131
Kelly, Terence, 4, 16, 40, 63, 64, 71, 101, 147
Kemplen, Ralph, 262, 269
Kennedy, Burt, 76
Kennedy-Martin, Troy, 284, 292
Kennaway, James, 48
Kennington, Jill, 223
Kerkorian, Kirk, 75
Kerr, Deborah, 3, 231
Kes (1969), 73, 351
Khartoum (1965), 72, 184
Kid for Two Farthings, A (1955), 286
Kidnapped (1960), 81
Kimmins, Anthony, 51
Kind Hearts and Coronets (1949), 172, 250
Kind of Loving, A (1962), 2, 3, 20, 48, 57, 146, 164, 181, 186, 310
Kine Weekly, 10, 22, 23, 45, 47, 48, 50, 54, 55, 70, 74, 75, 78, 82, 89, 110, 127, 164, 169, 183, 194, 227, 266, 287, 297, 335, 354, 356
King and Country (1964), 43, 57
King Rat (1965), 71
Kingsley, David, 22, 50, 52, 53, 97, 102, 107, 141, 146
Kinks, the, 336
Kinney National Services, 80
Kinnoch, Ronald, 74
Kiss of the Vampire (1964), 79
Kitchen, The (1961), 100
Klein, Allen, 74, 336, 339
Klinger, Michael, 14, 81, 120, 125, 126–32, 135
Knack . . . and How to Get It (1965), the, 3, 72, 166, 183, 212, 213–14, 216, 223, 247, 270, 272, 310, 316
Kneale, Nigel, 163
Knife in the Water (1962), 128
Koch, Howard, 165
Konga (1960), 47, 82
Korda, Alexander, 11, 49, 50, 97
Koscina, Sylva, 36, 37
Kotcheff, Ted, 38, 49, 71, 78, 187, 213
Kramer, Billy J., 334
Kramer, Larry, 42, 361
Krasker, Robert, 242
Krim, Arthur, 66
Krish, John, 52, 77, 143, 234, 311
Kubrick, Stanley, 15, 63, 71, 74, 75, 147, 187, 204, 361, 362
Kwan, Nancy, 52

L-Shaped Room, The (1962), 51, 124, 162, 251, 253, 254, 268, 353
La Frenais, Ian, 174, 352
Ladies Who Do (1963), 22, 51, 56, 114, 146, 263
Lady L (1965), 74
Lady Chatterley Trial, 122
Lancelot and Guinevere (1962), 79, 83, 86
Langlois, Henri, 193
Lassally, Walter, 242, 244–5, 250, 252, 270, 307
Last Year in Marienbad (1961), 166, 314
Latta, C. J., 42
Laughlin, Michael, 77, 88
Laughter in the Dark (1969), 73
Launder, Frank, 6, 13, 14, 49–50, 51, 52, 105, 185, 359
Lawrence, D. H., 42, 75
Lawrence of Arabia (1962), 3, 64, 70, 84, 165, 183, 204, 207, 229, 242, 261, 262, 267, 353, 356, 363
Lawson, Tony, 259, 266
Le Carre, John, 71, 78, 169, 248
League of Gentlemen, The (1960), 39, 58, 96, 99, 100, 162, 184, 355
Lean, David, 6, 64, 66, 74, 75, 165, 180, 183, 184, 207, 261, 267, 271, 306, 356, 359, 362
Leather Boys, The (1964), 22, 52, 56, 96, 114, 138, 145–7, 155, 312
Leder, Herbert, 82
Lee, Christopher, 153, 154
Lee, Jack, 310
Lee, Jennie, 17
Legend of Young Dick Turpin, The (1965), 81
Lelouche, Claude, 318
Lena, O My Lena (1960), 163
Lennon, John, 306, 340
Lenny, Bill, 266
Lesslie, Colin, 86
Lester, Richard, 63, 71, 72, 73, 80, 153, 166, 182, 183, 184, 187, 190, 204, 213, 216, 233, 246, 247, 249, 264, 270–1, 290, 306, 307, 310, 311–12, 314, 315–17, 340, 358
Let it Be (1970), 338
Levin, Bernard, 5, 6
Levin, Henry, 70
Levine, Joseph E., 48, 77, 81, 121, 362
Levy, Don, 18
Levy, Stuart, 22, 45–6, 48, 172

Lewenstein, Oscar, 52, 337
Leyton, John, 335
Lieberson, Sandy, 343
Life in Emergency Ward 10 (1959), 286
Life Magazine, 223
Life at the Top (1965), 71, 187
Life for Ruth (1963), 39
Light in the Piazza (1961), 74
Light Up the Sky (1960), 51, 56
Lion in Winter, The (1968), 81, 188–9, 226, 227, 255, 362, 363
Lippert, Robert, 76
Lipton, Ruth, 314
Liquidator, The (1965), 74
Littlewood, Joan, 43, 78
Litvak, Anatole, 70
Live it Up (1963), 170, 223, 330
Live Now, Pay Later (1963), 306
Lives of Harry Lime, The (1951–2), 291
Lloyd, Euan, 362
Loach, Ken, 48, 73, 96, 186, 212, 293, 294, 315, 360
Lock up Your Daughters! (1969), 71, 87
Lockwood, Margaret, 309
Lolita (1962), 74, 82
Lom, Herbert, 44, 144
Lombard, Carole, 231
London in the Raw (1965), 128
London Independent Producers, 20
London Palladium Show, 341
London Weekend Television, 291
Loneliness of the Long Distance Runner, The (1962), 51, 206, 262, 269, 318
Long and the Short and the Tall, The (1961), 43, 355
Long Day's Dying, The (1968), 78, 187
Long Distance Films, 52, 337
Long Duel, The (1967), 41, 58
Long Ships, The (1963), 70
Look at Life, 330
Look Back in Anger (1959), 80, 163, 244
Lord of the Flies (1964), 51
Lord Jim (1965), 71, 147
Losey, Joseph, 20, 43, 45, 47, 55, 63, 77, 79, 147, 163–4, 166, 181–2, 183, 187, 189, 207, 242, 252, 254, 255, 264, 306, 308, 309, 310, 311
Loved One, The (1965), 165, 351
Loving Memory (1970), 15, 18
Lucas, George, 90
Luckwell, Bill, 71
Luke, Michael, 43
Lulu, 330, 332

393

Lumet, Sidney, 71, 74, 80, 187
Lustgarten, Edgar, 141
Luv (1967), 193
Lyn, Vera, 194
Lyons, Stuart, 67, 76, 88

McCabe and Mrs Miller (1971), 248
McCarey, Leo, 76
McCartney, Paul, 194
MacDonald, David, 42
MacDonald, Richard, 207
McDonnell, Fergus, 264
McFarlane, Brian, 140, 231
McGrath, Joe, 71, 187, 213, 215, 216, 222, 292
McGrath, John, 79, 170
Mackendrick, Alexander, 52, 74, 147, 308
McKenna, A. T., 127, 128, 130
Mackenzie, John, 293
Mackie, Philip, 140, 297
Mackilliop, Ian, 8
MacLaine, Shirley, 215
McLoone, Martin, 284
MacMahon, G. H., 107
Macnee, Patrick, 6
McNay, M. G., 193
McShane, Ian, 37
MacTaggart, James, 297
Madwoman of Challiot, The (1969), 80
Madchen in Uniform (1931), 263
Mademoiselle (1966), 73, 226, 270, 352
Mademoiselle Strip Tease (1956), 127
Magic Christian, The (1969), 165, 212, 216
Magical Mystery Tour (1967), 338
Magna (Distributors), 50, 101
Magnificent Seven, The (1961), 355
Magnificent Showman, The (1964), 40
Magnificent Two, The (1967), 37
Magus, The (1968), 77, 189
Maibaum, Richard, 168–9
Maidment, Ken, 87
Main Attraction, The (1962), 82
Make Mine Mink (1960), 37
Man for All Seasons, A (1966), 3, 70, 71, 165, 209, 226, 242, 359, 361, 363
Man in the Middle (1963), 76
Man in the Moon (1961), 39
Man in the White Suit, The (1951), 250
Mancini, Henry, 308
Manfred Mann, 194, 330, 331, 340
Maniac (1963), 169
Mann, Anthony, 40, 71

Mankowitz, Wolf, 161, 162, 168–9
Marat/Sade (1966), 73, 247
Marguiles, Stan, 359
Mark, The (1961), 75
Mark of the Phoenix (1958), 84
Marks, Harrison, 127
Maroc 7 (1967), 40, 41, 58, 104, 109, 115, 223–4
Marowitz, Charles, 305
Marriage of Convenience (1960), 190
Marsh, Laurie, 129, 132–3
Marsh, Terence, 204
Marshall, Ted, 205, 207, 211
Martell, Edward, 102
Martinson, Leslie, 255
Marwick, Arthur, 4–5, 6, 7
Mary Poppins (1964), 226, 358
Mason, Hal, 355
Mason, James, 38
Masque of the Red Death, The (1964), 47, 82, 246
Masquerade (1964), 72, 184
Masters, Tony, 205
Matthews, Jessie, 309
Mayer, Louis B., 49
Mazzolo, Frank, 272
MCA, 67, 79
Medak, Peter, 78, 187
Medhurst, Andy, 343
Medwin, Michael, 15
Melly, George, 6, 331, 344
Melody Maker, 334
Mendleson, Anthony, 226, 227, 229, 232
Menges, Chris, 248, 292
Mercer, David, 166, 293
Mercenaries, The (1967), 74
Merton Park Studios, 11, 15, 45, 46, 47, 140–1, 243
MGM, 11, 24, 48, 67, 68, 69, 73–5, 82, 83–4, 89, 194–4, 230, 264, 350, 357, 358, 359, 361, 362, 363
MGM Studios (Borehamwood), 11, 66, 73–4, 75, 87, 246, 255
Midnight Cowboy (1969), 189, 273, 351
Mighty and the Mystical, The, 190
Miles, Christopher, 43
Miles, Sarah, 3, 242
Millar, Gavin, 267
Miller, Arnold L., 128
Millichip, Roy, 81, 103
Milligan, Spike, 308
Millings, Dougie, 232
Millionairess, The (1960), 76

Mills, Hayley, 39, 51, 81
Mills, John, 38, 355
Mills, Juliet, 36
Mills, Reginald, 260, 262, 264, 272
Mind Benders, The (1963), 48, 57, 114
Mingus, Charles, 332
Miracle (Distributor), 13, 121
Mirisch Corporation, the, 73
Mitchell, Warren, 53, 297
Modesty Blaise (1966), 53, 77, 224, 308, 310
Moffatt, Peggy, 223
Mohyeddin, Zia, 64
Moment of Danger (1960), 42
Monarch (Distributor), 39
Mondo Cane (1962), 127, 128
Mondial (Distributor), 121
Monitor (1958–), 186
Monkees, The (1966–8), 334, 337
Monkhouse, Bob, 47
Monopolies Commission, 4, 23, 45, 103, 106, 107
Monro, Matt, 255
Monster of Terror (1965), 47, 82
Monthly Film Bulletin, 140, 186, 295, 319
Moody, Ron, 3
Moon, Keith, 333
Moon Zero Two (1969), 80
Moonspinners, The (1964), 81
Moore, Roger, 292, 319
Moore, Ted, 242, 245, 246
Morahan, Christopher, 49, 293
Morahan, Tom, 204
Moral Rearmament (Distributor), 13
Moreau, Jeanne, 270
Morecambe, Eric, 37, 54, 273
More, Kenneth, 36, 319
Morgan, A Suitable Case for Treatment (1966), 20, 53, 56, 96, 104, 109, 166, 226, 227, 267, 268, 311
Morris, Oswald, 242, 243, 244, 245
Morris, William, 7
Mortimer, Penelope, 166, 293
Mosquito Squadron (1968), 73
Moss, Sandy, 224
Motion Picture Herald, 333
Motley (Designers), 226, 228
Mouse on the Moon, The (1963), 73
Mouse that Roared, The (1959), 71
Movie, 10, 180–2, 195
Moviola, 265, 271
Moynihan, Lord, 107
Moxey, Robert, 186

Mr Fish (Designer), 224
Mr Ten Percent (1967), 42
Mr Topaze (1961), 76
Mrs Brown, You've got a Lovely Daughter (1968), 74, 320, 339
Muir, Jean, 223, 224
Mullen, Barbara, 317
Mulligan, Gerry, 332
Mummy's Shroud, The (1967), 45
Mundy, John, 332
Murder Ahoy (1964), 74
Murder at the Gallop (1963), 74
Murder Most Foul (1964), 74
Murder She Said (1961), 74
Murdoch, Iris, 174
Murphy, Robert, 2, 7, 16, 46, 69, 73, 122, 138, 147–8
Music Lovers, The (1970), 255
Musicians Union, 16
My Fair Lady (1964), 226
My Generation (2017), 352
Myers, Ruth, 228
Myra Breckinridge (1970), 332
Mysterious Island (1961), 71

Naked as Nature Intended (1961), 127, 130
Naked Evil (1965), 84, 87
Naked Runner, The (1967), 80
Nanny, The (1965), 44, 82, 169, 353
Narrizano, Silvio, 71, 187, 269, 290
Nathans (costumiers), 227, 228
Nation, Terry, 294
National Archives (Kew), 10
National Film Finance Corporation (NFFC), 9, 13, 17, 20, 21, 22, 40, 49, 50, 54, 56–7, 58, 64, 69, 78, 95–113, 114–15, 132, 143, 146, 151, 191–2, 350
National Film and Television Archive, 10
National Film Theatre, 12, 125, 126
National Provincial Bank, 102, 146
National Screen Service, 288
National Telefilm Associates, 291
NATKE, 16, 286
Naughton, Bill, 15, 50–1, 185
Neame, Ronald, 72, 77, 79, 266
Ned Kelly (1970), 327
Negatives (1968), 78
Neilson, James, 81
Nelmes, Jill, 169
Nelson Keys, Anthony, 15
Never Let Go (1960), 38, 58, 294

Never Take Sweets from a Stranger (1961), 71
New Cinema Club, 125, 126
New Musical Express (NME), 332, 333, 334
New Realm Distributors, 121
Newbrook, Peter, 37, 47, 104
Newland, Paul, 8
Newman, Sydney, 292–3, 294
Newley, Anthony, 52, 79, 188
NFFC–Rank funding scheme, 58, 103–4, 105, 113
Nice Girl Like Me, A (1969), 81
Nicholson, James H., 82
Night After Night After Night (1969), 167
Night Must Fall (1964), 15, 74
Night of the Eagle (1962), 46, 143
Night of the Generals, The (1967), 70
Night Caller, The (1965), 104
Nightmare (1964), 169
Nine Hours to Rama (1962), 76
Nitzsche, Jack, 343
Niven, David, 360
No Kidding (1960), 46
No Love for Johnnie (1961), 37, 186
No, My Darling Daughter (1961), 36
No Trams to Lime Street (1959), 163
Nobody Runs Forever (1968), 37, 41, 58
Noone, Peter, 320
Norman, Leslie, 43, 51, 355
Nothing But the Best (1964), 48, 57, 96, 114, 162, 171, 172, 192–3, 312, 318
Nureyev, Rudolph, 103
Nurse on Wheels (1963), 46
Nuttall, Jeff, 6

O Lucky Man (1973), 90, 310
Oakes, Philip, 296
Oakhurst Productions, 15, 255
Oblong Box, The (1969), 82
O'Brien, Edna, 72, 103, 167, 172
O'Brien, Tim, 212
O'Brien, Tom, 286
O'Connolly, Jim, 39
O'Hara, Gerry, 104, 128
O'Herlihy, Michael, 81
O'Steen, Sam, 262
Obscene Publications Act 1959, 122
Observer, 123, 305
October Moth (1960), 142
Odeon Cinemas, 12, 21, 121, 133, 287
Of Human Bondage (1964), 82
Offbeat (1961), 269

Oh! What a Lovely War (1969), 78, 362
Oliver! (1968), 3, 70, 71, 90, 204, 208, 226, 242, 262, 329, 362, 363
Olivier, Laurence, 3, 43, 99
Oldham, Andrew, 334–6, 338, 341–2
On Her Majesty's Secret Service (1969), 72, 142, 268, 292, 363
On the Beat (1962), 37, 357
On the Braden Beat (1962–7), 309
On the Fiddle (1961), 47
One Million Years BC (1966), 45, 229, 360
One of the Missing (1968), 18
One Plus One/Sympathy for the Devil (1968), 327
One Way Pendulum (1965), 72, 183
Only Lovers Left Alive (unmade film), 340–2
Only Two Can Play (1962), 50, 162, 356
Only When I Larf (1968), 189
Operation Crossbow (1965), 74, 358
Orb (Distributor), 13
Ornstein, George H. (Bud), 72, 78, 80, 86, 89, 337
Orton, Joe, 341
Osbiston, Alan, 262, 269
Osborne, John, 13, 14, 51, 52, 72, 99, 163, 167, 337
Oscar Wilde (1960), 269
Oscars, 3, 48, 70, 72, 101, 128, 155, 161, 163–7, 169, 171, 180, 183, 184, 188, 189, 204, 205, 224, 226, 227, 231, 232, 242, 262, 274, 330, 350
Ostrer, Bertram, 355
O'Toole, Peter, 3, 64, 75, 147, 188, 231, 335
Our Man in Havana (1960), 71
Our Man in Marrakesh (1966), 49
Our Mother's House (1967), 75
Owen, Alun, 163–4, 213, 284
Owen, Cliff, 51, 52, 290, 357

Page, Anthony, 186, 293
Page, Genevieve, 234
Pallenberg, Anita, 343
Pallos, Steven, 52, 87
Panama, Norman, 356
Paramor, Norrie, 330
Paramount, 11, 41, 48, 49, 56, 65, 67, 68, 69, 77–8, 79, 81, 82, 83, 84, 89, 153, 154, 187, 254, 358, 359, 360, 361, 362, 363
Paris, Jerry, 71

Parish, Robert, 80, 87, 222
Parker, Alan, 273
Parkyn, Leslie, 14, 15, 38, 44, 141–4, 155, 171, 357
Parroch–McCallum, 50
Parsons, Jack, 15, 39
Party's Over, The (1965), 39, 123
Pasternak, Boris, 165
Paterson, Richard, 77
Pattinson, James, 75–6, 82
Pax (Distributors), 50, 52, 56, 101
Peeping Tom (1960), 46, 57, 96, 114, 122, 125, 127, 143, 249, 266
Pemberton, Reece, 213, 292, 308
Pennington, Jon, 53, 86, 362
Penney, J. C., 223
Pennington Richards, C. M., 47, 51
Penthouse, The (1967), 78, 132, 187
Peppard, George, 255
Percival, Lance, 152
Performance (1970), 80, 122, 188, 204, 246–7, 260, 271–2, 327, 342–3, 351
Perkins, Roy, 262
Perkins, V. F., 180–1, 182, 191
Petrie, Daniel, 73, 78, 82
Petticoat Pirates (1961), 42
Petulia (1968), 80, 166–7, 204, 246, 271, 272, 310
Phantom of the Opera, The (1962), 79
Phillips, Leslie, 104, 143, 223, 355
Photoplay, 10, 170, 334
Piccadilly Third Stop (1960), 58
Picker, Arnold, 72, 194
Picker, David, 72, 89
Pickfair Films, 337
Picture Parade (TV Show), 72, 289
Pilkington Committee, 290
Pinewood Studios, 11, 33, 36, 37, 76, 85, 102, 149, 151, 171, 190, 207, 208, 209, 228, 232, 254, 255, 264
Pinter, Harold, 43, 51, 166, 167, 192, 213
Pirates of Blood River, The (1962), 71, 356
Pitcher, George, 39
Pizer, Larry, 248, 316
Place to Go, A (1963), 51, 332
Plague of the Zombies, The (1966), 45, 208
Plane Makers, The (1963–5), 187
Planet (Distributor), 13, 121
Plaschkes, Otto, 71
Play it Cool (1962), 184, 330
Please Turn Over (1959), 149

Pliatzky, L., 107
Pleasance, Donald, 129
Pleasure Girls, The (1965), 128, 131
Polanski, Roman, 75, 120, 128–9, 187, 249
Poe, Edgar Allan, 47, 82
Point Blank (1967), 184, 351
Poll, Martin, 81
Ponti, Carlo, 74, 342, 358, 359, 362
Poor Cow (1967), 20, 48, 57, 96, 109, 112, 211, 293–4, 353, 360
Pop Gear (1965), 44
Pop Weekly, 332, 334, 335
Porteous, Emma, 228
Porter, Vincent, 8, 14, 36, 42, 46, 49, 66, 140
Postman's Knock (1961), 74
Pot Carriers, The (1962), 42
Powell, Dilys, 126, 172
Powell, Michael, 46, 76, 78, 104, 125, 127, 143, 182
Power Game, The (1965–9), 187
Preminger, Otto, 71, 180, 187, 339
Press for Time (1966), 37, 58, 115
Pretty Polly (1967), 79
Pretty Things, the, 339
Price, Vincent, 47
Priestley, Tom, 263, 267, 268
Prime of Miss Jean Brodie, The (1969), 77
Primitive London (1965), 128
Prince and the Pauper, The (1962), 81
Prince and the Showgirl, The (1957), 227
Private Potter (1962), 74
Private Property (1960), 127
Prize of Arms, A (1964), 52
Private's Progress (1956), 49
Privilege (1967), 15, 79, 340, 341
Probyn, Brian, 248, 292
Projected Man, The (1966), 104, 128
Promise Her Everything (1965), 82, 254
Proud, Peter, 210
Prudence and the Pill (1968), 77, 232
Psyche 59 (1964), 227, 232
Psychopath, The (1966), 78
Pudovkin, Vsevolod, 263
Pumpkin Eater, The (1964), 71, 166, 211, 226, 243
Punch and Judy Man, The (1962), 42, 296
Pure Hell of St Trinian's, The (1960), 50

Quant, Mary, 203, 214, 223, 224, 225
Quatermass and the Pit (1967), 45
Queen magazine, 305

Queen's Guards, The (1961), 76
Quiller Memorandum, The (1966), 41, 166
Quin, James, 18
Quintero, Jose, 80

Rachmil, Lewis, 358
Raddin, Paul, 359
Radio Caroline, 305, 334
Radio London, 305
Rainbow, The (1989), 310
Raising the Wind (1961), 46
Rakoff, Alvin, 290, 319
Rampling, Charlotte, 223, 231
Ramsay, Peggy, 165
Ramsbottom Rides Again (1956), 181
Rank Film Distributors, 33, 34–42, 354, 357, 358, 359, 361, 362
Rank, J. Arthur, 34, 36, 328
Rank Organisation, 6, 10, 11, 12, 13, 14, 21, 22, 23, 24, 33, 34, 36, 51, 54, 55, 58, 67, 72, 73, 100, 102, 103, 119, 121, 130, 133, 134, 142, 143, 145, 147, 149, 151, 152, 171, 184, 190, 231, 263, 283, 285, 328, 330–1
Ransohoff, Martin, 74
Raphael, Frederic, 161, 162, 170–5, 192
Rasputin, The Mad Monk (1965), 208
Rattle of a Simple Man (1964), 43
Rave, 334, 340, 341
Ray, Nicholas, 341
Reach for the Sky (1956), 185, 191
Reade, Walter, 52, 56
Ready Steady Go (1963–6), 334
Rebel, The (1960), 42, 282, 296, 355
Red and Blue (1967), 214
Red Berets, The (1953), 83
Redgrave, Lynn, 3, 223
Redgrave, Vanessa, 3, 247, 270
Redman, Joyce, 262
Reed, Carol, 6, 71, 184, 291, 362
Reed, Michael, 142
Rees, Al, 8
Reeves, Michael, 82, 127, 131
Regal (Distributor), 13
Reid Banks, Lynne, 124
Reisz, Karel, 17, 53, 74, 79, 181, 183, 187, 189, 307, 311, 337, 351, 355
Reith, Lord (John), 313
Relph, Michael, 15, 38–9, 48, 51, 72, 78, 99, 182, 355
Rennie, Michael, 291
Renown Pictures, 355

Reptile, The (1966), 208
Repulsion (1965), 3, 120, 129, 249
Resnais, Alain, 314
Reynolds, Charles, 87
Rhythm and Greens (1964), 332
Richard, Cliff, 15, 43, 55, 145, 184, 255, 330, 332, 333, 339, 343, 356, 357
Richard Schulman Entertainments, 13
Richard the Lionheart (1962–3), 14
Richards, Jeffrey, 3
Richards, Keith, 327, 341–2
Richardson, Tony, 13, 14, 17, 51, 52, 56, 72, 73, 85, 99, 147, 163, 167, 181, 183, 189, 206, 214, 244–5, 260, 262, 264, 269, 272, 337, 351–2, 355, 357, 361
Rickards, Jocelyn, 225–6, 227, 228, 229–30, 231
Rigg, Diana, 6, 292
Riley, Bridget, 203
Rilla, Wolf, 43, 312
Ring of Spies (1963), 51
Rise and Rise of Michael Rimmer, The (1970), 80
Ritchie, June, 2
Ritt, Martin, 78, 187
Rive, Kenneth, 120, 124–5
RKO, 286
Road to Hong Kong, The (1962), 356
Rob Roy the Highland Rogue (1954), 81
Robbery (1967), 15, 78, 255
Roberts, Rachel, 3, 38, 144
Robertson Justice, James, 36, 143
Robinson, Bernard, 208
Robinson, David, 189
Robinson, Robert, 289
Robson, Mark, 49, 76
Rock You Sinners (1957), 335
Rocket to the Moon (1967), 49
Roeg, Nicolas, 80, 188, 242, 243, 246, 250, 271, 273, 308, 310
Rogers, Peter, 13, 14, 37, 46–7, 48, 100, 135, 143, 148–152, 155, 263, 354, 355, 358, 361, 362
Rolling Stones, the, 74, 327–8, 332, 334–42, 343–4
Roman Spring of Mrs Stone, The (1961), 80, 82
Romeo and Juliet (1966), 40, 103, 104
Romeo and Juliet (1968), 78, 262, 362, 363
Romulus Films, 56, 283

Room at the Top (1959), 48, 122, 123, 172, 181
Roome, Alfred, 263–4
Rose, Reginald, 163
Rosenberg, Max, 15, 71, 128, 152–4, 155, 294
Ross, Herbert, 75
Ross, Robert, 48
Ross, Steven J., 80
Rothwell, Talbot, 148, 169
Rotten to the Core (1965), 51
Rough and the Smooth, The (1959), 206
Rouve, Pierre, 41
Royal College of Art, 224
Running Man, The (1963), 71
Russell, Ken, 42, 43, 73, 186, 189, 231, 255, 290, 304, 310, 316, 317
Russell, Patrick, 8
Russell, Shirley, 228, 231
Russell Taylor, John, 24, 77, 79, 205, 216, 255
Rutherford, Margaret, 74, 350
Ryan, Robert, 39
Ryan's Daughter (1970), 75, 248

Sailor from Gibraltar, The (1967), 18, 73, 227, 270, 352
Saint, The (1962–9), 292
St John, Earl, 36
Salt, Barry, 248, 259, 262
Saltzman, Harry, 13, 14, 18, 40, 72, 73, 78, 85, 168, 192, 356, 357, 358, 359, 360, 362
Sammy Going South (1963), 52, 56, 82, 147
Sampson, Anthony, 314
Sanctuary (1961), 351
Sandbrook, Dominic, 6–7
Sands of the Desert (1960), 42
Sands of the Kalahari, The (1965), 15, 77, 81, 83
Sandwich Man, The (1966), 40, 58, 103–4, 114
Sangster, Jimmy, 169
Santor Film Productions, 58
Sapper, Alan, 170
Sapphire (1959), 100
Saraband for Dead Lovers (1948), 250
Sarne, Mike, 77, 88, 188, 224, 332, 334, 335
Sarris, Andrew, 193
Sarron, Bernard, 212
Sasdy, Peter, 127, 132, 293

Sassoon, Vidal, 204, 231
Satan Never Sleeps (1962), 76
Saturday Night and Sunday Morning (1960), 20, 51, 56, 96, 100, 114, 123, 143, 146, 163, 244, 353, 355, 356
Saturday Night Out (1964), 128, 209
Savage, Norman, 262
Saville, Philip, 213, 293
Scales of Justice, The (1962–7), 141
Scarlet Blade, The (1963), 44
Schlesinger, John, 48, 52, 81, 164, 172, 174, 186, 189, 246, 264, 269, 273, 290, 306, 307, 310, 319, 351, 361
Schneer, Charles, 15, 70, 357, 361, 362
Schofield, Paul, 3
School for Scoundrels (1960), 355
Scott, Baillie, 215
Scott, Gordon L. T., 42
Scott, Hilary, 103
Scott, Peter Graham, 38, 41, 42
Scott, Ridley, 18, 307
Scott, Tony, 18
Schlesinger, John, 2, 20, 74
Scream and Scream Again (1970), 82
Screenwriter, The, 10, 167
Scrooge (1951), 190
Sea Shall Not Have Them, The (1954), 185
Seagull, The (1968), 80
Séance on a Wet Afternoon (1964), 39, 162
Searchers, The, 334
Searle, Francis, 141
Sebastian (1967), 78, 223
Secret Ceremony (1968), 79
Secret Place, The (1957), 190
Seekers, the, 330
Sekeley, Steve, 39
Sellers, Peter, 3, 38, 50, 51, 76, 83, 87, 143, 192, 335, 355, 356, 358, 360
Selmur Productions, 58
Seltzer, Walter, 76
Selznick, David O., 206
Serious Charge (1958), 333
Servant, The (1963), 20, 43, 55, 57, 96, 114, 147, 166, 169, 207, 242, 243, 252–4, 255, 353
Setton, Maxwell, 50, 67, 70, 99
Seven Arts, 14, 44–5, 52, 54, 67, 69, 77, 80, 81, 82
Sevenay, 330
Sewell, Vernon, 132, 186

S. F. Films, 121
Shadows, the, 332
Shail, Robert, 8
Shalako (1969), 362
Shampan, Harold, 330–1
Shapiro, Helen, 330
Sharif, Omar, 64
Sharp, Don, 44, 49, 142
Sharraff, Irene, 234
Shaw, Robert, 192
She (1965), 44, 82
Sheckman, Solomon, 12
She'll Have to Go (1962), 47
Shenson, Walter, 14, 71, 72, 73, 358
Shepperton Studios, 11, 33, 49, 50, 53, 102, 208, 255, 291
Sherwin, David, 166
Shipman & King Cinemas, 12, 117
Shipman, Gerald, 50
Shipman, Kenneth, 50
Shonteff, Lindsay, 49
Shot in the Dark, A (1964), 73, 227, 358
Showtime, 10, 187
Shuttered Room, The (1966), 82
Sidney, George, 78, 361, 362
Siege of Sidney Street, The (1960), 38
Sight and Sound, 1, 10, 63, 77, 79, 125, 147, 182, 186, 189, 192, 252, 289, 290, 292
Signoret, Simone, 43, 124
Sillitoe, Alan, 163
Silvester, F. J., 110
Silvers, Phil, 37, 151, 263
Simm, Ray, 233
Simmons, Anthony, 311, 316
Simpson, Alan, 296–7
Sims, Joan, 46, 151
Sinful Davey (1969), 73
Singer Not the Song, The (1961), 38
Singleton, Valerie, 194
Sinister Man, The (1961), 190
Sink the Bismark! (1960), 76, 355
Sinyard, Neil, 8
Sir Francis Drake, 190
Sir Gawain and the Green Knight (Arthurian story), 342
Skolimowski, Jerzy, 188
Skouras, Siros, 76
Skull, The (1965), 78, 84, 153–4, 263
Slater, John, 309
Sleep is Lovely (1968), 188
Sleeping Tiger, The (1954), 45
Slocombe, Douglas, 143, 242, 243, 250–6

Small Faces, the, 331, 338
Small World of Sammy Lee, The (1963), 52, 56, 82
Smashing Time (1967), 223, 319
Smedley Ashton, E. M., 51, 354
Smedley-Aston, Brian, 270, 272
Smight, Jack, 80
Smith, Adrian, 121
Smith, Bernard, 88, 154
Smith, Justin, 8
Smith, Maggie, 3
Smith, Roger, 292
Snake Woman, The (1961), 269
Snell, Peter, 41, 80
Snowball (1960), 142
Society of British Film Directors and Designers, 205
Society of Film and Television Arts, 16, 161 262
Some Girls Do (1969), 37
Some People (1962), 190–2, 193
Something Big (1971), 294
Sommer, Elke, 37
Sons and Lovers (1960), 75, 204, 242
Sorcerers, The (1967), 131
Sound of Music, The (1965), 76, 188, 329, 333, 359, 360
Southern Television, 283, 285
Southern, Terry, 165
Spare the Rod (1961), 51
Spark, Muriel, 77
Sparrows Can't Sing (1963), 43, 57, 114, 263
Speakman, Bill, 284
Spectator, 316
Speight, Jonny, 53, 297
Spencer Davis Group, the, 338, 339
Spicer, Andrew, 127, 128, 130
Spider's Web (1961), 72
Spiegel, Sam, 15, 66, 70, 83, 165, 356
Spikings, Barry, 55
Spring and Port Wine (1970), 15
Spy Who Came in from the Cold, The (1965), 78, 243, 248, 267
Spy Who Loved Me, The (1977), 20
Spy With a Cold Nose, The (1966), 78, 82
Staircase (1969), 77
Stamp, Terence, 3, 39, 48, 224, 246, 294
Stander, Lionel, 129
Stanley, Kim, 39
Star Cinemas, 12, 119
Star Wars (1977), 90, 351
Stark, Ray, 77, 78

INDEX

Starke, Frederick, 203
Starr, Ringo, 339
Steele, Tommy, 331–2
Steenbeck, 265
Steptoe and Son (1962–74), 297
Steptoe and Son (1972), 297
Steptoe Rides Again (1973), 297
Stevenson, Robert, 81
Steward, Ernest, 243
Stewart, Hugh, 15, 37, 357, 358, 359
Stitch in Time, A (1963), 37, 169, 357–8
Stolen Hours (1963), 73
Stranger in the House (1967), 41
Street, Sarah, 20, 363
Streisand, Barbara, 333
Strick, Joseph, 53
Stringer, Michael, 205, 210, 211
Stoll, John, 204
Stollery, Martin, 262
Stratford Films, 286
Story of Robin Hood and His Merrie Men, The (1952), 81
Stross, Raymond, 75, 145–7, 155
Stubbs, Jonathan, 66
Study in Terror, A (1965), 104, 128
Subafilms, 337
Submarine X1 (1968), 73
Subotsky, Milton, 15, 71, 128, 152–4, 155, 294–5
Subterfuge (1968), 41
Summer Holiday (1963), 43, 96, 184, 329, 332, 333, 343, 356–7
Summers, Jeremy, 42, 49
Sumuaru (1967), 49
Sunday Times, 230, 305
Sundowners, The (1960), 80, 355
Superman (1978), 274
Suschitzky, Peter, 248
Suspect (1960), 51
Sutton, Dudley, 138
Sweet, Matthew, 125
Swinging London, 2, 9
Swiss Family Robinson (1960), 81, 232, 355
Sword and the Rose, The (1953), 81
Sydney Box Associates, 58
Syndicate, The (1967), 44
System, The (1964), 52, 184, 246

Take a Girl Like You (1969), 333
Take Me Over (1963), 167
Talent for Loving, A (unmade film), 337
Tales From the Crypt (1972), 152

Tamahine (1963), 82
Tanner, Peter, 259, 260
Taste of Fear (1961), 169
Taste of Honey, A (1961), 51, 56, 143, 145–6, 163, 167, 181, 183, 206, 244, 269, 351
Taylor, Donald, 52
Taylor, Elizabeth, 20, 83–4, 189, 191, 234
Taylor, Gilbert, 242, 249
Taylor, James, 8
Taylor, Rod, 37
Technicolor, 246, 248, 250
Teddington Studios, 65
Teenage Command Performance (1964), 327
Television Mail, 314
Television Wales and the West, 283
Tempean Films, 291
Ten Little Indians (1965), 44, 82
Tenser, Tony, 14, 120, 125, 126–32, 133, 135, 155
Term of Trial (1962), 43
Terminus (1960), 189
Terror of the Tongs, The (1960), 71
Terrornaughts, The (1967), 81, 154
Terry, John, 97–9, 102, 103, 104, 107, 108, 112
Thames Television, 45, 283
Thank Your Lucky Stars (1961–6), 334
That Kind of Girl (1963), 128, 130–1
That Riviera Touch (1966), 37
That Was the Week That Was (1962–3), 5, 164
Theatre of Death (1967), 104, 109
There Was a Crooked Man (1960), 72
They're a Weird Mob (1966), 40, 58, 104, 109, 115, 352
Third Man, The (1949), 286, 291, 329
Third Man, The (1959–65), 269, 291
Third Secret, The (1963), 76
This is My Street (1963), 46
This Sporting Life (1963), 38, 143–4, 208, 310
Thomas Crown Affair, The (1968), 318, 333
Thomas, Gerald, 37, 46–7, 149–52, 186, 264, 349, 354, 355, 358, 361, 362
Thomas, Ralph, 36–7, 40, 149, 184, 186, 264, 354, 357
Thomson, Alex, 242
Thompson, J. Lee, 70, 74, 123, 184, 356
Thompson, J. Walter, 190
Thorpe, Richard, 79

Those Magnificent Men in Their Flying Machines (1965), 76, 169, 359
Three Hats for Lisa (1965), 46
Three Into Two Won't Go (1968), 79
Three Kings, 330
Three Lives of Thomasina, The (1963), 81
Thunderball (1965), 18, 20, 67, 72, 73, 268, 287, 330, 359, 363
Thunderbirds are Go! (1966), 73, 295
Thunderbird 6 (1968), 73, 295
Tiara Tahiti (1962), 38, 187, 287
Tiger Bay (1959), 100
Tigon British Film Productions, 132
Tigon, 13, 55, 82, 124, 131, 132–4, 135, 138, 155
Tigon/LMG/Classic, 134
Tigon Pictures, 132
Till Death Us Do Part (1969), 53, 54, 96, 112–13, 297, 362
Time Magazine, 9, 63, 230
Times, The, 112, 133, 140, 148, 164, 318
Tingey, Cynthia, 228
To Sir With Love (1967), 71, 330, 363
Todd, Ann, 309
Todd-AO, 76
Tom Jones (1963), 3, 15, 20, 53, 73, 83, 85–6, 100, 155, 163, 183, 205, 206, 230, 245, 260, 262, 269–70, 272, 337, 356–7, 363
Tomb of Ligeia, The (1965), 47, 82
Tommy Steele Story, The (1957), 46, 149, 331
Toms, Carl, 229
Tonight, 186
Tonite Let's All Make Love in London (1967), 318
Too Hot to Handle (1960), 43
Top of the Pops (1964–2006), 334, 342
Top Rank Records, 329, 330
Torn Curtain (1966), 164
Touch of Love, A (1969), 153
Touchables, The (1968), 77, 188, 208, 224, 317–18
Tourneur, Jacques, 47, 82
Towers, Harry Allan, 15, 44, 49, 82
Town Like Alice, A (1956), 310
Toye, Wendy, 43
Traffic, 194
Trap, The (1966), 40, 58, 104, 115, 352
Treasure Island (1950), 66, 81
Treasure of Monte Cristo, The (1960), 38
Treasury (HM Government), 103, 106, 107, 112

Trevelyan, John, 18, 122, 123, 126, 129, 130, 193
Trials of Oscar Wilde, The (1960), 163
Tronson, Robert, 51
Trouble in Store (1953), 36
Troy–Schenck Distributor, 232
Truffaut, Francois, 63, 79, 187, 246
Truman, Michael, 43, 51
Trumper, John, 264, 265
Truth About Spring, The (1964), 79
Tuffin, Sally, 223
Tully, Montgomery, 186
Tunes of Glory (1960), 72, 84, 266
Turner, Tim, 288
Turpin, Gerry, 233, 243
Tushingham, Rita, 3, 51, 145, 204, 244
TV Cartoons (Production Company), 309
Twice Round the Daffodils (1962), 46
Twickenham Studios, 14, 22, 50, 56, 215
Twiggy, 203
Twinky (1970), 274
Twisted Nerve (1968), 51, 189
Two and Two Make Six (1962), 51, 56, 114
Two for the Road (1967), 77, 171, 172–3
Two Gentlemen Sharing (1969), 49, 78, 187
Two Left Feet (1963), 51
Two Way Stretch (1960), 51, 56, 354–5
Two Weeks in September (1967), 40, 104
Tyne Tees Television, 283

Ulysses (1967), 18, 53, 56, 96, 109, 115
Un Homme et Une Femme (1966), 318
Une Femme Mariée (1964), 125
United Artists, 3, 11, 13, 20, 53, 66–7, 68, 69, 71–3, 78, 83, 84–5, 89, 100, 155, 168, 194, 195, 245, 295, 337, 343, 356, 357, 359, 360, 361, 362, 363
Universal, 11, 20, 33, 41, 54, 57, 58, 66, 67, 68, 69, 77, 79, 83, 86, 89, 99, 124, 188, 232
Unstoppable Man, The (1961), 269
Unsworth, Geoffrey, 242
Up Against It (unmade film), 341
Up Jumped a Swagman (1965), 43, 104
Up the Junction (1965), 284, 293
Up the Junction (1968), 78, 187, 288, 294, 330, 331, 360
Ustinov, Peter, 39, 74, 163

Valiant, The (1961), 72, 86
Vampire Lovers, The (1970), 82

van Eyssen, John, 70
Variety, 193, 195, 285, 291, 294, 296, 297
Vas, Robert, 261
Vengeance of Fu Manchu, The (1967), 49
Venice Film Festival, 232, 317
Very Edge, The (1963), 145, 146
Very Important Person (1961), 38, 143
Verushka, 223, 225
Vetchinsky, Alex, 209
Vic Films, 13, 310
Victim (1961), 39, 123, 147, 167, 184
Victor-Smith, John, 260
Victors, The (1963), 70
Viking Queen, The (1967), 229
Village of the Damned (1960), 74
VIPs, The (1963), 74, 83, 350, 357
Virgin Soldiers, The (1969), 362
Viscount Films, 331
Vitagraph, 65
Vogue, 224

Wald, Jerry, 75
Walkabout (1970), 272, 273
Walker, Alexander, 3–4, 6, 7, 24, 38, 49, 55, 63, 72, 78, 79, 89, 99, 105, 192, 315, 351
Walker, David, 230
Wallace, Edgar, 47, 243
Wallis, Dave, 340, 341
Wallis, Hal B., 15, 77, 79, 261
Wallis, R. J., 42
Walt Disney, 11, 66, 67, 68, 69, 80–1, 83, 232, 332, 355, 360
Walt Disney's Wonderful World of Colour (1961–9), 81
Walton, Tony, 226
Waltz of the Toreadors (1962), 38, 143
Wanamaker, Sam, 47
Wanger, Walter, 76
Wanstall, Norman, 274
War Game, The (1965), 291
War Lover, The (1962), 232
Warner Bros., 11, 34, 42, 43, 45, 54, 65, 66, 68, 68, 69, 80, 81, 86, 87, 89, 188, 343
Warner, David, 267, 268
Warner, Jack (Studio Head), 42, 80
Warner, Jack (Actor), 291
Warner Pathé Distributors, 11, 14, 33, 34, 35, 42–4, 47, 55, 80, 82, 121, 355, 356, 357, 358, 360
Warner–Seven Arts, 34, 56, 75, 80, 89

Warter, Philip, 42, 44
Warwick Films, 66, 70, 83, 185
Wassweman, Lew, 67, 79
Watch It Sailor! (1962), 71
Watch Your Stern (1960), 46
Waterhouse, Keith, 164, 341
Waterman, Denis, 142
Waterson, Chic, 251
Watkin, David, 242, 243, 247–8, 250, 255, 308, 309, 310, 316–17
Watkins, Peter, 15, 79, 291
Watson, Paul, 290
Watts, Charlie, 327, 336
Waugh, Evelyn, 77
We Joined the Navy (1962), 43, 232, 234
Webber, Richard, 148
Wedge, James, 223
Wednesday Play, The (1964–70), 292–3, 294
Welch, Raquel, 254, 255
Wellbeck Film Distributors, 58
Welles, Orson, 291, 304, 309
Wembley Studios, 65
We're Wrestling Tonight (1965), 104
Wesker, Arnold, 100, 337
Wessex (Distributors), 50, 101
West 11 (1963), 43
West, Sue, 224
What's Good for the Goose (1969), 339
What's New Pussycat? (1965), 193, 308, 330, 358
When Dinosaurs Ruled the Earth (1969), 80
When the Kissing had to Stop (unmade film), 342
Where Eagles Dare (1968), 75, 362
Where's Jack? (1969), 15
Whicker, Alan, 194
Whisperers, The (1967), 233–4
Whistle Down the Wind (1961), 39, 164, 355
Whitaker, W. A., 42, 355
White, Carol, 48, 96, 293
Whitehall, Richard, 170
Whitehead, Peter, 318, 338, 342
Whitehouse, Mary, 293
Whitfield, Graham, 129
Who, the, 194, 333, 336, 337
Wild Affair, The (1963), 52, 82, 223
Wild and the Willing, The (1962), 37
Wild One, The (1953), 127
Wilde, Cornel, 79, 83, 86
Wilde, Oscar, 342

Williams, Elmo, 76, 254
Williams, Kenneth, 46, 151
Williams, Richard, 193, 309
Williams, Billy, 242, 243, 248, 255, 310, 317
Williamson (Distributors), 109
Wilson, Freddie, 262
Wilson, Jimmy, 243
Wilson, Donald, 163
Wilson, Harold, 17, 112, 352
Wilson, Michael, 165
Winckles, Kenneth, 22
Windsor, Barbara, 128
Winner, Michael, 43, 52, 79, 183–4, 264, 304, 335, 351
Winter's Tale, The (1968), 80
Wintle, Anne, 142, 144
Wintle, Christopher, 143, 144
Wintle, Julian, 14, 15, 38, 44, 141–4, 155, 171, 357
Winwood, Steve, 194
Wisdom, Norman, 34, 36, 37, 72, 169, 273, 357, 359
Wise, Ernie, 37, 54, 273
Wise, Robert, 74, 76
Witchcraft (1964), 76
Witches, The (1966), 45
Witchfinder General (1968), 82, 132, 353
Withy, Alan, 208, 310
Wolff, Michael, 203
Wolff Olins, 203
Woman of Straw (1964), 72, 184, 227
Woman on Horseback (unmade film), 337
Women in Love (1969), 42, 73, 189, 231, 310, 317
Wonderful Life (1964), 43, 332, 333, 357–8
Wonderwall (1968), 212, 214–16
Wood, Charles, 166–7, 187
Wood, Duncan, 42, 297
Woodfall Films, 6, 13, 15, 18, 20, 41, 48, 51, 54, 72, 73, 78, 80, 83, 85, 99, 100, 103, 142, 145, 155, 163, 167, 183, 269–70, 337
Woolf, James, 15, 43, 51, 71
Woolf, John, 15, 71, 283, 362
World in Action (1963–98), 292

World of Suzie Wong, The (1960), 77, 82
World Ten Times Over, The (1963), 43
Worldwide (Distributor), 13
Work is a Four Letter Word (1967), 79, 332
Wright, Basil, 13
Writers' Guild, 16, 162, 163, 164–7, 170, 171
Wrong Arm of the Law, The (1962), 51, 56, 290, 357
Wrong Box, The (1966), 71, 227, 233
Wyman, Bill, 327
Wynn, Manny, 319

Yardbirds, the, 339
Yardley, 231
Yates, Peter, 43, 72, 78, 183, 184, 351, 357
Yeldham, Peter, 290
Yellow Hat, The (1966), 104
Yellow Rolls Royce, The (1964), 74
Yellow Submarine (1968), 337, 338
Yellow Teddy Bears, The (1963), 128, 130, 131
York, Michael, 194
York, Susannah, 224, 225
Yorkin, Bud, 73
You Only Live Twice (1967), 20, 72, 73, 84, 185, 209, 360, 363
Young Cassidy (1965), 74
Young, Freddie, 242, 246, 248, 250
Young Ones, The (1962), 43, 145, 191, 251, 332, 333, 356
Young, Terence, 43, 77, 168, 184–5, 356, 357

Zampi, Mario, 43
Zanuck, Darryl F., 76
Zanuck, Richard, 76, 77, 88, 188
Zefirelli, Franco, 78, 362
Zephyrs, the, 330
Zinnemann, Fred, 24, 71, 75, 80, 187, 355, 359, 361
Zombies, the, 339
Zsigmond, Vilmos, 248
Zorba the Greek (1964), 242
Zulu (1964), 15, 48, 77, 81, 83, 86, 358

EU representative:
Easy Access System Europe
Mustamäe tee 50, 10621 Tallinn, Estonia
Gpsr.requests@easproject.com

www.ingramcontent.com/pod-product-compliance
Lightning Source LLC
Chambersburg PA
CBHW070007010526
44117CB00011B/1458